SONG OF WRATH

SONG OF OF WRATH

The Peloponnesian War Begins

J. E. LENDON

BASIC BOOKS

A Member of the Perseus Books Group
New York

Published by
Basic Books, A Member of the Perseus Books Group
387 Park Avenue South
New York, NY 10016

Set in 10.5 point Sabon

ISBN 978-0-465-01506-1

Book Club Edition

The Wrath, sing, Goddess, of Achilles, Peleus' son,
that dire wrath which brought countless pains upon
   the Achaeans,
and sent to Hades many brave souls of heroes,
and made their bodies prey for dogs
and flocks of birds, and the will of Zeus was done.

To my teachers

Contents

INTRODUCTION

THEY LAY IN THE DARK in the temple of Ares, a brave handful led by Athens' boldest general. Swords and daggers and javelins were their arms—nothing heavy, nothing to make a noise or slow a man. Their mission was one of secrecy and stealth, "to steal just slaughters with a crafty hand." Beside the precinct of the war god, a fortification wall carved its arrogant course down to the water, a wall marrying a sleeping inland city to its harbor on the coast. That long wall was the Athenians' objective.

In the hour of ghosts, the hour before dawn, the Athenians sprang alert at the groan of a dray grinding its way up from the foreshore of the Saronic Gulf. Monstrous and heavy it showed in the moonlight, for upon the wagon was lashed a large rowing boat, a cumbrous and peculiar load. The boat had made this awkward journey before, to lull the complacency of the wall's guards. Every evening the boat was allowed to go out a gate in the long wall and down to the shore to raid the enemy—or so the crew claimed—and every dawn it was hauled back through that same gate. But this night, by secret arrangement, the boat's crew had armed friends lurking in the temple nearby. Would the wall's garrison suffer the boat to return on this one, most necessary night, or would they suspect a trick? Upon that the fate of a city depended.[1]

The ruse worked. Open swung the gate in the wall, and the tottering mass rolled halfway in, to block the closing of the door. Now the men hiding in the temple rose up to seize the obstructed portal. Grabbing their piratical armament, the crew of the boat at once cut down the gaping gate guards—those innocents who thought they were welcoming back their allies. Jolted by screams, more of the long wall's garrison stumbled up, only to be driven back by the in-comers with a storm of javelins. And finally there was heard the characteristic clank of heavy-armed infantry running, as a large body of stalwart hoplites of Athens, emerging from their hiding place in a ditch farther away, panted up with their shields and helmets and spears to reinforce their comrades.

1

Now the Athenians hastened to secure the stretches of wall to the left and right of their bridgehead in the gate. Some of the wall's garrison resisted and were killed; most fled. The defenders were confounded, for they, too, were strangers in that place. They were a mixed force of Sparta's allies from the Peloponnese, there both to fight the Athenians and to enforce the wavering loyalty of the city under attack. Who were friends and who were enemies? Had the whole city risen against them? Their suspicion of betrayal was confirmed when a clear voice from the Athenian darkness invited any Megarian who wished to join the invaders. For the city being attacked by treachery was Megara, whose territory spanned the land bridge between Attica, the domain of Athens, and the Peloponnese, the realm of the Spartans. It was a bloody summer night in 424 BC, the seventh year of the Peloponnesian War.

Dawn broke over a Megarian shore riven between three sovereignties. To the south, the garrison of Sparta's Peloponnesian allies held the city's port, Nisaea, which was their base. The Athenians, by now much augmented in strength, held the two long parallel walls that stretched from the port inland to the city of Megara itself. And to the north, Megara, behind her own walls, remained the property of the Megarians—but they no longer knew which side they were on. In principle Megara was an ally of Sparta—indeed, Megara's troubles with Athens had played a part in bringing on the great war between the two cities. But a faction in the city had schemed to bring Megara over to Athens and had connived with Athens' generals the trick of the boat in the gate. The pro-Athenian cabal had not the strength of arm simply to open the doors of the city itself to the Athenians, nor the strength of numbers to win a vote of the Megarian democracy to do so. Instead they had plotted with the generals of Athens another, darker scheme to get the Athenians into Megara.[2]

An assembly of the city's democracy was called, and the pro-Athenian cabal harangued their fellow Megarians, insisting that they must cast open the gates and march against the invading Athenians. Perhaps some of the audience noticed that the speakers' faces seemed to shine strangely and that their hair glistened and dripped; but then, it was summer, and the city was under attack: who would not sweat at such a time?

The cabal, in fact, were not perspiring. Rather, they had anointed themselves with oil as a secret sign. The instant the Megarians opened the gates, whipped to a fury to expel the hated Athenians, the Athenians were to fight their way into the city. Many Megarians, of course, would die. But the Athenians would recognize the members of the cabal by their unction and know to spare them.

The vote to march against the Athenians was carried, and the oleaginous conspirators gathered at the gates of Megara and were perhaps drib-

Megara and Its Environs, 424 BC

bling with anticipation on the very gate bar, when a stern body of men, quite dry, came up and thrust them away. These Megarians announced firmly that the gates would remain shut. It was too dangerous, they said, to go forth against the Athenians. And if anyone insisted on a fight, these dry men would happily oblige—here, inside the closed gates.

There were in Megara men just as anxious that the city should remain loyal to its alliance with Sparta as the pro-Athenian cabal was that Megara should defect to Athens. One of the pro-Athenian conspirators had disclosed their plot to their opponents, but those informed saw that announcing the conspiracy would reduce the city to pandemonium. So they simply pretended to know nothing about it, blandly insisting that their advice not to open the gates was better and posting reliable men at the portals to ensure that the conspirators could not let the Athenians in.

Thus the gates of Megara did not open: the Megarian betrayers were themselves betrayed. The generals of Athens waited anxiously outside, their men standing primed to charge into the city. But in time the Athenians came to guess that the plans of their allies within must have miscarried and that the gates would not be opening. Setting aside the immediate capture of Megara, then, the Athenians moved on to the next phase of their plan, the taking of Megara's more vulnerable port, Nisaea, still defended by its Peloponnesian garrison. For this the attackers were well prepared, with tools and stonemasons and iron that had all arrived quickly from Athens.

Setting to work with their tools and cutting down trees for logs, the busy Athenians first built a cross-wall between the two Megarian long walls—rather like the crossbar of a letter *H*—and then built walls outward in arcs left and right toward the sea, to isolate the port. In some places they built a stockade; in others, they simply incorporated sturdy suburban villas into the line of their wall by erecting a rampart on the roofs. In two days the port of Megara was nearly surrounded on the landward side by Athenian fortifications.

The Peloponnesian garrison in the port despaired. They thought that Megara itself was against them and foresaw no rapid succor from the states of their births, the Peloponnesian allies of Sparta that had sent them to Megara. Nor could they get away by sea: the Athenians had long blockaded Nisaea. They had no stores of food to withstand a siege because provisions had been sent down from Megara one day at a time. And so, in the evening of the second day, as the Athenian wall around them neared completion, the Peloponnesian garrison mutinied against its Spartan commanders and capitulated to the Athenians on terms, surrendering their arms and paying a ransom for the right to go free. The Athenians then moved their camp into the port itself, knocking down stretches of the long walls that connected the port to the city, so that the Megarians might not creep up on them along the wall walks.[3]

The Peloponnesian garrison of the port had despaired too soon, for great friendly powers were even now moving to the rescue of Megara. There abided nearby in those days a hero of the Spartans: Brasidas, son of Tellis, was his name. Brasidas was assembling an army for an expedition into distant parts, but hearing of the attack on Megara, he quickly marshaled an army of Spartan allies from both west and east and led it into the Megarid. On the way he learned that Nisaea, the port, had already fallen. Now, ahead of the rest of his force, he took three hundred picked men and marched straight for Megara, arriving from inland, unnoticed by the Athenians down by the sea. He shouted up to the walls of the city that the Megarians were to admit him forthwith, so that he might set about freeing their port from the Athenians.[4]

Inside the walls of Megara, all was confusion, division, and distrust. The pro-Athenian cabal dreaded the forceful Brasidas, fully expecting him to expel them as traitors to the Peloponnesian cause. Nearly as bad, Brasidas might restore the Megarians whom the Megarian democracy had exiled, the fiercest enemies of the pro-Athenian cabal, who intended to throw down the Megarian democracy and install an oligarchy—a "rule of the few"—in its place. On the other side, the opponents of the pro-Athenians feared that the cabal would resort to desperate acts to prevent that very scenario. Upon one thing, however, all the Megarians could agree: it was best, for the moment, not to let *anyone* inside the gates. If the great powers of their world wished to fight over the fate of Megara, let them do so *outside*.

After that, those friendly to the victors might trumpet their everlasting loyalty. Megara would be the trophy of the war, the Helen of Troy of the contest between Athens and Sparta. Turned away by the cautious Megarians, blustering Brasidas returned to his army.

To recover Megara for the Peloponnesian cause, Brasidas would have to win a victory over Athens. The next day the Spartan unleashed his cavalry into the plain before Megara, where the light-armed troops of the Athenians were looting, took them by surprise, and drove them in bloody flight to the sea. Then the Athenian horse came up, and there unfolded a huge, swirling cavalry battle.[5]

But Brasidas knew that little would be decided by the harrying of the light-armed or the inconclusive skirmishing of horsemen. To recover Megara for the Spartan alliance required some more certain triumph over the Athenians. And the curious nature of the triumph Brasidas was to achieve is a microcosm of the causes and course of the whole Ten Years' War between Athens and Sparta.

To us, the climactic encounter between Brasidas and the Athenians on the plains of Megara seems as strange as a confrontation between tribes of hooting apes or a standoff between feathered savages in a faded documentary. Its logic was not that of modern war, in all its glistening lethality, but that of drunks in a bar, eyes locked on eyes, shouting, "What *you* looking at?" and inching closer to each other, knuckles gleaming, until one drops his gaze and yields the victory. Under the rapt observation of the Megarians, watching from the walls of their city, Brasidas led out his army, arraying it for battle facing the port of Megara. Out came the host of the Athenians, deploying for battle opposite Brasidas. Time passed. Each side stood regarding the other. Then, finally, the Athenians filed back within the walls of the port. Brasidas led his army back to camp. And so it was that the Megarians opened their gates to Brasidas and the Peloponnesians. For Brasidas had recovered the loyalty of Megara.

The Athenians could have attacked the army of Brasidas, but their generals chose not to. And the reasons Thucydides, the historian who recorded these events, attributes to Athens' generals for their decision are strikingly modern. The generals had accomplished the minimum the Athenians had sent them to do—the taking of Megara's port (taking Megara itself would have been a nice bonus, but placing the city itself in Athenian hands was primarily the ambition of the pro-Athenian Megarian cabal rather than of the Athenians). The Athenians were somewhat outnumbered and therefore at a disadvantage. But most of all, Athens' generals were committed to force protection, to limiting their own casualties, even at the expense of full success. The army opposed to them, they reasoned, was made up of soldiers from several different Greek states: even in the event of a defeat by Athens, no one state would suffer crippling losses of men. But nearly all the soldiers on the Athenian side were Athenians, and so, win or lose, whatever casualties the Athenian side took, Athenian citizens themselves would suffer. There was good, practical logic, then, for declining to engage the Peloponnesians.[6]

Brasidas understood, however, that the Megarians viewed the conflict unfolding before the walls of their city as something far different, stranger, and nobler. They saw a trial of manhood being performed before them— a trial governed by tacit rules. According to the conventions of classical Greek war, one army might challenge another to battle by drawing up in a fair and open place. Then the other army was expected to answer the challenge by moving forward to attack the challenger. Both were expected to play their different parts like knights at a tournament: the one who thumped the shield of another with his lance to call him forth to fight, and the other who came forth from his pavilion to meet the challenger in the lists. In Greece such a challenge to battle might, of course, be refused, and in many, perhaps the majority, of cases, such challenges were indeed refused because the challenged state feared a bloody defeat. But refusing to fight was an act of cowardice and proved the challengers braver. And on this occasion, there was, on the walls of Megara, a keen audience to the contest, an audience whose loyalty hung in the balance, an audience resolved to ally itself with the better men.[7]

When Brasidas came forth first and drew up his army in the plain, he was delivering to the Athenians a well-understood challenge. To answer that challenge the Athenians had to draw up their army against him—and attack. The Athenians drew up, but for sound, rational, modern-sounding reasons, they did not advance to fight. And so it was that Brasidas won the contest of manhood, and with it Megara, in a victory without tears. Now at last the gates of Megara flew open, and Brasidas and his captains entered the city and sat down with their friends to make quite sure that the loyalty of Megara would never quake again.

The historian Thucydides did not trouble to explain exactly why the Megarians rejoined the Spartan alliance. Brasidas "had won and the Athenians had declined battle" was all the explanation he needed to give. The Megarian decision arose from a set of assumptions about the ways of men and states that Thucydides knew his ancient Greek readers shared with him. It is today's Western readers who need to fill in the logic because to us it is strange and shadowy.[8]

The logic of the Megarians was part of the heroic code of the Greeks. "Always to be the best and preeminent above others" was the aim of the heroes of the *Iliad*, and that aim was passed down the generations into later Greece, with only the respects in which an individual sought to excel changing over time. Like our society, then, Greek society was competitive. But Greeks—at least those of the upper classes, whose wealth freed them from want—competed primarily not for money but rather for honor or glory; "worth" they called it, *timē* being the Greek word. *Timē* was how the Greeks ranked themselves against each other: to be the best was to possess the most *timē*, which consisted of esteem by others and others' confirmation of one's lofty impression of one's own merits. Still, *timē* was not merely soap bubble popularity or gaseous celebrity: *timē* was glory made palpable and somehow separate from its possessor. *Timē* was thought to have a real, almost physical existence in the world: it could, for example, be taken by one man from another; it could be captured in war.[9]

The quest for *timē* drove or touched much of what we think of as characteristic of ancient Greece. Competition in athletics was propelled by lust for *timē*, for games had been a source of glory since the days of Homer. Rivalry powered literature, too: the dignified writer of Athenian tragedies waited anxiously to hear whether his was judged the best play of the festival. And, of course, Greeks from the age of Homer down sought *timē* especially in battle, for combat always remained the special arena "where men win glory." The ceaseless search for preeminence in *timē* is on display especially in Greek names, which nearly all have boastful meanings. The Peloponnesian War was populated by such characters as Pericles, "Very Glorious," and his ward Alcibiades, "Son of Violent Strength," whose father was Cleinias, "Famous," and whose mother was Deinomache, "Terrible in Battle."

Competition for *timē* was especially central to Greek politics. In the *Iliad* the assembly of warriors had been another field where "men win glory," and in classical times politics was still a ferociously rivalrous realm where *timē* was harvested. But victory in competition for *timē* also carried a strong entitlement to the deference and obedience of others and, therefore, lay at the basis of the loyalty of man to man. For it was simply in the nature of things, Greeks thought, for lesser men to respect and obey persons of the highest *timē*, worth, inasmuch as they were "worthy" of such treatment. Both gods and men paid automatic, unthinking respect to *timē*, and men paid respect to the gods at least in part because of their supreme *timē*.[10]

Yet in the political dimension of *timē* danger lay, for one Greek's giving a command to another usually implied the inferiority of the commanded in *timē*. If the commanded did not accept that inferiority, the command was an insult, an act of belittlement, an attempt to *deprive* the commanded of *timē* by acting as if he were of lesser rank in *timē* than the person who presumed to give the command. The Greeks had a fateful term for such an insult to *timē*, which they regarded as giving rise to much, or even most, human conflict: they called it *hybris*. *Hybris* was both the act of insult—whatever the reason for it—and the arrogant disposition that disposed a

Achilles clad as a fifth-century BC hoplite: the classical Greeks saw no sharp difference in either motives or methods between the *Iliad* and the wars they fought

man to the insult (it is from this second sense that the English "hubris" derives). And the normal Greek reaction to an act of *hybris* was overpowering wrath, which in turn propelled revenge. Only when revenge was achieved, the theory held, could the imbalance in *timē* be fixed; only then did wrath abate.

Greeks of all generations knew well the path that led from *timē* to *hybris* to wrath to revenge: no less a figure than Aristotle gives the standard analysis, fifth-century Greek tragedy seems fixated upon revenge to a nearly unhealthy degree, and in surviving speeches given in the courts of Athens, mostly from the fourth century BC, the cases frequently hang on *hybris*. These sentiments also underlie one of the founding legends of the Greeks, the strife between Agamemnon and Achilles, the conflict that drove the *Iliad*. Agamemnon claimed higher *timē* than Achilles—"since never equal to the rest is the portion of honor [*timē*] of the sceptered king to whom Zeus gives magnificence," as one of his supporters put it—and thereby the right to command Achilles as his inferior. Achilles, however, as "the best of the Achaeans," claimed higher *timē* than Agamemnon because of his undoubted supremacy as a warrior, and so refused to be commanded by him. As any Greek would, Achilles understood a command from a person without superior *timē* to be an insult—"I must be called of no account and a coward," he told Agamemnon, "if I must carry out every order you happen to give me." And when Agamemnon pressed his claim to be obeyed, Achilles was plunged into furious wrath,

> that dire wrath which brought countless pains upon
>   the Achaeans,
> and sent to Hades many brave souls of heroes.

Achilles sought revenge, first by trying to kill Agamemnon with his sword and then, when the goddess Athena thwarted him by grabbing the enraged hero by his hair, by angrily withdrawing himself and his retainers from the fighting and arranging for mighty Zeus to support Agamemnon's enemies, the Trojans. Hence unfolds the plot of the *Iliad*. All Greeks with any education knew this tale; it was their first tool for thinking about relationships of *timē*, *hybris*, anger, and revenge. Little surprise, then, that although contradictory and cross-cutting moral principles did exist in classical Greece—conceptions that one should *not* become angry and seek revenge—and although modes of revenge changed over time—from the blood revenge of the *Iliad* to the lawsuits of classical Athens—the road from *timē* to *hybris* to wrath to revenge remained open, well-paved, and frequently traveled by Greeks in all generations.[11]

Timē, *hybris*, wrath, and revenge played a parallel role in relations between the states of classical Greece. The Greeks had the habit of regarding their cities as gigantic conglomerate personalities, which were themselves ranked against each other by *timē*, *timē* that their citizens strove to defend and increase. This habit of ranking cities yielded a celebrated divine put-down when the tiny town of Aegium, after defeating an equally petty rival, applied to the oracle at Delphi to know who were the best of the Greeks (hoping perhaps for some encouragement to her own pretensions). Aegium was told,

> The best of all land has Pelasgian Argos,
> The best of horses the Thessalians, the best women the
>   Lacedaemonians,
> Those who drink the water of fair Arethusa are better men,
> But better still than they those who live between Tiryns and
>   Arcadia rich in flocks:
> The Argives, in their armor of linen, the goads of war.
> But *you*, men of Aegium, *you* are neither third nor fourth
> not twelfth: *you* are not on the list.

Regarded as humans and ranked against each other in this fashion, Greek states were naturally offended by *hybris*, became consumed with wrath, and sought revenge. Exactly how a collectivity could feel emotion was never a theoretical problem for the Greeks. "The Lacedaemonians were angry" and so went to war, writes a historian; "be angry," cries an Athenian orator to his countrymen, urging them on to fight.[12] We find this odd. Both the bloodless way we now write about relations between states and the whitewashed diplomatic language of our time have weakened our grasp of the power of emotion in foreign affairs. But to the ancient Greeks, affection, joy, and, especially and above all, anger were powerful and perennial forces in relations between states and men. Within the classical Greek city, there were many peaceful ways to settle conflicts over *timē* between individuals, many gentle sentiments opposed to settling them by violence, and many calming neighbors to urge the counsels of restraint. But outside the city, in the international arena, Greek states abided in a more primitive, Homeric world and often dealt with insults from other states as Achilles did when insulted by Agamemnon, by drawing their swords. So it is that the story told here of a ten-year-long war between states in classical Greece can share its theme with the *Iliad* and be called a *Song of Wrath*.[13]

Greek states went to war for many reasons. They fought for wealth, and they fought for power. They fought for freedom, and they fought to make others their slaves. But chief among the reasons that called Greeks to arms was the compulsion to determine the relative rank of two states when one felt that the other had inflicted *hybris* upon it. The Greeks had evolved a set of rough-and-ready rules for settling national rank in war. Victory in a stand-up battle proved the superior *timē* of the victor over the defeated. But frequently, fearing to lose, an army would decline to fight. And in such a case, the challenger was deemed the victor and thus the superior in *timē*.[14]

So it was that in the summer of 424 BC, Brasidas defeated the Athenians outside the city of Megara. When Brasidas drew up his army for battle, challenging the Athenians to fight, and the Athenians declined his challenge, they conceded higher rank in *timē* to the Peloponnesians. From this adjudication of relative *timē* followed the adhesion of the doubtful Megarians to the Spartan side. For just as Greek individuals were thought naturally to obey those higher in *timē*, Greek states naturally respected and obeyed other states that had proved their supreme rank in the contest of states. The Greek term for supreme *timē* among states was *hegemonia*, "leadership," the origin of the modern word "hegemony."[15]

In fact, hegemony, in the ancient Greek sense of superiority in rank and worth, was what the greater war between Athens and Sparta was about, the greater war of which this Megarian adventure is but a luckily fallen mirror shard: a small part, but one reflecting the whole. The greater war originated in the unwillingness of Athens to accept the superior rank of Sparta—and of Sparta to accept the equality of Athens. The struggle broke out amid an exchange of insults and was carried on by revenge and humiliation. So great was Athens' success that for a time she raised her ambitions from equality with Sparta to superiority—to hegemony. But peace came when both Athens and Sparta were finally so humiliated by different defeats that they were both willing to accept the equality in *timē* that had been Athens' ambition at the war's outbreak.

This may all make the relations of rank between Greek states sound very neat and predictable—a useful subject, perhaps, for social science modeling, with "rank points" assigned to the various Greek states and consequences blandly predicted. The reality was far from that. Just like Agamemnon and Achilles, Greek states often did not agree on their relative *timē*, and unlike in Homer's epic, there was no poet-umpire to settle the question for onlookers. Nor was there an easy way of canvassing Greek opinion about the relative standing of states. So states usually evaluated their own rank by reference to an imaginary audience—by asking themselves, What do the Greeks think of us?—and guessed the likely effect of their actions upon their rank in the same way—by asking themselves, What will the Greeks think? Naturally different states' imaginary audiences of Greek observers often returned different answers when consulted on these questions.[16]

The make-up of *timē*, too, was a puzzle. Although all the Greeks accepted that the *timē* of a Greek state was a mix of its ancient glory and its current power, they would not necessarily agree on the proportion that made up the mix (those with more glory than power naturally advocating glory, and those with more power than glory, power) or whose past was the most glorious, or what tales of mythical glory were to be credited, or how present power was to be measured.

Nor was it easy to agree when *timē* had been attacked and what the response should be. For Greek states also did not always agree on what constituted *hybris* and what constituted revenge for it. They naturally tended to regard their own acts as the latter rather than the former, since *hybris* was unjust but revenge for *hybris* was just. Moreover, although Greeks generally thought that revenge should be proportionate to *hybris*, they rarely agreed on when that equality was achieved. And some Greek authorities, the poet Hesiod for example, urged disproportionate, not equal, payback: "Who wrongs you first, with hateful word or deed, remember to repay him two-fold."[17]

Nor was establishing superiority in *timē* in war without its puzzles. For although the power of various methods of assailing the *timē* of an enemy—victory in battle, unanswered challenge to battle, ravaging an enemy's crops, or attacking the enemy's allies—was accepted, there was imperfect agreement as to the relative values of such methods and how they might offset each other. If one side ravaged the crops of the other, but the other destroyed an ally of the first, who was winning the war of *timē*?

Finally, the reactions of states to insult were unpredictable because, ultimately, they lay in the realm of emotion. The nexus between *timē*, *hybris*, and revenge, among states as among men, was not calm calculation of advantage but fiery anger, and subject to all of anger's chances and vagaries. "The events of war are hard to predict," says a wise man in Thucydides. "Sometimes great things result from small causes and enterprises arise from anger." For its part, the *Iliad* is full of warriors on the same side insulting each other and calling each other cowards, but such insults rarely result in brawls. Sometimes Greek states, like Achilles, took insults to heart, were furious, and drew their swords; sometimes they did not. Certain insults to their cities Greeks statesmen ignored, especially when they came from those far inferior in *timē*, but which insults could and should be ignored was never entirely clear, even to the Greeks. Context was all important—especially the past relations between given heroes or states, since both heroes and states tended not to perceive *hybris* in the tactless acts of those they considered friends. But in Greek interstate relations, as in the *Iliad*, the past relations between the actors may be hard to discern.[18]

There were rules for the struggle over rank between states, then, but the system was not wholly rule-bound: even to the Greeks the ranked relations between Greek states constituted a book of etiquette with a great many pages left blank. And we, today, with our imperfect evidence, are often quite at a loss to determine whether a given Greek state is acting in a way all Greeks would agree was according to the rules, or violating the rules, or trying to change the rules, or trying to get a new rule accepted, or acting in a zone where there were no rules. Part of the contest, indeed, was trying to establish one's authority over the rules themselves.

So today's historian must interpret, must imagine, must try to conjure sympathy for a strange and alien past from a mind in which today's assumptions about relations between states have already carved their tunnels and constructed their viaducts. He must look at the behavior of the Greeks, and read how the Greeks describe that behavior, and try to reduce that behavior to an approximate system, understanding that an imposed system can never be an entirely satisfactory way to understand a set of social regulations that were themselves often unclear, controversial, and evolving—and in which the actual operation of the rules was shot through with, and depended upon, violent emotion. Based as it was upon passion, we must accept, too, that the system often produced different outputs from similar inputs. Sometimes when you insult Achilles, he tries to kill you. Sometimes he shouts abuse at you. Sometimes he sulks in his tent. Sometimes he explains himself, rather apologetically. Sometimes he bursts into tears. So it was as well with the city-states of fifth-century BC Greece.[19]

IN THE LATE FIFTH CENTURY before Christ, ancient Greece was rent by a series of terrible wars. For ten years (431–421 BC), the Athenians and Spartans, and their respective allies, strove against each other. After those hostilities were ended by covenant, Sparta's old rival Argos tried to seize from her weakened enemy the lordship of the peninsula that they shared, the Peloponnese (421–418 BC). The Spartans prevailed in the resulting war. Then, in 415 BC, Athens launched a great expedition against Syracuse, in Sicily, an expedition that ended in cataclysm in 413. Even as those distant battles unfolded, a second ten-year war broke out between Athens and Sparta (414–404 BC), which ended with a starving Athens prostrate and at Sparta's mercy. To our eyes, this is a disquieting result, for Athens was a cheerful democracy, and Sparta, a grim totalitarian state. But, ultimately, Sparta was stronger.

These wars between 431 and 404 BC were given their unity by the man who first narrated them, a high-born Athenian by the name of Thucydides, son of Olorus. It was he who decided that the entire twenty-seven-year span, comprising four major wars and any number of petty ones, should be regarded as a single great war—what he called the "the war of the Peloponnesians and the Athenians," and what we, following the lead of later Greeks, call the Peloponnesian War (431–404 BC). Thucydides united these conflicts because a longer war would give him a grander

Bust of Thucydides

theme about which to write. But his main reason for yoking all the wars together was that Thucydides was a student of the ways of men, and the ways of men he wished to study extended beyond the limits of any one of the lesser wars. Thucydides combined the many wars into one, then, in order to learn from the whole, and so that his readers would learn from it as well. But this book redivides Thucydides' twenty-seven-year-long war, telling the story of the first of the wars that made it up. It does so for the same reason as Thucydides—to learn. Statesmanship is our study here. Thucydides could hardly object.

This volume concerns the origins and course of what Thucydides called the "Ten Years' War," the first decade-long fever of Thucydides' Peloponnesian War. Later Greeks called this conflict from 431 to 421 BC the Archidamian War, after Archidamus, the goodly Spartan king who commanded the earliest expeditions of the Spartans' Peloponnesian confederation. Well-reported by Thucydides, this early section of the greater series of wars is more amenable to being recounted as a single story than his sprawling greater congeries of wars. Moreover, although Thucydides lived to see the final surrender of Athens in 404, death or happenstance stopped his pen, in mid-sentence, as he was writing his account of the year 411. Parts of Thucydides' own account of the period between 421 and 411 BC seem rough and incomplete, and lesser men took up the story thereafter. Thus we know less about the years down to 404 than we do about the period before 420.[20]

But the particular significance of the Ten Years' War, and why it has been chosen as the subject of this book, is that the Ten Years' War and the period leading up to it provide the best opportunity we have in classical antiquity (and, indeed, one of the best from all of western history) to investigate how the causes of a war manifested themselves in that war's execution: the best place, in short, to study the relationship between foreign affairs and war strategy. It is this objective, then, that ultimately determines the chronological limits of this book.

Song of Wrath offers a narrative of the diplomatic and military history of ancient Greece from 480 BC, the year when Xerxes, the Great King of Persia, led his host into Greece, to 421 BC, when the Peace of Nicias finally brought an end to the Ten Years' War. The book begins with portraits of the two great antagonists, Athens and Sparta, pointing especially to the extremities of individual rivalry to be found in each state. Then, after a glance at the Persian War of 480–479 BC, the narrative traces in increasing detail the growth of rivalry between Athens and Sparta in the period after the Persian War, telling how that rivalry broke into war in the mid-fifth century and again in 431 BC. The early chapters examine how a democracy enters into war and investigate the diplomacy of pride, in which getting an opponent to back down comes to eclipse any other issues at stake.

After the outbreak of the Ten Years' War, *Song of Wrath* turns to the strategies, methods, and goals of the warriors. The book describes the ambition of the antagonists not to conquer but rather to *humiliate* the enemy: this was a war about national honor, about *timē*, which was carried on by acts of destructive revenge performed first by one side and then the other. Understanding the war in this way provides a compelling explanation for the general course of events, the logic behind the great motions of the conflict that generations of readers of Thucydides have found wanting in his account. The difficulty of convincing an enemy in a war without clear battle lines that he is defeated is a recurring theme, as is the dilemma of whether to persevere in a conflict when there is no easy way to judge the progress of either side. The early chapters also trace how the realities of the war changed both the aims and practices of warfare, as ancestral methods were eroded by the rough sandpaper of reality. The combatants searched for new metrics to judge who was winning this baffling struggle, and as they adapted their behavior to succeed according to those new metrics, they changed the nature of the war.

The story concludes by recounting the triumphal march of Athens and the humiliation of Sparta, Athens' vaunting ambitions for the hegemony of all Greece, and Athens' ensuing defeat in great battles on land. Once Athens was again willing to admit equality in rank with Sparta, peace was made between the two equally chastened powers. The later chapters explore how the initial reasons for war conditioned the strategies of both sides through all its years, just as they did the peace that ended the war. They describe the maddening difficulty of ending war when national honor is engaged, when an enemy must not only be defeated but be made to feel defeated and, most painfully, induced publicly to admit defeat in a treaty of peace.

In this book the story of the Ten Years' War is told by supplying to the narrative of events provided by Thucydides everyday ancient Greek assumptions about the behavior of states in the international arena—assumptions that, for the last decade or so, students of ancient Greek history have been busily excavating from the works of ancient Greek authors. Thucydides, although hoping that his book would be a "possession for all time," naturally assumed that "all time" would be inhabited by ancient Greeks. He thus took it for granted that his reader would bring those Greek assumptions to his work.[21]

Thucydides lived in a world in which Greek states had not only emotions but kin—mother cities, daughter cities, siblings—and in which these relationships often determined cities' actions and loyalties. The states of the Greeks belonged as well to one of several wider Greek "races," like the Dorian kindred that included Sparta and the Ionian kindred that included Athens. Expected to feel a lively sympathy for cities to which they were thus linked, states thought it natural to defend their ethnic brethren against the natural hostility of the other Greek races. In the world of Thucydides, states, like people, had "friends," one good turn from a state deserved another, and a state's sense of gratitude (or fury at ingratitude) or kinship might be far more powerful than her formal treaty obligations. Indeed, treaty obligations were often founded in, and thus secondary to, a state's feeling of kinship, of racial solidarity, of friendship, or its sense of gratitude. And all of this was tangled up with the ranking of Greek states against each other and their perpetual concern to defend that rank against insult, if necessary by war.[22]

Immersing Thucydides' narrative into the wider stream of ancient Greek thinking about foreign relations also lends refinement to our understanding of the intellectual contribution for which Thucydides is perhaps most famous today: his realism, his emphasis on fear of the power of others as a motor for the actions of nations. Contemporary realists, who dominate the academic study of international relations, avow Thucydides the progenitor of their similar doctrines. And not without justice. Power is all, Thucydides' characters frequently proclaim, and in relations between states, moral principles do, must, and should yield to the stark imperatives of power. "It has always been the law that the weaker should be subject to the stronger," Thucydides has a speaker say. Says another, "Right, as the world goes, is only in question between equals in power, while the strong do what they can and the weak suffer what they must." By placing Thucydides in the wider context of Greek thought, we can see why he had his characters, especially his evil characters, pronounce such sentiments. Such cold-blooded views were no doubt professed by some of Thucydides' contemporaries, but there were other, more traditional ways of thinking available, as well as other, less morally abandoned forms of realism. Thucydides wobbles between a traditional understanding of relations between states and a fatalistic, moralist realism, one that deplored the corrosive effect of fear and power on human ethics rather than crowing over their triumph. Thucydides places appalling realist sentiments in the mouths of his worst characters exactly to convince his readers that realism taken to such amoral extremes was both fruitless and wicked.[23]

Thucydides' account of the Peloponnesian War speaks to every generation who live under democracy, but in describing the confrontation of a democratic sea power with an authoritarian land power, the realist Thucydides seemed to speak especially to the concerns of the Cold War, when the democratic maritime United States faced the dour continental Soviet Union. The realist Thucydides so popular in that generation seemed to offer real solutions to real modern perils—or at least a reputable intellectual ancestor for such solutions.

Yet a Thucydides restored to his place among his Greek contemporaries, a Thucydides more comfortable in his ancient Greek context, also finds himself better suited to the post–Cold War world. Thucydides the realist was useful in his day: but now we need Thucydides the student of national honor and pride and vengeance. For very similar modes of understanding relations between states prevail today, especially among the nations and international actors whose aims and actions the contemporary West finds it hardest to understand and manage: the wrathful ones, those who seek symbolic victory regardless of consequences, those who seek revenge for ancient slights. It is not, therefore, only interesting to know how the Spartans and the Athenians once fought a great war over national rank by cycles of revenge and retribution. It may, alas, be useful as well.[24]

I

ATHENS AND SPARTA

The Birth of a Rivalry

O<small>N THE SECOND DAY OF</small> the solemn Mysteries of Eleusis, early in the soft Athenian autumn, the initiates purified themselves in the cleansing salt sea of the ancient harbor of Athens, and each washed in the water a writhing piglet to render it pleasing to Demeter and Corē, the mother-and-daughter goddesses of wheat. Then the pigs were gutted, squealing, and their carcasses brandished high to sprinkle their sanctifying blood upon the worshippers. This last step we deduce because it was dangerous to be among the very last to scrub one's piglet in the shallows, after the blood began to flow and sharks began to circle the slowest of the initiates.

A few days later unfolded the thousands-strong procession from Athens to holy Eleusis, when the initiates carried branches of myrtle tied with wool and bellowed as they marched the sacred roar *Iaccho! Iacche!* They passed by the place where Demeter gave figs to men, and the temple of bean sowing, and as they crossed into the ancient territory of Eleusis, it was the right of the local people to bind the right hand and left leg of each initiate with a yellow woolen thread. Farther along was a bridge to be crossed, and on it squatted men with veiled heads, who by curious but venerable custom made obscene mockery of any eminent person in the procession. By torchlight the votaries arrived at Eleusis—the old to sleep away the aches of the fifteen-mile walk, the young to regale themselves through the night. The next day the unutterable secrets of the goddesses would be revealed unto them.[1]

Visitors to Athens always remarked on the splendor of Athenian festivals. Even more splendid than the Eleusinian Mysteries was the mighty rite of the Panathenea with its pompous procession—depicted in relief on the mighty Parthenon, no less—when the new garment for the city's special goddess Athena was borne through the city hanging from the rigging of a ship crewed by priests. Attending it were basket bearers and chair bearers

MAP 1.1 Attica

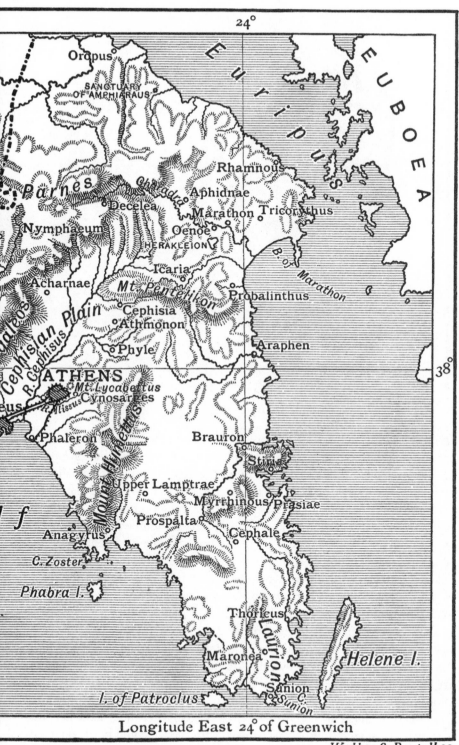

24°

EUBOEA

E
u
r
i
p
u
s

Oropus

SANCTUARY
OF AMPHIARAUS

Rhamnous

Parnes

Chradra

Aphidnae

Decelea

Marathon Tricorythus

Nymphaeum

Oenoe

HERAKLEION

B. of Marathon

Acharnae

Icaria

Cephisian Plain

Mt. Pentelikon

Probalinthus

R. Cephisus

Cephisia
Athmonon

Phyle

Araphen

38°

ATHENS

Mt. Lycabettus
Cynosarges

Ilissus

eus

Phaleron

Brauron

Mount Hymettus

Stiria

Upper Lamptrae

Myrrhinous Prasiae

Prospalta

Cephale

Anagyrus

C. Zoster

Phabra I.

Thoricus

Laurion

Maronea

Helene I.

Sunion
C. Sunion

I. of Patroclus

Longitude East 24° of Greenwich

Walker & Boutall sc.

FIGURE 1.1 Bust of
Athena, patron goddess
of Athens

and tray bearers, and bearers of green boughs, and the fire to light the sacrifice to the goddess was brought by runners in a ginger-stepping race up to
the Acropolis, for the torches bearing the sacred fire must not be allowed
to go out. The festival culminated in a sacrifice of so many cattle that all the
thousands of Athenians might feast upon the meat: eventually all of Athens'
subject cities, more than one hundred and forty in number, were obliged to
send a cow for slaughter and a set of hoplite equipment to dedicate to the
goddess. Our repulsion at such a rite—at hundreds of cattle ceremoniously
killed in public, dismembered, cooked, and joyfully devoured; at the Acropolis of Athens, now so harshly white, awash with gore—serves to remind
us of our distance from the rhythms of ancient life.

Once every four years, at the Greater Panathenea, there were games, too,
as well as musical contests and a regatta of war galleys. This was the greatest
competition in Greece given by a city (rather than by a pan-Hellenic sanctuary, as the Olympic Games were). And at several of the annual festivals of
Dionysus, plays were performed, and to one of them, the gigantic City
Dionysia, foreigners flocked from all over Greece. After the Panathenea, this
was the most splendid festival at Athens, with the wine god borne on a gal-

ley on wheels and a long procession of Athenians carrying holy phalluses, the cult object of Dionysus. Athens' many colonies, too, sent each a jutting phallus and its reverent bearer to the fest. And here the Athenians were invited to feast their eyes on the wages of their dominion, for the tribute of their maritime empire was set before them in bulging sacks, displayed in the theater of Dionysus.

The Eleusinian Mysteries, the Panathenea, and the City Dionysia were only the most opulent of Athens' rites. Every year the Athenians celebrated also ghost festivals, and bean festivals, and moon festivals, and washing festivals, and festivals where whores consumed lewdly shaped cakes. They jubileed at carnivals where ugly men were beaten and driven out of the city bearing the city's sins, festivals where men dressed up as women, festivals where women sat on the ground, festivals where young girls pounced like bears, festivals where young girls swung on swings, and festivals where baffled bulls were lifted bodily by teams of men before being thumped down for sacrifice upon the altar. And who knows what strange rites were performed at the altars of the Unknown Gods, or the altar of Love Avenging? At one sacrament dead piglets, snakes wrought cunningly of dough, and human penises (happily also wrought of dough) were cast into holes; at another, months later, they were dug up again to the sound of hand clapping (to drive away the snakes, *not* wrought from dough, who were thought to guard the holes) and placed on the altar of Demeter. And these were only the rites of the city as a whole. The many towns and villages of Attica, the territory of the state of Athens, had their own rites as well, to which they devoted care and wealth in their kind.[2]

At the somber city ritual of the *Bouphonia*, or "Ox-Slaying," the skin of a sacrificed draft beast was stuffed with hay and yoked to a plow, while the slaughtering axe was taken up and solemnly tried in the court of law the Athenians reserved to prosecute the crimes committed by inanimate objects. Upon being convicted—we may guess that few axes won acquittal—the felonious implement was doomed to exile and cast beyond the borders of Attica. And so the Athenians' much admired parade of festivals collided with the second thing Greeks noticed about the great city, although rarely with as much admiration: Athens' relentless litigation, which consumed so much of the energy of the grand and the humble alike.[3]

In the courts of Athens, the Athenian wealthy prosecuted each other and defended their names and estates, while the poor sat in panels of hundreds as paid jurors, so many that they could be said to represent the public opinion of the whole city. Here it was that the preening grandees of Athens—many of them claiming descent from the heroes of myth—jousted with one another over property and heiresses and slights. Of lawyers there were none (although there were plenty of speechwriters for hire), nor judges. As for law and evidence and relevance, they were no more or less than what the litigants could convince the mass jury to accept without prompting them to bellow in protest: an admirable venue, in short, for settling old scores and opening new wounds.[4]

In other Greek cities the rich fought out their rivalries in politics; at Athens, especially in the courts. In no other Greek state of which we know anything were the high so eager to commit their quarrels to the judgment of the horny-handed. And this is perhaps so because no other city had made governing so unsuitable for that competition instinctual to ancient Greeks. For Athens was a democracy, which to the Athenians meant that nearly all civil offices should be filled not by election but, instead, by lottery among the citizens. This aristocrats hated. With their wealth, connections, and hereditary fame, they usually won elections, but in the allocation of offices by lottery they fared no better than anyone else.

Even worse for the ambitions of the lofty to hold office, as Athens became rich in the course of the fifth century BC, Athenian office-holding by lottery was reinforced by the institution of salaries for officials, which allowed steadily humbler Athenians to offer their names to the lot; at the same time, the surviving property qualifications for office holding were increasingly ignored or swept away. Many hundreds of salaried, year-long offices filled by lot were created to administer Athens itself and its overseas dominions. Some of these officers formed committees administering Athenian festivals, providing the administrative manpower that, in addition to the wealth of the state and the piety of the Athenians, made those festivals so splendid. Finally, perhaps in the late 460s BC, pay was introduced for jurors, too, and with pay the roll of those registered as willing to serve grew to six thousand. Waged jurors were picked from these ranks in a daily lottery, to form the gigantic juries that provided a worthy audience for the battles of their betters.[5]

Thus the Athenian democracy excluded the aristocracy from preferential access to political office by the device of lottery and also blighted the attraction of offices themselves, since winning them was not the result of victory in competition over worthy rivals; nor were one's colleagues in allotted, salaried offices likely to ennoble the offices they held. At Athens the link between success in aristocratic rivalry for rank and the holding of political office, taken for granted in most Greek cities, was much enfeebled. In practice, only the very top rank in Athenian politics was open to rivalry, being marked by repeated tenure of the office of general, or *strategos* (ten of them being chosen every year, to serve for a year), one of the few elective offices to survive in the democracy, and so a real honor to possess. Nor could an Athenian of wealth and birth luxuriate, as in so many Greek states, in the deliberative council that actually managed the affairs of the city: at Athens, that, too, was selected by lot, and its members paid, and at Athens its functions were hardly elevated. The great decisions at Athens were made not by cozy councils of the rich and well-born but by the malodorous multitude in their assembly.

At Athens political prominence depended on speaking persuasively before that assembly and currying its favor—on being (for here was born that unlovely term) a demagogue, a "leader of the people." "Accursed race, those who seek a demagogue's glory. I know them not," sang the poet. For to many of the rich, the path of the demagogue seemed undignified, and one's rivals for the people's affection a dubious crowd of chancers: after all, in principle, *any* citizen could speak before the assembly. No wonder the Athenian rich were happier to battle for status in the courts, where their rivals were usually their relative equals, where victory and defeat were clear, and where the poor were their audience, not their opponents in debate. For the Athenian rich, courts were a far better *agōn*, an arena for competition in *timē*, than politics.[6]

Given the limitations placed on them by the democracy, the Athenian wealthy looked to different outlets for their rivalry. They eagerly contributed their wealth to sponsoring plays and choruses and teams of dancers: all such performances were competitive, with a victor chosen and the right to dedicate a public victory monument often going to the proud sponsor. And the rich, too, contributing to the fitting-out of warships for the fleet, in exchange got to command them in war. Where their wealth and admirable qualities *could* win them glory and durable marks of distinction, the rich of Athens rushed in, and with particular zeal, the democracy having closed off so many other options for contention. The singular literary and intellectual contributions of classical Athens did not precipitate merrily from the free air of the democracy. They are a by-product, and a symptom, of the Athenian democracy's constraint of the Athenian wealthy.[7]

The Athenian democracy was a jealous master. During the Peloponnesian War a group of rich men offered to erect a building for the democracy, but the democracy demurred. Nor could rich Athenians, so far as we can see, sponsor whole religious festivals, raise military units, or otherwise do the business the *demos* thought properly its own. There was a brittle intolerance in Athenian egalitarianism—as perhaps in all egalitarianism, ancient or modern—around which those who regarded themselves as the natural leaders of the Athenians had to step with a careful foot. But the greatest sign of this intolerance was the Athenian institution of ostracism, an election in reverse conducted by writing names on pieces of broken pots, *ostraca*, in which the man who won the most votes was sent for ten years into honorable exile. Over time this came to serve as a sort of general election, allowing the Athenians to choose between rival politicians by exiling

FIGURE I.2 View of the Pnyx at Athens, where the Athenian assembly gathered to deliberate

the less popular. But ostracism had originated as a way to banish aristocrats whose personal might threatened the young democracy, and any Athenian, politician or not, could in principle be ostracized. Ostracism served as a perennial threat to any Athenian who raised his head higher than the jealous democracy thought fit.[8]

The Athenian democracy was suspicious of the rich and well-born because they were, Athenians felt, particularly disposed to *hybris*, the insolent and cruel behavior that rose from the rivalrousness of the Greeks. And *hybris*, the taproot of political ills, was always in danger of burgeoning into *stasis*, or civil strife, the woeful but common sum of all dooms in Greek political thinking. "Insatiate of evils," the poet sang, *stasis* made "dust drink the black blood of the citizens." The democracy of the Athenians attempted to limit the power of those naturally disposed to *hybris* by making powerful elective offices as few as possible and by having as much of the state's business as was practical done by the people directly in their council and assembly or by committees of humble functionaries chosen by lot. *Hybris*, an Athenian would say, was a bane eternal, the simple lot of mankind; still, its perils could be limited by good laws. Good laws fettered the *hybris* of the wealthy, and good laws used the love of competition that

gave rise to *hybris* for good ends, harnessing the wealth of the rich to the provision of thundering tragedies in peace and swift galleys in war.[9]

A mere hundred road miles from Athens, men solved the problem of *hybris* differently, for a mere hundred miles from Athens, in the realm of Laconia, lay the rambling, unwalled town of Sparta, the capital of the state of Lacedaemon (but we usually call the state Sparta as well, our spirits wilting at Lacedaemon's maddening four syllables, and those the Greeks called the Lacedaemonians we usually call the Spartans). The plan of the Spartans was to root fatal *hybris* from the hearts of their men by harsh education. And so the boys of Lacedaemon were taken from their mothers at the age of seven and committed to barracks. Barefoot they went, and ill clad. They were starved and thrashed and made to kill puppies in sacrifice to the war god.[10]

The basis of Spartan education was relentless, brutal competition, and competition, too, was the Spartan cure for *hybris*. From childhood, and at every age thereafter, Spartans were set in rivalry with each other—a great part of which was in self-control, the art of beating down one's own *hybris*. Schooled to silence, the boys of Sparta walked with their eyes cast down

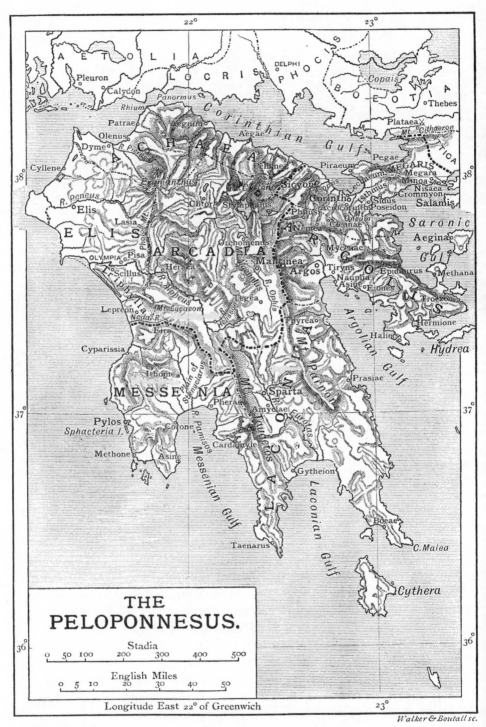

MAP I.2 The Peloponnese

and their hands beneath their cloaks. "You'd expect to hear a sound from a stone sooner than from one of them," wrote a fourth-century BC visitor. "You'd sooner catch the eye of a bronze statue." The great Spartan choral festival, the Gymnopaedia (or, the "Naked Boys") tested the boys' self-mastery, as they danced for hours beneath the sun of a Laconian July. Boys even competed in accepting insults from their elders with impassive calm. Spartan men of all ages competed, too, in their famous "Laconic" speaking, the technique of saying only what needed to be said, in as few words as possible. "Athens taken" would be the whole of the message sent by the Spartan admiral Lysander after the final surrender of Athens at the close of the Peloponnesian War. Whereupon the authorities back at Sparta (the story is told) frowned at his un-Spartan verbosity. "Taken" would have been sufficient.[11]

Self-control, however, was merely the first and most basic of the games of Sparta: with *hybris* restrained from childhood by one set of competitions, other competitions, the Spartans believed, made the Spartans excellent. So Spartan boys competed to be named captains of their companies, in contests of mocking one another, and, especially, in endurance of hardship and pain. This last competition gave rise to the celebrated story of the boy who, hiding a fox under his cloak when he was addressed by an adult Spartan, calmly allowed the fox to burrow into his vitals and fell down dead without showing any sign of anguish. Spartan boys even competed in stealing (and, in fact, were fed badly, so as to encourage them in it) but were whipped if caught, in order that they should learn to steal *well*. At the annual festival of Artemis, her altar was piled with cheeses, and boys set to trying to filch them while others pursued the would-be thieves with whips. By Roman times, the filching had become secondary to the whipping, which was Roman Sparta's chief tourist attraction, and a theater was built in front of the temple so that thousands could watch.[12]

Competition between Spartans did not end in childhood. Between the ages of twenty and thirty, Spartan men competed every year to be named among the "cavalry," an honor roll of three hundred, who, the name notwithstanding, made war on foot. The three selectors carefully explained why they had chosen those they chose and rejected those they had rejected. During the succeeding year, the chosen often got into fights with those excluded, and the outcomes of fights between the cavalrymen and those not chosen may have been considered in the selection process the next year.[13]

As year chased year, so the Spartans chased each other. Thirty-year-olds competed to be named one of the five "doers of good," sheriffs appointed from those aging out of the cavalry each year. From that age onwards, Spartans were required by law to practice gymnastics and devoted much of their time to competitive hunting (Spartan hounds being famous throughout the ancient world), offering what they killed to the common mess to display their prowess in the hunt. Lest there be any mistake, the mess cooks carefully identified the Spartan who had supplied each chunk of meat. Spartan men competed also in obedience to the laws and the authorities, running, not walking, when summoned: when summoned by the magistrates, one king of Sparta excelled by dragging along his clubfoot at a speedy trundle. Finally, in old age, the decrepitude of their sixtieth year, Spartans faced the ultimate test of election to the *Gerousia*, the Spartan senate: "Of all contests among mankind, this seems to have been the most striven over."[14]

The contests of Lacedaemon the Greeks traced back to the Spartans' primeval one-eyed lawgiver, Lycurgus, the "Wolf Worker." It was he, a twisting skein of often contradictory legends insisted, who had first created not only the singular Spartan way of life but also the peculiar Spartan constitution. From their coming into the vale of Laconia, the Lacedaemonians had rejoiced in not one but two kings, from different dynasties descended alike from the hero Heracles, son of Zeus. In classical times Sparta's kings served as the nation's leaders in war and were Sparta's most important priests; otherwise, their prerogatives were strictly limited. This was because Lycurgus had, some said, vested chief civil authority in five elected ephors (or "overseers"). The ephors were judges wielding what other Greeks saw as great arbitrary power and formed the permanent administration of Lacedaemon, such as it was. They were privileged not just to receive the envoys of foreign states but also to regard the hide of the ancient Cretan sage and sorcerer Epimenides, tattooed with strange letters, which dangled as a hanging in their hall. That the Spartans should "shave off their mustaches and obey the laws" was the stern ritual utterance of each board of ephors upon taking office. Every month the kings swore to reign according to the laws, and the ephors to uphold the power of the kings if they did.[15]

It was Lycurgus, too, the Spartans thought, who had created the *Gerousia* of twenty-eight ancients (for a total of thirty, since the kings were ancient ex officio), the council of advisors that also sat as Sparta's highest court. And for decisions on matters such as war and peace, Lycurgus had given the Spartans also an assembly of the citizens, which voted not by show of hands, as at Athens, but by shouting, and the presiding ephor decided which shout was louder. This was a perfect method of voting for the competitive, hierarchically minded Spartans, for in the *Iliad*, loud shouting was the special characteristic of the greatest heroes, and so voting by shouting might be thought to give the most excellent Spartans the most power over decisions.[16]

With power concentrated in the hands of officials (the kings, the ephors, and the members of the *Gerousia*), with those officials chosen by birth or election rather than lottery, and with the views of the rest of the Spartans infrequently and oddly consulted, Lacedaemon was not, by an Athenian definition, a democracy. Athenian democrats disliked and suspected the Spartans, and the Lacedaemonians, we may be sure, regarded the Athenian democracy with equal horror. Aristocratically minded intellectuals of Athens might admire Spartan ways, and Athenian aristocrats ape their long hair, their shoes, and their cups, but rarely did any of them take their emulation to the point of discomfort. For just about everything at Sparta was odd, and much of it highly uncomfortable. At Sparta, for example, marriage was by simulated kidnapping, yet with the bride shorn and dressed as a man for the consummation. Thereafter, young husbands had to sneak by night out of the barracks in which they lived to visit their wives: no doubt this, like the thieving of Spartan boys, was a contest of guile. Spartan men also borrowed each other's wives for the begetting of children. At Sparta, and only at Sparta, girls practiced athletics, and any long-time bachelor was publicly humiliated—forced to parade naked in winter, singing a mocking song at his own expense.[17]

The warriors of Sparta ate not at home with their families but in common messes of fifteen or so, to which each Spartan had to make a contribution of food. But Spartan citizens could not buy food, because they were supposed to live proudly above any practical economy. No precious coin was permitted in Lacedaemon, and when transactions were absolutely necessary, awkward and heavy iron spits were used. Nor could Spartans grow any food, for no Spartan citizen was allowed to plow or reap or practice any handicraft. The lot of the Spartans was to compete with each other in noble accomplishments and to live the life of the city, to rule and be ruled. It was left to the miserable helots to supply the Spartans with food for their messes.[18]

Like a hive of slave-taking ants, classical Lacedaemon could not exist without its thousands of toiling helots. The Spartans claimed that the original helots were a folk they had conquered, and reduced to servitude, when the sons of Heracles came to the Peloponnese. When the Spartans later conquered Messenia, the territory to the west of Laconia on the other side of Mount Taygetus, they reduced the inhabitants there to helotry as well. Marked out by their humiliating dress and dog-skin caps, the helots were compelled to perform antic dances, and the Spartans made them drunk to show their sons what a terrible thing it was to fail in self-control. According to one tradition, each helot received a set quota of beatings each year, regardless of his behavior, to remind him of his place. All Greek cities had slaves; some had unhappy serfs who inhabited the netherworld between slave and free. But nowhere in Greece, thought the Greeks, was the gulf between free and unfree so bottomless as in Lacedaemon.

Slave insurrections were nearly unknown in most of classical Greece. But they happened in Lacedaemon. And at Sparta, fear of the helots, who vastly outnumbered the Spartans, was rooted deep. Every year the Lacedaemonian nation declared war upon the helot nation, so troublesome helots could be killed as was convenient, without the killer incurring the blood guilt of murder. Young Spartans might be assigned to the *krypteia*, the "time in hiding," a public service in which they would lurk about the fields and dwellings of the helots, looking for traces of rebellion, and silently extirpate with their daggers any they found. But despite Spartan cruelty, and occasional helot uprisings, the helots were usually faithful to Lacedaemon—a beaten dog's love is so often its gift to its master. And the Spartans sometimes took advantage of this fearful loyalty: during the Peloponnesian War, the Spartans even enrolled helots as soldiers.[19]

The Spartans were constrained to make warriors of their slaves because the number of full Spartan citizens was in steady decline. At the exact causes of this waning, we can only guess—too much war? too much land in too few hands? too many curious customs?—but during the Great Persian War (480–479 BC), the Spartans were said to have had eight thousand full citizens, those who proudly called themselves the *homoioi*, the "peers" or "the similars." By 418 BC, a few years after our Ten Years' War ended, they probably had no more than twenty-five hundred. Fighting for Sparta alongside the Spartan citizens were also the *perioeci*, the "livers-around," freeborn men who dwelt in Laconia and Messenia, and served in the Spartan army, but were not Spartan citizens.[20]

However few the Spartans were becoming, their ways still made them strong in war. For Spartans were raised tough and brave and to dread above all things the shame of leaving their post in battle. Samurai-like, they charged blindly to their deaths or died by their own hands to avoid the humiliation of capture. Witness Thermopylae, in 480 BC, where three hundred Spartans stood and died rather than retreat before the myriads of Xerxes, the Great King of Persia. The words on the barrow of the fallen asked the passerby to tell the Spartans, "We lie here in obedience to their orders," because no one worthy survived to carry home the news. As for the families of Spartans who died in battle, they did not mourn but went about as proud as if they themselves were victors in public games.[21]

Individually brave, as a body the Spartans were even more formidable. For of the Greeks, only the Spartans all trained systematically for war, mostly by individual exercise but also with mass drill: the army of the Spartans alone was a biddable formation rather than an enthusiastic mob. In the fourth century BC, when such training was becoming more general, an observer could still note that "the Lacedaemonians conduct with the utmost ease [drill motions] that instructors in tactics regard as very difficult."[22]

The success in war that followed from these habits allowed Sparta, by the beginning of the fifth century BC, to establish her predominance in war over her chief rival in the Peloponnese, Argos. Lying in the Argolid, the next major plain to the north of Sparta's Laconia, ancient Argos had given its name to the whole Greek army that went against Troy, the Argives. This the men of Argos had not forgotten. In their territory lay the seat of Agamemnon, leader of the Greeks before Troy, while Sparta was no more than the seat of Menelaus, Agamemnon's weak brother, he who had allowed Helen to be seduced away from his halls. On the basis of Argos' standing in myth, Argos could claim the highest rank of any Greek state. And the Argives were anxious to vindicate that rank in every succeeding generation. Impossibly proud, the Argives were no cheerful and forgiving folk: they worshipped Apollo as a wolf and kept the head of Medusa under a mound in their city; on their citadel, priestesses drank the red blood of lambs and babbled dooms.[23]

In addition to securing for Sparta a much-resented military dominance over Argos, Sparta's success in war had allowed her, during the sixth century BC, to assemble an alliance of defeated, timid, or hopeful Peloponnesian states, what we call the Peloponnesian League (the Greeks called it "the Lacedaemonians and their allies" or "the Peloponnesians"). The members of the league were wards against the rising of the helots and allies against other enemies, especially against Argos, ever resentful, ever watchful, which they encircled. In the northwest of the Peloponnesian peninsula, Elis, home of the Olympic Games, was an ally of Sparta; in the center, the gritty towns of Arcadia, especially Tegea and Mantinea; north of Argos, there was wealthy Corinth and her western neighbor, Sicyon; and between Argos and the sea, lay sacred, medical Epidaurus. There were many other, smaller places, too, but these greater states were the brawn of the alliance. In the fifth century BC, Sparta would also extend her alliance beyond the boundaries of the Peloponnese. But the Greeks, rather confusingly, continued to call this larger body of Spartan allies "the Peloponnesians," and so do we.

Together, Sparta's league was stronger even than its mistress, for Sparta's allies commanded many times more soldiers than Sparta herself. Sparta could bully one town or a few, but not all at once, and not easily the greatest among them, a city like Corinth. To lead her alliance to war, Sparta had in practice to gain her allies' consent. Still, the consequence of Sparta's military prowess was that by the beginning of the fifth century, most Greeks admitted that Sparta was the highest in rank of the Greek city-states, that Lacedaemon was the *hegemon* of Greece. And Sparta's general *hegemonia*, in part the result of Sparta's Peloponnesian alliance, also played its part in holding together that alliance, for Sparta's allies naturally deferred to her supremacy in *timē* and did not feel slighted to take instructions from her. Wise, then, were the Lacedaemonians to keep at Sparta an ancient statue of the god of battles, bound in chains. If Ares could not run away, the Spartans would always be supreme in war.[24]

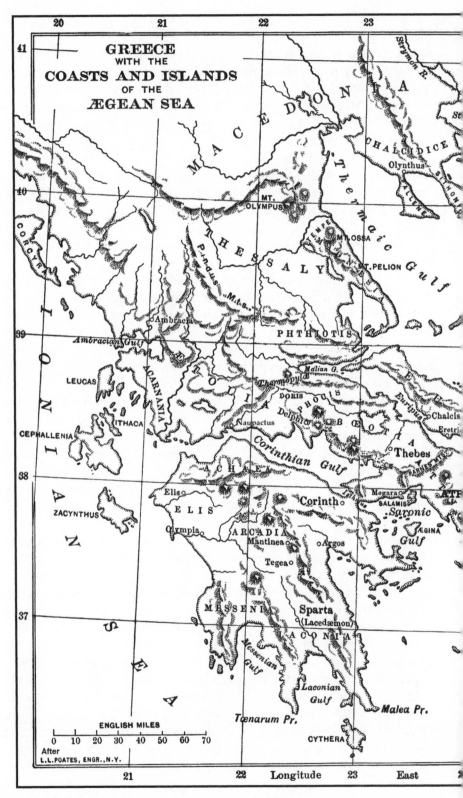

MAP 1.3 Greece and the Aegean

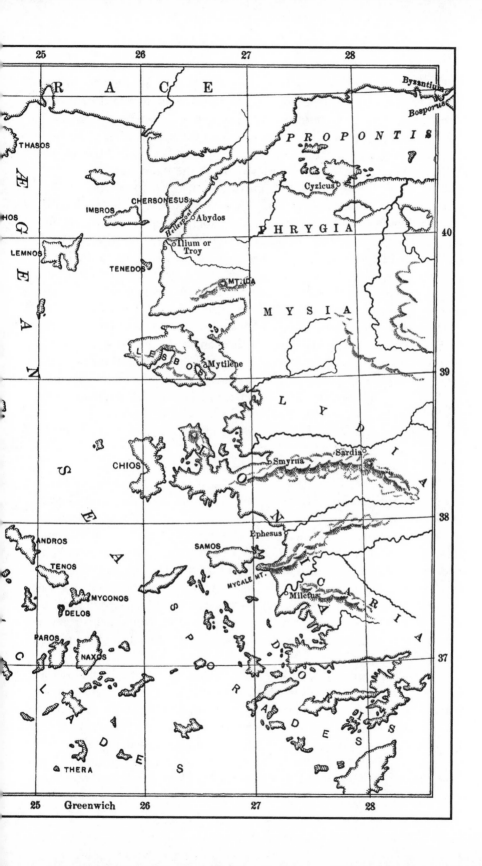

The lands of the Greeks that paid their respect to Sparta were, by the second decade of the fifth century BC, nonetheless limited in their extent. Lacedaemon was the *hegemon* of old Greece, but old Greece was merely a section of the horseshoe of Greek settlement around the Aegean, two-thirds of which was in thrall to the Great King of Persia. Old Greece was the left tang of the horseshoe, with Athens at the tip: a man going north from Attica walked over the hills into Boeotia, the land of Thebes, then over a second range into Thessaly, and then through the foothills of Mount Olympus into Macedonia. In Macedonia the land turned east, and the adjacent northern coast of the Aegean was also sprinkled with Greek cities, colonies of old Greece in an older time, running east to the Helle-spont and Bosporus, the sea passage from the Aegean into the Black Sea. Running south from that channel were the Greek cities on the west coast of Asia Minor (today held by Turkey), also colonies of old Greece, but some of them, like Ephesus and Miletus, antique and very wealthy. Since the middle of the sixth century BC, the Persians had come by stages to rule both the Greek cities on the coast of Asia Minor and those of the northern Aegean, and the Great King had also brought most of the major islands in the Aegean, which had also been colonized by the Greeks, under his sway. It would be no great thing, then, to add the Greeks who remained, the Greeks of the old Greece, to the world-spanning empire of the Persians.

WHEN IN 480 BC ALL the fury of the east marched against Greece, and the hosts of Xerxes marched over Hellespont on bridges of boats, the fractious Greeks saw the need to put aside their own battles and unite their efforts in the cause of Greek freedom. Great decisions would be made in great councils, yet someone must lead the allied forces to war. And the only state that could command the consent of most of the Greeks was Sparta, the *hegemon* of Greece. But since *hegemonia* was based in suprem-acy in rank, a state unwilling to admit its inferiority would neither enroll itself under the leader nor obey its orders, whatever the need of the rest of the Greeks.[25]

So it was that Argos, the ancestral rival of Sparta, refused to join the war against Persia if the Spartans were in command. Argos was not as strong as Sparta, let alone the Peloponnesian alliance Sparta had been assembling over the past decades; and some fifteen years before the Persian invasion, Sparta had defeated Argos bloodily in war. But rank depended only in part upon brute power. Great deeds in myth and history also contributed to rank, regardless of how much power might have been lost since those deeds

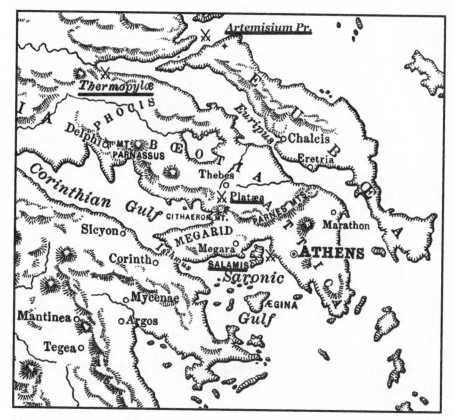

MAP 1.4 Greece in the Persian War, 480–479 BC

were done. And in the time of stories, the deeds of Argos had been second to none.

Argos insisted that she was entitled to lead all the Greeks to war, as had the Argives of old. But Argos would waive her rights and settle for sharing the command with Sparta, sharing it on the basis of equality—if the Spartans also bound themselves to peace with Argos for thirty years, until a new generation of Argives had risen to manhood to replace those the Spartans had slaughtered fifteen years before.[26]

The Spartans knew this ploy for what it was, an attempt to extort a revision of the ranking of the two states settled in Sparta's favor by their recent war, then freeze that revision in place until Argos was ready to joust again for outright supremacy. So the Spartans replied that, inasmuch as they possessed two kings and the Argives only one, any sharing of authority must be on the basis of two Spartan votes, and one Argive. "They would rather be ruled by the barbarians than yield a jot to the Lacedaemonians," replied the Argives in anger. The envoys of Sparta must leave the land of Argos before sunset, or they would be treated as enemies. Argos stood apart from the defense of Greece against the Persians.[27]

Athens, unlike Argos, was not a city unable to obey the Spartans out of rivalry and resentment. In the age of heroes, Athens had been a state of but second-rate glory (nothing to compare to Argos, say, or Thebes, the seat of Heracles), and she was only now emerging from a long period of shadow. In the middle years of the previous century, her tyrant Pisistratus had adorned the city with splendid works of man, but more recently Athens had been a place of no great might by land and, indeed, of great political turmoil, which had encouraged the Spartans to send armies in 511 and 508 BC. By 480 BC Athens' internal strife was over—the establishment of democracy in 507 BC had put a stop at least to the physical battles of Athens' aristocratic factions—and she had since enjoyed successes against her neighbors (and had a monument boasting that she had "quenched their *hybris*" to show for it). But Athens had unwisely supported a failed revolt by the Greek subjects of the Great King of Persia (499–493 BC), and when the Persians in 490 BC sent a punitive expedition against Athens, Athens' position in Greece was revealed by the fact that, with the exception of a single tiny neighbor, no Greek states came to help her. Nearly alone the Athenians had to throw back the Persians at the famous battle of Marathon.[28]

Athens in 480 BC could hardly claim to be a rival of Sparta for the hegemony of Greece. What Athens had, however—thanks to the fortuitous discovery of a rich vein of silver in her territory in 483 BC—was a great war fleet of two hundred galleys, much the largest among the Greeks. Even so, in the war against the Persians, the Athenians yielded command at sea to the Spartans, not least because the other Greeks would not follow the Athenians. The Greeks (Argos aside) might be willing to admit they were second in rank to Sparta, and so defer to her, but they would not yield place to a runner-up in rank like Athens.[29]

Athens, for her part, while willing to yield place to Sparta, was not willing to yield to Gelon, tyrant of the even less venerable Syracuse, a Sicilian colony of Corinth. Rich and powerful, the tyrant offered to make gigantic contributions to the war against Persia, but only if given command of the whole Greek force. The Spartans would not hear of it. "Much would Agamemnon, the descendent of Pelops, lament," the historian Herodotus has the Spartan envoy reply to Gelon, "if he heard of the hegemony being taken away from Sparta by Gelon and the Syracusans!" No, Gelon must place himself under Lacedaemonian command or not fight at all. So be it, rejoined Gelon: he would accept only half the command, either of the

Greek land forces or of the fleet. Since the Spartans would not give up the land command, Gelon turned his eyes on the fleet.[30]

Now the Athenians would not consent. Not only did they provide the largest naval contingent, they said, but "the race of the Athenians was the most ancient, and alone of the Greeks they had never changed habitation, and one of their countrymen [the very minor hero Menestheus, as any Athenian would know] Homer had identified as the best of all those who came to Troy at drawing up and disposing an army," thereby offering a perfect summary of how Greeks measured the rank of a state, by combining present power with ancient renown. The rank of Athens, the Athenians were saying, was higher than that of Syracuse, which was, however mighty in treasure and in arms, only a lowly colony in the distant west. It was unseemly, then, for the Syracusans to presume to command Athenians. In the end, neither Sparta nor Athens would yield place to Gelon, and so Gelon abided at home, counting his men and his money. "Report to Greece," he sniffed, "that the spring has been taken out of the year."[31]

Against Xerxes, then, the Spartans commanded the Greek allies both by land and by sea. When the Greeks settled upon the narrows of Thermopylae in central Greece as a choke point where an outnumbered army could defy the world, it was the Spartan king Leonidas who commanded the contingents the Greek allies sent to defend it. It was Leonidas who led the Greeks when they threw back the Persians from Thermopylae; it was Leonidas whose position was turned when a Greek traitor led Persian soldiers over mountain paths behind him; it was Leonidas who ordered the rest of the Greeks to withdraw to safety; and it was the doomed Leonidas who led the Three Hundred Spartans in their final stand, because the code of the Spartans forbade retreat.

In addition to the army that beat against Thermopylae, the Persians had brought a great fleet into Greece, one whose passage south had to be blocked, lest it land men behind Thermopylae. Another Spartan, Eurybiades, ruled the combined Greek fleet that guarded the sea flank of Leonidas, battling the Persians to two timber-shattering stalemates in the narrows off Cape Artemisium. This was before the fall of Thermopylae rendered the Greek harbors vulnerable by land and made the Greek navy withdraw toward the south.

After forcing Thermopylae, Xerxes marched south and accepted the submission of mighty Thebes, the head city of Boeotia and one of the powers of Greece. Then he marched south again against Athens—the Athenians would not surrender but evacuated their folk to the Peloponnese—and brought his fleet, much reduced by storms, around the horn of Attica. It was the Spartan Eurybiades again who led the Greek ships to face Xerxes in the waters off Athens. And it was the Spartan Eurybiades whom Themistocles, the guileful Odysseus of the age and admiral of the Athenians, tricked into facing the Persians in the tight strait between Attica and the island of Salamis, when Eurybiades and the rest of the admirals of the Greeks wanted to retreat. At the battle of Salamis, the Greeks prevailed, and the Great King's fleet was driven pell-mell back into Asia. Soon the Great King himself followed with part of his army, although a smaller force remained to face the Greeks the following year (479 BC) in Boeotia, on the fatal field of Plataea.

The array of the Greeks at Plataea, the climactic battle of the war against the Persians, is the fullest catalogue we have of the ranking of the states of Greece, since it was by rank that the allies were disposed by the Spartans. Naturally the Lacedaemonians themselves, as the hegemons of Greece, held the traditional place of honor on the right of the allied line. Second in honor was the extreme left, and for this place a quarrel broke out between mid-sized Tegea, Sparta's oldest ally in the Peloponnese, and swelling Athens.[32]

Tegea had brought fifteen hundred men to the battle; Athens came with eight thousand. But despite the disparity in their contributions, Tegea claimed preference because the city had always held the place of second honor in the joint expeditions of Sparta and her allies—and had held that position for a reason the Tegeans considered irrefutable. In the time before the Trojan War, the Tegeans explained, when the sons of Heracles were trying to invade the Peloponnese, the fate of all was pledged upon the outcome of a single combat between Hyllus, one of those doughty sons, and the king of Tegea. The king of Tegea had won, and so the sons of Heracles had been turned back. And in later times, the Tegeans went on to add, they had not only defeated other states in war but even prevailed several times over the Spartans themselves.[33]

Against the claims of Tegea to the position of honor, the Athenians urged not their eight thousand hoplites, their two hundred ships, or their chests of shining silver, but the fact that when the sons of Heracles were wandering in exile, it had been the Athenians who gave them refuge; that the Athenians had recovered by war and buried the bodies of the Seven Against Thebes; that they had prevailed over the Amazons, the appalling warrior women who invaded Attica—all this still before the Trojan War; that they had been glorious in the Trojan War (a wee fib); and that alone the Athenians had defeated the forty-six nations of Asia at Marathon eleven years before. This last achievement they mentioned not to claim any special expertise in fighting Persians but as if it were a supreme high deed that trumped the claims of Tegea to superiority in rank.[34]

Soberly weighing the claims of both parties, the Spartans awarded the honorable left flank to the Athenians, and the Tegeans the third place in honor, second after the Spartans on the right. To the left of the Tegeans, and so inferior to them, came the five thousand Corinthians (prominent, too, in myth and third in strength in the Peloponnese, after Sparta and Argos), then Arcadian Orchomenus, a small city that could send only six hundred men but had, in the time of heroes, been lord over Arcadia, and so still ranked high. Next came much larger Sicyon, with its three thousand men—but in myth, inferior to Orchomenus—and so on down the line, the Spartans carefully balancing the past glory of each state against its present strength. Mycenae, the seat of Agamemnon, and her neighbor Tiryns, now villages with but four hundred men between them, nonetheless ranked higher than the thousand of Phlius for their ancient fame. Finally the inglorious nadir of Corinth's northwestern colonies, Leucas and Ambracia, was reached. For as the mainlanders had made clear to Gelon of Syracuse, colonies were by their very nature inferior to the states of old Greece. Last of all there were two hundred men from Pale (where?), on the island of Cephallenia in the Ionian Sea: a place wholly bereft of either strength or fame, although Odysseus' Ithaca was thought to have lain nearby. But since in this array the extreme left was claimed as second in honor (this was not true in all Greek arrays), a second concentration of distinction built up beyond the men of Pale. Next to the Athenians stood the six hundred Plataeans; having the battle occur on one's territory gave a state a claim to preferment, and they were close friends of the Athenians, the only state that had come to help Athens eleven years before at Marathon. Then came the three thousand Megarians and then the five hundred Aeginetans, next to the men of Pale but, one suspects, shying fastidiously from their lowliness.

Counting inwards from both the glorious right and the only-slightly-less-glorious left allowed the perplexed Spartans—whose task was rather like that of a young hostess trying to work out the seating plan, honoring strict precedence, for a dinner with the Chancellor of the Duchy of Lancaster, the Graf von Kielmansegg, and the Panchen Lama—to reconcile with minimal offense the long-established relative rankings of states within the Spartan alliance and the claims of new and important allies from beyond the Peloponnese. And they seem to have succeeded, for nobody refused to fight—something that Greeks, as Argos and Gelon of Syracuse show, were perfectly willing to do if they felt their rank slighted. For this task the Spartans were actually fortunate that neither Argos nor Thebes fought on the Greek side at the battle: given the strength and ancient pomp of both of these powers, it would have been far harder to decide whom to put in second place. And, given mid-sized Tegea's willingness to joust for second place with enormous Athens, one suspects that those greater cities, if present, would have ranked a quarrelsome second and third, while Athens would have been pushed down to a humiliating fourth.[35]

Under the Spartan general Pausanias, the Greeks defeated the Persians at the battle of Plataea (479 BC), winning "the most famous victory of all those of which we know." On the right the Spartans and Tegeans turned the Persians to flight, while the Athenians on the left flank broke the Thebans, who were present as minions of the Persians. But if the Tegeans and Athenians were brave in the battle, the Lacedaemonians were braver yet, says Herodotus, once again reaffirming their rightful hegemony over Greece.[36]

At Plataea, too, the Spartans had their revenge for the death of Leonidas at Thermopylae. Obedient to the oracle at Delphi, the Spartans had made a formal demand upon Xerxes to make reparations for the killing of Leonidas, a demand that the Great King sneeringly referred for satisfaction to his general, Mardonius. Mardonius, who commanded the Persians at Plataea, was cut down by a Spartan in the battle. And so the debt was paid. Or was it? For the Persians had cut off the head of the fallen Leonidas and nailed his corpse to a board. Did exact revenge, a Greek ally cheerfully suggested, not require that the Spartans do exactly the same to the body of Mardonius? No, decided the Spartan commander: the field of corpses at Plataea was in itself enough to avenge Leonidas and those who had died alongside him. A queasy-making moment, this morbid calculation of revenge to such a nicety—but such logic, as we will see, could determine the course of a war.[37]

On the very same day as Plataea, the Greeks believed, a second victory had been won against the Persians, when a Greek army had descended from the Greek fleet beneath Mount Mycale far across the Aegean Sea. Here, although a Spartan was once again in command, the men of Athens carried away the palm for valor. This victory encouraged a general revolt from Persia of the Greeks in the islands and on the eastern coast of the Aegean. And it was the power and glory they gathered as the eventual leaders of the cities that rebelled from Persia that, in time, raised the ambitions of Athens to joust with Sparta for rank.[38]

IN THE IMMEDIATE AFTERMATH OF the Greek victory over Persia in 479 BC, Athens and Sparta were friendly. After Salamis the Spartans had honored the cunning Themistocles, who had commanded the Athenian ships, for his wise council. The Spartan "cavalry," that honor roll of three hundred who fought on foot around the Spartan king, escorted the striking carriage the Spartans had given Themistocles all the way to the borders of Laconia, "and of all men, he is the only one of whom we know whom the Spartans escorted in this fashion."[39]

Still, the Athenians were wary. In both years of the war, the Spartans had failed to prevent the Persians from invading Attica, which meant that the Athenians had twice been forced to evacuate their entire population to the Peloponnese and the nearby islands. In the year of Salamis (480 BC), after the fall of Thermopylae, when the Athenians expected the Spartans to lead the Greek allies to meet the Persian King's army in the field in Boeotia, safely to the north of Athens, the Athenians were appalled to discover that the Peloponnesians were instead building a wall across the narrow Isthmus of Corinth, the land bridge that connected the Peloponnese to the rest of Greece. The Peloponnesians would not protect Attica. And so, marching unhindered through Boeotia into Attica, the Persians took revenge for their humiliation at Marathon ten years before, and in the absence of the people of Athens, they took that revenge instead on its wood and stone, destroying the houses and burning the city's temples. In their wrath, so the story goes, they even tore down the walls of the city, by hand an unimaginable labor.[40]

Even after the Greek victory at Salamis, the Spartans were no less untrustworthy. In the next year, 479 BC, when a smaller army of Persians marched toward Attica, the Spartans and their Peloponnesian allies again failed to come forth from the Isthmus as they had promised. Indeed, even when all the Athenians had been evacuated for a second time, and the Persians had entered Attica, wasting what remained of Athens, the Peloponnesians showed no great eagerness to move, putting the finishing touches instead to their wall on the Isthmus. Eventually (as the story comes down to us) the Athenians sent envoys to tell the Spartans that unless they marched, Athens would be forced to make a private peace with Persia. But even then the Spartan authorities tricked the Athenian ambassadors, putting off their reply day after day for ten days. Finally the Athenian envoys approached the Spartan authorities with a furious ultimatum, only to be smugly informed that no fewer than forty thousand men—five thousand Spartans and thirty-five thousand helot attendants—had departed in total silence in the dark of the previous night and were now well on their way to make war on the "strangers," as the Spartans called the barbarians.[41]

The doleful lesson that Athens took from these Peloponnesian betrayals was that the Spartans could not be trusted and that states beyond the Isthmus must fend for themselves if the Persians returned—which there was every reason to suspect they would, if only to avenge their defeat. Thus it was that when the Athenians returned to Athens after Plataea, they began to build a new circuit of walls around their city (?479 BC[42]). Hearing of this, the Spartans sent envoys to bid the Athenians stop. It would be safer, they said, if no city beyond the Isthmus had walls so that the Persians would have no strong places to hold. Would the Athenians join the Spartans in tearing down all the walls outside the Peloponnese?[43]

Sparta's request to Athens was the instruction of a superior in rank—a *hegemon*—to an inferior in rank, who could be expected to defer to her superior's desires. But this, with her own protection at stake, Athens was no longer prepared to do. In fact, the Athenians took the opportunity to give the Spartans a gentle poke, a beautifully symmetrical jab in exchange for the trick the Spartans had played on Athens by delaying their reply to Athens' envoys from day to day while they finished their own wall on the Isthmus earlier in the year.

Themistocles had the Athenians send him to Sparta on the instant but told them to hold back the rest of the ambassadors until the walls of the city were high enough to defend—all Athenians, even the women and children, then labored to raise them as quickly as possible. Once Themistocles had arrived at Lacedaemon, rather than presenting himself before the authorities, he put the Spartans off day after day with the excuse that he was waiting for his colleagues; he was puzzled, he professed with wide, innocent eyes, that they had not yet arrived.[44]

When travelers reported to the Spartans in the most positive terms that the walls around Athens were nearly finished, Themistocles still denied it and prevailed upon his hosts to send a proper Spartan committee of inspection to verify the rumors—and when they did, he sent along a message telling the Athenians to keep the Spartan inspectors in comfortable custody until he and his colleagues returned. For he feared that when the Spartans learned the truth, they might not let him go.

Finally Themistocles' fellow envoys arrived at Lacedaemon, bearing to the cunning Athenian the happy news that the walls of Athens were, at last, high enough. Now Themistocles presented himself before the Spartans and told them the Athenians would no longer defer to Sparta on matters relating to their own safety. Hereafter Athens, Thucydides has Themistocles remark, intended to be "of equal weight in the common councils." And whether Themistocles actually said anything of the sort, this utterance is an early appearance of the idea of Athenian equality with Sparta—an idea that would prove of immense and sorrowful significance in the future.[45]

Soon after the Persian War, the Athenians began to accumulate the practical basis of their coming sense of equality with the Spartans: an alliance of their own. After the Greek victory at Mycale on the coast of Asia Minor

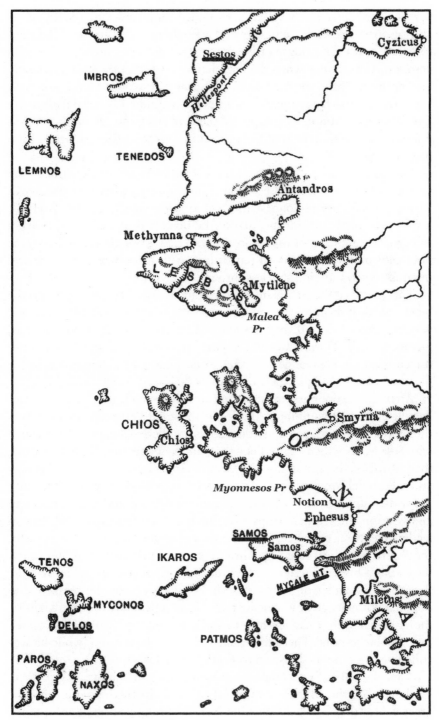

MAP 1.5 The Founding of the Delian League, 479–478 BC

(479 BC), the Greek allied fleet, surrounded on all sides by the joyful revolt of dozens of Greek cities from the Persians, sailed to the Hellespont to break down the bridges of boats that had brought the host of Xerxes across to Greece. But when the fleet arrived, it found the bridges already broken by a storm. So the Spartan king in command sailed home with the Greek ships from the Peloponnese, no doubt to the alarm of the Greeks of Asia Minor, who expected the Persians to put down their rebellion with energetic cruelty if the protection of the victorious Greek allies were withdrawn.[46]

Nor can the rebels have liked the tales they heard of the council the Greeks held on the Aegean island of Samos directly after their victory at Mycale, when the Peloponnesians urged that the Greek rebels of Asia Minor be uprooted and transplanted to the mainland of Greece. They were to occupy the houses of those Greeks who had given aid to the King (the Boeotians and Thessalians, in particular), with those wretches to be cast out and sent wandering shoeless through the world.[47]

This proposal the Athenians had defeated with vehement argument: the rebels, most of them Ionians, were their colonists, they said. They were the very children of the Athenian nation and no affair of the Peloponnesians, members of the Dorian race of the Greeks: in myth the Ionians had been driven from the Peloponnese by the Dorians and taken ship at Athens for the coast of Asia Minor, where the area of their settlement was called Ionia.

After the Peloponnesians departed the Hellespont, the Athenians, under their general Xanthippus (father of the great Pericles) remained with the rebels. The Persians had strong garrisons there—the greatest of which was Sestos, to which many Persians and their creatures had fled when they heard of the coming of the Greeks. To Sestos, then, the Athenians and their rebel compatriots laid siege, and under siege they kept it far into the winter, until those inside the city ran out of food and were reduced to gnawing on the leather straps from their beds, whereupon the Persian leaders crept out of the city, and the Greeks inside surrendered it. One of the Persians was captured by Thracians in the neighborhood and found his end as a human sacrifice in their uncouth rites. But no luckier was the Persian commander of Sestos, who had plundered temple treasures and even had knowledge of women within a holy sanctuary. Taken in flight by the Athenians, they carried him to the place where Xerxes had crossed over the Hellespont. There they nailed him to a board and, while he was still alive to see, stoned his son to death before his eyes.[48]

After the fall of Sestos, the season for sailing and fighting in 479 BC being long over, the Athenians returned to their city, taking with them the great cables that had held together Xerxes' bridges of boats in order to dedicate them in their temples. In the next year (478 BC), when the seas became friendly, the Spartans rejoined the naval campaign against Persia, although on a much smaller scale, another sign that they were losing interest in the Greek rebels against the King. To command the allied fleet, the Spartans sent Pausanias, the victor of Plataea. He led twenty Peloponnesian and thirty Athenian ships, but now a great part of the fleet was made up by the Aegean islanders and the Greeks of the coast of Asia Minor, those who had revolted against the Persians after Mycale.[49]

Sailing far to the south and east, Pausanias attacked Cyprus (settled by Greeks but long a possession of the Great King), and then made his way back to the Hellespont, where he assailed Byzantium, which was still under Persian control. But despite his vigor as a leader, Pausanias was still very much a Spartan. Expecting prompt obedience, when disappointed, as he often was, he turned harsh and cruel. Such discipline was foreign to the other Greeks, who regarded obedience to their military leaders much as they regarded their cities' attention to their *hegemon*, Sparta: as a form of uncoerced deference, that is, a tribute willingly given to the leader's admirable qualities. Certainly their obedience abided in a wholly different and gentler realm than Pausanias' walking stick, which the Ionian rebels were now amazed to discover bruising their freeborn persons. This seemed to them not like the tender persuasions of a true leader but the oppression of a despot. And so complaints, many of them exaggerated, were made to Sparta, and the Spartans summoned Pausanias home to answer them.[50]

In the absence of a Spartan chief, the rebels had to choose a leader of their own. While the Spartans had demonstrated but tepid interest in protecting the newly revolted Greeks the year before, the Athenians had persisted long into the winter. And so the rebellious states—many of them, at least in legend, colonists of an older Athens and sharers in the common rites of the Ionians on the holy island of Delos—now turned to Athens. The Athenians, for their part, accepted this leadership initially on the same terms as the Spartans had held the power, as a position of hegemony, in which the allies would obey Athens, uncoerced, out of respect for her rank.[51]

By the time the Lacedaemonians had finished acquitting Pausanias of the important charges against him—one of them the outlandish accusation that he, the victor of Plataea, was conspiring with the Persians—and sent out another commander in his place, the Athenians were firmly in control of the allied fleet. The Spartans did not press their rights, and the new Spartan commander, finding no one to obey him, simply returned home. Never enthusiastic about the naval campaign to begin with, the Spartans felt confident in the friendship of the Athenians. Even after being tricked in the affair of Athens' walls, says Thucydides, the Spartans "manifested no open anger toward the Athenians . . . because they were friendly toward them because of their zeal in the Persian War, but nevertheless, not getting what they wanted they were secretly vexed."[52]

"Open anger," had the Spartans felt it toward Athens as the result of Athens' behavior, might well, to Greek thinking, have resulted in war: between states, *hybris* produced anger that demanded a vengeance often sought in battle. And judging by the trick the Athenians used to forestall invasion while they were raising their walls, the Athenians must have considered it likely that the Spartans would interpret their disregard for Sparta's will as *hybris* and go to war over it. But here "friendship" turned away Sparta's wrath. Friendship between Greek states reduced sensitivity to acts that, on other occasions, might be considered *hybris* and result in war. This helps to explain why, although minor acts of disrespect between Greek states were constant and arrogant attitudes perpetual, war between Greek cities was not. States varied in their degree of sensitivity to insult, and that sensitivity depended, in large part, on the states' overall relationship with each other.[53]

There are hints that Sparta was not altogether happy to give up command of the naval war against the Persians. Perhaps most worrying to the Spartans about relinquishing the protection of the rebels to the Athenians was that the Greeks might interpret it as a loss of rank: would the Athenians (as a later author thought) be deemed to be "taking that glory from the Spartans?" Indeed, there may have been controversy about this at Sparta. Centuries later a story—perhaps nothing more than an invention—swims up from the murk, claiming that in the 470s BC the Spartans debated whether Athenian supremacy at sea was to be endured, and many Spartans thought not, arguing that naval power should be wrested from the Athenians, by war if necessary. But no action was taken, and the debate was bought to an end by the laconic croak of a Spartan elder: "it does not profit Sparta to dispute for the sea."[54]

While the Spartans consigned the defense of the Greeks by sea to the Athenians, there was much for the Spartans to do on the land, much unfinished business from the invasion of Xerxes. Thebes had been compelled to cleanse itself of those associated with the Persians. Not so horse-riding Thessaly, further north, which had joined the Persians with embarrassing alacrity, and where the powerful line of the Aleuadae still held sway, unashamed. And so to Thessaly the Spartans made an expedition; yet, victorious in battle, they failed to topple the Aleuadae, who were said to have bribed the Spartan king in command (certainly he went into exile after the campaign).[55]

Nor was Thessaly Sparta's only frustration in the 470s BC. Delphi, the seat of Greece's most important oracle, was a shrine rather than a city. In the absence of divine intervention (Apollo himself, the Greeks thought, had saved Delphi and her treasures from the Persians), the protection of Delphi was invested in a committee of Greek states, the Amphictyonic League. After the Persian War the Spartans tried to expel from the Amphictyonic League those states that had not helped against the Persians in the war: Thessaly, Thebes, and Argos. As in the case of the walls of Athens and the squabble over what do with the rebels in Asia Minor, here again Athens refused to defer, Themistocles (the story has it) leading the opposition. Once again the Spartans did not get their way.[56]

After the Persian War, the Spartans also encountered opposition in the Peloponnese itself. Back in ?494 BC, the Argives had been humiliated by Sparta at the battle of Sepeia: so many Argive warriors were killed in this war, the story was told, that the women of Argos had to drive the Spartans away. These losses were the reason Argos demanded that Sparta make a treaty of peace with her as a condition of fighting against Persia. And to make up these losses, the Argives had even been obliged to admit to citizenship the residents of some of their subject communities (agonizing to any city in old Greece, where the citizens thought they shared common blood, and especially to the proud Argives). Argos, we may believe, was eager to take revenge against Sparta, to reassert its rank, and to reestablish its power in the Peloponnese. And after the defeat of the Persians, Argos managed to recruit to her side Sparta's old crony Tegea—the city that had challenged the right of Athens to the position of second honor at Plataea and fought next to the Spartans in the battle—and perhaps others of the Arcadians who inhabited the mountainous center of the Peloponnese.[57]

The Spartans met the allies in battle in the territory of Tegea and prevailed. But although Argos now drops (briefly) out of the story, the Spartans soon had to fight another war against the better part of the Arcadians (Tegea included), defeating them as well at the battle of Dipaea. We see this Peloponnesian turmoil extremely dimly—most of this we have to deduce from a bare list of battles in which Sparta was victorious. But evidently Sparta, in the years after Plataea, was being made to fight for her lordship of the Peloponnese.[58]

WHILE THE SPARTANS WERE FIGHTING in Greece, the Athenians were fighting in the Aegean. To protect Greece against the return of the Persians, to uproot Persia's remaining holdings in the Aegean, and to take revenge upon the Persians for the invasion, Athens and her new allies needed to administer a common fleet, and they soon found it necessary to settle upon a quota system for contributions. The great Aegean islands—Chios, Lesbos, and Samos—contributed ships and rowers, but the great majority of the rebels against Persia preferred to contribute in silver alone. Aristides "the Just," an Athenian of exemplary character, assessed the contribution of each state (?477 BC). The silver was to be kept in the treasury of the temple of Apollo on the small Aegean island of Delos, a shrine sacred in common to the greater Ionian race, and was to be administered by officials from Athens called "treasurers of the Greeks." There, too, the allies would meet to mull the common weal. And upon the isle of Delos, the league was sworn, as blocks of massy iron were cast down into the sea, the alliance to last until they should surface once again.[59]

The first business of this new Delian League was to winkle out the last Persian forts on the Aegean coast and to clear the sea of marauders, always remaining in readiness should the Great King make a move. A sorrowful war, too, the league made in those early years upon Pausanias, the Spartan who had led the Greeks to victory at Plataea, only to be falsely accused by his fellow Greeks when he subsequently led the Greek fleet against the Persians. Disgraced by his recall and the charges against him, he had made his way back to the Hellespont and set himself up as despot in Byzantium; and now, in truth, he *was* intriguing with the Persians. Driven out by the Athenians and their allies, he then made his way back to Sparta. There, his crimes proved against him—and now he was accused of planning revolution with the helots as well—Pausanias took refuge in a hut in the precinct of a temple where he could not be touched without sacrilege. The Spartans simply took the roof off the hut to expose Pausanias to the weather, walled up the door, and starved him to death.[60]

The basic purpose of the Delian League was to maintain a powerful fleet in being in case the Great King made a move against the Greeks. In ?467 BC the Great King finally answered the Delian League's wondering anticipation, and a tremendous battle between Greeks and Persians was fought by land and sea at Eurymedon on the southern coast of Asia Minor. The Athenian general Cimon led the allied fleet (Miltiades, his father, had been the hero of the battle of Marathon in 490 BC). Two hundred of the King's galleys were captured or destroyed. Afterwards, the Athenians dedicated a great bronze palm tree at Delphi to celebrate the victory: from the top, a gilt statue of Athena surveyed the world.[61]

In time the Delian League lost its early luster and geniality. Some states attempted to withdraw, but since the league protected all alike, its members would not allow any one state to scant its contributions. And so the league of rebels against the Persians, ever more dominated by mighty Athens, fought small wars with small rebels against the league. Indeed, over time the league began to look more and more like a miniature version of the Persian empire itself, with the Athenians borrowing Persian methods of rule and exploitation. A later author rather breathlessly points out the implications of all these deeds for the rank of Athens: "The Athenians were far the first in glory and courage, famous through almost the whole inhabited world. They caused their *hegemonia* to grow to such a degree that, by themselves, without the Lacedaemonians and Peloponnesians, they defeated great Persian forces by land and by sea, and humbled the famous *hegemonia* of the Persians." The feats of the Athenians were raising the rank to which the Athenians thought themselves entitled. But what of the Spartans? An Athenian speaker much later in Thucydides draws the obvious conclusion: "After the Persian wars we had a fleet, and so got rid of the rule (*archē*) and supremacy in rank (*hegemonia*) of the Lacedaemonians, it being no more fitting for us to obey them, than they us, except insofar as they were stronger at the time."[62]

But not yet. In the years of Athens' eastern triumphs, her good relations with Sparta were preserved not least because Cimon, Athens' hammer of the Persians, was such a convinced admirer of Lacedaemon. "That's not how they do it at Sparta!" he would roar in frustration at his undisciplined Athenian countrymen. Playing an ever larger role in Athenian politics after the Persian War, Cimon was a political rival to Themistocles, Athens' other champion against the Persians at a different needful hour. Eventually Cimon won the struggle, and Themistocles was ostracized (?471/470 BC), settling into exile at Argos, Sparta's enemy. When the Spartans later brought against the exile absurd charges of conspiring with the Persians, Themistocles' political enemies at Athens were only too delighted to cooperate, and the Athenians were persuaded to lay him under a sentence of death. Now he was harried from Greece altogether, fleeing ultimately to refuge at the court of the Great King of Persia. On this occasion, unlike when Athens had rebuilt her walls, unlike when the Peloponnesians tried to evacuate the Greeks of Ionia to the mainland, and unlike when the Spartans tried to cleanse the Delphic Amphictyony of those who had not gone against Persians, what the Spartan *hegemon* asked, Athens deferentially did. Two of the three acts of Athenian opposition to Sparta were associated with Themistocles. But now friendly Cimon was in charge at Athens.[63]

THE FRIENDSHIP OF ATHENS AND Sparta was soon to be tested. A few years after Themistocles was driven from Greece, there was a great earthquake at Lacedaemon (?465 BC); the helots, taking this as a sign from the gods, revolted against their Spartan masters and were joined as well by some of Sparta's subject peoples, the *perioeci*. The Spartans dreaded a revolt of the helots above all things, and in their time of peril, they summoned all their friends and allies to help them, the Athenians included. The controversy that erupted at Athens over whether to send an expedition to assist the *hegemon* of Greece reveals the Athenians' new attitude toward their city's rank.[64]

The Athenian politician Ephialtes opposed the mission, we are told, arguing that Athens "ought not help or raise up again a city that was a rival to Athens, but to let the pride of Sparta be overthrown and be trodden underfoot." To Ephialtes the rebellion of the helots was an opportunity to surpass Sparta in rank. But his opponent Cimon carried the Athenians with the argument that Athens should "not allow Hellas to become lame, nor Athens to be deprived of her yoke-fellow." In Cimon's metaphors—a man with two legs or a yoke with two oxen—Athens and Sparta were equal in rank, and that was as it should be. Neither Athenian politician, however, not even the pro-Spartan Cimon, spoke of Sparta as Athens' *hegemon*, with any claim to deference. Athens' victories over the Persians, as well as the glory she drew from being *hegemon* of the Delian League, had raised the Athenians' own sense of the rank of their city. Athens would help Sparta as Sparta's equal, not as Sparta's subordinate.[65]

Seeking symbolic equality with a *hegemon*—Cimon's hope—was a characteristic ambition of Greek states. During the Persian War, both Argos and Gelon of Syracuse, as we have seen, sought equality with Sparta. And now that it had been sparked, Athenian yearning for equality with Sparta would long endure. In the next century, when Sparta was a shattered power, the Athenians were to debate how they could make an alliance with the Spartans on the basis of "perfect equality." Should the Spartans command on the land and the Athenians on the sea? No, that would not be quite equal enough, since Athenian citizens serving in the army would have to obey Spartan commands, while Spartan citizens, none of whom served in the fleet, would not have to obey those of Athenians. The solution was to trade the leadership on both land and sea every five days. Absurd, we think: hardly a way to run a war. Yet this compromise shows how overwhelmingly important the notion of equality could be to Greek states—to those states, at least, that were not in a position to claim and defend *sole* hegemony. For the Spartan reactions to Argos and Gelon reveal that the normal response of a *hegemon*, however great her need, to another state's request for equality was firm refusal.[66]

Victorious in the debate at Athens, Cimon led an Athenian army to help the Spartans, and with the aid of all their allies, the Spartans defeated the rebels in the field and besieged them upon Mount Ithome in Messenia. After their allies had departed, however, the Spartans discovered to their vexation that they could not dislodge the helots from Ithome. And so, after some years of desultory siege, they called for their allies once again, including Cimon and the Athenians (?462 BC).[67]

"The first open point of difference between the Lacedaemonians and the Athenians," recorded Thucydides, "was the result of this campaign." The Spartans besieging Ithome conceived a suspicion of the Athenians and sent them away, alone of those whom they had just summoned to help. Not that the Spartans voiced their suspicion; they politely told the Athenians that they were no longer needed. But the Athenians "took it ill and thought it unworthy of themselves to be treated so by the Lacedaemonians," and straight away, after they got home to Athens, they renounced the old alliance against the Persians that acknowledged Sparta's leadership and instead made a pact with Sparta's enemies, the Argives. And both Athens and Argos also made an alliance with Thessaly. Eventually—we are not told how soon—this break with Sparta led to war between Sparta and Athens, and this is all the explanation Thucydides seems to have thought he needed to give for the cause of the conflict. Yet this would have surprised no Greek reader, who would have understood such causation implicitly. The Athenians felt they had been subjected to insult, *hybris*, and *hybris*, the Greeks thought, was the cause of many wars in their world.[68]

Between cities, *hybris* could range from a military attack to any act of disrespect or failure to pay respect where respect was felt to be due. In the absence of any act at all, *hybris* could even be deduced from the suspicion that another party harbored an arrogant attitude—what the Greeks called "thinking big." Historians are sometimes puzzled to see overt acts of national aggression interpreted by the Greeks as *hybris*, since today's habit is the contrary one of interpreting insult, where possible, as aggression. We do not like to think we are going to war because we have been insulted; we prefer to convince ourselves that we are fighting a war to protect our families, our homes. But the Greeks much preferred to think in terms of wars of revenge for *hybris*: revenge was among the noblest possible motivations for war.[69]

For his Greek reader to understand the causes of the forthcoming hostilities between Athens and Sparta, then, Thucydides needed only to allude to the well-known road that led from rank to *hybris* to anger to revenge. The puzzle, then, concerns not the immediate cause of the trouble between Sparta and Athens: the cause fit in a well-worn Greek pattern. The puzzle is why Spartans insulted the Athenians, or if they did not mean to do so (as seems likely), why the Athenians had become so sensitive as to interpret being sent home, despite the Spartans' trying to put a polite face on their dismissal, as an act of *hybris*, as a blood insult to be avenged by war. At the end of the Persian War, after all, Athens and Sparta had been "friends," and friends ignored potentially insulting acts by their friends—as, indeed, the Spartans had done repeatedly.

In fact, since the end of the Persian War, Athens and Sparta had come to have profoundly different senses of their relative ranks. The Spartans were still acting as supreme in rank in Greece, as *hegemon*. Indeed, the alliance against the Persians that manifested Spartan primacy was still, notionally, in force. And the Spartans assumed that the Athenians still respected their superiority. The Athenians had sentenced Themistocles to death when the Spartans asked, after all, and the Athenians had also twice come against the helots when the Spartans called. These were the actions of a deferential inferior, one who would not feel insulted if sent home by its *hegemon*. But at Athens, neither anti-, nor even pro-, Spartan sentiment now accepted that Athens was still Sparta's inferior in rank: her successes against the Persians and her lordship over her own alliance made that impossible in Athenian eyes. Athens had come to Ithome as an equal of Sparta—so even friendly Cimon insisted. Athens saw herself as repaying a favor to Sparta or as doing a favor in order to be able to call upon Sparta in the future: that, after all, was how equals dealt with each other. And to dismiss an equal was to undercut the Athenians' estimation of themselves, to treat them "unworthily": in short, to inflict *hybris* upon them.[70]

Keenly did the Athenians feel the Spartan insult. Athens was unwilling to accept the Spartans' polite pretence that the Athenians were simply no longer needed. As a power pressing a claim to a new, higher rank, the Athenians were acutely sensitive to any perceived attempt to push them back down to their traditional, humbler place. A Greek senator of Rome, many centuries later, put his finger on the dynamic at work. Those whose rank is hallowed by time are hard to offend, he said, and do not look to the world for constant reassurance. But those whose rank is recently acquired are apt to interpret even the tiniest failure to pay respect as an intolerable insult. So it was with Sparta, the old *hegemon* of Greece, which had proved willing to ignore Athens' various impertinences, and up-and-coming Athens, which could not ignore even the slightest apparent lack of respect from Sparta.[71]

The Athenians were mortally offended by an act the Spartans did not intend as an offense. This war over rank arose not from an overt act of *hybris* but rather from the interpretation of a perhaps tactless act as such. And when a city had a chip on its shoulder, as Athens now did, events in the past were subject to reinterpretation as well, as the offended party searched for yet more *hybris* to stoke its anger. The Greeks had an unsettling fable about this habit, in which the brindled wolf, having cornered the fuzzy lambkin, labored to justify devouring him. "You insulted me last year!" cried the wolf. "I wasn't even born last year," replied the lamb. "Aren't you eating my grass?" "I'm too young to eat grass." "Didn't you drink from my spring?" "I drink only my mother's milk." But the wolf ate the lamb all the same.[72]

It is, therefore, like one of the suggestions of that wolf that we should probably understand the odd tale that Thucydides tells of a secret Spartan agreement to invade Attica in support of a rebellion from the Athenian alliance of Thasos, an island in the northern Aegean (?465 BC). The Spartans, he said, were conveniently prevented from keeping this engagement by the earthquake and the secession of the helots to Ithome. Thucydides no doubt thought the story true, but in fact it has all the signs of a manufactured casus belli: at once secret and stillborn, it was quite impossible to prove or disprove. Perhaps there had been messages sent between Thasos and Sparta: certainly it is easy to imagine the angry Athenian invention of, or elaboration upon, such contacts, in the hour of fury after Cimon's dismissal from Ithome.[73]

Cimon's association with the now-hated Spartans resulted in his own ostracism and exile upon his return to Athens with his insulted army (?461 BC). His rival Ephialtes, who had opposed helping the Spartans, was briefly supreme, but not long after Cimon's exile he was mysteriously murdered. The long war in Greece touched off by Athens' sense of insult, the war that dominated the middle years of the fifth century BC (?461–446/445 BC), would see the rise to power of Athens' greatest fifth-century statesman, Pericles.[74]

II

THE COMING OF THE
TEN YEARS' WAR

PERICLES, SON OF XANTHIPPUS, was an aristocrat of Athens. His father, whose name meant "Blond Horse" (horse names being the province of the grand since they implied the ability to afford the costly beasts), was a hero of the Persian War who had commanded Delian League expeditions in the years after Plataea and Mycale. Pericles' mother, Agariste (or "Very Best"), was descended from the line of the Sons of Alcmeon, a family so ancient and splendid that they had a two-century-old curse attaching to them, a distinction rather like a Victorian family owning a country house haunted by a particularly eminent ghost.

The manner of Pericles, like his family's position, was singularly lofty. He was a renowned master of the samurai-like impassivity that was a badge of rank among the Greeks. Never seen to laugh or become ruffled in any way, he did not weep at the funerals of his friends or even of his first-born son—though he did break down at the obsequies for his second, whose death threatened the extinction of his line. He dined at no man's house, for an iron reserve was hard to keep when the wine was poured; when forced by custom to attend a kinsman's wedding feast, he left before the drinking. Once a humble wretch was said to have shouted abuse at Pericles all day long in the market, but Pericles went about his business imperturbably and in the evening made his way home, still pursued by his screeching critic. Arriving at his own door, Pericles blandly bade a servant take a torch and escort the fellow safely home.[1]

A brilliant orator and hugely influential among the many, Pericles evoked mixed feelings among his peers. Some thought him arrogant, or his manner contrived simply for the sake of ambition. And so it may have been. For in early fifth-century BC Athenian politics, politicians often appear to have sought distinction by emphasizing a particularly admirable facet of their character, and Pericles' solemnity may have been in part a gambit to distinguish himself from his rivals. Themistocles had been known

FIGURE 2.1 Bust of Pericles

for his *mētis*, his cunning, the heroic quality of wily Odysseus that was so admired in ancient Greece. Aristides, who fixed the tribute of the members of the Delian League, was known for his singular justice. This was a good political choice, for it undermined Themistocles, so often Aristides' political opponent, whose displays of *mētis* encouraged rumors of corruption. The wealthy Cimon, in turn, pointed to his own admirable liberality through acts of public and private generosity. But this laid him open to suspicions that he was irresponsible and louche, something of an overgrown frat boy. Trying to make his name in a political world dominated by Cimon, it made sense for the younger Pericles to emphasize his distance from Cimon, and so polish his reputation for *sōphrosynē*, the outward self-control thought to signal inner wisdom.[2]

Over both the politics and the culture of Athens, Pericles exerted a singular sway. Educated in the new way by hired intellectuals, he was a patron of advanced thinking, and indeed of advanced thinkers, especially the cosmologist Anaxagoras and the sculptor Phidias—even though, in the way of advanced thinkers, they were apt to be prosecuted for impiety and fraud. In politics Pericles strove to close the gulf between the Athenian constitution, a participatory democracy, and Athenian reality, in which the poor were excluded from participation by virtue of their poverty. At his advice the Athenians built great structures that kept thousands in employment. It was Pericles who established pay for jurymen. Thanks to his influence, the Athenian fleet was sent out on maneuvers each year in peace, and the rowers duly paid. To far places the Athens of Pericles sent out colonies, where poor men were given land and became citizens of the newly founded cities. And Athenians were also given broad acres taken from defeated rebels from the Delian League, upon whom Athens imposed cleruchies, or "allotments," where Athenians received land without having to yield their Athenian citizenship.[3]

The perfect aristocrat in manner and the perfect democrat in politics, for the last fifteen years of his life Pericles was elected general every year (443–429 BC). The historian Thucydides, an admirer, described Pericles' reign as "a democracy in name, but in fact the rule of the first citizen." This was high praise, for to Thucydides, the Athenian democracy was undisciplined and bestial, much in need of a firm hand. The historian thought that Pericles commanded by his "worthiness," derived from his "rank and wisdom and outstanding integrity"—that he ruled his countrymen in the same gentle way in which a Greek *hegemon* was imagined to command the uncoerced respect and obedience of its allies. There was irony to this, because, however Pericles ruled at home, Athens' Aegean allies were no longer ruled in so kindly a fashion. The empire of the Athenians had become a dark thing, and under gentle, dignified Pericles, Athens' subjects were treated with great sternness. "Your empire," Thucydides has him say to the Athenians with appalling frankness, "is, to speak somewhat plainly, like a tyranny. To take it perhaps was wrong, but to let it go is unsafe."[4]

LONG PROMINENT IN ATHENIAN DOMESTIC politics, Pericles first appeared on the wider Greek stage during the war that convulsed Greece during the middle years of the fifth century BC. This war was not at first a struggle between the Athenians and Spartans; rather, it was an existing war into which both were eventually drawn. We do not know the ancient name for the whole conflict—if, indeed, it had one at all—but we call it the "First Peloponnesian War" (?461–446/445 BC) to distinguish it from the twenty-seven-year-long Peloponnesian War that began in 431 BC. That name is something of a pity, because it implies that this war was fought along the same axis of opposition—Athenians against Spartans—as the greater war. In fact, this earlier war was fought along at least two intersecting axes,

MAP 2.1 The First Peloponnesian War: Campaigns of ?458 and ?457 BC

Sparta against its longtime enemy Argos (with Athens as an ally of Argos) and Athens against maritime Corinth. And this was no fast-moving, targeted, toothy barracuda of a war: the First Peloponnesian War was more of a palsied octopus, with many tentacles, sometimes reaching out for enemies and sometimes at rest.

The war at mid-century arose out of local rivalries. Megara, strategically located on the Isthmus between the Peloponnese and Attica, was fighting over boundaries with Corinth, her neighbor to the west, and could get no aid or protection from Sparta, their mutual *hegemon*. Thus, to win help against Corinth, Megara left the Spartan alliance and joined herself instead to Athens, now—since the insult at Ithome—openly hostile to Sparta but so far (so far as we can see) inactive against Sparta in deeds.

The Athenians were delighted to accept the fealty of Megara: her adhesion added to the rank of Athens, and her defection detracted from that of Sparta. Besides, friendly control of the land bridge to the Peloponnese made an attack on Athens by Sparta and her allies substantially more complicated. The Megarians admitted Athenian garrisons to their city and its southern port of Nisaea, whereupon the Athenians built a set of long parallel walls to connect the two (the walls that they were later forced to take by

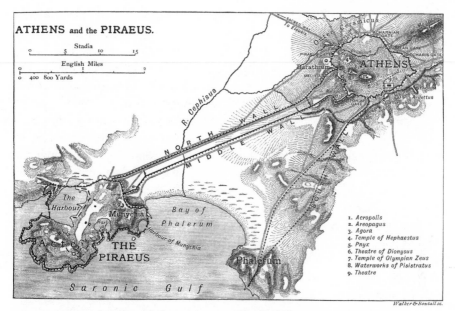

MAP 2.2 The Long Walls Between Athens and Piraeus, completed ?457 BC

subterfuge in 424 BC). Given their new hostility to Sparta and the rapid shifting of alliances, the Athenians also began to build their own set of long walls to connect Athens herself to her port of Piraeus, a distance of some five miles, extending the fortifications erected around Piraeus by Themistocles in the 470s BC.[5]

Corinth was fighting on two frontiers, for she was not only at war with Megara in the east but also with Athens' ally, Argos, across the hills to the south. Corinth and Argos had been fussing over Cleonae, a trifling enclave between them that was nevertheless desirable because it hosted the famous Nemean games, one of the four great pan-Hellenic festivals. In pursuit of her rivalry with Argos, Corinth also seems to have been supporting enemies of Argos on the Argolid peninsula, a hilly excrescence from the Peloponnesian coast that extended to the southeast of Argos and was occupied by a number of small Greek states.[6]

The conflict between Corinth and Argos seems the best explanation for the Athenians' first major reported action in the war (?458 BC), an attack on small Halieis, on the Argolid peninsula, which had evidently become allied to Corinth against Argos. There the Corinthians met, and defeated, the Athenians in battle. The Corinthians were accompanied by their smaller allies Epidaurus, their neighbor to the southeast, seat of the great temple of Asclepius, the healer (although on this occasion his votaries had anything

61

but healing on their minds), and by Sicyon, whose special cult was that of Dionysus, the god of wine and revelry, although now the men of Sicyon had exchanged the joys of Dionysus for the stern duty of war. The trio of Corinth, Epidaurus, and Sicyon will appear again: they were one of the massive solar systems of this war. And soon another considerable power was drawn in by their gravity: Aegina, an old naval rival of Athens.[7]

Aegina became involved in the war when the action moved from land to sea. After Athens' defeat by Corinth and her allies at Halieis, a naval battle was fought by the same parties in the Saronic Gulf, in which the Athenians prevailed. Aegina joined the war against Athens not long after. Aegina, an island off the Peloponnese, could be seen from Attica; Pericles therefore called it the "eyesore of the Piraeus" for its perennial hostility to Athens. Together with the feud between Sparta and Argos, that between Athens and Aegina was one of the old, fiery hatreds of Greece. Great traders, and not infrequently pirates, the Aeginetans paid special worship to Hecate, the fell goddess of magic and of ghosts. An earlier war between Athens and Aegina, and not the first, had been obliged to languish when the Greeks struck their truce to fight the Persians. But now Athens defeated Aegina at sea along with her allies, taking seventy ships.[8]

After besting their enemies on the water, the Athenians tackled the puzzle of landing an army on the island of Aegina itself, infamous for its rocks and reefs. Struggling ashore, the Athenians laid the city of Aegina under siege. Somehow the Corinthians and Epidaurians managed to transport three hundred mercenary hoplites into Aegina, but despite these reinforcements, they placed greater confidence in a plan to draw the Athenians away from their investment of the city. Athenian resources were stretched because, at the same time, Athens was also heavily engaged elsewhere on Delian League business, supporting a rebellion against the Great King in distant Egypt. And so, in the hope of compelling the Athenians to break the siege of Aegina, the Corinthians invaded the plain of Megara.[9]

The Corinthian plan failed. Rather than give up their stranglehold on hated Aegina to rescue Megara, the Athenians sent to Megara an army of boys and graybeards, those below or above the usual age of service and thus only called up in an emergency. This ragtag group fought the Corinthians, with both sides eventually retreating under the impression that they had lost. But upon realizing that the Corinthians had failed to erect a trophy to claim the victory—for such was the custom of the Greeks, and such trophies were acutely important to the rank of a state—the Athenians soon rushed out to claim it themselves. Back in Corinth the elders mocked Corinth's warriors for allowing the Athenians such cheap-bought glory, and twelve days later the Corinthians returned to set up their own trophy. But the Athenians sallied out of Megara against them and turned them to flight. A trivial, even comic, affair, this—but in the retreat some Corinthians strayed into a field surrounded by deep ditches, and once the Athenians had blocked the entrance with hoplites, there was no escape. Now the Athenian light-armed troops slowly stoned the imprisoned Corinthians to death: a massacre. Referring to this war against Athens, Thucydides gloomily notes that "the fierce hatred of the Corinthians for the Athenians arose first and especially from this." And a "hatred," in the lexicon of relations between Greek states, was a revenge owed but not yet collected.[10]

To Athens, too, the costs of the war were terrible. At the end of this year (?458 BC), the Athenians erected a series of lists of their war dead, one for each of the ten tribes into which their citizenry was divided. One of these monuments survives, and it lists one hundred and seventy-seven names. From this we may estimate over fifteen hundred Athenian dead in the year's fighting. The inscription somberly records, as well, where the fallen Athenians from that particular tribe fought and died: "Cyprus, Egypt, Phoenicia, Halieis, Aegina, Megara"—a reminder that, in addition to the full-scale war in Greece, the Athenians and their league were also fighting a tremendous war in the east against the minions of the Great King.[11]

Nor were Corinth and her friends Athens' only enemies in the Greek war. For the early years of the conflict may also have seen a battle between Argos and Sparta, in which the Athenians participated on the Argive side. This occurred near the town of Oenoe in the Argolid, and so delighted were the Athenians with their part in the victory that they commissioned a large painting of it, which even in Roman times could be seen in Athens' Painted Stoa, alongside pictures of the other victories of which Athens was most proud, her triumph over the Amazons in Attica and over the Persians at Marathon. Frustratingly, however, a report of this painting and of another monument for the victory set up by the Argives are the only evidence we have of the battle.[12]

Certainly the alliance between Athens and Sparta's enemy Argos was firm. The warm feelings between the allies can be seen in Aeschylus' *Eumenides*, produced in 458 BC, in which the Athenian playwright praises the alliance between the states to a degree that the more aesthetically minded modern readers of the tragedy sometimes find off-putting. Moreover, in the *Agamemnon*, the first play in the *Oresteia* trilogy of which the *Eumenides* is the third, Aeschylus firmly shifts the seat of Agamemnon (and so the very seat of Greek hegemony, Agamemnon having led the Greeks against Troy) from the Mycenae of Homer to Argos. Some earlier poets had, in an effort to adjust the myth to reflect current reality, shifted Agamemnon to Sparta, so as to honor the latter's hegemony. But by moving the scene to Argos, Aeschylus appears to reflect an Athenian hope that Argos would reclaim the hegemony of Greece from Sparta.[13]

Aeschylus also reveals an aspect of the alliance between Athens and Argos not hinted at by the fast-moving Thucydides: it could be thought that Athens had become an ally of the Argives not as an equal but as an inferior in rank. Certainly it must have looked that way from the Argive point of view: so proud and storied a power as Argos was hardly going to admit the equality of Athens; even in the crisis of the Persian invasion, they had been reluctant to admit the equality of a city as mighty as Sparta. And Aeschylus shows that, given Argos' supreme claims to glory in time of myth (only Thebes could match her; both Sparta and Athens were runners-up), at least some Athenians were willing to accept the natural superiority of Argos, as they were no longer willing to accept the superiority, and so authority, of Sparta. Understanding the relative status of Athens and Argos in this alliance is a key to understanding the rest of this mid-century war.

The Spartans had anxieties other than Argos and Athens. Deep in central Greece, in the hill country between Boeotia and Thessaly, lay the ancestral homeland of Spartans, wee Doris. In ?457 BC, the year after the war on the Argolid peninsula, Doris was attacked by a larger neighbor, piratical Phocis, and the Spartans felt obliged to rescue their tiny mother state. As their progenitors, the men of Doris were benefactors of the Spartans, and Greek states, as we will see during the Ten Years' War, took such moral debts extremely seriously.

Doris had attracted the covetous Phocians, and into Doris they came, seizing one of the three towns of which the small state was made up. For the delivery of Doris from her rude neighbors, the Spartans sent fifteen hundred hoplites of their own, as well as ten thousand allies from the Peloponnese—Doris being the mother of the whole Dorian race—and forced the Phocians to terms, compelling them to disgorge the town they had captured.[14]

Victorious, the Peloponnesians turned for home, only to find the Athenians blocking their way. The Athenians, the Peloponnesians learned, proposed to prevent with their fleet any Peloponnesian attempt to go home by sea, through the Gulf of Corinth. The Athenians had also garrisoned Geranea, the mountain dividing Megara from the Isthmus of Corinth, the mountain that the Peloponnesians would have to pass over or around if they went home by land.

The Athenians were blocking the Peloponnesians' homecoming because they had decided to challenge the Spartans to battle. To this end, they had summoned cavalry from allied Thessaly and sent for support from their Aegean allies and from Argos, which promptly sent one thousand hoplites. The Spartans accepted the tacit challenge of the Athenians, marching not southwest toward the Peloponnese but southeast toward the easiest road

MAP 2.3 The Tanagra Campaign, ?457 BC

into Attica. The Athenians came forth over their border and met the Spartans at Tanagra, in southeastern Boeotia.[15]

The battle of Tanagra was a bloody one, but the Spartans and their allies prevailed. Reliable details we have none, only indeed that the cavalry of the Thessalians defected to the Spartans in the middle of the battle. May we believe the splendid legend that the noble, exiled Cimon—despite his notorious affection for the Spartans—rode up to the Athenian array and offered the services of his strong right arm to his countrymen? And may we decline to credit the dreadful story that his political enemies among the Athenians drove him away? A very watery historical tradition speaks of engagements over two days, with Athens' Argive allies having the best of it on the first, but the Thessalians treacherously descending on Athenian supply wagons in the night, followed by a second pitched battle the next day, which the Peloponnesians won. After their triumph, the Peloponnesians marched into the plain of Megara, ravaged the land, and proceeded home over the mountain of Geranea. At Olympia, the great pan-Hellenic sanctuary of Zeus in the western Peloponnese that hosted the Olympic Games, and where, as at Delphi, the Greeks often put up proud monuments to their triumphs, the Spartans dedicated a shield to thank the god for the victory.[16]

Fuming at their defeat, the Athenians did not fail to notice that there had been some Boeotians fighting on the Spartan side at Tanagra. Sixty-two days later, the Athenians were back in Boeotia and met the Boeotians in battle at Oenophyta. Unable to take revenge on their principal enemy, the Spartans, it was perhaps appealing for the Athenians to do so upon an enemy who could be defeated and whose participation at Tanagra merited vengeance (as we will see below, the Athenians were also to attack Thessaly). The Athenian commander in this battle was Myronides, who had led the Athenians at Megara the previous year and upon whom the Athenians would look back with nostalgia by the century's end as one of their great fighting captains—a proper "hairy-assed" general, as Aristophanes called him. And legends of Myronides' martial cunning proliferated around Oenophyta, his greatest victory. He did not wait for those late to the muster before marching, the story was told, because he thought that the latecomers would be cowards anyway. Looking at the advancing clouds of Theban cavalry, he told his men that safety lay in holding their ground; if they turned to flight, they would surely be ridden down and destroyed. They harkened and held fast. "The left has won!" he shouted later in the fight, ordering his right to advance; this bellowed lie put spirit in his men and terrified the enemy, and so Myronides won the battle.[17]

Boeotia was divided among factions and, when struck a mighty blow by Athens, shattered into chips, which the Athenians proceeded to sweep up. The victory of Athens did not merely avenge Boeotia's role in Athens' defeat at Tanagra but made Boeotia Athens' dependency, probably to the surprise (and delight, given the implications of dominating others for rank) of the Athenians. As for the city of Tanagra itself, which may have been friendly to the Spartans and was the scene of the battle Athens had lost, the triumphant Athenians pulled down its very walls.[18]

Athens' victory at Oenophyta earned her a terrestrial dominion greater even than the broad plain of Boeotia. For so terrified were Boeotia's neighbors that they, too, yielded themselves to the Athenians. To the west of Boeotia, the wicked Phocians, so recently defeated by the Peloponnesians, may have felt in need of a strong ally and entered into Athens' protection. To the east of Phocis, on the Aegean coast north of Boeotia, dwelt the Opuntian Locrians, from whose realm the gigantic warrior Ajax set forth for Troy in the time of heroes. With no gargantuan protector in the present generation, the Opuntian Locrians consigned one hundred of their wealthiest men to the Athenians as hostages to guarantee their subservience.[19]

To add to these successes, Athens finished her long walls connecting the city to the sea shortly after the conquest of Boeotia (?457 BC). And finally, after a year and perhaps more of siege, Aegina, the eyesore of Piraeus and Athens' hated enemy, surrendered. Her walls were pulled down to render her defenseless in the future; her fleet of war galleys was confiscated; and once-proud Aegina was enrolled as a tribute-paying subject in Athens' Delian League.[20]

The Spartans reacted to none of these Athenian triumphs. But, then, neither had they acted against Athens in the years leading up to the battle of Tanagra. The Athenians, in fact, had to goad the Spartans to fight at Tanagra by obstructing their return to the Peloponnese, by cornering them in central Greece. Before and after that confrontation, the Spartans took no action against the Athenians because, in terms of rank, they had no reason to. This was a war the Athenians had entered, after all, to avenge an insult, so it was for the Athenians to march into Sparta's homeland of Laconia and challenge the Spartans to battle. And Athenian dread of doing so—indeed, of troubling the Spartans much at all, so far as we can see, before Tanagra—upheld Sparta's claim to superior rank.[21]

At Tanagra the Athenians saw their chance: the Peloponnesian army was footsore and no doubt reduced in numbers by its long campaign, upon which only fifteen hundred actual Spartans had set out in the first place. If ever Athens could hope to beat Sparta in a hoplite battle and claim supremacy in rank, this was the chance, and into that opportunity the Athenians sunk their claws. But in vain. At Tanagra, Sparta vindicated her rank against the Athenian challenge, and so, with her supremacy assured, Sparta went directly home and felt no need to act afterwards.

Athens was fighting, and defeating, allies of Sparta, and it might be thought that this would require the Spartans to act forcefully against Athens. But Athens' thrashing of Sparta's allies did not require action from Sparta if their wars with Athens were private, separate from Spartan affairs. Sparta's allies frequently fought private wars, even against each other (Megara and Corinth had been doing just that when the latter defected to Athens). Athens was fighting over Megara with Corinth, not Sparta, and Sparta had likely not sanctioned the Corinthians' going to war with either Megara or Athens.[22]

A state like Corinth, moreover, might not even seek Spartan help against Athens, even if entitled to. For then, of course, Sparta would be acting as *hegemon,* and thus it would be Sparta—not Corinth—whose rank was primarily exalted by victory. Calling for help, especially from great, hegemonal powers, posed a problem to proud Greek states. In patriotic orations at Athens, it was almost a tic to emphasize that the Athenians had won this or that victory "alone." Athens' near total diplomatic isolation in 490 BC, which compelled her to defeat the Persians at Marathon without any significant Greek allies, had, in retrospect, become a great source of pride. For fighting alone (or as *hegemon* of a coalition) gave the strongest proof of rank. Corinth may have gambled that she and her own small friends could beat Athens and Megara without Sparta's help, so that Corinth would get the full satisfaction of revenge.[23]

While Corinth may not have begged for Sparta's aid, Aegina may have begged in vain. Aegina had come to help the Spartans against the rebellious helots. Surely this gave the Aeginetans an unanswerable right, when Athens besieged them, to call upon the Spartans as their benefactors—the same sort of right enjoyed by tiny Doris. Sparta would, in fact, be anxious to repay this debt to Aegina in the first year of the Ten Years' War (431 BC), but for now the Spartans chose to disregard it. For, of course, Athens had also come to help Sparta against the helots, and that debt required Sparta not to act against Athens' interests. Furthermore, Aegina had been fighting Athens on and off forever, and Thucydides emphasizes that this new outbreak of war was a private matter between them. No, Sparta had decided that the war between Athens and Aegina was simply none of Sparta's affair. And Sparta would cleave to this decision; when at the end of this mid-century war Sparta finally had Athens at her mercy, she would not include the liberation of Aegina in the terms she imposed upon Athens. As for Boeotia, the Spartans had allowed a few friendly Boeotians to participate in Sparta's victory over Athens; Boeotia's meager contribution gave her no call upon Sparta.[24]

Sparta probably regarded the whole war swirling around Athens, Megara, Corinth, and Aegina as a monstrous distraction, a private enterprise that kept her allies from doing their duty by Sparta, and the Spartans thus felt little inclination to rescue the Corinthians and Aeginetans from their folly. For Sparta probably looked to her friends for support—which they presumably failed to provide, given their private warring—against the power Sparta regarded as her main rival: Argos. In Sparta's view Athens was only an occasional ally of the Argives, whereas the Argives were a real and constant danger. The main quarrel of Lacedaemon was with Argos, not Athens.

The armed rivalry between Sparta and Argos seems to have continued fiercely ever since Sparta's grave defeat of Argos at Sepeia in ?494 BC. Many of the dependencies of Argos appear to have taken that catastrophe as an opportunity to establish their independence. And their new liberty drew those former dependencies close to Sparta, their natural protector against Argive reconquest or revenge; small but proud Mycenae and Tiryns, for example, came to the battle of Plataea to fight under Sparta against the Persians, while Argos itself did not. Later, when the earthquake struck Sparta and inspired her helots to revolt (?465 BC), Argos took the opportunity to destroy Mycenae, implying that Sparta had guaranteed Mycenae's freedom. Even before that, Argos, allied with the Tegeans, had lost the battle of Tegea against Sparta, and the Tegeans subsequently helped Argos capture and destroy Mycenae. So for some years, Argos was allied to at least one rebellious subject of Sparta—and for all we know, she may have assembled an anti-Spartan league in the Peloponnese, as she was to do in the 420s BC.[25]

The state of long-standing hostility between Argos and Sparta made it natural for Athens, when she felt she had been insulted by Sparta, to seek an alliance with Argos. Allying herself with so high ranked a power inevitably came at some cost to Athens' own pretensions, but without the help of Argos, she had little prospect of achieving revenge by the traditional means of victory in a land battle. But at Tanagra, that ambitious land battle, although many Athenians and few Argives fought against the Peloponnesians, when the Spartans dedicated at Olympia their shield in celebration of this victory, they named the Argives first in the inscription, before the Athenians. To the Spartans, then, the main contender for Greek hegemony was still Argos, Sparta's rival in the Peloponnese. And so the Spartans could honorably concentrate all their efforts against Argos, as the *hegemon* of a coalition arrayed against them. After all, by joining Argos' anti-Spartan coalition, the Spartans would have told themselves, Athens had admitted that she was inferior in rank to Argos, and so hardly a direct rival of Sparta. Athens could be ignored.[26]

Sparta saw no need to act against Athens. It was Athens, rather, that was jolted into action by the defeat at Tanagra; she had marched forth to prove her superiority to Sparta, only to limp home defeated and humiliated. For Athens now to do nothing would have signified her acceptance that her pretensions had, indeed, been exploded and that she was nothing but the second-rate state the Greek world had long considered her. But even with Argos as an ally, Athens could hardly challenge Sparta to battle in the Peloponnese; Tanagra had been a singular opportunity to defeat Sparta on land, and even there Athens had failed.

Desperate for a way to avenge themselves on Sparta, the Athenians settled upon the strategy they would employ so relentlessly during the Peloponnesian War: that of naval raiding as revenge. Their first great raid, in the year after Tanagra (?456 BC), was led by the Athenian general Tolmides. His fleet sailed all around the Peloponnese, ravaging and burning the coast of Laconia and attacking Cythera, the large island off Laconia that was the mythological birthplace of Aphrodite, the callipygian goddess of love. Moving on around the Peloponnese into the northwest of Greece, Tolmides then took Chalcis, a Corinthian possession near the mouth of the

MAP 2.4 The Raids of Tolmides (?456 BC) and Pericles (?454 BC)

Gulf of Corinth, and sailed finally down the Gulf to Corinth's wine-loving ally Sicyon. Coming to land there, he accepted battle and triumphed. As a later author said of this raid, it was undertaken "to humble the fame of the Spartans."[27]

Tolmides humbled Spartan fame not only by destruction but also by a wily act of mercy. For ten grim years, the rebel helots had held out on Messenia's Mount Ithome, and for ten years the Spartans had besieged them. Finally, concluding that they might never win this war, the Spartans harkened to an old oracle to ease the shame of their failure: "Let go the suppliant of Zeus on Ithome," the god of Delphi had told the Spartans long ago. And so the Lacedaemonians made a covenant with the rebels that they should go out of the land, never again setting foot in the Peloponnese, and if any should be caught there, he would be the slave of his captor. Down from the mountain came the rebels, heads held high, their children and wives in their train—and lo! There, standing off the coast, were fifty ships of Athens, the fleet of bold Tolmides, who had been told to take the helots up. Tolmides carried the helots from their native Messenia to the mouth of the Gulf of Corinth and settled them there at Naupactus, where "the Messenians"—these helots' old name, predating their enslavement by Sparta—would long stand as firm allies of the Athenians. Naupactus was no bad place for Messenians to settle, for in a sense they had come from there: when the long-wandering sons of Heracles first crossed over from Naupactus—"where ships are built"—to conquer the Peloponnese, they divided the peninsula into parts, and Messenia, along with Lacedaemon and Argos, was one of those primeval portions.[28]

The Spartans made no response to Tolmides' raiding or to his cheeky deliverance of the Messenians. Any time a Greek state received a poke from another, it had two choices: to take revenge or simply to ignore the poke. The world, of course, was watching: to ignore a great poke, or a poke from a great adversary, was to accept inferiority and to lose rank accordingly. But one could fail to notice a small poke, or a poke from an inferior, and if the world interpreted that inaction as scorn born of strength and superiority (rather than weakness born of fear), then the failure to react could even be construed as an insult. For to react—to seek revenge—was, in a sense, to admit the relative equality of the other party, while to do nothing from a position of superiority was to deny that equality, to imply that the other was not even worthy of revenge. So Pericles had behaved when abused by the low fellow in the marketplace of Athens. A scornful refusal to notice was also the response of the Spartans to the raid of Tolmides, and naturally so, because to the Spartans Athens was merely an ally of Argos. The Spartans had always been higher in rank than Athens and had only proved that again at Tanagra. The Athenian raids along the Peloponnesian coast were pathetic, impertinent. Nor would the Spartans, by seeking vengeance in return, wish to give countenance to any Athenian claim that a scuttling raid from ships had the same status in honor as a solemn victory in a hoplite battle. The Spartans had every reason to ignore the Athenians, whatever their provocation—anything short of a land invasion of Laconia, that is, or some other enterprise too great in the eyes of the world to ignore.[29]

Ignoring the Athenians seems to have worked. A few years after Tolmides' raid, when the Athenians sent out another naval expedition (?454 BC), they ignored Laconia, suggesting that they thought Tolmides' raid there had not accomplished its goals well enough to merit repeating. Pericles himself led this second expedition, raiding instead along the coast of the Corinthian Gulf, and descended upon Sicyon, defeating her men in a pitched battle. In fact, both Tolmides and Pericles attacked Sicyon, which amounts to a considerable Athenian thrashing for a second-rate state. If the Spartans felt somehow bound to help Sicyon (which is suggested by a weak tradition that reports that the Spartans came to help Sicyon after Pericles' victory, when he had them bottled up in their city), this could explain Athens' attacks, for Sparta could be humiliated by its failure to protect such a state. Athens was exploring every possible form of vengeance for their disgrace at Tanagra.[30]

Raiding the Peloponnese and beating the Boeotians at Oenophyta were not Athens' only attempts to avenge Tanagra. The Thessalians had betrayed Athens during the battle; punishment must be meted out to them, too. And so, between the raiding expeditions of Tolmides and Pericles, the Athenians made an expedition to Thessaly (?455 BC) to try to impose an exiled Thessalian magnate as chief. Yet, even with the help of their new Boeotian and Phocian subjects, whom the Athenians took with them, the Athenians found it hard to prosecute a siege when harassed by the Thessalian cavalry, and so returned home in disappointment.[31]

Soon after these attempts to take revenge for Tanagra, the Athenians found themselves desperate for a suspension of hostilities with Sparta. The crisis was likely not in Greece but in the eastern Mediterranean, where the Athenians had, through all the years of the Greek war, also been fighting the Great King. An Athenian campaign in Egypt had ended in disaster (?459– ?454 BC), and in 454 BC the Athenians were so alarmed at the prospect of a Persian sortie into the Aegean that they moved the treasury of the Delian League from the vulnerable island of Delos to the safety of Athens.[32]

Three years after Pericles' naval expedition into the Gulf of Corinth, Cimon, who had finally returned from his ten-year exile, arranged for a truce of five years between the Athenians and Spartans (?451 BC). Cimon's challenge would have been to convince his own countrymen, not the Spartans, who were serene in their superiority over Athens and were likely delighted that their main adversary, Argos, should be stripped of a powerful ally. It was the Athenians who had failed to make good their claim for higher rank in Greece, and so might want to carry on fighting, and it was the Athenians who would also have been reluctant to abandon so staunch an opponent of the Spartans as Argos, with whom Athens had sworn solemn oaths of alliance.[33]

That war against the Great King compelled the perhaps reluctant Athenians to make this truce with Sparta is suggested by the fact that in the very next year after returning to Athens and brokering the truce (?450 BC), Cimon led an expedition of two hundred ships into the eastern Mediterranean, trying to overthrow the power of Persia in Cyprus while also detaching ships to support another anti-Persian rebellion in Egypt. Cimon died in the course of this campaign, but the Athenians nevertheless won a great sea battle off Cyprus, after which the war against the Persians seems to have come to an end.[34]

Back in Greece, however, Athens' private truce with Sparta constituted a black betrayal of Athens' ally Argos, and the Spartans took immediate advantage, likely defeating the Argives in battle, as they soon bound the Argives to peace for thirty years on terms that rankled their old enemy. (Under the terms of the treaty, the Spartans kept the territory of Thyrea, a strip of land between Laconia and the Argolid, possession of which had come to symbolize who was winning in their rivalry: Thyrea was the Alsace-Lorraine of ancient Greece). Sparta's hegemony was safe. But the life of this treaty with Argos would expire during the Peloponnesian War, and when it did, there was every reason to suppose that the Argives would seek a rematch. Indeed, this looming deadline would encourage the Spartans to make peace with Athens in 421 BC, ending the Ten Years' War.[35]

Even if Athens and Sparta were no longer actively fighting each other during Cimon's truce, this did not put a stop to Athens' rivalry with Sparta over rank. One of Sparta's traditional claims to supremacy was her guardianship of Delphi, seat of the oracle of Apollo and the most hallowed spot in Greece. In the time of Cimon's truce (?449 BC), the Spartans made an expedition—a so-called Sacred War—to free Delphi from the inevitable Phocians, those miscreants who had allied with Athens in the year of Oenophyta (?457 BC) and had recently occupied the sanctuary. The Spartans freed Delphi from the Phocians, but no sooner had their triumphant force departed than the Athenians marched out and placed Delphi back in Phocian hands. The Spartans had long enjoyed special privileges at Delphi, graven upon a bronze wolf: the Phocians now granted the Athenians identical rights, even carving the terms upon the same wolf.[36]

Delphi was not the only occasion for competition between Sparta and Athens during the truce. Around the same time as the Sacred War, the Athenians sent envoys to invite all the Greeks to a great pan-Hellenic congress at Athens, to weigh what should be done about the temples destroyed by the Persians, to mull the common sacrifices owed to the gods for the victory over the Persians, and to deliberate about freedom of the seas (?449 BC). The conference, however, was never held; the Spartans opposed the meeting, and thus Spartan allies throughout the Peloponnese refused the envoys' invitation. Little wonder the Spartans objected; for the Athenians to call such a meeting to their city was to claim to be the *hegemon* of Greece, and

FIGURE 2.2 The Parthenon at Athens, construction begun 447 BC

the summoning of ambassadors could only be construed as an invitation to other Greeks to acknowledge that supremacy. Plutarch says that Pericles proposed this meeting to get the Athenian people to "think big," a usual way of describing a Greek state's attempt to advance itself in rank, which itself could sometimes be a cause of war; whatever the value of Plutarch's testimony, the Spartans and their allies probably interpreted Athenian intentions in this way.[37]

Bigger still was the thinking that the Athenians launched upon soon after, when they decided to reinvent the city of Athens itself. During Cimon's truce (447 BC), Pericles and the Athenians began to build upon the acropolis of their city the temple of Athena whose gigantic ruins even today rule Athens' skyline: the Parthenon. This was to be the largest temple in mainland Greece—larger than the temple of any single city; larger than the Argive temple of Hera, which served an entire region; and larger even than the temples of Apollo at Delphi and of Zeus at Olympia, pan-Hellenic temples that served the entire Greek world. Indeed, the Parthenon was ever so *slightly* larger than the recently finished temple of Zeus at Peloponnesian Olympia, in the territory of Sparta's ally Elis, which may imply a calculated one-upmanship in its design. The edifice took sixteen years to finish, but the ambition of the enterprise would have been evident from the outset, and it was merely one part of an even vaster program, which included the immense Odeum, built to look like the pavilion of the Great King (or perhaps,

FIGURE 2.3 The Propylea at Athens

as a comic poet pointed out, a hat), and the ceremonial gate to the Acropolis, the Propylea, begun in the next decade once the heavy work on the Parthenon was finished. And there were great works undertaken, too, elsewhere in Attica, not least at the holy shrine of Eleusis.[38]

Athens' new buildings were huge, expensive, and flashy; in the rivalrous world of Greek states, a challenge. In Asia Minor and Sicily, Greek cities had long competed with one another by building larger temples than their rivals. And the physical transformation of Athens was nothing less than astonishing, for ever since the Persian War, Athens had been a workaday, mud-brick sort of place—certainly nothing much to look at. Whether it was because the Greeks had sworn a great oath to leave in ruins the temples destroyed by the Persians, or because the Athenians had simply never gotten around to building replacements, Athenians had lived and worshipped amidst the scorched, tumbled hulks of the edifices their ancestors had built a century before. The explosion of building sponsored by Pericles changed all that, putting a new face on a newly ambitious city.[39]

This explosion of construction marks the end of the evolution of the Athenian alliance, originally conceived as a voluntary league against the Persians, into a despotic Athenian empire, now subsisting chiefly for the profit and glory of Athens, whether or not the Persians required chastisement any longer. For much of the vast cost of the building program was paid for by the tribute contributed by the members of the Delian League and intended

FIGURE 2.4 The Acropolis at Athens, artist's reconstruction

to pay for the common defense. The debate within Athens over whether the tribute could rightly be spent in this way reveals a major goal of this building, for the debate was over what effect the decision might have on Athens' rank. Pericles' political opponents cried out that this was theft and that Athens would be disgraced because of it: it was an act of *hybris* against Athens' allies. But Pericles replied that not only would such projects provide work for the Athenians but they would bring the city "undying glory." And he won his point, both with the Athenians of his own time and with their posterity. Considering these buildings a century later, the orator Demosthenes knew perfectly well what they meant: "Once the Athenians had greater wealth than the rest of the Greeks, they spent it all in quest of honor. . . . The Propylea, the Parthenon, the porticos, the ship-sheds," these were all part of the "imperishable glory" that the Athenians of the fifth century had left their descendents.[40]

This Athenian striving for rank in time of truce irritated the Spartans far more than Athens' attacks in time of war. For with Argos humiliated and— thanks to the treaty with Sparta—knocked out of the contention for hegemony for thirty years, Athens was now for the first time Sparta's chief rival. While she was allied to Argos, Athens could be thrust behind the greater rival and slightingly ignored—but Athens alone could be dismissed no longer. And this arena in which Athens had chosen to compete with the Spartans was singularly well chosen, for in the realm of expensive piety,

MAP 2.5 The Campaigns of ?447 and 446 BC

victory over Sparta was nearly guaranteed. Sparta could hardly compete with Athens in the works of peace: Sparta's league contributed soldiers, not silver, and the crude villages of Laconia, lacking even a silver currency, could raise no Parthenons.

Finally forced to take notice of upstart Athens, as Cimon's truce went on the Spartans began to look for a means of humiliating her, of pushing the bumptious Athenians back down. Athens' new possessions in mainland Greece were unhappy—that much was clear—and Sparta saw opportunity in their discontent. While Athens spent the years of the truce striving for rank, Sparta, it seems, spent the last of them organizing a conspiracy against her presumptuous rival.

In the later years of Cimon's truce, the slow-boil resentment of Athens' new mainland subjects finally decocted a rebellion. While the truce still prevented direct Spartan action, there was a rising against Athens in Boeotia (?447 BC), likely with the tacit support of the Lacedaemonians. Athenian counsels were split: should they take the time to gather an irresistible force, or was haste more important? The general Tolmides argued for speed; Pericles, for delay and might. Tolmides prevailed, and the Athenians marched

77

out all unready, with whichever allies happened to be in town and only a thousand citizens of their own in the force.[41]

The Athenians' motley army took the unhappy city of Chaeronea and sold its inhabitants as slaves (no wonder Athenian rule was not loved in Boeotia), but on the way home they passed by the temple of Athena Itonia near the town of Coronea, a place of weird and eldritch rites—and here the Athenians were ambushed by a rag-tag force of Boeotian rebels, along with some Opuntian Locrians (whom the Athenians had subdued along with Boeotia some ten years before) and exiles from Euboea, where resentment of Athens was also seething. Tolmides was killed in the fight, following which much of the Athenian force surrendered.[42]

To recover their prisoners, Athens had to set Boeotia free. This was a fatal blow to the power of Athens on the mainland, for without Boeotia, there was no holding Boeotia's neighbors Phocis or Opuntian Locris either. When next they pop into view, in 431 BC, Boeotia, Phocis, and Opuntian Locris will all be allies of Sparta. But the loss at Coronea was also deeply humiliating to the Athenians. "The fame of Athens was cast down against the Boeotians," wrote an author in the next century, describing the consequences of this defeat for rank, "and the pride of the Boeotians against the Athenians was raised up."[43]

Embarrassed in Boeotia, Athens soon faced new alarms. With the turn of the year, the last sands of Cimon's truce with Sparta were running out (446 BC). And now alarming news came to Athens: Euboea, the long island to the east of Attica, had revolted against Athenian rule. The cities of Euboea had long been members of the Delian League, willing and unwilling, and now all were subjects of Athens. Pericles led most of the Athenian army over the water to suppress the uprising. But once they were there—the Spartans had planned well—the news gasped in that strategic Megara, which occupied the passage between Attica and the Peloponnese, had risen as well and rejoined the Spartan alliance. A great Peloponnesian host was gathering and would pass through Megara on the march for Attica. The Megarians had slipped into their city men from Corinth, Epidaurus, and Sicyon, cities that had ever been on the front line against Athens during the war. Then the Athenians in the city of Megara had been butchered, save those who fled to Megara's nearby Saronic Gulf port of Nisaea and made the port fast against their assailants.[44]

In the short run, with so much of Athens' army on Euboea, Athenian resistance to her enemies devolved upon a considerable body of Athenian soldiers posted at (or now sent to) Megara's other port at Pegae on the Corinthian Gulf. These were now cut off from home by Megara's defection. Sallying into the plain of Megara, these men surprised the Megarians in their fields, ravaged the country, and took some two thousand prisoners.

When the Megarians came out to face them, there was a fierce battle—a Megarian fighting on the Athenian side, we are told, slew seven of his countrymen, breaking seven spears in their bodies like a hero of old—and the Athenians prevailed. Then, upon the coming of the main Peloponnesian army into the Megarid, the Athenians left a garrison at Pegae, and the Megarian hero led the rest of the troops and their prisoners home by sly paths through hostile Boeotia. All this we know from the gravestone the Athenians erected in honor of this Megarian, Pythion by name.[45]

The retreating Athenians were soon followed by the Peloponnesian army, which marched through Megara and into the northwest of Attica, where it ravaged the plain around Eleusis, the major settlement in that district. After their defeats at Tanagra and Coronea, the Athenians did not believe they could win a battle on land; besides, vital Euboea was still in revolt. So Pericles brought his army back over the water and haggled for the best terms he could get, and a truce was agreed, whereupon the Peloponnesian army turned for home. Pericles quickly returned to Euboea, where he put down the rebellion and drove into exile the leading men of the Euboean city of Chalcis, as well as the whole population of Hestiaea. (Such treatment the latter had earned by capturing an Athenian galley and slaughtering its crew.) Finally, the Athenian army returned to Athens.[46]

After the suppression of the Euboean revolt, the agreement Pericles had made with the Spartans was ratified by both them and the Athenians: a treaty of peace to last for thirty years was struck in the winter of 446/445 BC. In territorial terms, this Thirty Years' Peace was humiliating for Athens. She was obliged to confirm her losses of Boeotia, Phocis, Opuntian Locris, and Megara, but she also had to withdraw from the bases she still held on the Peloponnese and in the Megarid, including both of Megara's ports. This second set of losses was deeply shaming to the Athenians; later, at the height of her success during the Ten Years' War, Athens would try to reverse them. Yet—and here is what makes this treaty so interesting—some Athenians would later look back upon this treaty fondly, the Athenians would adhere rigorously to its terms while it was in force, and the conduct of Pleistoanax, the young Spartan king who had led the Peloponnesian expedition, was bitterly unpopular in Sparta. Accused of having been bribed to lead his army away, Pleistoanax fled into exile (he will rejoin our story later in the Ten Years' War). These rumors of the bribery of Pleistoanax gave rise as well to a famous legend about Pericles, that he placed in his accounts for this year the tactful line item, "for what was necessary."[47]

It was not the treaty itself that irritated the Spartans. They ratified the agreement even after the Athenians used Pleistoanax' departure so ruthlessly to suppress the Euboeans and presumably after Pleistoanax himself had fled into exile. So it was not the fate of Euboea that vexed them; nor, for example, was it Athens' continued rule over Aegina. According to Thucydides, Pleistoanax' crime, rather, was that he "went as far as Eleusis and Thria . . . but withdrew again without going further." To Thucydides the inadequate *distance* of the Peloponnesian advance into Attica was the issue, the fact that Pleistoanax went no further than the northwest corner of Athens' territory. So the reason for Spartan displeasure with their king may have been that he did not advance far enough into Attica to challenge the Athenians to battle—the Athenians who were, after all, trickling back from Euboea and were presumably not ready to meet him so far from the city of Athens itself. Pleistoanax accepted Pericles' hasty offer of a territorial settlement (adequate in itself and which indeed the Spartans ratified), but unlike Brasidas' show at Megara in 424 BC (the episode with which we began this book), he did not advance far enough to prove that the Athenians were too timid to fight (or, of course, if they were willing to fight, to defeat them). He had made the Peloponnesian invasion of Attica look like a thieving raid rather than a solemn challenge to battle. Although Pleistoanax had satisfied Sparta's practical need to clear the Peloponnese of Athenian bases and attended to the security of Sparta's allies, he had missed the chance to humiliate the Athenians according to the customs of the Greeks. In the greater war that was to break out in fifteen years' time, the Lacedaemonians would not make that mistake again.[48]

Athens' territorial losses aside, other features of the Thirty Years' Peace were cheering to the Athenians' sense of rank, to their sense of themselves as Sparta's equals—and this is, no doubt, why some Athenians later regarded it with nostalgia. Lists of the allies of both sides were appended to the treaty, and it was stipulated that states not listed as belonging to either alliance could in future join either. So, although Sparta did not perhaps explicitly accept the legitimacy of the Athenian hegemony, the Spartans seemed in practice to admit its existence and to regard it as parallel to, and to be regarded in the same light as, Sparta's own hegemony. Future disputes between Athens and Sparta were to be handled by arbitration, which also might imply the equality of the parties. In formal terms, too, the treaty was an "equal" one. The Greeks tended to divide treaties into "equal" and "unequal"; unequal treaties had terms clearly subordinating one party to the other, like the pledge (later to be imposed upon Athens after her surrender in 404 BC) to "follow the Spartans wheresoever they may lead by land and sea." The Thirty Years' Peace lacked such a stipulation, and so it was, in the view of the Greeks, an "equal" treaty.[49]

The Spartans were content with these terms because they were certain, despite Pleistoanax's failure to challenge the Athenians to battle, that they had reasserted their superiority to Athens in rank. They had compelled

Athens to sue for peace, and they had stripped her of all her continental holdings outside Attica. Greek treaties of peace never addressed questions of rank directly; they merely dealt with the practical details that followed a war, although of course those practical details might be humiliating to the losers. But it was primarily the war itself that settled the rank of the parties.

In fact, the Spartans were unwise to allow a treaty with some clauses the Athenians could interpret as implying equality to settle the details of their equivocal triumph in Attica. For, as it turned out, the Athenians did not take to heart the humiliation that the Spartans were certain they had inflicted. Lacking in the Spartan victory in 446 BC was the crucial psychological component that made a victory "stick"—that made the defeated take their defeat, and therefore their inferiority in rank, to heart and thereafter behave with lowly deference toward the victor. "It is best not to puff yourselves up because of the misfortunes of the opponents," says a speaker much later in Thucydides, "but only be confident when you have conquered their spirits." The Spartans had failed to conquer the spirits of the Athenians; they had failed, in the vivid expressions of the Greeks, to "impose self-control" on the Athenians, to "wise 'em up." They had not inflicted the mix of shame and depression that Winston Churchill described overcoming the French high command after Germany's victory in 1940: "the tracks of invincible panzers have broken more than their villages, more than their massed infantry. They have smashed French will, hurled self-respect into the dust, humbled the glory of an empire."[50]

Failure to internalize defeat was quite common among defeated Greeks. Greek warfare had evolved conventions to make victory and defeat as clear as possible, partly to give defeat its proper psychological effect: the tacit challenge to battle that it was cowardly to decline; the straight-up battle fought head to head, providing no excuse for the defeated; the losers' formal admission of defeat by requesting the return of their dead; and the victors' erection of a trophy, formally to claim the victory. These practices served to strip Greek battle of its ambiguity.[51]

A multitude of possible outcomes in war, however, lay outside these Greek conventions and were therefore subject to interpretation; naturally, proud Greek states tended to interpret them as needed to save their pride. And so the Athenians seem to have interpreted the Peloponnesian campaign of 446 BC. In particular, Greek states that felt they had been defeated unfairly often failed to take their defeats to heart. If the loser felt she had lost merely by bad luck, or the winner had won by a trick (a "theft of war," as the Greeks called it), the psychological component essential for a victory to register fully in rank would be lacking. And in 446 BC, the Spartans had encouraged the rebellion of Megara, and likely of Boeotia and Euboea as well, and had therefore forced Athens to a truce by a theft of war.[52]

The habit of denying the greater validity of defeats that could be condemned as unfair is reflected in one of the oddest monuments to survive from classical Athens: a set of verses inscribed over the common tomb of a group of Athenian war dead. From what war they come, we do not know, although it may have been this very year of disasters, 446 BC.

> Wretches! What a contest of battle unexpected you fought
> to the end, and lost your brave souls in war.
> But 'twas not by the strength of enemy men that you were hurt,
> but some power half-divine stood in your road.
> Eagerly he hunted you and allotted you as prey—still
> unconquered—to your foes.
> And he brought this to pass for your ill, but laid it down for
> mortals to deem the outcome of prophecy certain.[53]

We may find it difficult to imagine being buried beneath an epitaph so defensive in tone, but Greek war-dead wished all the world to know if there was a reason for their defeat—here, it seems, the meddling of an oracle—that might clear them and their country of shame, while denying the victors their claim to pride.

Athens' refusal to take her defeat in 446 BC to heart was ominous for the long-term tranquility of Greece. The war at mid-century had made Sparta sensitive to Athens' pretensions to rank. Before the war, when Athens and Sparta were "friends," Sparta had been prepared to disregard slights such as the rebuilding of Athens' walls; during the war, feeling that her fight for hegemony was with Argos, Sparta was able scornfully to ignore Athenian insults, even the Athenian raid along the coast of Laconia. But after Argos bent the knee and Athens became Sparta's main rival, Sparta was to prove far more jealous of her honor and tender about her rank. Neither the cut-short Spartan invasion of Attica nor the Thirty Years' Peace—although the latter adjusted questions of territory—settled the question of pride. Yet the treaty did satisfy Sparta's allies, without whom she could not, in practice, make war on Athens. And in the years down to the outbreak of the greater war in 431 BC, it was Sparta's allies who would keep the peace.

For their part, the Athenians were still maneuvering to make Greece admit that Athens was the equal of Sparta. A few years after the conclusion of the Thirty Years' Peace, the Athenians led a colony to Thurii, in the south of Italy (?443 BC). The colony at Thurii was pan-Hellenic, with settlers drawn from the whole of Greece (including the Peloponnese), but those leading the expedition were Athenian. By founding Thurii, Athens was once again staking a claim to a pan-Hellenic hegemony like the Spartans enjoyed—a move parallel to Pericles' invitation to the pan-Hellenic congress at Athens to discuss the temples destroyed by the Persians. Thurii was a more modest gambit, but unlike the previous effort, it was successful. The point, however, was merely to launch a pan-Hellenic enterprise under Athenian auspices, not to establish a stronghold in the west. When the new colony soon got in trouble, first from civil strife and then from foreign war, Athens did nothing to help.[54]

With the Athenians still jousting for equality, and the Spartans feeling proud and touchy, any incident between them might easily lead to war. War, indeed, nearly broke out between Athens and Sparta only a few years after Thurii, when Athens' island ally Samos revolted against the Athenian alliance and called upon the Peloponnesians for help. The Spartans appear to have been willing to break the Thirty Years' Peace and go to war with Athens over Samos, but they were prevented by the unwillingness of their allies.

Powerful Samos was one of Athens' few island allies that still supplied ships for the common defense, and in 441 BC she got into a war of her own with wealthy Miletus, an Athenian ally on the nearby coast of Asia Minor that paid her tribute to Athens in money alone. Athens offered to arbitrate their quarrel, but the Samians refused. The Milesians complained loudly about the Samians—as well they might; they were losing the war—and in this caterwauling joined those Samians opposed to the present government of Samos, which was an oligarchy dominated by the island's great clans. Suddenly Pericles was at Samos with forty galleys and cast down the oligarchy, setting up a democracy in its place. Fifty men and fifty boys of the leading Samian families were taken as hostages, lodged on the distant isle of Lemnos, and Pericles left a garrison behind on Samos to ensure that Athens' wayward ally would not stray again.[55]

Pericles' triumph was short-lived. Some of the Samian oligarchs fled to the mainland, and hiring mercenaries and securing the support of the Persian satrap of the district, they intrigued with their friends back on Samos. In the next year (440 BC), crossing over to the island by night with seven hundred men, they overthrew the democracy. Then they spirited the hostages away from Lemnos and raised Samos in revolt from Athens. The Athenian garrison on Samos surrendered, and the forces of the oligarchy handed these Athenians over to the Persian satrap. And the tendrils of the rebels extended even farther than northerly Lemnos: Byzantium, on the strategic Bosporus, revolted as well. Populous Athens was not self-sufficient in food, and a great proportion of her grain imports were carried down from the Black Sea through the Bosporus and Hellespont. So the rebellion of Byzantium, or any

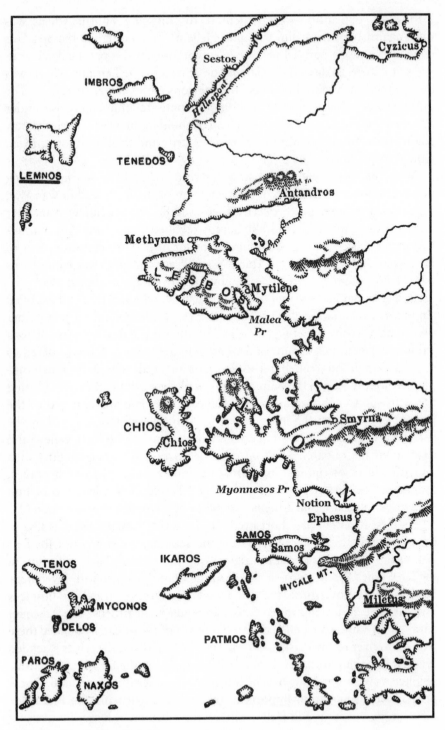

MAP 2.6 The Samian Rebellion, 440–439 BC

other subject city on narrow passage from the Black Sea, was a serious matter for Athens.[56]

By delivering the Athenian garrison to the Persians as hostages, the Samians seem to have thought they had guaranteed their liberty and safety from Athenian punishment (had not the Athenians abandoned Boeotia, after all, to get their prisoners back?). And so, with Athens checkmated, the Samians prepared an armament and sent it against hated, rich Miletus. But the Samians had misjudged the Athenians. On the way back from their attack on Miletus, the fifty Samian galleys were attacked by forty-four commanded by Pericles and all nine of the other Athenian generals. Athens' sending all ten of her generals with this fleet signifies just how critical the Athenians deemed the situation. And one of the generals hastening to war down the liberty of Samos was none other than playwright Sophocles, who had recently brought forth upon the stage of Athens his *Antigone*, that immortal paean to human freedom.[57]

The Athenians were not only anxious about the ramifying revolt in their empire but alarmed by the involvement of the Persians—indeed, the Athenians went so far as to send a squadron eastward to watch for the Persian fleet. For ten years the war with the Persians had dozed, and there could be no worse time for the slumbering King to reawaken.[58]

Fortune, for now, was with the Athenians. Assisting the Samians was a project of the local Persian satrap, not the distant Great King, and despite a Samian embassy to the east, no armada sailed from Phoenicia, seat of the Persian empire's naval power. Pericles defeated the Samian ships en route from Miletus, and when his force had been reinforced by more galleys from Athens and her island allies Chios and Lesbos, a landing was made on Samos, which the outnumbered Samians did not dare to oppose. The Athenians now surrounded the city of Samos with three siege walls and blockaded her from the water.[59]

Just when the Athenians seemed to have Samos safely cabined—panic! Upon a rumor that the Persians were at sea, Pericles sailed east with most of the Athenian fleet to confront this specter. Now the Samians rallied against the Athenian camp and sailed against those ships the Athenians had left, defeating them at sea. For fourteen days, the Samians ruled their own waters. But when Pericles returned he blockaded Samos once again, and more and more forces came in from Athens and her friendly islands to beleaguer the city. Eventually the Samians' hope for help from Persia faded, while of Greek help they had also seen none, and so the Samians realized that they would have to rescue themselves. Sailing out of their harbor, they met the Athenians in battle, but the Athenians prevailed. Finally, after eight months of siege, the Samians surrendered (439 BC). At well over a thousand talents—the Athenians eventually had one hundred and sixty ships involved in the war, not counting those of their allies—the war's charges had proved enormous (the total tribute Aristides had set for the Delian League had only been four hundred and sixty talents in the year). The terms of peace compelled the Samians to pay back the costs of the war by installments, as well as to give hostages to the Athenians, surrender their ships, and pull down their walls. Isolated Byzantium, too, came hastily to terms. The threat to the dominion of Athens had passed.[60]

The Spartans, it appears, had wanted to help Samos. At some stage during the rebellion, the Samians had appealed to the Peloponnesians. Of their claim we know nothing, but we do know the Samians had called upon the Spartans before, around 525 BC, to drive out their piratical tyrant Polycrates and, at that moment, had demanded that the Spartans requite Samos for services still further back in time, when the Samians had helped the Spartans conquer the Messenians. The Spartans had sent an expedition to Samos and besieged Polycrates in vain for forty days, before departing home in failure. And their failure meant, of course, that they had never repaid their old debt to Samos, and the Samians would surely have called upon it during their rebellion from Athens. It was a rather elderly debt, to be sure, but, then, we have seen the Spartans hasten to pay their even older debt to Doris.[61]

Whatever its basis, the appeal of the Samians to the Spartans during their revolt was well-judged. For after receiving the Samian plea, the Spartans summoned their allies to deliberate about going to war with Athens— a sign that powerful forces at Sparta were prepared to set aside the Thirty Years' Peace and make war themselves, if the essential aid of Sparta's allies could be secured. But the Corinthians—or so they would later claim— persuaded the allies to withhold their consent, and so no help was sent to the Samians. Without her allies, Sparta could neither undertake a naval campaign nor be confident of success on land. Only when Sparta's allies came to change their minds—as they soon did—would the major obstacle to war on the Peloponnesian side be removed.[62]

EIGHT YEARS AFTER THE SURRENDER of Samos, the Athens and Spartans were back at war. Thucydides' diagnosis of the origins of the Peloponnesian War that broke out in 431 BC is one of the most famous passages in his narrative and one of the most quoted passages from the ancient Greek historians today, for it encapsulates the cold principles of the contemporary realist school of international relations. "The truest cause of the war," wrote Thucydides, "was the growing greatness of the Athenians, and the fear that this inspired, which compelled the Lacedaemonians to go to war." Elsewhere he defines this "growing greatness" more exactly as the increase of the Athenians' power, *dynamis*, evident because "most of Greece was already subject to them," and goes on to expand upon the direction of the threat Athenian *dynamis* posed, which was to Sparta's allies. This cause is distinguished sharply from the immediate events that led up to war, which Thucydides terms the "charges" or "grounds for complaint" (*aitiai*) and "points of difference" (*diaphorai*), which are not the "truest cause" of the war. However the latter may have contributed, they were, to Thucydides, in some way less important.[63]

Most modern students of fifth-century BC Greece have accepted Thucydides' diagnosis of the causes of the Peloponnesian War. They have done so because Thucydides argues his point so skillfully, but also because the cause he offers fits so comfortably with contemporary expectations: our gut feeling is that fear of power *is* why wars break out. But this comfort is an artifact, an invisible result of the vast sway of Thucydides over later Western thought about relations between nations. Thucydides, after all, influenced Thomas Hobbes, who translated him into English; and not only are Thucydides and Hobbes together the progenitors of the theoretical realism that abides in today's universities and think tanks but, perhaps more important, they have molded the vulgate of the age. Power and fear are the tools for thinking about relations between states unreflectively employed in the media. Thus, if looking out the window we approve of Thucydides' description of the landscape, we do so unaware that it was Thucydides who sited the window in the first place.[64]

Even if Thucydides' realism seems perfectly natural to us, we can tell from Thucydides' own words that his account of the causes of the war would have struck his contemporaries as extremely surprising, because the way he presents his theory is argumentative: hence Thucydides' emphatic distinction between the "truest cause"—fear of power—and the mere "grounds for complaint" and "points of difference," which others evidently saw as decisive; hence Thucydides' admission that *his* cause was not much discussed at the time; and hence his subsequent account of the growth of Athenian power pressing harder upon the Spartans than their allies' appeals. And Thucydides' argument for his theory of why the war broke out is hardly limited to that theory's exposition. Thucydides' whole first book is, in fact, shot through with arguments for his understanding of the causes of the war. Speeches that Thucydides puts in the mouths of historical figures keep mentioning the power of Athens despite Thucydides' admission that the Spartans' fear of Athens' power had not been much discussed at the time. Had Thucydides' interpretation been as natural to his Greek audience as it is to us, he hardly would have had to prosecute so vigorous and ingenious a polemic.[65]

Other Greeks saw the coming of the war differently than Thucydides. In a passage in his *Acharnians* (425 BC), the Athenian comic playwright Aristophanes burlesqued the causes of the war by joking that, first, Athenians started harassing Megarian traders; then some Athenian youths went to Megara and kidnapped a whore, whereupon in revenge the Megarians stole *two* strumpets from the house of Pericles' mistress (ho! ho!); and then Pericles passed a decree banning the Megarians from Athens, whereupon the Megarians appealed to the Spartans—and so war broke out. In the *Peace* (421 BC), the same playwright gives another (quite different) comic history of the same events, summarizing the outbreak of the war as "one pot, whacked, kicking back in anger at another pot." And such a way of thinking about the causes of the war was hardly limited to Aristophanes. The Roman-period author Plutarch seems to have access to an earlier account, perhaps that of the fourth-century BC historian Ephorus, in which a sequence of revenges was similarly central to the outbreak of the war. Other Greeks, then, seem to have interpreted the origins of the war precisely in terms of the "grounds for complaint" and "points of difference" whose importance Thucydides insisted was secondary to the Spartan fear of the growth of Athenian power. And we can deduce the same from Thucydides' own argument. For why even aim a kick at the "grounds for complaint" and "points of difference" if other people did not think them the main cause of the war?[66]

Aristophanes' details, of course, are no use: his story is intentionally absurd. But his machinery of "pot kicking pot," a sequence of revenges, hews much more closely to how Greeks of the period expected war to break out than Thucydides' somber "fear of power." Thucydides himself, as we have seen, used exactly this thinking to explain why Athens split with Sparta at the beginning of the war at mid-century, when Athens felt insulted by being sent home from Mount Ithome and sought revenge by allying herself with Sparta's enemy Argos. And this more prevalent Greek conception of the origins of Greek wars—against which Thucydides struggled to make room for his own—is all the more appealing here for one important reason: as an explanation of the outbreak of the Peloponnesian War, Thucydides' fear-of-power formulation was simply wrong.[67]

Sparta had no cause to fear the growing power of Athens because Athens' power on land was not growing, and her power at sea was no more terrifying than it had ever been. On land, when she made the Thirty Years' Peace in 446/445 BC, Athens was far less powerful than she had been since ?457 BC, and nothing between then and the outbreak of war in 431 BC changed that. The Spartans, who in the Thirty Years' Peace had deprived Athens of all her mainland holdings outside Attica, knew this; indeed, they had planned the treaty so as to cripple Athens' terrestrial strength. Athens' power on the sea, meanwhile, was what it had always been: so much gigantically greater than that of Sparta and her allies that no addition could cause Sparta greater fear. Events like Athens' reduction of Samos or subsequent additions to Athens' power at sea (for such, indeed, there were) were buckets added to a roaring river—nothing to create fear, if the Spartans had not been fearful before.[68]

If Thucydides was wrong about the causes of the war, our next resort for explanation is naturally the prevailing theory that Thucydides was fighting against. We need, that is, to try to fit the "grounds for complaint" and "points of difference," for which Thucydides felt such contempt, into a "pot-kicking-pot" explanation, as apparently most of those who actually lived through the war did.[69]

In challenging Thucydides' power-and-fear explanation, it is useful to consider an explanation for another Greek war: the first-century BC Diodorus of Sicily's description of the outbreak of war between Argos and Mycenae in the 460s BC, which arose from rivalry over rank.

> At this time a war broke out between Argos and Mycenae for the following reasons. The Myceneans, because of the old worth/rank (*axiōma*) of their country, would not submit to the Argives, like the other cities of the Argolid, but rather when they were given orders they alone paid them no heed. And they disputed with the Argives about the temple of Hera [the Argive Heraion, the most important temple in the Argolid], and thought themselves worthy to conduct the Nemean games. . . . In sum, the Argives suspected them, fearing lest, if they grew more powerful, they would contend for the *hegemonia*, on account of the ancient pride of their city. The Argives, being estranged for these reasons (*aitiai*), having been eager of old to raise up their city, and thinking that this was a good opportunity, seeing that the Lacedaemonians were cast down and could not come to their aid . . . marched against the Myceneans.[70]

Great Argos and tiny Mycenae are rivals in rank, a rivalry manifested especially in the religious sphere, with wrangling over temples and games. The Argives think they have the right to give orders to the Myceneans; the Myceneans, thinking themselves equal in rank—for, however small, Mycenae had been the seat of Agamemnon, who led the Greeks against Troy—refuse to defer, refuse to obey, refuse even to notice. Combined with other insults, this failure of deference—itself an out-and-out insult in ancient Greece—leads to war. The Argives come to fear the power of the Myceneans, not because the power of the latter is inherently terrifying but because they diagnose a Mycenean thirst for rank, that they will try to take the *hegemonia* from Argos. This concern about rank makes the Argives sensitive to the growth of Mycenean power. Whether or not this particular account is true, the conventional Greek thinking represented here—the refusal of a proud state to defer to another that considers itself superior in rank constituting a cause of war—provides a useful tool for understanding the causes of the Peloponnesian War.

The Spartans were like the Argives in Diodorus' story, interpreting Athens' acts of rivalry and refusals to defer as insults and eventually going to war over them. Like the Argives coming to fear the Myceneans, the Spartans came to fear Athenian power, not because it was growing but because they increasingly dreaded the use Athens might make of it in their rivalry with Sparta.

The Athenians, on the other hand, were like far more powerful Myceneans in Diodorus' story, rivals for rank with the Spartans and unwilling to defer to them. This refusal to defer appears to have been the policy of Pericles in particular, who, Thucydides tells us, advocated consistent, even stiff-necked refusal to give way to the Spartans in any matter. "I have always held the same principle," Thucydides has him say, "not to yield to the Peloponnesians." In his own voice, Thucydides describes Pericles as "the most powerful man of his time, and leading the state he opposed the Lacedaemonians in everything, and he did not suffer them to yield, but urged the Athenians on to war." But although the attitude Pericles urged upon Athens might have encouraged the Spartans to attack them, the Athenians themselves did not break the treaty. Indeed, Athenian policy in the years before 431 BC reveals remarkable care in adhering to the terms of the Thirty Years' Peace, a fact attested to by none other than the Spartans themselves, who would later admit that when war finally broke out, it was they, not the Athenians, who had violated the peace. Rather than seeking war, Pericles rather seems to have been willing to accept the territorial losses embodied in the Thirty Years' Peace, while continuing Athens' rivalry with Sparta for rank. Indeed, Pericles' Athens used the treaty as a shield to protect herself against Spartan revenge for her continued pretensions to equal standing. But if Athens' rivalry made the Spartans break the treaty and attack, so be it.[71]

THE JANUS-FACED DIPLOMATIC STRATEGY OF Pericles manifested itself in the half-decade or so before the outbreak of the Peloponnesian War in 431 BC, the years that saw the accumulation of the "grounds for complaint" and "points of difference" between Athens and the Peloponnesians. Thucydides described or alluded to these events, only to dismiss them as the primary causes of the war, preferring his own diagnosis of

Spartan fear of Athenian power. But we suspect that these events were the primary causes of the war.

At some point after suppressing the rebellion of Samos, Athens fell into a dispute with Megara over the cultivation of sacred land on their mutual border, the harboring of runaway slaves, and, ultimately, a murdered herald: a perfectly unexceptional boundary dispute between Greek cities of the kind that frequently led to war. Athenian feelings ran high against Megara in any case, because of her betrayal of Athens in 446 BC, not to mention the Athenians killed in the streets of Megara when the Megarians defected to Sparta. Because Megara was now listed as a Spartan ally in the Thirty Years' Peace, however, Athens could not go to war against her without breaking the treaty, so instead she imposed a trade embargo upon the Megarians, barring them from the markets and harbors of Athens and her confederacy (?435 BC). In an overwhelmingly agricultural world, where few livelihoods depended on commerce, this Megarian Decree hardly reduced the Megarians to mass beggary. But that was not the intention of the embargo; rather, it was an insult, cunningly crafted, because the Megarians could not themselves avenge it in blood without breaking the Thirty Years' Peace.[72]

The Megarian Decree infuriated the Megarians, but Megara was a city of secondary importance. Holding the key to war or peace was great Corinth, the city that boasted of having prevented war between Athens and the Peloponnesians over the rebellion of Samos. An old hatred abided between Corinth and her colony, the island of Corcyra (now known in English as Corfu), in the northwest of Greece. A mother city expected deferential honor from her daughter, ceremonious precedence at sacrifices and in the acutely public common assemblies of the Greeks. Instead, the Corcyreans, wealthy in money and possessed of a powerful fleet, treated the Corinthians with contempt. "Raised up" by their nautical eminence, they renounced their Corinthian heritage, inventing for themselves instead a descent from the Phaeacians, the epic inhabitants of the island of Corcyra, who once had gloried in their ships and given shelter to the storm-tossed Odysseus. Such a rewriting of history was natural for a Greek colony with ambitions to rise in rank, since, as we are reminded by the quarrel over rank between Sparta, Athens, and Syracuse during the Persian War, colonies of other states were inevitably regarded as second-class.[73]

Between states locked in hatred as Corinth and Corcyra were—with so much pent-up desire for revenge—war was likely to burst out over any difference, as it certainly had before. The quarrel now was over Epidamnus, a colony of Corcyra's to the north on the mainland, assailed by Epidamnian exiles in alliance with the local barbarians. The Epidamnians asked Corcyra for help, but Corcyra refused. When they directed their pleas at Corinth instead, the Corinthians jumped at the chance, driven by their grievances

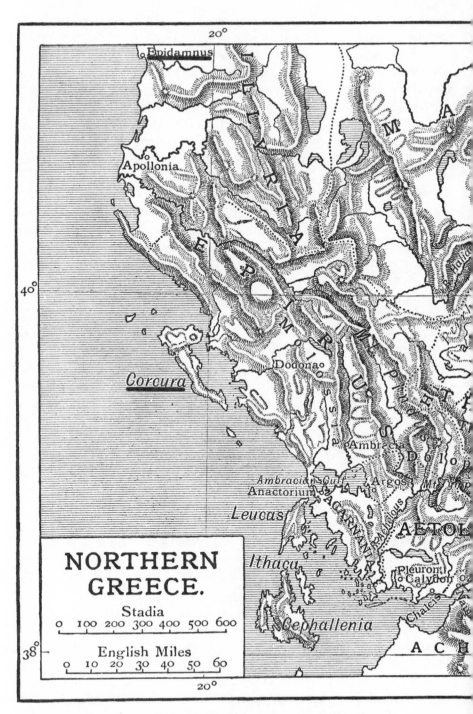

MAP 2.7 Northern Greece, Including Epidamnus, Corcyra, and Potidaea

against Corcyra for the contempt that she had shown them. This was a delightful one-in-the-eye for Corcyra, since Epidamnus would now hail Corinth, not Corcyra, as its founder—the grandmother city, as it were, grabbing the place and honor of the mother city. When the Corcyreans learned of this, they "flew into a rage"—note the rage, right where it should be as the link between insult and war—and sent a fleet against Epidamnus, also ordering the Corinthians to depart in what Thucydides calls "insulting language." Now there was war between Corinth and Corcyra—as nice a case of a war arising from rivalry in rank as survives from antiquity.[74]

Initially the Corcyreans had the better of the war, defeating the Corinthians in a sea battle (435 BC) and slaughtering many of the prisoners they took. They then sailed against and ravaged the lands of the nearby allies of Corinth who had aided Corinth against them. Meanwhile the Corinthians stoked their anger—their longing for revenge—and perhaps beseeched the favor of their cruel gods Necessity and Force, to whom stately altars stood consecrated at Corinth. The next year the Corinthians spent building a more formidable battle fleet, reports of which sent the Corcyreans to Athens to plead for an alliance. This Corcyrean plea the Athenians granted, although with great care for their obligations under the Thirty Years' Peace; after much deliberation, they consented to a defensive alliance only, sending but a small squadron to help, with Cimon's son Lacedaemonius, "the Spartan," as a commander, perhaps to emphasize Athens' lack of aggressive intent toward the Peloponnesians. And even that small squadron was forbidden to fight unless Corcyra herself, or one of her possessions, were threatened.[75]

Here Thucydides' identification of fear of other states' power as a driving force in international relations proves helpful for understanding Athenian willingness to help Corcyra against Corinth. Athens' dependence on naval supremacy made it impossible for her to allow the possibility that the two other significant fleets in Greece—those of Corcyra and Corinth—would, with a Corinthian conquest of Corcyra, be combined under a single head, whether at the outset friendly or hostile. So Thucydides presents the Corcyreans as arguing in the Athenian assembly. Greek ethics, however—the law that favors must be returned—backed Corinth's claim that Athens should not help Corcyra against her, and Thucydides portrays the Corinthians arguing ethics to dissuade the Athenians: at the very least, in exchange for old services and especially Corinth's recent intervention with Sparta's allies over Samos, Athens owed her neutrality. But in this case, fear of power—specifically Athenian fear of the specter of a combined Corinthian and Corcyrean fleet—trumped such ethical considerations. Driven by the cold imperative of fear, Athens sent her ships to Corcyra, and despite all her caution, her ships ended up fighting those of Corinth.[76]

The Corinthians set to sea with a fleet of one hundred and fifty galleys, ninety their own and sixty provided by their allies. These engaged Corcyra's one hundred and ten off Sybota (433 BC), near the southern tip of Corcyra, in the greatest sea battle ever fought to that date between Greeks. Both sides had shipped many hoplites, archers, and javelin men as marines ("the old, imperfect armament," sniffs Thucydides, since, in the interests of speed and maneuver, the Athenians had reduced passengers to a minimum), and as opposing ships came together, these marines fought it out on the decks. Soon, as more and more ships rafted up to one another, the sea battle became a vast and confused floating land battle.[77]

The ten Athenian ships, whose rules of engagement forbade them to attack the Corinthians outright, made mock charges wherever the Corcyreans seemed particularly hard-pressed, and so by play-acting tried to help their allies. The Corcyrean left flank defeated Corinth's allies on the Corinthian right, driving them to shore—but then, rather than return to help their

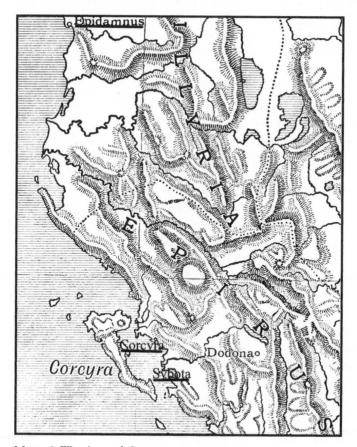

Map 2.8 War Around Corcyra, 435–433 BC

countrymen in the ongoing battle, the crews of the twenty pursuing Corcyrean ships disembarked to plunder the Corinthian camp. The Corinthians' left flank, meanwhile, prevailed over the Corcyrean right and began to force it back. The Athenians, who were licensed to fight only should their allies be losing and Corcyra itself fall under threat, first stepped up their frantic mumming and then, as it became all too clear that the Corcyreans were in flight, attacked the Corinthians in earnest—but too late to stem the Corcyrean rout.[78]

Such was the Corinthian hatred for the Corcyreans that, before towing off as booty the swamped wrecks (the usual by-product of a Greek sea battle), the Corinthians first sailed among the hulks, killing like seals the men clinging to the wreckage. They were likely taking revenge for the Corcyreans' slaughter of Corinthian prisoners two years before, and in the process the Corinthians slew by mistake not a few of their own allies. Afterwards they fetched the wrecks away to the nearby mainland. Then, in the afternoon, they put to sea again in the hopes of forcing a landing on Corcyra.[79]

Accompanied by the ten Athenian vessels, such Corcyrean ships as were still seaworthy now sailed forth to defend their coast. In the evening of the same day, a second sea battle was arraying. The paean to Apollo had been sung, and the sides surged together—when, suddenly, the Corinthians began to back water. A lookout, glancing over his shoulder in the dusk, had seen war galleys coming up behind the Corinthians. Nearly all the friendly warships in the Greek world were already fighting on the Corinthian side, so these had to be enemies, most likely Athenians. Failing light and rising terror conjured the whole of Athens' grand fleet, serried hundreds strong. The Corcyreans and their Athenian allies were also perplexed—and their perplexity consumed the precious minutes during which they might have taken advantage of the Corinthians' panic. Then, seeing the spectral fleet themselves, they, too, withdrew, suspecting an enemy reinforcement. Camping on the southern spit of Corcyra, the Corcyreans waited in alarm. Finally, late in the night, the ghostly craft revealed themselves as an Athenian squadron of but twenty ships, sent by the cautious democracy to reinforce the inadequate ten ships they had sent before.[80]

The next day the Corcyreans and Athenians rowed forth to challenge the Corinthians, who formed in line of battle against them. But the Corinthians needed a rapid decision—they had brought only three days' supplies and were having trouble repairing their ships and guarding their prisoners on the deserted beach that was serving as their harbor—and concluded that they could safely fight the Corcyreans alone but not the Athenians as well. And so the Corinthians now sent a skiff out among the Athenians as if visiting a friendly fleet. The Corinthian boat carried no herald's wand, a symbol that would have made it inviolable to combatants by cocooning it in the protection of the gods; only cities at war communicated by heralds, and the Corinthians did not wish to imply that they were at war with Athens.[81]

"You act unjustly in beginning war and violating the treaty," the brave envoys in the boat shouted up to the Athenians. "We are taking revenge upon our enemies, and we find you taking up arms to obstruct us. If your intention is to stop us sailing to Corcyra, or wherever we want, and so break the treaty, take *us* first and treat us as enemies."[82]

Witnessing this challenge, the Corcyreans shouted, "Take them and kill them!" But the Athenians' orders left them with no choice but to chop logic: they were not, they replied carefully, violating the treaty and beginning war. They were simply aiding their allies. The Corinthians might sail wheresoever they liked, then, excepting only to Corcyra.

Despairing of fighting the Athenians, either because they feared to lose or fearing that attacking the Athenians would break the Thirty Years' Peace, the Corinthians confined their energies to setting up a trophy—a stand of captured enemy arms—on the mainland to declare themselves victors in the battle the day before. Meanwhile the Corcyreans, towing off those wrecks that the Corinthians had neglected, set up their own trophy on a nearby island. The Corinthians, they reasoned, had refused to meet them in a second battle the day before, and they had refused again today, so the Corcyreans could rightfully claim victory.[83]

Finally, the Corinthians sailed home, but the contagion of Corinth's abiding anger had spread from her old enemy, Corcyra, to her new one, Athens. "This was the first ground for complaint that the Corinthians had for the war against the Athenians," says Thucydides, "that they had fought against them alongside the Corcyreans in time of treaty. Soon after this another point of difference tending toward war arose between the Athenians and the Peloponnesians: the Corinthians were devising to avenge themselves upon the Athenians, and the Athenians suspected their hatred."[84]

This new "point of difference" was yet another of Corinth's many colonies: Potidaea, on the northern coast of the Aegean, which was a tribute-paying member of the Athenian confederacy (the Delian League having admitted all Aegean states alike, whoever their original founders were). In the wake of the Corinthian frustration at Sybota (433 BC), Athens suspected Corinth of encouraging Potidaea to revolt and demanded that Potidaea send home the Corinthian officials stationed there. Potidaea took officials annually from her mother city, an unusual arrangement; for unlike Corinth's unloving daughter Corcyra, Potidaea still clung to her maternal city. In addition to expelling the officials from Corinth, the Potidaeans were also to give hostages to the Athenians to ensure their good behavior

MAP 2.9 The Revolt of Potidaea, 432 BC

and tear down their wall on the seaward side, which would leave them defenseless against the Athenian fleet. Athens was especially alarmed that Potidaea might revolt because Athens' subjects in this northern region were already wobbling in their allegiance. The Athenians had recently made a powerful enemy in that area, having angered Perdiccas, the subtle king of Macedonia, by supporting his brother against him: now Perdiccas was promoting a general rebellion against Athens on his borders and appealing to Corinth and Sparta to support him.[85]

Hoping that they would not have to revolt to Perdiccas, the Potidaeans sent envoys to Athens to plead their case—but they also sent emissaries to Sparta, in the company of envoys from their angry mother city, Corinth. The mission to Athens accomplished nothing. But the Spartans gave Potidaea a conditional promise of support: should Athens attack Potidaea, the Spartans, in turn, would invade Attica. Viewed in terms of power politics, this fateful guarantee is something of a puzzle. Distant Potidaea, after all, had nothing to do with the security of Sparta, or even with that of Corinth. Viewed in terms of rank, however, Sparta's guarantee makes perfect sense. By asserting an interest in Potidaea, Sparta was effectively demanding that Athens concede her inferiority by deferring to Spartan wishes. The vehicle for this demand, then, was irrelevant: Potidaea was simply an opportunity for the Spartans to press Athens. And it was a god-sent opportunity, moreover, because this time (unlike during the Samian imbroglio, when Corinth,

Sparta's greatest naval ally, prevented the Spartan alliance from coming to Samos' defense) Sparta enjoyed Corinthian support.[86]

Fortified by Sparta's assurances, Potidaea revolted from Athens (432 BC). An Athenian squadron that had been sent against King Perdiccas in Macedonia was now diverted to Potidaea, only to find the city in arms against them, and so returned in perplexity to fight Perdiccas. Many of the cities that shared the three-pronged peninsula of the Thracian Chalcidice with Potidaea revolted as well, allying themselves with Perdiccas, who helped them to empty the smaller and more vulnerable of their towns and resettle their inhabitants in a single large, strong city: Olynthus. Perdiccas even gave these Chalcidian rebels against Athens land to farm in his own realm, to replace what they had abandoned. And while the opportunity to help their imperiled kin offered, Corinth rushed "volunteers" to Potidaea (not official Corinthian soldiers, so as not formally to break the Thirty Years' Peace) and mercenaries from the Peloponnese, to the number of sixteen hundred hoplites and four hundred light troops. Their commander was the Corinthian Aristeus.[87]

In accord with the policy of Pericles to yield nothing to the Spartans, the Athenians simply ignored the Spartan threat to invade Attica if the Athenians attacked Potidaea. Athens soon sent a force against Potidaea, but this stopped along the way to fight Perdiccas, who, desperate to get rid of the Athenians infesting his territory, soon made a treaty with them. Next, the Athenians marched against the rebels, who had concentrated at Potidaea and Olynthus. There, the Athenians found the Corinthian Aristeus in command of the rebel infantry and—to the Athenians' surprise— Perdiccas leading the rebel cavalry, along with some of his own; the instant the naïve Athenians had departed Perdiccas' territory under the terms of the new treaty, that serpentine monarch had resumed his support for the rebellion he had fomented.[88]

Having distracted the rebels at Olynthus with a feint, the Athenians fought the Potidaeans and their allies before the very walls of Potidaea (?June 432 BC). The brave Aristeus, leading the Corinthian volunteers, turned to flight the Athenian force he confronted, but returning from the pursuit, he found that the rest of the Athenians had defeated the Potidaean army and driven it within the walls of the city. So Aristeus formed his men into a tight body and forced his way through the Athenian lines and into the safety of the town, to which the Athenians then laid siege. In the course of the battle, the golden Alcibiades, so powerful a spirit for good and ill in the later years of the war, was wounded, but his life and arms were saved by his friend and tent mate, the philosopher Socrates.[89]

The Potidaean affair further stoked the enmity between Athens and Corinth, offering more "grounds for complaint" (*aitiai*). Athens' attack on a colony of Corinth, and her siege of the Corinthians and Peloponnesians inside it, understandably angered the Corinthians; on the other hand, the Athenians were angry at the Peloponnesians' incitement of an Athenian subject to revolt and the Peloponnesians' open, if unofficial, fighting alongside the Potidaeans.[90]

Anxious about Potidaea and her men inside, Corinth summoned Sparta's allies to Sparta to urge the Spartans to go to war against Athens and so live up to their pledge to the Potidaeans (?July 432 BC). The Spartans needed little persuading: they had been willing to go war with Athens over Samos. Feeling at Sparta was hostile to Athens, as Thucydides repeatedly emphasizes. And this hostility was not known only in retrospect: "I see war rushing on us from the Peloponnese," Pericles was frequently heard to say.[91]

What had changed since Samos was that Sparta's allies were now behind her in her desire to fight Athens. The Spartans had been unable to go to war over Samos because their allies, Corinth in particular, had been unwilling. Now, because of Corcyra and Potidaea, the Corinthians wanted revenge against Athens. And the Megarians, too—who had a long list of "grievances" (*diaphorai*), chief among them the Athenian trade embargo (the Megarian Decree)—were eager for vengeance: this is how the "grounds for complaint" between the parties and the "grievances" produced a "pot-kicking-pot" situation, a chain of revenges, and led to war. Corinth, indeed, had already tried to take revenge on Athens in a way that did not directly violate the treaty, by subversion at Potidaea and then by unofficial support of the Potidaean revolt: Corinth's use of Potidaea was, thus, parallel in intention to Athens' trade embargo against Megara. But other cities, too, had cause for resentment. We are told especially of the eternal eyesore Aegina, an unwilling member of the Athenian confederacy since her surrender during the war at mid-century. At the great naval battle of Sybota, moreover, the Athenians had blocked the victory not only of Corinth but of Corinth's allies, too; these included Megara and considerable Elis in the west of the Peloponnese. *All* the major powers in the Peloponnese, and beyond the Peloponnese Megara and Aegina, too, now had reasons for wanting to take revenge on Athens. This angry atmosphere among Sparta's friends and allies also had implications for Sparta's own rank, for helping friends was an important way of proving rank. And now Sparta's friends wanted help.[92]

Opinion within Sparta itself was split, but primarily on the timing of the war, not the need for it. One of the Spartan kings, Archidamus, opposed an immediate declaration of war, and Thucydides imagined that he wanted to give the Peloponnesians more time to prepare for war against a maritime enemy, the Athenians more time to yield in the face of those preparations, and time for the arbitration required by the Thirty Years' Peace, which the Spartans could not scorn without offense to the gods. But

Archidamus' counsel of delay did not prevail at the meeting. Usually the Spartans voted by shouting, but the presiding ephor, one of the five "over-seers" who supervised Spartan public life, favored going promptly to war and pretended he could not tell which side shouted louder. He called upon the Spartan assembly to vote by separating into two groups, and a decided majority voted that the Athenians had, indeed, violated the treaty. The oracle of Delphi was consulted, and Apollo confirmed the judgment of the Spartans: "If they made war with all their might," the god affirmed, "they should have victory. And he would be with them both when asked and unasked."[93]

With Apollo's endorsement, the Spartans summoned all their allies to discuss going to war (?August 432 BC). In theory Lacedaemon had the right to command the members of her alliance, but in practice, as the deadlock over Samos had shown, she needed to secure their consent and active cooperation. Moreover, Sparta and her allies had to agree on how the war was to be conducted and, above all, on how it might end. "A war undertaken by an alliance to advance the interests of individual states," as Thucydides had King Archidamus say, "the outcome of which cannot be predicted, may not end easily or honorably." What would happen if the claims of some allies were satisfied while others suffered losses to their own property or pride? Sparta's allies had perhaps not forgotten how the Spartans had abandoned the Euboeans to their fate in 446 BC, when Pleistoanax had withdrawn from Attica and suffered Pericles to suppress their rebellion against Athens, or Sparta's decision in the 450s BC that the doom of Aegina was no affair of hers. And provision also had to be made lest an ally whose troops were away helping the Spartans were invaded by another Spartan ally, for private wars within the Spartan alliance were frequent. To prevent Sparta or any of her allies from selling out the others to Athens, and to protect Sparta's allies against each other, Sparta and her allies made an agreement—presumably at this meeting—that each ally must leave the war with the possessions she had upon entering it. Peace with Athens could not be made, that is, unless all territorial losses incurred in the course of the war were restored. And it was also agreed that the conclusion of peace with Athens should require the consent of a majority of the allies, whose vote should be binding upon all.[94]

Although the Spartans—and, subsequently, their allies—voted for war in 432 BC, probably toward the end of the summer, an actual attack upon Athens was still many months away. "During that time," Thucydides says, the Spartans "sent ambassadors to Athens alleging grievances, in order to have the best pretext for war, should the Athenians pay them no attention in any respect." Thucydides is dismissive of the protracted diplomatic exchange that separated the formal Peloponnesian decisions for war from the outbreak of the war itself. He felt that the Spartans had voted to go to war out of fear of Athenian power, and once the decision was made on that ample basis, every other Spartan gesture was but a sideshow, just bluster and delay.[95]

Viewed from the standpoint of rank, however, Sparta's diplomatic overtures to Athens appear far more significant than Thucydides acknowledges. Sparta had threatened war with Athens over Potidaea not because she cared about Potidaea but because she had chosen to test Athenian deference. The Athenians had not, as far as we know, openly defied Sparta over Potidaea; they had merely ignored her. Best for the Spartans to repeat forthrightly, then, the invitation to Athens to step down and concede the supremacy of Sparta in terms that could not be so easily ignored. Many Athenians, after all, might quail at an open challenge to Sparta, and thus the Spartans might well achieve the victory in standing they sought while avoiding war.[96]

During the winter of 432/431 BC, the Spartans sent three major diplomatic missions to Athens. First, the Spartans bade the Athenians to drive out the curse of the goddess—the hereditary taint attaching to Pericles through his mother's family, who incurred blood guilt two centuries before by killing some men who had taken refuge at the altar of Athena. The very strangeness, to modern eyes, of the Spartans' citing an ancient bane as an active grievance tends to confirm for the modern reader Thucydides' suggestion that the Spartans were merely groping for pretexts for war. Yet the content of the Spartan demand is less important than the *fact* of a demand. The question was whether the Athenians would climb down and obey Sparta's commands, whatever they were, or whether (as Thucydides put it) "the Athenians would pay them no attention *in any respect*." The Athenians, predictably, did not do as the Spartans ordered. Instead, they "retorted" with a demand that the Spartans drive out not one curse of their own but *two*. So not only did the Athenians refuse to yield, to admit their inferiority in rank, but they insulted the Spartans. They met the Spartans and raised them.[97]

Next, the Spartans returned with more down-to-earth ultimatums: "They commanded the Athenians to withdraw from Potidaea, to leave Aegina autonomous, and especially, most plainly of all, they said that there would not be war if they revoked the Megarian Decree." None of these commands had anything to do with the security of Sparta; none of these contentious issues inspired fear in the Spartans. Indeed, none of them had any direct bearing on even the pride of Sparta—although, indirectly, friends bruised and unhelped were an embarrassment—until Sparta chose to make them a test of Athenian respect for Sparta.[98]

Pericles' Athens refused to "submit" to the Spartans. Athens would adhere minutely to the terms of the Thirty Years' Peace, without acquiescing on any matter touching upon rank. One story has a Spartan envoy asking the Athenians whether, if they would not take down the Megarian Decree establishing the hated embargo, they might turn its face to the wall so that it could not be read. No. Athens must refuse to do anything commanded by the Spartans, be it great or small: so Thucydides makes Pericles say in the speech he writes for him on this occasion. And he has Pericles explain the logic behind Athens' behaving so. "We must not yield to the Peloponnesians," Pericles tells the Athenians. Only thus will the Spartans "learn to deal with you as equals." To the Spartans the Athenians replied that "they would do nothing at command"—an equal, after all, could not yield to orders—"but were ready to have their grievances settled in a fair and equitable manner by arbitration, according to the treaty."[99]

The Athenian offer of arbitration the Spartans refused, and so the arbitration clause of the Thirty Years' Peace, intended to stand between Athens and Sparta and war, failed of its purpose. The Spartans would in time feel that they had been wrong to refuse arbitration and that their neglect of this term of the treaty had offended the gods. But arbitration placed Athens and Sparta on the same level—exactly what Sparta was trying to avoid. When Corcyra had offered arbitration to Corinth during the wrangle over Epidamnus, Corinth had similarly refused, probably because arbitration implied exactly the equality between mother city and colony that the Corcyreans were trying to assert and the Corinthians to deny. At this stage of the rivalry, moreover, the Spartans could yield no more than the Athenians on any matter without seeming to back down, effectively sacrificing their claim to supreme rank. Accepting an offer to go to arbitration was itself humiliating in the world of Greek diplomacy; it might be resorted to if relations between powers were otherwise good, but when both sides were bristling, arbitration was abandoned in favor of trying to get the other party to take that one fateful, shameful step back.[100]

At the same time as they made their obstinate reply to Sparta's detailed demands and their offer of arbitration, the Athenians replied as well to a final Spartan mission, which bade them simply to grant autonomy to the Greeks—that is, to give up their naval empire. This last ultimatum was merely a slogan: the Athenians had not yielded to the orders of the Spartans, and now there would be war.[101]

WHY DID THE PELOPONNESIAN WAR break out? In seeking the cause of the war in Sparta's fear of Athens' growing power, Thucydides came close to the truth. It is likely that the Spartans had always viewed Athenian power with a certain concern, for it was a commonplace among Greeks that power and prosperity, especially if rapidly acquired, encouraged acts of *hybris*. Athenian power, any Greek would understand, would predispose Athens to challenge Sparta's supremacy in rank. It is also very likely that by the time war broke out between Athens and Sparta, Sparta did fear the power of Athens. But Spartan fear of Athens' power was not the cause of the war; it was but a by-product of Sparta's realization that Athens would not accept Sparta's supremacy in rank, the old hegemony over Greece that Sparta cast in the sixth century BC, forged in the Persian War, and tempered in the war at mid-century. Sparta feared not so much Athens' power but rather Athens' use of that power to dispute Sparta's rank—much, indeed, as Argos had feared the growing power of Mycenae in Diodorus' story of the outbreak of war between them. The Athenian challenge to Spartan rank, rather than Spartan fear of Athenian power, was the truest cause of the war.[102]

Who was responsible for the Peloponnesian War? Was it the Spartans, for being willing to go to war rather than brook any challenge to their ancient primacy? But there was no reason for Greece's hallowed *hegemon* to yield. Or was it the Athenians, as the dynamic party, for insisting on their equality in rank and being willing to go to war rather than yield the claim? But did not their victories over the Persians and their dominion over Greeks justify their pretension? There was nothing unnatural, nothing improper, about Athens' challenge to Sparta. However much Thucydides deplored the war he described, there is no hint of reproach in his description of the inflexible stance Pericles persuaded the Athenians to adopt as the war approached, no criticism of Athens' absolute refusal, in the words of a modern scholar, to throw Sparta a bone.[103]

To a Greek, the behavior of Pericles and Athens was entirely natural, indeed praiseworthy, in a state aspiring to rank. Likewise, the Spartan refusal to bow to a state they considered inferior would have been perfectly understandable. Are we, then, to blame the Corinthians, who began the chain of revenges and challenges to rank—of pot-kicking—that were the proximate cause of the war? No: few Greek states would have acted differently. We are in peril of ending up like Herodotus, when he pondered why the Persians fought the Greeks, tracing a chain of vengeances further back than the war against Troy.

In fact the Trojans, and the Greeks who fought them, may be as much to blame for the Peloponnesian War as Athenians, Spartans, or Corinthians. For with the story of the war against Troy, Homer also passed down to the classical Greeks the ferocious competitiveness of their forefathers. The transcendent cause of the Peloponnesian War was the culture of Greek foreign relations, which was deeply embedded in Greek competitiveness and the ethics of a heroic past. The principle that created the Olympic Games, the principle that inspired potter to outdo potter and poet to surpass poet, the competitive principle that drove so much of what is memorable about Greek civilization—that same principle drove Athens and Sparta to war.

III

THE WAR OF REVENGE,
431–430 BC

Mount Helicon, sacred to the muses, looked down upon the great marsh of Copaïs, graveyard of cities. In heroic times men had cleared the limestone caverns that drained Copaïs to the sea and tilled her smiling bottomlands and built their dwellings there. But with the passing of the heroes and the silting of the ways, the water carried in by the rivers Cephisus and Melas failed of escape, and the cities were drowned, and Copaïs became a mere—a sea of reeds, the haunt of waterfowl, rich pasture for lowing cattle and questing pigs. To her neighbors, the Boeotians, Copaïs gave their comfortable things: herbs and rushes, plump ducks and woodcocks, and—above all—tasty eels, grown fat from nibbling beneath the green-brown waters upon the inundated works of forgotten men.[1]

Sweating porters bore the eels from the huts of their snigglers to rich fanciers as far away as Athens, fifty miles to the south, where they were roasted over coals in leaves of beets. But only a morning's walk from Copaïs feasted the epicures of Thebes, lords of the Boeotian plain, whose character, it is nice to think, was formed over centuries by the very qualities of this writhing delicacy: strong, cunning, voracious. Here stern prince Cadmus, roving far from his Phoenician seat, had followed a queerly dappled cow in her wandering and founded a city where she toppled over in weariness. To people the land, he sowed dragon's teeth in the rich earth, and bronze-clad warriors grew up from them. Dreading their aspect, Cadmus cast a stone into their midst. Each of the dragon-born, believing the stone thrown by another, took fire at the slight; they smote each other until but five remained. And from those five descended the men of Thebes, a city born of guile and pride and slaughter.

In the time of stories, Thebes was second to none in grandeur: so we learn from epic, and especially from Athenian tragedy, with its Theban tales of Oedipus the damned, brave Antigone, and the doomed Seven Against Thebes. But in the fifth century BC, Thebes was a power of the second order, left to weigh her centuried glory against the dusty insignificance of her present. Ancient Thebes, the seat of Heracles, greatest of the heroes, should rule at least her own plain, thought the Thebans. But only eight miles from Thebes at the edge of that plain lay Plataea, the particular object of Thebes' treasured resentment, whose tiny independence mocked Theban pretensions. Clinging to the southern border of Boeotia, Plataea had been the site of the great Greek victory over the Persians in 479 BC and had ever refused to join the league of Boeotian cities of which Thebes was the *hegemon*. Although founded by Thebes—or so the Thebans claimed and the Plataeans no less firmly denied—Plataea had by April 431 BC for nearly a century been the fast ally of mighty Athens to the south—Athens, long an enemy of the Thebans.[2]

Tired after a festival day, little Plataea lay asleep in the arms of Mount Cithaeron beneath a narrow moon. In the first watch of the night, Plataean traitors opened a gate, and the men of Thebes crept in. The plan was for a massacre: the Thebans, three hundred and a few, were to kill the political rivals of the natives who had admitted them, whereupon those traitors were to bring the city over to Thebes, its rightful master. And so, as soon as the Thebans grounded their spears in the marketplace, poisoned whispers told them the doors they must break down and named the men they must slay.[3]

But no: to the horror of the betrayers, the Thebans had settled upon a gentler course. There would be no killing. Instead the Plataeans were to be invited to abandon their allegiance to Athens and instead join Thebes' Boeotian League. Not the crash of falling doors, not the screams of new-made widows, but the pure notes of a herald's voice roused the townsfolk and bade them in mild words to turn out in the square and compact with their kinsmen in the Boeotian union.

Night concealed from the Plataeans the scantiness of the Thebans, and so the leading men of the town, whey-faced with despair, came forth to agree to what the Thebans said and to bargain for the best terms they could. But they also sent a runner to their great ally Athens, pleading for rescue.

As the night grew older and rain began to fall, the Plataeans came to realize just how few the Thebans were and resolved upon resistance. By burrowing through the clay walls of their houses, they collected in armed groups and quietly rolled wains to block the streets. Then, just before dawn, the men of Plataea threw open their doors and rallied against the Thebans. Again and again the Thebans, formed close in their phalanx, threw the Plataeans back; but the women and slaves of the town raised eerie cries from the roofs and threw roof tiles and stones among the tight-grouped invaders; and the rain came down, and still the maddened Plataeans charged out of the dark. Suddenly all was panic and flight among the Thebans as they fumbled for a way out of the mud and the maze of alleys. The gate they came in—now closed, spiked with a javelin. Another gate—barred. But here was an axe to cut through it! A few got out that way, but the Plataeans, who knew every shadowed lane, quickly shut the door again. In desperation some of the Thebans cast themselves from the town's high walls, to be crippled as they landed; others were slain stumbling alone in the dark. Finally, an open gate! But rather than a passage to freedom, it was the great portal of a structure built onto the town wall, and with the groan of the door behind them, the frantic Thebans were entombed.

By torchlight the Plataeans deliberated on whether to set fire to the wooden hulk that confined the Thebans. Meanwhile a second messenger was sent to Athens to report the victory. Elsewhere in the dark, shouting streets, lost Thebans were cut down or yielded themselves and were made prisoners. As for the mass of Thebans in the building, they surrendered before the Plataeans could decide how to dislodge them. But now a cry from beyond the walls: the whole Theban army was outside in the rain. Supposed to arrive soon after the seizure of the town to confirm Theban control, they had gotten lost in the dark, become mired in a flooded river, and only now approached the city.

Instantly the Plataeans understood their new peril. The Thebans had attacked in time of peace: there had not even been a guard upon the gate when their men slipped in. Plataea's livestock and many of her citizens slept in the countryside. How easily might the Thebans seize these outliers and hold them hostage. But the Plataeans, of course, had hostages as well. And so they sent their herald out into the dawn to warn the Thebans: lay a hand on our possessions, they said, and we will slaughter our Theban prisoners. Frustrated, the sodden Theban army turned for home. The Thebans later claimed that the Plataeans had promised to release their prisoners, should the Plataean territory be left inviolate; naturally the Plataeans denied any such promise. Whatever the truth, the next act of the Plataeans was to kill their prisoners in revenge for the Theban attack. So perished one hundred and eighty men of Thebes. Too late came a runner from Athens, gasping for the Thebans' lives.[4]

With their carefully concerted plot, the Thebans could have established a prompt and bloody grip upon Plataea. But they chose not to, probably in order to plant what they considered a vital quibble to allow them to retain—not just seize—control of the city. For Sparta had agreed with her allies (of which Thebes was one) that peace with Athens could be made only if Sparta's allies received back everything they might lose in the course of the war. And from that agreement, it could be deduced that any war between the Athenian and Spartan confederacies was likely to end on terms whereby both sides received back what they had held at the beginning. If so, Thebes

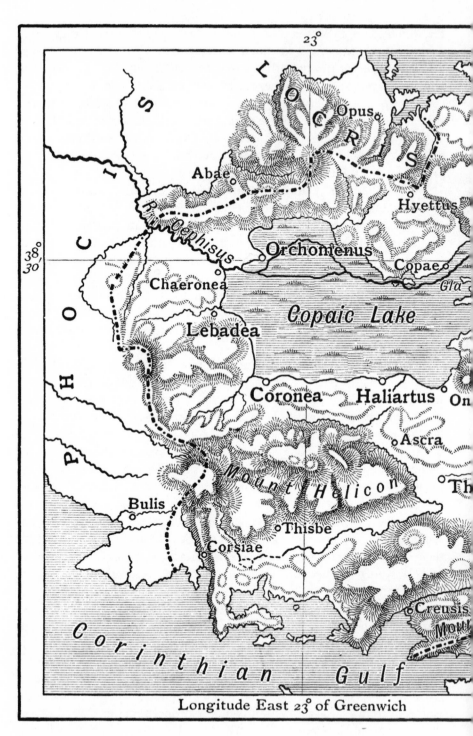

MAP 3.1 Boeotia

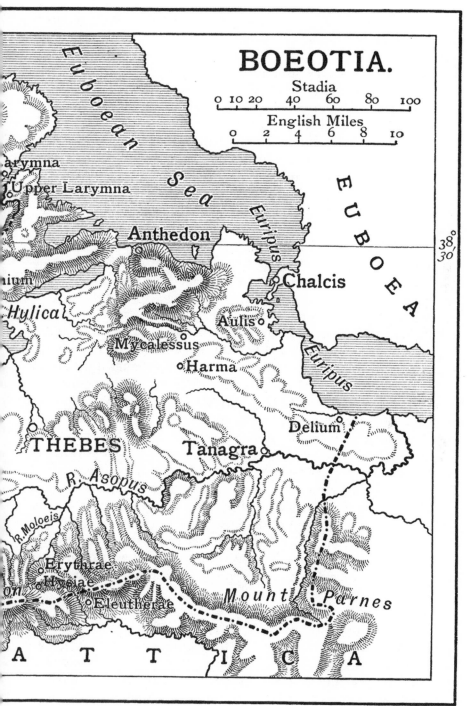

BOEOTIA.

Stadia

0 10 20   40   60   80   100

English Miles

0   2   4   6   8   10

Euboean Sea

Euripus

EUBOEA

38°
30'

arymna

Upper Larymna

Anthedon

Chalcis

ium

Hylica

Aulis

Euripus

Mycalessus

Harma

Euripus

Delium

THEBES

Tanagra

R. Asopus

R. Moloeis

Erythrae

Hysiae

on

Eleutherae

Mount   Parnes

A T T I C A

Walker & Boutall sc.

hoped to claim that Plataea had not been conquered but rather had chosen their side, and so was theirs by right, not the Athenians', and need not be returned. The Spartans, then, had unwittingly encouraged Thebes to turn pickpocket. Years later, the Spartans would think that this Theban attack on Plataea had put them in the wrong with the gods: perhaps the Thebans also hoped that if Plataea came over voluntarily, all would be right with gods and men.[5]

On the Plataean side, if the Plataeans had chosen not to kill their captives, those captives might have guaranteed the safety of their city. One hundred and eighty Theban prisoners, some of them no doubt prominent, would have been an admirable bond for Thebes' good behavior in future, especially if—as was likely—they were lodged at mighty Athens. So the Athenians seem to have thought, in any event, for they arrested all the Boeotians they could find in Attica as soon as they heard of Thebes' descent on Plataea and begged the Plataeans to keep any prisoners they took alive. But it was not to be: after a night of blood, dawn broke upon wrath and vengeance.[6]

The Theban attempt upon Plataea ended as if it had been a Greek battle, with the rituals of victory and defeat: the Thebans sent a herald to ask for the return of their dead for burial (thereby admitting defeat, according to the customs of Greek war), whereupon the Plataeans granted the bodies to the Thebans to bear away under truce. A tense and strange business, to be sure: for on a field of battle the victors could move away to allow the losers to remove the corpses, but at Plataea the defeated had to carry their kinsmen's murdered bodies from the very thresholds of their murderers. Now there could be no doubt that a state of war existed, that the treaty between Athens and her allies and Sparta and hers had been, in the words of Thucydides, "glaringly violated." By killing the Thebans, the Plataeans had made Plataea the indisputable first battlefield of a wider war. No soft, winking words, no portrayal of the Theban incursion as unofficial, as a friendly visit gotten out of hand, might now keep the peace. Accordingly the women, the children, and the weak of the Plataeans were removed to safety in Attica, while Athens sent a garrison to support the warriors of Plataea in the defense of their city.[7]

The Plataeans' decision to indulge their anger shows that they, like the Thebans when they planted their quibble, expected any greater war between Athens and Sparta to be a short, low-stakes affair, a sharp but temporary distraction from the eternal business of Greeks hating their neighbors. The power of protective Athens, Plataea seems to have thought, would not be broken; nor would Sparta be so weakened as to lose her hold over Thebes. A settlement would be negotiated between the powers (in no longer time than Plataea could hold out in hostile Boeotia) that would give to each his own, thereby returning all the parties to the status quo before the war. Plataea's killing of the Thebans would, therefore, go unavenged. Plataea did not think to hazard her existence by killing the Theban prisoners: she could, she calculated, satisfy her ire with impunity. She was wrong, of course. The seed of the dragon would have their revenge.

I N THE GENERAL WAR THAT the Thebans had unleashed and the Plataeans had not prevented, Lacedaemon and her allies would fight Athens and hers. On the land, the strength of Sparta far outweighed that of Athens. For in time of war, Sparta could in principle draw support from nearly all the powers in the Peloponnese, other than Argos, which she had bound to peace for thirty years in 450 BC. Sparta's alliance extended, too, through the Isthmus of Corinth—the peninsula that connected the Peloponnese to the mainland and that Corinth shared with Megara—and further east into Boeotia, subservient (Plataea excepted) to friendly Thebes, and then northwest into unruly Phocis. South of Boeotia, Athens was isolated on the heel of Attica, her only nearby mainland allies small, like Plataea, or weak and faintly comic, like the tribes of Ozolian—"Smelly"—Locris and various of the sombrero-wearing barons of Thessaly.[8]

Athens' power lay in the string of old Greek colonies across the Aegean Sea, on the west coast of Asia Minor, cities that pebbled the skin of the western provinces of the gigantic Persian empire, whose center was three months' walk away to the east. These Athenian subjects were connected to the Greek mainland by the Thraceward region, the string of Greek colonies along the north coast of the Aegean; up-country from the coast lay the wastes of the Thracian barbarians. The Thraceward cities, too, bent the knee to Athens, as did the multitude of Aegean islands; the Aegean Sea was the blue road that joined the possessions of Athens together. Under tribute of treasure she laid them, and that tribute fed a great and hungry fleet, a ward against the Persians but also the heart of her naval supremacy; with three hundred seaworthy war galleys, the naval strength of Athens was greater than that of the rest of Greece together. These ships and the silver to pay their crews—for Athens had long turned a profit on her confederation—were the true power of Athens. But Athens' home strength in soldiers was great as well: with the largest free population in Greece, Athens could herself put thirteen thousand heavy-armed infantry into the field, along with twelve hundred horsemen and archers to match, without cheating her forts and garrisons. Unlike Sparta's, Athens' allies contributed mostly money or ships. But those Athenians who had gone overseas to receive allotments—to places where Athens had established cleruchies—were called upon to fight for

Athens on land. The cleruchs of Lemnos and Imbros, islands in the northern Aegean, seem especially to have been valued for their military qualities.[9]

Brave Sparta herself could not field so many soldiers as Athens: around six thousand heavy-armed men is the largest number the Spartans were ever reported to send on campaign during the Peloponnesian War. But Sparta had her allies—weak, with a few exceptions, in money and in ships but strong in infantry. Had Sparta assembled all her friends for a single great battle, their full force must have numbered at least forty or fifty thousand hoplites. And more than men, Sparta had her iron legend, mined in the course of her long struggle against Argos and forged in the war against the Persians. Sparta's soldiers, the Greeks thought, might be killed in combat, but they could not truly be vanquished. In a world where battles were won by men thrusting at one another with spear and shield, fame in war was every bit as potent as numbers: for if a warrior knew the man set against him would not flee, so much greater was the temptation to flee from him.[10]

U NTIL THE NIGHT FIGHT IN PLATAEA, the great antagonists Sparta and Athens had been noisy in words but quiet in deeds. Now both sides began formally to request aid from their Greek allies and sympathizers and also attempted to secure the help of the Great King of Persia, as well as other, lesser barbarian powers. From friendly Greek states in Italy and Sicily, the Spartans begged money and ordered the construction of five hundred ships of war—an astonishing total, if understood as a realistic program of building; less so if the purpose was merely to rattle the Athenians and make them fear for their naval superiority when they got wind of the request, since the Greeks of the mainland were quite ignorant of the actual resources of their western kin. In fact, no ships were built, and no money sent from the west, and this was no disaster: for Sparta's strategy depended neither upon war galleys nor upon silver.[11]

The main effort of the Spartans was to assemble at the Isthmus of Corinth an army of allies to invade Attica, the very territory of Athens itself. As in any war not aimed at the brute extermination of the foe, the strategy of the Spartans was premised upon a theory about how the enemy might be forced to yield. This theory, shared by the Greeks in general, required that the Spartans invade the home territory of their enemy. At that point—or even while the Peloponnesian army was en route—the Athenians might sue for peace. If they did not and accepted the Spartan challenge, a battle would be fought on the plains of Attica. After the Spartans won that battle—as they expected they would—the Athenians would sue for peace. And if the Athenians did not emerge from their walls to fight, the Peloponnesian army would ravage their agricultural land, doing what damage they could to the grain in the fields, the olive groves, the vineyards, and the various structures outside the city walls. After this, according to the Spartan theory, the Athenians would yield—if not right away, then certainly once the process was repeated. These outcomes were commonplaces among the Greeks, and the Spartans' predictions were justified in part by the observed behavior of Greek cities generally and in part by the behavior of Athens itself. For when the Spartans had invaded Attica in 446 BC and ravaged only a corner of the land, the Athenians had, in fact, soon made peace.[12]

Despite these historical precedents, the Spartans' expectations for victory are slightly puzzling. The confidence they placed in ravaging is especially curious, for in a world without chainsaws and gasoline, trees were exhausting to cut, and grains could only be burned at the right time and in the right weather. Even if a harvest could be damaged, ancient Greek cities—like most agricultural societies known to history—kept reserves of food against the failure of harvests in the event of bad weather or blight. Ravaging the crops of a normal Greek city, then, while costly for its population, would not usually bring it to the verge of starvation. And Athens was hardly a normal Greek city. She was a trading power with a large population and great public wealth and had for decades imported much of her grain from abroad. Moreover, Athens had walls connecting the city to its port, Piraeus, and these defenses would allow her to sustain herself through commerce even if wholly deprived of the yield of Attica. So long as Athens had access to the sea, she could not be starved out, whatever momentary financial hardship the ravaging of her fields might bring to Athenian individuals. The Greeks, including the Spartans, knew this.[13]

Defeat in the field, moreover, was often no more decisive in practical terms than ravaging. Losers' casualties in Greek battles, while considerable, were rarely of demographic significance. It was not, then, that the loser could not fight on. In practice, rather, defeat in the field—for Athens or nearly any other Greek state—meant being forced behind the walls of the central settlement. But unlike in Roman times or the Middle Ages, this did not lead to assault or to siege and eventual reduction by starvation. For in fifth-century BC Greece, the technology of fortification had so far outstripped the tools available for attacking fortified places that all but the smallest were impervious to assault. Greek armies in the field, too, lacked a central commissariat, surviving instead on food carried by individual soldiers, bought from merchants, or seized from the granaries or farms of the enemy. This meant that long sieges of great cities were usually impossible. The practical outcome of a Greek defeat in battle, then, was much the same as a refusal to fight in the first place: the loser would retire behind his walls, while the victor spent a few days ravaging the loser's territory before, perforce, returning home.[14]

It may seem strange, then, that the Spartans expected the Athenians to yield after defeat in battle or after having their fields ravaged. Yet even if a loss in battle did not present danger of extermination or if being ravaged did not usually pose the threat of starvation, these acts had profound significance in the realm of symbols, in the realm of the rank of states. They were (depending of the point of view of the onlooker) acts of either *hybris* or revenge: they asserted the superior rank of the victors, or ravagers, because they proved their superiority in manhood and showed the inferiority of the ravaged, who did not have the courage to come out and fight but looked on impotently from their walls.[15]

Humiliating the victim and boosting the pride of the victor in battle, or ravager, generally sufficed to settle the relative standing of the parties, which was often the main issue of the war. Beating the enemy in the field and ravaging, then, were not so much methods of coercion as victories in themselves. The defeated, or ravaged, party, taking to heart its proven inferiority, was expected to agree to a treaty that ratified that decision and adjusted the practical consequences accordingly, sometimes awarding the victor a strip of disputed borderland, like Thyrea, which lay between Sparta and Argos, itself primarily symbolic of the precedence over which the two states fought.

Such was the Spartans' strategy in 431 BC: they hoped that the mere threat of financial loss or humiliation might force the Athenians to yield before the Peloponnesians arrived in Attica. But if the Athenians did not, then by fighting or ravaging the Spartans would confirm their superiority in rank, and that would itself constitute victory. Perhaps the Athenians would beg for peace right away, as indeed they had done in 446 BC; perhaps they would not. It made little difference: the Spartans trusted they would win anyway. Invading Attica and ravaging the fields of the Athenians would win the war. "In a few years of ravaging the land," the Spartans thought, "they would destroy the power of the Athenians." And invading Attica would win the war in a relatively short time: "some of the Greeks thought that the Athenians might hold out one year, if the Spartans should invade their land, some two, and some longer, but no more than three years."[16]

As soon as the fight at Plataea was reported, runners went out with instructions for Sparta's allies to assemble at the Isthmus; two-thirds of the full levy of each state was summoned. It took the allies more than a month to gather. Command over them was held by Archidamus, one of Sparta's two kings. Archidamus himself had advocated delay before going to war with Athens, wanting to give diplomacy a longer time to work and the Peloponnesians more time to prepare for a war against a power so unlike their own. But with Sparta's other king, Pleistoanax, in exile—for leading the Peloponnesians home in 446 BC, bribed, it was alleged, by Pericles—and his successor yet a child, Archidamus put his reservations aside and did his Spartan duty.

Once the army had come together, Archidamus sent ahead a lone messenger to see if the Athenians would yield now that the Peloponnesians were on the march. We must imagine this envoy, with his red cloak and herald's wand, pacing through the dusty, semiabandoned villages of Attica, bearing somber witness (for Spartan self-control brooked no gawking) to the ruin the Athenians were preemptively wreaking upon their own countryside. They were herding their beasts in long, protesting lines to the coast, to be carried across in boats to the safety of nearby islands, deep-soiled Euboea in particular—safety, that is, as long as Athens commanded the sea. And perhaps the Lacedaemonian's unstirred visage was momentarily heated by the angry gaze of an Attic farmer, his children whimpering in his wagon, piled high with food and furnishings, as the rustic painfully broke down his house to take the valuable beams and doors and windows behind Athens' walls, the roof of his home already sagging and the walls of mud, now ungirded, caving in.

Even as the Peloponnesians gathered at the Isthmus, the Athenian democracy had voted not to come out and fight them, not to defend the countryside. And the country dwellers, which is to say, most Athenians, had used the time to save what they could of their substance—other than the still-ripening crops themselves—from the coming of the enemy. But discontent with this policy was sharp, and at any time the assembly might vote to reverse it and send the Athenian army forth to fight; or quailing before shame or hardship, the assembly might instead seek a settlement with the Spartans. To fortify Athenian resolution, Pericles had urged upon the assembly a supporting measure that no emissary was to be received while the Spartan army was in the field.

And so it was that when the dust-shod Spartan envoy arrived at the gate of Athens, he found it shut against him. He might not enter the city and address the Athenians. No, the Athenian authorities said, he must be beyond the borders of Attica before the sun arose again, and they sent him off with grim men to ensure that he talked to no one on the way. Back through the empty fields of Attica the Spartan stalked with his silent escort, frowned down upon by abandoned paddocks, gaped at by the empty doors of empty houses. And just as he crossed the frontier and his escort turned away, he brought forth a laconic prophecy: "this day will begin great evils for the Greeks."[17]

MAP 3.2 Peloponnesian Invasion of Attica, 431 BC

Now at last Archidamus and the army of the Peloponnesians came forth over the Isthmus of Corinth. Attica was bounded not only by Boeotia to the north but also by Megara to the west. In this northwestern corner was the Thriasian plain (Eleusis was its biggest place), which ended to the north in the ridge of Cithaeron—and over Cithaeron, on the hostile Boeotian side, lay friendly, embattled Plataea. But in the debatable land between Boeotia and Attica, in a glen of Cithaeron, nestled the fortified border town of Oenoe. The Athenians held Oenoe, but this was a place upon which the Boeotian League had an old claim. And so we may justly detect the eel-fed hand of Thebes, master of the Boeotians, twining around Archidamus' decision to attack Oenoe before advancing into Attica proper.[18]

The Thebans' logic will have been a variation on that which guided their nighttime descent on Plataea. For, in a formal sense, the war between Athens and Sparta would only commence when the Peloponnesians crossed into Attica itself. The Boeotians could construe the taking of Oenoe, then, as merely driving some deracinated squatters out of a small quarter of Boeotia. And when the war came to be settled on the terms Sparta had promised her allies—the return to each of their holdings at war's beginning—Thebes' claim to Oenoe would be fortified by the fact that Oenoe had, in truth, been in Boeotian hands when the war between Athens and Sparta technically began.[19]

Archidamus would have to harken to Theban desires, even to Theban quibbles. For not only did Boeotia provide a significant part of his force, including all the cavalry (so necessary to protect Archidamus' footmen against the Athenian cavalry, when the Peloponnesian army spread out to ravage), but any supplies that made their way to the Peloponnesian army in Attica were also apt to come from Boeotia. But Archidamus, Thucydides tells us, was not unhappy to dally at Oenoe. He felt that the Athenians were most likely to yield with their crops yet unravaged and hoped that they might come to their senses while he thus delayed. All he needed to put a stop to the war was the Athenians "yielding anything." Any sort of climbdown would do, so long as it implied that Athens acknowledged Sparta's superior rank—for it was rank, after all, that Athens and Sparta were fighting over.

Alas for Archidamus and the Thebans, the Peloponnesian attack on Oenoe served chiefly as proof of the power of fortifications in classical Greece. A great army strove against a mite, cutting down trees, building rams, and trying every means at its disposal—but in vain. Archidamus was ever more roundly reproached, in the mouthy way of Greek armies, for his delay at the Isthmus, for the slowness of his march, and, above all, for this futile diversion at Oenoe. The Peloponnesians were furious at being deprived of the plunder of Attica. For the Athenians had been slow to strip the countryside of their goods, in the manner of coastal dwellers waiting for the last minute to flee a hurricane, and Archidamus' delay had given them the precious time they needed to finish the task.[20]

Finally, since the Athenians gave no hint of humbling themselves, Archidamus abandoned the frustration of Oenoe and descended into Attica itself. Thus it was that the war between Athens and Sparta commenced in earnest some eighty days after the Theban attack on Plataea, in late June 431 BC, when the grain was ripe. And upon that ripe grain in the northwestern corner of Attica, in the fields around Eleusis (sacred to grain's gracious goddess and, in story, the very first ground to be cultivated by man), and then west into the Thriasian plain, the army of the Peloponnesians slaked its concatenated ire. It was a devil's harvest: the grain not cut and stored but rather devoured and trampled and burned; vines torn from their supports; olive trees hacked about with hatchets; the barns that looked for a festive harvest instead set afire or simply thrown down. And all the time there were Peloponnesian watchers on Athens—watchers, we must imagine, on the ridge of Aegaleus, which sundered northeastern Attica from the town.[21]

Would the Athenians come out to meet the Peloponnesians in battle? Then—an open gate! A cloud of dust! But it was only the Athenian cavalry, riding forth to harry the ravagers. A quick fight near Eleusis, and the Athenian horse fled back inside the walls. On came Archidamus, unopposed by footmen, destroying ever eastwards, and then, all at once, as he rounded the end of the ridge, the army of the Peloponnesians could be seen from Athens' walls and her acropolis. Archidamus camped in full view of the city, around the abandoned town of Acharnae, the largest town in Attica other than Piraeus and the city of Athens itself. And there, at last, Archidamus drew up his army for battle, goading the Athenians to come out to fight, challenging them just as brave Brasidas was to do before Megara in the seventh year of the war and as shunned Pleistoanax seemingly failed to do in 446 BC.[22]

Now the Athenians felt shame—that overwhelming shame that begins in the face and rushes hot down the backbone. For the Athenians were a proud people, with much to be proud of. In a speech he writes for the Spartan king before the departure of the Peloponnesians from the Isthmus, Thucydides has Archidamus describe the Athenians as "deeming themselves worthy to invade and ravage their neighbors rather than to witness the same happen to them." The Athenians, Archidamus says, esteemed themselves superior in rank to other Greeks and deemed it in the course of nature to visit such superiority upon the lesser. For men of such pride, to be ravaged and do nothing was the most abject humiliation. The Athenians had set themselves up as rivals to the Spartans, and now the Spartans could claim to have shown, in a time-honored Greek way, that they were better men than the Athenians.[23]

In the streets, Athenians gathered in clots, hotly disputing what should be done. Oracles of strange purport were recited. The young men in particular, never having seen an enemy from their own walls, were furious to march out and come to grips with the impertinent foe, while Pericles was blackguarded for cowardice—for having kept the Athenians within their gates.[24]

Not least passionate among the Athenians were the men of Acharnae, over whose fields the fist of Archidamus even now hovered. Thucydides reports that Archidamus had chosen to camp at Acharnae precisely because it was so large a place, and its men, therefore, were powerful in the democracy. He hoped they might tip the Athenians toward fighting. And perhaps they would have, had an assembly been called. But Pericles, by methods legal or not, prevented such a meeting and so forestalled any vote on whether to march forth.[25]

Refusing to fight for the fields of Attica had been Pericles' plan all along. And to reinforce the Athenians' confidence in him, Pericles had offered to sacrifice his own property to the city. Suspecting that the Spartans

FIGURE 3.1 Greek cavalryman

would exclude his lands from the general destruction, either to make the Athenians mistrust him or because of his personal connection to Archidamus (they were "guest-friends," a relationship between prominent men of different states that had survived among the Greeks from the days of Homer), he proclaimed to the Athenians that he would surrender his holdings, should they be spared, to the Athenian state. Nor was land the only sacrifice Pericles would make for his strategy. When the Peloponnesians ravaged northern Attica, in silent dignity Pericles took upon himself the whole wrath of the scandalized Athenian people. Silent he endured the savage mockery of the poets and suffered the waxing of a shrill politician, Cleon, who swelled like a leech upon the people's anger.[26]

Despite popular fury, Pericles prevailed, and the gates of Athens remained shut, except to cavalry patrols that went out to cut off those Peloponnesians who strayed too far from their host. There was another skirmish, this time between Boeotian and Athenian horse, who were accompanied by some Thessalians; the Athenians had the best of it until Peloponnesian infantry came up and drove them away. Avoiding the ritual admission of defeat, the

Athenians were able to recover the bodies of their dead without asking for a truce, but the Peloponnesians erected a trophy to mark the spot anyway, making the ritual claim to victory. This was, after all, a war of pride, a war for symbolic dominance, and thus a war in which such tokens mattered.[27]

The challenge to battle at Acharnae did not bring the Athenian infantry out; nor, while the Peloponnesians remained there, did the ravaging of Acharnae's fields. So Archidamus broke camp and continued slowly east, across the northern reaches of Attica, wasting the land between Mounts Parnes and Pentelikon. By now the invaders' provisions were close to exhaustion (it shows the simplicity of Greek logistics that an army could fear starvation while spoiling ripe grain), and the Peloponnesians had to head for friendly territory. And so they marched northeast, out of Attica into Boeotia, ravaging the land of Oropus, an Athenian possession beyond the Attic border and another place upon which, like Oenoe, the Boeotians had an old claim. Nor did the Thebans fail to indulge their private wrath, for while they had provided both cavalry and foot for the inroad into Attica, the rest of their forces had avenged the humiliation they had suffered earlier in the year by ravaging the territory of Plataea. Once it had similarly ravaged Oropus, the Peloponnesian army marched back west across the Isthmus, whereupon its contingents were dismissed to their homes, hastening to gather in their own harvests. They had despoiled Attica for perhaps a month.[28]

Once the Peloponnesian army was gone, the Athenians sat themselves in assembly to consider their defense for the future. Garrisons were sent by land and sea to fortified places in Attica and the Athenian empire, while what were judged the hundred best warships of the year and a thousand talents of silver (imagine a talent as being worth a million of today's dollars) were set aside to defend against the only thing that might endanger Athens' existence: an enemy attack by sea. Death was decreed to any man who proposed to use the money for any other end. Such arrangements accorded well with the strategy of caution Pericles had prevailed upon the Athenians to adopt: one of "keeping quiet, taking care of their navy, and not trying to add to their empire or running any risks during the war." Both the Athenians' cautious measures and Pericles' plans reflect anxiety that the war against Sparta might transform itself into one for national survival—but they show that it was not a war of that nature yet. Greek cities sometimes did destroy each other, especially when actuated by revenge. A war over rank might well escalate into a war of extermination.[29]

Even as Archidamus' army was slashing its way through Attica, Pericles' counterstrategy was set in train. A war fleet of one hundred ships, each carrying the usual ten heavy-armed marines and four archers, was fitted out at Piraeus and dispatched upon a raiding expedition around the Peloponnese.

Such an expedition had been well prepared, over years, by a series of alliances between Athens and states on the far side of the Peloponnese—particularly with Zacynthus, an island guarding the outlet of the gulf of Corinth; with Corinth's estranged colony Corcyra to its north; and with Acarnania on the mainland between them, where men cultivated the art of hurling stones at their enemies from whirling slings. Thus the Athenian fleet would have safe havens at the far hinge of its expeditions—places to rest, refit, and resupply before sailing back around the unfriendly Peloponnese.[30]

Coastal raiding was not a new strategy. It was exactly what Athens had done in its earlier war with Sparta, probably in 456 and 454 BC, when she had sent great fleets around the Peloponnese, stopping here and there to ravage and destroy, to "humble the fame of the Spartans." And such was the purpose of the Athenian raid in 431 BC. Thucydides has Pericles, contemplating this technique for the present war, describe it as a means of "reprisal" and "revenge." The comic playwright Aristophanes, as well, confirms that the Athenians understood their raids as revenge for the Spartans' invasions of Attica.[31]

Athens could inflict less economic damage upon Sparta and her allies with raids from ships than Sparta could inflict upon Athens by ravaging the fields of Attica. But just as Sparta's strategy was ultimately symbolic, rather than economic, so was that of Athens. Nor was there any exact calculus of shame; humiliation was not measured by bushels of wasted grain. A ravaging was a ravaging. More than the economic impact, it was the manner of the ravaging—the insolent insouciance with which it was carried out and the hand-wringing inability of the ravaged to prevent it—that made the impact, that filled full the barns of enemy shame. The degree of pain caused was important, too; Thucydides has Pericles argue that even if Athenian ravaging destroyed less, it caused more pain because the Peloponnesians lacked Athens' ability to import supplies. Speed, too, was vital: the best revenge was one taken right away. As far back as the *Iliad*, the debt of revenge was one that "should not go long unpaid." It was for this last reason, as well as the convenient absence of so many of the Peloponnesian defenders, that the Athenian expedition set out while the Peloponnesians were still in Attica. And if Sparta could conduct one ravaging of Attica, Athens, with the mobility provided by her ships, could ravage both the land of Sparta and that of her allies.[32]

In the war over rank, Athens' great strategic advantage was that she did not need to outdo Sparta in causing humiliation. Rather, it was the Spartans who, emphatically, had to outdo Athens, for they were the ones who began the war; they were the ones who sought to show their superiority and make the Athenians admit their inferiority. Pericles' war aim was not to assert Athens' superiority in rank but simply her equality with Sparta—to make

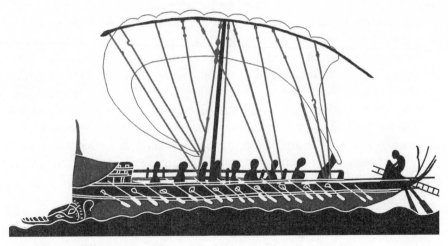

FIGURE 3.2 Greek warship under sail

(as Thucydides has Pericles say to the Athenians) the Spartans "deal with you as equals."[33]

In this war, achieving equality simply meant that the Athenians had to prevent the Spartans from gaining any insuperable advantage in rank—by winning a great battle, say, or by ravaging Attica unavenged. If Athens could achieve that, she would get what she wanted out of the war. In principle such a war might go on forever; neither the Spartan nor the Athenian strategy was aimed directly at forcing their opponents to make peace; rather, both strove to impress their conception of the relative rank of the two states upon their enemy and upon the Greek world. Neither party expected the war to be eternal, however; both sides assumed that once their claim to rank was made good, peace would naturally follow because there would be nothing further to fight about. That was how, Greeks knew, wars worked.[34]

Along with fifty ships provided by her ally Corcyra, Athens raided the coast of Sparta's own territory of Laconia; Messenia, Sparta's possession to the west; and Elis, Sparta's ally in the northwestern Peloponnese. "Doing ill as they sailed around" is the historian's terse shorthand for the great Athenian raiding expedition of the first year of the war. But what naval skill lies behind that clipped description![35]

The Peloponnese—its three craggy southern peninsulas in particular—is a sailor's nightmare of harborless rocks and suddenly threatening lee shores. Nor would any modern captain care to make a passage on the quick-to-anger Mediterranean upon the warships of fifth-century BC Greece. These were tall galleys with three stacked banks of oars—*triereis*, or "three-ers," to the Greeks; we call them triremes, after the Latin—with a few officers and

FIGURE 3.3 Reconstructed trireme under sail

marines and archers perched on deck, and one hundred and seventy rowers crammed in as tightly as possible in the three tiers beneath. Every comfort and sea-keeping quality was sacrificed to speed under oar: the rowers, although for the most part free men, were enslaved to the great destroying bronze ram at the bow. Triremes were top-heavy, with little or no keel, no ballast, and round bottoms: under sail (for they set up masts and hoisted sails when the wind was friendly), they were wallowing beasts in any wind, but even with the masts and sails taken down to fight, they were hard to manage, their high sides offering a welcome purchase to any peevish gust. The trireme also had a perilously low freeboard to allow the plying of the oars (indeed, the lowest bank of oars sported leather sleeves to keep out the water), no rudder, and clumsy sweeps for steering.[36]

In the inevitable Mediterranean squalls, triremes ran before the wind, relying on their elegantly upswept sterns to prevent the sea from crashing in aft—but should human strength fail at the steering oars, the unballasted ship would slew sideways to the storm and capsize in an instant. Some six hundred Persian triremes, the Greeks believed, had been wrecked in tempests during Xerxes' great invasion in 480 BC. The number is no doubt exaggerated, and perhaps the Greek winds were less angry at the Greeks than at Xerxes. Still, the fate of the Persians provides a sense of the peril the Greeks faced any time they went to war in triremes.

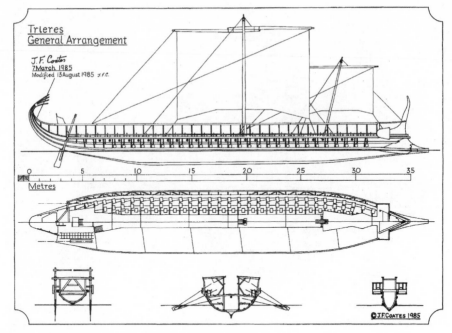

FIGURE 3.4 Lines of the reconstructed trireme *Olympias*

Dangerous vessels on the sea, triremes redoubled the hazards of their crews because they were bound also to the land. On a trireme there was nowhere for the crew to sleep save at their oars, no place to cook, and little room to carry food or water. On a hostile shore, the Greeks could hardly have landed every night, but frequently they did risk anchoring in the shallows and sending the rowers ashore to sleep, cook, and fill great vases with sweet water—an anxious respite, and perhaps a deadly one, should the locals gather to ambush the foragers. When ravaging was intended, then the marines and archers and (we presume) many of the rowers left the ships and struck off inland. But, given the mercurial temper of the sea, there was no guarantee they would find the fleet still there when they returned—no assurance they would not be cast away in an enemy land. In 431 BC the Athenians' circumnavigation of the Peloponnese brought them to the land of Elis on the west coast, which served as steward over the Olympic games every four years. The Athenians ravaged the fields of Elis for two days, their marines putting to flight a force of three hundred picked Eleans who came against them. But upon returning to the shore, they found that a storm had driven most of the fleet to shelter. Stoutly the soldiers marched across the nearby peninsula—taking the

MAP 3.3 Athenian Fleet Raids on the West Coast of the Peloponnese, 431 BC

small town of Pheia on the way—and rejoined the fleet where it lay at anchor in the lee. Only then did the main force of the Eleans come up, and the Athenians, abandoning shattered Pheia, sailed away to undertake further depredations elsewhere.[37]

Even when this troublesome mating of land and sea operations was successful, the raiders' endeavors on the land might not be. Early in their circumnavigation of the Peloponnese, the Athenians assailed weak Methone in the south of the Lacedaemonian district of Messenia, an isolated place with a good harbor, an old temple to Athena of the Winds (for on the south coast of the Peloponnese, even great Poseidon needed help safeguarding mariners), and a well of curiously dark-looking water. But nearby was a Spartan garrison commanded by Brasidas, son of Tellis (here he makes his debut in history), and with a hundred men he ran through the Athenian attackers, throwing himself into the town of Methone to save it. At Lacedaemon he was publicly honored for his daring and, shortly thereafter, elected to the high office of ephor.[38]

The fuss made over Brasidas for his saving a subject town reveals that Pericles' strategy of reprisal was having its intended effect upon the Spartans. For Pericles' plan depended on the raids of the Athenians being received not indifferently—as a weak threat to the Peloponnesian economy—but passionately, as a threat to the standing and honor of Lacedaemon. And Sparta's extravagant reaction to the thwarting of the Methone raid tells us that the Athenian raids were so received—that the Spartans did, indeed, feel humbled by the Athenians' ability to land so swiftly and "do ill" upon the inviolate soil of Sparta and her possessions.

The shame of Sparta was twofold: her inability to defend her own territory from ravaging was ignominious, of course, but so was her inability to protect her allies. The Athenian raiding was not likely to press the allies to such economic discomfort as to encourage them to pursue a separate peace. No, the raids upon Sparta's allies were intended to humiliate them, too, but above all to shame Sparta, who was largely unable to assist them. For any friendly relationship between Greek states was built upon the exchange of good offices, and failure to return those offices brought disgrace. Many of Sparta's allies had helped Sparta in the past, and all were helping her in the present war: failure to protect them in exchange was shameful.[39]

While failing to support an ally was shameful, eagerly returning an ally's friendly deeds was highly honorable and advanced one's state in the competition for rank—or might at least lessen shame incurred elsewhere. Thus it was that when the Athenian fleet left the Peloponnese and sailed up the northwestern coast of Greece, its purpose was not only to secure safe harbors for Athens but also to help Athens' friends. On that coast lived the friendly Acarnanians, those men so skilled with slings, and for them the Athenians captured Sollium, a Corinthian possession, afterwards capturing and retaining the coastal town of Astacus—"the Lobster"—for themselves. Finally, they headed out to sea to the island of Cephallenia—twin guard with friendly Zacynthus of the mouth of the Gulf of Corinth—which joined their confederation without a fight; it would be a useful base when the Athenian fleet came to those parts again. Corinth was the traditional *hegemon* of the Greek northwest—the area was thick with her colonies

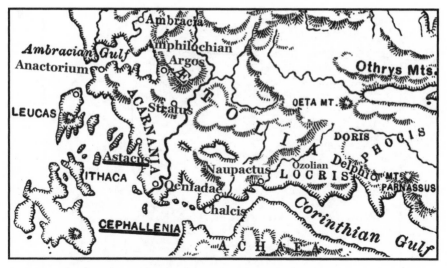

MAP 3.4 Athenian Fleet in the Greek Northwest, 431 BC

and friends—and Athens' activities there also served as revenge upon Corinth for all her recent hostile works against Athens.[40]

Athens' helping friends and harming enemy allies was not confined to the west coast of Greece. On the other side of the mainland, the Athenians sent thirty ships north to trouble the men of Opuntian Locris, to the north of Boeotia and across from the northern end of Euboea. Athenian-allied Euboea was where most of the beasts of Athens had been taken to protect them against the Peloponnesian invasion of Attica, and the Opuntian Locrians, who were allied to the Spartans, had a raffish, even buccaneering reputation. The Athenians ravaged the Locrians' land, captured one of their towns, and took hostages to ensure the Locrians' good behavior in future. Later the fleet fortified the small desert island of Atalanta, off the Locrian coast, to serve as a garrison against Locrian raids on Euboea. Thus the allies of the Athenians were well protected (along with Athens' livestock), and those of the Spartans—to their *hegemon*'s shame—assailed.[41]

It was the Spartans, however, who mounted the early pinnacle in the one-upmanship of helping friends and harming enemies when the Athenians decided to expel the men of Aegina from their homes. This island to the west of Attica in the Saronic Gulf, an old maritime rival of Athens, had finally been reduced to subjection during the war at mid-century (?457 BC). But the Aeginetans, gnawing at the Athenian bit, had secretly sent representatives to urge the Spartans to go to war with Athens, hoping that Spartan

MAP 3.5 Athenian Activity in Opuntian Locris, Aegina, and the Megarid, 431 BC

victory would improve their lot. The Athenians came to know of Aegina's representations to Sparta. And to punish the Aeginetans, and because Aegina was so close to the Peloponnese and so vulnerable to subversion, the Athenians in the first year of the war exiled the population of the island and settled their own folk there instead.[42]

The Spartans, feeble as they were at sea, could not protect the islander Aeginetans from their fate; yet they managed to rescue some honor from their disgraceful incapacity by offering the expelled Aeginetans territory of their own to settle upon, proclaiming that they were doing so because the Aeginetans had come to their aid during the rising of the Messenian helots thirty years before. We *do* requite our benefactors, the Spartans were crying out to the world, and even if we cannot now restore Sollium to the Corinthians—or their crops to the men of Elis, or their hostages to the men of Locris—we will never forget what we owe. This shrewd response to Athens' counterstrategy of humiliation was especially pointed because the territory the Spartans gave the men of Aegina was hallowed Thyrea, a tract famed and valued by the Spartans for their age-old conflict over it with Argos. Sparta had won the land at the fabled Battle of Champions around 550 BC, when three hundred paladins of each side strove against each other; the sole survivor and victor—the Spartan story went— was a Spartan. Giving Thyrea to the Aeginetans was deft, too, because the Aeginetans were old friends of Argos, that dangerous neutral on the Peloponnese, and the Argives still yearned to win back Thyrea. Filling the territory with the exiled Aeginetans, friends of both parties, might mollify the Argives and discourage them from taking the Athenians' side.[43]

At summer's end, Athens made her final move of the campaigning season, calling up her full force of thirteen thousand heavy-armed infantry— three thousand of them resident aliens—as well as a multitude of light troops, and marching through her own ravaged fields in northwestern Attica into the neighboring territory of Megara. These borderlands were places of dark memory. Here monstrous Cercyon had once wrestled all comers to their deaths, until wrestled to his own by Theseus, the hero of Athens. And here men pointed to the tombs of the Seven Against Thebes, the heroes whom one son of accursed Oedipus had led against another and whose bodies the Theban ruler Creon had commanded should be left to rot where they had fallen, the sport of dogs and birds. Antigone, sister of one of the seven, had buried her brother against Creon's orders and so was doomed to die, while the Athenians had gone to war to compel Creon to surrender the other bodies and gave them pious burial on the borders of Attica.[44]

Along with Corinth and Aegina (both already punished this year, the former by the taking of Sollium, the latter by the expulsion of her population), Megara had been the main source of pressure upon Sparta for war. And now that the Peloponnesian army had been dispersed at the end of its own campaign, Athens could take revenge upon hated Megara without hazard. Outnumbered, the Megarians declined to come out from behind their walls to fight—the long walls between Megara and her port had been built, it may be recalled, by the Athenians when Athens and Megara had been friends—and so the Athenians ravaged their land. The Athenian fleet that had gone around the Peloponnese was just returning when Athenian troops set foot in Megara; the triremes anchored at empty Aegina, and their sailors and marines came over to the coast of the Megarid and joined in the ravaging. The large scale of this expedition by land and the salt-stained fleet's junction with it, combined with the fact that Pericles himself led the land march, suggests the terrible magnitude of this invasion in the minds of the Athenians. And so events confirm, for this incursion was to be repeated in subsequent years of the war, sometimes with foot, sometimes only with horse, and eventually not once but twice a year.[45]

Sore pain did this sustained harrying bring to the Megarians, who lacked Athens' wealth and rich maritime supplies, but neither in the first year nor after, while the Athenians confined themselves to ravaging Megara, did the Spartans or any other ally come to help the Megarians. To be sure, a force could have been stationed in Megara itself, and given the tiny distances involved, the Corinthians or Boeotians could have arrived with their levies in a day or so—Megara being only thirty miles from the former and twenty from the latter. But there was something private and passionate about the conflict between Athens and Megara. Their enmity was contained within the wider war but not exactly a part of it, for the decree that commanded the Athenians to invade Megara was propelled—we understand from a later author—by the Megarian killing of an Athenian envoy who had come to complain about some previous Megarian misbehavior. Just as with Sparta's apparent neglect of her allies during the war at mid-century, not all wars involving allies of the great combatants were neatly swallowed by the greater one between Athens and Sparta. Sparta (and the rest of her alliance) could, without shame, ignore harm to an ally if she deemed that ally's conflict with Athens not to align with her own. And so it was that Sparta stood by as Athens avenged herself on Megara, not once but year after year.[46]

As the campaigning season came to an end in September 431 BC, when the rains came to the land and the sea became stormy, as ships and shields were put away for the winter, both at Athens and Sparta the question will have been asked, Are we winning? This was no easy question to answer. In a war in which armies did not clash in the field and battle lines did not shift on maps, it could be hard to judge who was ahead.

In similarly perplexing wars, today's armies establish artificial—and often futile—measures to gauge their progress, trying to count (as in Vietnam) enemy dead, or the volume of enemy equipment captured, or (as in Iraq) the frequency of enemy attacks on friendly forces. Sometimes such methods prove useful, although sometimes their result is to divert warriors from actual fighting to subverting the metric (thus the gruesome game of body count in Vietnam). But in the war between Athens and Sparta, victory had to be judged not by a statistical exercise, but in the gut.

The strategies of both parties depended on humiliating the enemy while accepting a lesser degree of humiliation themselves. How much, then, had the enemy been humiliated thus far? And, for that matter, how much had one's own side? Honor and humiliation were a mix of the objective and the subjective. Having one's lands ravaged, for example, was certainly a humiliation—but both sides had suffered this fate. And the impact of the ravaging—not the acreage ravaged but the enemy's actual experience of shame—was hard to judge. Nor was it obvious how to assess the contribution of other blows in the boxing match of honor and humiliation:

minor victories and the superiority they proved; aiding one's allies and harrying the enemy's. That such things played a role, everyone agreed. But there was no agreement on the value or weight of any of these acts. As long as humiliation did not bring one side or the other to sue for peace, progress in a war of pride and humiliation could not easily be assessed.

What *could* be watched and fretted about was the disposition of one's own side. Keeping one's own side proud was itself part of victory, for if one's own folk did not feel humiliated, did not feel they were losing, then—at least in doubtful cases like that of the Athenians and Spartans in 431 BC—they were not. We do not know how the Spartans discussed these issues, but since they followed much the same strategy in the second year of the war as in the first, we can guess that they did not think their strategy had been unsuccessful or that they had fallen behind. Indeed, the Spartans' unresisted invasion of Attica, their unanswered challenge to battle, and their unhindered ravaging of the Attic countryside were no doubt thought to have proved their superiority well enough. In Sparta's eyes, Athenian counterraids (not, a Spartan would hasten to point out, accompanied by a proper challenge to battle) and assaults on Sparta's allies, while not exactly pinpricks, did not fundamentally alter the picture. Indeed, Athens' need to raid by sea and her decision to attack Megara only after the Peloponnesian army had disbanded may only have served to reemphasize Athens' inferiority by proving that she could not meet the Spartans in the field. If the Athenians wished to claim superiority or even equality, the Spartans would have thought, let them march into the Peloponnese and face their foe on his home soil, as the Spartans were doing in Attica.

But both sides probably thought that they were winning at the end of the war's first year. More can be deduced about public sentiment at Athens than at Sparta, thanks to the speech with which Thucydides ends his account of the first year of the war: the famous Funeral Oration of Pericles, which eulogizes the Athenian dead by enfolding them in the glory and power of contemporary Athens. The state's institutions and the character of the Athenians have created this unique glory, Pericles declares, and the history of the city is portrayed as a progression toward it. This address, like all his characters' speeches, was of course written by Thucydides himself (Thucydides' speeches are discussed the appendix). But if we cannot believe that these exact words were necessarily spoken by a given speaker, we can believe the shadows that events cast upon the words Thucydides wrote. For if the words cannot be seen as strictly historical, the situations that the words address can be, and so the speeches in Thucydides reveal much about their historical contexts. And the triumphal tenor that Thucydides gives to Pericles' Funeral Oration would be out of place in an Athens that thought it was losing the war against Sparta.[47]

Pericles' speech also suggests the reasoning behind Athenian satisfaction. For Thucydides has Pericles undermine the main claim of the Spartans to superiority in the war: their invasion of Attica, where the Athenians did not dare to meet them in the field. Pericles counters that the Spartans only dared to come against Athens with an overwhelming number of allies, while the Athenians faced their invasion alone; nor were the Athenian home forces even complete because of the need for garrisons and marines for the fleet. This was not, he implies, a fair challenge.[48]

As the Spartans' ultimately unsatisfactory defeat of Athens in 446 BC has already suggested, a conflict that settled the rank of the contending states was supposed to be fair. The Greeks, of course, went to war for many reasons, used all sorts of strategies in war, and called upon allies when they could: fairness was not an issue in a war for plunder, or a war for domination, or a war against helots. But if a war was to settle issues of standing between cities, a strong current of Greek thinking maintained that the victor had to deny the defeated any way to claim that they had been defeated by anything other than by the victor's superior manhood. The Spartan invasion, Pericles implies, would have been a fair fight only if the Spartans had come alone to face the Athenians; otherwise, the Spartans had no right to feel proud, and the Athenians no reason to be humiliated for not fighting them. Moreover, if the Spartans did happen to defeat some small contingent of Athenians, Pericles says (perhaps alluding to the Athenian setback at Methone), they absurdly seemed to feel that they had defeated the whole state. And Pericles pointedly contrasts the behavior of the Athenians with that of the Spartans. The Athenians, he says, thinking of Megara in particular, do go alone against their adversaries. Thus when the Athenians win, theirs has been a fair fight, by which they *have* proved their superiority. The Athenians, then, thought they were holding their own in the war of standing. Yet the historian's decision to have Pericles conclude the speech by urging the Athenians to rededicate themselves to the war hints at just how fragile he felt that confidence was.[49]

In the winter after the first season of the Ten Years' War, the main warlike activity took place in the northwest of Greece. Earlier in the year the roving Athenian fleet had turned the tyrant of Astacus, Evarchus (whose name, ironically, means "good ruler" in Greek) out of his crustacean stronghold in friendly Acarnania. Yearning to be restored, he convinced the Corinthians to mount an expedition of forty ships and fifteen hundred hoplites to accomplish that end. Safe beyond the normal season of sailing from the Athenian fleet, they were nevertheless in great peril from the winter's gusts and seas as they buffeted their way the eighty miles down the Gulf of Corinth. At the mouth of the Gulf, the Corinthians hauled their wind and sailed northwest into the Adriatic, to Acarnania, where they succeeded in returning Astacus to the obedience of its unlovely lord. They had other ambitions in Acarnania, too—designs on strong places—but in these they failed. Then, from Acarnania they sailed southeast to Cephallenia, the island that had joined Athens during the Athenian expedition of the previous summer. The Corinthians' attempts to ravage, however, were defeated by a trick, and set upon by surprise by the locals, they lost some men and returned with difficulty to Corinth. This dangerous adventure reveals about the Corinthians the same thing the Spartans' honoring of Brasidas had revealed about the Spartans: Athens' strategy of shaming her enemies by picking off their possessions and friends was working.[50]

T HE GREEK SPRING YIELDS AN explosion of flowers to herald the end of the rains and the calming of the seas. The shepherd and the soldier alike can sleep in the fields without shelter. The hard northerlies of winter, which practically cut off Athens from her northern possessions, are finally spent, and the winds become friendly and various: the sea breeze and her merry sister, the land breeze, breathe in and out day by day, and happy ships reach along the sparkling shores of Hellas.

At the outset of the next campaigning season, in May 430 BC, the Peloponnesian levy, two-thirds of the full contingent of each Spartan ally, gathered promptly and marched into Attica. There were to be none of the delays of the year past—no futile siege or waiting for the Athenians to yield. This time such minimal logistical preparations as the Greeks knew were more stringently enforced upon the individual soldiers, and the army was able to spend forty days in Attica: their longest invasion of the Ten Years' War. The Peloponnesians ravaged the plain around Athens itself (coming far closer to the city than they had the previous year), then marched south on a path of destruction all the way down the west coast of Attica to its tip and then north again, along the other coast up the eastern side of the ridge of Pentelikon.[51]

Even in the course of this bellicose processional, the Spartans did not destroy every stalk of wheat they could. The extreme northeast of Attica they did not ravage, for once upon a time that region had offered shelter to the fleeing sons of Heracles after the hero's death, and from two of those sons the Spartans had sprung. The story is told, too, that during the Ten Years' War the Spartans held their hand from the Attic village of Decelea and its lands, in thanks for Decelea's help to Sparta before the Trojan War. This was assistance given when easy-to-misplace Helen, before she ran away to Troy, had to be rescued from Attica by her brothers Castor and

MAP 3.6 Peloponnesian Invasion of Attica, 430 BC

Pollux—the latter of whom had been born with her from a single large egg, since Leda (of the swan) was the mother of all three. And the story must have been true, for at Sparta was preserved the egg itself, dangling from ribbons in a temple. But Sparta's mercy to Decelea and the Attic northeast was no product of quaint sentimentality. With her allies suffering more than she from Athenian raiding and with Sparta unable to protect them, acts like these were similar to rescuing Doris from the Phocians and settling the Aeginetan refugees at Thyrea: they were messages to all that the Spartans would remember their debts to those who did well by them, even if these debts were not redeemed for centuries. If anything, the older and stranger the debt, the louder its repayment spoke to the honor of Lacedaemon.[52]

"Ravaged the whole country" is how Thucydides describes this Spartan invasion of Attica. And geographic expansiveness, rather than thorough destruction, was exactly the Peloponnesian goal. By the standards of Greek city-states, Attica boasted an enormous extent of land—some thousand square miles—and ravaging, if done properly, was slow. This year the Spartans and their allies purposed to march over at least thrice the acreage they had ravaged the year before, although by so expanding their scope, they must have correspondingly lessened the actual damage to any one field. But destruction itself was not the whole point; rather, the goal was for the Peloponnesians to set their muddy feet on every undefended rod of Attic soil, to make the Athenian refusal to come out of their strongholds—as Pericles once again prevailed upon the Athenians not to do—even more mortifying than the year before. What could be destroyed quickly was: all the fine houses of the rich near the city were burned. But no less important was to challenge the Athenians to come forth and protect the ancestral tombs and rural temples of Attica, for the Greeks thought about the sanctity of their countryside in terms of tombs and shrines. The Athenians did not. So Spartans wandered craggy Sounion, at the tip of the land, where they rested in the shade of the temple of Poseidon, and they entered holy Brauron, where in peace little girls in honey-colored robes ran races for Artemis and brides dedicated to her the toys of their childhood before going to the marriage bed. And if the Spartans did not loot these holy places—revering the gods too much for that—it was shaming nevertheless to have the shrines of Attica held by the Peloponnesians. It was shaming, in short, that not a rod of Attic soil outside the very walls of Athens and her garrisons should be untrampled by her enemies.[53]

Even as smoke writhed from the manses and fields around Athens, it mated with serpents of smoke coiling up from behind the walls of the city. Balefires were burning, and escaping slaves soon brought their meaning to the Spartans. Soon after the Peloponnesians had set foot in Attica, a contagion had broken out within the city, a distemper brought by ship from the east, which—spreading from person to person first among the walled-in folk of Piraeus, then those of Athens itself, and killing in thirsty agony those it afflicted—quickly took on the terrible character of a plague. Thucydides, who suffered from the illness himself, describes its symptoms: the burning sensation in the head, the inflammation of the eyes, the coughing, the vomiting, the convulsions, the pustules, the consuming heat, the quenchless thirst, the bloody flux, the despair. It has become a morbid game among modern doctors to try to diagnose the exact ailment he describes—but in vain. The disease has expired, it is to be hoped, of its own virulence, for even the dogs and ravens who fed upon the corpses died, while their more fortunate mates cawed and barked in hungry frustration, warned away by their instincts.[54]

That Thucydides could cast a clinical eye upon the plague's effects on eaters of human carrion reveals the breakdown of law and custom that followed the onset of the disorder. Corpses were often dumped unburned—that is how the hounds and birds got at them—or simply tossed upon other men's pyres. The malady was fiercely infectious, and soon the sick were abandoned to die alone in their houses or died as whole families from nursing one another. Those conscientious about visiting sick friends were soon carried away by the disease, and so, to the horror of the snobbish Thucydides, "those claiming excellence"—those at the top of Athenian society—suffered in disproportion to their numbers. Just as bad to Thucydides' way of thinking, the poor and wicked often inherited the property of the rich and good, while the rich who survived were demoralized and hastened to satisfy their lowest desires in anticipation of inevitable death. For death was everywhere; those sufferers with enough strength crashed through the streets in search of water, throwing themselves into cisterns and collapsing at fountains. The worst conditions of all were in the great shantytowns that the rural poor had built upon seeking refuge within the walls from the dreaded Spartans; there the dying lay upon each other and rolled in the dusty passages between the huts. Into the city's towers and temples, too, the poor had removed, so that men found themselves imploring the gods for aid amidst the piled corpses of those the gods had not aided.[55]

To most Greeks, plague was not a phenomenon of nature but a visitation of divinity—above all the archer Apollo, bringer of plagues, who had brought the pest upon the Achaeans before Troy and so unleashed the action of the *Iliad*. It escaped no one's notice that Apollo sided with the Spartans in this war, having cheerfully volunteered "to cooperate with them asked or unasked" when the Spartans inquired of his oracle at Delphi whether they should go to war against Athens. Thus the Athenians understood the plague at Athens not as a matter of bad luck, bad sanitation, or overcrowding, but rather as the victory of a powerful—indeed, a divine—Spartan ally over Athens. Nor was this victory easily balanced by a comparable Athenian victory (as, for instance, Spartan ravaging might be balanced by Athenian ravaging). It was exactly the kind of large, unanswerable Peloponnesian triumph that the conservative strategy of Pericles had aspired to avoid.[56]

It was under sooty auspices, then, that the Athenian fleet set out on its raiding expedition once the Peloponnesians had marched into southern Attica. Pericles' plan was likely the same as that of the year before: to make a slow, plundering circumnavigation of the Peloponnese. Athens had sought to confirm her position in the northwest the year before (and had consolidated her alliances there in the years prior to that) precisely in order to repeat such expeditions, and this Athenian fleet was certainly equipped for the task, indeed on a somewhat larger scale than that of 431 BC. The number of ships had not changed; Pericles led a hundred from Athens, and Athens' allies, the men of the great Aegean islands Chios and Lesbos, accompanied the expedition with fifty more. But this time the Athenians sailed with four

MAP 3.7 Athenian Fleet Raids on the East Coast of the Peloponnese, 430 BC

times as many heavy infantry—some four thousand in total—as well as three hundred cavalry, whose steeds were conveyed in newly devised horse transports adapted from decayed triremes. Taking along the cavalry, so useful in defending ravagers, particularly suggests a repetition of the previous year's ambitions. Laconia, of course, would have to be prodded again—tit for tat after the ravaging of Attica. But since the far coast of the Peloponnese had received the raiders' chief attention on their last expedition, this year it would be the near coast's turn. For the Athenians sought the same geographical exhaustiveness in their raiding as the Spartans. Their point was to ravage everywhere, to show that there was nowhere the Spartans could defend, that there was no ally they could protect.[57]

The first landfall of the Athenians was just across the Saronic Gulf, in the territory of Epidaurus, where they wasted the land. But here Pericles also detected an opportunity to make an attempt on the city of Epidaurus itself, a considerable place. This risky decision—involving an extended stay in a hostile land and the very real possibility of meeting a rallying enemy in the field—is something of a mystery because it seems so contrary to Pericles' risk-avoidant strategy. But perhaps the Athenians had a spiritual motive, for

FIGURE 3.5 The Athenian hero Theseus clad as a hoplite in linen cuirass

Epidaurus was home to the great shrine of Asclepius, the divine healer suck-led by goats in the hills around and a divinity who drew men's thoughts in time of plague. Pericles hardly intended, like a Roman general after the cap-ture of a city, to bundle a useful god into a wagon and take him home to worship there; Greek gods do not seem to have liked such rough wooing. But the so-called Sacred Wars (?595–?585, ?449, 356–346 BC), fought in part over access to the oracle at Delphi, remind us that Greeks did go to war over their right to approach specific gods in their chief temples. In Athens' inva-sion of Epidaurus, therefore, we may detect a wish to beseech the divine healer in his own place. (In fact, soon after the Ten Years' War, the Athenians did establish their own shrine to Asclepius.) At the same time, the attack on Epidaurus may be explicable as a purely secular attempt to conjure an unde-niable triumph for Athens with which to offset the shame that Apollo's plague arrows had inflicted. And if the Athenians thought this year's invasion of Attica more insulting to their gods in their undefended temples than last year's (last year the main cult center threatened by invasion, Eleusis, was an Athenian fort, which the Athenians held against the Peloponnesians), this at-tack on a Peloponnesian religious center might serve as a tit-for-tat response.

As it turned out, however, Pericles' attempt to seize Epidaurus failed, and the Athenians returned to their ships.[58]

After failing at Epidaurus, the Athenians fell upon the lands of Troezen, Halieis, and Hermione, further south on the Argolid peninsula. These were small places, all of them, but rich with lore and ancient fame. Troezen had a temple of Artemis boasting a hole said to reach all the way down to hell: from this very chasm, Heracles had dragged to the surface Cerberus, the three-headed watchdog of Hades. In the same land, Heracles had leaned his club against a statue of Hermes, whereupon it grew into an olive tree, a tree that might still be visited. Near Halieis, Zeus himself had been transformed into a cuckoo—thus the glowering Mount Cuckoo, which stood north of the city, topped by Zeus' shrine. Hermione possessed a temple to Demeter into which a full-grown cow was released untethered, to be leapt upon in the twilight by four crones, who slashed at its throat with sickles. Once the cow was slain, another was let in, and another, and a fourth. And lo! Just as the first cow fell to the right or the left in its death struggle, the three others fell always on the same side. The men of Hermione, too, had their own hole down to hell and insisted that Heracles had dragged Cerberus up through it, not the orifice at Troezen.[59]

Having ravaged these storied places, the Athenians struck south along the coast of Laconia and, coming to Prasiae, just twenty-five miles from inland Sparta, not only wasted the land but also captured and sacked the town itself. "Oh! Prasiae!" sang Aristophanes of this memorable destruction, "Thrice wretched, five times, aye, a thousand times wretched!" Pericles had no doubt expected to sail on around the Peloponnese and to end the tour by resting his squadrons with Athens' allies in the northwest of Greece, at Zacynthus, Cephallenia, Acarnania, or Corcyra. But the plague had broken out in the fleet, and since the Athenians knew it to be contagious, it would have been ill diplomacy indeed to inflict it upon their northwestern allies. No, the ships could only turn for home. When they returned, they found the Peloponnesians gone from Attica. The Athenian expedition had lasted perhaps twenty days.[60]

The Athenians still needed a triumph to counterbalance the heavy hand Apollo had laid upon Athens. And with the journey of their fleet into the northwest cancelled, the Athenians hoped to find this triumph at Potidaea, the northerly city that had played an evil role in the events that led to the war when she had secured a Spartan pledge of protection and rebelled from Athens. Ungentle masters and cruel avengers of rebellion, the Athenians had already beleaguered Potidaea for two years at colossal expense. The Spartans had committed their honor to defending Potidaea, so finally capturing the town to which Sparta had made such guarantees, and about which Corinth was so anxious (many of her men were inside as "volunteers"), would be a noble victory for the Athenians; "the people, in their ambition for honor, yearned to take Potidaea by force" is how a later historian interpreted the Athenian motive. Moreover, the taking of Potidaea seemed to be the only significant victory available to the Athenians to offset the triumph of Apollo.[61]

No sooner, then, had the plague fleet returned from its abortive expedition around the Peloponnese than it was quickly dispatched again, under other generals, north to Potidaea. All was militant energy there—the newly arrived Athenians roused their war-weary comrades, built devices, and undertook great efforts to capture the city—but, again, in vain. And all the while the plague galloped through the Athenian camp. In forty days, more than a quarter of the fleet's four thousand hoplites succumbed. And not only were the newcomers of no help to the besiegers already present, but they infected them with the disease as well. It was with relief, one suspects, that the old blockaders of Potidaea beheld that futile fleet wafting away down the wind.[62]

When the Athenians had turned back from their raiding expedition in Laconia—when they had decided to sail back to Athens rather than on around the Peloponnese—they left their allies in northwestern Greece plague-free but unguarded. Now, late in the campaigning season, the Spartans took the opportunity to launch a considerable expedition to try to detach the island of Zacynthus from Athens. If the Gulf of Corinth looks like a watery crocodile crawling east into Greece, then Zacynthus and her neighbor, Cephallenia, are the mangled prey it has left behind in the Ionian Sea. Cephallenia had been raided by the Corinthians during their weather-beaten expedition of the winter before. Now, against Zacynthus, Sparta's allies assembled one hundred ships, very likely their whole strength, while the Spartans themselves contributed a thousand Lacedaemonian hoplites, whose bristling presence further underscored the gravity of the expedition, for the Spartans were ever stinting of their own soldiers. Commanding the whole was a Spartan.

In the symmetry-seeking world of Greek warfare, the great Peloponnesian attack on Zacynthus was certainly a response to Athens' raiding of Sparta's confederates: a humiliating demonstration that Athens herself could not always protect her allies. But it shows also the impact of Pericles' strategy of naval raiding because Zacynthus was so useful a base for that enterprise. Since the Peloponnesians were unable to stop Athenian raiders on the beaches of the Peloponnese, the Spartans were trying to forestall a repeat of the plundering circumnavigation by depriving Athens of her most useful harbors in the northwest, first with the Corinthian attack on Cephallenia and now with this even greater movement against Zacynthus. The loss of Cephallenia and Zacynthus would compel the Athenians to rest in harbors more distant and less commodious and so might put them off their raiding entirely. But the Peloponnesians would have to find some other means to accomplish this, for though they made a thorough job of ravaging Zacynthus, the Zacynthians scorned the terms they offered, remaining loyal to Athens.[63]

At Athens the political situation had become stern; indeed, it is possible that Pericles declined to lead the expedition to Potidaea in order to manage affairs at home. For the war by now was pressing hard upon the Athenians. As the weeks passed and Athenians died atrocious deaths from the plague, ill-omened tidings began to spread to the effect that, although the disease had arisen in the wicked lands of the Great King of Persia and afflicted other populous places in the Greek world, it had not spread to the enemy in the Peloponnese. That rumor, and the uncanny arrival of the plague in Attica at the same time as the Peloponnesian army, would have discouraged naturalistic explanations of the phenomenon, should any have been offered.[64]

No, the Athenians thought, it was more obvious than ever that the plague was the work of that malevolent deity Apollo. Thus, while the respective ravagings could be viewed as balancing each other (the Spartans "did the Athenians much ill by land, but they suffered from them much ill by sea," as a later author put it), Athens still had nothing to offset the awe-inspiring intervention of a god on Sparta's side. Indeed, Athens' bold attempts to secure offsetting victories at Epidaurus and Potidaea had proved embarrassing failures. And so humiliation was piled upon humiliation.[65]

The mood at Athens was gloomy. By now, a great number of Athenians had died of the disease; many others had been crippled or blinded. Medicine having failed, the only thing that might stop the sickness was appeasing Apollo—which might require peace with Apollo's friend Sparta. Many of the rich were feeling the pinch from the destruction of their rural homes and crops, while many of the poor were hungry. And so the Athenians sent emissaries to Sparta to ask for terms of peace.[66]

Why the Athenian envoys' efforts came to naught, Thucydides does not say. But the terms the Spartans offered the envoys when they inquired can be deduced from the speech Thucydides places in the mouth of Pericles, urging the Athenians not to blame him for the plight and under no circumstances to send further envoys to Sparta. Unlike the triumphal funeral oration, this speech of Pericles' is embattled and defensive in tone: it would make little sense unless the Athenians believed they were now in danger of losing the war and being forced to give up their pretensions to equality. In his address, Pericles inveighs against "submission," against paying "obedience" to the Spartans, and goes so far as to say that the Athenians are in danger of exchanging freedom for slavery. It is not, of course, literal slavery and freedom he has in mind: these are but code words in the language of rank, "slavery" being a metaphor for symbolic submission to the Spartans and "freedom," the staunch refusal of such submission. From this we can deduce that the Spartans had asked for some symbolic submission in exchange for peace.[67]

In his speech, Thucydides has Pericles inveigh against the Athenians' acquiescence to a peace that acknowledged Sparta's superiority in rank. Pericles thunders about the high rank of Athens and the need to uphold it: the Athenians were not to mar the good name of Athens or to make the Greeks think their previous reputation was based on presumption. Do not shame your fathers! cries Pericles. Glory in your empire! Feel only contempt for the foe! Regard the plague as bad luck, and so an opportunity to burnish the reputation of Athens by enduring it manfully. Lord unchallenged of the nautical realm, Athens is the greatest power in the history of Greece! Even others' hatred for us proves our glory! Such sentiments, whether or not the historical Pericles uttered them, must have prevailed at Athens, if only because the Athenians made no further overtures to the Spartans. Although at the moment they sent envoys to Sparta they must have been prepared to make some symbolic submission, Pericles' powers of persuasion, simple lapse of time, or (perhaps most likely) an arrogant reply from Sparta convinced the Athenians that they could not in the end yield their claim to equality in rank.

Whatever effect Pericles may have had on the Athenians with his oratory, he did not succeed in turning their wrath away from him personally. Prosecuted for corruption by his political enemies (one source names Cleon among them), Pericles was convicted and mulcted of an immense fine. As a result he was dismissed from the office of general, although he was reelected the following year.[68]

The Spartans, as the second campaigning season drew to a close, will have been well content with the course of the war. Not only had they twice proved their superiority in rank with unopposed invasions of Attica, but their divine ally had driven Athens to beg for peace. In 446 BC the Spartans had, they thought, humiliated Athens, but Athens had not felt that humiliation. Now, once again, the Spartans had humiliated Athens, and now the Athenians did feel it, along with misery. It was curious that they were unwilling to humble themselves before the Spartans long enough for peace to be made, but the Athenians were nevertheless showing signs of returning to their senses. A treaty was the only unfinished business, and a treaty could be achieved by means other than humiliating the enemy: a treaty could be achieved by arm-twisting.

The Spartans' immediate resort in the wake of the second campaigning season of the war was, indeed, to prepare for arm-twisting. After Athens' refusal to agree to satisfactory terms, the Spartans undertook to press upon not only Athens' pride, but also her safety. But since the city of Athens itself was invulnerable, the Spartans had to fight the Athenians at sea, and to do that they needed ships. For a fleet that could face the combined might of Athens' three hundred triremes, the Spartans needed an ocean of money. When he told of the beginning of the war, Thucydides noted in passing that both sides had tried to recruit the Great King of Persia to their side. Now the Peloponnesians tried again, sending a mission consisting of the heroic Corinthian Aristeus (it was he who had saved northerly Potidaea when the Athenians first attacked it), three Lacedaemonians, a Tegean, and a stray Argive who could disavow the pro-Athenian sympathies of his neutral state and was no doubt prepared to tell the Persians astonishing lies about how Argos would join with Sparta if only the King opened his coffers (the Argives, too, claimed an old kinship with Persia, which might ease the embassy's reception: because of the similarity of names, the line of the Persians could be traced to Perseus, the hero of Argos). How hopeful the Spartans were that the Great King would actually open his treasury we cannot know, but any hint that he might—or even, given their pessimism, the mere knowledge that the Peloponnesians had sent an embassy to him— might be enough to move the Athenians the little way they needed to go to make peace with the Peloponnesians. The Spartan mission to Persia was much like the Spartan request to the Greek states of Italy and Sicily for money and ships at the very beginning of the war: the very sending of it was intended to terrify the Athenians.[69]

The Peloponnesian ambassadors never reached the court of the Great King. So keenly did the Spartans feel the danger to Potidaea, having plighted their honor to its safety, that they hoped to wheedle the mighty Thracian king Sitalces into giving over his Athenian alliance and sending an army to deliver the besieged city on the Chalcidice. To the northern court of Sitalces, then, the Peloponnesian envoys made a detour on their way to Persia. But the Thracians were not so easily swayed, and Athenian envoys prevailed upon Sitalces' pro-Athenian son to ambush the envoys in Thrace, whereupon they were promptly handed over to the Athenians. Taken to Athens, they were executed, and their bodies cast into a pit: a nice piece of revenge, for the Spartans had themselves been killing and casting into pits Athenian and allied traders they happened to take on the coasts of the Peloponnese. Vindictive? It was a vindictive war.

In this famous deed of revenge, moreover, the gods, too, played their vengeful part. For more than sixty years before, the Spartans had murdered emissaries from the Great King of Persia and cast them into a well (they had asked for earth and water as symbols of submission, so the Spartans gave them water). The gods had been angry, and the Spartans could gain no favorable omens thereafter. So the heralds of the Spartans went up to the Great King and invited him to kill them in exchange, to cleanse Sparta of the bane. The King refused and sent them home, not wanting to incur the same curse of herald-killing as the Spartans had. At Sparta the office of herald was hereditary, and it was the very sons of the envoys the Great King had spared whom the Athenians now captured and cast into the pit. The revenge of the gods was slow, but it was certain. The same clattering loom-shuttle of revenge that wove the events of the Ten Years' War wove, too, the acts of high Olympus.[70]

IV

ODYSSEUS' WAR,
429–428 BC

IN THE NORTH, BELEAGUERED POTIDAEA had endured alone. She had been under close siege by the Athenians for two and a half years, without help from the Thracians, the Chalcidians or the Peloponnesians. The siege had cost the Athenians two thousand talents (their cash reserve at the beginning of hostilities was six thousand). Now, in the winter after the second campaigning season of the war (the winter dividing 430 from 429 BC), food within the walls of Potidaea had entirely run out, and the townsfolk implored the Athenian generals for safe passage out of the city. Considering the expense of the siege and the suffering of their own army, the generals granted the plea. And so the Potidaean survivors filed out of the gates, clutching the coins that would keep them alive on their trip into exile, the men allowed by covenant of surrender to retain one garment apiece, the women two. All starveling thin were they, except for a few who, we may guess, walked unwithered but alone and shunned—for they had filled their bellies by devouring the dead.[1]

Ill news for the Spartans was the fall of Potidaea: long-suffering Potidaea, to whose aid Sparta had pledged herself before the war broke out. Athens' taking of Potidaea went a long way toward balancing the account books of this strangely symmetrical war. The fall of Potidaea brought shame upon Sparta, a debt that itself required vengeful repayment in the form of an achievement as famous as the taking of Potidaea. Ambitious to show their superiority in rank—not merely equality, as the Athenians sought—the Spartans could not just shrug Potidaea off as simply offsetting the plague.

Determined to make return, Sparta now began to scan the landscape for a town in which Athens' honor was as invested as Sparta's had been in Potidaea: Potidaea, to which the Spartans had given their fatal guarantee before the war; Potidaea, upon which the Spartans hoped their invasions of Attica might make the Athenians release their grip (or so Thucydides implies);

Potidaea, for which the Spartans had doomed their mission to the Great King to beg for a Thracian rescue. There was only one possibility, only one place at once famous, weak, easy to reach, and closely bound to Athens: Plataea, the small Athenian ally in Boeotia whose travails had ushered in the war.[2]

This year, then, there would be no invasion of Attica. All the strength of the Peloponnese would crash upon the flint of Plataea. Largely evacuated after the Theban incursion (just four hundred Plataean warriors remained, along with eighty Athenians and a hundred and ten women to tend house), Plataea was of no great military significance, so Sparta's interest in her was not born of any practical strategic need. Nor will the Spartans have imagined that the Athenians were more likely to march forth to deliver Plataea than to defend their own fields from ravaging—so the Spartans did not choose to attack Potidaea as a lure to draw out and defeat the Athenian army. No, if Sparta suddenly hungered for Plataea, it was to deal a blow to Athens as retribution for the fall of Potidaea.[3]

The Spartan decision to forgo an invasion of Attica and attack Plataea hints that the Greeks, and now even the Spartans, were coming gradually to accept the Athenian view that Athens' reprisal raids on the Peloponnese from ships were full and adequate revenge for the Peloponnesian invasions of Attica; that they cancelled out the Spartan ravaging of Attica in the war over rank. For if the Spartans had been wholly confident that they were gaining ground by their ravaging, despite Athens' reprisals, they would have been unlikely to suspend their invasions for a year. And if the Spartans felt that they had established an overwhelming advantage in honor through their ravaging, they might not have even felt the need to avenge the fall of Potidaea tit for tat.

As it was, however, the Spartans had to seek revenge for Potidaea through Plataea, despite the problems that presented. For not only was Plataea well fortified, but an outright attack on her posed almost insuperable challenges to the good faith of Lacedaemon. At Sparta's own bidding, in around 520 BC, Plataea had allied herself with Athens against Thebes, because Sparta considered herself too distant to protect Plataea against Thebes' neighborly detestation. The battle of Plataea, the climactic battle of the Persian War and Sparta's most famous victory, had also unfolded in the city's territory. There, in heroes' barrows, lay Sparta's glorious dead, and there the Plataeans reverently tended them, making to the warriors' illustrious shades offerings of raiment and the first fruits of the year. In honor of the victory, at which Plataea's plucky six hundred had stood in the line beside Athens' thousands, the leader of the Spartans had proclaimed Plataean soil independent, neutral, and inviolate, and Sparta's triumphant allies in the Persian War had agreed to defend Plataea against any impious assailant. At Plataea, in the wake of the battle, the Spartans had even set up an altar to Zeus Eleutherius—Zeus, Bringer of Freedom. It was the Spartans themselves, then, who had made Plataea sacred to Greek liberty.[4]

Very well, the Spartans reasoned: they would be hard-pressed to justify an attack on Plataea. But if they yearned to set off the shame of Potidaea with Plataea, there were ways by which that might be done other than violent capture. After all, Potidaea had not been stormed either; it had yielded on terms. The Plataeans might join the Spartans. The Spartan king Archidamus suggested as much when he met Plataea's delegates at their border. Alternately, he said, Plataea might remove herself from the fight, proclaiming herself neutral, and receive all as friends. If the Plataeans feared that Athens would punish the former choice, the king said, or that the ruthless Thebans might take advantage of the latter (as the Plataeans earnestly predicted), then the Plataeans might simply walk out of their land and go wheresoever they willed. The Spartans would hold Plataea's houses and fields in trust (protecting them against the Thebans) and pay its displaced citizens an allowance for their upkeep during the war, after which they would be free to return. Such a compromise—an evacuation on terms— was, of course, exactly how Athens had captured Potidaea (although the terms Archidamus offered the Plataeans were decidedly more generous), emphasizing the symmetry between the two situations in the Spartan mind. Sparta's offer to serve as steward over the territory of Plataea also renders it unlikely that Sparta's aim was purely to gratify the Thebans, since this plan would deny Thebes possession. No, the Spartans did not want Plataea for themselves or for the Thebans. They simply wanted the triumph of detaching Plataea from Athens, ideally without breaking their own ancient ties and guarantees to the famous little city.[5]

The Plataean garrison gave their consent to evacuation, but they could not in conscience act without Athens' agreement; their families, after all, had already been removed there. So Archidamus' army remained in camp on the Plataean border while the garrison's messengers passed to and fro from Attica. Alas, the Athenians refused to agree to Archidamus' plan, recalling in their reply Athens' past protection of Plataea, promising to protect the city as ever, and sternly adjuring the Plataeans not to betray their oaths of alliance. The plan of evacuation, of course, offended the Athenians for precisely the same reason it appealed to the Spartans: for Athens to surrender such an ally would be a humiliation, and Athens did not intend so easily to sacrifice the increment of standing that she had just earned with the capture of Potidaea.[6]

Thus it was that the Plataeans somberly announced from the battlements of their city that they were unable to do as the Lacedaemonians bade them. And Archidamus in turn called upon all the gods and heroes of the land to witness that the Spartans were not first in doing wrong: their proposals had been fair, he said, and by fighting alongside the Athenians in the war, the Plataeans had departed from the neutrality to which they were bound by the common oath. Thus the attack of the Spartans was just revenge upon them. The Spartan king's conscience, it would seem, was troubling him, and he feared the punishment of heaven. Here, and not for the first time, we find that, to today's sensibility, Archidamus is perhaps the most sympathetic character in the Ten Years' War: a Spartan warrior who was reluctant to fight but fated by birth to lead Sparta to war; a friend forced to make war against a friend, Pericles; and a man of justice and piety who was quietly appalled by what war compelled him and his city to do. But Archidamus' archaic-seeming pronouncement also stands as a reminder that the Greeks crafted their international relations not out of twisted fragments of social science, as we do today, but rather out of notions of wrongdoing and just revenge.[7]

Once diplomacy had failed and justification of blood had been rendered to gods and men, the Spartans and their allies marched into the territory of Plataea, cutting down the trees and wasting the land. The wood they used to build a stockade around Plataea so that none of its defenders might escape and nothing might be brought in. But starving out Plataea was not the Peloponnesians' plan. Rather, they intended to take the city with siege works. And so they began to build a ramp up to the wall of the city, cutting wood from looming Mount Cithaeron to make a wooden lattice on either side of the intended slope, then hauling wood, stones, and dirt to fill up the space between. At this the Peloponnesians labored day and night under the stern eyes of the Lacedaemonian commanders of the allied contingents: for Spartan soldiers themselves were, apparently, excused from such low work.[8]

As the ramp slowly rose, the Plataeans realized their peril and began to raise their own wall opposite with wood and bricks, covering their work with hides to protect the builders from missiles and the structure itself from flaming arrows. But doubtful as to whether they would win the race for height, the Plataeans also took measures to thwart the Peloponnesian building, cutting through their own wall where the ramp leaned against it and carting away the very stuff of which the ramp was built. The Peloponnesians, despairing at the sight of their sinking earthwork, cast into the depression hard clay that could not so easily be carried off. Undiscouraged, the Plataeans abandoned their hole through the wall, digging instead a mine deep under wall and ramp alike, and from this they surreptitiously carried away earth for many days, so that although the Peloponnesians brought ever more to pile upon the ramp from above, the Plataeans steadily mined it away from below, and the structure failed to increase in height as much as the Peloponnesians expected.

Nevertheless, dreading that they were falling behind in the building, the Plataeans finally abandoned their attempts to make their own wall higher and to thwart the Peloponnesian ramp. Instead they built a second, crescent-shaped rampart behind the first, walling off a pocket within the city: thus, even if the Peloponnesians took the outer wall, they would have to extend their ramp to this inner wall, all the while exposed to missiles from their flanks. This was a wise provision, for as it climbed toward the sky, the outer city wall was becoming dangerously unstable. Eventually the Peloponnesians managed to seat a battering ram on their ramp, and it rattled down much of the wall's wood-and-brick addition. But the second Plataean wall still lurked behind the first, and although the Peloponnesians subsequently built more rams, the Plataeans were equal to them, sending down from their walls nooses to haul the engines up and away and cunningly attacking the Peloponnesian rams with perpendicular rams of their own, which they suspended by poles from the battlements to break the heads off the enemy machines.

All this construction might seem a somewhat dainty plan for an attacking army that must have outnumbered the besieged by at least twenty to one. With such a preponderance of troops, a Napoleonic general would just have thrown up ladders and accepted casualties until all the defenders were dead or exhausted. But there was more at stake than merely capturing the town. The symmetry between the rock-paper-scissors tactics and counter-tactics of the assault on Plataea and the strategies of one-upmanship in the greater war is not accidental: both reflect a common pattern of Greek culture. In either case the contest for victory was at once directed, and partly consumed, by a contest for rank.

The primary contests between Athens and Sparta in the wider Ten Years' War were in display of *andreia*, or courage, superiority in which was shown by fighting or ravaging, and *charis*, or effective reciprocation of what was owed, shown in one's ability to help friends and harm enemies. But at the siege of Plataea, the contest was one of ingenuity and invention, of guile, of *mētis*, the display of which had contributed to rank since the age of Odysseus, the craftiest of men. Since the days of myth, *mētis* had been associated particularly with ingenious craftsmanship and construction. The pattern of behavior in all these competitions was the same: first came an action constituting a challenge to an honorable quality of the opponent's, then a symmetrical reaction, whereby the opponent tried to trump the action to show that he was, in fact, superior in the quality over which they were competing. Then that countering move was countered, and so on. Once the competitive back-and-forth was begun, it was very hard for the participants to escape its logic, for leaving off would be an admission of defeat. Since the Peloponnesians had begun to attack Plataea by ingenious construction, and since they had been countered by ingenuity, the siege would likely continue in the same mode. The assault on Plataea, therefore, was not merely a fight over the fabric of the city and the safety of those inside it. It was a contest of one-upmanship between Plataea and the Peloponnesians, one that reflected upon the rank of each. And to the fury of the Peloponnesians, the Plataeans were winning.[9]

Despairing finally of their ramp and their rams, the Peloponnesians devised to burn Plataea down, assembling a small hillock of wood on their side of the city wall, dousing it with sulphur and pitch, and then setting it alight in the most gigantic conflagration the Greeks of Thucydides' day had ever seen. So fierce was the heat that the Plataeans could not even approach the section of wall the fire abutted. But the wind the Peloponnesians had counted on to carry the sparks over the wall and into the city did not stir that day—and then, suddenly, with a crack of thunder, a torrent of rain came in, utterly quenching the blaze. Zeus' rain had saved Plataea before, when the Thebans tried to capture it by subterfuge. Now Zeus had saved the town again. King Archidamus, already suspecting that the Spartans were doing evil by attacking Plataea, must have slept poorly that night.[10]

Martial guile and its engines having failed to take the city in an acceptable period, the greater part of the Peloponnesian army was finally sent home. Plataea was now to be starved out. But an extended siege was not without its risks to the Peloponnesians; their new plan would take the siege into winter, beyond the season of war. And the Athenians, so close, might easily come to deliver the town while the majority of the Peloponnesians were absent. So the remaining invaders improved the stockade of logs that the Peloponnesians had drawn around the city when they first came, transforming it into an elaborate double wall, constructed of bricks and outfitted with battlements pointing both inward toward the city and outward to ward off any Athenian relief. It was a formidable tire-shaped fortification, itself no little triumph of *mētis*. In mid-September, when the building was finished, the remnants of the Peloponnesian army were dismissed to their homes, save for a small garrison to keep the Plataeans in and the Athenians out.[11]

In the third year of the war, while the Peloponnesians exasperated themselves at Plataea, the Athenians did not raid the Peloponnese. The Athenian strategy of raiding was strictly one of reprisal for Peloponnesian ravaging; thus, if the Peloponnesians did not ravage Attica, as they did not in this year, there was no call for the Athenians to take revenge. There were rules, after all, governing revenge: it was supposed to be both reciprocal and proportionate. A just act of revenge should only occur in reaction to an act of *hybris*, and it should answer precisely the magnitude of that *hybris*. Excessive revenge was punished by the gods; so important was exact retribution to the Greeks that the Spartans even had a temple to the principle of appropriate revenge, a shrine to Athena of Worthy Requital. And men, too, stigmatized excessive revenge: it placed the avenger in the wrong in the eyes of his peers, when being in the right was itself part of rank.[12]

Athens wished the world to believe that the first Peloponnesian invasion of Attica was the war's precipitating act of *hybris*. To maintain this position, and thus her rank, Athens had to avenge Sparta's *hybris* and the *hybris* of any further Peloponnesian invasions—but she had to do this exactly and not out of proportion. For if she went beyond just revenge, then Athens, not Sparta, would be guilty of *hybris*, and any future Spartan invasion would be a justifiable act of revenge against her. Besides, the Athenians believed—and were indeed prevailing upon the world to believe—that their reprisal raiding, although it was conducted from ships and did not offer a formal challenge to battle to the Spartans, was nevertheless adequate revenge for Peloponnesian ravaging of Attica. Their raiding, when the Peloponnesians had not, would be as good as admitting that they needed to catch up. At the moment, the Athenians thought they had made good their equality in rank with the taking of Potidaea and the Peloponnesians' copycat attack on Plataea, which implied that it was the Peloponnesians who were trying to catch up. So the Athenians must do nothing to imply they thought themselves in any way behind, lest they surrender their advantage.

Besides wanting to maintain an air of equality with the Spartans, the Athenians would also have been relieved not to have to raid the Peloponnese in this, the third year of the war. The pest still held sway at Athens: eventually the plague would kill off a full third of the Athenian soldiery. Raids were also enormously expensive. A hundred ships—which was how many Athens sent out in both the first and second years, with her allies adding a total of fifty more—carried seventeen thousand paid rowers. Financially, it was a reprieve for the Athenians not to have to raid the Peloponnese.

A reprieve was especially welcome, moreover, because the Athenians were beginning to show signs of financial stress. During the previous winter the Athenians had sent six triremes to southern Asia Minor to watch out for Peloponnesian privateers, but also to do some looting of their own in the land of the Great King. The official dispatch of such a piratical mission indicates Athenian concern that they were running short of money. For raiding the land of the Great King was dangerous. Not only were many Athenians, the commander included, killed in the course of this expedition, but such raiding might disastrously transform the nature of the war, were the Great King, neutral thus far in the conflict, to be irked into supporting the Spartans with his gigantic wealth.[13]

For their part, even if unraided this year, the Spartans were intensely anxious to prevent future Athenian expeditions around the Peloponnese. And so they launched a war against one of Athens' allies in the northwest of Greece, the Acarnanians, who held the coast above the elbow of land where the Gulf of Corinth meets the Ionian Sea. By attacking Acarnania, the Spartans were also honorably aiding an ally, for to the north of Acarnania lived the Ambracians, colonists of the Corinthians and longtime local rivals of the Acarnanians. Perhaps sensing an opportunity to use the greater war to their advantage, the Ambracians (in company with some of their barbarian allies) asked the Spartans to help them attack Acarnania. And the Spartans were more than happy to oblige.[14]

In explaining Spartan involvement in this distant conflict, Thucydides attributes to the Spartans a domino theory about the northwest during the Ten Years' War: if the Peloponnesians could prevail over one of the states there, the other Athenian-allied states would be likely to fall into line as well. "And after that," says Thucydides, "the Athenians would not find it so easy to sail around the Peloponnese." This domino theory explains why, even though the Athenians had many allies in northwestern Greece, the Peloponnesians thought it worthwhile to attack them individually, as they already had Cephallenia and Zacynthus (in vain), or in this

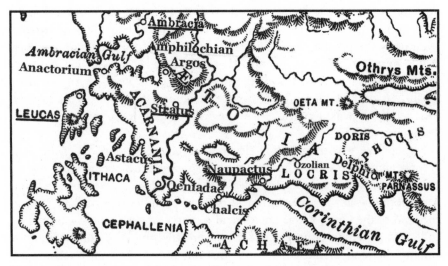

MAP 4.1 Peloponnesian and Ambracian Campaign in Acarnania, 429 BC

year Acarnania. Indeed, if held by both Spartans and Athenians, the sense that the northwestern states were flibbertigibbet allies explains much of the activity of the northwest during the war. And there were reasons to suppose that they might be, reasons even beyond southern-Greek prejudice. For Cephallenia had indeed come over to Athens without a battle in the first year of the war. In 426 BC the Ozolian Locrians would flop over just as easily in the face of a Peloponnesian force marching through their territory. And, as time was to show, Athens' ally Corcyra was politically unstable, while the Peloponnesians had many friends there.[15]

The best way for the Athenians to protect their allies in the northwest was to guard the mouth of the Corinthian Gulf, to keep the Corinthian fleet out of the Ionian Sea. The past winter, in the wake of the previous year's Peloponnesian attack on Zacynthus, the Athenians had stationed a squadron of twenty ships under their general Phormio at friendly Naupactus, the home of the former Messenian helots whom the Athenians had settled there during the war at mid-century (?456 BC).[16]

Sparta's naval resources in the Ionian Sea, supplied by friends like Elis, Leucas, and Anactorium, were far inferior to those inside the Gulf, but at least their way north to Ambracia was not blocked by Phormio at Naupactus. Using these ships the Spartan admiral Cnemus avoided Phormio and landed a thousand Peloponnesian hoplites in Ambracia. From there his force, along with that of the Ambracians and their wild allies, marched south into Acarnania, heading for Stratus, the greatest town of the Acarnanians. But the Acarnanians laid an ambush for a contingent of the Ambracians' barbarian friends and slew many of them, leaving Cnemus and the rest of his force to retire in discouragement, much pelted by the slings of the Acarnanians.[17]

Although the first thrust of the Peloponnesians' northwestern campaign had failed, help was on the way. While Cnemus was leading his campaign

MAP 4.2 Phormio's Victories in the Gulf of Corinth, 429 BC

FIGURE 4.1 Greek warship, possibly a trireme

against Acarnania, the Peloponnesians had been fitting out a considerable fleet to reinforce him. Forty-seven triremes strong, this expedition finally departed from Corinth and Sicyon without undue concern about the twenty Athenian galleys stationed at Naupactus. West along the southern coast of the Corinthian Gulf the Peloponnesians sailed, fat and slow, packed with soldiers and supplies. And then, suddenly, as if a mirror had been dropped from heaven, they were confronted with a fleet steering parallel upon the north shore: Phormio's twenty triremes, sleek and ready for battle. Reaching the point where they hoped to cross north over the strait in the direction of Ambracia, the Peloponnesians turned into the passage, expecting the outnumbered Athenians to give way—but instead the Athenians immediately turned their rams south to challenge them.[18]

The Peloponnesians, fearing a battle in open water against swifter, less laden foes, turned back to shore to anchor for the night. Before dawn the next day, they attempted to escape their tormenters by slipping their anchors and rowing across the strait in the dark, only to be detected (had Phormio stationed a keen-eared scout nearby?), and soon after dawn battle was joined in the middle of the channel.

With its long bronze snout of a ram and eyes painted above to drive off evil spirits—which made the vessel appear even more bestial—a trireme in battle was like an agile rhinoceros, maneuvering to propel its nose into the side or stern of an enemy ship. If two triremes bent on war met upon a lonely sea, their natural tactic was to circle each other like sharks or like fighter planes in a dogfight, each ship trying to go faster and turn more tightly so as to ram the other while avoiding the other's ram. The Greeks had a term for this tactic, the *periplous*, or "sailing-around." And, just as with warplanes, the natural resort of the slower and less maneuverable party was to place a number of triremes in formation so that they could protect one another. Thus the elementary array of a trireme fleet was a line of parallel ships (a "line abreast," in naval terms), for if an enemy turned to ram any one of the ships in the line, he would expose his vulnerable side to his target's neighbor. This formation, moreover, was easy to form out of the follow-the-leader column that triremes generally took up while rowing

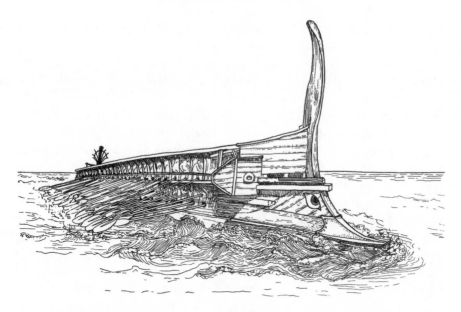

FIGURE 4.2 Trireme ramming

or sailing from place to place. Greek sea battles, then, were usually fought between two facing rows of triremes in line abreast, friends lined up alongside friends, rams pointing at enemy rams.[19]

Given the vagaries of wind and water, however, skilled seamanship was required to maintain even intervals between the ships in line of battle. And this station-keeping was even harder when the line was supposed to remain stationary, since (like all ships before the invention of modern thrusters) triremes had no efficient way of maneuvering directly to port or starboard without going either ahead or astern. In practice, a battle line of parallel triremes quickly developed large gaps as some drifted away from their neighbors or were forced to row forward or back to adjust their intervals. And while uneven spacing was a problem to be avoided in one's own fleet, it could also be exploited in an opponent's. Greek naval tactics prized the maneuver of the *diekplous*, the "sailing through and out"; as soon as a tempting hole in the enemy line was spotted, one's ships would leap into it from one's own line, turning and crashing into the enemy ships to either side to put them out of action, but also to widen the hole and thereby let yet more friendly ships in, whereupon the attackers would "sail out" the back and turn upon the vulnerable sterns of the enemy ships still in line to either side. A successful *diekplous*, requiring great skill and practice, had something of the character of a nautical blitzkrieg. And so, to prevent just such disastrous breakthroughs, a sufficiently large fleet might deploy in multiple lines, one behind the other, especially if its commanders feared their ships were less practiced than those of the opposition.[20]

The dreaded *diekplous* was precisely what the Peloponnesians at the mouth of the Corinthian Gulf feared from the salty Athenian Phormio. Less practiced in sea fighting, deep-loaded and slow, and almost certainly encumbered by their masts and sails (ideally left on shore before a battle), the Peloponnesians reasonably expected the Athenians to have the advantage, were both sides to line up in the conventional line abreast. Thus they decided to minimize the danger of a *diekplous*—and obviate that of being outflanked—by forming a circle, rams out and sterns close together. The small cargo boats that had accompanied the fleet gathered in the center, as did five of the fastest triremes, to reinforce the circle anywhere it might be threatened and to ram any Athenian trireme that did manage to break through the ring—acting, in short, as something of a mobile second line. If the Peloponnesians could deny the Athenians good ramming angles, the Athenians would either have to abandon their attack or ram front to front, damaging both ships and leaving the more numerous Peloponnesians, at the very least, with a victory by attrition. A head-to-head attack, moreover, might well foul the opposing ships together, allowing boarding—and the Peloponnesian triremes, unlike the agile Athenian galleys, were weighed down with troops.

The defensive circle was a venerable tactic of less handy trireme fleets. The Greeks, indeed, had used it to fight the more maneuverable and more numerous Persians to a draw at Artemisium in 480 BC. What the Peloponnesians near the Gulf of Corinth forgot, however, was that it is far easier to keep ships in station when moving than when stopped. Phormio's fleet of twenty began to circle the Peloponnesian ring, faking in as if to ram only to haul off again, just grazing the bows of the Peloponnesians. This had the effect of pushing the Peloponnesian triremes back, closer together and toward the gaggle of cargo boats at their center. None of Phormio's ships was to attack until he gave the signal—and Phormio was waiting for the morning breeze that usually arose at the mouth of the Gulf.[21]

When the wind stirred, just as Phormio predicted, it assured the doom of the Peloponnesians. The Athenians, in motion, could constantly adjust their positions relative to each other. The Peloponnesians, frozen in place by the need to preserve their circle—each of them at a different angle to the wind, with some protected in the lees of others, so that each ship was affected differently by the gusts—were blown into each other. Soon they were pushing each other off with poles and trying to keep clear of the cargo craft, which, lower than the towering triremes and more heavily laden, would drift to leeward more slowly than the warships, and so find the wind driving the galleys into them. Hoarse cries and shouts arose, drowning out the commands of the rowing masters, while the long oars fouled one another, meeting disastrously like the legs of tipsy, colliding centipedes. It was hard to row in chop at the best of times, and the Peloponnesians, not nearly as adept as the Athenians, were soon quite unable to maneuver.[22]

Phormio had been inspecting the plight of the Peloponnesians from but a few yards away as his ships continued their sinister circling, and just as the confusion reached its height, he hoisted his signal, and the Athenians turned in to the attack. It was hardly even a battle. The Athenians rammed and swamped the trireme of one of the Peloponnesian commanders and were rapidly disabling any number of other ships, when the survivors all at once turned to flight, rowing as fast as they could for the Peloponnesian shore. The Athenians captured twelve more ships before the rest made good their escape.

The Athenians towed one of the captive ships to the narrowest point of the strait—the very mouth of the Corinthian Gulf—where they hauled it up on land and dedicated it to the sea god Poseidon. And forever thereafter (for such dedications could not be dismantled, lest the gods be enraged, and few were as dreaded for their vengeful whims as Poseidon), whenever Corinthians sailed west from Corinth, they would have to avert their eyes from this symbol of their defeat, gazing down upon them with reproach from its own great, blind, painted eye. Such a monument, thought the Athenians with some justice, matched the magnitude of their victory over the multitude of their foes.

Even after his triumph, Phormio was in peril. He was still badly outnumbered even by the fleet he had defeated; worse, he knew that a second Peloponnesian fleet lurked as close as Leucas, the third misshapen island at the mouth of the Gulf of Corinth, under the command of the Spartan Cnemus, who had made his way back from Acarnania. And the Peloponnesians were gathering more ships yet, sending commissioners to investigate their defeat by Phormio and to assist Cnemus in making sure the like did not happen again. The chief of these commissioners was Brasidas, hero of Methone and ephor in the previous year. Urgent, then, was Phormio's message to Athens that he needed reinforcements, and just as urgently was a second fleet of twenty ships prepared to reinforce him.[23]

But then a friend from the southerly island of Crete appeared at Athens, with a tale of strange doings in his homeland: if a squadron were sent there promptly, it was reported, one town might take another by coup de main and make it an ally of Athens. Alas, the only immediately available squadron was that bespoke for Phormio, and so it was ordered to detour to Crete on its way to the Athenian station at Naupactus, a diversion of some three hundred miles—and a diversion made worse for Phormio by the considerable time the fleet spent at the island, ravaging the land of one petty Cretan city to gratify another. And so it was that Phormio and his twenty triremes were left to face the massing fleets of the Peloponnesians without help.[24]

It is easy to wonder at Athens' apparent willingness to endanger Phormio for what would have been, even if successful, a tiny strategic gain in a rather distant place. But that is to forget the symbolic importance in this war of being seen to help friends, no matter how small or distant or how dated their own services—that very principle of which the Spartans, by succoring the exiled Aeginetans or holding their hands from Decelea and the villages of northeastern Attica, were showing themselves masters.

We are not told how this Cretan had earned the right to call upon the Athenians—all Thucydides says is that he was the *proxenos*, the hereditary Athenian resident consul in the important Cretan town of Gortyn (where he was a citizen, in the usual Greek way), which was itself not apparently involved in this intrigue. But such a right the Cretan evidently had, and the Athenians, fighting a war of symbols, necessarily vindicated that right in a prompt and spectacular fashion. Perhaps it all went back to the visit to Athens by the strange, tattooed Cretan wizard Epimenides nearly two centuries before, when Athens (in one story) had been stricken by an earlier plague, and the mystic had purified her of the curse that had brought it on. The current plague at Athens will have given a plea for requital of that ancient Cretan service a particular force.[25]

By the time the Peloponnesians were finally ready to face Phormio's squadron of twenty for the second time, they had accumulated an overwhelming force of seventy-seven triremes. To the narrow mouth of the Corinthian Gulf they sailed, anchoring off the southern coast. Opposite them, a mile across the strait, Phormio came west from Naupactus to anchor beneath the trireme the Athenians had dedicated after their recent victory. And there the fleets waited for six or seven days, eyeing each other across the water and coming out to practice their drills day after day, but nothing more. Despite their greater numbers the Peloponnesians were unwilling to fight in the open sea to the west, outside the Gulf, where the more maneuverable and skilled Athenians would have had the advantage, while Phormio was reluctant to fight in the narrows or the close quarters of the Gulf further east, where space to maneuver would be limited, and the greater numbers of the Peloponnesians would tell.[26]

The Spartans had assembled an army on the nearby coast of the Peloponnese, to guard the beaches on which the trireme crews ate and slept, while behind Phormio on the northern shore of the Gulf camped the brave Messenians of Naupactus. None hated the Spartans more than they, for they were the Spartans' former helots.[27]

It was the Peloponnesians, in the end, who forced action, fearing the arrival of Athenian reinforcements. To compel the Athenians to fight in the close quarters of the Gulf, the Spartans sailed toward Phormio's undefended base at Naupactus. Having lain at anchor in four rows, the Peloponnesians now made their way east along the friendly southern shore in four parallel columns: should the Athenians pursue them and attack, and the Peloponnesian fleet turn north to face them in lines abreast, the Peloponnesian line would be nearly as long as the Athenian but protected by its fourfold depth against even the most diabolical *diekplous*. Leading the four columns, to prevent the swift Athenians from escaping down the Gulf to the east, were the twenty fastest Peloponnesian triremes.

The Athenians gave chase just as the Peloponnesians had expected. Phormio had to protect Naupactus, which he had denuded of its menfolk in order to line the shore behind his fleet, and so when the Peloponnesians started toward Naupactus along the south coast, Phormio steered along his north coast in single file, while the Messenians panted toward home on the land.

The Peloponnesians, treated to the agreeable spectacle of the outnumbered Athenians in narrow waters and close inshore, were not slow to exploit their long-sought advantage. The signal hoisted, the four columns now turned north to become four lines of battle and rowed for the Athenians at their best speed. Sensing their peril, the Athenians tried to outrow the Peloponnesians to the east, just as predicted, but despite the Peloponnesian precautions, eleven Athenian triremes escaped in the direction of Naupactus. The rear nine, however, were caught—one captured with its crew and the rest run onto the north shore of the Gulf by their captains, who leapt off with their men to swim or wade to safety. Of these craft some were towed off by the Peloponnesians, but the fast-marching Messenians came upon others while the Peloponnesians were still dragging at them, and mounting the triremes in their armor, they fought the Peloponnesian sailors from the decks, thus saving the ships. With the exception of the twenty fast-sailers who had pursued the eleven escaping Athenians eastwards, the rest of the Peloponnesian fleet became entangled in this trophy hunt.

Phormio and ten of his surviving ships, meanwhile, had won through to Naupactus, and in the shallows beneath the temple of Apollo, they turned their rams outward to await the Peloponnesian attack. One Athenian craft lagged behind, closely pursued by a single trireme from the island of Leucas, a speedy vessel that had pulled ahead of the Peloponnesian squadron. The rest of the twenty, thrilling with victory, sang their battle hymn to Apollo as they came on in a gaggle.

Outside the harbor at Naupactus, a plump merchantman lay at anchor. Behind her high hull the tardy Athenian for a moment vanished from the rapt eyes of her pursuer. But then, even as the ship of Leucas put over her helm to pass the merchant, the Athenian shot out from the other side at ramming speed, having invisibly circled around, and took the trireme of Leucas amidships with her ram, swamping her.

At a thunderstroke, the Peloponnesians rowing hard behind realized that, far from pursuing a terrified foe, they were facing Athenian ships awaiting them quietly in order of battle. Newly wary, those in front backed their oars to await those behind—thus sacrificing the very velocity that made a trireme dangerous—while others ran aground in the shallow anchorage. Taking advantage of the chaos, the Athenians gave a cheer and sped out to attack, and the Peloponnesians resisted only momentarily before turning to flight. Seeing their élite squadron streaming back toward them appears to have panicked the greater mass of the Peloponnesian fleet, which now abandoned the Athenian hulls they were towing and set off west out of the Gulf at speed. The Athenians not only recaptured most of the ships they had lost but also managed to capture six Peloponnesian galleys in the course of the chase.

This second victory of Phormio was even more shaming to the Spartans than his first. The Athenians returned the dead to the Peloponnesians under truce and set up their second trophy on the north shore of the Gulf, this time at Naupactus, where they had turned the tide of the battle. A splendid, cruel irony was an Athenian trophy at Naupactus, a town with deep ties to the Spartans. Naupactus was hallowed among the Dorians as the place where the sons of Heracles embarked on their final, successful invasion of the Peloponnese; the Spartans, like most other Peloponnesians, claimed to be the sons of these invaders, while the Athenians who triumphed at Naupactus claimed to be the ancestors of the Ionian race of the Greeks, the Dorians' ancient foes.[28]

The Peloponnesians, however, tried to salvage what honor they could from the battle in the Gulf. Having driven the Athenians to the beach before the battle went so wrong, the battered Peloponnesians claimed a victory, too, and set up a trophy on their shore, opposite the Athenian trophy from Phormio's previous battle, dedicating there the single Athenian trireme with which they had escaped. The strange laws of symmetry that ruled this war were honored once again as the unblinking eyes painted on the bows of two triremes regarded each other from across the narrow mouth of the Gulf of Corinth.

Now the harbor at Naupactus, so recently the scene of fatal action, fell silent. Clinging to the swamped wreck of their broken trireme, the sailors of Leucas waited to be picked up and captured, while others swam ashore into captivity. One of the Spartan commissioners had been aboard that ship—Timocrates, "Strong in Honor," was his name—and in the way Spartans sometimes did after a defeat, he took his own life upon the wreck, his body washing ashore. And it would have been wise for the elated Athenian sailors, seeing Timocrates lying heavily upon the foreshore in his wet red cloak, seaweed strewn in his long hair, to ponder how, in the end, they could defeat a folk who held their lives so cheap and their honor so dear.

I N THE WIDER WAR OF STANDING, Athens was pulling ahead. The taking of Potidaea remained unavenged because Sparta, despite her efforts, could not capture Plataea. Nor had Attica itself been ravaged this year. And now the Athenians had won not one but two victories at sea, against great odds. Just as the Athenians had sought victories at Epidaurus and Potidaea to set against the plague, the Spartans now had to gamble after some equalizing success. Poor Megara, which had been ravaged by the Athenians for three years running, was of the same mind. And so it was that, once the season for great expeditions was over, when the Peloponnesian fleet had returned to Corinth and Athens' ships were laid up for the winter, Cnemus, Brasidas, and the other Peloponnesian leaders contrived with the Megarians to launch a surprise attack on the Athenian port of Piraeus, only twenty miles from Nisaea, Megara's port on the Saronic Gulf, the gulf of Athens.[29]

In preparation for the assault, the Megarians had retrieved from retirement at Nisaea forty leaky triremes. Crewing them required nearly seven thousand oarsmen. Those Cnemus and Brasidas would gather from Corinth and march rapidly with their oars to Megara, where they would throw themselves into the waiting galleys and heave for Piraeus. So confident were the Athenians in their control of their home waters that no squadrons or fortifications protected Piraeus, and the Peloponnesians hoped to come ashore by surprise and make a pyre of Athens' dockyards before the Athenians could even organize a defense. The resulting victory over Athens would be as cheeky as it was spectacular.

The expedition miscarried. The surprise was well-enough managed, and the rowers passed undetected to the port of Megara. By night they boarded their ships and set forth. But it was not to Piraeus they steered. They made landfall instead on a nearby promontory of the Athenian-settled island of Salamis, where the Athenians had a fort and kept three triremes to blockade Nisaea. Thucydides attributes this diversion to cowardice and sneers at the excuse that the wind was contrary. Yet how could forty ships, rowing in

MAP 4.3 Abortive Peloponnesian Attack on Piraeus and Raid on Salamis, 429 BC

the dark, all lose heart independently and end up in the same place? The Megarian pilots must have been responsible, for they were in their home waters, and the change of objective was perhaps concerted among them in advance. Certainly the outcome agreed well with the Megarians' own wants, for having attacked the blockading fort and towed off the three triremes, and so avenged Athens' blockade of Nisaea, the crews of the raiding fleet proceeded to plunder the island of Salamis. Unlike evacuated Attica, this was a fat place taken unsuspecting, with its animals in their bowers and its folk polishing their treasures in their houses. And since it was by ravaging that the Athenians had made war upon the Megarians, it was—in keeping with the rule of symmetry—by ravaging that the Megarians got their revenge.[30]

It was the Peloponnesians, not the Megarians, who needed to attack Piraeus—for only a great success there could avenge their great defeats elsewhere. The Megarians had used the promise of that general revenge to secure instead the Megarians' own private one. But while the Peloponnesians were perhaps disappointed, they will not have been wholly dissatisfied by the outcome of the wayward expedition. When beacons told the Athenians of the descent on Salamis, they were thrown into a panic, fearing—ironically—that the enemy was already in Piraeus. Piraeus, in turn, flew into an even greater panic, fearing that the enemy was about to enter the harbor.

To arms! To arms! At dawn the Athenians marched down to Piraeus as if to battle, launched their ships in confusion, and sailed for Salamis, leaving their infantry to guard the Attic shore. With long warning of the Athenians' coming, the Peloponnesians gathered their captives, their plunder, and the three captured triremes at their leisure, before sailing back to Megara. It was good they had not delayed longer: the hulls of the Megarian triremes, so long beached on the shore at Nisaea, were full of holes and taking on water. From Megara the rowers walked back to Corinth, many of them, no doubt, with booty swinging from their oars.

This was hardly the end the Peloponnesians had sought: rather than charring the dockyards of Athens, they had looted the farmyards of Salamis. But victories in the contest of standing depended largely on the subjective reaction of the defeated, and by displaying such histrionic terror—a spectacle no doubt soon discussed all over the Greek world—the Athenians had managed to humiliate themselves.[31]

As the Peloponnesian attempt on Piraeus shows, sailing and fighting were only the first of the challenges of trireme warfare. Thucydides' account of the attack contains two telling details about the severe practical constraints facing trireme fleets: the Megarian ships, so long on shore, had become too leaky for safe use, and the Athenians were obliged to launch ships from the shore to chase these sinking Peloponnesians back to Megara. Both were consequences of making war in lightly built wooden ships, designed above all for speed.[32]

We shake our heads that the Athenians did not have a guard squadron at Piraeus in the water and ready to go, but it was not overconfidence that kept the Athenians on the shore. The planks of a wooden boat left in the Mediterranean too long fall victim to aquatic pests, especially shipworms, which eat them away from within, leaving them dangerously flimsy. "I'd rather be gnawed by teredo worms!" says a talking trireme in Aristophanes, imagining the worst possible fate for an Athenian galley. Nor were worms the only problem. Triremes left in the water too long became slow because of marine growths, waterlogging, and leaking—modern experts estimate that a knot of speed might be lost as a result. Triremes were performance craft, and their effectiveness in battle depended upon speed, so this lag put them at a potentially fatal disadvantage in combat. To keep triremes safe and speedy, Greeks had regularly to haul the ships out of the water, scrape their hulls, and dry them out—long drying being the only way to kill the greedy worms.[33]

Keeping triremes out of the water, however, presented its own challenges. As the leaky Megarian ships show, triremes left out of the water for any long period developed leaks as the planks shrunk. This is the case with any wooden boat, and before it can be launched again, its seams must be stopped: this, evidently, the Megarians had failed to do with their triremes at Nisaea. And this is no surprise, since surprise was the Megarian goal during this adventure: given the labor involved, stopping the seams of a fleet of triremes may have been one of the largest industrial enterprises known to the ancient world. It was a process quite impossible to keep secret from the Athenians watching from their fort on Salamis a few miles away, whether or not it involved, as stopping ships' seams did in later eras, clouds of reeking black smoke.[34]

Here, then, was the governing dilemma of trireme warfare: to preserve their performance and fabric, triremes needed to be taken out of the water whenever possible, but once out of the water for more than a few days, they took an immense effort to render seaworthy again. Athens naturally kept her fleet on the shore over the winter, and recaulking ships assigned to expeditions in the spring would have taken weeks of labor for thousands of men, many of them highly skilled and naturally, therefore, expensive.

The fact that keeping triremes in the water was so bad for their fabric, as well as the expense of putting them in the water once they had been hauled out, had predictable consequences at Athens. Anchoring idle triremes in the harbor at Piraeus was apparently not Athenian practice, except when a specific threat was detected—thus the lack of ships in the water when the Peloponnesians descended by surprise on Salamis. This also explains why the Athenians seem to have had no sea-ready reserve earlier in 429 BC, when they diverted Phormio's reinforcements to Crete, or later, as in 428 BC, when a fleet intended to raid the Peloponnese was diverted to respond to an emergency in the Aegean. In 425 BC, when an emergency was reported in Corcyra, a Sicily-bound fleet was assigned to deal with it on the way. If ships already prepared for another expedition were not available, the Athenians suffered considerable delays in dispatching fleets on unexpected missions, even in cases of stark emergency: in 427 BC it took the Athenians some two weeks to get a fleet of sixty ships to sea; in 406 BC it would take them thirty days to launch a fleet of one hundred and ten.[35]

Despite the danger of slow response to emergency, the maritime Athenians had decided that keeping ships on shore was the safest, most cost-effective option available for them during wartime. The reserve of the "hundred best triremes of the year," which Athens established in 431 BC to protect her against an enemy coming by sea, was certainly not kept in the water. These ships sat on the land with most of the rest of Athens' three hundred triremes, days or weeks of labor away from launching. During the Ten Years' War, Athens kept no "home fleet" crewed and ready for action at Piraeus. It may be that the only Athenian ships kept in the water and crewed throughout the sailing season were the two state galleys *Salaminia* and *Paralus*, which is why they so frequently pop up by name during emergencies: only the *Salaminia* and the *Paralus* were always ready for sea.[36]

Despite the military disadvantages of not keeping a ready squadron at Athens, the Athenians' practice of keeping the fleet drawn up on shore explains how Athens could afford her naval war effort. One usual method of estimating Athens' naval costs is to take the total number of ships she is reported to have sent out in a given year and assume that the rowers in each of those ships cost one talent per month for the eight months of the sailing season. So if in 431 BC the Athenians sent out one hundred and thirty ships, their wages cost alone would have been one thousand and forty talents; if in the second year of the war the Athenians sent one hundred ships, these would have cost eight hundred talents. But Athens' treasury at the beginning of the war contained only six thousand talents, while the income from her empire was six hundred, and there were also the land army and the expenses of the democracy to pay for. Calculations on this basis produce a miserable prognosis for the Athenian treasury— Athens is only able to afford Pericles' strategy for three years, or five, or six, depending on the assumptions made—and make deliberate Pericles seem like a foolish optimist, since the war lasted for ten.[37]

It is, in fact, likely that Athens was not as talent-strapped as this and that Pericles was not such a fool. Athenian naval expenses have been overstated. It was in time of peace, according to a later author, that Pericles would send out sixty ships a year to train for eight months: such a luxury was not available in war time, as is signaled by the fact that the Athenians by 425 BC had become anxious about their fleet's lack of practice. And if Athenian triremes were only launched and crewed for expeditions instead of for the entire sailing season, then the cost of wages during wartime would have been only a fraction of what has been estimated. In 431 BC, assuming that the hundred-ship raid around the Peloponnese took a leisurely three months, and the thirty-ship expedition to Opuntian Locris a month, the cost of naval wages for the year would have been closer to three hundred and thirty than one thousand and forty talents; in 430 BC, on the same assumptions, the cost would have been three hundred rather than eight hundred talents. Crew wages, moreover, were only one naval expense. Ships must be built and equipped, reequipped, and maintained, and Athens' gigantic shipyards had their own fixed costs. All in, and including the fixed costs at home, a trireme on campaign may have cost the Athenians as much as two talents a month (rather than one, the conventional figure used above). If so, the Athenian war effort seems far more financially practical if the Athenians kept the number of triremes at sea to a minimum.[38]

Athenian reluctance to keep triremes in the water for extended periods, and their very high costs when they were crewed and sent out, also helps to explain why Athenian expeditions expected to last a long time were often so small. It was cheaper, in wages at least, and created far less wear on the ships to send a hundred triremes out for a month than ten ships out for a year. A mere ten ships were sent out to Corcyra with Lacedaemonius in 433 BC; a mere twenty reinforced him. Phormio had only twenty ships at Naupactus in 429 BC; his delayed reinforcement was only twenty more. Athens would have to pay the rowers in detached squadrons like these all year round, whether they were fighting or not, and so the Athenians tried to keep such year-round payments to a minimum. And the ships, in distant and less well-equipped ports than Piraeus, might also have to spend far more time in the water, which slowed them in the short run and rendered them dangerous to their crews in the long run. Little surprise that fleets the Athenians posted away from Piraeus were as small as possible.[39]

The realities of trireme warfare also reveal what was at stake in the aborted Peloponnesian attack on Piraeus: not merely the sack of the port itself, the greatest market and cheaping-town of the Greek world, but the destruction of Athens' dockyards, Athens' ship sheds, and almost the entire Athenian fleet, drawn up empty on shore. A successful attack on Piraeus would have been a far more thorough-going Pearl Harbor. No wonder the Athenians panicked. And perhaps their alarm was increased by a sense that they lacked a leader equal to the crisis. For only a few weeks before the raid, Athens' great steadier, Pericles, had succumbed to the plague—one of the last to do so in this first two-year onslaught of the disease.[40]

What would the great statesman have thought as he lay dying? How Athens stood in the war? Pericles, Thucydides says, had told the Athenians that "they would win through if they would keep quiet, take care of their fleet, make no attempts to expand their empire during the war, and not place the city at risk." In detail this meant that "they should prepare for the war, and bring their property in from the country. They should not go out to battle, but come into the city and protect it. They should make ready their fleet, in which their strength lay, and keep control of their allies . . . because the strength of Athens depended on the revenue of money that came from the allies."[41]

Pericles' strategy of avoiding dangers and protecting Athenian resources has been controversial at least since 1888, when the formidable Julius von

Pflugk-Hartung reproached the Athenian as a mere "mayor," a parochial politician whose passive policy offered no clear route to victory. And Pflugk-Hartung knew about such things: he had fought the perfidious French in 1870. No, responded the great Hans Delbrück: Pericles' plans were well conceived. Pericles' "strategy of exhaustion" had every prospect of winning the war by wearing out the resources and spirit of Athens' opponents. After one hundred and thirty years, the debate has not shifted a great deal. Many have despaired with Pflugk-Hartung, while others have offered scenarios whereby Pericles' passive strategy might lead to triumph: Athens' mere survival would inevitably bring the Peloponnesians to treat for peace, or Sparta's failure promptly to defeat Athens would by itself cause the Spartan league to dissolve. But, in the just words of an eminent contemporary interpreter of these events, "These expectations seem far too optimistic."[42]

Staying inside their walls and watching over their allies is not, of course, all the Athenians did. The Athenians also raided the Peloponnese, but because the purpose of these raids has proved so hard to fathom, these undertakings have tended to take a subordinate place in discussions of Athenian strategy. Thucydides did not trouble to reconcile these more active measures with his descriptions of Pericles' more passive plans. But the historian realized that the Athenians thought the raids important: if the Athenians "could firm up their friendships with Corcyra, Cephallenia, the Acarnanians, and Zacynthus," they believed, "they could wear down the Peloponnese by warfare round about it." And by sending one hundred and fifty ships on these raids, the Athenians themselves signaled that they considered them of the first significance. But these raids were not, we now think, an economic blockade of the Peloponnese, although that theory was modish once upon a time. Nor are they likely to have caused enough economic hardship to split the Spartan league. So were the raids intended not to cause much damage in fact, but to signal, rather like the U.S. bombings of North Vietnam, that Athens could cause damage if she chose?[43]

In fact, Pericles' strategy was never a modern one of "exhaustion," aimed at the physical, economic, or psychological wearing-out of the Peloponnesians; nor was it intended to divide the Peloponnesian alliance; nor was it designed to communicate the mere potential of Athenian strength (although Pericles would hardly have objected if any of those ends were achieved). But Pericles' strategy was indeed one of communication: by carefully judged reprisals for the Spartan ravaging of Attica, by humiliation of the Spartans through attacks on Sparta's allies, and by exaltation of Athens by helping Athens' allies, Pericles planned to impress the rank and renown of Athens upon the Spartans and upon the wider world of the Greeks.

Pericles' strategy was primarily intended to justify Athens' claim to equality in rank with Sparta. For to Pericles and the Athenians, just as to Archidamus and the Spartans, this was a war of pride, of standing. No modern logic makes sense of the strategies in the Ten Years' War—of the ravaging, of the raiding, of the strange episodes of generosity to exiles and friends from the days of legend, of the symmetries and tit-for-tat campaigns. Only a logic of rank and revenge explains such things.[44]

In the first three years of the war, both sides had, for the most part, abided by their initial strategies of waging war by humiliation and one-upmanship. Diversions from those strategies—attempts to break the power of the enemy rather than simply to bespatter his honor—were but few, halfhearted, and incubated mostly on the Spartan side: adventures like the Spartan embassy to Persia, intended to raise money in order to wrest the sea from Athens, and the abortive attack on Piraeus, intended to strike a real blow at Athens' naval strength (although destroying Athenian naval power, would, of course, cast down her rank along with her power). Even the fighting in the northwest was primarily a function of the Athenian strategy of revenge, as the Athenians were determined to protect their bases for future raiding circumnavigations of the Peloponnese, and the Peloponnesians, we are told, were fighting to prevent the same.

It was not in the interests of Athens, Pericles felt, to adopt a more ruthless strategy: by the time of his death, with the capture of Potidaea and Phormio's victories at the Gulf of Corinth, Athens was winning the existing war of pride. Athens was doing better, in fact, than the sober Pericles had hoped—for Pericles' strategy had been aimed simply at defending Athens' claims to equality in rank rather than at seeking the clear superiority toward which events were propelling her. Not only might a more aggressive strategy prove dangerous, but it would also certainly encourage the Spartans to adopt similar measures, tit for tat, with incalculable consequences.

We can think of (and splenetic critics like Pflugk-Hartung have roundly reproached Pericles for his failure to employ) more forceful methods that one or the other side might have adopted. The Athenians might have quickly occupied the island of Cythera, off Laconia, and harried the Spartans from there. They had, after all, fortified Atalanta off Opuntian Locris during the first year of the war, and they would finally get around to capturing Cythera in 424 BC. The Spartans might immediately have built a fort in Attica and so denied the Athenians access to their fields the year round as they would do in 413 BC. This hardly required military genius: Thucydides says that even before the war both sides had considered building forts in enemy territory.[45]

If neither side had yet taken such drastic measures against the other, it was not because these measures had not occurred to them but because they were not suited to the type of war being fought. Neither the Athenians nor the Spartans were as yet fighting a war of economics, a war of conquest, or a war of extermination; rather they fought a war of symbols, in which the fact and geographical extent of ravaging or raiding were held to be more important than their economic impact. As the season of battles drew to a close in 429 BC, the war so far seemed to be very much the rather staid, predictable, old-fashioned affair that the Thebans and Plataeans had both guessed it would be back on that rainy night of slaughter in April 431 BC— the night when the Thebans decided not to kill the Plataeans they had at their mercy, while the Plataeans felt free to butcher the Thebans they had at theirs. Not yet the cry of trumpets, but the moan of low bassoons.

THE WEST COAST OF ASIA Minor crumbles into the Aegean Sea in a chaos of islands, some of them the old habitations of men, some no more than grazing for a handful of affable sheep, and some mere rocks tyrannized by a single arrogant lizard. Of the greater islands, Lesbos imposed itself most upon the sentiments of the Greeks—Lesbos, the mother of poets, where once Sappho had sung of Eros the bittersweet, and where ivy-crowned Alcaeus had reeled with the unmixed wine. Here, even the working women were poets and added their milling song to the canon of Greek verse: "Grind, mill, grind! For even Pittacus grinds, and he is king over great Mytilene!" Mytilene was indeed great—she was the first city of Lesbos—and Pittacus, one of the Seven Wise Men of legendary Greece, had indeed ruled over her, in the old days when tyrants and poets and wise men walked the land.

In the fifth century BC, Mytilene was still strong, one of the few subjects of imperial Athens privileged to contribute ships rather than silver to the common defense, one of the few privileged to keep her power at home rather than build up that of Athens. But anxious that Mytilene should not become stronger still, Athens had prevented her from bringing all of Lesbos under her sway, and this Mytilene resented. Sometime before the outbreak of the greater war, Mytilene had asked Sparta for help were she to revolt from Athens. The Spartans had been discouraging: either they had not then wished to endanger their relations with Athens, or they had simply had no help to give. Mytilene, after all, brooded upon a distant island surrounded by Athenian allies and would be as hard to help as northerly Potidaea. Still, the Mytileneans pressed forward with their plans to make all of Lesbos theirs and prepared also in case of an angry Athenian reaction. At the beginning of 428 BC, the people of Mytilene were extending their walls, blocking up the harbors around which their city was built, and sending for grain and mercenary archers from the north. If they had to fight, they wanted to be ready, but their preparations might equally

MAP 4.4 The Rebellion of Mytilene, 428 BC

well prevent a fight. Athens was already fighting a sprawling war, and if Mytilene looked strong enough, its leaders perhaps calculated, Athens would think it best to let them do as they liked on their island home.[46]

The particular object of Mytilene's hunger was Methymna, the second city of Lesbos and a rival of old, situated on the far coast of the mountainous, clam-shaped isle. Fearing their insular enemy's plans, the men of Methymna wasted no time in warning Athens of the Mytileneans' dark preparations, claiming that Mytilene was plotting to revolt in cooperation with Sparta and the Boeotians, the founders of their race. In this warning Methymna was joined by Tenedos—a speck of an island to the north of Lesbos, sacred to Apollo and long on bad terms with Mytilene—and also by the Athenian *proxenoi*, or honorary consuls, who lived in Mytilene itself.[47]

So horrid a rumor about Mytilene, however, the Athenians were loath to believe. They dreaded adding another considerable war to the one they were already fighting. And so, somewhat carelessly, they sent envoys to Mytilene, much in the manner of a parent who hears unexplained thumping from the children's bedrooms upstairs: "whatever you're doing, quit it!" But the envoys returned with an astonishing report: the Mytileneans had declined to desist. Swinging now from lassitude to panic, the Athenians overreacted and sent a naval squadron to descend on Lesbos by surprise during the festival of Apollo on Cape Malea, when the population of Mytilene would be outside the protection of their walls, celebrating the rites of the god upon the point of the land. The fleet of forty triremes sent to Lesbos was that voted by the democracy and launched to make vengeful descents upon the Peloponnese; keeping no ships in the water at Piraeus, in time of emergency the Athenians had to rob Peter to pay Paul.[48]

The swinging of the seasons had once again brought the Peloponnesians into Attica when the grain came ripe, in the middle of May. Their desire for revenge, in this fourth year of the war, had perhaps been rekindled by Athens' great victories in the Gulf of Corinth the summer before. The Peloponnesian invasions of 431 and 430 BC were intended to humiliate Athens, to prove Sparta's superior rank. But after a year's hiatus, when the Peloponnesians had suffered much ignominy, the resumption of ravaging Attica in 428 BC was more likely intended as a means of catching up.[49]

Making camp some distance from Athens itself, the Peloponnesians issued forth to rip and burn. They were met and harried by the horse of the Athenians, sallying forth from the city as usual; thus the light-armed troops, to whom much of the hot business of ravaging was consigned, were confined to their camp, and only the hoplites could come forth, prepared to form a prickly clump should the horsemen of Athens approach.

After a month or so, when the provisions of the Peloponnesians were exhausted, the army quit Attica and lumbered back to the Peloponnese. In terms of crops destroyed, this had been a singularly futile invasion. But these invasions were not, of course, primarily economic in purpose. So long as the Athenians did not dare to come forth with their hoplites, the campaign was a victory for the Spartans. Even so, the boldness of the Athenian cavalry hints that the horsemen of Boeotia, who had previously countered the Athenian cavalry, were absent from Attica during this year's invasion—unlike in the first year of the war, when skirmishes between Athenian and Boeotian cavalry were reported, or the second, when the Peloponnesian ravaging was so extensive as to imply that it overcame all opposition. Perhaps all the attention of the Boeotians was focused this year on Plataea, still under siege, Plataea, Thebes' abiding itch.[50]

Clearly, if the Peloponnesians had invaded Attica, the logic of revenge demanded that the Athenians raid the Peloponnese. This year the planned fleet of reprisal was, at forty ships, smaller by far than those of the first and second years of the war, both of which had boasted a hundred Athenian vessels reinforced by fifty more from their allies. A smaller raiding fleet may signal the dilapidated state of Athens' finances, but it also may reflect an inflated Athenian confidence that, after Phormio's victories the year before, a smaller squadron would be ample to defeat any ships the Peloponnesians might send against it. Indeed, it may even have been intended to belittle this year's Peloponnesian invasion of Attica, the implication of the smaller fleet being that there was less to avenge; that each successive Peloponnesian invasion was somehow less shaming than the one before it; that, in short, so great was the Athenian advantage in honor after the fall of Potidaea, and after Phormio's double victory in the northwest, that it hardly needed topping off.

This Athenian fleet of vengeance never sailed west to the Peloponnese as planned, but rather headed east on foaming oar to Lesbos to preempt the rising of Mytilene. There were things more important to Athens than her rank, and the Aegean empire upon which both rank and power depended was one of them.

Of the Athenians' hoped-for surprise, however, there was none: the coming of the Athenians had been reported to Mytilene. The democracy of Athens could as yet do no great deed in secret, relying upon the assembly in its thousands to vote on its expeditions. And although the Athenians had rounded up and interned the crews of the ten Mytilenean triremes that were stationed at Athens in accordance with the treaty of alliance between Athens and Mytilene, a Hellenic Paul Revere hastened from Attica as soon as he heard the plans of the Athenians. Crossing over to Euboea, he panted through the hills to the island's southern tip, where he caught a merchant ship just pulling up its anchor. Within three days of leaving Athens, he was in Mytilene, unfolding the designs of the Athenians.

So it was that when the jaws of the Athenian fleet closed upon Cape Malea and its temple of Apollo, they clashed upon no one at all; or, if the suspension of his rites had not been reported to Apollo, perhaps they champed upon the descended nimbus alone, puzzled by the absence of feast and song and peering about for his priests and lowing sacrifices. But of the Mytileneans themselves there was no trace: they were even then in the city, where they were busily finishing their walls with stockades and preparing for war.[51]

Thwarted in their guile, the Athenians delivered an ultimatum to Mytilene: the Mytileneans were to give up their ships and tear down their walls. They were to be degraded, that is, to the same status as Athens' lesser, tribute-paying allies. The Mytileneans were troubled: their preparations for war were far from complete, and they were also, we suspect, divided in their councils. Most—if they had any sense, at least—would hardly have looked forward to fighting a war against mighty Athens. Their preparations had been but a bluff to secure license to dominate Lesbos. Yet a fiery minority had indeed yearned for revolt and was in fact in contact with both Lacedaemon and Thebes. Even as the Athenians arrived, envoys from those cities were struggling to cross the sea to Lesbos.[52]

From the divided councils of the Mytileneans, then, emerged a feeble conspiracy of bluster. The majority still hoped to scare the Athenians with their strength; the minority, to commit their countrymen to open rebellion, however unwilling. What the two sides could agree upon, we guess, was a charade, a show of force. Out of her harbor the fleet of Mytilene sailed, as if to give battle to the Athenians. But the Athenians would not be bluffed: they attacked. The pantomiming Mytileneans, appalled by the enormity of their own daring and unprepared in spirit for an actual fight, resisted little and were driven to land. Their sham having failed, the men of Mytilene now implored the Athenian generals to let them send envoys to Athens that they might explain themselves. This was granted them, for the Athenian fleet, having been sent off in a panic to attempt a coup de main, had few soldiers aboard and was quite unprepared to prosecute the siege of so considerable a city.[53]

Envoys of Mytilene were now sent to humble themselves before the Athenians. But envoys were sent in another direction as well: to Sparta, to appeal for help in the event that no good agreement could be reached with the Athenians. To this end a trireme darted out of the city, eluding the Athenian fleet anchored along the shore to the north, and made a stormy, hungry passage all the way to the Peloponnese, never touching land (for all the islands that spotted the Aegean between Lesbos and the Peloponnese were friendly, or subject, to the Athenians).[54]

The Mytilenean envoys to Athens returned soon enough to report that no kindly settlement could be achieved with the Athenians: now that there had been fighting, however desultory, the furious Athenians likely insisted on terms of grim subjection. So now, in desperation, Mytilene and all her friends on Lesbos—all the island towns, that is, except for loyal Methymna—declared war on Athens. The Athenians brought in soldiers from the nearby islands of Imbros and Lemnos, among other places, but still they lacked the strength to lay siege to the city by land. Instead, it was the Mytileneans who, seeing the weakness of the Athenians, marched out against them with all their forces. North the Mytileneans marched toward the camp of the Athenians, and when the latter came out to accept the challenge, the Mytileneans defeated them and their islander allies in a pitched battle. Yet despite their victory, the Mytileneans could not pluck up the courage to camp on the battlefield and instead withdrew back into the city, thereby sacrificing the symbolic reward of their victory—or, just as possibly, showing a shrewd modesty. For a formal defeat by the Mytileneans, with the Athenians forced to apply for a truce to recover their dead, the Athenians might well feel obliged to avenge in blood; and so a formal defeat, perhaps the careful and the wise at Mytilene decided, would make terms with mighty Athens impossible to secure. Better to retire into the city and, leaving the bodies, let the Athenians save their pride.[55]

After the battle there came yet more encouragement to the most militant of the rebels at Mytilene. The messengers sent from Sparta and Thebes before the revolt had finally managed to slink into Mytilene in a trireme and evidently made extravagant promises of aid, for the Mytileneans now ceased attacking the Athenians to await Peloponnesian relief. The chastened Athenians, although they dared not advance from their camp to approach Mytilene by land, summoned more triremes from their allies and laid the city under close blockade by sea, rounding off their naval cordon by establishing smaller fortified havens north and south of Mytilene, supplied by the larger camp farther north. But while there was no Athenian blockade of Mytilene by land, even that by sea was hardly perfect: the Spartan and Theban messengers, along with yet more Mytilenean ambassadors, soon made their escape to Sparta in a trireme.[56]

The first set of envoys from Mytilene arrived at Sparta in mid-July at the latest. But if they hoped for rapid action from the Lacedaemonians, they were to be disappointed. For rather than take any immediate, practical steps, the Spartans instructed the envoys to present themselves at the Olympic Games, in the middle of August, and there to make their plea for aid before Sparta's allies. Nor would their plea be delivered before Sparta's allies alone. For the festival of Zeus at Olympia was the greatest in-gathering of all the Greeks, to which athletes and spectators came from Asia Minor, Sicily, Italy, and even farther afield—wherever in the world, that is, the venturesome Hellenes had wandered. The Athenians would be there, too, of course, as would their allies, protected by the sacred Olympic truce, just like all the other visitors, even enemies locked in bitter war. We scratch our heads to think of the Greeks on opposite sides of the conflict who may have met at Olympic feasts and sacrifices. Did cunning Phormio and brave Brasidas replay with olive pits the sea fights of the year before? Did somber King Archidamus of Sparta, as he nodded a countryman's horses to victory in the race of the four-horse chariots, miss his old friend Pericles?[57]

To parade the rebel Mytileneans before such a congregation—to bid famous Mytilene cry out against the iniquity of Athenian rule and plead with the Spartans and their allies for rescue, while the Athenians could do nothing but glare, lest they incur the curse of Zeus—was a magnificently contrived humiliation. The decision of the Spartans to follow such a course (rather than, say, tumble a fleet to sea as swiftly as possible in hopes of surprising the Athenians besieging Mytilene) shows that they were still thinking of victory over Athens in terms of harvesting honor and imposing shame—and that, moreover, in the wake of Potidaea and their losses in the Gulf of Corinth, they thought they were losing the war of rank and could only begin to even the balance by shaming Athens in the most public forum in the Greek world.

Making such a display of Mytilene was stormy with perils, for in throwing themselves behind the Mytileneans, the Spartans were risking another Potidaea. In time, it could be predicted, Athens would grind Mytilene down with her maritime power, and as with Potidaea, Sparta would be shown false in her pledges and futile to her friends—and would sink even lower into ignominy. Wiser, perhaps, to give no public guarantee to the Mytileneans, yet privately suckle them with such practical help as was possible. Then, should the men of Lesbos succeed in establishing their own independence, the Spartans might be received with pipes and trumpets when all peril was past.[58]

The Spartans did the opposite. So hungry were they for an immediate victory in honor that they took the extravagant gamble of making a spectacle of Mytilene, thereby making a hostage of their honor in the time to come. And so it was that after the god had been honored and the races run, even as the merchants were striking their stalls and the whoremasters counting their gains, the envoys of Mytilene were brought into the hallowed temple of Olympian Zeus—the most public place in all of Greece—where Sparta's allies sat in solemn council in their festival robes, to beg to be allowed to join the Spartan alliance. Their pleas were granted, and energetic

FIGURE 4.3 Ancient Olympia, artist's reconstruction

measures were announced on the spot for their succor: a second invasion of Attica in the fall of the year and, more daring yet, a naval expedition into the Saronic Gulf, Athens' home waters.[59]

Although these bold new designs were to follow Sparta's bold flaunting of Mytilene at the Olympics, they were based not upon the flashing-eyed reckoning of honor but upon sober calculations about money. In the months past, the Athenians had given many signs of financial debility. The year before, in 429 BC, the Athenians had not raided the Peloponnese at all. Their strategy of reprisal had demanded this restraint, and the Spartans no doubt understood that—but, at the same time, inaction might imply a failure of strength. This year, moreover, the Athenians had reduced the size of their ravaging fleet; from the reports from Lesbos, the Spartans would have known that the fleet appointed to raid the Peloponnese—the one diverted to meet the emergency of Mytilene—was only forty triremes strong. And, while the Spartans were gloating over the Mytilenean envoys and burnishing them for display at Olympia, the replacement fleet that the Athenians later sent in reprisal for the Peloponnesian invasion of Attica was, at thirty triremes, even slighter. What a fall from the first and second

years of the war, when a round century of Athenian warships, supported by allies and cargo craft as well, had made their stately circumnavigations of the Peloponnese! Even if the Spartans had no good knowledge of Athenian finances (as it turns out, they overestimated Athenian stringency), from what they and their allies could see for themselves, the Athenians had the look of men turning over their coffers and thumping them in the hope that a few neglected obols might fall out.[60]

The Peloponnesians conjured a twofold plan from their deduction of Athenian poverty. First, they would drag a fleet of triremes by land over the Isthmus from the Gulf of Corinth and unleash it into the Saronic Gulf. Should Athenian finances permit no more ships to be sent out from Piraeus, the Spartans reasoned, the Athenians would be forced to recall their fleets from besieging Mytilene and raiding the Peloponnese to protect Athens from blockade. And so, for a time at least, the Peloponnese would be spared, and the siege of Mytilene would be lifted. At the same moment, the Spartans and their allies would make a second land invasion of Attica, in the fragrant autumn season when olives and grapes were gathered in. Even the rumor of such an expedition would, the Peloponnesians hoped, confine Athens' infantry to Attica and prevent them from perfecting the siege of Mytilene by land.[61]

In its basic purpose, the Spartan plan succeeded before it ever began. The Athenians did not recall their ships from Mytilene, but mere knowledge of the plans of the Peloponnesians—blared forth at Olympia, they were soon known to all the Greeks—did bar the Athenians from sending land reinforcements to Lesbos. So unconstrained were the Mytileneans on their island that while the Peloponnesians were making their preparations at the Isthmus, the islanders marched forth to attack their hated insular enemy, Methymna. The main interests of the men of Mytilene had, of course, always been local—it was, after all, their desire to dominate all Lesbos that brought them into conflict with Athens. And taking Methymna would also release the soldiers of Mytilene's small allies on Lesbos, all of them physically closer to Methymna than to Mytilene, to fight the Athenians. But the traitors in the city of Methymna, upon whom the Mytileneans were relying, failed them, and the Mytileneans were thrown back. This encouraged the men of Methymna, in turn, to attack one of Mytilene's small allies on the island, but they too were defeated, leaving many dead. The Mytileneans remained masters of the dry land. So the Peloponnesian distraction of the Athenians had been a success, even if the Mytileneans had made but a parochial use of it.[62]

Yet, however successful the twofold plan of the Peloponnesians was as distracting bustle, the actual land-and-sea campaigns were an ignominious failure. This was a consequence, in part, of a lack of support from Sparta's allies. After Olympia the Spartans themselves hastened with their forces to the Isthmus and began there to prepare the haul-ways used to draw triremes over the narrowest point of the land. But Sparta's allies, who were already bringing in their fall harvests, had no stomach for a second campaign and dawdled. The Athenians, meanwhile, had guessed that this new Spartan boldness must have arisen from a sense of Athenian financial infirmity. Sensing now the opportunity for a victory in honor by proving their enemies wrong, they strained all the sinews of their treasury and set to sea from Piraeus with one hundred shining ships. Even the proud hoplites of Athens—who usually swanked on deck, excused from lowly rowing—were embarked, as were the resident aliens, many of them wealthy. Rowing well in battle, of course, required untold hours of practice. Thus, setting well-off novices to the oar is a strong indication that the Athenians did not really expect to fight: rather, this was a show of force, and a successful one at that. The Athenian fleet cruised in its dread magnificence along the coast of the Isthmus and insolently put ashore to plunder here and there along the near coast of the Peloponnese.[63]

Sparta's high designs were collapsing, and final proof came when her army at the Isthmus received news that the remnant of the earlier Athenian raiding fleet of thirty ships, which had ravaged the coast of Laconia on its way out to the northwest, was—rather than hurrying home to ward the menaced strands of Attica—raiding Laconia again on its way back. That was enough for the Spartans. They had wholly underestimated the resources of the enemy. The summons to their allies, most of whom had yet to arrive, was cancelled, and the Spartans, too, marched home.[64]

Not being ancient Greeks, it is hard for us to estimate the combatants' progress in the war for rank in a year of equivocal results like 428 BC. But the Greeks themselves may have been just as puzzled and come to different estimates. On one hand, the Peloponnesians had proved futile in their siege of Plataea all through the campaigning season. They had invaded Attica once, but the Athenians had sent two ravaging expeditions to the Peloponnese: the fleet of thirty that had replaced the fleet sent against Mytilene and, in the autumn, the emergency fleet of one hundred ships. The Spartans could still try to convince themselves that no number of naval raids was equal to even one proper ravaging by land, with its implicit challenge to hoplite battle, but the fact was that, just as in 429 BC when they had attacked Plataea rather than invade Attica, now, by attempting a second invasion of Attica in the year, they were tacitly endorsing the Athenian position that a ravaging was a ravaging and that ravagings were to be counted rather than measured.

The defection of Mytilene, on the other hand, had embarrassed the Athenians—indeed, the Spartans had wrung out of it every ounce of embarrassment—as had Athenian setbacks on the island. And the Athenians had suffered, too, a minor defeat in the northwest, when an attack on the Spartan-allied island of Leucas failed, and the Athenians had to recover the bodies of their dead, including their admiral, under truce. These Athenian mishaps, however, were arguably offset by the collapse of the Peloponnesians' land-and-sea campaign. For the abortive double campaign was twice again as mortifying for the unique publicity with which it was launched: proclaimed at Olympia in the very wake of the games, with all of Greece peering curiously in at the doors of the temple of Zeus. Best, then, to call honors even in 428 BC—but that left Athens in the lead as the captors of Potidaea and two-time victors in the Gulf of Corinth, whereas both of Sparta's attempts to equalize the account, at Plataea and Mytilene, were still hanging fire as the campaigning season approached its end.[65]

Any Spartans who foresaw the risk of parading the Mytileneans at Olympia, when no aid could easily be brought to them, were soon offered the spectacle of their new ally—sworn into alliance on the very altar of Olympian Zeus, no oath being more sacred or infamous to betray—transformed into an appalling simulacrum of the ally they had previously failed to help, Potidaea. For once the failure of the Peloponnesian expeditions by land and sea had become apparent, the Athenians finally did send enough soldiers to Lesbos to dominate Mytilene from the land. Under the command of the general Paches, a thousand hoplites were sent, themselves serving as rowers for the passage (thus saving the Athenian treasury the cost of a thousand additional men), and with this addition of strength, the Athenians cast a wall around Mytilene and made it bristle with forts. Now Mytilene, like Potidaea before it, was closely blockaded both by land and by sea. The lives of the people of Mytilene and the honor of the Peloponnesians were intertwined in peril.[66]

Yet, even as Athens completed the investment of Mytilene, she was showing yet more strain to her finances. The Peloponnesians had gambled that Athens was wholly out of money; they had been wrong. But if their impression of Athenian poverty was exaggerated, it was not without basis. Using hoplites to do their own rowing was one sign of this stringency, as was sending smaller expeditions to raid the Peloponnese. To pay for the war on Mytilene, Athens also imposed an emergency property tax upon her richest citizens in 428 BC, raising two hundred talents; the richest Athenians were excused from rowing in the emergency fleet of one hundred ships, presumably in order to gather the money. And the Athenians dispatched a naval expedition of twelve ships commanded by the general Lysicles to plunder the land of the Great King in Caria on the coast of Asia Minor. Four colleagues from Athens' board of ten generals accompanied Lysicles, which suggests the importance of their mission. But Lysicles and his army were attacked by the locals and a body of Samian exiles—those who had settled on the mainland after fleeing Samos in the wake of her failed revolt from Athens in 440 BC. Rather than bringing home shiploads of blood-stained Persian gold, Lysicles and much of his force were slaughtered.[67]

Lysicles' sojourn in Hades under the reproachful glare of Pericles (he had taken up with Pericles' mistress after the latter's death) may have been lightened by better news from other felled Athenians who would stagger off Charon's boat in years to come: the year of Lysicles' piratical expedition to Caria appears to have been the nadir of Athens' financial condition during the Ten Years' War. We hear no more of property taxes, no more of hoplites doing their own rowing. Nor did Athens' enemies act again on the presumption that Athens was in financial stress. In the first years of the war, the Athenians had borrowed enormous sums from the treasuries of their gods (when the Athenians lodged their surplus tribute in temples, as was their custom, it became, in some sense, the property of the gods, and Athens called upon it by "borrowing"). But after 428 BC, this borrowing appears to have dropped off. Somehow—most likely by raising the tribute she charged her subjects—Athens' finances seem to have been put back in order after 428 BC and to have remained relatively tidy for the rest of the Ten Years War.[68]

THE WINTER BETWEEN THE CAMPAIGNING seasons of 428 and 427 BC brought a reminder to Athens that, in addition to wasting her treasure, she had also made a hostage of her honor by refusing to allow her vulnerable friend Plataea to escape into neutrality. Plataea had been besieged by the Peloponnesians since early summer of 429 BC, and now the garrison was running out of food. But the perils of a breakout appealed to only half the defenders, some two hundred and twenty brave souls. Little surprise, for the Peloponnesians had striven to make such an undertaking altogether perilous by building an elaborate fortification around Plataea, consisting of two walls: an outer one to keep the Athenians from relieving the town and an inner one to immure the Plataeans. Between the walls—a mere sixteen feet apart—stretched a parapet roof, and beneath that roof, between the walls, lived the besiegers. Connecting the walls at close intervals were towers. The more spirited of the Plataeans, noticing that the Peloponnesian watchmen sheltered in these towers in bad weather, waited for precisely such conditions to attempt an escape.[69]

First, the Plataeans made careful preparations: they could slip out a gate in their own city wall, but they would need ladders to scale the inner Peloponnesian wall; yet how high should these be? Too short, and they would not reach the top of the wall. Too long, and the Peloponnesians, noticing the ladders rising, might take alarm; moreover, too long a ladder would offer the enemy an easy grip, the better to push the damn thing over. The Plataeans could hardly stroll out to measure the offending wall. So the escapers laboriously eyeballed the number of bricks in the enemy wall, counting them to arrive at the precise height of the ladders and then pooling their counts, so there would be no mistake.

With their ladders in readiness, the Plataeans waited for a suitably diabolical night: moonless, windy, and raining. Then—quietly, and with one foot bare, to keep human flesh in contact with the ground as a plea to the kindly gods of earth for protection—they edged out of a town gate and over the ditch that the Peloponnesians had dug for clay to make the bricks of their wall. The escapers had been instructed to walk apart: the jostling of one man's gear against his neighbor's was the under-melody of Greek battle, but silence, on this night, was all. Up quietly went the ladders, and up them twelve men in breastplates with daggers to hand. The roof was empty, dark, and rain-washed. The climbers pressed against the nearest towers, ready to waylay anyone who came out. Now men with javelins crept up the ladders, followed by men carrying shields for them—but suddenly there was a scrape, a terrible gulf of hopeful silence, and a sounding splash, as a tile dislodged by a climber fell into the mud beneath. From the towers came cries. Discovered![70]

Now the Plataeans' resort was blood and craft. They had never expected to get away unseen, after all, and they had laid their plans well. On the far side of the town, as arranged, a gate was thrown open and those Plataeans without the heart to attempt the escape stormed out, whooping and shouting, pretending to attack the wall opposite. This froze the Peloponnesian watchers at their stations atop the walls, while thoroughly bamboozling the Peloponnesian reaction force of three hundred, which lived inside the wall: toward the noise they rushed, away from the real breakout. Beacon fires were kindled to tell Thebes of the emergency, but for this the Plataeans had prepared as well; their own fires leapt from the walls of Plataea to muddle whatever simple message the Peloponnesians were trying to send.

Now the escapers, no longer needing silence, crashed their way into the towers on either side of the stretch of roof they had mounted. Quick and bloody work with daggers cleared the rooms where the guards had been sheltering from the storm. But some of the sentries had climbed to the tops of their towers when the alarm sounded and, hearing the killing beneath, shut the trapdoors. So ladders were then manhandled up onto the walls and set against the towers. Soon the tops of the towers were clear of living foes, and Plataean javelins could sweep the exposed stretches of wall beyond. Guards were set inside the towers, before the doors leading to the wall-walks still in enemy hands. And more men with javelins—escapers who had not yet made the ascent to the wall—spread out in the mud beyond the towers so that anyone attacking along the walls would be transfixed from both above and below.

With the approaches secured, the main body of the Plataeans now threw up more ladders and climbed the inner wall, then crossed over the roof and jumped down the outer. Beyond that, as further defense against an Athenian relief, the Peloponnesians had dug a second ditch, deep and full of icy water nearly head-high. Through this water the Plataeans now plunged, stopping only when they had crossed to shoot arrows and hurl their javelins at any Peloponnesians who appeared along the outside of the wall. When the main body of escapers was finally through the ditch, the order went back for the guardians of the towers to follow.[71]

Only now did the Peloponnesian reaction force of three hundred, having discovered their error around the other side of the town, run up with torches. These were hoplites, heavy-armed with shields and spears, who should have made short work of the light-armed escapers. But they could not locate an enemy so effectively cloaked in night, while the lights they carried made them easy targets for the missiles of the Plataeans. Before the heavy-armed Peloponnesians could find and crush their enemies, the last of the Plataeans from the towers had forged his way through the water of the ditch to emerge shivering on the outside bank.

Now the Plataeans turned to flight, as had always been their plan. Without heavy gear to slow them down, they managed to break contact with the Peloponnesian hoplites—only a single Plataean archer was captured—and set out in the murk along the road to enemy Thebes, a direction no one would imagine them going. They were soon gratified to see Peloponnesian torches in the distance, bobbing along the direct road to Athens. After half a mile the Plataeans turned off at a crossroads and followed a different path over Mount Cithaeron into the warm safety of Attica.

In a war over reputation, famous acts of cunning and military art, like the Plataeans' escape or their thwarting of the earlier Peloponnesian assaults on their city, raised the pride of the perpetrators while humbling that of their opponents. This was especially important for the Athenians and their allies, for every year the Athenians declined the formal challenge to land battle that the Spartans delivered by invading Attica, because they feared they would be defeated by the incomparable hoplites of Lacedaemon. If the strategy of the Spartans was grounded in proving their superior *andreia*, or bravery, then the strategy of the Athenians emphasized their superior *mētis*, or cunning; this was a war, in short, of a brash Achilles against a guileful Odysseus. Not without reason, then, does Thucydides' depiction of the escape from Plataea form one of the most detailed stretches of his narrative: it was not merely an adventure but a palpable hit in the war of rank.[72]

We should probably also score the victories of Phormio in the Gulf of Corinth in 429 BC as triumphs of *mētis*. We are surprisingly ill-informed about how helmsmen and captains of triremes and leaders of trireme fleets regarded what they were doing. But helmsmen at least could be regarded as competing in skillful maneuvering against the helmsmen of enemy and friendly craft alike. And heroic competition in practical skill fell into the category of *mētis*, as did the competitions of generals in outsmarting their enemies—and Greek naval warfare, as Phormio's victories reveal, was highly tactical.[73]

The same conception of war as a contest in trickery explains why Thucydides digresses from the story of the next year of the Ten Years' War to report on an episode of superlative Athenian cunning—at Notion, on the coast of Asia Minor, near Mytilene—that had no practical bearing on wider events. Paches, the sly Athenian general, lured a mercenary commander in Persian employ out of his fortress for a conference by promising (no doubt with tremendous oaths to the gods) to restore him to his ramparts "safe and healthy." When the man came forth, Paches proceeded to have him seized—although not placed in chains, which, chafing, would have violated his oath—then attacked and took the fortress and slaughtered those in it. His bloody work finished, Paches had the enemy commander carried delicately back within the fortress and set down "safe and healthy," thus fulfilling the exact terms of his promise. Then Paches had him grabbed again and shot to death with arrows, a nasty and slow way to die.[74]

We may think this treacherous little *conte* rather unappealing. Not so Thucydides, however, nor his intended Greek audience, to whom it represented an enjoyable example of craft, very much worth recording for the admiration of the ages. Not everyone, of course, reveled in the *mētis* of Athens and her allies; the Peloponnesians at Plataea, who found themselves repeatedly hoodwinked by such wiliness, were greatly humiliated by it: thus the escape from Plataea was a very real defeat for the Spartans in the war the Athenians and Spartans were fighting. And in a war so bare of battles on land and of clear indicators of who was winning, events like the Plataeans' escape likely took on an exaggerated importance in estimating the martial progress of the combatants. In 431 BC it might have been regarded as trivial; not so in 428 BC. Victories of *mētis* took on such weight because the original plot of the war—the ravaging of Attica and the raiding of the Peloponnese—had failed to produce unequivocal results, and the attention of the Greeks was pulling away. Men were casting about for other ways to discern who was ahead. The Athenians, then, were not only winning the war according to the Greeks' existing standards of evaluation, but they were beginning to transform the very criteria in their own favor. Odysseus was overcoming Achilles.

V

THE DYING OF THE BRAVE,
427 BC

A WINTER'S DAY IN EMBATTLED MYTILENE. The hungry guards looked out from the walls at the Athenian stockade surrounding the city; the cold Athenians on the stockade gazed resentfully at the city walls topped with cozy towers. All the long winter, Mytilene had been blockaded by darting ships upon the deep and by soldiers from the landward side: food was running short, and once again there was talk of begging Athens for terms. But suddenly a knock on a postern or a low cry from no-man's-land revealed the impossible: someone wanted to get *into* the city.

Opening a gate in the city wall, the astonished guards admitted a drenched figure whose long hair and red cloak—and no doubt his chilly equanimity at having crept through the Athenian lines—revealed him as a Spartan. Salaethus was his name, and in a trireme he had crossed the stormful February Aegean to land at one of Mytilene's small allies on Lesbos; then on foot to Mytilene he had come, slipping under the Athenian fortifications by crawling up the bed of a torrent. Now, having rattled the ice out of his beard, he spoke his message to the besieged. The Peloponnesians were coming![1]

A fleet of forty Peloponnesian ships had been prepared in the Gulf of Corinth that winter, and as soon as the weather allowed, it would cross the Aegean to rescue Mytilene and her allies on Lesbos. In order that Athens' home navy should not intercept the expedition, the Peloponnesians would distract the Athenians with their usual invasion of Attica, and the ravaging was to be extended until good tidings from Lesbos brought word that Mytilene had been saved. (A similar distraction had, after all, prevented the Athenians from sending troops to Lesbos the previous autumn.) In the meantime, Salaethus told the men of Mytilene, he would take command of the city's defense. With relief the Mytileneans placed their fate in his hands, all talk of surrender silenced by his promise of deliverance.[2]

The war's fourth Peloponnesian invasion of Attica (427 BC) got under-way according to plan—but unlike the three previous invasions of Attica, it was not led by King Archidamus of Sparta's Eurypontid dynasty. The command fell rather to Sparta's other line of kings, the Agiads (the Spar-tans had two kings at once, it will be recalled, one from each house). The new commander was Cleomenes, regent for his nephew, King Pausanias, who was still a child. With this change of command we bid farewell to King Archidamus, whose otherwise unreported sickness or death this ap-pointment must signal.³

Archidamus had represented what was best about Sparta. With hard-won wisdom he had opposed immediate war against Athens, foreseeing that it would.be difficult to win and long to end—but when his countrymen rushed to war heedless of his counsel, he did his Lacedaemonian duty, lead-ing three forays into Attica. Archidamus had set aside his personal connec-tion with Pericles in the interests of his state (not so obvious a decision among the Greeks, whose pan-Hellenic aristocracy was older than the states themselves, and its personal claims strong). And Archidamus' conscience had tormented him when the Spartans forswore their oaths to attack Plataea. A noble being was Archidamus, but he was duty-bound in the way of the Spartans. We find him far more sympathetic than the stiff-necked Per-icles, "who opposed the Lacedaemonians in everything, and he did not suf-fer them to yield, but urged the Athenians on to war." Yet Pericles and Archidamus both basked in the ardent admiration of Thucydides. And the gap between our estimation of these two characters and that of the historian reflects the gap between today's soft sentiments and the harsher ones of an-cient Greece.⁴

To his severe path Archidamus had schooled his two sons: first, his suc-cessor, Agis, who would grow gray in the last years of the Peloponnesian War commanding a fortress in Attica that warded a permanent force of ravagers. And much of Archidamus can be discerned, too, in his other son, the great Agesilaus. Succeeding his half-brother Agis as king in the next century, Agesilaus dragged a club foot up and down the dusty ways of Greece for decades to preserve the dying power of Sparta—and when that power was lost, and Lacedaemon a pauper, he was to die at eighty-four as a mercenary captain in North Africa, even then striving to gather money and restore the fortunes of his homeland.

Archidamus and his sons were Eurypontids. The other Spartan royal line, that of the Agiads, here emerges for a moment to lead the Pelopon-nesians into Attica. The Agiad line was one of fractured gold—of heroes and of madmen. In the late sixth century, the Agiad king Cleomenes (whose name the Spartan regent in the current war shared) had finally established Sparta's supremacy over ancient Argos, only to take his own life in a fren-

FIGURE 5.1 Tegean hoplite, late fifth century BC. Spartan hoplites probably used similar equipment.

zied attempt to flay himself alive. His blameless brother Leonidas, on the other hand, had died the perfect Spartan death at Thermopylae, where he had led the famous Three Hundred to their fate. Leonidas' nephew (who, like the current king, was named Pausanias) had led the Greeks to victory over the Persians at Plataea but became a plotting minion of the Great King of Persia, whereupon the Spartans—as we have seen—walled him up in a hut in a sacred precinct to starve to death. The resulting curse was one of those the Athenians had bade the Spartans to expel in the months before the war. The son of that Pausanias, King Pleistoanax, now languished in exile, convicted of accepting a bribe from Pericles in 446 BC—which is why his young son, also called Pausanias, now perched on the Agiad throne, even as Pleistoanax was intriguing to return.

With a new commander at its head, the army of the Peloponnesians marched into Attica, intending a long stay. For it was the army's mission to distract the Athenians—to blind them, as it were, with smoke from their burning crops, to the Peloponnesian fleet churning toward Mytilene. Regions ravaged before were ravaged again, while districts previously neglected were neglected no longer. For the Athenians, other than the long-drawn-out second invasion of 430 BC, this was the most painful

Peloponnesian incursion of the Ten Years' War. The Peloponnesians were wasting Attica with rekindled zeal, for the honor of all was engaged in Mytilene. Yet, as they cut and as they burned, the invaders would pause from time to time to stretch their wits eastward, listening hopefully for the friendly rustle of the sea breeze carrying in a trireme bearing news of the liberation of doughty Lesbos. Long did the Peloponnesians ravage, and devoutly did they hope, as if hope itself could drive warships and win sea battles. But no tidings came, and when the soldiers' food was finally exhausted, this invasion, like the ones before it, ebbed as it had flowed.[5]

The tale of Mytilene, when the ravagers finally heard it, grumbling around their hearths back in the Peloponnese, was one both of infuriating lassitude and cursed ill luck. The rescue fleet had indeed been ready at the outset of the sailing season, as the brave Salaethus had assured the men of Mytilene it would be. Having set out from the Gulf of Corinth, however, the Spartan admiral Alcidas led his ships languidly in their hazardous circumnavigation of the Peloponnese, and once they had passed into the Aegean, he steered a slow and timid course (likely far to the south in the open water toward Crete) so as not to be spotted from the Cycladic islands, allies of Athens. Indeed, any craft the Peloponnesian fleet encountered upon the deep they seized and emptied of its crew to preserve the secret. As far as holy Delos the Peloponnesians gained without being reported to foe or friend.[6]

Whether born of cunning or timidity, the Peloponnesians' stealthy slowness proved their undoing. The Mytileneans, being a seafaring folk, knew exactly how long it should take a fleet of rescuers to reach them from the Gulf of Corinth: they had, after all, made the same trip in reverse, as allies of the Athenians. And, alas, the exquisite care Alcidas took that his coming should not be known denied the men of Mytilene even a reassuring trickle of rumors. They sank again into despair: there was nothing more to eat, and the rescue fleet must not be coming after all. Soon the brave and practical Salaethus had to agree.

But Salaethus did not despair at the lack of reinforcements. The Mytileneans would just have to break the siege with their own right arms, he said, by making a sally from the city. Pleased to discover great magazines of hoplite equipment—far more than was needed for the ruling oligarchs of the town—Salaethus distributed the equipment to the commons, only to be thanked with an immediate insurrection. The oligarchs had locked up the arms for good reason; as the siege worsened, the commons had become convinced that their rulers were hoarding food. Now armed, they demanded that the food be disgorged and distributed, lest they surrender the city to the Athenians (confident, of course, that the revenge of the Athenians would fall upon the rulers of the town and not themselves). But the oligarchs had not, in fact, been

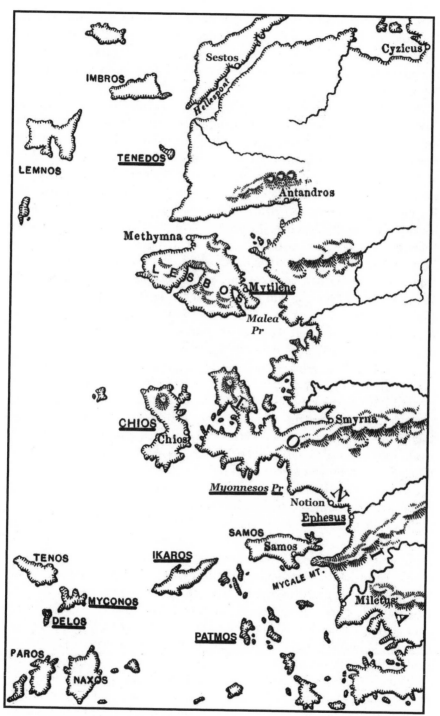

MAP 5.1 The Fall of Mytilene, 427 BC

regaling themselves in secret feasts; they had no tidbits to give, not even humble grain. And so, to preempt the surrender of the town by the commons and their being excluded from whatever terms might be struck, the oligarchs joined the people in a hasty parley with the Athenians for the capitulation of Mytilene.[7]

The Athenian commander Paches agreed to inflict no woe upon the Mytileneans out of hand: envoys would be sent to Athens, and the Athenians would decide upon the city's fate. Nonetheless, when the gates were opened, and the Athenians marched in, the terrified oligarchs took refuge at the altars of the gods. Paches attempted to reassure them, pledging that they would come to no harm before the decision of the Athenian assembly. Perhaps in part to protect them against their own commons, he sent the oligarchs to nearby Tenedos, the sacred isle and Athenian ally that had informed upon Mytilene in the first place. The indefatigable Salaethus, for his part, had long since escaped the doomed city; before the gates of Mytilene were even opened he was gone, no doubt splashing again down the brook that had brought him in, and as he squeezed under the Athenian stockade, perhaps reflecting, as Spartans so often had cause to do, on just how unworthy other Greeks were of Spartan leadership. He found refuge at one of Mytilene's small allies on Lesbos.[8]

From the isle of Delos, where they were spotted by the enemy, the Peloponnesian fleet of slow deliverance was now steering northeast in its course toward Lesbos, weaving through the islands of the Aegean. It was at Myconos and Ikaros that the Peloponnesians first heard rumors of Mytilene's fall as they luffed toward her. Horrified, but determined to find out the truth, they proceeded north toward Lesbos along the coast of Asia Minor, touching the continent across from the island of Chios (a dangerous place, because the Athenian-allied Chians boasted their own fleet). Here the fatal tidings were confirmed: Mytilene had surrendered seven days before.[9]

It was proposed to Alcidas that the fleet should surge the last sixty miles to Mytilene anyway, in the hope of catching the Athenians unready in the relaxation of victory. He refused, no doubt wisely. For now the Athenians would be inside the Mytilenean fortifications, which the Peloponnesians were quite unprepared to assail. Given the recent course of the Peloponnesian fleet between the close-set islands of Athenian allies, Alcidas had to assume that Paches was well aware of his coming; south, then, away from Paches and his fleet, and at best speed, shedding all unnecessary weight, including that of prisoners.[10]

The fleeing Alcidas peopled with ghosts Cape Myonessus—in later years a haunt of pirates—when he came to land there and butchered most of the captives he had seized from ships and coastal villages on his secretive journey toward Mytilene. Of the latter there were many, because none of the Athenian-allied coastal dwellers had expected a Peloponnesian fleet in their waters and, thinking the ships to be friendly, ran up to sell their wares wherever they came to shore. To lighten his ships for flight, Alcidas might as easily have set his prisoners free ashore rather than killing them, and in doing so he might have spared Sparta the hatred of the Aegean. But that was only a consideration if Alcidas thought the Spartans had future interests in this part of the world, which apparently he did not. Most of his prisoners, moreover, came from allies of Athens and so were clear enemies. And if he needed further justification for his slaughter, since the beginning of the war the Spartans had considered anyone sailing on the high seas an enemy. Yet, with that curious Spartan mixture of brutality and religion, Alcidas did not just throw his captives overboard to drown, and for fish to nibble on the fat around their livers, but rather took them ashore and had them laboriously killed by hand so that the bodies could be buried and the spirits of the dead make their orderly way to the underworld.[11]

His load sufficiently lightened, Alcidas preserved a few of his prisoners, including those from Chios, with whom he no doubt hoped to bargain for his squadron's escape should the formidable Chian fleet pursue him. He then continued twenty miles on to the great city of Ephesus—quick! quick!—to get in supplies for the long trip home. Undefended Ephesus no doubt agreed to supply a market rather than suffer the Peloponnesians' simply taking what they needed.

While Alcidas was in Ephesus, he was approached by a group of brave exiles from Samos, the same men who had fatally ambushed the Athenian general Lysicles when he came to plunder nearby Persian holdings the previous year. But even men so passionate against Athens upbraided Alcidas for killing his captives. "No very noble way of freeing the Greeks," they called his act, their irony making bitter allusion to the proclamation that the Spartans had made at the outset of the war. The men Alcidas had killed were allies of the Athenians by compulsion, the exiles explained, not choice, and Sparta would hardly win friends among the Greeks at large by such murder. Abashed, Alcidas released his remaining captives, including his Chian hostages.[12]

Although moved by the reproaches of the Samian exiles, Alcidas had no wider interest in "freeing the Greeks." His murder of his prisoners shows that Sparta was not looking for allies in the Aegean. Thucydides has characters suggest to the Spartans a policy of promoting revolt in Athens' empire. He has the Mytileneans mention in their pleading speech at Olympia the possibility that their revolt, if successful, might provoke a wider uprising in the Athenian empire and possibly help the Spartans to win the war. Thucydides also has exiles from Ionia, as well as the envoys of Lesbos whom Alcidas was trying to take home, suggest that the Peloponnesian fleet should seize a city on the coast of Asia Minor after the discovery that Mytilene had already fallen to the Athenians. Perhaps even the Persian satrap, they speculated, would then join the war against Athens.[13]

Despite these optimistic suggestions, however, at no point in the mournful story of Alcidas' journey do the Spartans show any ambitions greater than the liberation of Mytilene. Perhaps an impatient Thucydides is anticipating tactics the Spartans were indeed to employ much later in the Peloponnesian War, or perhaps such suggestions were actually made at the time. It does not much matter. For from Alcidas' massacre of his prisoners, it is certain that encouraging a wider rebellion in the Athenian empire was at this stage not part of the Spartans' plan. Still fighting a war of symbols, they had accepted the alliance of Mytilene—and made the rebels beg for it at Olympia—in order to humiliate the Athenians. They had pledged their faith to help the Mytileneans, and the Mytileneans alone. Having failed to fulfill that pledge, it was hardly the duty of their commander to risk further humiliation in, say, a sea battle against an Athenian fleet or by raising in revolt yet other distant states—states to which the troth and honor of Sparta would then be plighted and who would be every bit as hard to help as Mytilene. Already the Spartans had seen their triumph over the defection of Mytilene transformed into the mortification of a second Potidaea. They had no interest in raising up yet more Potidaeas to mock them. And so Alcidas washed his hands of the blood of the innocents he had slain and steered his fleet for home.[14]

Paches and the Athenians chased him. Paches had heard reports of the Peloponnesian fleet's presence only sixty miles from Lesbos, as far north as the mainland coast across from Chios. Indeed, terrified reports—many, no doubt, wholly fanciful—of Peloponnesian ships were now coming in from all sides as panic gripped Ionia. (Mostly located near the water and unwalled on the seaward side, the Ionian cities were also ungarrisoned by the Athenians, and so a hostile fleet might sail up and plunder them at its pleasure.) Struggling to sort through these conflicting reports, Paches finally received sound tidings: as Alcidas had been resting at anchor on the way south to Ephesus, he was spotted by the Athenian state triremes *Salaminia* and *Paralus*, fast sailers crewed entirely by Athenian citizens, who turned instantly north to report to Paches.[15]

Hearing reliable news of Alcidas' location, Paches now set out in pursuit, his crews pulling heroically after the marauders. They gave up only at Patmos, after a blistering row of one hundred and twenty miles. There was no catching the Peloponnesians, who were now clearly steering southwest, away from Ionia. And Paches was far gladder to see them depart than to have to besiege the Peloponnesians in the harbor of an Ionian city, should they decide to hole up in one.

All of Alcidas' old timidity—never far from the surface—now returned, and to avoid being seen, he skirted the Cyclades altogether, denying his crews a restorative landfall by steering south for Crete. There, to add to their miseries, his luckless ships were caught in a storm. Slow and painful, then, was the fleet's homecoming to the Peloponnese. Paches, for his part, returned to Lesbos and completed his reduction of Mytilene's minor allies on the island, in the process capturing the Spartan Salaethus, who had found sanctuary in one of them. Paches dispatched him to Athens, along with the thousand Mytilenean oligarchs he had been holding on Tenedos. Now their fates lay in the hands of the Athenian assembly.[16]

The assembly, to which the rebellion of Mytilene seemed a knife driven into the back so hard the hilt quivered, was furious. Lesbos had been a favored subject, caressed by Athens, allowed a near equality with her. And *she* had made an alliance with the Spartans! *She* had called a Peloponnesian fleet into tender Ionia! The envoys sent from Mytilene to plead their case craved the mercy of mighty Athens. In moving against Methymna—let us imagine their pleas—they were merely exercising the freedom Athens had graciously given them. Might the Athenians have been swayed by the lies of Mytilene's enemies when they tried to attack Mytilene by surprise? After that, surely, Mytilene's resistance could be excused as self-defense, conducted as demurely as possible and with many pleas for reasonable terms. Finally, if some of the Mytileneans had acted ill, it was but a wicked few: the hated oligarchs. Indeed, the instant the people themselves had arms in their hands, hadn't they arranged the surrender of the city to their Athenian friends? How could the virtuous many be held responsible for the actions of an evil handful? Yes, that's a good argument at democratic Athens![17]

In vain. With unabated fury, the Athenians pronounced their verdict. All the men of sorrowing Mytilene, not only the thousand oligarchs held in Athens, were to be put to the sword. All the women and children of Mytilene were to be sold as slaves. Nor would anger wait: that very day a trireme was dispatched to Paches to tell him to execute the Athenians' horrible will. And so did the day of wrath revolve toward evening. We can guess how the immortal Turner would have painted the coming of that night: mist diffusing a blood-red sunset and a tiny, ominous ship scudding over obscure seas.

But the rays of morning lit misgivings on the features of the Athenians. More than a few must have lain awake pondering the edict of their assembly; others may have wondered how the fickle gods would receive such a deed of blood. And those peering longest into the dark of the future may have imagined Athens, now so proud, one day as prostrate as Mytilene. The fates of the Greeks, after all, worked by cycles—"create a desolation, and be destroyed yourself thereafter," sang the poet—and what was wrought now upon the weak might some day rebound upon the strong. Seeing pity in the eyes of the Athenians, the envoys from Mytilene and their Athenian friends begged that the assembly be recalled to reconsider yesterday's terrible decree. The presiding officials were soon prevailed upon: they, too, felt the change of feeling among their countrymen; they, too, felt the warm breeze of mercy. Here, the informality of Athenian democracy should earn the praise of those accustomed to a more deliberate way of government, for what was done wrong at Athens could very quickly be set aright.[18]

Of the speeches given that fateful morning in the Athenian assembly, Thucydides offers up two—two of the most famous in Greek literature, in fact, although they are among the least likely in Thucydides' work to represent what was actually said at the time. The first address is given to the politician Cleon, introduced here by Thucydides as the "most violent of the citizens" (and very rarely does the historian commit himself in this way—Thucydides detested Cleon), who is made to deliver a whisker-twirling harangue in which he calls for the decree of the day before to be upheld and for the death of Mytilene. To act thus, he says, is both just and expedient: ethically proper as an act of revenge and pragmatic as a deterrent against rebellion in future. As an imperial people, he says, the Athenians must suppress dangerous feelings of mercy.[19]

Thucydides puts the reply to Cleon in the mouth of Diodotus, an otherwise unknown Athenian. Diodotus grants that it would be just, certainly, to destroy Mytilene, and joins in Cleon's counsels against soft sentiment. But he goes on to argue that so fell a course would not be expedient for Athens because, faced with the example of the fate of Mytilene, no rebellious state—and such, given the frailty of men, there would always be—would ever surrender.

Taken together, the speeches of Cleon and Diodotus offer a Thucydidean essay on the moral abandonment of the Athenian imperial democracy, that topsy-turvy universe in which the unjust is warmly agreed to be just and human mercy can only triumph by cost-benefit analysis. And the speeches are better taken as Thucydides' commentary than as history, for Thucydides himself tells us that the debate did not really unfold along such lines. It was not expediency that compelled the reconsideration, he reveals, but moral revulsion. And whatever was actually said in the assembly, repentance triumphed and the vote of the previous day was overturned—by a narrow margin, notes Thucydides censoriously. But the repeal was, for the time being, hollow—for the previous day's fatal decree had a full night and day's start on its dolorous voyage to Lesbos, where thousands of lives were at hazard.[20]

Lucky is he who has never felt the torments of the envoys of Mytilene as they waited the long minutes for the new order to be written out, then sprang to horse and galloped with foaming muzzle down between the long fortification walls that led from the city to the port, through the vast shantytown of the refugees from the Attic countryside. In the harbor waited a second trireme, crewed and victualed for instant departure. Now all the envoys could do was encourage the rowers and promise them rich rewards, feeding them with barley cakes kneaded with wine and oil as they rowed, so that they need not stop to eat. But even as they hastened, they caught no glimpse of the first-departed trireme. The rowers took turns sleeping, so the ship never had to halt, and the gods sent winds friendly to so good and urgent a cause. But still the horizon gave no hint of the first trireme. Finally Lesbos' Cape Malea rose in the distance, and on it the temple of Apollo, where first the Athenians had tried to seize the men of Mytilene during their festival—but still the sea was empty of the other ship. Then, with a final burst of speed, the trireme swung into the harbor of Mytilene, to be greeted there by its passengers' greatest fear: the ship of cruel destiny bobbed quietly at anchor, its message of death already delivered. The envoys and their crew must have shuddered with exhaustion and despair. If ever the great painted eyes of a trireme could weep, this was their moment.[21]

What first hinted that all was not lost? The unexpected calm over the town? That they heard no shrieks of dying men, no keening of women, widowed and enslaved? Or did they see the first trireme still casually disembarking its rowers (for its crew had not rushed upon their horrid errand)? However they learned, their message bearing mercy's edict found the Athenian commander Paches just as he had finished reading the earlier decree, with his brow furled over the arcana of killing a city full of men in their houses. "By just so much," intones Thucydides, "did Mytilene escape its danger."[22]

Mytilene had not escaped bitter chastisement, only utter annihilation. The thousand and some captives at Athens—those Paches had selected as "most guilty of the uprising"—were indeed put to death. Athens' victims will have been all the prosperous partakers in the oligarchy of Mytilene and a large proportion of the total citizenry. That revenge would be taken on Mytilene was never in doubt: the only question was how much revenge Athenian conscience, and the gods, would allow.[23]

Although the lives of her humble were spared, Mytilene herself was ruined. Her walls were pulled down and her fleet confiscated by the Athenians; her possessions on the mainland were likewise seized. But rather than reducing Mytilene to a tribute-paying ally (as Athens had done with Samos in 440 BC), Athens confiscated all the agricultural land of Lesbos, except that of loyal Methymna. That seized land Athens divided into three thousand allotments and, giving three hundred of those to the gods, assigned the remainder by lot to Athenians. The unhappy folk of Lesbos, reduced nearly to the status of helots, would still cultivate the land but pay their new—probably absentee—landlords a set rent of two hundred drachmae a year for each tract, a sum that was something like the cost of subsistence for a family.[24]

If the new arrangement brought Lesbos to her knees, it also helped Athens after her period of financial hardship. The wealth of Lesbos was to relieve the poor of Athens, many of whom had suffered from the Peloponnesian ravaging of Attica. But that is not to say that Athens, in time of war, was unwisely surrendering a source of state income into private hands. For the total amount of the annual rents paid to the Athenians for Mytilene, one hundred talents, was far higher than the highest known tribute from any city in the Athenian empire, which was thirty talents. And we have evidence from the next century that Athenian allotment holders, or cleruchs, paid special taxes to Athens in exchange for the land they held. So imposing cleruchs upon Lesbos may have been the most efficient and ruthless method of exploitation the Athenians knew.[25]

Soon after the fall of Mytilene, the Athenians turned their gaze upon a much closer threat, one that soured their very home waters in the Saronic Gulf. Minoa, a small island off the southern coast of the Megarid, was home to a Megarian outpost whose watchtowers warded Nisaea, the port of Megara. In the third year of the war, the Peloponnesians had sent a fleet forth from Nisaea to take Piraeus by surprise; they had failed, but cozy Salamis had been plundered, and the episode had been terrifying to the Athenians.

The threat from Nisaea had not abated since that first Peloponnesian attack by sea. Megarian privateers were slipping out from Nisaea and pestering the bustling waterway that brought trade in and out of Piraeus. And only last year, in 428 BC, the Peloponnesians had tried to put a fleet into the Saronic Gulf by pulling it over the Isthmus of Corinth, and had their allies not dallied and spoiled the plot, that fleet's most natural course toward Athens would have taken it right by Nisaea and Minoa. No question, the waters around Athens would be far safer were Minoa in Athenian hands and Nisaea more closely blockaded than was possible from the Athenian post on Salamis. Perfecting the blockade of Nisaea also had the added appeal of rendering the Megarians—who were still ritually invaded and ravaged every year by the Athenians—more miserable yet by preventing even smugglers from entering their southern port.[26]

The expedition against Minoa was to be led by Nicias, son of Niceratus. No blue-blood he (we do not even know the name of his grandfather), Nicias had nevertheless become rich as a contactor in the hellish Athenian silver mines at Laurion. His diffident and slightly bumbling manner appealed to the people (not least in its contrast with the aristocratic ice of Pericles). To top it off, Nicias was generous and pious and a careful and crafty soldier. In the years after the death of Pericles, Nicias and Cleon—whose father, like Nicias, had become rich through trade, his the tannery kind—were the most prominent politicians in Athens, and often in opposition to each other.[27]

Nicias set forth and promptly captured two of Minoa's watchtowers directly from the sea—possibly with newfangled scaling ladders reaching from his ships. He then fortified the island against recapture by the Megarians, with a wall on the landward side as well as a fort, and, leaving behind a garrison, returned home to Athens.[28]

The taking of Minoa was a true-born sprout of Athens' previous strategy of maritime security and revenge. And so was the fact that the Athenians did not send a raiding fleet around the Peloponnese this year. The Spartans had invaded Attica with historic ferocity. But the Athenians had raided the Peloponnese twice in the previous year (428 BC), the second time in preemptive reprisal for the Peloponnesians' abortive second invasion of Attica, an expedition that had never reached the fields of Athens and therefore did not count. So the logic of revenge barred the Athenians from raiding the Peloponnese in 427 BC because they began the year one ahead, and when the Peloponnesians ravaged Attica, the balance was restored and honors were even. For the Athenians to raid in 427 BC would imply that their previous raids had not been full and equal revenge for the Spartan invasions. And were the Athenians to raid again in order to stay ahead, they would sacrifice their claim to being the wronged party merely avenging attacks upon them. Besides, the Athenians had built up a formidable advantage in other respects. For to the glorious capture of Potidaea and the double defeat of Peloponnesian fleets in the northwest had been added the Athenian capture of Mytilene, to which the Spartan alliance had pledged itself with the greatest possible solemnity. Twice foresworn, then, were the Spartans; and many times victorious, the Athenians.[29]

Around the time that they were celebrating their capture of Minoa from Megara, the Athenians received word of a humiliation of their own: the fall of besieged Plataea to the Peloponnesians. This the Athenians had long dreaded; when Salaethus, the brave Spartan captain from Mytilene, was brought prisoner to Athens, he offered, in exchange for his life, to induce the Peloponnesians to withdraw from Plataea. How he proposed to do this we do not know, and the Athenians seem not to have believed him because they executed him despite his promise; but even if born of wily desperation, his offer signals Athenian anxiety about Plataea.[30]

The Athenians had foreseen the fall of Plataea. They had known at least from the time of the daring breakout from Plataea the winter before just how scanty the provisions in the city were. Even with the number of mouths reduced by half after the escape, the Athenians could predict that those who remained—two hundred Plataeans, twenty-five Athenians, and such as survived of the one hundred and ten women who had stayed to cook—would soon have to yield if not rescued. But the formidable double wall the Peloponnesians had built around Plataea prevented any easy help. A relieving army would have to lay the besiegers themselves under siege. The Athenians would soon face a land battle against the nearby Boeotians and, were the Athenians to extend their stay, against the massed soldiery of the Peloponnesians as well. Besides, even if they did breach the Peloponnesian ring around Plataea, the Athenians could do no more than spirit the survivors away and cede the city, or resupply it, only to face the same perplexity again.[31]

Unless the Athenians could find the courage to face the Peloponnesians in the field, there was no real promise of victory at Plataea—that is, of reestablishing the Plataeans as masters of their land and borders. But they were absolutely unwilling to risk a hoplite battle, which they feared they would lose: for not only would many Athenians be killed but victory in such a battle was the gold standard of warfare over rank. And so a loss would be another Tanagra: Athens' claim to equality would be exploded.

In fact, the garrison of Plataea held out longer than anyone expected, surrendering only around the time of Nicias' expedition to Minoa. The Peloponnesians had made an assault on the wall of the town, an assault that the starving defenders were too feeble to repel. But the instant he sensed that the town was at his mercy, the Spartan commander recalled his attackers. This he did out of deference to the Thebans, the Spartan allies who expected to receive the conquered town and its territory. For the Thebans were still wedded to their original quibble, the one that had thwarted their capture of Plataea at the outset of the war: they required that Plataea should seem to come over voluntarily so that, when the war ended on terms of "to each his own" (as the Spartans had pledged their allies), they would not have to return Plataea to the Athenians. That this quibble had persisted this far shows that neither Sparta's own goals nor her allies' predictions for the war's outcome had changed: the Lacedaemonians sought not to destroy the power of Athens or to abolish the Athenian empire, but simply to vindicate their rank and then negotiate a settlement with Athens, part of which would allow Sparta to honor her agreements with her allies.[32]

The Spartan commander, seeing that the Plataeans could no longer resist, proposed that the city should yield itself "willingly" to the Spartans and promised in exchange to refrain from an offhand massacre of the defenders: instead, their fate would be decided by judges sent from Sparta, with only the guilty punished. The Plataeans, no doubt relieved that they were not simply to be handed over to the Thebans for slaughter, promptly surrendered the city to the Spartans. They were rewarded with meals and awaited the arrival of five judges from Sparta.

When the Lacedaemonian judges came, the skeletal Plataeans were arraigned before them and grimly asked to volunteer whether any of them had done any service for the Spartans or their allies in this war. Balancing good deeds against ill underlay the Greek sense of justice, and since the Plataeans had done evil against the Spartans and their allies by fighting them, the Spartans naturally wanted to know whether any of them could speak of any good deeds that might outweigh the bad and so earn them the right to live. We shake our heads at these ethics: this is one of those moments when we are reminded that the Greeks were not like us. But they remind us, too, that we must always be prepared to supply a Greek logic of balancing good and ill, grace and revenge, if we are to understand the events Thucydides describes.[33]

The Plataeans saw no profit in answering the question posed by the Spartan judges and instead made a wider plea for mercy, appointing among their spokesmen the Spartan honorary consul, or *proxenos* (a Plataean citizen, in the usual Greek way), Lacon ("the Laconian"), whose father had marched alongside the Spartans at the battle of Plataea, in order to emphasize the old and warm relationship between Plataea and Sparta.[34]

Heartfelt and muddled were the pleas of the Plataeans, and cynical and sophistic the arguments of the Thebans—at least as Thucydides presents them. The speeches that Thucydides writes for both sides inspire mournful pathos in his reader and drive home the fact that the Plataeans were nothing less than the heaven-picked heroes of the Ten Years' War: the Plataeans, who had defended their homes in the storm that brought war to Boeotia; who had repelled the Peloponnesian attacks upon their city in the third year of the war, when rain quenched the fire that was to consume the town; and who had broken out of the prison of their city in the tempest the winter before. Zeus himself had judged them worthy, for his weather had aided the Plataeans each time.[35]

If such a debate as Thucydides presents did in fact occur, it changed nothing. The Spartan judges summoned up their captives one by one and again asked each whether he had done any good for the Spartans and their allies in this war. Upon receiving no sufficient answer from any of them (and we may be excused for indulging our modern longing that each replied with a dignified no), they were led out and executed, to the number of two hundred, along with the twenty-five Athenians. The surviving women were sold as slaves, while the city itself and its lands were handed over to the Thebans, who happily leased the fields to their own countrymen, although they could not for some time decide what to do with the town itself.[36]

The gratified Thebans first gave the city of Plataea to some exiles from Megara, expelled after an intestine quarrel there, and bade them share it with the handful of pro-Theban Plataeans (who had no doubt been plumping themselves in exile in Thebes since the beginning of the war). After a year, however, they changed their minds and razed the buildings of the town, using the wood to build a large inn (what a small place Plataea must have been!) on the grounds of the temple of Hera, one of Plataea's monuments to Greek freedom. It was while gazing at that very temple, in the heat of the battle against the Persians, that the Lacedaemonian general Pausanias, hitherto unable to secure favorable auspices for an attack, had been inspired to appeal to Hera—whereupon, lo! the auspices turned fair, and the Spartans charged, driving the long-haired Persians from Greece. This had been during that earlier, greater struggle at Plataea, when the Thebans had fought *against* Greek freedom on the side of the Persians; yet the Thebans, with their fathomless, eel-fed cynicism, were perfectly happy to exploit its memory anyway.[37]

The Athenians had to do everything they could to reduce the shame of the loss of Plataea, Plataea, to which they had pledged themselves and which they had forbidden to agree to the Spartan proposal that its hallowed territory be neutral in the war; Plataea, a self-inflicted shame not unlike that of Sparta's Potidaea or Mytilene. Most of the people of Plataea had been evacuated to Athens at the beginning of the war, and slightly more than two hundred more had escaped in the breakout the previous winter. When, earlier in the war, the folk of Sparta's benefactor Aegina had been driven from their homes by the Athenians, Sparta had settled them upon her own borders to emphasize that she never forgot those who had helped her. But in the wake of the fall of Plataea, the Athenians went even further. They granted the Plataeans the privilege of Athenian citizenship, folding them into their own citizenry.[38]

This was, in ancient Greek terms, a profound gesture. Greek cities believed that their citizens were descended from common ancestors—that they were a family as well as a state. The Athenians in particular believed that they had abided in Attica since before the time of heroes—indeed, that the first of them had squirmed up out of the very earth of Athens on legs of snakes. No alien—no matter how long he might have lived at Athens, no matter how perfectly Athenian his Greek or his manners—could ever become an Athenian citizen unless (and this was very rare) he performed some stupendous act of bravery or princely act of generosity for the city, for which he was made a citizen by a special vote of the people. Since the middle of the century, not even those Greeks with only a single Athenian parent had been admitted to Athenian citizenship—to qualify, both of one's parents had to be citizens. When the Spartans settled the Aeginetans on their own borders, no one ever imagined that they would be admitted to Lacedaemonian citizenship; nor were they. And so, as they so often did in this to-and-fro war, in making the Plataeans citizens of Athens, the Athenians were going the Spartans one better.[39]

THE ATHENIANS WERE PERHAPS STILL salving their consciences and bandaging their honor after the fall of Plataea, when envoys arrived at Athens from Corcyra, Athens' great island ally in the northwest of Greece. The Corcyreans wanted nothing more of the war, they declared, or of the Athenian alliance. There had been a change of rulers at Corcyra, and the new authorities proposed to withdraw the island into the shell of her ancestral neutrality. Hereafter, the envoys said, neither of the combatants would be received if they came in force; no fleets or squadrons from either side would be admitted to the harbor of Corcyra, only single triremes. Knowing there was more to the story, the Athenians arrested the envoys.[40]

The Athenians were right to be suspicious. Athens had protected, perhaps even saved, Corcyra from Corinth at the battle of Sybota in 433 BC, before the greater war began. In 431 BC, the first year of the war, the Corcyreans had with fifty ships accompanied the Athenian raiding expedition around the Peloponnese. But the Peloponnesians, particularly Corcyra's old enemies the Corinthians, had long been scheming to bring about the defection of the island to their side. During Corinth's fight with Corcyra in 433 BC, the Corinthians had taken a great number of Corcyrean prisoners. Of these they kept two hundred and fifty, many of them rich and well connected. As in most Greek states, these were men of oligarchic sympathies, with no great love for democracy. Held in gentle custody at Corinth, they were cultivated by the Corinthians and finally released without ransom upon an agreement that they would try to convert Corcyra's democracy to an oligarchy and bring her into alliance with Corinth. Returning to Corcyra, the oligarchs had spent several years scheming and flattering. Finally, in 427 BC, their mighty conspiracy against both the Athenian alliance and the Corcyrean democracy slid down the slipway into the bright Ionian Sea.[41]

By the time the Corcyrean envoys arrived at Athens, the oligarchic conspiracy at Corcyra had already run its course. First, in the presence of envoys summoned from both Athens and Corinth, the oligarchs had prevailed upon the Corcyrean popular assembly to reaffirm their island's ancient "friendship" with the Peloponnesians. At the same time, the assembly reaffirmed the city's more recent alliance with the Athenians. Neither the oligarchs nor anyone else, we guess, knew exactly what this contradiction signified: it was merely one step in a longer process of detaching Corcyra from Athens and the strongest measure the oligarchs could extract from the assembly at the moment. At the same time as they were muddying their homeland's diplomatic position, the oligarchs also launched their attack on the democratic regime at Corcyra by prosecuting one of its chiefs, who also happened to be an honorary consul of the Athenians, for "trying to enslave Corcyra to Athens." If they could destroy this popular leader in the popular court, the oligarchs will have reasoned, no other Corcyrean would dare to raise up his head against them—their legal success rendering a violent coup d'état unnecessary.[42]

In prosecuting this particular politician, however, the oligarchs over-reached. The democrat Peithias—"the Persuader" as he was aptly named—was acquitted and promptly countersued five leaders of the oligarchs on equally trumped-up charges: they were accused of cutting down holy trees, although any accusation would do in such a test of strength. And in court the persuasive democrat again prevailed, driving the oligarchs to desperation with the size of the fine imposed upon them. Might they pay by installments? they asked from the safety of the altars of the gods, where they had taken refuge after their conviction. No, replied the council of the democracy, at the bidding of the triumphant democrat.[43]

Faced with ruin and the prospect of the democrats' not merely reaffirming but extending the scope of Corcyra's compact with Athens—for such was Peithias' announced plan—the oligarchs determined upon violence. Breaking into the council chamber with daggers, they killed swaggering Peithias and around sixty others, some of them councilors, some not. A few escaped the slaughter to take refuge on the Athenian trireme in the harbor, the same one that had brought the envoys who had listened, bemused, to the Corcyreans' warmly affirming their friendship at once with Athens and with Athens' enemies. Whatever suspicions the Athenians had brought with them were now confirmed by the wild-eyed politicians who heaved themselves on deck, their tunics sprinkled with the blood of their fellow democrats.[44]

Summoning the Corcyrean popular assembly, the oligarchs now harangued their partisans and those brave enough to venture out of their houses. They would save Corcyra from slavery to Athens, they promised. The cabal forced the assembly to vote that Corcyra was hereafter to be neutral in the war, with envoys to be sent immediately to tell the Athenians that the men of Corcyra had withdrawn from their alliance. These were the men the Athenians arrested, for they already knew about the coup at Corcyra when the envoys arrived. It was perhaps the very trireme upon which the democratic survivors of the massacre in the council took refuge that rushed to Athens to tell them. And the Athenians did more than arrest the ambassadors of the Corcyrean oligarchs. They ordered an expedition of sixty

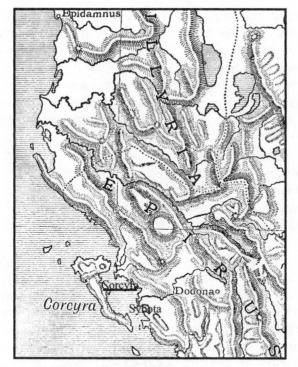

MAP 5.2 The Corcyrean Revolution, 427 BC

ships to sail at speed for Corcyra, to restore the democracy and preserve the Athenian alliance. On its way to Athens, moreover, the trireme bearing tidings and democrats may have detoured to raise the alarm at Naupactus, for twelve triremes from the Athenian base also set to sea, swinging north out of the mouth of the Corinthian Gulf and frothing toward Corcyra.[45]

Back at Corcyra, the confidence of the oligarchs had been fired by the arrival of Spartan envoys in a Corinthian ship (waiting just over the horizon, we expect, for tidings that the coup had succeeded). Now the oligarchs set upon the democrats with arms and by evening had driven their rivals to refuge in the acropolis and the high places of the city. The next day saw a lull, as the oligarchs brought over eight hundred mercenaries from the mainland—proof, if any were needed, that their coup (and its violence) had been planned long in advance—and both sides sent messengers out into the Corcyrean countryside to offer freedom to any slaves who would join them; most joined the democrats.[46]

We read casually enough over appeals to slaves, but to an ancient reader of Thucydides this detail would have stood out from the page as if embossed in blood. All citizens of Greek cities, rich or poor, whatever their politics, dreaded the idea of slaves with weapons in their hands. Slaves were, after all, the natural enemies of all free men in a society that kept them shackled. In a poor world, too, much of a city's wealth was tied up in its slaves, because buying slaves and putting them to work was one of the few ways free capital could be invested for a profit—capital that would be consumed in the holocaust of a single moment were the slaves to be set at liberty. For men locked in civil strife to bid for the support of slaves, then, signaled that an unnatural frenzy had come upon Corcyra: there was nothing the men of the island would not do or waste, if it helped them to overcome their foes.

The next day the democrats, with their advantage of increased numbers and advantageous position (and of their wives, who, perched on the roofs, flung down heavy roof tiles on their enemies), began to press back the oligarchs. As their resistance broke around dusk, the oligarchs set fire to the shops around the marketplace, and even to their own grand houses, to stop the democrats' advance; so the fighting claimed yet more of the city's old abundance. That night, each party guarded its alleys against the other, but all could see that the democrats had won the day. Most of the oligarchs' mercenaries now slipped away to the mainland in boats, while Corinth's trireme—whose arrival had set off the battle in the streets—stole off into the murk. In the darkness the vessel passed the twelve ships of Athens' Naupactus squadron rowing fast in the opposite direction.[47]

Nicostratus, the Athenian general leading the squadron, arrived at Corcyra the next day and landed the five hundred intimidating Messenian hoplites he had brought from Naupactus. With them he tried to bring peace to the city—no easy task, to calm men bent to the point of madness upon killing each other. Nicostratus essayed to soothe them by limiting the blame; let only five of the ringleaders on each side stand trial, he suggested, and let everyone else live in harmony. Should the chosen ten vanish into exile rather than face judgment (as in the event they did), that would only make things easier. The rest were to be bound to tranquility with mighty oaths. And let the happy, reunited city form the closer alliance with Athens that the Corcyrean democrats had hoped for before this recent unpleasantness. The Corcyreans of both parties, under the hard eyes of the Messenians, mumbled their agreement.[48]

His mission of reconciliation accomplished, Nicostratus ordered his ships back to sea, for vital Naupactus had been left uncovered—but his departure was halted by the pleas of the Corcyrean democrats. Would he not leave five of his ships to overawe the oligarchs? In exchange the democrats would send five Corcyrean ships to help in the defense of Naupactus. Gentle Nicostratus agreed, but he had been hoodwinked: for the sly democrats began to enroll oligarchs as crew upon the ships. Nicostratus would sail with a squadron of the damned—a fleet of exile bearing the oligarchs away from Corcyra, or even, as the oligarchs came to fear, into Athenian fetters. Those oligarchs chosen as crew sat themselves as suppliants in the temple of Castor and Pollux, where they could not be touched without invoking the twin heroes' wrath. The manning of the ships came to a halt. In vain did Nicostratus plead with the suppliants to leave the temple, for not only were they delaying his return to Naupactus, but now they were endangering Corcyra's fragile peace as well. The democrats, taking the oligarchs' refusal to board the ships as proof of wicked intent, had begun to gather and arm themselves.[49]

Now Nicostratus found himself interceding for the lives of the very oligarchs who had so recently attempted to carry Corcyra into the Spartan alliance, when they encountered armed democrats in the streets. Then word was brought that in response to this renewed violence, the rest of the oligarchic party, four hundred men, had also sat themselves as suppliants—these in the temple of Hera. So many assembled, no matter how seemingly suppliant, was a danger; anything might respark the fighting. To remove them from the city, the democrats offered the oligarchs safe passage to a small island right off Hera's shrine, where they would be housed and fed: Nicostratus, no doubt, agreed to guarantee their safety and their provisions so that order on Corcyra would be restored and her alliance with Athens preserved.[50]

And so it was that, day after day, Nicostratus abided away from his Naupactus station, keeping an unquiet peace between the oligarchs on the island and the democrats in the city. Uneasy would he have slept at night, thinking of the cruel fates of Athenian generals who failed the democracy in important offices; uneasy would he have puzzled through his days, seeing the disquiet on the war-beaten faces of his Messenians, whose wives and children were back in Naupactus, with neither Athenian ships nor Messenian men to guard them. Nicostratus' troops knew as well as he did that the Peloponnesians had a squadron near Naupactus, at Cyllene, the port of Elis. One energetic Peloponnesian admiral could place the folk of Naupactus—and Athens' position in the northwest—in peril.[51]

Relief and horror must have warred in the heart of Nicostratus when, four or five days after the removal of the oligarchs to the island, he received word that the Peloponnesians at Cyllene had in fact sailed not for Naupactus but instead for Corcyra—and that their fleet, fifty-three triremes strong, was now less than a day away. For only now, perhaps, did Nicostratus learn that the contemptible thirteen Peloponnesian ships at Cyllene had been joined by Alcidas' ill-fated forty, which, having been too late to rescue Mytilene, had finally made their way back from Ionia by way of stormy Crete. At Cyllene the deliberate Alcidas had been joined by the aggressive Spartan Brasidas, hero of Methone in the first year of the war, ephor in the second, and one of the devisers of the bold attempt upon Piraeus in the third; now he was to assist Alcidas. With only twelve ships, Nicostratus was badly outnumbered. The Corcyreans, of course, had ships aplenty. But would their internecine quarrels spoil the use of them?[52]

If the Spartans could finish what the friendly Corcyrean oligarchs had started and secure the adherence of Corcyra and its fleet, they could up-end the strategy of Athens: far harder for the Athenians to raid around the Peloponnese if a great, hostile fleet awaited them when they arrived in the northwest, wounded and windblown, at the end of their journey. Taking Corcyra, then, would go far toward thwarting Athenian reprisals against the Peloponnese, or at least compel the Athenians to return to the huge, costly, impervious armadas they had sent against the Peloponnese in the first two years of the war—if, of course, Athens could even afford them any longer. But the taking of Corcyra from the Athenians would also be a victory to avenge Sparta's humiliation at Mytilene, for the Athenians were sworn to Corcyra's protection as surely as the Peloponnesians had been to Mytilene's. Already the Spartans had their capture of Plataea to set against their loss of Potidaea. Were they to take Corcyra, the loss of Mytilene would be cancelled out as well.[53]

At daybreak the Peloponnesians set out from the mainland against the island of Corcyra. And when the Corcyrean fleet came forth to face them, sixty shabby triremes straggling out of the harbor one by one, it was plain to both their Athenian friends and their Peloponnesian enemies that confusion was in command. The Corcyrean command structure was likely to blame. Corcyrean warships were probably financed like those of Athens, with a combination of public and private money: at Athens the city provided the hull, basic equipment, and salary for the crew, while a rich man paid for much other gear and recruited the rowers (often paying bonuses out of his own pocket) and so was entitled to command the ship in battle. Most of Corcyra's experienced captains would have been wealthy men; thus many would have been oligarchs, sitting out the battle on the little island off the city. Other captains with oligarchic sympathies had recruited friendly crews or even manned their ships with their own slaves—unlike other Greek fleets, rowed mostly by free men, the Corcyreans used many slave rowers—and once out of the harbor, two Corcyrean triremes promptly defected to the Peloponnesians. On other ships, fighting broke out between oligarchs and democrats. In a trireme battle, where speed and discipline were all, there was little to fear from such a cockeyed assemblage of craft. Contemptuously, the Peloponnesians told a mere twenty of their triremes to face the Corcyrean sixty, while the remaining thirty-three bore down upon the twelve Athenians.[54]

Just as when shrewd Phormio had led the outnumbered Naupactus squadron to victory in the Corinthian Gulf in the third year of the war, all the hopes of the Athenians off Corcyra were pinned on their nimbleness. They were also fortunate to have in the squadron the élite of the Athenian fleet: Athens' state galleys, the *Salaminia* and the *Paralus*, with their stalwart citizen-sailors. Fearing encirclement by greater numbers, the Athenians did not meet the whole force of the Peloponnesians head on. Instead, they rowed rapidly around one of the Peloponnesian wings and rammed a single Peloponnesian ship, shattering it. Here paid the psychological legacy of Phormio's unlikely victories in 429 BC. A commander on the Spartan side panicked and sent the thirty-three Peloponnesians into a defensive circle, rams facing outwards. And just as when Phormio had led them, the Athenians rowed around this circle, brushing by the enemy and trying to throw him into confusion. But the twenty Peloponnesian ships detailed to sheepdog the chaotic Corcyreans—the Corcyreans had engaged but feebly, in penny packets, and thirteen craft had already been taken or swamped—saw what was happening on the far flank of the battle and, recalling Phormio's victory under similar circumstances, rowed to the rescue of their larger division.[55]

Checked by the approaching Peloponnesians, the Athenians had to give over their circling. And so, in line and facing the entire Peloponnesian fleet, the bullying Athenians slowly withdrew, rowing backwards, rams to the front, to give the remaining Corcyreans a chance to escape—just as the Athenians had done in these very waters, at the battle of Sybota, before the war. The Corcyreans fled into the harbor, while the Athenians backed water until dusk brought peace to the sound. Then, in the gloom, the Peloponnesians rowed back to their camp on the mainland with the thirteen Corcyrean triremes they had taken.

The democrats of Corcyra, their fleet pummeled and humiliated, feared an attack on the city by the Peloponnesians. Accordingly they brought the oligarchs back from the island (lest the Peloponnesians rescue them from there) and shut them once again in the temple of Hera. The next morning there were agitated talks between democrats and oligarchs in an attempt to put a more efficient fleet to sea, and with some of the oligarchs persuaded to go aboard, thirty ships were eventually manned. But Corcyra and the Athenians were blessed once again by the strange lassitude of Alcidas. For on the day after the battle, despite tumult in the city—and in the face of bitter remonstration by the forceful Brasidas—Alcidas did not sail forth to renew naval combat, or try to land men near the city, or establish a blockade by sea. Instead he disembarked men on the extreme southernmost peninsula of Corcyra in the morning and ravaged the countryside until about midday. He then sailed back to the mainland, but not, we may guess, before erecting a trophy for his victory over the Corcyreans the day before.[56]

As dusk approached, the Peloponnesians considered their plans for the day to follow—we can imagine Brasidas booming angrily once again—when a beacon shone bright upon a mountain to the south. Watchers on the friendly isle of Leucas had spotted an Athenian fleet, sixty strong, faring north to Corcyra; these were the ships that the Athenians had hurried to sea upon hearing of the island's defection from their alliance. This fleet was led by the Athenian general Eurymedon—an auspicious name for a commander, for he was named after the great battle the Athenians had won against the Persians at mid-century.[57]

The prospect of fighting a fleet of sixty Athenian ships confounded Alcidas, who had been frustrated by twelve. Orders were accordingly given for instant flight south, in the hope of passing the Athenians unaware in the night. The next day, so as not to be seen rounding Leucas from Athenian-allied Cephallenia, the next island south, the Peloponnesians hauled their ships by hand over the sandy isthmus connecting Leucas to the mainland. Safely escaped, the Peloponnesians left the Corcyrean oligarchs to their fate.[58]

After the flight of the Peloponnesian fleet from Corcyra, the Corcyrean democrats did not even wait for the Athenian admiral Eurymedon to make landfall before they turned their hands to the slaughter of their fellow citizens. Those oligarchs whom the democrats had just enticed to lend their skills to the Corcyrean fleet (enticements garlanded, no doubt, with terrific oaths guaranteeing their safety) were now killed as they disembarked, while oligarchs who ventured into the streets were cut down when met. The largest body of oligarchs was besieged in the sanctuary of Hera, preserved from violence at least by the democrats' healthy fear of the goddess. Yet not even grim Hera could preserve the oligarchs from democratic wiles. Upon a guarantee that they would be allowed to stand trial, some fifty came forth, those no doubt wholly confident of their blamelessness. And stand trial they did, as promised, then and there, whereupon all were condemned and all were promptly slain.[59]

Now no one would come out from the temple of Hera, and the democrats would admit no food or water. In their desolation the oligarchs sought the only revenge in their power: to pollute the temple by suicide and so bring upon the city the wrath of the vengeful goddess. Some of the suppliants hanged themselves to trees within the precinct or begged comrades to stab them; the remainder sought whatever mode of self-murder the ingenuity of anguish proposed. Nor was the defilement of temples confined to the oligarchs: in other shrines democrats dragged oligarchic suppliants from the very altars or even slaughtered them where they clung, and some were walled up by their foes in the temple of Dionysus, to die of thirst and of starvation in the precinct of wine and of plenty. For all the seven days of this butchery, Eurymedon's sixty ships lay in the harbor, and his Athenian crews, camped upon the welcoming foreshore, did nothing to stop the killing.[60]

The cataclysm on Corcyra foreshadowed a greater darkness creeping over Greece. Thucydides points to this spreading evil right after his account of the slaughter on Corcyra, when he turns to his reader and offers what has become his most famous passage of political analysis. The strife at Corcyra, he explains, was but the first example of what became a monstrous habit in the course of the war. For civil strife, he says—*stasis* is the Greek word—has a fearful dynamic of its own. Whatever its spark, civil strife burns high and soon consumes within it all other forms of division between men, giving license to wickedness under the cover of party and enforcing by a principle of tit-for-tat escalation ever more fearful methods. It is war itself and the resulting scarcity, says Thucydides, that destroys human morals and ideals. "War proves a teacher of violence that brings most men's characters to a level with their fortunes." War is why "the ancient simplicity into which honor so largely entered was laughed down and disappeared."[61]

For centuries men have looked upon Thucydides' description of the internal workings of civil strife and found that he describes what they themselves have seen, not merely when nations are sundered but, indeed, when the apple of discord is cast into any assembly of men. Justly, it seems, did the historian claim that the course of *stasis* would be similar "as long as the nature of mankind remains the same." Yet Thucydides' diagnosis of the cause of *stasis*—his argument that domestic strife is usually the child of foreign war—was not true as a rule even in Thucydides' own time, and was certainly not true in the case of Corcyra, which was untouched by the wider war and hardly, in 427 BC, confronted with "imperious necessities."

Foreign war, in fact, does not reliably create civil strife. Nor, when such strife arises, is foreign war reliably its cause. But the frailty of Thucydides' theory has not prevented men from acting upon it in the after time, or coming independently to Thucydides' conclusion and essaying with force of arms to invoke domestic unquiet in their foes, forgetting that foreign war can just as easily draw a people together as thrust them apart. And when men strive with arms to divide an enemy, they, too, often forget what they might have learned from Thucydides' sound description of the inexorable march of *stasis*. For even a conqueror may find it impossible to rule a folk who have spun into civil strife—when moderation has fled, when all are plotting, when violence is manliness, when blood is a weaker tie than party, and when the bloody factions have "carried to an excess the refinement of their inventions, as manifested in the cunning of their attacks and the atrocity of their reprisals."[62]

AFTER SLAUGHTER HAD RESTORED PEACE to Corcyra, and before the turn of the season made long passages perilous, the Athenians sent a fleet of twenty ships west, across the Adriatic. Athens had kinsmen in Sicily and the south of Italy, where some of the cities belonged to the greater Ionian nation. And from friendly Leontini had come the greatest orator of the age, Gorgias, to beseech the Athenian assembly for aid with his perfect, pointed periods. Leontini was losing a war in Sicily against neighboring Syracuse, the mighty colony of Dorian Corinth, and Leontini was allied to Ionian Rhegium, just at the tip of the toe of Italy, which was fighting a war against her neighbor, Dorian Locri; indeed, all eastern Sicily and the toe of Italy were split between two great, embattled parties, one Ionian and the other Dorian. Athens had been in formal alliance with Leontini and Rhegium at least since the year before the outbreak of the general war in Greece, although neither had helped her in the war. And although they had similarly provided the Spartans with no actual aid, Syracuse and her Dorian kin were allies of the Peloponnesians.[63]

The Athenians had many reasons not to become involved in the affairs of the west. Athens had a great war to fight in Greece. Fighting in Sicily meant long voyages and high charges; it also meant goading powerful, seagoing Syracuse, the Athens of Sicily, which had not hitherto helped her Peloponnesian allies—but might well do so if herself attacked. Thucydides suggests that kinship and alliance with the Ionian Greeks was merely a pretext for this expedition and that one of the real reasons for it was that the Athenians "wanted to prevent the exportation of grain into the Peloponnese from there." In a day when learned men believed that economics was all, this passage was leapt on as by cheetahs: it might explain the whole importance of the west in the war, and the northwest; nay, it might explain the war itself, as a conflict between Athens and Corinth over trade. Even now, when we deny such causes automatic precedence, Thucydides' explanation remains a puzzle.[64]

It is unlikely, we now think, that the Athenian plan in the west was one of economic blockade of the Peloponnese. The Peloponnese, after all, was almost certainly self-sufficient in food, so preventing the carrying in of grain was hardly a war-winning military objective. Besides, if it were desired to put economic pressure on the Peloponnese, perhaps the first thing to do would have been to prevent imports from Athens herself. For archeology suggests that trade in luxuries, at least, between Athens and enemy Corinth,

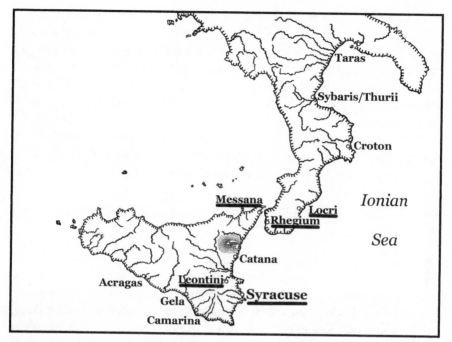

MAP 5.3 The Athenian Expedition to Southern Italy and Sicily, 427 BC

continued merrily throughout the war. If this surprises us, it would not have the Greeks themselves, for why should trade suffer in a war over rank, unless one party had decided (as had Athens with Megara) to make blocking that trade a form of revenge? Nor was sending a fleet to Sicily the obvious way to stop imports of grain to the Peloponnese in any case: that would have been accomplished by stationing a squadron at friendly Corcyra or, more aggressively, at Cape Iapygium, on Italy's boot heel. For while Greek merchant ships could sail the open sea, most clung to the shores of the mainland, lest they sacrifice the strong sea and land breezes, the most reliable airs in a Mediterranean summer.[65]

When the Athenians arrived in the west, they seem, in fact, to have shown little interest in establishing a blockade of Sicilian grain; instead they plunged right into the existing war, proving admirable and energetic allies to their local friends. They participated in sea battles against the Syracusans and Locrians, in the course of which one of the Athenian generals was killed. Enemy cities were taken—most notably great Messana, right across the strait from Rhegium—only to be lost again. Battles on land were won and lost, and fields were ravaged. Soon the Sicels, the non-Greeks who abode in the high fastnesses of the island, were drawn into

213

alliance, and the Athenians fought for their interests as well. When at the end of 426 BC a small reinforcement was received from Athens and the surviving Athenian general was superseded, his renown was such that he returned home to star in the *Laches*, the early dialogue of Plato that takes his name for a title; in the dialogue, Laches is offered as an exemplary general, although somewhat baffled, in the way of Socrates' interlocutors, when Socrates calls on him not merely to *be* courageous but to *define* courage.[66]

The Athenian expedition to Sicily, then, was not intended to establish a blockade as we understand it. It was rather a crocus bud of a new Athenian strategy—a new way of humiliating Sparta that would bloom in the next year of the war.[67]

A THENS HAD ENTERED THE SEASON of war in 427 BC ahead in the calculus of honor, and as the autumn of that year turned to winter, she still had an advantage. If honors were equal from ravaging (as the Spartans seemed to admit when they skipped ravaging for a year to attack Plataea), Athens had won more military victories. Sparta's capture of Plataea might have avenged Athens' taking of Potidaea, but Athens' victories in the Gulf of Corinth remained unanswered, and now there was the debt of Mytilene as well. And if the Peloponnesians had in this year won a sea battle off Corcyra, they had fled yelping right after, once again abandoning their friends, whom they left to die in an orgy of unholy slaughter.

But if Hera had refused to rescue the oligarchs of Corcyra, then Apollo must still have been angry at the Athenians, for that winter the plague returned to Athens and continued to rage through the next year. Thucydides calculates that, between its previous depredations and the present, the plague killed forty-four hundred men from the hoplite list (which at the outbreak of the war had numbered thirteen thousand), as well as three hundred of the thousand well-heeled Athenians who formed the cavalry.[68]

The return of the plague in the winter of 427 BC seems to offer the best context for an event we see but dimly and that comes to us without a date: an offer of peace to Athens from Sparta, alluded to by Aristophanes. One of the offer's conditions (no doubt there were others) was that the Athenians restore Aegina to the Aeginetans. The puzzle is not so much to find a juncture when the Spartans might have hoped for an honorable peace—they had slowly been losing ground in the war over rank since 429 BC. Rather, it is to find a moment when the Spartans might have thought the Athenians would accept a peace that required Athens to step down—for that is what the liberation of Aegina would imply—and therefore clearly signaled the continued preeminence of Sparta. The terrible plague winter after 427 BC and the resulting gloom that afflicted the Athenians—for "nothing cast the Athenians down more than this," observes Thucydides somberly—would have been the most likely moment. After all, when plague had last come upon the Athenians, in 430 BC, the Athenians had themselves appealed to the Spartans for peace.[69]

It was most likely during this winter, then, that the Spartans took the opportunity afforded by Athenian dejection to propose a treaty. And Sparta likely offered to Athens the same terms that in 432 BC she had promised her allies would be the minimum terms for peace: that each state would get back what it had held at the beginning of the war. So far as Athens was concerned, this would involve surrendering some Corinthian possessions in the northwest and returning Minoa to Megara, but chiefly, of course (although Aegina was not formally party to the agreement between Sparta and her allies), it would entail letting the Aeginetans return to Aegina. Nearly all the sacrifice, then, would be on Athens' part—for she had enjoyed the most military gains to date and thus had the most to give up. But as it turned out, the Spartans misjudged the mood of their opponents: cast down the Athenians might be, but they were not prepared to make peace on any conditions the Spartans were prepared to offer—especially not if it involved admitting Spartan superiority.

Athens was ruled by sorrow and pride: sorrow for those felled by the returning plague but pride in her own victories. The Athenians felt confident that they were winning the war over rank, as they had been doing now for three years, ever since their capture of Potidaea. Indeed, they were doing better than Pericles had hoped, for he had merely schemed to establish equality in honor with the Spartans. In principle, the Spartans should long before this have been prepared to treat with Athens and grant her the equality in rank she yearned for. Although they were battered, however, the Spartans would not admit defeat—just as the Athenians, in the end, had been unwilling to give way in the plague year of 430 BC. If the Spartans were offering peace in the winter after 427 BC, it was still a peace that implied their superiority. So, just as with the Spartans in 430 BC, the pride of the Athenians in 427 BC was veined with frustration. They had won battle after battle; they had, at the very least, proved their equality. Why did the Spartans not understand?

With only a few small floods beyond their banks, the channels by which the war had flowed up to this time were the venerable ones of reciprocal and proportionate revenge. Those old ways had produced the war's strange symmetry: the carefully balanced ravaging expeditions and the tit-for-tat structure of events, with the combatants looking to avenge their own humiliations by shaming the enemy. At the war's outset, the Peloponnesians

seemed to accept that the crimes of the Athenians might require several ravagings of Attica to avenge—or at least that several invasions would be
necessary to convince Athens of her inferior place in the world. But the
Athenian response was perfectly symmetrical: every time the Spartans invaded Attica, the Athenians ravaged the coast of the Peloponnese. When the
Peloponnesians did not, the Athenians did not. And as Athens repeated her
expeditions, over time the Peloponnesian, too, would have come to think of
their own invasions as acts of revenge for Athens' raids—for that is how revenge works, drawing both sides into symmetry. In recent years, moreover,
the Athenians had by simple repetition prevailed upon Greek opinion in
general (and finally even Spartan opinion in particular) to accept that raiding from ships was equal in the calculus of rank to ravaging by land. Here
again, both sides were drawn into symmetry, to the great advantage of the
Athenians.

Outside the symmetry of ravaging, the war's other great events had by
427 BC formed a symmetry of their own. To avenge the shame of the
plague inflicted by Sparta's ally Apollo, the Athenians made an expedition
to take Potidaea, already under siege. To avenge the fall of Potidaea, the
Peloponnesian attacked Plataea. When Plataea would not fall, the Peloponnesians received Mytilene into alliance. Then Plataea did fall, and Potidaea was avenged, but in the meantime Mytilene had already been lost,
and as revenge the Peloponnesians tried to secure the defection of Corcyra.

This crosshatch patterning of events answers the question that forces itself upon today's observer more and more as the war develops: Why did the
two antagonists not do more to win the war? For despite much experience
with limited war, our tidy minds are still most comfortable with total war.
We expect two nations locked in combat to fall upon each other pitilessly,
to seek every opportunity to damage each other—in short, to behave in the
bestial fashion Thucydides attributes to the parties in the civil war at Corcyra. But that was hardly the story of the Peloponnesian War at the close of
its fifth year. The war's progress had been gradual, stately—choreographed
even, like a court dance in a ruffed and brocaded castle.

However odd, the methods of the combatants were dictated by the initial aims of both sides in the war. No conspiracy of caution kept the antagonists to their rote design; nor did any naïve sense of "fair play"; nor was
it simply because the Greeks were old-fashioned and could not think of
better ways to fight. Rather, it was because, in fighting for rank, they must
adhere to the rules of war over rank. Ultimately, rank was a question of
reputation, after all—both as it really existed in the gathering places of
Greece and, at least as powerfully, as it shrank and swelled in the imagina-
tion of the actors themselves. The combatants felt Greek opinion in their
viscera as pride and shame, and that opinion punished serious departures

from the symmetrical patterns of war, stripping the offenders of exactly the honor, pride, and rank they were fighting for.

In Greek terms this was a war in which both sides thought of themselves—and wished to be thought of by others—as just avengers, as having been injured by their enemy's *hybris*: the Peloponnesians by the arrogance of Athens before the war, and the Athenians by the Peloponnesian invasion at the outset of the war. Both could hardly be right, we think, but rarely among Greeks or moderns does anyone ever go into a war thinking they are in the wrong; both sides adjust the backstory to frame the other. And in so doing they trap themselves. For it was exactly because both parties thought that they were in the right in the Ten Years' War that their fighting was subject to the rules of reciprocity and proportionality, the laws of just revenge. Should these rules be violated, the combatants would crash over the boundary of just revenge into the dark realm of *hybris*. And *hybris* was wrong and shameful, punished by gods and men.[70]

The patterns of rule-bound warfare were traditional and powerful, but the symmetry of action in war constantly risked breakdown, because other forces, including other symmetries, pulled the combatants away from purely symmetrical behavior. Escalation was a perpetual temptation. Had it succeeded, the second Peloponnesian invasion of Attica planned for 428 BC would have broken the symmetry of the Ten Years' War by escalation, by trying to insert two ravagings in a year. Certainly that is what Athenians thought, because they preemptively avenged that second planned invasion with a ravaging raid of their own, only to find that they themselves had accidentally broken the symmetry of the war when the Peloponnesian invasion did not materialize. In that instance, in their need to help Mytilene, the Peloponnesians were willing to sacrifice one of the war's symmetries (that of ravaging) in order to achieve symmetrical revenge for the loss of Potidaea.

With the Peloponnesians' planned second invasion of Attica in 428 BC, the possibility of a new, more ruthless type of war yawned for a moment. Yet, the Athenians, by declining to raid the Peloponnese in 427 BC, decided to restore the endangered symmetry of the war. No surprise, because they were winning the war under the rules prevailing; they were getting the best of the symmetries. The end of 427 BC brought the third year of their winning to a close. States that were being humiliated were supposed to admit the fact and settle, as had been expected of the Athenians themselves, who were never expected to last longer than three years. But now it was the Athenians who were becoming impatient.[71]

VI

THE NEW SPEAR, 426 BC

FROM THE HILT OF EUBOEA off the coast of Athens, the greater islands of the Cyclades slash cross the Aegean like a sword: Andros, Tenos, Myconos, Naxos. The lesser isles gleam beneath them like drops of blood. Of the Cyclades only two were not subjects of Athens at the outbreak of the war: Thera (the Santorini of today's tourists) and Melos. Both were, rarest of things, insular colonies of the stay-at-home Lacedaemonians. Melos was small and weak, an insignificant island one hundred miles south of Athens on the way to Crete. Thus far she had taken no part in the hostilities between her mother state and Athens. But in 426 BC, the sixth year of the war, the Athenians decided to attack her.

Thucydides, ever alive to the iniquity of the post-Periclean Athenian democracy, attributes Athens' attack on Melos to sheer aggression, but the true cause was almost certainly Melos' close connection to Sparta. This is implied, too, by the large size of the fleet Athens sent against the small island: at sixty ships, it was a number nicely calculated to overtop the fifty-three-ship fleet the Peloponnesians had sent to Corcyra just the year before, implying that the Athenians foresaw the possibility of the Peloponnesians putting to sea to rescue Sparta's colony. Certainly sixty ships were more than were necessary to assail Melos. Whether the Athenians could force the Melians to surrender or, as the event proved, they would succeed merely in ravaging the Melian land, either outcome would be a clear humiliation for the Spartans, who would be proven impotent or unwilling to protect their children.[1]

There was more cruel novelty to Athenian activity this year than the attack on Melos. The Athenians raided the Peloponnese without a ravaging of Attica to avenge; for while the mainland campaign of 426 BC began in the usual fashion, with the Peloponnesians assembling at the Isthmus under the command of the Spartan king Agis, son of Archidamus, the invasion of Attica was abandoned before the army marched, when the Spartans interpreted a series of earthquakes as an evil omen. Always ones to take religion

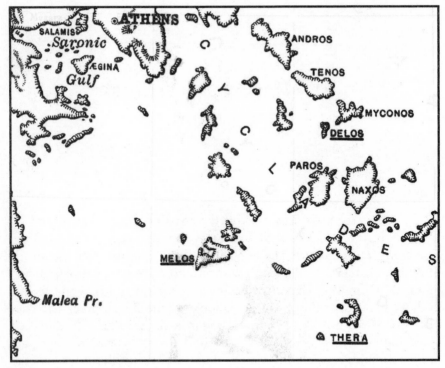

MAP 6.1 Athenian Attack on Melos, 426 BC

seriously, the Spartans did so now with especially good reason, for the return of the plague to Athens was a reminder that the gods were with Sparta in this war. And if the Athenians had been as mindful of the heavens, they would have stuck to their previous strategy, in which their own raiding served only as reprisal for Peloponnesian invasions of Attica. This would have dictated a suspension of Athenian raiding in this year, just as in 429 BC, when the Spartans had not invaded Attica, and in 427 BC, when the Athenians found themselves a ravaging ahead, having raided the Peloponnese twice in 428 BC, the second time in revenge for a second Peloponnesian invasion of Attica that never transpired. Great would be the relief at Athens, moreover, if the treasury could be spared the expense of yet another expedition around the Peloponnese. Nevertheless, in 426 BC, a raiding expedition of thirty ships was sent to plunder the enemy's coasts.[2]

In choosing to raid the Peloponnese in the absence of a Peloponnesian invasion of Attica, the Athenians were abandoning the exacting Periclean tit-for-tat that had previously governed their incursions. Attacking unoffending Melos also represented something new in Athenian strategy: not merely avenging an insult but bringing into the world a fresh and unprompted source of shame for the Spartans. The Athenians had, of course, attacked friends of the Spartans before, during their ravaging expeditions, but those friends had also been combatants in the war against Athens and so deserving of revenge themselves. Melos was not.

Why the Athenians changed their strategy is not hard to guess: they had, they thought, been winning the war for three years, but the Spartans still would not admit it. The inadequate Spartan peace offer of the previous winter (if we are right in our guess about its date and significance) only reconfirmed Spartan intransigence. The Spartans were still very far from humbling themselves and acknowledging Athenian equality in rank—the equality that perfectly symmetrical revenge was intended to convey. But perfectly symmetrical revenge had not brought an end to the war, and now the Athenians were trying something new.

The event that precipitated the Athenians' new strategy was perhaps the fall of Plataea during the previous year, in 427 BC. In a mechanical sense, the Athenians were still ahead in the war over rank—they could still boast, at least, of their captures of Potidaea and Mytilene and the naval victories of Phormio. But rank existed in the minds of men, and men were apt to forget; rank was also more a matter of emotion than of calculation, and emotion had to be stoked: thus the most recent great, unequivocal victory will often have been the one men looked to. Corcyra in 427 BC was a puzzle: the Athenians had lost the battle but won the war. So the most recent great, unequivocal victory in the war was the Peloponnesian capture of Plataea, and given the Athenians' remarkable reaction to its taking—granting the surviving Plataeans Athenian citizenship—the Athenians were acutely humiliated by its loss. In the wake of Plataea, the Athenians may have thought, the Spartans might never climb down from their hauteur. It was time to try something different.

Whatever the exact triggers, the change of Athenian strategy is clear: Athens determined that in her attempts to humiliate Sparta, she would no longer be constrained by reciprocity and proportionality. The Athenians would still, of course, seek revenge for Spartan offences. But they would seek to humiliate the Spartans even beyond the bounds of revenge carefully calculated to be equal to the Spartans' offence, and also in realms (such as that of poor Melos) where there was no revenge to take, because the Spartans had not acted in them. In short, the Athenians were gambling that their actions could bring upon the Spartans more shame than the Athenians would incur themselves by breaking the rules of just revenge—indeed, that a deluge of shame would force the Spartans to a settlement that would finally enshrine Athenian equality in standing. A hostile critic would insist, of course, that Athens was thereby plunging into the realm of *hybris*. And an unbiased critic, if such a one could be found, might well agree.

Looking back at the last campaign of the previous year, this new Athenian strategy helps to explain the Athenian decision to send twenty ships to Sicily. For great Sicilian Syracuse offered Athens the same opportunity as tiny Melos: a Spartan ally whom the Spartans were in no position to help. Whether the Syracusans and their friends in Sicily and southern Italy had in fact provided practical assistance to Sparta in the war was neither here nor there in the world of rank: attacking them shamed Sparta all the same. Besides, Athens had been summoned by her western allies Leontini and Rhegium, and helping friends and harming enemies were honorable acts in themselves, the former perhaps honorable in proportion to the perceived selflessness of the intervention.

Nor were attacks on her allies the only way to humiliate Sparta in the west. The Athenian expedition, Thucydides said, was intended "to prevent the importation of grain into the Peloponnese" from Sicily and southern Italy. As we have already noted, this makes little sense as an attack on the Peloponnesian economy; nor did the Athenians in fact try to establish a blockade. But just as before the war, when the Athenians insulted Megara by denying the Megarians access to the ports and markets of Athens and her empire, Athens' proclamation that grain might not pass to the Peloponnese and Athenian ships' busy capture of a few merchant craft (this is probably all that their activity came to, in fact; Thucydides does not say) were not economic in purpose, but chiefly an insult at once to those who sought to import grain into the Peloponnese and to those western allies who sought to export it to them.[3]

Like the attack on Melos, troubling the grain for the Peloponnese was but another move on the chessboard of rank, a knight's move into a realm where Sparta could not help her allies. It was an artfully contrived insult to Sparta, an attempt to inaugurate a whole new genre of humiliation. As such, the mission to Sicily fits well into the new Athenian strategy of not merely taking equal reprisal for the dishonor the Spartans inflicted on the Athenians, but setting aside the demure rules of proportion and reciprocity to inundate the Spartans with shame.

After ravaging the territory of Melos—with over ten thousand men, probably wasting Melos' sixty-odd square miles far more completely than the Peloponnesians ever did Attica's nearly fifteen hundred square miles—the Athenian fleet sailed north again, back in the direction of Athens. But it did not return to the port of Piraeus. Instead, the fleet made its way up the west coast of Attica to Oropus, in the debatable land on the Boeotian border. At nightfall the ten hoplites carried by each trireme were disembarked, and this élite corps crossed the Boeotian border toward the city of Tanagra, just ten miles away.[4]

MAP 6.2 Athenian Incursion into Boeotia, 426 BC

The Athenians had fought the Spartans at Tanagra in ?457 BC and had been ignominiously defeated by them. This the Athenians had certainly not forgotten, but the other Greeks knew rural Tanagra for less alarming traits: as the birthplace of the poetess Corinna, for its curious fowls, and because its coast had once been beset by a triton, a monster upward man and downward fish, whom the wily folk of the town had made drunk on wine, then beheaded as he snored, later erecting a headless triton statue to celebrate their high deed.[5]

Once the vanguard from Athens' ships had signaled that all was quiet—no enemies about, no tipsy tritons—the entire Athenian hoplite levy, thousands strong, marched through the night from the direction of Athens to meet them in the Boeotian countryside. Then, having made their rendezvous, the two bodies made camp. The Athenians spent the next day ravaging the territory of Tanagra and that night returned unmolested to their tents. No doubt like the Melians, the Boeotians seem to have been genuinely surprised by the Athenians' choice of targets. Only the day after the ravaging were the men of Tanagra ready for battle, and even then the Thebans, only ten miles away, were unable to send their full levy to help, but only a handful of fighters. Yet this small combined force—the Athenians must have outnumbered them at least five to one—nevertheless issued forth from Tanagra against the host of the Athenians and pluckily offered battle: so strong among the other Greeks was the drive to hoplite battle, which the sea-loving Athenians scorned by immuring themselves in their city.[6]

The Athenians naturally defeated the Boeotians and, having set up their trophy, withdrew into Attica—the marines to their ships at Oropus and the rest to the city—before the whole force of the Boeotian League could descend upon them. The Athenian fleet then sailed north to raid Opuntian Locris, Sparta's ally immediately to the north of Boeotia, just as Athenian triremes had done in the first year of the war. Finally they returned to Piraeus.[7]

The incursion into Boeotia was the first that the Athenians had made during the entire war. This despite the fact that Athens and Boeotia shared a common border; that the Boeotians had, in fact, begun the war by attacking Athens' ally, Plataea; that the Boeotians had helped to tempt Mytilene into revolt; and that the Boeotians had participated in some—indeed, perhaps all—of the Peloponnesian invasions of Attica. Even if the Athenians were reluctant to face the full Boeotian armament in the field (as their prompt departure from Tanagra on this occasion perhaps suggests), they could have raided over the border, or from their ships as they did around Peloponnese, and so brought woe upon the Boeotians.[8]

But rather than harass the Boeotians, Athens had chosen to disregard them entirely. In the first year of the war, when they had sent a fleet to raid Opuntian Locris, north of Boeotia, they sailed right by Boeotia itself and had likewise ignored Boeotia ever since. This is another of those strange acts of passivity that makes the strategies of the war so difficult for today's observer to fathom. There were others, too, equally puzzling: we never hear of the Athenians raiding the territory of Corinth, for instance, although the Corinthians had done so much against Athens. Nor had the Peloponnesians done anything to protect Megara, which continued to be invaded and ravaged by the Athenians every year.[9]

If the Athenians neglected Boeotia, it was not because they did not consider her a threat. But just as when a southern gentlemen, jostled by another in the streets of old Charleston, could coolly decide not to construe the contact as an insult and thus avoid the duel, so did an ancient Greek state in a war over rank, as we have seen, enjoy a certain latitude to fail to "notice" acts of their adversaries—by deeming the acts or their actors too trivial to deserve revenge. Indeed, with enough insouciance and public emphasis, this very failure to notice was itself an effective insult, an ostentatious signal of contempt suggesting the unworthiness of an adversary even to compete. Such had been the response of Sparta to the raid of the Athenian general Tolmides around the Peloponnese in ?456 BC, when by ignoring the Athenians they implied that the Athenians were no more than subordinate allies of Argos, Sparta's proper rival.[10]

In the present war, the main rivals, Athens and Sparta, could hardly ignore each other, but both could, if they wished, ignore each other's allies. To prove her equality with Sparta, Athens had long chosen to avenge Sparta's attacks, but she had declined to notice the antics of Thebes and Corinth—for to return the blows of these lesser states might imply that Athens was equal to them rather than to lofty Sparta. Athens had concentrated her Peloponnesian raiding instead on pettier allies of Sparta, the cities of the Argolid peninsula in the east and Elis in the west. Raiding those allies embarrassed Sparta just as well—because Sparta could not protect them—and was less subject to misinterpretation than raiding Corinth or Boeotia, for, unlike those greater states, no one could think that tiny Hermione, say, rivaled Athens in rank, and thus that Athens' raiding her might imply Hermione's equality with Athens. For her part, Sparta long chose to regard the Athenian war against Megara as a sideshow, something separate and independent from her war against Athens, and so declined to notice the annual invasions of Megara's land.

Failing to acknowledge an opponent was a gambit in the game of reputation: one could not be certain in advance whether the Greeks would accept failure to respond as the scorn of the higher or the fear of the weaker (in which case the gambit rebounded, disgracing the state that had attempted it). The party who failed to notice insisted on the former, while the ignored party insisted on the latter. In doubtful cases, since there was no way of consulting Greek public opinion, both parties would believe their own stories and behave as if their interpretation was right. Until 426 BC, the Athenians were evidently happy with their policy of ignoring the deeds of Boeotia and thereby belittling the Boeotians.

The capture of heroic little Plataea by the Peloponnesians in the previous year and the absorption of her territory into that of Thebes changed Athens' attitude to the Spartan ally. Given Athens' long alliance with Plataea and her guarantees of Plataea's safety, the capture of Plataea would have passed the threshold for acts that Athens could fail to notice (much as Sparta had not been able to ignore the fall of Potidaea in the winter of 430/429 BC, as tempting as it must have been to do so). Choosing to take revenge against not the Spartans but the Boeotians, moreover, implied that they were the ones responsible for hurting Athens' pride. This was a shrewd piece of statecraft; for other than Sparta's annual ravagings (so carefully avenged, one for one, by the Athenians) and the divine intervention on her behalf in the form of the plague, the Peloponnesian capture of Plataea was the single unquestionable victory the Spartans could point to in the war. If that victory could be transferred in the minds of the Greeks from Sparta to Thebes, Sparta would lose a major claim to pride.[11]

Particularly clever about this Athenian slight of hand was that the Boeotians could be counted on to cooperate in it. And they did. It was in fact as an admission that Boeotia had scored a hit upon Athens that the Boeotians treated the Athenian incursion into Boeotia. For, apart from some cattle reiving and thieving over the border (which we deduce from mentions in Aristophanes' *Acharnians*), the Boeotians did not respond to the Athenian invasion of their lands with their own public act of revenge. They did not march their hoplite levy into Attica, although the quick departure of the Athenians from Tanagra was practically an invitation to do so, suggesting as it did that the Athenians considered themselves unequal to the Boeotians on land. No, the Boeotians did not react at all. In their eyes, the Athenian incursion had elevated them in standing by admitting, finally, that they were an enemy worth taking revenge upon, an enemy one could no longer fail to notice. The Boeotians, then, were delighted to accept Athens' revenge as a proportionate response to the Theban seizure of Plataea. Honors were even, the Boeotians thought, and Boeotia had been admitted to the top division. There was nothing more for the Boeotians to do except quietly exult.[12]

In the same summer that Athens and Boeotia came to their curious agreement to consider the capture of Plataea a matter between them and so exclude the Spartans, the Spartans also began to feel the favor of divinity slipping away from them. A series of earthquakes throughout Greece (those that had prevented Sparta's invasion of Attica were merely the last of a singularly tremorous winter) had made the god-fearing Lacedaemonians anxious that they had offended the gods. Nor, despite the reassuring return of the plague to Athens, did the overall course of the war suggest the favor of Olympus. Missions to the oracle at Delphi, on any subject, brought back a disturbing confirmation of Spartan fears: they had done wrong by driving their king Pleistoanax into exile nineteen years before, when they convicted him of having been bribed by Pericles. Through his babbling prophetess, Apollo kept nagging Spartans who visited Delphi with the same command: "to bring home from abroad the seed of Zeus' son, the demi-god [Heracles], lest you plow with a silver share." (In time the Spartans came to ponder exactly why the god chose to interest himself in such a matter and wondered whether Pleistoanax had not bribed the Pythia, the priestess who pronounced Apollo's prophecies.)[13]

All the time of his exile King Pleistoanax had abided in high Arcadia, in the holy sanctuary of Zeus on Mount Lycaeus (Wolf Mountain). His very house was bisected (for fear of the Spartan violence) by the sanctuary boundary, so that in a flash Pleistoanax could flee into the protection of the god. And through his years in that high fane, the banished king would have seen sights strange and uncanny: for there on Wolf Mountain Zeus was worshipped as a wolf god; no man born of woman might pass within the innermost sanctum lest he die within the year; and in that forbidden spot, it was said that neither man nor beast cast a shadow. Upon the yearly rites of Zeus Lycaeus, so the story went, one of his human votaries was transformed into a wolf. And off into the wilds of Arcadia that werewolf loped, to be tested whenever he came upon a lone shepherd or a humble mountain croft, with its curl of smoke arising: could he summon his old humanity enough to hold himself from tasting man-flesh? If for nine years he did so restrain himself, in the tenth he was changed back into a man. But if he lost himself to his lupine nature, a wolf he would remain to the end of his days.[14]

It was from such a haunted place that Pleistoanax, elderly and likely addled, was brought back to Lacedaemon after so many years, for the oracle would not be denied, and the Spartans feared the wrath of Apollo. And so, with the sacrifices and dances that attended the accession of a Spartan king—rituals harking back, the Spartans believed, to the coming of the sons of Heracles to the hollow vale of Lacedaemon—did the long-exiled Pleistoanax make his late return to the land that had raised and rejected him.[15]

Perhaps this same atmosphere of deepened piety at Sparta, brought on by the trembling of the earth, also played a part in the Spartan decision to send forth in 426 BC a colony named Heraclea to the region of Trachis, near Thermopylae, north of Boeotia. An appeal had been made to the Spartans by their allies, the Trachinians, who were being pressed in war by a neighboring tribe. The envoy they sent to Sparta was named Tisamenus, "the Avenger," perhaps to indicate the service sought. But far more important, the southern neighbor of Trachis, tiny Doris, who was suffering depredations from the same tribe, joined in this appeal of the Trachinians. No more than Delphic Apollo were the men of Doris, the diminutive ancestors of the Dorian Peloponnesians, to be denied. Some thirty years before, in ?457 BC, the Spartans had marched to help the men of Doris against a different neighbor, on the expedition that eventually led the Spartans to defeat the Athenians at the battle of Tanagra, when the Athenians challenged the Spartans to battle on their way home.[16]

Now the Spartans consulted the god at Delphi, returned to his good humor by the restoration of Pleistoanax, and Apollo endorsed their designs for a colony. The Spartans dispatched a few of their own citizens (one of the three leaders being the luckless Alcidas), as well as more of their Laconian subject folk, and called far and wide for colonists from friendly divisions of the Hellenic nation.

Sending the colony appealed to the Spartans not just because it offered them the chance to gain honor by helping their northern allies and ancestors

MAP 6.3 Spartan Foundation of Heraclea in Trachis, 426 BC

but also, as Thucydides observes, because Heraclea was usefully situated for raids by sea against the island of Euboea, where Athens had sent her beasts to protect them from Peloponnesian invasions of Attica: the closest cape of Euboea was but twenty miles from Heraclea. Indeed, since Athens had adjusted the rules of revenge so that seaborne raids were equal to land-borne ones, the prospect of turning Athens' principle against her by doing some seaborne raiding of their own was no doubt very appealing to the Peloponnesians.[17]

We require no considerations beyond these, then, to explain the Spartans' establishment of a colony in far Trachis, in this year when the earth shook. And yet, if we imagine the Spartans gloomily receiving the tidings of the year—the news of the harrying of Melos and the Athenian rampages in the west, of bloodied Tanagra and the ravaged fields of friendly Locris—and devising to ease the shame of their inability to help their wider-spread allies, we can easily imagine them sending the colony to Trachis for this reason as well. So Thucydides implies: he places his account of the colony right after he has mentioned the Athenian raid on neighboring Locris. Any Greek reader would assume a relationship.

In 426 BC Sparta would have relished any chance to assist wee Doris, the mother of the Dorians, because, as Athens widened the war in search of ways to humiliate Sparta, the Ten Years' War was taking on an increasingly Dorian-against-Ionian complexion. The war in Sicily, for instance, was fought between the races of the Greeks—the Dorians led by Syracuse and the Ionians led by Leontini and Rhegium, who in turn had called in Athens, the mother city of their race. Bewildered Melos, too, was Dorian and the child of Sparta herself. Just as the Spartans held their hands from villages in Attica that had helped Sparta in the time of heroes, to remind all of Greece that services to Sparta would never be forgotten, so helping Doris, the ancestor of all Dorians, broadcast to the world the same message: no matter how old the debt, the Spartans would treasure it through the extremities of time.

The Dorian connection of Heraclea was emphasized because not only did Doris join in calling for the colony but the colony itself had a peculiarly Dorian quality. Most of the colonists will have been Dorians because, despite a wide call for colonists, the Ionians—and members of certain other races of the Greeks—were excluded from joining. The colony's very name—"the city of Heracles"—linked it to Dorian mythology, for the sons of Heracles had led the Dorians into the Peloponnese. In fact, according to one legend, Heracles had lived for a time in Trachis, and according to another, he had died there. The Spartans may even have emphasized their devotion to Heracles by choosing as the leaders of the colony men named Alcidas, "Son of Force," which was an epithet of Heracles, and Leon, "the Lion," whose name inevitably called to mind Heracles' slaying of the Nemean Lion, after which he memorably girded himself with the pelt.[18]

The colony was perhaps also intended specifically to relieve the suffering of Sparta's Dorian friends within the Peloponnese. Thucydides says that a great many colonists joined the new colony in search of security. Many of these will have been citizens of Sparta's allies ruined by the accidents of war and Athenian raiding—which, even if it was not of general economic significance, could certainly destroy the property of individuals.

To these men, then, and to their states, the colony was a clear act of gratitude for their losses, and to the whole Dorian nation, a promise of Spartan gratitude for all time. If so, the colony to Trachis also tells us that the
new, unrestrained Athenian strategy was working, shaming the Lacedaemonians to a degree that they felt compelled to make some visible and un-
precedented response. Much like the Spartan adulation of Brasidas after
he had saved Methone in the first year of the war, Sparta's new mission to
colonize hints that Sparta felt a deepening shame.

Needless to say, in this year of explosive Athenian activity, not even a
Spartan gesture to her allies like Heraclea could be allowed to go unanswered. If the Spartans were signifying their gratitude to the Dorian nation, then Athens could do the same to the Ionians, making a competition
even of thanks, loyalty, and piety. Thus, in the winter following the fighting season of 426 BC, the Athenians ritually purified Delos, the tiny Cycladic island sacred to Ionian Apollo, by removing all the graves from it
and decreeing that thereafter no one should give birth or die there—both,
in Greek thinking, bringing impurity—and that those who showed any inclination to do either should promptly be conveyed over to a smaller island
nearby until they were finished. In times past there had been a regular festival with games on Delos, a great in-gathering of all the Ionians, but the
old rites had declined. The Athenians now revived them, restoring the contests and adding extravagant horse races.[19]

It was wise for the Athenians to attend to the gods in this year of earthquakes. In purifying Delos and reviving its festival, they renewed their devotion to Apollo the Far Darter, bringer of plagues—a prudent petition, in
this year when the plague had also, alas, returned to Athens. But in the
wider scheme of the war over rank, it was wise as well for the Athenians to
trump the Spartans' gesture to the Dorians with an opulent gesture to their
own Ionian kin.

THE ATHENIANS WERE COMMITTED ANEW to the strategy of raiding
around the Peloponnese, although now their intention was to shame
the Spartans regardless of whether the Spartans invaded Attica or not.
The northwest of Greece, therefore, needed putting right to ensure that
the Athenian expeditions found safe harbors at the far end of their raiding
voyages.

Four major islands, all now havens for yachtsmen and heavens for
tourists, adorn the Ionian Sea. Northernmost is Corcyra, which in 426 BC
had recently been brutally reconfirmed in its alliance to Athens after being
led astray by its oligarchy. The two most southerly isles, Zacynthus and

MAP 6.4 Northwestern Greece

Cephallenia at the mouth of the Gulf of Corinth, had a cleaner record of friendship with Athens. But there was a taint in these friendly waters: for between Cephallenia and Corcyra lay Leucas, a colony of Corinth loyal to Sparta. Nearby on the continent (to which Leucas was attached by the sand spit over which the Peloponnesians, fleeing from Corcyra in 427 BC, had dragged their ships) lay the realm of the Acarnanians, who occupied the elbow and bicep of the land where the coast outside the Corinthian Gulf turns north toward what is now Albania. The sling-wielding Acarnanians were friendly to the Athenians. To their north, divided from them by a gulf, lay the city of Ambracia, colonists of the Corinthians, friendly to the Lacedaemonians, and traditionally the greatest land power in the northwest.

The ancient Greek sailor could continue to trace a similar patchwork of allegiance as he passed from the Ionian Sea into the Gulf of Corinth. To the east of the Acarnanians, along the northern shore of the Gulf and extending further north into the hills, lay the Aetolians, who fancied the Spartan side. Next along that shore came the Ozolian—or "Smelly"—Locrians, who favored the Athenians. Many were the tales of how these folk won their name: Was it by the rotting of a famous corpse or the reek of a native river? Or that once upon a time they wore the untanned pelts of beasts? So the uncharitable insisted. But perhaps the aroma was that of the pleasing asphodel, the flower of forever; or perhaps there was no smell—from the verb *ozō*—at all. Perhaps they were merely the "Branch"—from the Greek *ozos*—Locrians, for it was admitted by all that soon after the great flood, the king of the land had kept a bitch that famously gave birth to a stick. Next, heading east along the coast, came Phocis, uncomfortable home to holy Delphi and ally to the Spartans, where the wind told tales on the hillsides to the black hellebore. And Phocis bordered upon Boeotia, another Spartan ally.[20]

This checkerboard of loyalties in the northwest was no creation of the Athenians and Spartans but simply reflected the inveterate hostility of Greek states to their immediate neighbors: thus when one, perhaps on the basis of ancient kinship, called in the Athenians or Peloponnesians for assistance against a neighbor, that neighbor naturally allied itself to the other great power. Although Greek in language and habits, for the most part these continent dwellers lived as tribes and clans spread over the land, rather than owing their loyalty to individual cities, as was the custom in southern Greece. They were, then, an old-fashioned folk, their men still carrying weapons on their daily rounds, leading to a more forthright, rambunctious, even Homeric notion of mine and thine than prevailed in the city-states to the south. The southern Greeks thought that a visit to the northwestern tribes was rather like taking a journey into their own past. When the Acarnanians in 428 BC had been told that the Athenians were sending a raiding fleet around the Peloponnese, a fleet that would assist them upon its arrival in the northwest, they had begged the Athenians, since their hero Phormio was not available, to send a son or relative of his in his place. This detail the sophisticated Thucydides reports with an ever-so-slightly raised eyebrow, as reverence for heroic blood that recalled a more ancient, more innocent time.[21]

Just as the region was rent by conflict between the tribes, so did the very tribes of northwestern Greece lack unity: in the winter after his famous 429 BC naval victories in the northwest, Phormio had marched through friendly Acarnania, driving out of her towns men hostile to the Acarnanian confederation, and so to Athens. The Acarnanian city of Oeniadae, long hostile to the rest of the Acarnanians, had actually ranged herself on the Lacedaemonian side in the greater war, and so the Athenian fleet of 428 BC (commanded by Asopius, the requested son of Phormio) attempted, but failed, to assist the Acarnanians in conquering it. But Oeniadae was supported in its independence by its location in the riven and pestilent delta of the Archelous River: many centuries later the poet Byron would die of fever in this district while fighting for the freedom of the Greeks.[22]

Not all the settlements among the tribesmen were inhabited by those tribesmen. Over the generations, southern Greeks had settled fortified cities among the coastal tribes, cities that the ancient rulers of the land naturally detested. Among the hostile Acarnanians, the Corinthians had settled Sollium, which the Athenians had captured and given to the Acarnanians in the first year of the war. By the Gulf of Ambracia, where the fields of the Ambracians and the Acarnanians met, strong Peloponnesian Argos had in the time of heroes settled a weak daughter city, Amphilochian Argos. Needing help many generations later, the men of Amphilochian Argos invited the Ambracians to have a share in their city—which they took, and soon more than a share, for the Ambracians drove the settlers from Argos out. This impelled the colonists in turn into the arms of the Acarnanians, who together with Phormio and the Athenians recaptured Amphilochian Argos and made slaves of the Ambracians they captured there. This joint expedition of Athenians and Acarnanians, some years before the outbreak of the Ten Years' War (although we do not know exactly when), was the origin of the alliance between Athens and the Acarnanians. But the men of Ambracia still looked upon Amphilochian Argos as their own and, wanting revenge, had attacked her without success in 430 BC.[23]

In the larger war, Athenian-allied Naupactus was by far the most important of the embattled fortress cities in the northwest. Naupactus was Athens' naval base and home to the Messenian exiles who had already proved such valuable auxiliaries to the Athenians. Lying near the narrows at the mouth of the Corinthian Gulf, the Gibraltar of Greece, Naupactus was well placed to torment Peloponnesian ships coming and going. But by land Naupactus was less well situated, for it lay upon the borders of the Ozolian Locrians and the Aetolians, the former friendly, the latter emphatically not.[24]

The Athenian commander to whose lot it fell in the summer of 426 BC to safeguard the allies of Athens in the northwest was Demosthenes, son of Alcisthenes, who now set off around the Peloponnese with a fleet of thirty triremes. He was to become a leading Athenian general in the later stages of the Ten Years' War. Thucydides did not much like Demosthenes and subtly belittles his achievements. Was he a political ally of the hated Cleon? Or did the aristocratic Thucydides simply loathe his rather too democratic bumper sticker of a name, which meant, literally, "People Power"? Or could Thucydides simply never find it in his heart to forgive Demosthenes for his unpunished bumbling in this, his first major command?[25]

Demosthenes saw that the chief hazard posed to Athenian interests in the northwest was the Spartan-allied island of Leucas, which lay nudged up against the coast of friendly Acarnania on the route north to Corcyra and was forever hostile to the Acarnanians. Leucas had served as the assembly point for the ill-fated joint Ambracian/Peloponnesian invasion of Acarnania in 429 BC and had also provided soldiers and ships for that effort. Demosthenes was right to see the danger posed by Leucas; in 428 BC, Asopius, the son of Phormio, had met his death raiding there.[26]

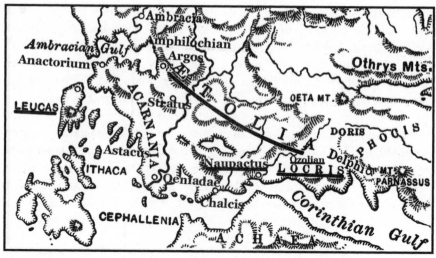

MAP 6.5 Campaigns of Demosthenes Against Leucas and Aetolia, 426 BC

Now Demosthenes, perhaps to avenge the misfortune of Asopius, perhaps hoping to force the island to yield, summoned the whole force of the Acarnanians (except, of course, pesky Oeniadae), as well as men from the southerly allied islands of Zacynthus and Cephallenia, and fifteen ships from Corcyra. Together these landed on Leucas and proceeded to ravage its countryside, the men of the place not daring to come forth from their walls to face Demosthenes' superior numbers. The Acarnanians now urged Demosthenes to wall off the hated town of Leucas itself, which was set upon a tip of the land, and to besiege it. But the Athenians knew from Samos, Potidaea, and Mytilene how expensive and laborious such a siege could be, and Demosthenes refused.[27]

Demosthenes contented himself with the ravaging of Leucas (in the course of which some ten thousand men trampled just over a hundred square miles of island), then turned his ambitions upon another enemy: the Aetolians, who held the stretch of coast between friendly Acarnania and the Athenian base at Naupactus but also occupied a large expanse of the continent inland of Naupactus, to the north of the Gulf of Corinth. It was the Messenians of Naupactus who urged Demosthenes to attack the Aetolians, for they were a perpetual threat to the Messenians' adopted city; Athens, for her part, would take any measure to safeguard Naupactus so as to protect her base. And it would be well also to clear the land road between Naupactus and the friendly Acarnanians further west: then Athens would dominate the whole of the elbow of northwestern Greece, from Mount Parnassus on the eastern border of the friendly Ozolian Locrians all the way to the Gulf of Ambracia. Besides, by attacking Aetolia Demosthenes could "do a favor for the Messenians," who, having helped Phormio so bravely in 429 BC and Nicostratus on Corcyra in 427 BC, had, to Greek thinking, every right to call in a favor.[28]

Aetolia would be easier to attack than Leucas—at least, so said the Messenians of Naupactus. Fighting the Aetolians, they urged Demosthenes, threatened none of the intractable difficulties presented by a siege of the town of Leucas: the Aetolians' settlements were not walled; nor, if it should come to battle in the open, did the Aetolians fight as hoplites but as light-armed troops, flinging javelins and rocks and fighting hand to hand individually, not in the mass of the phalanx. In their eager advocacy the Messenians presumably neglected to tell Demosthenes that the Aetolians were so fierce a folk that even their women had names like "Battle Leader" and "Good Battle."[29]

Having resolved to attack Aetolia, Demosthenes sailed back to Acarnania to report his decision and to try to enlist the cooperation of the Acarnanians for his new venture. Furious that he had balked at perfecting the destruction of hated Leucas, they, however, refused. The Corcyreans, presumably summoned against Leucas alone, also departed for home. Demosthenes now sailed to Ozolian Locris and prepared to march north against the Aetolians with only his Messenian friends, the islanders of Zacynthus and Cephallenia, and the three hundred hoplites from his Athenian ships. The Ozolian Locrians, light-armed like the Aetolians, were to join him too, but they took time to assemble, and the Messenians were pressing upon Demosthenes the need for haste. The Aetolians were a numerous folk, they said, and were best defeated in detail before they could rally from their far-flung settlements. Nor were the Messenians wrong in this. Neither they nor the Athenians knew, however, that the Aetolians, having long known of Demosthenes' plans against them, were even now gathered to await him.[30]

Before crossing the border into Aetolia, Demosthenes camped in a precinct of Zeus, ill famed as the place where the men of that region had killed Hesiod, the second bard of the Greeks. This was a luckless omen. Then, north into Aetolia the oblivious Demosthenes led his small army, plundering unfortified places and sending the booty back into the coastal strip of Ozolian Locris. None resisted him. Those whose homes the Athenians were looting kept a grim watch from the heights, their eyes reflecting the fire devouring their houses. Then, some nine miles north of the sea, while the Athenians were moving through a valley . . . an ambush.[31]

From the hills surged light-armed Aetolians, flinging their javelins at the Athenian force massed below. A storm of Athenian arrows—arrows were a peril to the ill-protected light-armed—threw them back. The hoplites charged to drive off the Aetolians, who fled before them. But the heavy-armed Athenians could not catch the swift tribesmen, and when the hoplites turned back to their formation, the Aetolians reversed course and pursued them in their turn, still casting javelins. Demosthenes must have seen cold reproach in the eyes of his comrades in the phalanx, reproach that he had not waited for the aid of the light-armed Ozolian Locrians. The archers on the Athenian side were running out of arrows; when the captain of the bowmen was killed, the archers quickly scattered.[32]

The Athenian hoplites in their heavy gear, for their part, were exhausted by the length of the fight, but still the Aetolians ran in, and still the Aetolians hurled their javelins. The enemy seemed beyond number, for the Aetolians had summoned to battle even their very least presentable cousins, baying savages from the northern clans who (Thucydides was told) spoke a hooting gabble and gnawed upon raw meat. And finally, with a terrible simultaneity, a mass contagion of spirit, the Athenian phalanx collapsed, and Demosthenes' whole force was in flight: some down the roads, to be pursued and killed by the fleet-footed Aetolians; some by mistake into dead-end ravines (for their Messenian guide had been killed in the fighting); many into a dense forest nearby, to which the ingenious Aetolians, who knew that the woods had no exit, promptly set fire.

Of the three hundred Athenian hoplites who had set out, only one hundred and eighty made it back to the sea. Procles, Demosthenes' colleague in the generalship, was among the dead. Casualties among the allies were equally grave. The Athenians asked for their dead back under a truce, then rowed their doleful way back to Naupactus. The widows of the Messenians mourned their husbands, the survivors from Zacynthus and Cephallenia slunk home, and the fleet of thirty Athenian ships returned to Athens. Demosthenes, however, knowing how the Athenian democracy often received its defeated generals, prudently chose to stay behind at Naupactus.[33] Athens' shock over the disaster in Aetolia rumples the very texture of history. To those Athenians who fell in Aetolia, Thucydides delivers a remarkable, Homeric epitaph. "So great a number died," he says, "and all of an age, and they were the best men that the Athenians lost in this war." So unusual an outburst from the somber Thucydides compels conjecture. Did Thucydides lose a son or a friend in this shambles? Grief would explain why he could never reconcile himself to Demosthenes, despite Demosthenes' later successes.[34]

Savage Aetolia was never a target of the Athenians for its own sake. Athens' unfolding campaign in the northwest, so far a bloody failure, was primarily an auxiliary to the revived strategy of raiding around the Peloponnese. It was with an eye to ravaging that Athens essayed to fortify her important northwestern ally, Acarnania, and to protect strategic Naupactus from enemies in its hinterland. At the same time, the efforts against Leucas and Aetolia fit well into the new Athenian strategy of trying to humiliate Sparta by attacking Spartan allies—Melos, Syracuse—to whom the Spartans could not easily bring aid. As it happened, of course, it was the Athenians who were humiliated—a source of some satisfaction for the Peloponnesians, although, alas, they had not administered the drubbing themselves.

Unlike seagirt Melos and far Syracuse, however, the Spartans could actually protect their friends in northwestern Greece—and with them, Spartan honor—from Athenian attack. The Peloponnesians could send an army to northwestern Greece by way of Boeotia or even, if they were feeling bold, across the Gulf of Corinth. Indeed, as soon as the Aetolians heard rumors of Demosthenes' plans against them, they had sent envoys pleading for aid from Sparta and Corinth. Help proved unnecessary, as the Aetolians defeated Demosthenes themselves before the Peloponnesians could act. But now, in the wake of their lonely victory, the Aetolians urged the Spartans to send a force to help attack Naupactus, which had summoned the Athenians against them.[35]

To the Spartans, an expedition against Naupactus seemed rich with opportunity. Not only would success make Athenian raiding of the Peloponnese more difficult by denying Athens her best-located base in the northwest, but it was also a chance for Sparta to help an embattled ally, thus countering the new Athenian strategy of humiliating Sparta by attacking her undefended friends. Finally, given how weak Naupactus was and how celebrated for Athenian victory Naupactus had become, an expedition offered the opportunity for a real, glorious, avenging victory.

Late in the summer of 426 BC, therefore, the Peloponnesians assembled at holy Delphi a force of three thousand allied hoplites under a Spartan commander, Eurylochus. Six hundred of these men were drawn from recently founded Heraclea, the new Spartan colony in Trachis. In total this was a formidable force, likely made up of several times as many soldiers as Demosthenes had taken into Aetolia. It certainly unnerved the Ozolian Locrians, the allies of Athens through whose territory the Peloponnesians had to march—although, with the defeat of Demosthenes in Aetolia, the Ozolian Locrians no doubt also felt a wider shift of fortunes in their part of the world. Whatever their reasons, they placed no bar to the Peloponnesians marching through their land, even surrendering some of their own folk as hostages to guarantee their good behavior and in many instances going so far as to send contingents to help the invaders. Only a handful of Locrian towns near Naupactus remained loyal to the Athenian alliance, and two such places were seized by the Peloponnesians on their march. Approaching Naupactus itself, Eurylochus and the Peloponnesians were joined by the triumphant Aetolians, and the teeming host captured Naupactus' unfortified

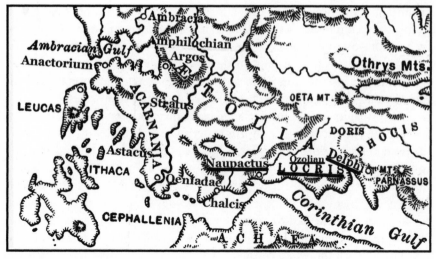

MAP 6.6 Campaign of the Peloponnesians Against Naupactus, 426 BC

suburbs as well as another small Athenian ally close by before laying the port town itself under siege.[36]

The hazard to Naupactus was critical. The walls of the city were extensive, built large enough to accommodate a large Athenian expedition, but the Athenians were absent and the Messenians of Naupactus were too few to defend their walls alone. One stalwart assault and the place would fall, and the Messenians and their wives, former helots of the Spartans, and their children—the first generation born in freedom had recently come of age—would perhaps be returned to the meager mercy of their one-time Spartan masters and to the dog-skin caps and arbitrary executions that had marked their enslavement. Alas for the Messenians! To Thucydides the Plataeans were the heroes of the war, free men defending their ancestral ground; but today's sympathies lie rather with the Messenians, the runaway slaves forging a new freedom for their children, exiles in an enemy land. We are horrified at the snuffer looming over the Messenian candle. But just as the Peloponnesians sensed victory—and of victory they had seen little enough in this war—dark ships were sighted in the offing, wallowing triremes crowded to the rails with hoplites. These were Acarnanians, come in the nick of time to save Naupactus.[37]

When the overland approach of the Peloponnesians was first reported, the disgraced Demosthenes had left Naupactus with the Athenian squadron and sailed north to beg the Acarnanians for help. This must have been keenly gratifying for the Acarnanians, whom Demosthenes had jilted earlier in the same year when he abandoned the siege of Leucas. Nor did they now allow themselves to be persuaded easily, delaying nearly long enough to doom Naupactus—but when the Acarnanians had wrung out of the chastened Demosthenes all the pleading of which he was capable, they unbent and gave the Athenian a thousand hoplites. These he landed in a rush in the harbor at Naupactus, and with them he manned the walls, delivering the city. The hopes of the Peloponnesians were obliterated, for properly defended Naupactus could not be taken. And so the attempt was abandoned, and parched Sparta still croaked for a victory.

The Spartan failure at Naupactus, however, pointed the Spartans at another target, where victory might be easier. For the misadventure taught the Spartan commanders that Acarnania, not Naupactus, was the anchor of Athens' power in the northwest. And so when envoys from Ambracia, Sparta's ally to the north of Acarnania, appeared at the disgruntled camp of the thwarted Peloponnesians and urged the Spartan chiefs to join them in an attack on Acarnania, they secured an eager hearing. First, the two forces would go hand in hand against Ambracia's old bane, Amphilochian Argos. Held by the hated Acarnanians, who had seized it from its rightful Ambracian conquerors, it blocked the road from Ambracia into Acarnania. Having recaptured that city, the Ambracians and Peloponnesians would march south together into Acarnania itself.[38]

The season turned before the Ambracians could assemble for war and hire mercenaries from the tribes north of them in Epirus; the Peloponnesians abided meanwhile in Aetolia, in the cold and rain of the autumn. But before winter made fighting impractical, the Ambracians descended in the company of those tribesmen upon Amphilochian Argos and captured Olpae, a coastal town in its territory; soon after the Peloponnesian army of Eurylochus received word to join them there.[39]

To oppose the Ambracians, the Acarnanians sent reliefs into Amphilochian Argos, but camped most of their forces on the road somewhat to the south of the city to block the Peloponnesians from making their rendezvous with their allies. The Acarnanians called for Demosthenes to be their leader (perhaps the disputatious Acarnanians found it easier to follow a foreigner than to bend the knee to an Acarnanian chief from another valley), and he hastened to their aid with two hundred Messenian hoplites and twenty ships. These twenty ships had just arrived in the northwest, presumably sent out from Athens when word was received that the Peloponnesians had not gone home after their failure before Naupactus but were still hovering close by in Aetolia, devising ill. Formally, the two generals the Athenians sent with the ships would have superseded Demosthenes in command of the Athenian forces, but he was still in charge of the whole campaign as war chief of the Acarnanians, a position it is nice to imagine was outfitted with a rude finery of torques and feathers.[40]

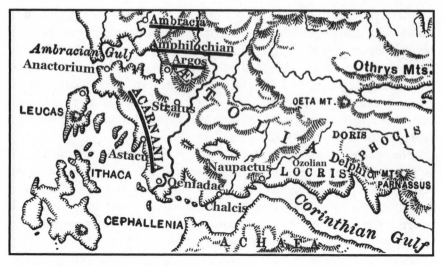

MAP 6.7 War Around Amphilochian Argos, 426 BC

The Peloponnesians, meanwhile, had been waiting in Aetolia, and when they finally received their summons from the Ambracians, they marched directly north through hostile Acarnania. But the way of their going they found abandoned and eerie. All the fighting men of the Acarnanians were in Amphilochian Argos or awaiting the Peloponnesians on the road near there, to prevent them from uniting with the Ambracians. Aware of the Acarnanian blocking position, the Peloponnesians passed it on another road, marching unseen by night between the city of Amphilochian Argos and the Acarnanian camps, and so they met their Ambracian allies at Olpae.[41]

A few days after the Peloponnesians succeeded in joining the Ambracians, Demosthenes joined the Acarnanians in Amphilochian Argos, disembarking from his ships sixty Athenian bowmen and perhaps two hundred Athenian hoplite marines to add to his two hundred Messenians and the army of the Acarnanians. And he led these combined forces—along with some light troops of the non-Greek natives of the country around, the Amphilochians—toward Olpae to challenge the Ambracians and Peloponnesians. The Athenian fleet, moreover, laid Olpae under blockade from the sea so that no additions could be made to the forces of their enemies from Ambracia, across the gulf, forces that already outnumbered those of Demosthenes.[42]

For five days the armies camped across from each other, enemies separated by a deep ravine. During that lull Demosthenes scouted the fields nearby to find what the Greeks called a dancing ground of Ares—a field of battle. But the place he chose, near an overgrown, sunken road, would not normally appeal to the general of a smaller army, for it was not hemmed in close on either side with trees or water courses or hills, obstacles that would prevent the smaller phalanx from being outflanked by the larger. When dawn broke on the sixth day and Demosthenes led his army out to challenge his enemies to battle on this ground, Eurylochus the Spartan must have honored his adversary's fighting spirit: for he was offering true, fair hoplite battle—the delight of the war god. The armies would fall to combat nose-to-nose, on an open plain, where the loser could plead no excuses and fortune would favor the brave.

Demosthenes arrayed his Messenians and Athenians on the right while Acarnanian hoplites and the Amphilochian light troops formed the rest of the line. Eurylochus will have considered this deployment odd, since the ally in whose territory a battle was fought—in this case the Acarnanians—usually claimed the prestigious right wing. Just like the arrogant Athenians, Eurylochus may have thought, to hog the place of honor! The army of Demosthenes was faced by a mixed phalanx of Peloponnesians and Ambracians, but Eurylochus deployed against the Athenians and Messenians on the right the soldiers in his army in which he had most confidence. So Eurylochus' left wing consisted of a contingent from Mantinea, Sparta's ally in the Peloponnese, and beside them holding the end of the line, an élite Peloponnesian contingent led by Eurylochus himself, which may have been made up of the former Laconians who had colonized Heraclea.[43]

When the two armies finally came together, Eurylochus' force clasped Demosthenes' in a bloody embrace, and the greater size of the Peloponnesian host immediately told. Eurylochus' left wing, extending well beyond the forces of Demosthenes, began to lap around it. The contingent led by Eurylochus took the Messenians in the flank. A dour struggle ensued, and the Peloponnesians knew they would soon win.

But then, like an angry river in the *Iliad*, like some slice of nature possessed of its own terrible volition, the sunken road seemed to rise from its bed, as four hundred brave men of the Acarnanians—hoplites and light troops both—emerged from the brush where they had been lying in ambush. Leaping to the charge, they fell on the rear of the Peloponnesian flanking force and broke it at first blow. Demosthenes had predicted that Eurylochus would mirror the Athenian's unusual deployment—since the Peloponnesians would want to defeat the Athenians themselves, for the honor of it, and defeat the Messenians, too, to feed their hatred—and so Demosthenes' deployment had lured Eurylochus' contingent into the killing zone of his ambush. Eurylochus and his second in command fell in the slaughter, and the panic of the ambushed ran like a squall along the Peloponnesian lines, for those shattered were the best men on their side. Soon the larger part of the army was in flight.[44]

On the other flank of the battle, the Ambracians had prevailed over the Acarnanians and put them to flight toward Amphilochian Argos, but no sooner had they returned from the brief pursuit of which gear-laden hoplites were capable than they realized all was lost. Now the Acarnanian center began to press upon the Ambracians, and they, too, soon fled. Alas, there were light troops enough on Demosthenes' side to pursue and make the general rout a bloody one; only the Mantineans kept their nerve (and their ranks) in the retreat, and so fared better.

The battle and pursuit lasted into the evening, and it was not until morning that a Peloponnesian emissary with a herald's wand emerged from Olpae asking Demosthenes for a truce to recover the bodies of the vanquished's dead. And the herald bore another question, too: would Demosthenes and his generals allow the defeated to go home? For Olpae, which had seemed so usefully secure when the Peloponnesians and their allies invaded the territory of Amphilochian Argos, had now—with enemies holding the field before it and the Athenian fleet circling behind it—become a prison. Eurylochus was dead, and with him his understudy, who would otherwise have assumed command. Instead, authority had devolved upon the understudy's understudy, the Spartan Menedaius, and he was at a loss as to how to extract his army.[45]

The request to recover the bodies was granted, and Demosthenes and the Acarnanians set up their trophy on the field, taking up their own three hundred dead. The request for safe passage for all the defeated, however, was denied. At the same time, messages were slipped to forlorn Menedaius and to the other leaders of the Peloponnesians that if they could slip away, they would be allowed to pass. This was no course of charity; it was, rather, a guileful plan to isolate the Ambracians and their barbarian mercenaries and, above all, to disgrace the Spartans and the Peloponnesians in the eyes of those in the northwest as betrayers of their allies and slaves to their own interests.[46]

As suggested by the enemy, the Peloponnesians began to slink away from their Ambracian allies, on such rustic pretexts as gathering firewood and cooking herbs. But the escapers inevitably drew many Ambracians along with them, and in larger and larger bodies as it became clear that a breakout was underway; soon there was a general exodus from the Ambracian camp. Quickly discerning that not only the covenanted Peloponnesians were fleeing, but unable to tell one group from the other, the Acarnanians attempted to pursue, and when their chiefs tried to hold them back in order to uphold the private truce, the leaders found themselves dodging their own men's javelins, being thought traitors. Nevertheless, the Acarnanians captured a goodly number of those escaping and then fell to disputing which were Peloponnesians, and thus must be let go, and which, as Ambracians, they might have the pleasure of killing. Urbane Thucydides allows himself a cruel smile at these Acarnanian antics: this, he seems to say, is how people behave when they do not live the life of the city. In the end the Acarnanians killed some two hundred captives.[47]

The great mass of those making their escape, Ambracians and Peloponnesians alike, safely reached the friendly kingdom of Agraea to the west because Demosthenes and his army were already on the move in another direction. For even while the Peloponnesians and Ambracians were taking up and burying their dead and the former were planning their escape, word had been brought to Demosthenes that the remaining forces of the Ambracians were marching south along the Gulf of Ambracia to join their countrymen at Olpae, oblivious to their defeat. (This was yet another reason to break up the survivors at Olpae, lest the arrival of their friends put them back in courage.) Demosthenes promptly dispatched his ships north along the coast of the gulf and, sending parties to occupy strong positions and prepare ambushes on the road, followed with his main Acarnanian force as soon as he could.[48]

On came the fresh Ambracians, unconscious of the hostile forces now gathering. They camped for the night on a low hill at Idomene, twin to a higher one quietly occupied by Demosthenes' scouts. These soon enough reported the Ambracians' location to Demosthenes, who now marched his army through the night to reach the still unsuspecting enemy.[49]

In the darkness before dawn, the Ambracians' sentries heard movement, but their somnolent challenges were quickly answered by reassuring Dorian voices identifying themselves as their own countrymen. A moment later the guileful Messenians—whom Demosthenes had posted to his front precisely because they were Dorian speakers—were close enough to cut the sentries down. Now Demosthenes and his Acarnanian troops were among the tents and bivouacs of the sleeping Ambracians, killing all they came across. The survivors fled into the dark, only to fall headlong into ravines and into the ambushes that Demosthenes had so carefully laid upon the road. This was not their country, after all—but it was the country of the Acarnanians' barbarian allies, the fleet-footed Amphilochians, and these hunted the fleeing Ambracians through the hills like rabbits. The tale was later told that, with the coming of day, not a few of the despairing Ambracians, seeing Athenian ships sailing north along the coast, flung themselves into the water and swam out to them—not expecting their lives to be spared, but wanting at least to die at the hands of Greeks.

Demosthenes and the Acarnanians set up their trophies, stripped the bodies of the enemy dead, and returned to Amphilochian Argos. To that city there soon came a herald from the Ambracian survivors of Olpae, now safe in Agraean country, to treat for the bodies of those who had been captured and killed during the escape. Witnessing a seemingly limitless thicket of captured arms and armor, the herald could not mask his shock.

"How many of yours did you think we killed?" asked those who received him.

"About two hundred," he answered.

"But there are more than a thousand here."

"So they are not ours?"

"Yes they are, if you fought yesterday at Idomene."

The herald was baffled by the date and the mention of the hill, which was quite some distance from Olpae. "But we didn't fight anybody yesterday; our losses were the day *before* yesterday, on the retreat from Olpae."

"Ah, but *these* are the arms of those we killed *yesterday*, coming to your aid from Ambracia."

Only then did the herald realize that both armies of the Ambracians had been defeated and the one surprised at Idomene nearly wiped out. Thucydides tells us how the exchange ended. The herald "cried out in woe, and was so stunned by the magnitude of the disaster that he departed straight away, his errand of asking for the dead forgotten."[50]

"This was the greatest disaster to befall a Greek city in the span of two days during the entire war," observes Thucydides somberly. The number of dead he does not record, lest, he says, his reader scoff at him for lying. Scythed, scythed low, was the manhood of Ambracia. The colony of Corinth was now forced to make peace with the Acarnanians, who had vetoed Demosthenes' suggestion that the allies march on Ambracia immediately, preferring an independent but weak Ambracia as a neighbor to a possession of strong Athens. So poor was Ambracia in men that she had to appeal to her mother city, Corinth, for a garrison. Peace was followed by an alliance for one hundred years between Ambracia, Amphilochian Argos, and the Acarnanians—an alliance whose equal and reciprocal terms Thucydides lovingly outlines. The terms show—as no Greek reader would have to be told—that proud Ambracia had been forced to admit the equality in rank of Amphilochian Argos, long the punching bag of the northwest and previously Ambracia's subject, and also of the ridiculous, sling-wielding Acarnanians, those sword-carrying yokels who did not even live the life of the city. Such was the degradation of Ambracia.[51]

After so great a victory, Demosthenes could at last safely go home to Athens without fearing punishment for his earlier defeat. In gratitude the Acarnanians gave to Athens a third of the captured war gear (although the city's share of the loot was later lost on the way home around the Peloponnese), and the Athenian commander himself made his triumphant return to Attica accompanied by three hundred other panoplies of arms, taken from the enemy dead, which the Acarnanians gave him in person. These he dedicated to the gods of Athens. An Athenian inscription hints that the other Athenian spoils of these northwestern victories may have been sold and the proceeds spent on two golden statues of the goddess Victory.[52]

Well might the Athenians celebrate and thank their gods. For despite Demosthenes' early disaster in Aetolia at the hands of Sparta's allies, the year had been one of successes for Athens. The founding of Heraclea in Trachis already hints that the new Athenian strategy of embarrassing Sparta by more vigorous depredations upon her allies, however far-flung, was working: the Spartans were embarrassed by Melos and Syracuse and perhaps by the Athenian incursion into Boeotia as well. But this most recent humiliation was far worse: for the first time in the long war, a land force containing many Peloponnesians and led by Spartans had met in hoplite battle a land force containing Athenians led by an Athenian—and the Athenians had won. Perhaps there were only a handful of true Spartans or true Athenians at the battle; perhaps Demosthenes had won by a dishonorable ruse. Yet, the fact remained. Certainly the capture of Plataea by the Peloponnesians in the previous year had been avenged, and over-avenged: the new strategy of the Athenians, their new unconstrained shaming of the Spartans, was working, and the Athenians were again pulling further ahead in the war over rank.

The northwestern campaign extended the fighting of 426 BC long into the fall. It may have been but a few weeks after the triumphant return of Demosthenes to Athens that the rites of the Lenaea came upon the city. And so the dignified thanks of the Athenians to the stern gods of their city and the solemnity of hymns and dedications gave way to a festival of flatulence. For at this late-February carnival of the wine god Dionysus, comedies were performed, and Athenian comedy was a maelstrom of fart, belch, and anatomically exacting buggery jokes. First prize in the spring of 425 BC was won by the *Acharnians*, the earliest of Aristophanes' plays to survive.

The main character in the *Acharnians*, a war-weary Athenian farmer named Dicaeopolis, "Chastiser of the City," goes to the Athenian assembly, hoping to hear proposals for peace with Sparta. But the only speaker who advocates peace is frog-marched away, and the assembly is occupied instead by the report of a lengthy and comfortable embassy to Persia. "They *made* us drink unmixed wine from cups of glass and gold!" protest the envoys, who have also brought back a Persian ambassador bearing, they allege, promises of treasure for Athens. But no: "No gold for you, you gaping-assed Ionian!" he says. And one of his accompanying eunuchs turns out to be an Athenian imposter, discovered only because, in a moment of lewd absentmindedness, he had shaved his buttocks rather than his face.[53]

Frustrated by the operations of democracy, Dicaeopolis makes a private treaty with the Spartans, but his messenger returns chased by the play's chorus, the very Acharnians of the title. These doughty dotards from the largest country town in Attica see treason in a treaty and splutter with rage at the damage the Peloponnesians have done to their crops, crying out for revenge. They begin to pelt Dicaeopolis with stones—"throw! throw! throw! throw!"—but he saves his hide by taking hostage a basket of charcoal and threatening it with a knife, for—ho! ho!—the Acharnians are charcoal burners by trade and "that basket is a fellow-villager" (the sort of feeble jest one might once have made, say, with a can of beans in Boston or a scuttle of coal in Newcastle).[54]

Before Dicaeopolis pleads his case to the Acharnians, he borrows from the playwright Euripides a pitiful costume and a great number of beggarly props—a stick, a basket, a broken cup, a bottle, rotten greens for the basket—so desperate is Euripides to get rid of him. "What rents of garments seeketh the man? The filthsome robings that Bellerophon the crooked wore?" Euripides is made to ask, in tragic fustian that mocks his own style. Attired finally as a pathetic beggar, Dicaeopolis addresses the Acharnians somewhat gingerly to justify the Spartans' going to war, reminding them that it was the Athenians ("It was our men—I don't say the city! Remember, I don't say the city!") who started the chain of slights and revenges that led to war. Some of the Acharnians are convinced, while others continue to threaten. But then Dicaeopolis converts them wholly to his side by pointing out that the profits of the war, the luxurious embassies in particular, go to but a few (like his neighbor, the general Lamachus) and never to humble men like himself—nor, for that matter, to the Acharnians in the chorus.[55]

Having reconciled the Acharnians to his private peace, Dicaeopolis then sets up a private market in which to buy himself the delicacies the war has denied to Attica. First, there are piglets from Megara—actually the seller's daughters, so hungry are the relentlessly ravaged Megarians, "and the meat of these piglets is delicious when skewered on a spit" (ho! ho!). Then a merchant from Boeotia enters accompanied by pipers who (for reasons obscure to scholars but naturally of acute interest) are playing a jaunty air called "The Dog's Asshole." The merchant has fowls to sell, and hares and tasty moles, and, best of all, toothsome Copaïc eels.[56]

Now Dicaeopolis and his family regale themselves, and he grandly dismisses the petitions of those who wish a share of his imported delicacies or even a single drop of his peace, including a wretched herdsman whose oxen have been rustled over the northern border of Attica by the Boeotians. But to one young beauty, a bride, he does give a small bottleful of peace so that her new husband will not be called away to war: whenever an army is enrolled, she is to rub some peace on his virility. Then Dicae-opolis is invited to a feast at the house of the priest of Dionysus, for which he makes greedy preparations ("bring me my sausage!"), even as his next-door neighbor, the general Lamachus, makes his own preparations ("bring me my spear!") to chase Boeotian raiders in the snow. "Fare-thee-well on your campaigns twain! But how unlike the paths you'll go," says the cho-rus with that witlessness to which choruses were prone, "he'll drink wear-ing a garland, and you'll stand guard and freeze! He'll lie with a blooming lass, having his Big One squeezed!" Finally Lamachus returns home, in-jured from the war—"Oh ah! Oh ah!" he moans—while Dicaeopolis re-turns drunk from his party, fondling two girls—"Ooh aah! Ooh aah!"[57]

To the modern reader, altogether too used to the axe grinding of mod-ern political drama, a play that harps so relentlessly on the miseries of war and the joys of peace must seem like a plea for Athens to make peace with Sparta. But when the chorus turns to the audience to speak for the poet himself, Aristophanes turns out to be quite against making a treaty with Sparta. Indeed, insofar as the play offers a vision of the state of opin-ion at Athens, that opinion was ardently in favor of continuing the fight: that is why Dicaeopolis has to make a private peace in order to remove himself from the fighting, and why he is in such danger of being thrashed by his countrymen. Dicaeopolis himself is war weary, certainly, but even his is a strangely triumphant war weariness: he mocks the Megarians, for instance, whom the Athenians have reduced to starvation.[58]

No, the war weariness of Athens was well mixed with a stern determi-nation to see the war through to victory. Nor should this surprise: a na-tional willingness to abandon a war being won is even in our society a very recent decadence. The Athenians of early 425 BC thought they were win-ning the war. Fighting might be miserable, but giving up while ahead was unthinkable.[59]

VII

AS HONORABLE AS
CIRCUMSTANCES PERMIT, 425 BC

LIKE A RELATION ABANDONED IN the pain ward of a distant, squalid hospital, Corcyra suffered on. The mutual slaughter of democrat and oligarch in 427 BC had not ended the agony of that tortured isle. During the bloody turmoil in which Athens' friends the democrats had seized control of the city, some five hundred of the oligarchic faction had escaped to the mainland, seized forts, and made themselves masters of the Corcyrean territory there. Their confidence waxing, they had begun to cross back over to the island of their birth in boats and to prey upon the rustics, preventing them from working the fields: so famine now held the city in its implacable grasp. To Sparta and Corinth the oligarchs had sent messengers, begging for another expedition to help them recover their homeland.

No immediate help was forthcoming from the Peloponnese, and so the oligarchs hired a hundred barbarian mercenaries and crossed over to the island, establishing posts in its mountainous north. Perhaps the democrats in the city saw the smoke from the oligarchs' burning boats, their pyres a somber pledge either to conquer or to perish. From their inaccessible strongholds, the oligarchs descended from the hills upon the fields to the south and made themselves lords of the countryside. Upon receiving tidings of these events, the Peloponnesians now calculated that an expedition might swing the balance in the oligarchs' favor and bring Corcyra into friendly hands. And so, during the winter of 426–425 BC, the Peloponnesians fitted out a fleet of sixty galleys to hasten north as soon as the seas turned calm.[1]

The Athenians also came to know of the peril to their democratic allies on Corcyra and the plans of the Spartans to exploit it. So Athens, too, must send a fleet, to arrive before any power sent out of Peloponnese might decide the island's fate. The squadron the Athenians had available was one they had prepared for Sicily that winter: forty ships to add to the twenty that had been fighting there these last two years, with varying success. Athens' allies in Sicily had warned her that Syracuse and her minions were getting together a fleet of their own and that a larger force was needed to contain them.[2]

If Athens was glad to have a chance to help her Sicilian friends, she was also eager to put more men out upon the sea. A Sicilian expedition afforded her a good opportunity to practice her fleet, which had seen little actual action thus far in the war. With Pericles' program of peacetime training suspended for reasons of economy during the war and the Athenians sending out smaller fleets on expeditions than they had in the war's first two years, the Athenians evidently felt that their body of skilled rowers was diminishing. The Athenians, too, had not yet been involved in a major fleet action in this war. Such sea battles as there had been were fought by diminutive squadrons of Athenians, however many the Peloponnesian ships involved. Thus, by this time many more Peloponnesian crews than Athenian had actually taken part in a sea battle, and the Athenians may well have worried that their fleet was losing its edge. If the Sicily-bound fleet could find an educational sea battle in the west, that would be all to the good; but even if not, the novices would certainly learn to row.[3]

The luxury of sending a fleet of forty ships across the Adriatic, with simple training as part of their mission, also confirms that Athens had, by the spring of 425 BC, solved the financial problems that had troubled her so deeply in 428 BC. Athens had, of course, sent out greater fleets than this during the war, but only for short periods: never more than three months. Squadrons intended to be away for longer periods were small, never more than twenty ships. But the length of a mission to the west was impossible to predict, and its being sent shows that Athens must now have felt able to support not merely the squadron of twenty ships that had been fighting in the west in 427 BC but a fleet of sixty ships on a distant mission of indefinite duration.

The campaign of 425 BC began in what had become the conventional way, when the Peloponnesians marched into Attica to ravage, King Agis, son of Archidamus, leading them. The previous year the gods had forbidden this expedition with their earthquakes, and as the Spartan fell steadily further behind in the war of rank, every year there was more to avenge. In 426 BC not only had Sparta's colony Melos been attacked by the Athenians, but the Peloponnesians had endured the exquisite humiliation of losing a land battle in the northwest to them as well.[4]

In addition to launching and anticipating this vengeful invasion, both sides knew that they had to rush to bleeding Corcyra. And so, at much the same moment as Agis marched into Attica, the Peloponnesian fleet of sixty triremes set sail, and the Athenian fleet of forty departed from the Piraeus. The Athenians were led by Eurymedon, who had frightened the Peloponnesians away from Corcyra in 427 BC, and a colleague—but the fleet also car-

MAP 7.1 The Pylos Campaign, 425 BC

ried Demosthenes, the unlikely hero of the previous year's campaigning in the northwest. Although not an elected general, Demosthenes had been given the power to use the fleet to raid as it passed along the Peloponnesian coastline. This unusual mandate was likely granted before the exigency of Corcyra became known—when the fleet's mission was merely a leisurely cruise to Sicily—but was nevertheless a logical extension of the new Athenian policy of unrestrained shaming of the Spartans.[5]

Off the southwestern tip of the Peloponnese, Demosthenes attempted to exercise his authority, urging the Athenians generals to put in at the desert promontory of Pylos, on the Messenian coast of the Peloponnese, and launch a raid from there. The generals flatly refused. Corcyra could not wait: they had just received word that the Peloponnesians were already there. The generals may also have just been informed of a gloomy turn of events in the west: Messana, the city perched on the Sicilian shore across the strait from Italy—and an ally whose defection from Syracuse had been the great Athenian success of the previous year—had, it seemed, defected back to the Syracusans. Meanwhile, on the Italian side of the strait, Syracuse's Locrian allies had invaded the territory of Athens' ally Rhegium. The generals knew that their fleet must hurry before the situation in Sicily became worse yet.[6]

There the dispute between the Athenians might have stood, the fleet's oarlocks groaning in harmony with the frustrated grinding of Demosthenes' teeth, had not a storm arisen—winter's storms stayed unusually late this year, Thucydides says—and forced the Athenian fleet into Pylos anyway. Here the nearly three-mile-long island of Sphacteria, the Isle of Slaughter, sunders from the Ionian Sea the vast half-moon of Navarino Bay, which is the only good harbor in the southwestern Peloponnese. A narrow but navigable strait of some four hundred and fifty feet divides Sphacteria island from the rocky promontory of Pylos to its north, and a much broader strait of some four thousand feet separates the southern end of the island from the continent.[7]

Now, as the storm raged out to sea, the rowers of Athens wandered the Messenian foreshore. But Demosthenes had a plan to beguile their idleness: he wanted to fortify the headland of Pylos. So far as we can make out, this had been his original plan: he would sail with the Sicily-bound fleet to Naupactus and there pick up enough Messenians and tools—no tools had been carried from Athens—to establish a fort at Pylos. This would serve as a base with a good harbor for raiding the interior of Messenia. Perhaps reports of the oligarchs on Corcyra issuing forth from their hill castle—the very oligarchs from whom the Athenian fleet was ordered to rescue Corcyra—gave Demosthenes the idea.[8]

The Athenian generals resisted Demosthenes' suggestion, jokingly pointing out that there were plenty of other desert headlands in the Peloponnese if Demosthenes wanted to waste the treasure of Athens fortifying them. The generals, after all, were in a hurry to reach Corcyra and then Sicily; surely this was more urgent than indulging one ex-commander's strategic fancies. It is clear that Demosthenes was operating under no explicit directives from home to undertake such a fortification. No surprise: for to fortify Pylos and garrison it with Messenians would be to create another Plataea, a place to whose protection the Athenians would be committed in honor but that, given its location, they could not easily rescue. Unlike Plataea, of course, Py-

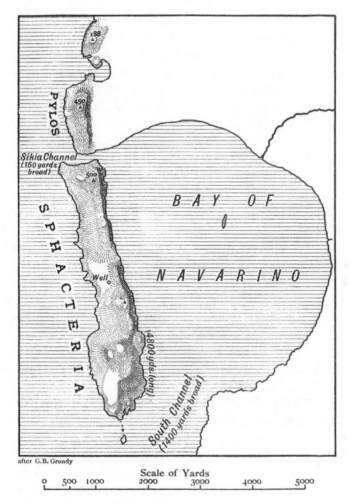

MAP 7.2 Navarino Bay, with Pylos and Sphacteria

los lay on the coast, but that coast was a distant one, and when the tempests of winter sent triremes to sleep in their sheds, Pylos would be isolated. If the little fort survived there, it would be as a besieged speck. And if it were lost to the Spartans, the loss would be a humiliation. Little wonder the Athenian generals said no.[9]

Yet while the generals of the Athenians did not want to waste time at Pylos, they had little choice. The winds did not slacken; nor did the waves cease hurling themselves against the headland. Eventually, generals and rowers alike realized that hurrying to Corcyra was the least of their worries: they were in peril of losing their very lives in the bet Athens had made by sending them into the Ionian Sea so early in the season. Forty ships carried only four hundred hoplites; soon enough the Spartans would arrive with a larger force than that, even if the better part of the Peloponnesian army stayed behind in Attica to carry on with their ravaging. The Athenians were struck with well-justified terror. "An impulse fell upon the inactive soldiers to surround and fortify the place," writes Thucydides. "In every way they hastened to antici-pate the Lacedaemonians by completing the fortification of the most vul-nerable points." With bleeding hands—for they had no proper tools—the Athenians began to pile up rocks at the accessible points in the bluff, and great clods of dirt and clay they carried stooping on their backs.[10]

Over six days the Athenians managed to fortify the promontory at Pylos, preserved from immediate attack by good fortune, for the Lacedaemonians were celebrating a festival at home. By the time the fort was completed, the seas had calmed enough for the generals to feel confident in departing for Corcyra. But they left Demosthenes with five ships at Pylos; he had presum-ably invoked his special commission and claimed the five ships on the grounds that he planned to raid out of the fort. Likely the generals expected, as Thucydides says the Spartans did, too, that Demosthenes would evacuate the promontory as soon as the Lacedaemonians approached. But Demos-thenes was of no mind to abandon his new stronghold. If the gods had al-lowed him to put his plan for Pylos into action before he had intended, that was all the more reason to carry it through. And so, rather than heading to Naupactus himself to fetch his Messenian friends, he sent for them—as many as could leave on an instant—to join him where he was, and bade them to bring any hoplite equipment they could lay hands upon, for he pur-posed to arm the rowers of his five ships as well.[11]

At Sparta, where the gods were occupying the people's first attentions, the Athenian landing at Pylos was received with indifference, dismissed as merely a more extended instance of the tit-for-tat raiding the Lacedaemoni-ans had suffered many times before. But when the Pylos fortification was re-ported to Agis and the army in Attica, they interpreted it quite differently. Agis and those with him saw in this fortification a profound danger to the safety of Sparta, what in our own embattled times would be called an "exis-tential" threat. An Athenian station in Messenia, Agis feared, might animate the menace that Spartans dreaded most: a desperate uprising of the helots, as had happened after the earthquake forty years before. Agis feared, in other words, a revolution in the nature of the war, an escalation from a war over rank to a war over existence. And his alarm was probably prompted in part by the shift in Athenian strategy the year before, in 426 BC. Athens' de-parture from Pericles' policy of rigorously tit-for-tat revenge upon Sparta made the Athenians suddenly seem far less predictable and potentially far more dangerous. In his fear, however, Agis certainly overestimated the ambi-tions of the Athenians and probably even the hopes of Demosthenes himself.

To Demosthenes and the Athenians, the war was still about shaming their rivals, not eradicating them, and the fort at Pylos was merely an additional means to that end.[12]

The Athenians were still fighting, and indeed winning, a war over rank. Ravaging and raiding were parts of that war, as were helping friends and harming enemies, both by fighting and by guile. But inciting other men's slaves to revolt played no role in the calculus of rank. Who, after all, would wish to have it known that he could not win a war without the help of rebellious slaves? Such a victory was hardly likely to vindicate the honor of freeborn Greeks. Indeed, Thucydides used the Corcyrean factions' courting of slaves during the civil war there to signal just how subhuman that conflict had become and to show that honor was meaningless to the combatants. Had the Athenians intended to threaten the existence of Sparta, they could have set forts around the Peloponnese in the first year of the war, teasing the helots with lofty promises. If they did not do so, it was not because they lacked the ability or could not grasp the idea: it was because they were fighting the war to an entirely different purpose. The importance of raiding was chiefly symbolic, and where rank was concerned, the Athenians saw no advantage to raiding from fortifications on the coast. The risk of loss and disgrace—in the event that they were expelled from a place that they had fortified—was simply too great.[13]

All these things were perhaps understood at Sparta itself, where the leaders were confident that the nature of the war had not changed. But King Agis did not feel that he could take the risk that the helots might rise, with or without active Athenian encouragement. So, after only fifteen days in Attica, Agis turned his army around and began the march back to Sparta. The withdrawal was a relief to his troops, who were running short of food; the seasons had not cooperated with the Peloponnesians' plans, for the grain of Attica was not yet ripe, preventing the Peloponnesians from supporting themselves by devouring what they did not destroy. Besides, it was stormy—presumably they suffered the same bad weather that drove the Athenian fleet into Pylos—and the Peloponnesian soldiers were wretched.[14]

When Agis' returning soldiers reached the Peloponnese, they were dismissed, but Sparta's allies were instructed to assemble fresh contingents and hurry them to Pylos. A summons was also sent to the Peloponnesian fleet, which had reached Corcyra and had set to work helping the oligarchs in beleaguering from the heights the democratic city of the plain.[15]

To the thousand Athenians on the point at Pylos, the seaward storms had given way to a no less unnerving landward calm. Where were the Spartans? The silence persisted, growing louder day by day, and was broken only briefly by a pair of boats from Naupactus, bearing forty Messenian hoplites, now finally restored to their homeland; the boats also carried some weapons and a mass of willow branches grabbed up in the emergency for the rowers of the triremes to weave into makeshift shields.[16]

And then, perhaps a week after the Athenian fleet had departed, those waiting on Pylos had their answer: the Lacedaemonian host swarmed over the horizon of the land, and soon thereafter the Peloponnesian fleet from Corcyra speckled the waters off the promontory. By hauling their triremes over the isthmus of Leucas, just as they had in their flight from Corcyra two years before, the crews of the sixty ships had avoided being spotted by the Athenian fleet, which the general Eurymedon had led to friendly Zacynthus, likely to refit his galleys from the damages of the storm that had driven them into Pylos. The Athenians would not be at Zacynthus for much longer; between the coming of doom from the land and death from the sea, Demosthenes had time to send a pair of his ships to Zacynthus to report the peril of his station. We can imagine the fury of the Athenian generals when they received the message: this was precisely what they had warned would happen if Demosthenes fortified Pylos. But soon more cheerful thoughts must have prevailed, for if the Peloponnesian fleet had sailed south, then it was no longer so urgent for the Athenians to get to Corcyra. And perhaps—just perhaps—the Peloponnesians might be enticed into a sea battle.[17]

The Spartans' immediate plan was to attack the fortified promontory of Pylos from both land and sea, while keeping watch for the arrival of the Athenian fleet from Zacynthus. When the Athenian ships arrived, the Peloponnesians hoped to offer them battle only in the narrows to the north and south of long Sphacteria island, which barred most of the mouth of the bay. They hoped that the Athenians, discouraged by the strong position of the Peloponnesians in the straits, would be unwilling to attack and, in the absence of any other large harbors in the area, could be kept away long enough for the Spartans to take Pylos—which they expected to do in a matter of hours, not days.[18]

Reconstructing the details of how the Peloponnesians proposed to block the straits with their ships reveals much not only about this campaign but also about trireme warfare in general. The Peloponnesian fleet was certainly large enough to fill the passages if drawn up in normal Greek battle order, because considerable gaps were necessary between triremes. Estimates that cloistered scholars have sometimes made of the minimum distance between triremes drawn up parallel in order of battle, as low as "4 ft. 3 in. on either side for a safety margin," are quite hilarious to anyone with much familiarity with boats: high-sided ships one hundred and twenty feet long, like triremes, cannot possibly be kept stationary so close together without colliding. Sailboat racers know the same, for they have seen what happens when boats set up for the start of a race too early and must try to hold their positions: they quickly slide into each other. In the real world, wind and waves and currents hit each ship in a line differently, and some ships shelter others, so all drift about in different directions and at different speeds— requiring great separation between ships to avoid collision. Triremes lined up too close together would have met their fate in the sort of pileup that cost the Persians the battle of Salamis or that the Peloponnesians fell victim to—as many of them will have remembered—because of the tactics of Phormio outside the Corinthian Gulf in the third year of the war.[19]

In the real world, therefore, triremes lined up stationary in battle order needed very large gaps between them. One salty sort who has considered the question of how large that gap was suggests that triremes traveled over distances in single file a full trireme length apart (the closest safe distance), and so they naturally turned into line of battle two full lengths apart (say two hundred and forty feet) with a gap of some two hundred feet between their oars. As it happens, there is confirmation of gaps of roughly two hundred feet between triremes in line of battle: when fortifying their harbor at Syracuse in 413 BC, the Athenians anchored merchant ships as obstructions two hundred feet apart, between which Athenian triremes were to retreat if pressed.[20]

If triremes were arrayed two hundred feet apart in normal battle order, the southern passage of Navarino Bay would thus fit a mere sixteen triremes; the rest would form lines behind, probably covering the gaps. Of course, even with such gaps preventing collisions, holding position for hours in a seaway would have been as arduous as it was boring: far better to anchor (the bottom is about two hundred feet deep), ready, of course, to cut in an instant as the enemy approached. We happen to know from elsewhere that Greek triremes might indeed anchor in battle formation. And this habit allows a second estimate of spacing between the triremes in order of battle: for to prevent the triremes at anchor from swinging into each other, at least the hundred-and-twenty-odd-foot length of a trireme would be required as a gap between ships, along with forty more so that the anchor line would not become entangled with the neighboring trireme. Anchored, then, a maximum of twenty-five triremes could safely have formed a line in the passage to the south of Sphacteria.[21]

Ships so spread out would hardly constitute an impenetrable barrier against the Athenians. But the Athenians' advantage in battle depended on their superiority in maneuver. And maneuvering to outflank a fleet so deployed would be impossible. Indeed, lining up in a narrow place was a well-known trireme tactic to prevent being outflanked. And if the Athenians came head on? As Thucydides portrays the great Phormio warning his crews in the Corinthian Gulf in 429 BC, "a confined space is not to the advantage of ships that are fewer but experienced and better sailors." Ramming angles would be bad, and other tactics favored by Athenian captains—the *diekplous* maneuver and circling around individual enemy ships—would be perilous, not least because the Peloponnesians had enough ships to have a second line behind their first, which was the traditional counter to the *diekplous*.[22]

If the Athenians at Pylos persisted in their attack, the result would be a land battle on the sea, like Sybota had been before the war, with opposing ships rafting up to each other and marines fighting across the conjoined decks of the triremes. Such a battle the larger fleet, that of the Peloponnesians, would be likely to win. Besides, Athenians forced overboard at Pylos—their ships being rammed, sunk, or seized—would find no nearby friendly coast to swim to, and damaged ships would have no convenient beach to withdraw upon. The combination of the straits filled with ships and the land bristling with soldiers would have been intimidating indeed, and the Athenians might well decline to attack. The Spartan plan to discourage the Athenian fleet while the Peloponnesians attacked Pylos by land was a sound one.[23]

There was one problem. Although the Spartans controlled the shoreline of Navarino Bay itself, there was some danger of the Athenians' using the long seaward beach of Sphacteria as a makeshift harbor; running west as it runs north, the island provides some protection from the prevailing northerly winds coming down the coast of the Peloponnese, especially if they have some easterly in them. To prevent the Athenians from taking refuge on the far side of Sphacteria, the Spartans stationed a force of hoplites upon the island, along with their helot attendants, while posting others on the shore of the mainland to guard against the Athenians coming to anchor either to the north or south of Navarino Bay.[24]

Their preparations made for a defense against Eurymedon's Athenian fleet, the Spartans now beset Demosthenes' fort at Pylos. Peloponnesian troops came against the Athenian defenses from the landward side—against the bluff the Athenians had labored to make even harder to ascend—even as their commanders ran triremes aground on the promontory behind those defenses, at the one location where a few triremes could easily be brought to land: the western, seaward side of the headland. More Peloponnesian soldiers were aboard these triremes, preparing to leap down and attack the Athenians.[25]

Most of his force, especially his badly equipped rowers, Demosthenes placed on the land wall, but he himself led sixty hoplites (probably nearly all he had) and a few archers to oppose the Peloponnesians attempting to climb down from their ships. The very size of the Peloponnesian fleet—forty-three ships jockeying for position—hampered these craft, as did the reluctance of their captains to run them on the rocks that lined the shore of the promontory. When they did ground, the ships towered thirteen feet above the sand, an alarming jump in armor, and climbing down the boarding ladders in the face of Demosthenes' men took courage as well.[26]

Captain of one of the Peloponnesian ships was brave Brasidas, hero of Methone and indignant advisor to overcautious Alcidas in the Corcyra expedition of 427 BC. Brasidas bellowed to his fellows not to "allow the enemy to fortify himself on our land by being stingy with lumber," and promptly ran his own ship aground as an example. Then, just as he was mounting the landing ladder to descend to the beach, he was struck senseless by an Athenian. He fell backwards into his ship and lost his shield into the sea.[27]

Every time a trireme grounded, Demosthenes' men waded out into the surf to ensure that no one should get down from it alive. Eventually the trireme's hoplites would falter, victims of wounds or exhaustion, and the ship's oarsmen would row it back off the beach, to be replaced by another, cheered on by those waiting their turn. Time and again the bloody scenario was enacted, and time and again Demosthenes' hoplites, in a welter of gore and spume, denied the Peloponnesians the firm footing they needed to win a beachhead.

For one long day and part of the next, the Spartans assailed the fort from land and sea. It seems to have appealed to Thucydides' sense of paradox that the Athenians, famed for their prowess on the sea, were fighting so well on the land, while the Spartans, unbeatable on land, were struggling to attack from the sea. But his mention of this fact was no mere literary flourish, for it helped Thucydides' Greek reader value the fight in the war over rank. Thucydides tells us that "it was the special glory of the continental Spartans that they were superior by land, and of the sea-going Athenians that they were superior with their ships"—but as the combatants were each working outside their area of expertise in this fight, victory would have an exaggerated impact on the rank of the victor. As the battle ground on, and the Spartans made no progress, it became clear just who that paradoxical victor would be.[28]

At length the Spartan attacks dwindled, and the Athenians—proud, relieved, astonished—raised a trophy on their promontory, adorning it with the shield of Brasidas, which they had fished out of the surf. The Spartans had finally despaired of taking the fort by direct, unaided assault—but they were not through with Demosthenes. Instead, they hoped to bring their ships up at another point of the promontory, an easier place to land, where they could ascend with ladders a section of wall the Athenians had built there. The next day they sent some ships away to secure the timber for those ladders.[29]

Busy as they were with preparations for a new attack on Pylos, the Spartans were evidently not expecting the Athenian fleet to arrive soon. But

arrive it did—now fifty ships strong (for nine had been added from Naupactus, and four ships of allied Chios had come late from the Aegean). Just
as the Peloponnesians had foretold, the Athenians were looking for a harbor rather than a fight, but they saw only Peloponnesian hoplites on the
beaches of the mainland and Sphacteria island as they sailed along the
coast. And in the straits to the north and south of Sphacteria, they spotted,
we may guess, the Peloponnesian fleet lined up in order of battle, determined to deny the Athenians entry to the haven of Navarino Bay. For into
such position the Peloponnesians would have hastened at the first sighting
of the triremes of Athens, if they were not already at anchor in the straits.[30]

The Athenians were discouraged—at least for the moment—by the
Peloponnesian array and could no more force a landing against the stout
soldiers on the shore than the Peloponnesians had been able to force a
landing on Pylos. The Spartans' plan was a success. And so the Athenians
drew off to the barren island of Prote, eight miles north of Pylos, whose
harbor was far too small to accommodate all of them and where, we may
assume, they spent an uncomfortable and anxious night.[31]

The next morning the Athenians steered back down to Pylos in search of
a fight, intending (according to Thucydides) to force a sea battle whether
the Peloponnesians sailed out against them into the open sea or stayed to
defend the straits. But the Spartans had decided on battle as well. For rather
than taking up yesterday's blocking positions in the straits, they began to
deploy inside broad Navarino Bay.[32]

Now the Peloponnesians did not want merely to discourage the Athenians; they, too, needed a battle. At the first appearance of the Athenians the
day before, the Peloponnesians had naturally put into action the plan they
had practiced. But the Athenians had returned, and events had overtaken
the Peloponnesians' previous plan: lining up in the straits had been a short-
term tactic of delay, based on the assumption that the Peloponnesians
could use the time gained by warding off the Athenians to capture Pylos
quickly by assault. But now that their assault had failed, to besiege Pylos at
length with a hope of success required that the Athenian fleet instead be
defeated. And it had to be defeated quickly, before the landing of marines
from Athens' ships had a chance to change the balance of the land battle—
for although there was no harbor to protect the Athenian fleet on the seaward coast of Demosthenes' Pylos promontory (a fact Thucydides says the
Spartans considered when they manned the coasts around it), the Athenians could certainly land men and supplies on Pylos' seaward face, where
Brasidas and the Peloponnesians had tried to force their way ashore.[33]

In opting to challenge the Athenians to a sea battle, the Peloponnesians, although they could hardly be confident of victory against such
foes, had some grounds for modest confidence. In 427 BC, off Corcyra,

the Peloponnesian fleet had been victorious over a larger Corcyrean fleet accompanied by some Athenian ships. Over all, the Peloponnesians also had far more recent experience in battle than the Athenians (as, indeed, the Athenians had admitted by sending their fleet to Sicily in search of a nautical education). And at sixty ships, the Peloponnesians slightly outnumbered their enemies—an advantage that would be especially telling in the confines of Navarino Bay, where Athenian maneuverability would be limited and the surrounding shores were held by Spartan troops. If ever there were circumstances in which a sea battle against Athens might be won, surely this was it. The Peloponnesians would yield their blocking positions, then, and array against the Athenians in the interior of Navarino Bay. This was to be a straight-up battle, the kind where honor was most starkly won and lost.

The Peloponnesians' decision to offer honorable battle in Navarino Bay set their thinking along a comfortable channel that would ultimately bear them to their doom. For the Greeks carried in their minds a set of expectations about how such battles would unfold, expectations that, in this case, blinkered the Peloponnesians to danger. "Fair and open" Greek battles were not held by formal appointment, at agreed times—but there was nevertheless usually considerable waiting around before combat. There was no formal rule that both sides should let their opponents form up for battle at leisure or any requirement that fighting be delayed until both sides were ready—but it often happened thus, and on land there was usually even time for the opposing generals to give speeches to their armies.[34]

These expectations that a "fair and open battle" would have an unhurried opening, themselves the result of decades of empirical experience in Greek warfare, settled silently over the Peloponnesians like a nighttime snow. Once the Peloponnesians had resolved upon a regular battle in the bay rather than a blocking defense of its entrances—once they had decided to fight on the basis of courage rather than craft—they lost their sense of urgency about putting to sea on the day of the battle. They lapsed, as Greek armies often did, into a sort of competitive tunnel vision, assuming that they knew the limits of behavior between which events would play out; this tunnel vision was why playing tricks on Greek armies was often so easy and so effective. After resolving to do battle, the Peloponnesians assumed that they would have plenty of time to form up for combat before the Athenians attacked.[35]

In the event, the Athenians appear to have sailed into Navarino Bay before the Peloponnesians were ready for them and put them at once to flight, driving them back to the nearby shore, where their crews abandoned their ships. During the pursuit the Athenians rammed many vessels and captured five, including one with its crew; the crews of the other four swam to safety. At the shore, some Peloponnesian ships were still being manned, and these, too, the Athenians rushed in and rammed, lashing to their own ships those whose crews had fled and bearing them as prizes out into the bay. Trying to haul their abandoned triremes up out of harm's way, the Peloponnesian hoplites ran into the surf in their heavy equipment, and a grim tug-of-war ensued as the Athenians tried to tow the ships out into deeper water. Thus a confused and bloody battle broke out between the Peloponnesian soldiers on the land and the Athenians on the ships, a sort of morbid replay, Thucydides noted, of the attempt of the Spartans to land men from triremes at Pylos.[36]

The outcome of the battle in Navarino Bay was an easy and total victory for the Athenians. The Peloponnesians managed to save many of the abandoned ships, drawing them far up the beach, but the damage was done: the Athenians towed away the carcasses of the ships they had rammed, gave back the Peloponnesian dead under truce, and set up their trophy. Now the shield of another Spartan gleamed across to that of Brasidas. The Athenians had won a great triumph, and without losing a ship.[37]

The triumph of the Athenians was no mere watery one. On Sphacteria island, as the Athenians had seen the day before when they sought to land there, was an outpost of Lacedaemonian hoplites. After their victory in the bay, Athenian ships quickly began to circle the island of Sphacteria like barracudas to ensure that none of those hoplites were borne away. The full value of their prize the Athenians perhaps only in time came to realize. Of the four hundred and twenty hoplites on the island, perhaps one hundred and seventy were full Spartan citizens, the rest being members of the classes living in Laconia that fell between full Spartans and the despised helots. And these one hundred and seventy Spartans constituted perhaps one fifteenth of the entire male Spartan citizenry of military age: were the same proportion applied to the contemporary United States, the number would be over four million. And among these soldiers, moreover, were members of Sparta's highest and most influential families.[38]

The isolation of the Spartan hoplites on Sphacteria changed the course of the war. When their predicament was reported at Sparta, Thucydides says, the Spartan authorities rushed to the scene and concluded that the men could not be rescued. And so a herald was sent into the Athenian fort and there, beneath the glinting shield of Brasidas, begged the Athenians for a truce in order that Sparta might send to Athens proposals for a lasting peace. Concern for the men on the island was no doubt their paramount motivation, but the Spartans had other reasons to seek a treaty. There would have been a growing sense that the Spartans were not likely to dislodge the Athenians from Pylos—a stronghold that some, like Agis, might have considered a threat to the very existence of Sparta—as well as a sense that the Spartans were only falling farther behind in the war of rank (Melos, then a land battle in the northwest lost in the previous year, and now trophies raised against them in Messenia for defeats both on land and on sea). Were Athens to agree to a peace on the basis of equality in rank, that would certainly be better than the Lacedaemonians' performance in the war merited.[39]

The Athenian generals granted the Spartans their truce, but on the harshest of terms: the Spartans were to surrender, empty, all their triremes in Navarino Bay, and indeed all their warships in Laconia, for the duration of the truce, and they were to cease attacking Pylos. In exchange, the Athenians would neither land on Sphacteria nor attack the Peloponnesians gathered around the bay. Under Athenian watch, the Spartans might send rations to the soldiers on Sphacteria and half shares to their attendants, but they were not otherwise to approach the island. Sparta's envoys were to be conveyed by the Athenians to and from Athens, where their proposals for peace would be heard. When the envoys returned, the Athenians were to return the Peloponnesian triremes in the condition in which they had received them, and the truce would expire unless a lasting peace had been reached.[40]

The terms of this truce betray how desperate to achieve a settlement the Spartans were, but their agreement to hand over their Navarino Bay fleet was not a very dire concession. The ships the Spartans surrendered had been pulled up high on shore in the bay and were little better than driftwood so long as the Athenians were triumphant at sea. If, moreover, the Athenians refused to return the ships on some pretext, the Spartans would gain as firmer allies the gods of their oaths (a welcome change, as the Spartans must have been puzzling how they had offended the gods for them to have granted the Athenians such victories), and the world would know the Athenians as oath breakers: hardly a bad exchange, in the currencies of divine wrath and honor among men, for ships the Spartans already counted as lost.

The downcast envoys of Lacedaemon were delivered to a delighted and wondering Athens. Thucydides gives the Spartan ambassadors a speech that he sets in the Athenian assembly, a speech so unlaconic in its length and the intricacy of its argument, so sententiously moralizing, and so obviously a rehearsal of what the Athenians already knew, that Thucydides himself seems to have been embarrassed by it, for he prefaces the speech by having the Spartan speakers apologize for speaking in such a strain. Rarely in reading a Thucydidean speech does the reader feel so little of the shouting assembly of the Athenian democracy and so much of the calm study of the historian, in the company of his friendly circle of abstract nouns.[41]

The speech of the Spartan envoys at Athens is a chance for Thucydides to analyze what he thinks the issues were at this stage of the Ten Years' War. And whatever reasons he assigned to the war's outbreak, Thucydides now makes clear that he thinks the coming of peace would depend on reaching a settlement about the respective rank of the parties. Nowhere else, indeed, does Thucydides have so much to say about the ranking of states and its role in their relations. The Athenians, he allows the Spartans to say, now have the opportunity not only to maintain their strategic position but also to obtain "honor and fame." The Spartans, their envoys say, have "the greatest reputation among the Greeks" and are accustomed to give, not ask for, favors. But now they are asking, which is in itself an act of self-abasement. So the Spartans are climbing down from their superiority in rank and making way for the Athenians to ascend. And in exchange the Spartans are to get protection against further loss of honor. For them a treaty with Athens is "as honorable as circumstances permit."[42]

The Athenians, the Spartan envoys says, would have much to gain from making peace with Sparta. They would be elevated in honor by their victory, their undamaged reputation for strength, and their wisdom for deciding to make peace—not to mention the gratitude of the Greeks for putting an end to the war. Moreover, they would finally get what they wanted—for the Spartans would concede that the Athenians were equal to them in rank. From their positions of inferiority, the rest of the Greeks would honor both of them alike. In fact, to guarantee that equality in honor, the Spartans and Athenians should make not just a treaty but an alliance.[43]

The Spartan suggestion of an alliance with Athens may seem strange to us, since the two states had just been fighting an increasingly brutal war, but we should not forget that the relative standing of Greek states was expressed most clearly in terms of alliances—as it had been, for example, just the year before, when Ambracia, denuded of her men, was forced to conclude an equal alliance for a century with the Acarnanians and the Amphilochian Argives—an equal alliance that represented a descent for the Ambracians, just as this alliance the Spartans were now offering would represent a descent for them.[44]

It was revenge that stood in the way of peace, the Spartans said, but that, too, could be overcome if the Athenians—admittedly, by an act of grace—would grant the Spartans an equal peace. Such a concession would not only break the terrible chain of vengeances (unlike an unequal peace, in which the losers would still hunger for revenge) but bind the Spartans to reciprocate not ill but good. (This idea—of granting favors and using the resulting sense of debt as a tool in foreign affairs—was conventional among the Greeks.) On the other hand, were this proposal to be rejected and the Athenians to cause further humiliation to the Spartans (by killing the men on the island, that is), no debt for favors would exist, but rather an implacable debt of revenge, Spartan hatred for Athens that would be eternal.[45]

A Spartan peace offer stipulating equality of rank between Athens and Sparta would at one time have been sure to end the war. Certainly it was an offer that Pericles would have accepted: to him the war was all about making the Spartans admit the equality of Athens—precisely what the Spartans were finally doing. And, as Thucydides observes, the Spartans expected the Athenians to accept: they were, after all, giving the Athenians what they thought Athens wanted. Thucydides has little to say about the specifics of the Spartan offer: the Spartans ask for nothing more in the speech itself than the recovery of the men on the island. Thucydides is trying to convey that any territorial arrangements were but secondary to the politics of pride—and that, for the first time, Sparta was prepared to cry to the world that Athens was her equal.[46]

We puzzle at the Spartan offer because it makes no sense to us. The rank, the *timē*, of a Greek state was a summation of the massed opinion of the Greeks. But the Spartans proposed to grant the Athenians equality, as if giving them a trinket. One city was offering to bestow fame on another city; one entity proposed to make a commodity out of the esteem of all and give it to another. But the Greeks would never have seen this problem, because they regarded *timē* as a nearly physical thing that, just as it could be taken by violence, could also be given away. "Be king equally with me: take half my *timē*," says one hero in Homer to another. Men and cities that possessed *timē* could grant *timē* in proportion to their possession of it. This the Greeks knew as "honoring," and it was a perfectly normal social function.[47]

It was perfectly natural, then, for two Greek states such as Athens and Sparta mutually to agree on their relative standing, and the opinion of the Greeks at large would adjust itself to match. This process of agreement, rather than warfare itself, was regarded as the surest way of adjusting questions of rank between states. And that is why Greek states were so anxious not only to win in war but to make the losers admit publicly that they had lost and confess to the world the consequences of their defeat for their rank. And that is why Greek states—like Athens in the plague year of 430 BC and Sparta ever since Athens began to win the war of rank in 429 BC—resisted doing exactly that: it is why Athens, even in the depths of her suffering, ultimately refused to admit her inferiority to Sparta, and why Sparta long refused to admit the equality of Athens.

Sad but confident, then, came the Spartan envoys to Athens: sad that they had lost the war to defend their sole possession of supreme rank among the Greeks but confident that, with the concessions they were prepared to make, the war was over. To the Athenian assembly they said their piece (no doubt much pithier than the piece Thucydides wrote for them) and then stepped down from the speaker's platform to listen—perhaps, being Spartans, in some amazement—to the freewheeling debate that followed. And only gradually, as the meeting went on, would they have become aware that many Athenians opposed the peace the Spartans had come to offer. More unsettled still would they have been when they realized that Cleon, the most prominent voice in the assembly, was the leader of the opponents. And finally, they would have been both amazed and appalled when the Athenian democracy, following the counsel of Cleon, rejected the terms the Spartans offered.[48]

The Athenians replied that the Spartans might have peace—but only if Athens were to receive back every single one of the possessions she had given up in the Thirty Years' Peace of 446/445 BC. The Athenians wanted back both of the ports of Megara: Nisaea, on the Saronic Gulf near Athens, and Pegae, on the Corinthian Gulf. They wanted back Troezen, too, on the near coast of the Peloponnese. And they wanted Sparta to allow the men of Achaea in the northern Peloponnese to become the allies of Athens once again.[49]

Athens' demands for these territories did not represent a practical strategic plan to make her safe; the city of Megara itself, for example, was not asked for, and Troezen would be less a bastion of protection than a glass vase of vulnerability. Nor were there any demands about nearby Boeotia—not even for the surrender of sad, heroic Plataea. Athens' demand was instead for a peace perfectly symmetrical to, and perfectly reversing, the Thirty Years' Peace that the Spartans had imposed upon the Athenians in 446/445 BC (which is why Plataea and the city of Megara were not mentioned, since Athens did not give them up in that peace). It was an exquisitely calculated revenge for Sparta's previous victory over Athens two decades before, a demand intended to humiliate the Spartans utterly; it was like Hitler, in 1940, insisting that the defeated French sign the armistice in the very same railway carriage where the defeated Germans had signed the armistice of 1918.[50]

The ambitions of Athens had changed since the death of Pericles. Now, in their hour of victory, the Athenians no longer sought equality in rank with Sparta. They wished the Spartans to admit that they, the Athenians, were first in honor—that Athens, not Sparta, was the *hegemon* of Greece. And the first demonstration of this *hegemonia* was to be that the men on the island could not go free: they must surrender and be brought to Athens. Only once the Spartan soldiers had done the unthinkable, only once they had shamed Sparta, could the Spartans begin to reverse the judgment of

446/445 BC. And after that was done, the men on the island would be granted their liberty—and their lives.[51]

Thucydides was disappointed by the Athenian response: by going beyond Pericles' goal of equality with Sparta, the Athenians, he felt, were foolishly "grasping for more." Yet his own writing tacitly supports the Athenians' attitude. By making the Spartan envoys beg and wheedle in their speech to the Athenians, he presents them as anything but equals; he presents them, rather, as inferiors asking the favor of being treated as equals. To oblige them might have been statesmanship; it might even, as the Spartans insisted, have brought about a firm peace. But it was hardly natural for the Greeks.[52]

Once the assembly had confirmed the terms proposed by Cleon, the Spartan envoys were, in the relaxed way of the democracy, hustled back up upon the speaker's platform to reply to them. This they refused to do, asking instead for a smaller body of Athenians to be appointed to confer with them. The Spartan envoys were not prepared to admit Athens' superiority in rank but hoped that a compromise might yet be reached on the basis of equality and the satisfaction of more down-to-earth demands. While they were willing to adjust their offer, however, they were not prepared to haggle before the entire Athenian assembly, since the new details might include surrendering the land and interests of their allies, and the betrayal of allies is always best done in private.[53]

Cleon inveighed against this request for private discussions—crying out, Thucydides reports, that the Spartans' desire to negotiate in secret indicated their wicked intentions: honest men should be happy to speak in public. But Cleon, however ghastly, had a point; his insistence on public negotiation was only consistent with his hopes for Athens' gains from the war, and Pericles might have insisted on the same, to achieve his lesser goal of equality with Sparta. For the whole point was that Sparta, through her envoys, should abase herself in public. A private conference might settle matters of territory, but it could not settle questions of pride: that required public performance. If they wanted to win peace, in short, the Spartans must grovel in the dust of the Athenian assembly.[54]

Concluding that no satisfactory terms could be obtained from the Athenians and that effective negotiations would be impossible without endangering the loyalty of their allies, the Spartan envoys somberly left the city and walked the long, fortified corridor to Piraeus, from which an Athenian trireme carried them back to Pylos. The embassy to Athens having failed, the Spartans now demanded that the Athenians return the ships they had surrendered under the terms of the truce, but the Athenians offered a series of quibbles and, in the end, refused to comply. To keep the ships perhaps was wrong, but to let them go would have been unsafe. So Athens added sixty more hulks to the veterans' hospital of triremes she already tended in Piraeus and risked the wrath of the gods by breaking her oaths. The Peloponnesians, on the other hand, could once again be confident that the gods, who had become fickle since Apollo had so boldly volunteered to help them at war's beginning, were once again enraged against their oath-breaking foes. The truce between Athens and Sparta had lasted for twenty days.[55]

Had anyone thought to polish the shield of Brasidas decorating the Athenian trophy on Pylos in the summer of 425 BC, it would now have reflected a curious double siege. The Spartans and their allies fruitlessly assailed the fort of Pylos, even as Athenian ships carefully patrolled around the island of Sphacteria to guarantee that no men escaped and no food was carried in to those trapped there, for the provision of agreed-on rations had expired along with the short-lived truce. But the Athenians were hardly less miserable than the Spartans on the island, for with the coming of twenty additional ships to help in the blockade, the Athenians had over fourteen thousand men at Pylos and nowhere for them to live (the size of this fleet, seventy ships, is another indication of Athens' financial recovery). Their ships lay at anchor all around Sphacteria (except on the seaward face when the wind blew stiff and westerly), and all food had to be borne in from faraway allies of Athens. To allay the thirst of such a host, there was but a single sad spring high on the promontory of Pylos and such brackish groundwater as could be found by digging into the beach at the base of the bluffs. There was not even enough room on this meager promontory beach for the crews to cook, so ships had to come into Pylos in rotation, while the crews waiting their turn looked on hungrily from their anchorages. So desperate did they become that they landed on the ends of Sphacteria island to cook their meals, setting guards against the Spartans in the brush.[56]

The Spartans on the island were at once nourished and cheered by the ingenuity of the efforts to bring provisions to them. Freedom and reward were offered to any helot who could breach the blockade, and some sailed in by night with boats crammed with flour, wine, and noble cheeses, successfully running in from seaward when the wind was strong from the west and the Athenians had to take shelter in Navarino Bay. Others swam to the island from the mainland, towing supplies on lengths of line. Eventually these swimmers were noticed and hunted like turtles from boats. And so, "each side kept employing every possible trick," observes Thucydides, "the one to get food in, the other to catch them doing it." This was a competition in *mētis*, like the Peloponnesian attack on Plataea. And, like the resolute Plataeans did for so long, the trapped Spartans gave no signs of capitulation.[57]

As the summer wore on, the Athenians began to realize that the endurance of the men on the island might outlast the sailing season. Given the lack of dock facilities for Athens' triremes and the difficulty of supplying food through the tempests of winter to so considerable a body of men (who were poorly enough fed in the summer), the blockade would have to be abandoned and the trapped Peloponnesians let go.[58]

The Spartans sensed that time was on their side and made no more pleas for peace. Interpreting this as a sign of growing confidence among their enemies, the Athenians began to grumble at Cleon for urging them not to accept the Spartans' offer. Cleon tried to shift the blame first to the messengers coming from Pylos, accusing them of not telling the truth about conditions there, and then to the generals. When the general Nicias was assigned to take a force of reinforcements to Pylos, Cleon baited him before the assembly. "If the generals were men," he said, it would be easy enough to capture the Spartans on the island once and for all. If it's so easy, Nicias responded, why don't you do it? In fact, he would happily resign his command to Cleon so that he could lead the troops himself. Fine, responded Cleon, getting into the spirit of the thing; he would.[59]

This all might have seemed innocent fun, but Nicias meant it. Now Cleon began to wriggle, and Nicias, seeing his advantage, pressed him. The Athenians, who loved a good wrangle, bellowed at Cleon to take the command, and finally he had to accept. He blustered that with but a few reinforcements to the troops already at Pylos, he would kill or capture the Lacedaemonians on Sphacteria within twenty days. The assembly erupted in laughter, but "sensible men" were delighted, said Thucydides, because either way, they won: in twenty days, they would be rid of either the Lacedaemonians on the island or Cleon himself.[60]

Few moments in the history of the Athenian democracy—at least when the Athenians were not busy sentencing Socrates to death, as they would in 399 bc, or executing the generals who had just won them a great battle, as they would in 406 bc—have inspired such scowling from moderns as this. Cleon is bratty, while Nicias, who so often seems the embodiment of statesmanlike gravity, seems willing to endanger any number of Athenian soldiers and sailors simply to embarrass a political opponent. The assembly is feckless. And the "sensible men"—along with Thucydides—chortlingly place their hatred of a single politician before the interests of their country. This story unites two of Thucydides' sincerest dislikes—Cleon and the post-Periclean Athenian democracy—so we may believe as little or as much of the tale as we like. But perhaps the peculiarity of this anecdote derives not so much from Thucydides' hatred of Cleon or his general contempt for democracy as from his love (and that of his intended Greek audience) for a contest of wits. For that is how Thucydides recounts this episode: almost as a mirror for the contest of wits at Sphacteria over the smuggling in of food for the Spartans. In any event, this circus at Athens had very real consequences; Cleon ended up leading a reinforcement of hoplites, peltasts (light troops, mostly javelin-armed, named for the small shields they carried), and four hundred archers, with instructions to attack the island as soon as possible and to capture or kill the men upon it. As his colleague in this mission, Cleon wisely chose the intrepid Demosthenes, who was now a general de jure as well as de facto, either by virtue of having been elected in absentia in an extraordinary midyear election or of finally having succeeded to a generalship to which he been elected back in Athens in the spring, but whose term of office did not begin until mid-summer.[61]

The situation of the men on the island, meanwhile, had become bleaker. Day by day Athenian rowers had been cooking their nervous meals on the island's far reaches. One day there was an especially strong wind: to the dry brush their fire leapt, into the trees the wind lashed the flames, and soon the whole island was alight. Sphacteria's scrubby trees and thorn bushes—well known to anyone who has wandered from a path in Greece—were quickly reduced to gray skeletons, and every step raised a choking cloud of ash. At long last the Athenians could see, and count, the Spartans on the island. There were more of them than Demosthenes had thought, for during the twenty-day truce the Spartans had carried over less food than they were allowed to in order to keep the Athenians guessing. (How the recipients of these short rations regarded this piece of cunning we are left to wonder, especially since the Spartan commander hoarded against a hungry future much of the food that did come over during the truce; but no doubt the helot attendants cheerfully volunteered to go without.)[62]

This accidental fire stirred the confidence of the Athenians. Having had his army driven to slaughter in the trackless woods of Aetolia in the previous year, Demosthenes had naturally been chary of fighting blind in thickets again. But now, with the brush burnt, both friends and enemies could be seen, and the Spartans could no longer fight the Athenians from concealment. Such in war is the dread of the unknown, and such the confidence bred of certainty, that Demosthenes now girded himself more readily against a larger visible enemy than he had against a smaller hidden one.[63]

Demosthenes was already planning his attack on the island when Cleon and his reinforcements sailed up. Now the Athenians sent to the Spartans on the mainland a herald bearing an ultimatum: if they wished to avoid a battle on the island, the men isolated there were to surrender with their arms, to be treated kindly as captives until such time as a general peace

Figure 7.1 Hoplite and light-armed soldier throwing a stone

could be agreed. The Spartans refused. They expected their men on the island to hold out or to die there with Spartan valor. Besides, an Athenian ultimatum proved that the Athenians were becoming desperate, fearing the change of seasons and the storms of autumn. The Athenians might be bluffing. Hopefully would the Spartans have recited to each other Hesiod's verses, which closed the season of safe sailing fifty days after the summer solstice, in mid-August, for that deadline was close if not already past.[64]

One day passed after the Athenian ultimatum. Then eight hundred Athenians, all heavy-armed with spears, shields, and helmets, landed by night on the southern end of Sphacteria. Rushing the watch post there, they killed thirty Spartans as they lay in their blankets or fumbled in the dark for their weapons. Then, at dawn, the rest of the Athenian host landed: the trusty Messenians, eight hundred archers, eight hundred javelin throwers, and more than seventy-five hundred rowers from the Athenian fleet—all but those who plied the lowest bank of oars, the minimum required to move the ships. The rowers, although armed with no more than knives and cooking spits, could make ready use of the countless rocks offered by the island's blighted hillsides.[65]

Soon enough, the main force of the Spartans came forth to fight for the island—only to march into bewilderment. All Spartans were heavy-armed; it was a point of honor with them. But the Athenian heavy-armed would not come up to meet them in combat (craven dogs! the Spartans must have

271

thought). Rather, the Spartan advance brought only swarms of arrows, javelins, and stones hurled from the sides and rear: for Demosthenes divided his masses of light-armed fighters into mobs of around two hundred and instructed them to occupy high points, to swarm around the flanks and rear of the Spartans, and to pelt them from there. The Athenian general had learned much, evidently, from the tactics of the flitting Aetolians, who had defeated him on their native heath. Although easily driven off by Spartan charges, the light-armed Athenian rabble would not take their defeat to heart, and as soon as the Spartan pursuers were recalled to their formation, the throng cheekily turned to pursue them. Surging forward, the Spartans were bombarded from the rear, and when they struck to the right or left, the crowd on that flank would scatter before them, even as the crowd opposite redoubled its hurling. As Euripides sang, imagining the victim of such an attack (perhaps thinking of this very moment),

> They cast stones with their hands:
> he was pelted by a thick hail storm,
> and he used his kit to hold off the attacks,
> turning his shield there! and there! with his hand.
> They couldn't hit him, but a host of missiles flew together,
> arrows, javelins, light, doubled-edged,
> oxen-piercing sacrificial knives:
> you would have seen a grim war-dancer
> warding off the weapons.

Eventually the Spartan counterattacks seemed to flag, as the Lacedaemonians grew tired and discouraged, while the Athenians—their confidence soaring as they discovered that Spartans were not the invincible sons of Ares they had so long feared—ran up with a joyful shout and cast their missiles from just beyond the Spartans' reach. Now the ash the harassers kicked up drifted over the Spartans in blinding clouds, so they could hardly see the men standing next to them.[66]

The Spartans' commanders could not extricate them. Most Greek armies were armed mobs with but one or a handful of lofty commanders leading by example; of all the armies in classical Greece, only the Spartans had what we would call a chain of command: "leaders over leaders," as the Greeks admiringly described it. But in this crisis the Spartan commanders were dying, and the orders of those who remained were drowned out by the noise, so that the Spartan soldiers were frozen in their places. More and more of the Spartans fell, as missiles found gaps in their gear—the Spartan helmet offering but poor protection to the face and neck. Finally, the Lacedaemonian soldiers took command of their own fate, closed their ranks, and retreated in

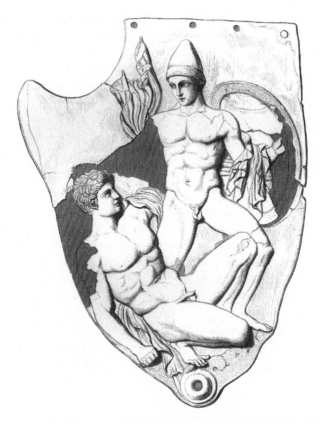

Figure 7.2 A Greek soldier in a *pilos* helmet, the kind that Thucydides says the Spartans wore. Such helmets provided poor protection against missiles.

a bunch to the north end of the island, harried all the way and stumbling over friends and shield mates, shot down and abandoned.[67]

On the northern tip of Sphacteria, in a commanding position difficult of access, stood an ancient, tumbledown fort, a gaunt survivor from the age of heroes. The Spartans had manned the fort with a garrison in case their fighters were forced to withdraw from the rest of the island. Into that fort the Spartan survivors now threw themselves, and from it, for many hours, they repelled the direct attacks of the Athenians, who were elated by the knowledge that they had made Spartans—Spartans!—turn tail and run. Eventually, however, the Athenians' Messenian friends—who hated the Spartans more than anyone—found a way around the back of the fort and led archers to high ground, from which they could ply their bows downward at the Spartans' backs. Picked off one by one, the Spartans began to falter, and as they fell back from the walls, the Athenians seized the entrances. Soon they would be inside the fort, their numbers would tell in the mêlée, and the Spartans would die.[68]

But the generals of the Athenians preferred not to kill the remaining Spartans: instead, they wanted to capture them. A Spartan surrender—unheard of!—would humiliate the Spartans most and give the Athenians the greatest claim to glory. To badger a body of Spartans to extinction with mobs and arrows was no inglorious feat, to be sure, but this was a war of pride, a war of symbols—a war that had broken out precisely because the Spartans had deemed that they were better men than the Athenians. Were the Spartans to die well in combat, a handful against a host, the Spartan legend would only gleam brighter. Thucydides even compares the situation of the Spartans in the fort to that of the Spartan contingent at Thermopylae: the opportunity for a heroic death on Sphacteria, he thought, was the same. If the Spartans died like Spartans should, the reward in honor for the victory on Sphacteria might go to the vanquished rather than the victors. All around Greece the lyres of the poets were being strung to sing the brave deaths of the Lacedaemonians on the Isle of Slaughter.[69]

The Athenians were therefore acutely eager to capture the remaining Spartans rather than kill them. This was, in fact, no less than the third time the Athenians had asked the men on the island to yield themselves. They had demanded it in their reply to the Spartan peace offer and again before they had attacked Sphacteria. In a war without battle lines, it was by just such tokens that winning and losing were gauged.

The Athenians accordingly sent forward a herald to bid the Spartans surrender, and, amazing to say, some of the Spartans grounded their shields and gestured that they were willing to do so. But they were still men under discipline. The Spartan commander had been killed, and his replacement had been left for dead. The surviving third in rank now begged the Athenians to let him consult the Spartans on the mainland as to what he and his soldiers should do. Spartan heralds accordingly crossed from land to the island three times to take messages from the besieged to the Lacedaemonian authorities and to bring back their replies.[70]

The final edict of the Spartan authorities was laconic: "The Lacedaemonians command you to do as you will, but nothing disgraceful." Since anything but death was disgraceful, the authorities were telling their comrades on the island to die. But the message did the men in fort great honor, for it allowed them to die of their own free will: to make, like Achilles in the *Iliad*, the heroic choice of an heroic death. Such a choice had not been given to the Three Hundred at Thermopylae. "Go tell the Spartans that we lie here according to their orders" read their epitaph, for it was under orders that they had died.

The Spartans did their soldiers on Sphacteria the honor of letting them choose the noble way, as well as the manner of their death: they might die fighting, then, or, as Lacedaemonians so often did to save their honor, by their own hands.[71]

Once the edict of the Spartan authorities was delivered, so honorable, so stern, the Spartan survivors gathered within the ruins of the shattered fort somberly to deliberate upon their fate. Four hundred and twenty hoplites had gone to the island, of whom perhaps one hundred and seventy had been full Spartans. Now two hundred and ninety-two warriors remained, of whom one hundred and twenty were citizens of Lacedaemon. The hoplites assembled, they deliberated, they decided, and they conveyed their answer to the waiting Athenians. Their resolution sent a shock wave of surprise rolling through Greece. "Of all the events of this war," writes Thucydides, "this came as the greatest surprise to the Hellenic World." The Spartans surrendered.[72]

The Spartans on Sphacteria surrendered for the same reasons any soldiers might surrender: they were wounded, thirsty, hungry, and exhausted; they stood with one foot set already on the rail of Charon's barge. But they surrendered also for a reason singular to Greeks, for the Athenians had flagrantly breached the odd Greek customs of warfare that made fighting a test of personal excellence. Heavy-armed were supposed to match their courage against other heavy-armed in the close grind of hand-to-hand combat. Archers and javelin throwers were not meant to take a decisive part, let alone stone throwers. "Were the brave men all killed?" one of the Spartan prisoners was taunted. The Spartan shot back that an arrow could hardly tell a hero from a coward.[73]

The battle for Sphacteria had not, in Spartan terms, been a "stand-up battle." It was as worthless for testing excellence as a football game would be in which one team was armed with revolvers. And if winning was not brave, then surely surrender was not cowardly—for the whole structure of honor in warfare had been cast down. Thus perhaps did the Spartans reconcile their capitulation with the authorities' injunction that they do "nothing dishonorable."[74]

But the personal hurt of the Spartans and the trampling of the Greek warrior code by the Athenians were not the only forces at play in the Spartan decision to surrender. A singularly Spartan factor also contributed. For Spartans, far more than other Greeks, looked to be commanded in war, and in the absence of command, forced to form a tiny parliament of the wounded and to debate their own fate, they proved different men from those who, under the certainty of orders, were so dauntless. The Spartan authorities had expected their men to behave like Achilles, to choose a noble death. But Spartans had not brought up their sons to act like Achilles;

they had brought them up to obey orders. Never does the strange contradiction at the heart of Spartan society show so clearly as here: Spartans were expected to live the *Iliad*, but an *Iliad* set in totalitarian Sparta.

The Spartans surrendered on the seventy-second day after the sea battle in Navarino Bay, in the middle of August, in the year 425 BC. To express the astonishment of the Greeks and the humiliation of Sparta, Thucydides pretends to read the minds of the greater Greek nation as they savored every appalling detail. Like mere humans, the Spartans had surrendered because they were *hungry*. They had yielded their very weapons to the Athenians: they had not been disarmed and helpless but had surrendered *with weapons in their hands*. They had not fought until they were killed. The very root of Spartan power, the martial mystique of the Lacedaemonians that the Athenians had both so long feared to confront on the field of battle and feared to encourage by compelling the Spartans to die fighting, was given a mighty yank halfway from the ground by this surrender. And as for the rank of Sparta, the primacy that Athens and Sparta were fighting over? The answer was obvious to any Greek. "The glory of the Lacedaemonians was cast down," wrote a later author, "because of their loss of their men on the island."[75]

Back at Athens, Cleon was honored by vote of the democracy with a front seat at the theater and, like an Olympic victor, awarded meals for life in the Prytaneum, the public dining room for representatives of the democracy who minded the affairs of the state. "Cleon's undertaking, however mad, was fulfilled," reports Thucydides bitterly. "He brought the men back within twenty days, just as he promised."[76]

Cleon did not rejoice alone. In commemoration of the battle on Sphacteria, a bronze statue of Victory was erected on the Acropolis, while the shields captured from the Spartans were displayed in Athens' Painted Stoa alongside pictures of the victories of which Athens was most proud, where they could still be seen nearly six centuries later (indeed, one of them can still be seen in Athens' Agora Museum). Nor was the glory Athens' alone. The Messenians of Naupactus—and now of Messenia as well, because they were to garrison Pylos—commissioned at Olympia a famous statue of Victory by the sculptor Paeonius, set up on a pillar thirty feet high. Much battered, it, too, survives to this day.[77]

THE SPARTAN PRISONERS FROM SPHACTERIA were charily divided among Athens' thirty homebound triremes to avoid their being misplaced in a mass in the event of nautical misadventure; again, Demosthenes was surely remembering what had happened to Athens' share of the

FIGURE 7.3 The *Nike* of Paeonius, commissioned by the Messenians of Naupactus to celebrate the victory over the Spartans at Sphacteria

panoplies from his northwestern campaign of the year before, lost on the journey around the Peloponnese. But the forty ships of Eurymedon's original Corcyra- and Sicily-bound fleet resumed their long-delayed expedition and soon raised the hills of long-suffering Corcyra.[78]

All through the summer the Corcyrean oligarchs, from the safety of their robber-knight castle in the hills, had been descending upon the fields of Corcyra. Alongside the Corcyrean democrats, the Athenians now attacked and took the fort, but the oligarchs got away, fleeing to even higher ground. From temporary safety there they negotiated their surrender—to the Athenians, rather than to their furious countrymen. The oligarchs were to be taken to Athens, where their fate would be decided by the Athenian assembly. In the meantime—for the Athenians to whom they had yielded were, in fact, sailing to Sicily, not home—they were to abide on a small island off the coast of Corcyra (probably not the same one where the oligarchs had been quarantined in 427 BC) under terms of sworn truce, and none should try to escape lest the truce be deemed broken by all of them.[79]

But the democrats on Corcyra did not trust in the consistent cruelty of the Athenian democracy, and the Athenian generals in command of the fleet were heard to grumble that they resented any other Athenian ships carrying the prisoners home and harvesting the glory from a crop the generals had sown. Already they had been cheated out of one victorious homecoming, when Johnny-come-lately reinforcements had carried back to Athens the Spartans captured on Sphacteria. And although Eurymedon and his ships had won the decisive battle in Navarino Bay, their reward was not the homely hearths of Attica, decked for heroes, but a cold cruise west into the doubtful and dangerous fall. The democrats of Corcyra thus guessed that the embittered Athenian generals would enforce the terms of the truce to a nicety and would hardly be inclined—should the oligarchs appear to break the truce—to look into the details with disagreeable curiosity before departing west.[80]

And so it was that the democrats began to play upon the terrors of the oligarchs on their island of confinement, whispering to them that the Athenians were sure to surrender them to their enemies on Corcyra: if any wished to be saved, they must escape. Upon a few the democrats prevailed, and to that few they supplied a truce-breaking boat, and when the fearful few set sail, they were promptly seized and delivered, blazing with apparent guilt, to the Athenians. As expected, the Athenian generals did not pry but simply handed the Corcyrean oligarchs over to their democratic fellows, who now shut them into a building in the city. They were all to be killed, but how to do it in a fashion that at once gratified both public and private vengeance?[81]

The soldiers of the democracy were invited to form two lines, and twenty of the wretched oligarchs, having been brought forth tied together in a coffle, were driven between those lines, flogged lest they inconveniently tarry. Any of the soldiers of the democracy might beat or stab anyone he recognized or against whom he nursed private bile. In such a fashion were three bands of twenty merrily dispatched. But now the remaining oligarchs in the building conceived a suspicion that their comrades were not merely being moved to another place, as they had been told. No more would come forth from the building, and they would attack with their bare hands anyone who tried to come in. They set up a tragic cry to the Athenians, who were witness to all, that if they wished to kill the oligarchs, they should do so themselves rather than rely on sadistic agents.[82]

Although the oligarchs were unarmed, the democrats were reluctant to storm the makeshift prison and confront the desperate captives. Instead, the democrats climbed upon the roof and began to tear holes in it, throwing heavy roof tiles down upon those within and shooting them with arrows. The oligarchs defended themselves from this fusillade as best they could, but not because they expected to survive. No, die they would, but they wanted to die as free men and by their own hands. For even without a temple to defile, self-murder was more monstrous to Greek piety than killing, and so the wrath of the gods might yet bring the oligarchs their revenge. Some thrust the arrows that had been shot at them into their own throats; others hanged themselves on bed cords or strips made from their own clothing. This collaborative slaughter extended to nightfall, and even through the night, as the democrats slowly clawed through more and more of the roof and the oligarchs plied their suicidal innovations. But by morning, all was quiet, and the democrats, entering the fatal building, piled the dead on wagons like logs, lengthwise and crosswise. The women captured in the oligarchs' castle in the hills were sold as slaves. So ended the civil war on Corcyra. The oligarchs had honored the pledge they made to die or conquer when they burned the boats that carried them over to the island. There were none of them left to carry on the fight.[83]

Now the Athenian fleet sailed west for Sicily, but overhung by ill portent. And it may be that on some desolate strand, when the rowers of Athens kindled their cooking fires, a silence fell upon them as their general, Eurymedon, walked his evening round. For Eurymedon had now been the midwife of not one but two godless slaughters on Corcyra. And perhaps even by day his men cringed away from him, fearing the pollution of a curse.[84]

Strange indeed was the doom that the gods turned in their lofty minds for Eurymedon and the Athenian generals who shared his expedition with him. At the beginning of the year, the state of things in the west had seemed critical: Sicilian Messana had defected back to Syracuse, and friendly Italian Rhegium had been invaded by Locri. The Athenians had at first rushed to help—but then the fleet they were sending wore out nearly the entire summer at Pylos. Getting word of the Athenian delay, the men of Syracuse conceived the idea of engaging by sea the Athenians already present in the west. For if they could win a sea battle, the Syracusans could blockade Rhegium entirely—their Locrian allies acting from the land; the Syracusans, from the sea. And if strategic Rhegium on the strait could be made to yield, one of the major forces of the western war would fall silent, and the Athenians would by the same stroke be robbed of any convenient port from which to carry on the conflict in the west. And so the Syracusans brought up their ships, some thirty in number, to Messana. Only a few miles away on the other side of the strait that divided Sicily from Italy, the Athenians lay at anchor at Rhegium, the city infested from the landward side by the soldiers of Locri.[85]

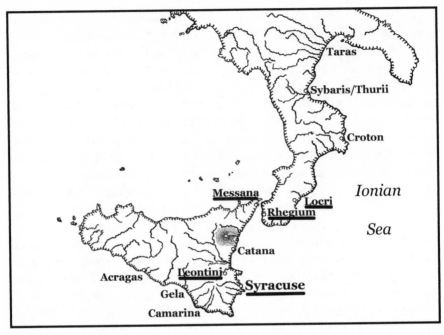

MAP 7.3 The War in the West, 425 BC

Still, when it came, it was the Athenians who forced the sea fight. One day in the afternoon, a fat merchant ship passed down the strait, no doubt bucketing along with the powerful current, which can reach six to eight knots—enough to push backwards a trireme rowing hard against it. The Athenians came out to intercept the speeding bark, the Syracusans and their allies to defend her, and soon both fleets were committed to battle, swirling north in the current. The Athenians, with sixteen ships of their own and eight from Rhegium itself, were somewhat outnumbered. But their fathomless maritime experience—and the local knowledge of the Rhegians—proved far more important than numbers in so treacherous a passage. For not only is the main current in the strait between Italy and Sicily as irregular in its habits as it is powerful in its spate, but it is bounded on either side by rip currents rushing the other way to create violent whirlpools. Soon the Syracusans were put to flight, losing a ship in the process, and night brought an end to the chase.[86]

The Athenian victory delivered Rhegium, for the men of Locri now went away, and the next day the Athenians sailed forth to complete their naval victory over Syracuse. They probably timed their arrival on the enemy shore for slack water, lest they be carried away from an anchored foe by the current. There they found the Syracusan fleet on the Sicilian coast north of Messana, uncrewed but garrisoned by the Syracusan land army, which had marched to join its navy. But the Athenians, trying to tow off some of the enemy ships, succeeded only in losing one of their own when it was reeled in by a grappling hook—what the ancient Greeks with splendid literalness called an "iron hand." Its crew had to jump into the water to save themselves.[87]

The Athenian attack had failed, but it drove the Syracusans to seek better shelter. Immediately the Syracusans drew their fleet back to the safety of Messana, manning their triremes and using the land army to tow the ships south, against the coastal current. By exploiting the main current, which runs opposite the shore current, the Athenians could get in front of the Syracusan tow, then angle in for a ramming attack before the inshore current carried them north beyond their prey. But such unusual conditions gave the advantage to the Syracusans, and when the Athenians approached (no doubt in some confusion), the Syracusan triremes simply slipped their tows, charged, and drove the Athenians off, capturing another ship. The Syracusan fleet finally made it safely to Messana and finished the adventure with one more ship than it had started with.[88]

Messana had become the key to the war in the west. Later that same summer, Messana was bloodily defeated while attacking a Sicilian neighbor, and so the Athenians and their landlocked Sicilian ally Leontini essayed an attack on the weakened city, hoping to reclaim it (the city had briefly defected to the Ionian alliance in 426 BC before reneging a year later). But the men of Leontini were beaten by land, and many slain, and although the Athenians came ashore and won a victory, the attempt to recapture Messana failed. The Athenians sailed back to Rhegium.[89]

It was only after the conclusion of all this campaigning in the west—a whole war's worth crammed into the summer of 425 BC—that Eurymedon and his fleet finally, and very tardily, arrived, still flushed from their successes at Pylos and Corcyra. There was yet some small time left for fighting after their advent, but they appear to have accomplished little before the turn of the seasons suspended the war.[90]

In the next year, 424 BC—we are jumping ahead to complete this story—just as the Athenians began to polish their weapons and caulk their triremes for war, a terrible contagion of peace began to steal over the island of Sicily. First, it was two minor towns, and then a general conference that hammered out a general agreement between the mass of warring parties in both Sicily and southern Italy—Syracuse and Leontini, Rhegium and Locri, the Ionians and the Dorians. The Athenian generals, called in by their allies and invited to join in the treaty, had no choice but to agree. They must have been appalled. For, whatever their reason for being in the west—to practice the fleet in battle, to tamper insolently with the supply of grain to the Peloponnese, to support their allies or bring shame upon the Spartans for their failure to defend theirs—it could hardly be accomplished with their western friends all wandering doe-eyed through the gardens of tranquility.[91]

The Athenian people were certainly furious at the outcome of their western expedition when the western fleet slunk back to Athens in 424 BC. They sentenced two of the fleet's generals to exile and fined Eurymedon, charging that all three had been bribed to depart Sicily. But bribery was frequently the charge lodged to punish unsuccessful generals, when cowardice or treason or impiety did not precisely fit. It was in the parochial interests of Athens, of course, that the war in the west should go on: perhaps the generals' underlying crime, then, was that they had not successfully disrupted the search for peace. Thucydides thinks that the soaring spirits of the Athenians in the wake of the victory at Sphacteria resulted in the unjust conviction of the generals: the Athenians, he says, were now so arrogant that they even expected their generals to accomplish the impossible. But whatever the charges or their causes, the generals certainly had failed in their mission, and the Athenian democracy was never tolerant of generals who failed.[92]

THE CAPTURE OF THE SPARTAN hoplites on Sphacteria in 425 BC opened a new epoch of the Ten Years' War. Conveyed safely back to Athens late that summer, the prisoners were kept there as hostages to safeguard the fields of Attica: for the Spartans were made to know that if the Peloponnesians again invaded Attica, the prisoners would be put to death. And so, for the rest of the Ten Years' War, Athens was secure from invasion.[93]

It is curious that the Spartans allowed themselves to be stymied in this way. When the men were isolated on the island, they were still Spartan warriors, and Sparta's eagerness to recover them is explicable. But after they surrendered to the Athenians, they became something quite different: Spartan cowards. According to the law of Sparta, cowards were stripped of their citizenship, ostracized (in our, rather than the Athenian, sense), beaten in the streets, and (in one tradition) transformed into a cautionary spectacle, required to wear cloaks of rags and tatters and to shave off half their beards, while the other half grew long and cockeyed. Why the Spartans should want such men back at all is a puzzle, and it is doubly so that they should regard their survival as so important as to suspend their main strategy in the war. But Thucydides notes elsewhere that many of them were high-born and well connected, and, in fact, when finally returned to

Sparta, they were apparently not subjected to any immediate punishment. But the Spartans came to fear that, dreading some disgrace, the recovered prisoners might try to overthrow the Lacedaemonian state and so temporarily disenfranchised them as a precaution. And this fear speaks to the sinister power of these men far more than Thucydides' statement that they had important kin. It was not the noble Sparta of Lycurgus that wanted the men back but the real Sparta that so often seemed to behave like a perfectly normal Greek oligarchy.[94]

There was no question that after the surrender of the Spartans on Sphacteria, the Athenians were victors in the war of pride. All that remained was to compel the Spartans to accept a peace that asserted Athenian superiority in rank. So hereafter, Athenian strategy aimed not merely at humiliating Lacedaemon but also at twisting Spartan arms to compel the Spartans to admit the fact of their humiliation. Messenians from Naupactus were settled at Pylos, from which they raided not only into their ancestral homeland of Messenia but even across the mountain into Laconia as well. Perhaps the appearance of former slaves fighting the Spartans gave hope to the helots, for some now began to flee to Pylos, and the Spartans dreaded that those remaining might rise.[95]

The war for honor was over. The Athenians' actions by late 425 BC were no longer the ceremonious raiding for revenge of earlier in the war—for a city should take revenge itself, and here the Athenians were relying on the Messenians to do their work. This was finally the kind of war that the Spartan King Agis had feared when he rushed back from Attica to assail Pylos, war as we today usually think of it: a ruthless conflict to crush an enemy or force him to make a wretched peace. The Athenians had won the contest of rank; now they were fighting to enforce the judgment of the gods.

Still, there was more to Athenian planning than mere coercion of the Spartans. In late August, after the Spartan prisoners were brought back from Pylos, the Athenians made an attack on the territory of Corinth, which abided at the Peloponnesian end of the Isthmus, west of Megara. In this war Athens had frequently fought and defeated Corinthian ships, as well as seized and raided and fought against Corinthian possessions and colonies in the northwest: Sollium, Ambracia, and Leucas. Later in 425 BC the Athenians at Naupactus and the Acarnanians together would also take Anactorium by treachery, a Corinthian town in the north of Acarnania near Leucas. But as far as we can tell, until 425 the Corinthiad itself, like the territory of Boeotia until 426, had been left untouched by the Athenians. The reason for this would have been the same as that behind the long tranquility enjoyed by Thebes: Athens was asserting that Corinth was beneath notice in the contest for honor, unworthy of revenge raiding. It was a shift of

MAP 7.4 Athenian Attack on Corinth and the Argolid Peninsula, 425 BC

Athenian strategy, then, this descent in force upon Corinth's coast on the Saronic Gulf. The expedition was a sizable one as well: eighty ships under the command of Nicias, two thousand Athenian hoplites along with other detachments from several of Athens' Aegean allies, and two hundred cavalry carried in horse transports—the horse transports that we last saw the Athenians using during the raid on the eastern Peloponnese in the second year of the war, providing another example of Athens' return to financial health.[96]

Thucydides does not tell us exactly why the Athenians invaded the Corinthiad in 425 BC. But unlike their previous descents on the Peloponnese, here for the very first time in the war, so far as we know, the Athenians were willing to fight a hoplite battle against a significant Peloponnesian force on Peloponnesian soil. There is no reason to suppose that they were compelled to do so. So whether their plan was a ravaging raid with orders to accept battle if offered or the Athenian instructions had been to challenge the Corinthians to battle, battle must have been regarded as likely, even attractive. Why this new willingness to fight? It was the first sign of a larger new strategy that would guide Athenian action in the next year of the war, and it will

FIGURE 7.4 Detail of Athenian cavalry from the Parthenon Frieze

only become fully clear then. For the moment, however, the reader is urged neither to bear too much in mind, nor wholly to forget, that in (probably) 458 BC, during the war at mid-century, the Athenians had lost a hoplite battle to Corinth on the Peloponnese, when they met at Halieis.[97]

The plan of the Athenians to come against the Corinthiad in 425 BC was betrayed to Corinth by friends at Argos, and so the hoplite forces of the Corinthians—except for her garrisons in distant Leucas and Ambracia and those who dwelt in the furthest recesses of the land—were already gathered at the Isthmus, ready for battle, by the time the Athenians arrived. Leaving half their army to garrison needful places, the Corinthians marched toward the Athenian beachhead. But the Athenians did not withdraw to their ships in the face of this considerable force, as they had before the less numerous Eleans at Pheia in the first year of the war. Instead, they offered stern battle on the beach, the hoplites fighting hand to hand.[98]

This battle of Solygeia—named for a hill nearby, famous in Dorian legend because the sons of Heracles had made camp there—was an unusual

Greek land battle because of its multiple shifts of advantage. First, the Athenian right wing pushed back the Corinthians, who retired behind a stone wall on the slope behind the beach and restoked their shaken courage by flinging rocks down upon the Athenians. Recovering their boldness (a rare event in a Greek battle, where broken men, like crockery, usually stayed that way), the Corinthians charged again, singing their paean. Fighting was renewed on that flank, and when a tardy company reinforced the Corinthians, the Athenians were turned to flight and driven into the shallows. There, wading through the reddening tide, they rallied in their turn and repulsed the Corinthians. Long and bitter was the battle, but eventually the Athenian cavalry (the Corinthians, like most Peloponnesian folk, had none) tipped the scales, and the Corinthians fled. A few months later, in his comedy the *Knights*, Aristophanes would hymn the heroics of the Athenian horsemen at this battle—sort of. For he actually praised the cavalrymen's horses in their place and did not hesitate to suggest that the horses' main achievement—and by extension that of their aristocratic riders—consisted mostly of being willing to force down normal military food rather than the exquisite delicacies to which they were accustomed.[99]

Most of the two hundred and twelve Corinthian casualties at the battle of Solygeia were on the Corinthian right wing, where their general, Lycophron, fell as well. The survivors fled to the high ground beyond the beach, and the Athenians did not pursue them. Instead, they set up their trophy, stripped the Corinthian dead, and took up their own. But then they saw a new army marching upon them from the north—the other half of the Corinthian hoplite force, as well as the older men from Corinth, summoned for the emergency. They had seen the dust of the battle billow toward the sky and were rushing to reinforce their comrades.[100]

The Athenians imagined that these Corinthian reinforcements were an overwhelming force sent from neighboring Peloponnesian states, and so the victors hastened aboard their ships, hauling with them their spoils and their fewer than fifty dead, and put out to sea. But then—crushing disappointment—a head count revealed that exactly two Athenian corpses had been left on the beach in the confusion. And that meant that the Athenians, who had won the battle on the battlefield, were obliged to send a herald to shore and humbly ask for a truce to recover their dead, thereby playing the part of the defeated. And so, by the curious rules of Greek battle, it was the Corinthians who were the victors. But the Athenians sped to take their revenge that same day: outpacing the Corinthian land forces, they rowed to the opposite end of Corinth's coast, where they landed, ravaged the land, and spent the night.[101]

Nothing obliged Thucydides to tell his reader that the Athenians set up their trophy after their victory at Solygeia, so claiming victory, and then had

FIGURE 7.5 Greek cavalryman

to send heralds to apply for a truce to recover the two bodies they had left behind, so admitting defeat. But Thucydides is usually quite fastidious about mentioning to his reader the setting up of trophies and the sending of heralds, if he has described an engagement in any detail. These were symbols of victory and defeat in the war over rank, and Thucydides thought such things worth recording. But Thucydides is also quick to mention occasions when both sides put up trophies, or one side put up a trophy without having won, or (as here in the Corinthiad) the defeated ended up being able to claim victory by a technicality. War made men bad, Thucydides thought, and the cynical manipulation of these venerable tokens, which had deep religious significance, was an aspect of that moral decline. But from such episodes we take away a sense of how fiercely the Greeks cared about such symbols, the participants caring enough to seek them by cheating and observers (like Thucydides) caring enough to comment when the system failed for other reasons, as it did, because of Athenian bad luck, at Solygeia.[102]

Having satisfied themselves against the Corinthians, the next day the Athenians sailed toward the site of the battle they had lost against Corinth in ?458 BC, toward the Argolid peninsula, which was crowded with small allies of Sparta whom the Athenians may not have raided since the second year of the war. They landed and ravaged the coast of Epidaurus, then settled down on Methana, which stuck out from the larger peninsula on a smaller peninsula of its own, with a narrow land bridge to the mainland. This land bridge the Athenians walled off, making for themselves a second, more luxurious Pylos in the country of Sparta's allies, and from here they raided into Troezen, Halieis, and Epidaurus. After fortifying Methana and garrisoning it with troops, the Athenians sailed home. All three places the Athenians raided had fought in the war against Athens in the 450s BC, and Troezen, which had yielded to Athens in that war, then been returned perforce to the Peloponnesians in the Thirty Years' Peace of 446/445 BC, had been demanded back again by the Athenians in response to the Spartan peace proposal earlier in 425 BC. Just as in their descent on the Corinthiad, the Athenians seemed no longer to be fighting this Ten Years' War but to be fighting over again the war at mid-century. They had found an itch, and in their hour of triumph over Sparta, they were scratching it. In the next year, the itch was to become an all-consuming rash.[103]

VIII

THE BRONZE DREAM,
424 BC

T HE SPARTANS WANTED PEACE. Ever since the Athenian capture of
the hoplites on Sphacteria, Sparta had been sending envoys to Athens,
hoping to end the war and recover their men. They were also driven,
Thucydides tells us, by the defection of helots to Pylos and fear of a general helot uprising—which, should it occur, would threaten the very existence of Lacedaemon. Three times after the surrender on Sphacteria did
the Spartans send to treat with Athens, and three times the treaties they
offered were voted down in the Athenian assembly.

The Spartans kept offering the Athenians peace on the basis of equality
in rank, no doubt with different concessions each time, in the hope of finding a winning combination that would appease the Athenians or perhaps
that the simple passage of time would ease Athens' inflexibility. But now
that Sparta's hoplites were prisoners in Attica, the Athenians had a mind
to demand more than they had when the hoplites were merely isolated on
the island—and even then they had wanted a treaty humiliating to Sparta,
with terms implying Athens' outright supremacy in rank. Each time, then,
the envoys returned to Sparta to report that the Athenians still would not
accept terms to which proud Sparta could possibly agree.[1]

The problem, as the Athenians saw it, was Sparta's stiff-necked pride.
The Athenians, after all, had proved their superior rank. Very well: if the
Spartans would not agree that they had lost, perhaps they could be forced
to confess it. The Athenians fixed their eyes on a considerable island that lay
off the southern coast of Laconia, Cythera, which a sage had once told the
Spartans would be better for them sunk under the water than protruding
above it, so obvious a base was it from which to torment Lacedaemon; indeed, Herodotus supposed that the Persians had considered doing just that
when they had invaded Greece earlier in the century. The Athenians had
in fact seized this strategic prize during the earlier war in the 450s BC. But
through this current war, the Athenians had scorned to occupy the island,

MAP 8.1 Athenian Attacks on Cythera, Laconia, and Thyrea, 424 BC

seeing just as much good—and much less risk—in raiding Laconia directly from the sea. Now, however, their purpose was not merely revenge but coercion as well, and so it was time for the Athenians to take Cythera.[2]

In early May 424 BC, the dutiful Athenian general Nicias, having been given one hundred talents of silver by the treasurers of Athena to pay his men, set off for Cythera with two colleagues and a fleet of sixty ships, carrying two thousand Athenian hoplites and some provided by the allies, as well as a handful of cavalry. Landing on the island, Nicias took the city's port with a detachment, then, advancing upon the city itself, fought a battle with its inhabitants. These were Spartans of the inferior class of the *perioeci*, or "livers-around," as opposed to actual Spartan citizens, but their governor and no doubt commander, the Judge of Cythera, was sent out every year from Lacedaemon.[3]

The Cytherans put up a stern defense of the unwalled town but eventually broke and fled to the acropolis, the town's most defensible point. Negotiations ensued, much eased by previous discussions that Nicias had apparently had with the folk of the island. And so, when the men of Cythera surrendered, they were left in possession of their homes and folds, and the Athenians—while taking hostages to ensure Cythera's good conduct and garrisoning her harbor—left the town in the hands of its people and enrolled the island as a tribute-paying subject of the Athenian empire.[4]

Using acquiescent Cythera as a base, Nicias next led his fleet against the coast of Laconia and ravaged for some seven days. The Spartans did not mass their strength to drive the Athenians away or to offer battle but instead yielded the shore and divided their forces into garrisons about the country—not merely on the coast but in the interior, too, far from the marauding Athenians. For their chief fear now was not of the Athenians but of their own subject peoples. Pinned by dread of revolt, the Spartans even formed bodies of horsemen, of whom they enlisted four hundred, and archers, whose cowardly way of fighting made them long unimaginable in hoplite-proud Sparta. The archers, presumably, were not full Spartan citizens, but the cavalrymen may well have been. These arrangements signaled an astonishing loss of nerve for a folk who prided themselves on being the finest infantry in Greece and whose ancestral three-hundred-strong "cavalry" fought on foot around the king.[5]

The Spartans were paralyzed: by fear of their subjects, by dread of a further calamity like Sphacteria, and by widespread failure of initiative and confidence in the wake of the disasters they had already suffered. Each isolated garrison felt outnumbered, and none would come forth when the Athenians approached—except for one, that is, which rushed out to drive away some light-armed Athenians and was in turn driven away itself by the sudden appearance of Athenian hoplites, losing a few men and their arms in flight. And so, for the first time in their history, the Athenians erected in hollow Laconia a trophy celebrating victory over the Spartans. There seemed no end to Lacedaemonian shame.

In their time of fear, the Spartans happened upon an irresistible opportunity to remove the most dangerous of their helots a long way from the imperiled realm of Lacedaemon. In the north, in the Thraceward region, the rebellion of the Chalcidians against Athens still smoldered—these were the cities that had joined the rebellion of Potidaea, and although Athens had recaptured that city, the others still resisted. Sparta was receiving appeals from these Chalcidian rebels and from others in the district who hoped to join them. All were alarmed at what Athens' recent success over Sparta might mean for them. To the pleas of the Chalcidians, shrewd King Perdiccas of Macedon added his whispers as well. Thrace was weeks of marching away from Sparta, sundered from southern Greece by broad Thessaly, with its quarrelsome sun-hatted dynasts and its divided friendships. A march through Thessaly's sun-bleached fields might prove impossible or deadly. No bad destination, then, the Spartans thought, for a body of Spartan helots of military age, who would otherwise be the natural leaders and warriors in any rebellion in Laconia. And if these helots actually managed to reach Thrace and to provide the rebels some assistance against Athens, so much the better.[6]

So it was, then, that when the inevitable Brasidas volunteered to lead north a force of seven hundred helots armed as hoplites and as many Peloponnesians as he could recruit with promises of pay when they arrived, the Spartans jumped at the offer. Should Brasidas make it to Thrace and rekindle the war against Athens in that far world, he might distract the Athenians from Laconia. Or, should his helots die on the way, devoured by wolves or killed by Thessalians, abandoned forlorn and unburied in ditches by the road, well, that would be no bad thing either.[7]

The Spartans had so little confidence in the military prospects of this mission that they did not even assign Brasidas the two Spartan-citizen subordinates who regularly accompanied the Spartan commander of expeditions in order to take command in succession in the event of their chief's demise (as, indeed, had proved necessary at Olpae and on Sphacteria). No, of all the Spartans, brave Brasidas, with his long hair and red cloak, went alone. With his helots jangling in their unaccustomed gear (the law at Sparta was that shields could not even be stored with their handles attached, lest the helots get hold of them), Brasidas hastened to the area of the Isthmus, to recruit the rest of his army from Corinth and Sicyon.[8]

The Athenians withdrew at last to their ships after about seven days of ravaging Laconia, feeling they had made their point. Despite the Spartans' fear, the Athenians seem not to have gone ashore to intrigue with the helots or the *perioeci*. This was, rather, an entirely conventional ravaging raid. But it was not a raid in reprisal for a Peloponnesian invasion of Attica: now that Athens kept the Spartans from Sphacteria as hostages, there would be no more of those. And with the contest over rank already won by Athens, ravaging to establish superiority in rank over Sparta was superfluous. But ravaging Laconia could still bring honor to the Athenians. Greek states, after all, frequently ravaged the land of other states whose inferiority was assumed, not only by the aggressor but often by the victim state itself: Athens' relentless ravaging of sad Megara was probably of this type. Ravaging was driven by anger. It was not limited to relative equals or confined to rival states striving to determine relative rank. Ravaging an inferior could be done to embarrass some more important ally or connection of the lesser city, as Athens had done when ravaging Melos, and as she did whenever she raided Peloponnesian states other than Sparta. Ravaging could be done, too, in the hope of forcing a political settlement (as here and, again, as at Melos). But even in the absence of such motives, ravaging was often done because it added to the honor of the ravager, even if the ravaged was an inferior.

The Greeks preserved from their earliest days a sense that the rank-honor of a man or state could be stripped from a victim and added to that of the vanquisher. In Homer merely killing a foe was not the end of the quest for honor. The custom was to loot the body, stripping it of its armor, and often to vaunt over the corpse, "staking a claim for glory" with boasting words: "carrion birds will drag at you, beating their wings hard about you!" This was a process of sapping glory from the defeated and transferring it to the victor. That is what the Athenians were doing in prostrate Laconia, fashioning for themselves an ever more glorious persona on the wider Hellenic stage while the Spartans looked on.[9]

Like a Homeric hero taunting a dead body, the significance of the labor of ravaging the fields of one's enemy is not immediately obvious. Since ravaging was chiefly symbolic in purpose—largely a matter of *timē*, of rank-honor—we wonder why it was such hard work. The Greeks could have chosen any number of safer, easier ways to symbolize the humiliation of an enemy who would not come out to fight. Failure to accept a challenge to battle was itself a humiliation: it is a puzzle, then, why the aggressor went on from the unmet challenge to ravaging. Ravagers might find some profit in the contents of the houses, to be sure, and there was innocent joy in arson, but when ravaging, most of an army's time was spent in the exhausting and unprofitable work of trampling and burning grain (or harvesting and grinding it for the invaders to eat), tearing down vines, and cutting down trees.

In fact, much of the power of ravaging lay in the strange humanity of Greek cities—in the Greek insistence on regarding their cities as metaphorical men. Cities were subject to the same forms of humiliation and exaltation as men were. Not only Homeric but classical Greeks stripped the war gear off the bodies of the defeated dead as a claim to glory, and while cities did not wear armor, they did have crops to strip and rural houses to plunder. And when a city was captured, as Tanagra was by Athens in ?457 BC, the victor might tear down the actual walls of the settlement to make the metaphorical stripping of the corpse even more vivid.

The imagined humanity of the Greek city, as well as its liability to be stripped like a corpse, also solves another niggling puzzle about Peloponnesian strategy in the war. In 431 BC the Peloponnesians came into Attica with an overwhelming force. The Athenians refused to come out against them and justified their refusal on the grounds that the Peloponnesian force was so large: without the prospect of a fair battle, they argued, there was no dishonor in refusing to fight. The mystery, then, is why the Peloponnesians, eager to establish their superior rank, did not send smaller forces into Attica in subsequent years. For the smaller the force the Peloponnesians sent, the more shame the Athenians would incur by not fighting, and if numbers were equal, the Athenian sense of shame might well have goaded them out to fight a hoplite battle. The answer lies in the fact that ravaging the fields of an enemy was not only a challenge to battle but also a form of harvesting *timē* in its own right, and for that second end, because the geographical extent of the destruction mattered, as many men as possible were needed. The two ways of gaining rank through ravaging suggested different, and potentially contradictory, strategies to ravagers.[10]

Athens' reinvention of herself as a hero state in 424 BC was not limited to ravaging Laconia. Finally quitting the Spartan shore, the Athenian fleet sailed back toward Athens and, rounding Cape Malea, raided a community on Laconia's eastern coast. The fleet then sailed north into the Gulf of Argos and descended upon Thyrea, on the Peloponnesian coast south of Argos, Argos which, although bound by oaths to neutrality in the war, was ever hostile to Sparta. This was hallowed ground for the Spartans, the place where they had prevailed in the Battle of Champions over Argos, in which—so Spartan legend held—three hundred picked men from each city had fought to their mutual destruction, with only a lone Spartan surviving to claim the victory. To attack Thyrea was, then, another humiliating act of vaunting over Sparta's sometime renown.[11]

But there was another reason for the Athenians to attack Thyrea. For at Thyrea dwelt the exiled people of Aegina, those the Athenians had expelled from their island in the first year of the war and whom the Spartans had settled there. Athens might have attacked the Aeginetans at Thyrea at any time but decided to attack them now. This fit into the broader pattern of Athenian activity in late 425 and 424 BC. Aegina, so long a bitter rival and enemy of Athens, had played a large part in the war in the 450s BC, until, in (probably) 457, Athens had conquered her, taken her ships, and engulfed her in the Athenian empire. So Thyrea fits in with Corinth and Troezen and Halieis and Epidaurus: it is as if the Athenians were following a script from the 450s and reopening the war with her enemies from long ago.[12]

Having foreseen the Athenian attack, the Aeginetans of Thyrea were busy building a fort on their shore when the Athenian fleet appeared in the offing. Fleeing to the town itself, a little more than a mile inland, they implored the local Spartan garrison, which had been helping them with the construction, to join them in its defense. But in vain did the Aeginetans appeal to the dauntless spirit of Thermopylae. The Spartans refused to help, being badly outnumbered and dreading being cut off inside the city (Sphacteria, presumably, was much in mind), and instead watched from the safety of high ground nearby. But one Spartan awaited his fate with the Aeginetans: when the Athenians came up from the shore and stormed Thyrea, killing, sacking, and burning, they wounded a Spartan official named Tantalus and took him alive to Athens to join the other Spartan hostages. (In myth, of course, Tantalus served up his son to the gods to eat and so was one of the few illustrious villains forever tormented in Hades, consumed by hunger and thirst, with food and drink ever just out of reach. What can the Spartan's parents have been thinking when they named him?) The Aeginetan survivors of the sack, too, were carried away to Athens, but upon arrival they were executed "because of the old eternal hatred," as Thucydides put it. As far as the Athenians were concerned, it was the 450s again, and they were exercising old grudges.[13]

NEXT ON THE LIST FROM the earlier war was Megara. Athens had continued to invade and ravage Megara's flaxen plain every year, and in recent years not once, but twice. And the Athenians were proud of the destruction they wrought: in his 425 BC play, the *Acharnians*, Aristophanes had cruelly mocked the desperate hunger of the Megarians, portraying one of them as having to sell his own daughters so that he himself could eat. Adding to Megarian misery, in 427 Athens had thought it worthwhile to seize the island of Minoa, right off the harbor of Nisaea, to perfect the blockade of Megara's port on the Saronic Gulf. The contrast between Athens' thrashing of Megara and her indifference to Corinth and Boeotia is striking: Athens had not acted against Boeotia until the sixth year of the war, and not against the Corinthiad until the seventh. The Athenians, then, had for the most part been content to roll up their resentment of those foes into the war against Sparta and therefore to ignore them. Not so Megara: against Megara, Athens treasured an abiding, separate fury.[14]

Megara was troubled as well by home quarrels. For Megara was a democracy—a rare thing in the Spartan alliance—and recently, as the result of civil conflict, some of her people, presumably oligarchs, had been expelled. The Boeotians had settled these exiles at Plataea, after Plataea's capture. Now, in 424 BC, the Megarian exiles had returned to seize Megara's other port, Pegae, on the Gulf of Corinth, at the northern end of the Megarid plain (Mount Geranea dividing the Megarid from Corinth to the

MAP 8.2 Athenian Attack on Megara, 424 BC

west and Mount Cerata separating it from Attica to the east), and in the fashion of the oligarchs of Corcyra, they were now making raids to the south, toward Megara itself.[15]

Doubly wretched, then, were the Megarians, and now many within the city began agitating to recall the exiles and thereby put an end, if not to foreign woe, then at least to the domestic. But the democrats dreaded letting their opponents within the gates—as well they might, had they received any tidings from Corcyra, whose calamitous history theirs seemed to be tracing. And so it was that, driven by fear of their exiled countrymen and now of their city neighbors as well, a number of the Megarian democrats entered into communications with Athens and proposed to betray their own city to the Athenians, thinking an alien tyranny preferable to the embrace of domestic foes. In these negotiations they dealt with the wily veteran Demosthenes, as well as a second Athenian general, the aristocratic Hippocrates, a nephew of Pericles.[16]

Bringing about the defection of Megara to Athens was no simple task. Only a small Megarian cabal was willing to betray their state to Athens for their party interest; the great mass of citizens were indifferent or opposed to the idea of abandoning the Peloponnesians. Indeed, the Peloponnesians had a garrison in Megara's port of Nisaea, exactly intended to ensure the loyalty of Megara, whose fidelity the Spartans had come to doubt. (A cruel irony this, since the Megarians, having suffered the most pain for the Peloponnesian cause, had seen so little help from their allies.)[17]

Any plan to change the allegiance of Megara must cope with these Peloponnesians, driving them off or isolating them in Nisaea. But just as Athens and the Piraeus were joined, so Megara was connected to Nisaea and the sea by a set of long walls, extending about a mile, built for the Megarians by the Athenians themselves in the 450s BC when Megara and Athens had been allies. The conspirators determined that these long walls should first be seized; with the Peloponnesians' route to the city preemptively cut off, it would be easier to bring Megara over.[18]

The plan for capturing the long walls of Megara in 424 BC, already recounted in the adventure that introduced this book, casts a rare light upon the day-to-day experience of the war for those who endured it. A rowboat on a cart was to block the gate and admit the Athenians. The captain of the gate had given the boat permission to come and go because the crew of the boat claimed they were privateering against the Athenians in the Saronic Gulf. So small a craft, of course, can hardly have preyed upon shipping: the gate captain's acceptance of this ruse shows, rather, that it was perfectly normal for two or three men to slip over to Salamis, the closest point of which was but two miles across the water, and slink through the darkness, robbing and murdering Athenians in their houses. This glimpse jibes well with complaints in Aristophanes' *Acharnians* about repeated smash-and-grab raids from over the Boeotian border, as well as the passing mention of Athenian border guards in Thucydides' narrative of this Megarian venture (they were part of the force Demosthenes led against the gate). Taken together, all these details yield a vision of a nasty, dirty, small-scale war, an irregular war of ambush, private plunder, and skullduggery, fought between the combatant states that bordered upon each other or were separated by narrow water—a war carried on quite separately from, and beneath, the stately expeditions of the great powers' armies and fleets.[19]

The Athenian part in the plot illustrates the lessons the Athenians, and Demosthenes in particular, had learned from their earlier failures in the war. Hippocrates would steal to Athenian-held Minoa by night in ships with six hundred hoplites, along with a light-armed contingent under Demosthenes to rush the gate; that same night another four thousand Athenian hoplites and six hundred cavalry would march over the Attic border, to be followed by day with wagons full of artisans and gear to build a wall around Nisaea. All this required secrecy, and secrecy had not previously been an Athenian specialty in this war: the Athenians, after all, were the people whose surprise descent upon Mytilene in 428 BC had been betrayed to its intended victims, and whose surprise attack on Aetolia in 426 BC had been met by formications of unsurprised Aetolians.

Unlike in Athens' prior bungles, however, secrecy was faultlessly preserved in the 424 BC action in Megara—no small feat for an expedition of more than five thousand men, approaching in two separate bodies (one of them carried in ships, involving yet more men), which required a mighty magazine of fortification equipment and the men to use it. All of these forces were assembled and delivered to their destinations in perfect quiet. For the successful surprise, we must credit the ingenious Demosthenes, whose expedition in Aetolia loose lips had sunk: he did not propose to allow that mistake again. Better than any man, Demosthenes, too, knew what it was like to build fortifications without the proper gear, as his men had to do at Pylos. No clods, this time, would be carried on the backs of soldiers, their hands linked low to prevent them falling off.

The Athenian attempt on Megara also offers a portrait of the active resistance to Athens in 424 BC and how, with the paralysis of hegemonic Sparta, that resistance had become at once more diffuse and more collaborative. The first of Brasidas' acts against the Athenians was to unleash the Boeotian cavalry upon them. The Athenians were taken by surprise, Thucydides says, because never in seven years of Athenian harrying of the Megarid had Megara's notional allies ever come to her aid. Hitherto, all had seemed to agree that the war between Athens and Megara was a private feud, set apart from the wider war. The Athenians expected this latest clash to be no different, failing to grasp the consequences of their own success against the Spartans, which now compelled Athens' other enemies to form new constellations of enmity against her.[20]

Brasidas' allied army charts those new anti-Athenian constellations. The Peloponnesian garrison in Nisaea surrendered in part because they expected no speedy rescue from the Peloponnese—an interesting indication that Sparta's confoundment was by now only too well understood by Sparta's allies and the troops she commanded. But now Brasidas was able to rally soldiers quickly from Corinth, Phlius, and Sicyon, while the Boeotians rushed to help Megara, Thucydides says gnomically, "because the danger was not foreign to them." The paralysis of Sparta had created a sense of mutual protection against Athens among the rest of the Peloponnesian alliance, a sense that had been far weaker before.[21]

Finally, Megara in 424 BC is also a study of the rules of Greek warfare and the limits of Athenian strategy earlier in the war. For at the same time as they had been fighting a war over rank, the Athenians had been battling to change the definition of rank, to move the rank of states away from being regarded primarily as a function of victory in, or challenge to, a hoplite battle. In this the Athenians had been successful. Although they had been challenged to battle five times by Peloponnesian invasions of Attica, they had always refused to accept the challenge; in the greater war, however, even before Sphacteria, the Athenians had long been winning the war over rank despite the shame this policy of calculated obliviousness brought them. What the Athenians had been doing to humiliate the Spartans, the Athenians had established, shamed the Spartans more than what the Spartans had been doing to the Athenians. Both sides imagined that the rank of their city was a product of the opinion of Greece as a whole, but there was no way to consult Greece. In practice, therefore, much depended on appearing to convince the enemy himself, on getting him to behave as if he accepted your valuation of your attacks on him. This he admitted by trying to avenge them. So Sparta's repeated attempts to avenge Athens' successes during the war went a long way toward proving that the Spartans accepted the Athenians' valuation of Athenian attacks on Sparta.

Athens' expectation that she could at once win the war of rank and the war to define rank was disappointed at Megara because there the audience to the acts of the combatants was real, not imaginary. When the Athenians at Megara avoided battle according to their normal Athenian logic, their plan backfired, because at Megara, Athens could not twist the rules to her benefit. For at Megara there was a referee to the war over rank: the Megarians lining the walls of their city. And that referee awarded victory to Brasidas and the Peloponnesians, and with it, the loyalty of Megara.[22]

The competition for rank between Greek cities was neither wholly governed by rules nor wholly lawless. But the power of the rules as they existed independent of the combatants, as well as the ability of the combatants to change them, varied by situation. The confrontation between Brasidas and the Athenians before Megara in 424 BC was the high point of the power of the rules.

Now that his strict observation of the rules had brought Megara back into the Peloponnesian alliance and he had made the city secure, Brasidas sent the Boeotians home and himself returned to Corinth to continue recruiting mercenaries for his expedition to Thrace. The Athenians, too, returned home, leaving a garrison in Nisaea, which they would hold until 409 BC. Soon the Megarians demolished the remainder of their long walls so that the Athenians might not use them to approach the city. The leaders of the pro-Athenian cabal at Megara soon withdrew from the city into exile, while the friends of the oligarchs brought back their own exiles from the northern port of Pegae. These latter were bound by terrible oaths not to remember the discord of the past, but power obstructs oblivion, and once elected to office, the oligarchs used the pretext of a military review to disarm their opponents. Then they compelled the people to sentence their

enemies to death, as well as those on the outskirts of the pro-Athenian cabal who had not left the city, one hundred in number. And so it was that an
oligarchy was established at Megara—an oligarchy that Thucydides regarded as admirably long-lasting and estimably exclusive.[23]

All through the winter, as Demosthenes and Hippocrates were weaving
their subtleties in Megara, they were whispering, too, with malcontents
from Boeotia hoping to arrange pro-Athenian risings in their cities as well.
The pair made a good team for this work, Demosthenes providing proven
courage and cunning and Hippocrates the important things Demosthenes
could never have: a thoroughly aristocratic name ("Horse Conqueror"), the
intercity connections of a family claiming to date back to the age of heroes,
and, no doubt, the sort of high-born manner that eased the suspicions of
conspirators in aristocratic regions like Boeotia—places where even the
leaders who favored democratic regimes were likely themselves to be high-
born. This remained true even in Athens, where politicians and generals of
humbler birth, like Cleon and Demosthenes, remained in the minority.[24]

Whatever the talents of Demosthenes and the connections of Hippocrates, however, conniving at revolution in Boeotia's main city of Thebes
was likely to be futile. The Athenians had no powerful friends there who
could attempt a coup. In Thebes, indeed in Boeotia generally, there had
been no ever-escalating misery to make the folk eager for peace. For of all
the major combatant states, Boeotia had been luckiest in the war. Unlike
Corinth, she had lost no ships or men on expeditions to the northwest. She
had devoured hated Plataea and participated happily in the plundering of
Attica, but apart from the brief Athenian incursion in 426 BC, and perhaps
some trivial raiding over the border, her own lands were as yet untouched.
To pass from the blasted, beastless farms of Attica into the garden that was
Boeotia, snortling with merry swine, would have been like a visit to the
Elysian Fields from the dark realm of Hades, where Sisyphus rolled his rock
and where Tantalus gaped with hunger and with thirst.

Still, even in untroubled Boeotia there were discontents for the Athenians to encourage. Some in that region of oligarchies, Thucydides says,
longed for democracy in the style of Athens—a longing that Athens'
proven success in the war no doubt strengthened. We know, too, that the
lordship of Thebes had always been hateful to certain of the other states
in Boeotia and that conflict might yet be coaxed out of these resentments.
Not least of Thebes' Boeotian rivals was Orchomenus, to the north, sitting on a spit of land driving into Lake Copaïs, a city antique beyond the
memory of man. The sway of Minyan Orchomenus over Boeotia had
been shattered by the parvenu Heracles, hero of Thebes. But the supremacy of Thebes ever rankled because Orchomenus was older than Thebes.

Indeed, to Orchomenus, the Trojan War itself was little more than a tardy footnote, a distant clatter in the tenth generation after the city's founding. To worthy visitors the men of Orchomenus showed the treasury of Minyas, their greatest early king, who had ruled three generations before Heracles and was the first man so rich that he needed such a depository. We, too, can visit the treasury, a Mycenean beehive tomb from the thirteenth century BC, although it has long since lost its roof. Justly, it would seem, did Orchomenus preen herself upon her rich stock of centuries.[25]

Orchomenus and Thebes had ever disdained each other, and the road between them was strewn with monuments to their mutual spite. Close to Thebes stood the statue of Heracles the Nose-Docker, which celebrated the Theban hero's response to a visit from heralds of Orchomenus, who came to Thebes with haughty calls for tribute. (They returned home sorry and noseless.) But with the march of years, Orchomenus had lost more than the snouts of her heralds; now the ancient city languished in shame as the subject of Thebes, and her patriots brooded in exile, despairing of raising the city herself in revolt against its Theban overlords. Yet subject to Orchomenus in turn was Chaeronea, on the road north to Phocis and, beyond that, to broad Thessaly; in later days Chaeronea was the field of terrible battles, for she lay at a strategic point in central Greece. Now, as part of a wider Boeotian conspiracy against Thebes, and with the help of mercenaries hired out of the Peloponnese, sympathizers in Orchomenus itself, and a party of Phocians from across the nearby border, the exiles of Orchomenus hoped to capture Chaeronea and hand it over to the Athenians.[26]

The conspiracy's second tentacle wrapped around Siphae, a Corinthian Gulf port of inland Thespiae, which was to be surrendered by traitors there to Athenians arriving by sea. With the Boeotians distracted by these risings, the Athenians were to leap over their northern border into the territory of Tanagra, which they had invaded in 426 BC, and fortify the seaside temple of Apollo at Delium. Even if a general revolution did not roll immediately over the Boeotian League, "things would transpire in a suitable fashion," it was hoped, as long as these strongholds could be held and used as refuges and stations for ravaging, and the forces marshaled against the rebellion divided on many fronts.[27]

From an Athenian perspective, the Boeotian plot seems needlessly complicated and devious. Many sound objections might have been made by the generals of Athens to the list of places in Boeotia to be seized: Chaeronea, for instance, lay in the most inaccessible corner of the land, twenty miles from the coast of the Corinthian Gulf, and most of those miles were draped over the heights of Mount Helicon—it was hardly an easy place for the Athenians to hold or even get to. Delium, on the other hand, might be regarded as too close to Athens and her possessions to be

MAP 8.3 Plan for Risings in Boeotia, 424 BC

worth having: only a little more than a mile from the Athenian-held border territory of Oropus and a mere seven miles away by sea from Athens'
subjects Chalcis and Eretria on the nearby island of Euboea. Whatever
one wanted done from Delium could be done more easily from Euboea or
Oropus. And were the temple at Delium indeed desired by the Athenians,
it could be had far more easily than by this complicated plan for a three-
fold simultaneous revolt and invasion. The Athenians could just walk half
an hour over their border and grab it.[28]

It was not the Athenians, then, but the Boeotian rebels who initiated
this campaign and named its objectives—the Athenians were their helpers,
not their guides. And the ultimate aim of seizing Chaeronea, Siphae, and
Delium was not to establish three Athenian outposts in hostile Boeotia—
three copies of Pylos, that is to say, or of Methana or Cythera—but rather
three rebel encampments, three "convenient refuges," as Thucydides calls
them, such as oligarchic Pegae had been in the Megarid and on Corcyra
the oligarchic steep. The Athenians would give any necessary help, but at
the outset (if the eventual occupation of Delium is anything to go by), the
main Athenian effort was to consist mostly of building: improving the de-

fenses of the places quickly so the Boeotian rebels, however few in number, might hold them. No doubt the rebels, too, wanted the Athenians involved as little as possible. For insofar as this was a rebellion of democrats against oligarchs and of other Boeotian cities against Thebes, it would be easier for the rebels to bring over their countrymen if the old Boeotian hate for Athens were not pricked into full wakefulness but allowed instead, however uneasily, to slumber.[29]

The intrigue of the democrats and the Athenians in Boeotia failed in all its parts, for its parts were all too many. A man of Phocis, hearing perhaps of the part his countrymen were to play at Chaeronea, soon reported the design to Sparta, and the Spartans passed word on to Thebes. (However split in its sympathies and thieving its folk, Phocis, to the northwest of Boeotia, was still in principle allied to Lacedaemon.) According to the plan, the two Athenian generals were to take up their stations in Boeotia on the selfsame day: Demosthenes coming by sea from the Gulf of Corinth and his colleague, Hippocrates, by land from Attica. It appears, however, that the Boeotian rebels at Siphae and at Chaeronea, perhaps hearing that they themselves had been betrayed, concerted to advance the day of action, before the Boeotian League's gathering strength might obliterate their hopes. The rebels no doubt sent messages to Demosthenes to hasten as he might. But Demosthenes had only four hundred Athenian hoplites, the ten who served on each of his forty triremes. Before Demosthenes could land in Boeotia, he had to collect an army. The main force of his footmen in Boeotia was to be supplied by the friendly Acarnanians, who lived beyond the mouth of the Gulf of Corinth. But they had needs of their own to attend to, needs for which they expected Demosthenes to fight before the date appointed for him to receive the betrayal of Siphae by the sea.[30]

In particular, Demosthenes had been asked to help the Acarnanians capture Oeniadae in the south of their realm, so long estranged from their nation and hostile to Athens. But when he arrived, he found that the Acarnanians had already by themselves forced Oeniadae to yield and join the Athenian confederation. Having mustered all of Athens' allies in the neighborhood, Demosthenes then marched against the Agraeans, inland neighbors of the Acarnanians, in order to make them contribute warriors to his force as well. Only then did he complete his preparations for his descent on Boeotia. But by the day Demosthenes finally dropped anchor at Siphae, although arriving before the date agreed with Hippocrates, he found it armed against him by the forces of the Boeotian League. The Boeotians had had time enough to act upon the information from Sparta. With both Siphae and Chaeronea inundated by preventive soldiery, the rebels, unsurprisingly, had attempted nothing.[31]

MAP 8.4 Demosthenes Approaches Boeotia from the West, 424 BC

Away, then, the thwarted Demosthenes sailed and, in passing, made a descent upon Corinth's western neighbor Sicyon on the northern coast of the Peloponnese, a town that in seven long years of war Athens had never before touched. But even before all his ships had come to land, the men of Sicyon were at the landing place and routed Demosthenes' force, killing some and making others captive. The locals set up their trophy and returned the Athenian dead under truce: Demosthenes had been defeated. Well might he have remembered that the coins of Sicyon bore upon them the monstrous chimera, "a thing of immortal make," according to Homer, "not human, lion-fronted and snake behind, a goat in the middle, and snorting out the breath of the terrible flame of bright fire."[32]

Come the beginning of November and the long-appointed day, Hippocrates marched into Boeotia with the soldiery of Athens. He knew nothing of Demosthenes' turning back from Siphae and the implosion of Athenian hopes; nor that the Boeotians had already secured their wobbly towns and, having since returned home from that mission, were fully expecting his invasion of their land. And so into Boeotia crunched the martial automaton that was Hippocrates, with citizens, allies, and resident aliens rattling in his train. Athens' hoplite force was the strength of the invasion, but most of the crowd had light arms or no arms at all: in addition to the warriors, many hands were needed to build the fort at Delium.[33]

Marching into the territory of the Boeotian city of Tanagra, the force from Athens encountered no opposition, but no Athenian found this odd: their attack, after all, was supposed to be a surprise. Wise Athenians, however, perhaps thought it strange, and in time perhaps more ominous than strange, that no friendly natives capered along their line of march, welcoming them as liberators from Theban tyranny and bringers of democracy. Still, to the tumbledown temple of Apollo at Delium, in all the pomp of war,

MAP 8.5 The Delium Campaign, 424 BC

came the Athenians. Their masses proceeded to dig a ditch around the sanctuary, and the earth they piled up into a wall behind, cutting the vines around the holy place and clawing down houses stone by stone for matter to hold in the dirt and build the wall higher. Towers, too, they built of wood, where the temple itself did not crane over their defenses. And atop the temple itself they likely erected battlements as well—an act of no little sacrilege to a god who had already twice smitten the Athenians with his plague.[34]

The Athenians spent two and a half days at their labors, perhaps spicing them with a little ravaging of the countryside, and then on the third day, when the heavy work was done and the temple was fit to be defended, they turned for home. A mile and a half from Delium, the hoplites stopped—even as the great mob of unarmed builders streamed on down the road to Athens—to wait for their general, who was still back at the fort with a body of cavalry, arranging a garrison of some hundreds to hold the fort and putting finishing touches to its defenses. Hippocrates was no doubt perplexed by the absence of friendly Boeotians to occupy the fort, but even now he had no idea that the general rebellion in Boeotia had never begun. These conspiracies were a clutch of puzzles, he must have thought; no doubt

Boeotian democrats would present themselves in due time. And until then he simply garrisoned the fortified temple with Athenians.[35]

Such was Hippocrates' position when he was suddenly informed that the whole army of the Boeotian League was approaching. For three days they had been massing at Tanagra, a short distance inland. With the Boeotian conspiracy exploded and the Athenians' plans known, the Boeotians had prepared at leisure; indeed, they had taken advantage of the long notice to summon allied cavalry from Opuntian Locris to the north of Boeotia, horsemen who were just now finishing their ride to join them. Still, by the time the Boeotians approached the Athenian army where it was waiting for Hippocrates, the hoplites of Athens' main body were already over the line into the southern land of Oropus, a boundary territory controlled by Athens but long claimed by Boeotia.[36]

There were good reasons for the Boeotians not to pursue the Athenians across the border. Were the Boeotians to lose a battle, the rebellion they had just doused might rekindle. Even now their first duty was to drive the Athenians out of Delium, which was certainly in Boeotia, lest undetected traitors flock to them as originally planned. Of the eleven officials, the Boeotarchs who represented the Boeotian League, only one, the Theban Pagondas, son of Aeolidas, wished to pursue and attack the Athenians.

The other commanders may have worried that, if the Boeotians were to defeat the Athenians in what the Athenians considered their own land, they must (unless they broke the power of Athens utterly, a most unlikely outcome) look forward to the revenge of their arrogant neighbors, the neighbors who had warred the very Spartans to their knees. Far better to ignore the Athenian incursion, as the Boeotians had done when the Athenians ravaged Tanagra in the sixth year of the war. For even a victory would lock Boeotia into a chain of revenges, like that which Athens and Sparta had just concluded—with the humiliation and near ruin of proud Lacedaemon.[37]

Pagondas, however, prevailed over his skeptical Boeotian colleagues. Thucydides gives him a speech of encouragement to the league's army in which he stresses the need to deter future Athenian aggression. There is no end to Athenian appetite, he is made to say; thus only by defeating Athens would the Boeotians be secure against the Athenians. So high did Athens now fancy her merits that inaction was no longer an option: it would simply be an invitation to the Athenians to press harder. Whether the real Pagondas convinced the Boeotians by his eloquence or compelled them by some constitutional power, the Boeotians now marched over the border of Oropus to fight the Athenians.[38]

Alerted to the advancing enemy, Hippocrates sent a message to the seven thousand Athenian hoplites awaiting him in Oropus, ordering them into line of battle. Then he rushed from Delium to join them. In addition to the garrison, he left three hundred horsemen at the fort with instructions to fall upon the Boeotians, should an opportunity present itself: a stratagem much like that Demosthenes had used so well at the battle of Olpae in the north-west, except that here there was no secrecy, and the Boeotians quickly sent a detachment to bottle up this cavalry; they would play no role in the bat-tle. Meanwhile, the hoplites in Athens' main force were marshaled eight men deep, with the rest of the Athenian cavalry holding either flank.[39]

Behind a concealing hill, Pagondas perfected his arrangements, intent on guarding his dispositions from Athenian eyes. For Pagondas had a plan, one not without danger to his own army. He, too, had around seven thou-sand hoplites, roughly the same number as Hippocrates. But rather than spread them out to equal the length of the Athenian line, he decided to mar-shal his own Thebans—massed on the right, in the place of honor, and no doubt the largest contingent—twenty-five men deep, as opposed to the Athenians' depth of eight. The rest of the Boeotian contingents each lined up as deep as they liked, probably for the most part to a depth of eight shields, like the Athenians. Pagondas' decision to deepen his Thebans short-ened the Boeotian line, which therefore risked being outflanked by the Athenians. But Pagondas may have judged that his flanks would be pro-tected by natural features, for the likely fighting ground on the other side of the hill was bordered by deep streams and therefore too narrow for encir-clement to be a real peril. Besides, his flanks were held not only by the ex-cellent Boeotian cavalry, a thousand strong, but by a horde of light troops as well—Thucydides guesses ten thousand and adds to that five hundred peltast skirmishers, probably mercenaries. Of light troops as a regular part of their home army, the Athenians now had none—so Pagondas' swarm of harriers had no counter on the Athenian side.[40]

The most striking feature of Pagondas' deployment was the twenty-five-deep array of his Thebans. And the advantage he sought from that deep ar-ray is a celebrated puzzle, one hinging on one of the most enjoyable perplexities in military history. For all their knowledge of Greek warfare, historians do not know exactly what happened when two bodies of hostile hoplites collided on a field of battle. Here and there—the classic instance being in this very battle—ancient authors refer to a hoplite "push," and more specifically, to a "push of shields." So did the hoplite lodge his shoul-der in his bowl-like shield and *push* his hoplite foeman back? And did the friendly men behind him, in turn, push upon his back? Is that the reason for Pagondas' twenty-five ranks—to form a sort of bulldozer to force back the eight-deep Athenians? Such is the orthodox view.[41]

Impossible! cry critics. The men in the middle of such an affray would be squashed between friends and enemies like so much waffle batter. And

Figure 8.1 Hoplites running in three lines. The charge of a phalanx will have looked similar.

we know that somehow wounded men could be extracted from a hoplite fight—hard to imagine if thousands of men were pressing on each other. No, hoplite fighting was more individual and more spread out—a matter of spear fighting, not a gigantic, demented rugby scrum. Hoplites carried spears as their main weapon, after all, and we hear about phalanxes meeting "at the length of the spear." So they must have been using these weapons at the instant of attack. As for the "push," sometimes the "push" of Greek armies is clearly metaphorical, as it is when ancients apply it to ships and when moderns refer to "pushing forward" in war. And when Greek authors mention more exactly the "pushing of shields," this must not have been a mass push either but a sort of individual flicking of the hoplite shield to knock an enemy off balance.[42]

If mass pushing was not its purpose, the critics of hoplite orthodoxy argue, a deep formation like Pagondas' was surely devised instead for a psychological end, to terrify those it charged—for however many men in it were killed, there would always be more behind. And a deep formation would also serve as a psychological crutch for its own members, since the men placed at the rear, so far from the fighting, would not be inclined to run away, and with so many behind them, the men in the front ranks could not run away. Thus the front fighters' will to resist was bucked up like that of Wellington's cringing allied infantry at Waterloo, behind whom he pointedly placed his cavalry.

Hogwash! respond the orthodox. For one thing, historical accounts do seem to refer to mass pushing. If the "pushing of shields" was just a technique used by individual hoplites, it would hardly be mentioned in the all-at-a-glance descriptions of battles ancient authors give us. And what

FIGURE 8.2 Hoplites fighting with spears

about the step-by-step descriptions of these pushes, the phrases like "pushing them back little by little they followed after them," which succeeds the "push of shields" at this very battle of Delium? That doesn't sound like a metaphor! And what about the later Greek general who is reported to have cried out, "Give me one more step, and victory is ours!" That sounds like real pushing is involved. And what about other periods in ancient history, where the pushing seems to have been quite literal— once even described as "pushing with the pressure of their knees"? And how would a dainty stabbing combat produce that gigantic, seemingly simultaneous collapse of an army, the "turning to flight" of the defeated, that Greek authors describe, which was memorialized by placing the "trophy" (the Greek word means "turning") at that point on the battlefield?[43]

Even leaving aside the ancient written evidence, the orthodox go on to say, there is nothing impractical about the mass push. Critics who insist that the frontline fighters in a hoplite battle would be squashed to goo in a push are absurdly overestimating the force that one human can exert upon another by pushing. And look at hoplite gear! The massive, awkward shield ("the size of a small bridge table," as one controversialist puts it);

309

Figure 8.3 Hoplite with detailed representation of armor

the helmet—especially in the centuries before the Ten Years' War, when the engulfing Corinthian helmet was in vogue—which made it hard to see and impossible to hear; the bronze breastplate and greaves (also mostly abandoned by the late fifth century BC but still equipment for which an interpretation of hoplite fighting must account). A warrior equipped like that could hardly leap about like an agitated earwig, fighting in an individual style: he would soon be exhausted, and sooner blind, as his motions knocked his helmet out of position so that it covered his eyes. No, the prodigious hoplite panoply must have been designed for lining up and pushing. And finally the orthodox can call upon the formidable authority of Chief Inspector Claus Olsen of the Copenhagen Police. This grizzled veteran of a hundred battles with toilet-flinging squatters confirms that there is really very little that can be done by armored men with large shields, except line up and try to preserve the shield wall. Individual fighting is out of the question.[44]

On the basis of the ancient evidence, the orthodox who believe in the hoplite push should win this controversy: that there was frequently actual mass pushing in the combat of Greek hoplites seems, on balance, likely. Nor is there anything impractical about such mass pushing, as can be deduced rather easily from modern parallels. The best contemporary parallel to hoplite battle, however, is not the Copenhagen Police rousting the straggling anarchists of Christiana but the police of Japan and South Korea fighting the highly organized, helmeted, and staff-armed rioters of their cities in the past half century. In Japan (where there was much rioting in the 1970s and 1980s) and in Korea (more recently), both police and rioters often form in deep masses, and those masses may meet at a run (usually when the rioters charge the police), producing a mass push—without, apparently, crushing to death those caught in the middle. In film footage, the venerable noise of co-operative effort in the East—"Oysha! Oysha!"—can be heard as the two swarms strive against each other.

Such Japanese and Korean rioting also offers an analogue to the spear fighting of hoplite combat. For both rioters and police are armed with long staves, and both use them vigorously; staff fighting proceeds on either flank of those pushing and, when the pushers finally pull back, between those who had just been pushing. In practice, a mass push usually dissolves into a battle with staves—this can happen almost instantaneously—and staff combats break out in the inevitable eddies that form even during a mass push. Not that this staff fighting always accomplishes much; somewhat ineffectual staff fighting when the lines are about two yards apart—what the Greeks would call fighting "at length of spear"—is, in fact, the most common mode of combat when the two sides are not pushing. It can extend for long periods. Frequently, too, both sides pull back out of staff range (or just stop fighting within staff range) for a rest, by tacit consent; such private truces, sometimes bringing quiet to part of the line only or even to just a small clump of fighters, seem surprisingly easy to strike.[45]

The combat of Greek hoplites is likely to have operated along much the same principles as East Asian rioting. If two hoplite armies approached each other slowly, then the hoplites might stop at spear point and fight man to man with spears. But if either or both sides approached at a trot or a run (which seems to have been more usual), then there was no way to stop everyone at once, and front rank would have met front rank shield against shield, simply because both mobs would have crashed into them from behind and pushed them forward. In such a way, a real mass push might naturally develop (as it develops when charging rioters meet the police). But once the momentum of such a charge was exhausted, opposing soldiers would pull apart again, to spear's length, and fight from that distance. Or they might pull back further, by a tacit mutual consent, to rest, or simply stop fighting and rest in place.

Pushes did not always require a charge, but without one they were usually consigned to a smaller scale, at least initially. Perhaps a body of men within earshot might be rallied by a leader (for leaders fought in the phalanx beside their men) to draw together and surge forward, which might produce another push. And during a push at the front of the line, no doubt some of the men behind would push as well. The force as a whole did not begin to push all at once, however, unless a push developed from a mass charge. Still, if a push began to succeed, it might well ramify left and right and even backwards as more soldiers joined it, and thus become the decisive mass push that turned the enemy to flight. But at any given moment, pushing, spear fighting, and resting might all be going on at once at different places along the battle line.

The motions of both rioters and police in a riot suggest that the distribution of troops would have been quite irregular in a hoplite battle. In a Japanese or Korean riot, the density of the fighting throngs on both sides rapidly changes, with fighters massing with comrades to push or—if police—to form a static shield wall; or spreading further apart to fight with staves; or dispersing even further to rest, which many do simply by stepping backwards a few yards behind their comrades. In a Greek battle, too, hoplites would mass and scatter, sometimes "drawing together," as Greek historians describe it, to deliver or receive an attack. Undrilled or poorly drilled hoplites came together in tight clumps when they needed to, either because they anticipated a push or to protect each other with their massed shields (much as Homer described humble warriors doing in the *Iliad* to protect a wounded leader or to defend against the onset of an enemy hero). During the frequent periods when the density of the fighters was less, however, the injured on both sides would likely be helped away, just as we can see happening in riots.[46]

A deep hoplite array, like that in which Pagondas drew up his Thebans at Delium, is best understood in terms of this practice of hoplites' "drawing together" and the normal level of disorganization that the need to "draw together" suggests. The goal of such an array as Pagondas' was primarily neither physical nor psychological and was intended neither for practiced mass pushing nor to scare the enemy nor to encourage the soldiers. Rather, Pagondas' aim was an organizational one: to secure higher density at the point of impact. On the advance to battle, especially during the charge itself, a hoplite army lost density, as some men rushed ahead and some fell behind, while others clumped up left and right, leaving larger gaps elsewhere along the line (characteristically, the one fifth-century BC Greek hoplite army that seems to have been systematically drilled, that of Sparta, walked, rather than ran, into battle). A deep array solved this problem of scattering. It was an imperfect means of hitting the enemy line with a relatively compact body of men: a pre-made "drawing together." Pagondas' deep array would not, of course, arrive at the enemy line as a neat rectangle twenty-five deep but as a rather deeper mob, tight at the center, the rear of which would quickly splatter in both directions, like a raindrop hitting a windshield. But if a more compact mass met an enemy force already scattered from a charge, it might simply bowl it over by virtue of its greater concentration, while if the enemy tried to mass to meet it, the friendly soldiers would already be massed for the first crucial seconds of the push. Again, modern riots provide a clue here. For modern Western riot police send out clumps, or "snatch teams" as they are called, to seize a leader of the rioters, and they push their way through with their shields, not because they outnumber the rioters but because, massed, they are able to push aside the more scattered rioters at any given point. Such advantages of density, of bowling over and pushing through, will have been Pagondas' aim when he drew up his Thebans twenty-five deep.[47]

Having disposed his army to advantage on the battlefield of Delium, Pagondas then led it over the crest of the hill and down toward the Athenians. Beneath the wave of Boeotians, Hippocrates was still delivering his harangue as he passed along the Athenian lines. Pagondas shouted encouragement to his own army, and the Boeotians struck up their paean to Apollo—with special passion, one suspects, because it was Apollo's temple at Delium whose desecration the Boeotians were avenging. The Athenians, with no time to spare, now surged forward and met the Boeotians at a run.[48]

Pagondas had been right not to worry about his flanks, for the battlefield was constrained on both sides by streambeds, and as the two armies advanced, both of the main bodies of hoplites were denuded of the other troops on their left and right, as the advance of those troops was blocked by the terrain. Then the hoplites ground into each other, the collision resolving itself into a "pushing of shields." Pagondas' deep mass did not bowl over the Athenians out of hand, as the commander had perhaps hoped. But successive pushing by the massed Thebans soon began to drive the Athenians slowly back, perhaps first with the benefit of their greater density and subsequently by virtue of their moral and physical momentum as they continued to gain ground. On the other wing of the hoplite battle, however, where the non-Theban Boeotian contingents faced the Athenian right, many of those less deeply arrayed Boeotians soon turned to flight. They left behind only the unmoved hoplites of Thespiae, isolated with their flanks exposed on either side.[49]

The men of Thespiae were the most famous soldiers in Boeotia, renowned as the only men of the Greeks to join the Spartans in their last stand at Thermopylae. Above all other gods they revered Love—but this was no flower-sniffing Love, for the Spartans, too, sacrificed to Love before they went into battle. This was the love that held men together in the maelstrom of Ares, as it held them together now in the face of the triumphant Athenians. Even as the victorious line of the Athenians lapped around them on both sides, the Thespians would not flee, and forming a sea urchin sharp in every direction, they died fighting hand to hand, some three hundred in their number. Around the back of the doomed Thespian clot, Athenians caught sight of a blaze of boastful shield emblems. Hoplites advancing against them! They threw themselves upon those who dared to oppose them, and some were slain before they realized that they were fighting fellow Athenians who had come around the Thespians the other way, completing the circle.[50]

Pagondas, seeing his left flank of hoplites beginning to crumble, quickly dispatched a contingent of his idle cavalry, blocked from the fighting by the landscape's streambeds, to attempt a desperate ruse. He ordered them to vanish quietly behind the hill over which the Boeotians had come and then to reappear over the same hill in a cloud of dust and equestrian glitter. The ruse worked. The Athenians' victorious right, which had slaughtered the Thespians and driven away the rest of the Boeotians arrayed against it, thought that a whole other enemy army had arrived, and was cast into terrified perplexity.[51]

At the same time that the Boeotian cavalry panicked Athens' successful right flank, the Theban mass on the Boeotian right finally broke the Athenian left, and suddenly the whole army of the Athenians was in flight and scattering—some to Delium to the north, some to the town of Oropus to the east, and some toward Mount Parnes to the south. Now the well-rested cavalry of the Boeotians had their chance and rode down the fleeing Athenians, joined in their effort by the horse of Opuntian Locris, whom the gods had ordained should arrive just when they might prove useful.

In the strew, one tiny body of Athenians withdrew in good order: the men who had gathered around the imperturbable philosopher Socrates, whose inhuman calm amid the turmoil warned pursuers off to seek easier prey. Some of the pursuing cavalry moved on to the unfortunate Athenian light-armed and unarmed builders, many of whom had dawdled on the way home and were now overtaken. Only the coming of the early dark of November—for the battle had been fought in the afternoon—brought an end to the pursuit. The Boeotians had lost somewhat more than five hundred hoplites, the majority of them the stalwarts of Thespiae, and the Athenians just under a thousand, including Hippocrates, their general.[52]

With the Athenians dispersed and humiliated, the Boeotians reveled in their victory. They proceeded to strip the Athenian dead of their war gear, place a guard over them, and set up their trophy. The victorious Thebans took home their share of the hundreds of panoplies and nailed the booty to their public buildings, so that the city looked all of bronze or as if a gigantic shrike of uncommon acquisitiveness were nesting nearby. From the loot and the ransoms of captives, the Thebans would fund a great portico in their market, adorned with bronze statues, and endow a festival in honor of

Delian Apollo, the defilement of whose shrine they had avenged by their victory.[53]

The day after the battle, those of Athens' fleeing men who had managed to reach Oropus were picked up by ship, as were those in the fortified temple at Delium—all except the garrison that was to remain there, whose soldiers no doubt watched with some envy as their comrades sailed away. For the Athenians knew they had been beaten, and in accordance with the Greek rules of war, they sent a herald to ask to recover the dead under truce. But a bizarre wrangle now arose over the bodies of the fallen Athenians: on the road to the Boeotian camp, the Athenian herald met another bearer of Hermes' wand coming the other way, who turned him back. The Athenians, this Boeotian visitor explained, had committed sacrilege by fortifying the temple at Delium. Now they dwelt in the shrine as in a barracks, farting and burping in a holy place just as they might at home, while as their daily drink they slurped down sacred water, water that might only be used for holy lustration. So the Athenians must abandon the seat of Apollo before they might recover the bodies of their dead.[54]

The exchange of sophistries that followed Thucydides reports with the deepest and most pleasurable irony. Delium, a tiny landlocked island won by the spear, was no longer any business of the Boeotians, the Athenians claimed. It was now part of Attica. And if the Athenians had presumed to guzzle holy water, it was in order to defend this new-won speck of Attica against Boeotian aggression; thus, if anything it was the Boeotians' fault for threatening a shrine! Shame on *them*! Under the circumstances, the god would forgive the Athenians. It was the Boeotians, instead, who were committing impiety by refusing to return the Athenian bodies.[55]

Very well then, the Boeotians responded wryly. If dubious parts of Attica are nothing to do with us, then you may naturally recover your dead (which lay in the territory of Oropus, which Athens controlled) without our permission. That is, if you can.

Acutely must the Athenians have felt the barbs of Boeotia's response, and acutely must the Greeks have enjoyed the story. The clever Athenians had been defeated in cleverness—in the cut and thrust, that is, of *mētis*, of cunning. Not only had the Boeotians won the battle, but they had won glory from this test of wits as well, much as the Plataeans had from outwitting the Peloponnesians besieging their city. Euripides' play the *Suppliants*, which many date to around this time, takes as its theme a myth about Thebans refusing to allow the women of Argos to recover their dead; many think the play is an allusion to the wrangle over the dead after Delium. In any case, in the winter that followed the battle, many a hearth in Greece surely chortled at the twofold guile of the victorious Boeotians.[56]

But this battle of wits over the Athenian dead was not the end of the Boeotians' cunning. The Athenians were still disgracefully fortified in the temple of Apollo at Delium, and to dislodge them the Boeotians called upon their allies. The list of those who came to Boeotia's aid—Corinthians, some Megarians, and the disgraced garrison of surrendered Nisaea—points to the active opposition to Athens in this time of Spartan paralysis. The Boeotians also summoned down javelin men and slingers from the north, no doubt for pay. All of these, and yet the Boeotians would strive in vain against the fortified temple, until some latter-day Daedalus contrived a strange device: a long wooden pipe made from a beam cut in two, hollowed out within, and then restored, attached at one end to a cauldron of coals, sulphur, and pitch, along with a bellows to drive the fire through the conduit. This contraption was rolled up on carts to where the Athenian wall was mostly wood and vines and worked to blow fire upon the structure. Alight, the wall could no longer be defended. Boeotian wits had again outmatched those of the Athenians.[57]

Seventeen days after the battle of Delium, after much vigorous bellows-pumping, the Boeotians broke into the fort at Delium, capturing two hundred Athenians beyond those they slew. The Athenian fleet managed to rescue the remainder of the garrison from the burning fort, presumably hustling them back to Athens. Only when the temples and fields of Boeotia were finally both free of Athenian taint did the Boeotians give the Athenians back their battle dead. Gaily must the eels of Copaïs have thrashed their tails, that they fed so cunning a race as the sons of the Boeotians.[58]

The whole war was transformed on that afternoon in November 424 BC when the Athenians fought and lost the battle of Delium. As an author in the next century would say both of Delium and Athens' earlier disaster at Coronea, in ?447 BC, "the fame of Athens was cast down against the Boeotians, and the pride of the Boeotians against the Athenians was raised up." The Athenians forfeited their claim to be *hegemon* of Greece when they lost a hoplite battle—a proper, stand-up hoplite battle, which the Greeks still considered the most powerful way of settling the rank of states. Athens, moreover, had been defeated by a power that did not even claim first place itself but that admitted Sparta as its chief—so Athens, logically, could rank no higher than third. Perhaps the worst outcome of Delium was that Athens had been defeated by humble Boeotia, which the Athenians had for most of the war sneered at as unworthy even to compete with them and which they had disdained for so long even to attack. From that instant on, an admission of equality from the Spartans, which Athens had so flatly rejected when the Spartans offered it in 425 BC, held much more appeal. At least it would compel Sparta to endorse Athens' superiority over grinning, gloating Boeotia![59]

A THENS' DISASTER AT DELIUM WAS a result of the new strategy the Athenians had been pursuing ever since their victory on Sphacteria. That strategy failed at Delium, but the strategy was not itself illogical—even if to us the logic is an alien one. For in great and in small, the plans of Athens in late 425 and 424 BC echo her deeds and accomplishments in the 450s BC, during her earlier war with the Peloponnesians.

The war at mid-century had pitted Athens largely against Sparta's allies, rather than against Sparta herself. And now, again, the Athenians had decided to assail Sparta's allies—the same ones and sometimes even in the same ways. In the 450s BC, Megara had defected to the side of Athens—just as Athens now plotted that Megara might do the same. Then Athens had dominated Boeotia, perhaps by exploiting divisions among the Boeotians—just as now Athens hoped to do. Then a hoplite battle against the Corinthians had been fought, and lost, in the Peloponnese—just as now the Athenians, having left the territory of Corinth alone through the long years of war, landed and sought a battle against the Corinthians in the Peloponnese. Then Cythera had been captured, just as now Cythera, so long a neglected prize in this war, was captured—indeed, one of the generals who seized it may even have been a relative of Tolmides, who had captured it in the 450s BC. Then, as now, raids were made on Sicyon, hitherto untouched in this war. Then, as now, a raid had been made on small Halieis on the Argolid peninsula, and then, as now, nearby Troezen had been pressured to defect—and had just indeed defected or would soon do so. Then Aegina had been fought and conquered, and now the Athenians pursued the Aeginetans even into their exile refuge at Thyrea, that their destruction might be made complete. Then Athens had been an ally of Argos, and shortly before the spring of 424 BC, Cleon had been at Argos negotiating. The match is hardly perfect—for these are the real affairs of men—yet the correspondence of events seems far too striking to be entirely accidental.[60]

So close is the parallel between the 450s and late 425 and 424 BC that it can even be used to understand certain Athenian operations that Thucydides did not take the pains to describe in detail but only mentioned in passing. During Tolmides' celebrated campaign in the 450s, the Athenians had burnt the Spartan arsenal on the coast of Laconia before capturing Cythera. And in 424 we find the Athenians, after capturing Cythera, trampling around in the same area of Laconia. Demosthenes' fateful acceptance of battle at Sicyon—indeed, his whole Corinthian Gulf expedition in 424—seems an eerie mirror image of Pericles' expedition in the 450s. Then, Pericles had sailed from Megara's port of Pegae to ravage Sicyon, defeated the Sicyonians in battle at Nemea, and, after setting up his trophy, gathered up allies from Achaea (then friendly to the Athenians), in the north of the Peloponnese, whereupon he sailed over to assail Oeniadae. Demosthenes in 424 began at Oeniadae (discovering that the Acarnanians had already taken it), after which he traced a route rather like Pericles' in reverse, gathering allies, then sailing deep into the Gulf of Corinth to Siphae, ten miles from Pericles' Pegae, finally returning from there to attack Sicyon, where he was attacked on the beach by the locals and defeated.[61]

This relationship of present Athenian behavior in late 425 and 424 BC to the past may indeed have been so obvious to contemporaries that it alerted Athens' enemies to what the Athenians were planning: for many of their enemies seem to have expected them. At least the Corinthians (whose information was from Argos), the Aeginetans at Thyrea, and the men of Sicyon all seem to have anticipated the Athenian attacks on them. The Peloponnesians, too, saw the pattern behind Athens' actions.[62]

It is one thing, however, to notice the pattern of similarity between the acts of Athens in 425 and 424 and those of the 450s, and quite another to explain it. Imperial Athens was hardly an historical reenactors' club, determined to re-create the victories of the past for the mere sport of it. Moreover, any Athenian strategy that looked beyond a crippled Sparta was bound to appear somewhat similar, Corinth, Boeotia, and Megara being Athens' next natural targets after Lacedaemon.[63]

A general trend toward a more aggressive Athenian strategy has often been detected in the period after the death of Pericles. And if such a strategy was not followed consistently, it may have been largely because of politics at Athens: the conservative-minded Nicias, it is argued, championed a more cautious, Periclean strategy, while the more adventurous Cleon was only able to put his bold plans into action in the wake of his unexpected triumph on Sphacteria. So, indeed, it may have been—although we have no evidence for such strategic disagreement in Athens at this time, and that sort of party-political analysis of Athenian politics, smacking as it does of the stately combinations of Whigs and Tories, is now regarded as rather old-fashioned. But even accepting the general trend toward a more aggressive strategy and allowing the likelihood that politics played a role in it, we must still explain why this new, more aggressive Athenian strategy took the form it did. For the fit between old and new is just too weirdly exact for the Athenians not to have had the 450s BC very much on their minds.[64]

Beyond the Athenians' actions, their own words confirm that they were dwelling on the past. This is most apparent in the odd terms Athens returned to Sparta in response to the Spartan 425 BC peace mission after the battle in Navarino Bay, when Athens demanded to get back exactly what she had surrendered in the Thirty Years' Peace of 446/445 BC. Recall the curiosities of that diplomatic rejoinder: the Athenians wanted Megara's ports (which they had given up in the Thirty Years' Peace), but not Megara, which they had lost earlier; they wanted weak Troezen, in the Peloponnese, because they had given it up in the treaty. And they wanted to resume their alliance with the region of Achaea in the northern Peloponnese, also yielded in the treaty—although there is no reason to suppose that the Achaeans themselves wanted to become allies of the Athenians. When the Athenians made those demands upon Sparta before their great triumph on Sphacteria, they were, without doubt, attempting to undo the past.[65]

The Athenians had become even more ambitious since they rejected Sparta's first peace offering. But what differed between the Athenian offer in 425 BC and the goals of the subsequent Athenian actions in 425 and 424 was only the moment of the past to be re-created: now they wanted to revive the more glorious period before their losses of Boeotia and the city of Megara in 447 and 446 BC, rather than the dimmed splendor represented by the day before the Thirty Years' Peace of 446/445, which was struck after they had lost those places. The Athenian triumph on Sphacteria is, of course, the reason for this waxing of ambition, and it no doubt lies behind the ever less acceptable demands that Athens made to the stream of Spartan envoys asking for peace in Sphacteria's wake. After the capture of the Spartans on Sphacteria, Sparta's wondering envoys may have heard not just about Athens' wanting tiny Troezen and the ports of Megara, but Megara herself and Boeotia, too, which the Athenians had ruled in the 450s. At the same time, Athenians with more modest views may still have looked back to re-creating the day before the peace of 446/445 as a resolution to the war satisfactory to the honor of Athens and certainly easier to force Sparta to consent to.

Surviving affection for the day before the Thirty Years' Peace would explain, for example, the decision of the Athenian generals at Megara in 424 BC not to fight Brasidas for the city of Megara itself but rather to content themselves with Nisaea. That decision is a real head-scratcher for anyone who thinks that Athens wanted Megara primarily for strategic reasons— say, to block Peloponnesian invasions—rather than reasons of pride. But Athens had already lost Megara by the time of the Thirty Years' Peace of 446/445: it was Nisaea that, humiliatingly, they had to return in the peace. And so Nisaea was the necessary minimum of what they wanted to recover in 424. In soaring 424, the vengeful terms the Athenians offered the Spartans before their triumph in 425 had become, for some Athenians at least, an acceptable fallback position.[66]

So the Athenians were indeed, it seems clear, trying to re-create the past. Simple revanchism will have been a great part of their motive. Athens was striving to avenge herself on cities that had humiliated her, either by their own actions or as Sparta's allies when Sparta finally won the war at midcentury. Now that Sparta was essentially removed from the current conflict, Athens had the opportunity and the power to take revenge on others to whom a debt of revenge was owed. The customs of Greek war over rank allowed a competitor to ignore the allies of an enemy *hegemon*, but they did not require it. And Greek memories, when it came to revenge, were long.

The pattern of Athenian actions, however, suggests a motivation even beyond that of inflicting revenge upon individual states. It suggests that the Athenians were pursuing another course toward being accepted as *hegemon* of Greece, the first city in rank-honor. For no matter how desperate and how cruelly coerced, the Spartans might never concede superiority to Athens. It was perfectly possible to imagine tight-lipped Lacedaemon being extirpated by helot rebellion or external invasion without yielding a jot of her overweening pride. Getting the losing side in this struggle over rank formally to accept that it had lost had, after all, been the problem in the war all along. It had been Sparta's perplexity in the winter following 430 BC, just as it was Athens' in 425 BC, and it remained a puzzle. So the Athenians must take their case for superiority to the wider Hellenic nation.

To achieve her goal of primacy, then, Athens must build herself up—must raise her own standing in the full sight of Greece, quite independently of pushing Sparta down. And other than strength and the ability to humiliate rivals (which Athens had already shown), Greeks thought about the honor of cities in terms of great deeds in the past.

Athens, for all her present might, was not a city of top-of-the-line mythical cachet. For all the earnest labors of her later poets, Athens had been but a runner-up in the age of heroes (remember that before the battle of Plataea, Tegea could urge her mythic glories against those of Athens). The single historical moment of which the Athenians were most proud—when they had stood nearly alone against the Persians at Marathon—was not, in time of Greek war and Persian quiet, suitable for emulation. But in the years before Athens had lost Boeotia at Coronea in ?447 BC—then, *then* Athens had stood astride the world. Then she had been sovereign over central Greece and marched unchecked through the Peloponnese. Then she could tilt with fair fortune against Persia's lofty King, the greatest power the Greeks could conceive, and compel the King to stay his angry bow. That was the time of Athens' greatest historical glory, and if Athens sought to be supreme in honor among the Greeks, that was the period of her past she must evoke now. What Athenian strategy after Sphacteria looks like, then—a grab for the past with both hands—is precisely what Athenian strategy after Sphacteria was.

There are other indications, too, in other realms, that the eyes of Athens in the 420s BC were fixed upon her mid-century past. Then Pericles had established payment for jurors at two obols; now Cleon raised it to three obols. Then Pericles had built mighty buildings on the Acropolis; now his program may have been revived with the building of the sprightly

FIGURE 8.4 The Temple of Athena Nike on the Athenian Acropolis, likely commissioned by the Athenians to celebrate their victory over the Spartans at Sphacteria

temple of Athena Nike, for which the victory at Sphacteria seems the best context. At mid-century the Athenians built their long walls; now, too, Cleon may have improved the wall system. A new temple to Apollo at Delos may have been built after Sphacteria, and a new portico for Artemis at Brauron, while the theater of Dionysus at Athens was remodeled. Nor does the vengeful spirit of the Athenian reply to the Spartan plea for peace in 425 BC provide a bad juncture for the rebuilding of the temple of Nemesis, the very goddess of vengeance herself, at Rhamnous, in the northeast of Attica. Taken individually, these various building projects are a mass of dating perplexities, but leaning on each other for support, they imply an ambition—however constrained by Athens' present reality—to return to the glories of mid-century.[67]

A parallel policy of looking back to the mid-century may also be visible in Athens' relations with her imperial subjects. The project of assigning dates to the undated inscriptions on stone that reveal how Athens administered her imperial subjects must be regarded with pervasive doubt (see appendix pp. 426–30 below). But one currently fashionable reconstruction concentrates a series of important inscriptions—inscriptions regulating the collection of tribute and imposing Athenian coinage and weights and measures on the empire—in exactly the period 425 and 424 BC. If the inscriptions do indeed date to these years, they may imply a spate of imperial reorganization intended to return Athens' empire to its mid-century splendor as well.[68]

A warped and comic reflection of this 420s BC historical mindedness, above all in its military aspects, may, finally, be seen in Aristophanes' *Knights*, produced in February 424 BC, just before the most ambitious of Athens' new plans were attempted. In this play a figure representing the politician Cleon competes with a sausage seller (who defeats even Cleon in vulgarity) for the affection of an old man named Demos ("the People"). When the sausage seller finally wins the contest, he—for no reason arising from the plot up to that point, but, then, this is a comedy—boils up old Demos in a pot. This restores Demos to his youth "in the violet-crowned Athens of yore," when "Aristides and Miltiades were his messmates." "O Athens, shining, violet-crowned, envied of all," sings the chorus, in delight, "show us this monarch of Greece and of this land!" And out comes Demos resplendent, his hair adorned with a golden cricket (as Thucydides tells us were worn by the Ionians of old).[69]

"Greetings, O king of the Greeks!" sings the chorus to Demos, "worthy of the city and of Marathon's trophy!" The rejuvenated Demos then pledges to carry on the current war against Sparta as Athens fought wars in the good old days: money will be spent on triremes, not on the teeming functionaries of the Athenian democracy; the rowers will be paid on time; and corruption in the enrollment of hoplites will be stopped. Finally the sausage seller brings out a girl wantonly clad as the Thirty Years' Peace of 446/445 BC, and Demos swoons, "Wow, isn't she pretty! I'll spend thirty years with that one!" Demos' vision of the good old days goes further than that of some of his countrymen, who were exactly trying to reverse the verdict of the Thirty Years' Peace. But this joke shows that the Thirty Years' Peace might be regarded as the end of an Athenian golden age extending back to Marathon. And boiling Demos back into his youth makes a joke of Athens' contemporary attempts to re-create the glories of her past, the period when the Athenian *demos* was (as the chorus says) king of Greece.[70]

The military strategy of Athens after Sphacteria was merely one aspect of a wider movement in Athenian culture, a brief silver age launched by the Athenian triumph over the Spartans, during which the Athenians looked into their recent past and tried to re-create, especially, the golden age of Pericles in the 450s and early 440s BC. The strategic part of this program was brought to an end by the Athenian disaster at Delium. And not only by Delium. For by the time the battle of Delium had been lost, Athens had also suffered defeats in an unexpected realm, among the northern cities of the Thraceward region, where revolt from the Athenian empire, long asleep, now reawakened with a snort.

IX

THE BLOODY MARCH OF PEACE,
424–420 BC

B EYOND THE NORTHERN SHORE OF the Aegean, beyond the roof of
Greece and the Greek cities clinging like droplets to its eaves, lay the
abode of the Thracians, a people consecrated to war. Red-haired, scorn-
ing the plow for the sword, the highest among them marked their rank
with strange tattoos. Rude and quarrelsome the Greeks thought them: at
a Thracian banquet, it was manners to eat little from one's own plate and
graze instead on food flung at one by other diners. Those Thracians who
lived up north, toward the Danube, sent memoranda to their god in this
wise: by lot a messenger was chosen and charged with the needful com-
muniqués; then, while three men steadied their javelins in the ground,
others took the messenger by his hands and feet and swung him—up! up!
and away!—to land upon the javelins' waiting points. Were he to die
pierced through, the messages were guaranteed a friendly reception. If
not, the messenger was much reproached, and a more reliable envoy was
chosen in his place.[1]

Among the squabbling tribes of Thrace, greatest in these days were the
Odrysians and their king, Sitalces. It was his father, Teres, who had first
made an empire in the north. Few Greeks would have had much knowledge
of this savage land—but of those few, one was Thucydides. His father's
name, Olorus, was after all Thracian, which bespeaks a bond between his
own proud family and a royal Thracian line—most likely the very one that
once gave a wife to Miltiades, the victor of Marathon. The historian himself held a contract to work mines near the river Strymon and was influential, he tells us, among the people of the region.[2]

To the east, the domain of the Thracians stretched away to the Hellespont and Bosporus, the conduit through which the urgent waters of the
Black Sea—which the nervous Greeks pleadingly called the Friendly Sea—
rushed south to mingle with the more complacent Aegean. To the west of

Thrace, the waters of the Strymon formed the border with Macedonia, another power of this northern world.

In less than a century Macedon would bring Greece into thrall and cast down the storied empire of Persia, but in these early days she was both weak and palsied, divided between the rival claimants to a tottering throne. Truculent, too, and unobeying, were the lords of Macedonia's rude uplands: those regions that in latter days, under the stern lordship of King Philip II and his son Alexander the Great, were to furnish the heart of an unconquerable army, the dauntless warriors who would march east to graffiti the pyramids of Egypt and tame the pachyderms of India. But as yet Macedon lacked even good roads and strong places of refuge. Like that of Thessaly, her old enemy to the south, the strength of Macedon lay in her feudal cavalry; the stalwart infantry of Macedon's heyday was still unimagined.[3]

The Greeks could not decide what to do with Macedon, just as Macedon did not seem to know what to do with herself. The Macedonians spoke Greek—very badly, a southern Greek would hasten to add—but the Greeks could never quite resolve whether they were in truth a branch of the Greek family. The tactful Greek solution was to trace the line of the Macedonian kings to Argos, so that Macedonian royalty at least might compete as Hellenes at Olympia.[4]

Suspended between—or, more accurately, below—the Macedonians and the Thracians was a realm of cities of the Greeks. From the Aegean shore west of Strymon, there extended to the south a fat outthrust of land, terminating in three slim and eccentric peninsulas: this was the Thracian Chalcidice, three slanting icicles suspended from the roof of northern Greece. This region contained no fewer than forty Greek states, most of them tiny.[5]

The Thracian Chalcidice's westerly peninsula, which held the Greek cities of Mende and Scione, was called Pallene. This peninsula was joined to the mainland by a thin neck, and the choke point was held by ill-fated Potidaea, the anvil of troubles. In the elder days Pallene had been named Phlegra, and here primeval Earth, the first of all, bore the terrible Giants to take revenge upon the late-born gods of Olympus.

The central peninsula of the Chalcidice held the Greek city of Torone. The easterly peninsula, called Acte, was tipped by the inaccessible Mount Athos, today the aerie of bearded monks and muttering hermits. But in those days, Acte's considerable cities were Sane and Dium. Once upon a time the Great King of Persia had cut a canal through this peninsula to ease the journey of his ships when he led his hosts against Greece.

North of the peninsulas of the Chalcidice, on the strip of land that linked them, were Olynthus and Acanthus. Further north and west, in the

MAP 9.1 The Greek North

wider outcropping of land where the Chalcidice ended and the region called Bottice began, were more Greek settlements, Spartolus chief among them. And further east, once this broad Greek insult to the smooth-running coast was exhausted, there was the mighty river Strymon, and at her mouth the port of Eion. Up Strymon, in a bend on the river's Thracian coast, was the city of Amphipolis. With her bridge over the river, her shipbuilding timber, her mines, her eel fisheries, and her bustling folk, Amphipolis was the most important city in the region, and Athens held her tight.[6]

Before war shook through this region, all of its Greek cities, great and small, had been members of the Athenian empire. They might have stayed that way, too, had Athens not decided to tamper with the local order. In the time before the war, Macedon's King Perdiccas had been a friend of the Athenians, but for a reason lost to history, the Athenians had preferred to see Perdiccas' brother Philip on his throne. In 432 BC the Athenians prepared a fleet against Perdiccas, to act in cooperation with Philip's incursion by land. In response to this threat, Perdiccas began to treat with the Spartans and Corinthians and to urge the Athenian allies in the region—Potidaea and the rest—to revolt.[7]

Perdiccas' plots were successful. In the year before the war, when Potidaea, encouraged by the Macedonian king and with guarantees of support from Sparta, rebelled from Athens, she was indeed joined by some of the other Chalcidian towns. Some cities of Bottice joined the rebellion, too, despite the old song the Bottiaean maidens sang, which began, "Let us go to Athens." Perdiccas gathered the people from all the small, weak places in Chalcidice and settled them all in one strong, well-protected inland city, Olynthus. Because they were giving up their own land at his bidding, Perdiccas gave the Chalcidians soil of his own to till, so long as the war with Athens should last. But all those friends and allies could not protect Potidaea herself. In the winter after the second fighting season of the war, Potidaea had surrendered on terms, and her folk, released to go where they might, took refuge with their fellow Chalcidian rebels in nearby towns.[8]

Having emptied strategic Potidaea of its inhabitants, the Athenians sent out some of their own people and made a colony of it so that it might be safe in the future. The next summer (429 BC) the Athenians tried to suppress what remained of the northern rebellion. They sent two thousand hoplites and two hundred cavalry to take Spartolus, in Bottice, but they were driven back into Potidaea by Chalcidian rebels from the stronghold of Olynthus. After the fall of Potidaea, Olynthus had become the heart of the rebellion, the very center of a rebel Chalcidian federation.[9]

After this failure in the north, with the exception of a tiny failed adventure in 425 BC, the Athenians let the northern rebels alone. How their zeal had flagged since their gigantic labors to capture Potidaea! For that project two thousand talents (a third of Athens' prewar reserve) had been exhausted, and as many lives. There was a reason for this difference: the honor of the Peloponnesians was engaged in Potidaea, to whom Sparta had promised her support and whose mother city, Corinth, was acutely interested in her welfare. And so capturing Potidaea would humiliate Athens' greater enemies, a precious Athenian goal. The other rebels were just that—rebels—and might be dealt with at leisure when the greater war was done.[10]

When the Athenians came against King Perdiccas in 432 BC, acting in cooperation with his brother Philip, they captured the Macedonian city of Therme. But the nearby Chalcidian rebellion had begun to press on the Athenians, so they formed an alliance with Perdiccas to secure his help and departed from his realm. Wily Perdiccas promptly betrayed his new allies and campaigned alongside the rebels against the Athenians. In the next year, the first of the wider war, Athenians managed to trade Therme for the renewed support of Perdiccas, and he joined the Athenians against the Chalcidians. But by 429 BC, Perdiccas was quietly sending forces to support the Peloponnesian efforts in the northwest.[11]

Perdiccas also faced dangers closer than the Greeks. In the winter following the campaigns of 429 BC, Sitalces the Thracian descended upon Macedonia and upon Athens' northern rebels. This intervention came about because in 431 BC, the first year of the war, the Athenians had by deft diplomacy made Sitalces their ally, hoping to use his forces against the rebellion and against Perdiccas, who was then fighting the Athenians. And as an ally, Sitalces had done even better than fight Perdiccas: it was he who had brokered the 431 BC return of Perdiccas to the Athenian alliance in exchange for Therme.[12]

As a condition of reconciling the hard-pressed Perdiccas to the Athenians, Sitalces had extracted from that slippery king some tremendous pledge. This promise—Thucydides is coy about what it was—Perdiccas naturally had not fulfilled, and finally, in 429 BC, Sitalces resolved to replace the forsworn monarch with Perdiccas' nephew Amyntas, son of the would-be usurper Philip, a Macedonian heir whom Sitalces kept in his train.[13]

At the same time that he had determined to topple Perdiccas in Macedon, Sitalces proposed to honor his alliance with the Athenians by putting down the rebellion against them in the Chalcidice. It may be that he had been supposed to cooperate with the failed Athenian attack on Spartolus in the summer of 429 BC but had not been able to assemble his host in time. Yet it may also be that the calling of his host was itself Sitalces' true purpose, as it would show his titanic strength to subject and enemy alike. For Thucydides numbers the Thracian horde at one hundred and fifty thousand, unrolling it with the flourish of Homer telling the ships of the Achaeans or Herodotus the multitudes Xerxes led against Greece, and if the army of Sitalces was anything near so huge, it could hardly be kept long in the field.[14]

Sitalces first led this multitude into the old realm of Perdiccas' hated brother Philip. Some strong places he captured, and others came over to him readily out of love for Philip's son, Amyntas. But outside that district, all the Thracians did was plunder Macedonia, while the Macedonians cut off stragglers with their cavalry. Sitalces also sent some of the Thracian host into the Chalcidice, where they plundered the lands of the Chalcidian and Bottiaean rebels from Athens. He expected the Athenians to send a fleet to join him (was this to have been the Spartolus expedition, now long gone home, or a different one?), but they failed to appear, "not believing that he would come" despite all their gifts and their envoys' pleading that he should do so.[15]

After a month of plundering, but only eight days among the Chalcidians, the Thracians turned for home. They had probably run out of food, for even the less numerous and better organized Peloponnesians had never, even in time of harvest (rather than a Thracian winter), been able to spend more than forty days in Attica without running out of provisions. But Thucydides reports a more nefarious reason for their withdrawal: the devious Perdiccas had bribed the heir of Sitalces, the Thracian king's nephew Seuthes, with the promise of marriage to Perdiccas' dowered sister if Seuthes could convince his barbarous uncle to depart. Perdiccas' pledge, which he for once actually carried through on, was surely wasted if intended as a bribe to prompt Sitalces' departure, for the Thracians would not have been able to carry on their invasion much longer in any event. But if, on the other hand, Perdiccas' purpose was instead to forge a bond between the lordly houses of the north, his offer was entirely successful. For after the death of Sitalces in late 424 BC, his mighty kingdom descended to the same Seuthes. By now Perdiccas had once again turned against the Athenians, and Sitalces' domain, now ruled by Perdiccas' brother-in-law, was to play no further part in the war, just when Athens again needed allies in the north.[16]

The titanic expedition of Sitalces had, then, little immediate effect upon northern affairs and in the long term proved ill for Athens' northern interests. But as a display of Thracian power, it was nevertheless astounding. When the Thracians appeared in the Chalcidice, all the Greeks south to Thermopylae, the Thessalians chief among them, flew to arms, dreading that Sitalces might march upon them. Even further south, rumors marched through Greece of an invasion by numberless Thracians, led by the Athenians against the Peloponnesians.[17]

From these alarms in the north, Thucydides draws one of his beloved ironies. In that chilly realm, where the wily Perdiccas set the moral tone and where Greeks scorned their pledges, there was one man of iron principle: Sitalces, the barbarian. He had come upon his great campaign in 429 BC "to enforce one promise, and to fulfill another"—to enforce Perdiccas' nameless but weighty promise to him, that is, and to fulfill his undertaking to help the Athenians in the Chalcidice. His arrival in winter—freezing his own men to fulfill his pledge—signals his simple honesty, while the dishonest Athenians doomed his expedition by failing to come, unlike Sitalces more mindful of the weather than their oaths. The "ancient simplicity," that reverence for honor and custom that Thucydides saw being driven out of Greece by war, had taken flight to barbarian lands.[18]

Come Sphacteria in 425 BC and the crippling of Sparta's will, the rebels against Athenian power in the north justly suspected that Athens would soon be at leisure to deal with them. Other cities in the Chalcidice, which yearned for freedom from Athens but had not the courage to revolt openly, were also full of dread at the impending attention of their mighty overlords. And although Perdiccas, Macedon's serpentine king, might for the moment be at peace with Athens, the long-term interests of Macedonia could hardly be reconciled with Athenian domination of the Greek cities on (or, as a Macedonian would no doubt insist, within) her borders. Perdiccas, too, had not forgotten how, before the war, the Athenians had tried to replace him with his detestable brother. And Perdiccas, finally, had need of speedy martial help because he was fighting a civil war with Arrhabaeus of the Lyncestians, a hedge-king of the Macedonian highlands. And so these needy parties in Chalcidice and Macedonia joined in imploring Sparta for help, help which the Spartans, for their own reasons, dispatched in 424 BC: the seven hundred helot hoplites who had been sent to die far away rather than endanger Sparta; their leader, Brasidas; and a thousand Peloponnesian mercenaries.[19]

Brasidas had recruited his sell-swords at Corinth and Sicyon. While his fledgling force was still aborning in the Peloponnese, he had used it to avert the betrayal of Megara to Athens. Soon after that, and before the Athenian adventure in Boeotia, Brasidas and his small army set out for the north, first passing through Boeotia to the new Spartan colony of Heraclea in Trachis. Before him now lay the fields of Thessaly, divided among its barons, some favoring Athens (as did the commons), and some Sparta.

Boldness and speed would be required for Brasidas to win through Thessaly before Sparta's enemies could gather to block his way. Brasidas summoned his Thessalian guest-friends to provide an escort (a reminder that such archaic relationships were still powerful in classical Greece), along with a friend of Perdiccas and a representative of the Chalcidians—whose own ties and friendships, he perhaps hoped, might ease his passage. When all was ready, Brasidas stepped off north, but soon after crossing into Thessaly, he was challenged at a river ford by a party of hostile Thessalians, who said that without official consent he might not pass.

With wide-eyed innocence, Brasidas' Thessalian escort explained their presence as no more than that of hosts entertaining unexpected guests who came in a private capacity (and so had naturally not asked anyone's permission): seventeen hundred was a considerable party of guests, certainly, yet the laws of hospitality were exacting. Of course, if the Thessalian authorities objected, they would go no further. With this Brasidas warmly concurred—he would await official permission—and the men rode away. Then—fast! fast!—Brasidas drove his force north at a jog-trot, before the thundering lie could be punished by the massed forces of the Thessalians. (This is another of those tales of victorious guile that Greeks so loved to hear, and the experience itself was good practice for Brasidas, who would soon be passing into the realm of Perdiccas—that master of perjury, the king from whom, in the words of the poet, ships brought to Athens "cargoes of lies.") In just three days, Brasidas marched his army the entire length of Thessaly, some seventy miles.[20]

Poignant it must have been for the Peloponnesians, forced to pass so quickly through the hallowed hills and plains of Thessaly. For Thessaly was the oldest habitation of the Greeks, where the traveler preferred to dawdle, to wander, and to crane. This was the kingdom of old Deucalion, who during the Flood—for the Greeks, too, knew the Flood—had survived by floating with his wife in a large chest, so much less slovenly than a

MAP 9.2 The March of Brasidas, 424 BC

beastly ark. Coming to land, the couple repeopled the earth without undue fatigue by casting over their shoulders stones, which grew into folk where they fell. Their more conventional acts of repeopling yielded a son: Hellen, father of the Hellenes, from whose sons and grandsons were traced all the Greek peoples.

The first district of Thessaly through which Brasidas led his men was Phthiotis, where Hellen had once kept his state. Here in later days dwelt the Myrmidons, and here the exiled Peleus raised his hall and captured the sea nymph Thetis for his bride—no easy task, for she transformed herself into many an aqueous wriggling form. Their wedding was the last banquet gods would share with men, the banquet to which the goddess Strife came uninvited and cast her golden apple among the goddesses as the prize for the fairest, so kindling the Trojan War. And in that war the son of Peleus and Thetis came to his glory: Achilles, the champion of Phthia; Achilles, the hero of the *Iliad*; Achilles, by far the best of the Achaeans.

To the east of Brasidas' course now rose the land of Iolcus, the kingdom of Jason, who had quested for the Golden Fleece. Along with the fleece, Jason had brought back from far Colchis the sorceress Medea, who gained the hero a throne with her ruses and her runes. The wicked old monarch who then held it had grown old: to show how he might be saved, Medea cut up an old ram, boiled it in a pot, and out it sprang young again. She bade the king's daughters to do the same in piety to their elderly father. But the daughters had not the knack—they managed the cutting and boiling but not the reviving—and so Jason claimed the throne. It is this famous tale of which the boiling of Demos back to youth in Aristophanes' *Knights* makes a joke.

As Brasidas' footsore troops hurried north, they saw high Pelion rising in the distance. There the men of old had lived with the centaurs, proud and sad. The mountain's slopes were home to hemlock and henbane, mandrake and yarrow; here Asclepius, the first healer, had learned the lore of simples. And on Pelion men had once summoned a bride's centaur kin to a great wedding, whereupon the beast-men, taking fire from unfamiliar wine, tried to carry away the bride. In the battle that followed, the centaurs were driven from Thessaly. So wide have they wandered, and so shy of men become, that centaurs are now but rarely seen.

North and ever north the Peloponnesians marched, and now Ossa loomed, and behind her stormy Olympus. When the twin giants, Poseidon's sons, attacked heaven—having eased their task by imprisoning warlike Ares in a jar—they piled Ossa upon Olympus and Pelion upon Ossa to make a stair to reach the sky. In vain: now the giants languish in Hades, lashed to columns by bonds of snakes, tormented forever by the screeching of an owl. And perhaps brave Orpheus saw them there, for the gorge between Ossa and Olympus was the Vale of Tempe, a valley sacred to Apollo and the fairest spot in all of Greece. Here a god's son had chased the dryad Eurydice, wife of Orpheus, and here she had died, bitten by a snake. And so her husband, the inventor of music, played such dolorous airs that all the gods did weep, and sent him to the underworld to recover his beloved. The dark lord Hades, melted by Orpheus' strains, consented to give Eurydice back, but on the black condition that Orpheus might not gaze his upon love until they both emerged into the light. Yet such was Orpheus' fondness that he glanced back at his bride—and so lost Eurydice forever.

To visit Tempe, sacred to the gods, hallowed by myth, and blessed by nature, was like a return to Hesiod's Age of Gold, when men lived like

FIGURE 9.1 Centaur with female captive

gods, without sorrow, without toil, abounding in justice, and when the rich earth yielded its fruits without stint.

But the flowers of Tempe the men of Brasidas did not admire; nor did they breathe deep of the valley's fragrant airs. Their stern and unromantic chief led them west around Olympus instead, and so they passed into the realm of twisting Perdiccas and into the Age of Iron.

Now that he had a Peloponnesian army in his hire (he was to supply one half of the costs of paying the mercenaries and feeding the helots, and the Chalcidian rebels the other), the Macedonian king showed little concern for the fears of the Chalcidians, little anxiety at their tiny shuddering under the cocked fist of a vengeful Athens. Nor did Perdiccas seem particularly concerned about far-reaching Athens itself, though Athens had now declared war on Macedon. Athens was suffered to set guards over her northern subjects, while Perdiccas led Brasidas northwest, toward Lyncestis to fight his private war with "King" Arrhabaeus. But before descending

332

MAP 9.3 Brasidas in the Thracian Chalcidice, 424 BC

the high pass into the wild vale of Lyncestis, Brasidas halted the expedition. Arrhabaeus had contacted the Spartan in secret and offered to let him arbitrate between himself and Perdiccas. Brasidas already had reason to be unhappy with his mission; as the Chalcidians accompanying Brasidas observed, if Arrhabaeus were destroyed out of hand, Perdiccas would no longer need Brasidas and would be less likely to support either him or the northern rebels in the fight against Athens. Better, Brasidas thought, to enroll Arrhabaeus as an independent ally of Sparta, who might be played against Perdiccas in case the slippery king proved trying.[21]

Perdiccas was furious: it was not for a hireling army to decide whom to fight. But Brasidas prevailed and made a private peace with Arrhabaeus, then marched away toward the Chalcidice to make trouble for the Athenians. Perdiccas fumed, but Brasidas had estimated to a nicety the king's need to preserve his link with the Spartan in case he needed to call on him in the future. Perdiccas could only swallow his anger and reduce his support for Brasidas' army from half to one third—no huge loss, since the Chalcidians were still paying the other half. Brasidas, it seemed, had outwitted the slyest of men.[22]

Upon his belated arrival in the Chalcidice in the late summer of 424 BC, Brasidas began inciting rebellions against Athens. Just before the vintage—in late August, still before the battle of Delium—Brasidas and his Chalcidian allies presented themselves before Acanthus, a wine-making city near the neck of the most easterly of the Chalcidian peninsulas and still under Athenian domination. Brasidas ordered the men of Acanthus to admit his army into the city. The Acanthians were torn. On the one hand, they feared for their grapes, which Brasidas threatened to destroy if they did not comply. On the other hand, should the Acanthians revolt against Athens, they might soon have much more than grapes to worry about. The grapes eventually won, their juicy cause no doubt much strengthened by the Acanthians' sympathy with the Chalcidian rebels and the proven success of Brasidas, who had seen off the Athenians at Megara, not to mention the Athenians' long failure to suppress the existing revolt in the north. And so Acanthus opened its gates, joining the rebellion against Athens. Soon Stagirus, north up the coast, followed suit. Sixty years later there would be brought to birth in that obscure town a squalling infant with a large forehead: his parents named him Aristotle.[23]

With Acanthus and Stagirus raised in revolt, Brasidas now cast his eye eastward, beyond Chalcidice, to the greatest city of the region: bustling Amphipolis, set in a winding of the Strymon. This colony of Athens was so great a place, and so closely watched, that Brasidas was obliged to take it by betrayal, and so some months were spent in scheming and secret sendings. In the south during this time, the Athenians made their bid for Boeotia and lost the hand at Delium. The rebels of the north rejoiced to hear of Athens' defeat and no doubt thrilled to the tale of their former masters paddling away from the desecrated temple, an angry Apollo scowling at their backs.[24]

Brasidas' target, Amphipolis, boasted a near embarrassment of potential traitors to help the Spartan get through the gates; some of them were loyal to Perdiccas, and others to the Chalcidians. But those in whom Brasidas placed the most confidence were the men of Argilus, a small town on the coast near Amphipolis. The Athenians had long treated Argilus with suspicion, perhaps because its inhabitants did not conceal their anger at having gigantic Amphipolis founded in their rightful territory. Many resentful Argilans lived in Amphipolis, and it was they who were to open the gates to Brasidas.[25]

It was winter, and snowy, when Brasidas set out for Argilus and Amphipolis. To take the city by surprise, he covered half the distance from Chalcidice in a single day and finished the journey by night. He reached Argilus in darkness, and the town revolted to him on the instant; the Argilans then led his forces through the dawn to the great bridge over Strymon, so large in the importance of Amphipolis. Overcoming a guard weakened both by surprise and treachery, Brasidas crossed the river to the eastern side, where Amphipolis lay. There his troops began to plunder the homes just outside the city, taking many Amphipolitans prisoner. Not a few of the locals, oblivious to Brasidas' coming, had passed the night outside the pro-

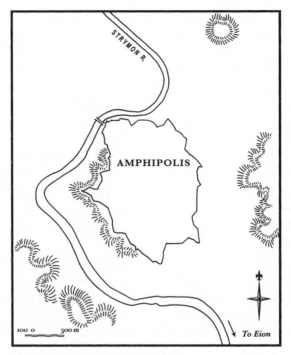

MAP 9.4 Amphipolis and Environs

tective city wall—the rich in their villas, the poor in their dumbles—just as so many of the folk of Plataea had done when the Thebans came calling at the outbreak of the war. But all this looting thwarted the planned betrayal of Amphipolis, as those flocking into the city for safety brought news of the enemy in their neighborhood. Now well-alerted, inhabitants loyal to Athens prevented the traitors from opening the gates. And so Brasidas was forced to camp his exhausted army outside the city walls as day broke over the north.[26]

Just like Megara in similar circumstances, Amphipolis was in turmoil, with Brasidas without and rent within by the conflicting suspicions of the people. Earlier, when they had heard of the coming of Brasidas to the Thraceward region, the Athenians had sent a squadron to the area under the command of one general and sent a second general to hold Amphipolis itself. The Athenian general in command of the city now sent an urgent message to the nearby island of Thasos, where his colleague happened to be, to summon him and the squadron.[27]

Brasidas knew that it was only a matter of time until a considerable force could be assembled against him and that the town's resistance to him would

335

only wax as the power of Athens gathered. Thus, the betrayal of the city having failed, that same day he offered its inhabitants soft terms if they opened the gates and joined the northern rebellion. Any of Amphipolis' occupants—including Athenians—might stay and enjoy their property, or they might leave within five days, carrying with them such wealth as they could.[28]

Brasidas' offer made a surprising impact on the nervous crowd within the city. The men of Amphipolis could not have anticipated an invitation to join the northern rebellion as friends. Rather, as an Athenian colony, with Athenians in the city and with an Athenian general in command, they would have expected an enemy to sack and slaughter if he got within the walls; at best, if the city were forced to surrender, its folk would be expelled into the snow. And so they might still, if terms were not agreed and the traitors in the city could force open a gate.

There were other reasons, too, that Brasidas' offer was appealing to the people of Amphipolis. Many fellow citizens, relatives of those within, were in the Spartan's hands, having been captured outside the walls when Brasidas first marched up. Nor was the number of Amphipolitans with close ties to Athens large—so the connection that Brasidas hoped to sever was already thin. And the Athenian citizens within Amphipolis were wavering as well, knowing that it would take time for the generals of Athens to assemble a force capable of facing Brasidas in the field. Now those who had promised, but failed, to betray the city to Brasidas harangued the assembly, urging the Amphipolitans to accept Brasidas' terms. And, exploiting the astonishment of the citizenry that the enemy army outside meant them no harm, the argument for revolt from Athens prevailed. Amphipolis opened its gates.[29]

Such was the situation when the Athenian general from Thasos sailed into the mouth of the Strymon, on the evening of the day whose dawn had seen Brasidas arrive before Amphipolis, three miles upriver. Putting into the estuary city of Eion, the general received news of the capitulation of Amphipolis. The great city could hardly be recaptured by the seven ships he had with him, so he put Eion into a state of defense—just in time, as it turned out, for the next morning Brasidas' army bobbed down the river in a collection of boats they had found on the docks of Amphipolis, hoping to seize the breakwater, and so the harbor, of Eion. Troops of Brasidas' arrived by land, as well, and these combined forces attacked the town. But the alert Athenians drove them off, and Brasidas was forced to return to Amphipolis.[30]

For the next five days, Amphipolis witnessed the departure—and Eion the arrival—of Athenians and their loyalists leaving under the generous terms of Amphipolis' capitulation, floating their goods and kin down the river or rattling them away on wagons. And soon rebellion crashed through the region, like an avalanche kicked off by man but gathering its own force in its fall. Two Greek coastal towns to the east of the Strymon, colonies of Thasos, came over to Brasidas, and—wonder of wonders—the Spartan received also the tattooed headmen of a nearby settlement of the Thracians, never subject to Athens. These warriors were disgruntled, Brasidas learned, because their rightful king had recently been killed in a conspiracy involving his own wife. No doubt to the accompaniment of much snorting and scratching, they yielded themselves to Brasidas' power.[31]

Many other subject cities of Athens, thrilled at Brasidas' success and having heard of the humiliation of the Athenians at Delium (which seemed to eclipse the Athenian sun that had shone so hotly in the year since Sphacteria), sent messages to Brasidas, pledging to revolt if he should come to them. The kindly terms he had given at Amphipolis urged along this movement, as did the earnestness of his proclamations that he had come to free the Greeks from empire rather than simply to replace Athenian rule with Spartan. For he pledged to leave the constitutional arrangements of the rebels unchanged and to impose no garrisons or governors. After a seven-year pregnancy, Sparta seemed finally to have brought to birth a son who was in earnest about freeing the Greeks from Athens, the slogan under which Sparta had gone to war in 431 BC and that had brought Sparta such goodwill at war's beginning. Even the cynical Perdiccas appeared at Amphipolis to find out what profit he might draw from these remarkable events.[32]

The gods were friendly to a northern rebellion in winter. Day after day the wind blew hard and stormy from the north—even against the Athenians, who claimed Boreas, the north wind, as their kinsman. Thus no great northbound expedition by sea could be mounted against Brasidas. But what ships the Athenians could get through they did, to place garrisons in the northern cities the Athenians still held and so prevent these towns from yielding to the attacks, or enticements, of Brasidas.[33]

As they worried over their northern possessions in the winter of 424/423 BC, the Athenians beguiled their frustration with a favorite amusement: putting a failed general on trial. And so the wrath of the Athenians fell upon the unlucky commander at Thasos, who had so terribly failed to prevent the defection of Amphipolis. His crime, we may guess, was less sloth for failing to save the city when he heard that Brasidas was outside than inattention for allowing Brasidas to fall upon Amphipolis by surprise. For the Athenians had known that Brasidas was less than forty miles away in the Chalcidice, and yet he had managed to sneak up and rob them of the greatest city in the region. Sentenced to exile, the Athenian general would return to Athens only after the end of the Peloponnesian War, in 404 BC. The name of the general was Thucydides, son of Olorus.[34]

With friends holding the country of winds and the Aegean entrenched with storms, Brasidas moved his affairs in the north. On Strymon's bank he

MAP 9.5 Fighting in the Thracian Chalcidice, 423 BC

began to build triremes—an absurd endeavor considering the nautical might of the Athenians, yet perhaps he could snatch a local mastery while Athens' fleet was windbound in Piraeus. Sailing out past Eion, he could cruise along the coast, safe in the lee of the south-smiling land, and perhaps even sail east to Thasos, whose colonies had just revolted to him. But Brasidas' main plots lay on terra firma, back in the Chalcidice. First he marched to Acte, the easternmost of the three Chalcidian capes and the closest to Amphipolis; most of the small cities there joined him. The two largest, however, Sane and Dium, clung to Athens. So Brasidas ravaged their territory, which in winter was more a matter of destroying farm buildings than wasting actual crops, although olive trees and vines could be damaged in any season.[35]

After Acte, Brasidas marched to the middle jut of the Chalcidice, where Torone, its greatest town, was held by an Athenian garrison. A peaceful community rising up a hill from the sea—"quieter than the harbor of the Toroneans," said the Greeks to describe a scene of utter stillness—Torone was known for its tasty dog sharks, its curious white sea urchins, and its men who dove for sponges in the shining sea. The quiet was hardly broken by Torone's would-be rebels, for they treated with Brasidas in whispers and duly promised to betray the place.[36]

Another night march, then, and Brasidas' men quietly grounded their spears at the temple of Castor and Pollux outside the walls of Torone.

FIGURE 9.2 Torone from the sea, present state, with the Oil Bottle in the foreground

There, in the dark and cold, the Spartan held a nervous colloquy with the conspirators from the town. Twenty of Brasidas' men, armed with daggers, followed Toronean guides to the seawall, and although thirteen of them balked at the peril, seven slipped into the city. These tiptoed through the blackness of the town, but they lost their way in the dark. Finally, spotting a tower at the highest point of the steep city, they crept upon the garrison, broke in, and slew those within. Then these brave seven opened the nearby gate—which was, however, on the wrong side of the town because of their earlier miscarriage. If they made their signal, they made it into the un-answering dark. For Brasidas had posted his peltasts near the lower-down market gate to rush into the city as soon as they saw it open and a beacon was lit to signal that all was in readiness within. It was now long past time, and Brasidas' men outside kept creeping closer and closer to the walls.[37]

It was the Toronean co-conspirators, waiting inside the city, who guessed the infiltrators' error. Cutting through the wooden bar, these Toroneans broke open the market gate. All was silent: the town's garrison still dozed. Brasidas' peltasts were primed to charge the gate, but there was no need for haste. And so the unflappable Toroneans turned the muddle of Brasidas' infiltrators to advantage by leading more of Brasidas' men around to the rear gate, wrongly opened, so that they could attack the town from that side as well. Justly did the proverb of the Greeks name the men of Torone sponges, for not only did they harvest them from the sea, but like sponges they changed shape to adapt to events.[38]

Finally, the conspirators struck their flame at the market gate, and the peltasts came running from the nearby dark. Brasidas, too, saw the flare, and he and his troops surged toward the market gate with a mighty roar. Some crushed their way through the narrow portal; others ran up beams left leaning against the wall in the process of repairs: so little had the Athenians been expecting an attack.

Now the unsuspecting people of Torone awoke to discover that their town was in peril. Now quiet Torone was quiet no longer. The incomers assailed from all sides the fifty Athenian hoplites who had been camped in the marketplace, killing a few of them. But Brasidas' orders were for his soldiers to take the high places of the city, while others scattered unordered, presumably in search of loot. Thus most of the Athenians—and the men of Torone loyal to them—had time to escape to the two Athenian triremes in the harbor or to flee on foot to the citadel of Torone, on a narrow peninsula off the city called the "Oil Bottle" for its shape. This strong place they held against Brasidas.[39]

Come morning, Brasidas tried to take the Oil Bottle without fighting, by resorting to the diplomacy that had served him so well in the past. He promised the Athenians safe conduct away and pardon for the Toroneans who had taken refuge with them, but the Athenians merely replied with a request for a day's truce to take up their dead. Brasidas gave them two, and the Athenians occupied the time feverishly improving their fortifications, even as Brasidas fortified nearby houses against them. He also addressed the assembly of the Toroneans, fishing for the loyalty of the majority by promising to treat them, like the privileged men of Amphipolis, not as his war captives but rather as voluntary adherents to the lofty cause of Chalcidian liberty.[40]

When the two-day truce expired, Brasidas proceeded to attack the Athenians on the Oil Bottle, but was beaten back. The next day the Athenians saw Brasidas' men slowly preparing an infernal engine to burn down their defenses—something very like the monstrous bellows with which the Boeotians had taken the fort at Delium. Knowing where this contraption must approach, the Athenians leapt to counter it by erecting a wooden tower on the roof of a house just inside the Oil Bottle and conveying up water in containers and stones to drop, as well as men to drop them. Too much! With a groan and a crack, the house beneath collapsed into splintered driftwood and powdered clay. The defenders nearby knew this for an accident and that their position remained secure. But those further out on the Oil Bottle, hearing the crash, imagined that Brasidas' men were within the wall and ran for their boats. Brasidas saw the panic out on the peninsula and promptly ordered an attack. His men now took the citadel at a rush, killing all those left inside it—in great part Toroneans, since most of the Athenians had escaped to their triremes.[41]

Before the panic, Brasidas had offered a cash reward to the first man to scale the Athenian wall—but the citadel, it seemed, had fallen by no human hand. A temple of Athena stood upon the Oil Bottle, and Brasidas determined that she had intervened on his behalf. He cleared the entire peninsula of other buildings and dedicated the whole as a holy precinct to the goddess. The cash reward he gave to her as well, in thanks for making the house fall down. Honor properly done to Athena, Brasidas then sat himself down to ponder what other mischief he might make for Athens in the north.[42]

By the end of March 423 BC, another of Brasidas' plots came into flower. Scione, near the tip of Pallene, the westernmost arm of the Chalcidice, revolted against Athens. Proud of their Peloponnesian origin—they had been blown into the north on their way back from Troy, they claimed—the Scionians would have considered themselves by nature braver than the Ionians and sundry mongrels in their neighborhood. And their revolt was an act of courage, indeed, for they were cut off from the rest of the northern rebellion: Potidaea, now full of Athenian colonists, quite closed off the cape on which Scione stood, leaving no way for Brasidas to get there but by sea. Yet by sea he went, with one of his new Strymon-built triremes in the lead, to serve as protection against a weak enemy and as bait for a strong one, the guileful Spartan skimming along in a boat behind.[43]

Arriving on Pallene, Brasidas enrolled Scione in the Spartan alliance with much praise of the courage of its folk (and not a little secret trepidation, one suspects, about how he was going to defend the inaccessible city against Athens). Received as a hero, Brasidas was crowned with a wreath of gold, and men hung him with ribbons as if he were a victorious athlete who might share with them his divine blessing. The fame of Brasidas was now Sparta's most potent weapon in the north—a refutation of the rumors about Sparta's downfall and itself an incitement to revolt against the Athenians.[44]

The safety of Scione depended upon opening a road to the mainland: upon taking Potidaea, which blocked the way off the peninsula, and the town of Mende, which lay between the two cities. And all this must be done quickly, for the season of tempests was drawing in, and the Aegean would soon present a direful calm, allowing the galleys of Piraeus to convey

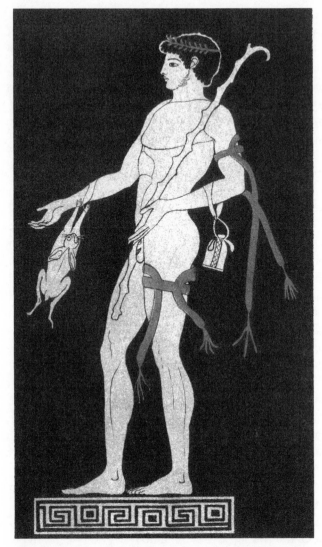

FIGURE 9.3 What Brasidas would have looked like when
adorned with the ribbons of an athletic victor

the immeasurable strength of Athens to this quailing northern strand. Brasidas understood this exigency all too well; he carried soldiers over the water to garrison Scione and now began to intrigue for the betrayal of Mende, halfway up Pallene, and to lay plans against Potidaea. But the last blast of winter carried into Scione's harbor a trireme carrying commissioners both Athenian and Spartan. Such strange collaboration could mean only one thing. Brasidas' homeland had betrayed his efforts. Athens and Sparta had made a truce.[45]

Brasidas listened with incredulity to the terms of the year-long truce. Each side was to hold what they held on the day the truce came into effect in southern Greece and take nothing more. And a quick count on his fingers revealed to Brasidas the fearful truth: Scione had rebelled two days after the truce was struck. So Brasidas must surrender his brave new ally to the wrath of an avenging Athens.

EVER SINCE THE BLOCKADE OF the men upon Sphacteria in 425 BC, Sparta had been pressing for peace, but peace only under acceptable conditions. The most elementary of those conditions was the return of the Lacedaemonians captured on the island and Athenian withdrawal from Spartan territory, namely, from Pylos and Cythera. When the Peloponnesians had entered the war, moreover, they had sworn to each other high oaths that all should leave the war with what they had held going into it; that is, Athens would have to return anything she had captured from Sparta's allies. This meant that the Athenians must agree to give up all the places they held in Peloponnese and depart from the Argolid peninsula before the Peloponnesians could confirm any peace treaty. Megara's port of Nisaea, also, must be returned, as must her island of Minoa and the places that Athens had captured from Corinth in the northwest of Greece, especially Sollium and Anactorium. Finally, as the Spartan offer in 425 BC signaled, the Spartans would accept no peace that implied the symbolic inferiority of Sparta to Athens, although they had reconciled themselves to Athens' equality.[46]

As for Athens, she had good reasons to make peace, if a satisfactory peace could be negotiated, and ever better reasons for a temporary suspension of hostilities. In the wake of Sphacteria, when Athens preened herself as *hegemon* of Greece, she had scoffed at the terms that Sparta offered her. But her pretensions to supremacy had been left a broken corpse upon the field of Delium. After that debacle, Thucydides implies, the Athenians were willing "to make peace on the basis of equality." And now, for the first time in the war since Mytilene had almost succeeded in turning Lesbos against her, Athens feared not merely for her honor but also for her empire. A good part of the north had already defected, and with the bridge at Amphipolis lost to Athens, there was nothing to keep Brasidas from marching east and collecting up, one by one, Athens' subjects on the coast of Thrace. Dryshod he might arrive at the very Hellespont itself, seat of a second important assemblage of Athenian allies, and a waterway that was, of course, important to the trade and grain supply of Athens as well.[47]

Apart from the specific threat of Brasidas on the rampage in the north, Athens could not wholly discount the possibility of a general revolt throughout her empire. The Athenians were suspicious even of those who had been steadfast friends; in the winter after Sphacteria, for instance, the Athenians had bade the men of Chios, their last remaining ally who provided ships, to pull down the wall they had just built around their town, suspecting that it betokened plans for an insurrection; wall building had, after all, preceded the revolt of nearby Mytilene.[48]

Athens' suspicions of her friends aside, the Chalcidice was not the only region of the empire where a long-smoldering rebellion might take fire. After Athens' bloody suppression of the revolt of Mytilene in 427 BC, many of the folk of Mytilene and Lesbos had escaped to the mainland of Asia Minor. They were wealthy enough to hire mercenaries, both locally and from the Peloponnese. With these forces, they took a city near the Hellespont in 424 BC, returned it to Athens for a ransom, and then took Antandros, a mainland city right across the water from Lesbos and one of the places on the coast of Asia Minor that the Athenians had stripped from Mytilene when her insurrection had failed. A full-scale rebellion was growing on that coast, and the rebels were trying to make themselves masters of the mainland cities round about, while also building ships to raid Lesbos. Later in 424 BC the Athenians turned these miscreants out of Antandros, but they were still a peril elsewhere on the mainland. And, to add to Athens' woes in this region, graying exiles from Samos (refugees from Athens' suppression of their rebellion in 440 BC) had their own station on the mainland across from Samos, further south from Antandros; from there they harassed the island and had the impertinence to send their experienced steersmen to man Peloponnesian triremes in Sparta's naval battles against Athens.[49]

The notional purpose of the truce struck between Athens and Sparta in 423 BC was the negotiation of a general peace, and emissaries buzzed back and forth during the year. That general peace was not achieved. Yet both sides had accepted the suspension of hostilities. We should perhaps accept, then, Thucydides' hint that while the Spartans were eager for a long-term treaty, the Athenians regarded the one-year truce in the first place as an instrument of war, almost a ruse, a way to halt immediately and without risk the growing avalanche of rebellions from Athens in the north. The use of truces as weapons was, of course, nothing new in the world: the Spartans had used the five-year truce Cimon struck in 451 BC to assemble a conspiracy against Athens. Now the Athenians saw a dangerous wave building against them, and freezing all in place would certainly, whatever else it did, break the wave's momentum.[50]

Freezing the combatants is exactly what the truce of 423 BC did. Neither side was to give up any territory, and neither might stray from its current

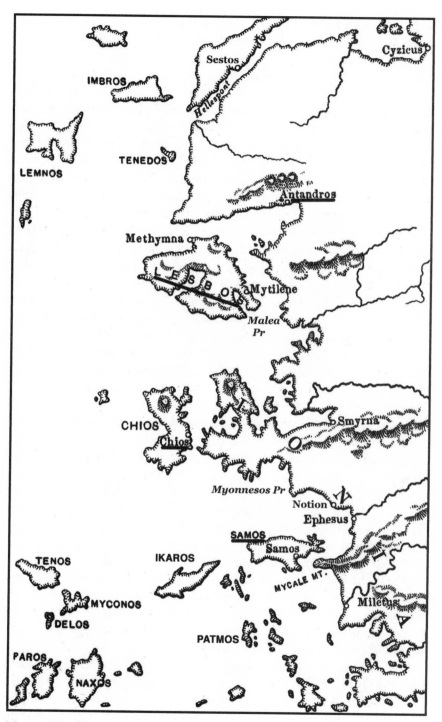

MAP 9.6 Trouble in the Athenian Empire, 423 BC

holdings. Near the fort at Pylos, on the western coast of the Peloponnese, a line was drawn between two points, over which the Athenians might not pass into the rest of Messenia. Nor might any cross from Cythera to the mainland. Nor might either side receive deserters from the other—so the Athenians at Pylos could take in no more defecting helots. Between Megara and her Athenian-held port of Nisaea, a wandering boundary was carefully drawn across the land—along a road from a shrine to the temple of Poseidon, then on to the bridge to the tiny southern island of Minoa, prickly with watchtowers—which neither side was to transgress. All the warlike sea fell to Athens, so while the Peloponnesians might trade along their coast, they must not set out in warships, and the maximum size of oared vessels was carefully specified so that they might not try to pass off a trireme as a bumboat.[51]

Although happy to suspend her war with the Peloponnesians for a year, Athens was not yet willing to make peace with Sparta on the terms Sparta was offering. Judging by the terms agreed to in the eventual peace two years later, although she was willing to yield up the prisoners from Sphacteria and her conquests in the Peloponnese (Pylos and Cythera and Methana), Athens was not willing to surrender her extra-Peloponnesian gains, especially not the Megarian port of Nisaea or the Corinthian towns in the northwest. In other words, she was willing to make a peace equal in honor—and territorially a peace on the basis of status quo ante bellum—with Sparta alone. Athens was not, however, about to yield anything to Sparta's greater allies. And why should she? She was hardly prepared to admit the equality of Megara or Corinth; as for Boeotia, Athens had been humiliated in that territory, and her defeat there she might yet want to avenge.

A peace on the basis of equality might be made with Sparta, then, but not with the other members of the wider Peloponnesian alliance. This effectively prevented any lasting peace from being struck in 423 BC. Earlier in the war, when Athens had concentrated her attention on Sparta and Megara, scornfully declining to "notice" Corinth and Boeotia, it might have been possible to continue to ignore them as well in a treaty. But since 426 BC Athens had been treating Boeotia and Corinth as independent opponents in the war of pride, whose rank in relation to Athens must be adjusted in any peace; so Athens was unwilling to satisfy their demands, lest she concede an inch of honor. Either Athens must change her views, or Sparta must betray her allies. Otherwise, there was no way forward—and war would continue once the one-year truce ran out.

With our vast power of retrospect, and knowing how cynically a "peace process" may be exploited by those with no real interest in peace, we might have advised the Spartans to have refused the year's truce of 423 BC. But to blame the Spartans for accepting the truce would be to demand from them foolish overconfidence or extrahuman foresight. They could expect the summer of 423 BC to bring more incursions from Pylos and Cythera—if, indeed, they had not suffered raids by land from Pylos all the past winter—not to mention more defections of the helots and likely more attacks upon their Peloponnesian allies. The great helot rebellion they had feared the summer before had failed to transpire, but they could hardly be sure that, with further Athenian goading, it would not break out this year or the next. A year's respite, whatever the future might bring, would allow Sparta to make things safer at home.[52]

The Spartans were not worried about bringing a halt to Brasidas' series of triumphs in the north. Further campaigning in the north might make peace harder to achieve, not easier. For if fighting went on and Brasidas were defeated, then Sparta would lose all the leverage that holding Amphipolis and the northern cities currently gave her, while if Brasidas won, Athens might then feel obliged to avenge the defeat. Then the war would surely continue, and the Spartans might never recover their captured men.

Curiously, the defeat of Sparta at Sphacteria and of Athens at Delium had created a parity of humiliation that was no bad basis for peace. Especially conducive to a settlement was the fact that the Athenians had been defeated by someone other than Sparta, so the pride of Athens was lowered without that of Sparta being unduly raised. A balance seemed to have been struck, although it was tenuous indeed. For if the principals were themselves to fight again, and if Athens were to win, she might no longer be willing to make peace on the basis of equality in honor, which would preclude a treaty, as both sides must have known. If, however, Brasidas won, although he might achieve a military parity with Athens (the most that could be hoped for, given the hostages that Athens held), his victory would also imperil the parity in honor between Athens and Sparta, the parity that was the fragile foundation upon which the Spartans now hoped to make peace: if the Athenians were to fall behind again, the war might go on for years as they tried to catch up.[53]

That the Spartans regarded Brasidas' success in this equivocal light the commander already knew, because over the winter (424/423 BC) they had refused to send him reinforcements when he sent to ask for them. The unabated eagerness of the Lacedaemonians to recover the men captured on Sphacteria had been one of their reasons for that decision. The fact is, the Spartans were afraid lest Brasidas succeed too well.[54]

Informed of the truce between Athens and Sparta by the trireme carrying commissioners from Athens and Sparta, Brasidas' immediate anxiety was for Scione, which, in ignorance of the truce, had revolted to him two days after the truce came into effect. Mytilene was surely on his mind as a model for what would happen to the people of Scione, were Brasidas to return it to the Athenians, and Brasidas felt that both he, and the Spartans, were committed to the city's safety. Besides, surrendering Scione would have incalculable consequences for the reputation of Brasidas in the north as a staunch champion of Chalcidian liberty. But while the Athenian commissioner consented to Brasidas' retaining all his other holdings, as Athens and Sparta had agreed, Scione was very pointedly excluded from the truce.

In such a predicament, all Brasidas could do was draw himself up to his full height, take a deep breath, and lie. He insisted that Scione had revolted *before* the deadline and wrote to Sparta asserting the same. When his claim was reported to Athens, the Athenians prepared an expedition to sail north and retake Scione by force, even as envoys from Sparta, trusting Brasidas, insisted that attacking Scione would violate the truce. Let the matter be put to arbitration, they pleaded, as the truce required of dubious points. But the Athenians were impatient with the cunctations of debate. Sinister indeed, in their minds, was the march of the rebellion to Scione, for it was the first place to revolt that Brasidas could not reach by land. Practically and politically, Scione was an island. What insular ally of Athens would turn on her next? Thasos? Chios? Euboea? Indeed, there may have been some trouble on Euboea this year. And the whole point of the truce, in the eyes of Athens, had been to stop the momentum of the rebellion, which now seemed to roll on regardless. No, an example must be made of Scione, and straightaway. Thus Cleon swiftly passed a decree that, upon the recapture of Scione, the city was to be destroyed and its men executed.[55]

Brasidas' bold lie at Scione had a keen audience in Mende, northward up the cape from Scione—Mende, famous for its wine and divided in its loyalties. There a small cabal rejoiced upon learning that Brasidas would not give up Scione and soon approached him with an offer to betray their city as well. Would he accept them after the truce had come into effect? He would; and when Athens challenged his decision, he put forward several cavils that the Athenians had violated the truce's terms. The Greeks must have chuckled, remembering the Athenians' equally weak excuses for failing to return the Peloponnesian fleet in Navarino Bay in the wake of the twenty-day truce of 425 BC.[56]

Brasidas may have defended his reception of Scione by bluffing the Athenians and lying to the Spartans, but receiving Mende in the teeth of the truce between Sparta and Athens was quite another thing. Now Brasidas had cast away his Lacedaemonian discipline and seemed to be acting as general of the Chalcidians rather than an officer of the Spartans. Although this no doubt alarmed the Spartans, their rage was nothing compared to that of the Athenians, who now marked down Mende along with Scione for chastisement and prepared their armament. Knowing that their coming would not be long delayed, Brasidas garrisoned the two cities and evacuated their women and children by sea to Olynthus, headquarters of the Chalcidian rebellion. And so it was that, although the truce of 423 BC was observed in southern Greece and the rest of the north, conflict still flamed on the peninsula of Pellene, where the very stones remembered the footsteps of the Giants who had once made war upon the gods.[57]

The wrath of Athens would break upon Scione and Mende without the sheltering presence of Brasidas. For months Perdiccas had been paying Brasidas' army, while getting little in return. And Perdiccas was at war again with his rebellious subject Arrhabaeus of Lyncestis; Perdiccas' previous campaign had been thwarted, for diplomatic reasons, by Brasidas when he first arrived in the north. Now Brasidas, his Peloponnesians, and the men of the Chalcidice—three thousand in total—had to pay their debt to Perdiccas and march with the Macedonian king back into the dale of Lyncestis.[58]

As soon as the allies entered the land of Arrhabaeus, the Lyncestians offered battle. There was first a vast, whirling mêlée of horsemen in the Macedonian manner. It was inconclusive (of course it was, a Greek would say; all cavalry battles are). Then the sturdy Greek hoplites fought the Lyncestian hoplites and drove them away (not surprising, a Greek would say). Perdiccas wanted to advance to plunder the villages of Lyncestis, but the multitude of Illyrians, piratical barbarians from the west whom he had hired to help, had not yet appeared (typical, a Greek would say). Brasidas did not want to stray further into the wastes of Macedonia: he feared for Mende and Scione. Perdiccas and Brasidas wrangled. Now it was reported that the Illyrians had betrayed Perdiccas and joined Arrhabaeus (of course, a Greek would say). Both leaders then agreed that the allies must retreat. But in the meantime nightfall had come upon them. In the gloaming the Macedonians conjured visions of Illyrians loping through the night. And in the dark the Macedonians and their barbarian allies fled away (naturally, a Greek would say), sweeping King Perdiccas with them. Brasidas had camped apart. Only with the coming of morning did the Greeks realize that they had been abandoned among enemies, and now Arrhabaeus and altogether real Illyrians were coming against them.

Thucydides dwells upon the running battle by which Brasidas extracted his army from Lyncestis because it was a successful fighting retreat (unlike, for example, that of Demosthenes in Aetolia in the sixth year of the war) and a successful defense by hoplites against light-armed enemies (unlike that of the Spartans at Sphacteria). Part of Thucydides' purpose in writing was, after all, to arm his reader with useful know-how, in case some later student of great affairs found himself in a similar situation. Here, then, is what to do if surrounded by barbarians at the extremity of the world:

First, form your hoplites into a square. Put your outnumbered light-armed troops (and no doubt your baggage as well) in the middle. Establish a fast-reaction force of the youngest hoplites to dash out and counter-attack if the enemy presses at any point of the perimeter. Establish another picked force as a rearguard, for theirs will be the post of greatest peril. Should you need to pass through a narrow place, send your picked men to seize the heights. When you encourage your troops (Thucydides gives Brasidas a speech), attempt no literary novelty but rather remind them of their advantages: contrast the inborn bravery of Greeks with the innate cowardice of barbarians. Contrast the steadiness of hoplites with the leap-ing of the light-armed. Scorn their savage numbers, and warn your men against their gasconade hooting and their brandishing of arms. Then set the square in motion toward safety. Calm is all: the enemy onset will be worst at the outset, when they think you are in flight. When they discover their error, they will soon become discouraged.[59]

And so it was, teaching Thucydides' readers no bad lesson for eternity, that Brasidas and his men returned safe into the land of Perdiccas. But they were furious at Perdiccas' flight, and once their enemies fell away, their march became an invasion of his realm. They pillaged the abandoned Mac-edonian baggage on the road and slaughtered the draft oxen. Now it was Perdiccas' turn to be angry, and, Thucydides says, his thoughts turned to yet another reconciliation with Brasidas' enemy, Athens.[60]

Once his army had sated its rage against Perdiccas and the Macedonians, Brasidas marched straight out of Macedonia into the Chalcidice, only to dis-cover that what he dreaded had indeed transpired: in his absence, Mende had fallen to Athens. The Athenians had sailed against the rebels on Pallene with forty ships of their own and ten from Chios, carrying a thousand hop-lites and six hundred archers. They were commanded by Nicias, conqueror of Minoa and Cythera, who had led the Athenians against Corinth at Soly-geia in 425 BC, and Nicostratus, the goodly soul who had tried to reconcile the Corcyrean factions in 427 BC. At Potidaea they had picked up a host of local light-armed auxiliaries. Coming to land near Mende, they found their route to the city blocked by a steep hill held by Mende's defenders: a Pelo-ponnesian garrison, the soldiers of Mende, and three hundred fellow rebels from Scione—seven hundred men in all. Two Athenian attempts to dislodge the defenders from the hill failed. At nightfall the Athenians camped, and the defenders returned to Mende.[61]

The next day the Athenians circumvented the hill position by landing their soldiers from ships on the other side of the town. After disembarking they took the unwalled suburb on that side and ravaged the land. None came against them because there was an uproar within the walls. Strife had developed in Mende over whether the Athenians ought to be resisted at all. The cabal that had betrayed Mende to Brasidas was small: only those few, the Peloponnesian garrison, and the men of Scione wanted to keep fighting. And that night the three hundred of Scione crept home in disgust, no doubt cursing the cowardice of their neighbors.[62]

On the third day, half the Athenians ravaged the territory of Mende south toward Scione, at the tip of the peninsula, while the other half kept Mende under watch. The leader of the defenders, Polydamidas, saw in this division of forces an opportunity to make a sally against the Athenians. At the gate nearest to the enemy, he drew up his remaining troops and began to harangue them—only to be answered by a weedy voice piping up from the ranks: "I won't go! There's no need to fight!" The furious Polydamidas rounded on the heckler and began to pummel him—and that alone was required, in ancient Greece where the skin of a free man was held sacred, to touch off a civil war.[63]

The people of Mende, who had never wanted to revolt from Athens in the first place, caught up their arms and charged the Peloponnesians and the cabal. They fell on them, routed them, and drove the Peloponnesians back to the acropolis—the more easily because the Peloponnesians thought that the Mendean counterrevolutionaries had arranged their counterrevolution with the Athenians. Then the men of Mende did indeed open the gates to the Athenians, but the Athenian contingent outside waited—bemused by the tumult within—until the other half of their army hurried back from its ravaging. Then they burst into the city and—because there had in fact been no communication between the Mendeans and the Athenians—proceeded to plunder it, their commanders holding them back from general massacre only with difficulty. Once calm was restored, the Athenians walled off the acropolis, set guards over the Peloponnesians who still lurked inside, and bade the people of Mende to go about their affairs as they had before Brasidas came and to place any surviving members of the cabal on trial. Then the main force of the Athenians marched off to deal with Scione.

Scione would not be so easy to take. Its folk were not divided. Like the defenders of Mende, the men of Scione occupied a hill on the approach to the town, but unlike at Mende the Athenians drove them off it and behind the walls of the city. Now the Athenians began to encircle Scione with a siege wall, but before they could complete it, the Peloponnesians confined on the acropolis of Mende broke through their Athenian guards, marched by night along the shore, and reached Scione. Most of them got through the Athenian lines and into the town, where they joined its defenders. Now Scione would be harder than ever to storm. And so, once the Athenians had safely invested Scione at the end of the summer of 423 BC, there was nothing for them to do but leave an ample watch around the city and go home. Scione would hold out until after peace was made in 421 BC, but when she fell, the Athenians did indeed inflict upon her the awful punishment that Cleon had devised. All the men they killed, and they sold the women and children as slaves. But for now, the Athenians had accomplished the goal of their mission: for even if they had not extinguished the rebellion on the cape of Pallene, they had damped and banked the blaze.[64]

The fall of Mende and the siege of Scione were not the end of Brasidas' woes. King Perdiccas had now openly taken the Athenian side. Thucydides attributes this to hatred for Brasidas arising from the disaster in Lyncestis. There is no reason to discount that motive, but at the same time it was in the underlying interest of Perdiccas that none but he should be strong in the north, and he surely felt that Brasidas was becoming overmighty there, so it made sense for him to back the Athenians—only to betray them again, of course, if they began to prevail. In the summer of 423 BC, Perdiccas made an alliance with the Athenians. He had presumably already stopped paying Brasidas' army after the disaster in Lyncestis.[65]

This new Athenian alliance with Perdiccas promptly showed its utility when Perdiccas prevented a Peloponnesian reinforcement intended for Brasidas. Although the Spartans had refused to reinforce Brasidas when he called for help in the winter (424/423 BC), by the following summer they evidently thought the danger of his rout more perilous than that of his triumph and began to assemble in the Peloponnese an army to send north. But any reinforcement for Brasidas must pass through Thessaly, and in Thessaly Perdiccas had many friends. Under the influence of the Macedonian king, the lords of Thessaly made it very clear that a Peloponnesian army was not welcome in their land. And so the Peloponnesian march to reinforce Brasidas was abandoned. But, alas for unbridled Brasidas, the Lacedaemonian leaders of this abortive expedition took advantage of the truce to sail the sea without fear and presented themselves in the north anyway: a commission of three inspectors to look over Brasidas' shoulder and a flock of keen young Spartans to govern the cities that had rebelled to Brasidas, no doubt without Brasidas' tact. This was, of course, quite against the repeated promises that Brasidas had made to the cities that had revolted to him, that they should govern themselves and that he had come to liberate them from Athens rather than to establish a Spartan empire in the north. Yet the governors were installed.[66]

In the summer of 423 BC, all was quiet between Athens and Sparta in the south of Greece. But if conclusive proof were needed of the eclipse of the Spartan sun, it came the following winter, when Tegea and Mantinea, both allies of Sparta, fought a war against each other, one that concluded in a very bloody battle. Tegea and Mantinea were the two most considerable cities of the region of Arcadia to the north of Sparta and (naturally) traditional rivals, and both summoned allies of their own to their sides.

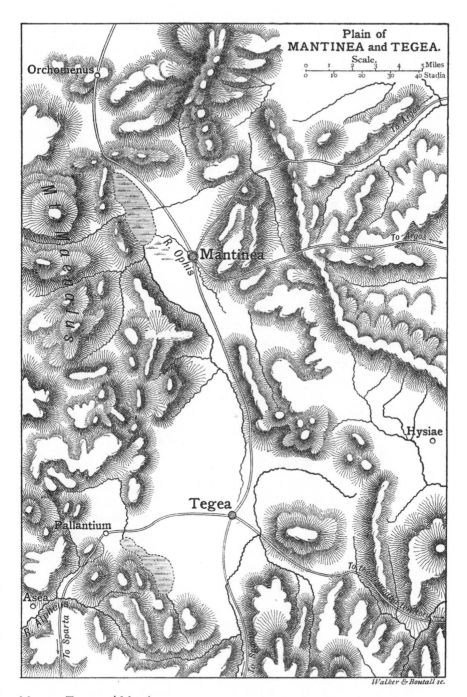

MAP 9.7 Tegea and Mantinea

The Spartans must have been appalled, not only by the loss of manpower upon which they might yet need to call but also because making peace with Athens might depend on Athens' sense that Sparta could control her allies and compel them to make peace as well. Nor was this the only sign of disobedience to Spartan will: the terms of the truce in 423 BC had acknowledged that small Troezen, on the Argolid peninsula, had made a private peace with Athens.[67]

It was the interests of Sparta's allies that had so far prevented the Spartans from agreeing to terms of long-term peace satisfactory to the Athenians. It is attractive to suppose that at this point, when Sparta's allies seemed to have forsaken her (with a haughty disregard to which tender Sparta would have been keenly sensitive), the Spartans began rethinking their previous commitment and allowing that they, too, might have to go their own way.

Brasidas, who had never loved the truce, seems nevertheless to have kept it after Mende. Certainly his new chaperones from Sparta would have tried to ensure he did. But in the early spring of 422 BC, besieged Scione called to him, and the only way to get an army to Scione was right through the truce—by breaking through the twin walls of Potidaea, the city that sealed the Pallene peninsula. Another night march in winter, then, and another wait in the cold and dark before the walls of a city. But at Potidaea Brasidas had no co-conspirators within: the old population that had so bravely resisted the might of Athens had been replaced by Athenian colonists. This place Brasidas must take with his unaided guile.[68]

Ladders had been prepared for the assault on Potidaea. On the city's northern wall, Brasidas had learned, a bell was passed slowly from sentinel to sentinel to make sure all stayed awake. After the bell was heard to clank close by, its bearer left his post to hand the instrument on to the next station. So just after the bell was heard was the moment to raise the ladders. And so attackers did, but in vain. The guards were alert, the alarm was given, and Brasidas did not even send his men up the wall. Still in the dark, he led his force away. Brasidas had emphatically failed.

The one year's truce expired at the end of March 422 BC, but Athens and Sparta agreed to extend it until after the games of Apollo at Delphi's Pythian festival in very late July or August of that year. The first two conditions of the year's truce had also concerned Apollo—namely, access to Delphi and detecting thefts from Apollo's treasures there. This was not usual in Greek diplomatic documents; rather, it seems that Apollo had become uneasy. And, indeed, during the extension of the truce in 422 BC, the Athenians undertook an elaborate repurification of Delos, the isle sacred to Apollo, from which they now expelled all its inhabitants as impure.

The appointment of the Pythian Games as the new end to the truce fits too well with these other Apollonian anxieties to be accidental.[69]

So evidently the Spartans and Athenians both knew something was amiss with Apollo, but here Thucydides' severe secularism fails us—for as with so many of the religious phenomena he reports, he declines to explain the reason for their fears. Had the plague reappeared at Athens and the Athenians become anxious to placate Apollo? Or did the Athenians feel guilty at having debauched his temple at Delium? And were the Spartans reluctant to seem behindhand in their obsequies to the god who had favored them in the war? But whatever the origin of the divine disquiet, it surely manifested itself in rivalrous displays of devotion to Apollo, as had happened in time of armistice before: during Cimon's truce, after 451 BC, Athens and Sparta had also jousted for the favor of the god at Delphi, an earlier contention to which stood witness a much-suffering bronze wolf, inscribed on both flanks with the privileges the competitors had earned. Now, with both sides trying to outstrip the other in piety, it will have been easy for one—we suspect the Spartans, for they were the ones more anxious for peace and that the Athenians should be paralyzed through most of the sailing season—to propose that the god be honored by an extension of the truce through his great four-yearly festival. Trapped in the logic of the rivalry, the other party could hardly refuse the suggestion to honor the god.

And so it was that the spring and summer of 422 BC passed in tranquility, and Apollo's races were run on the mountainside of mighty Parnassus. But to the Athenians the position in the north was intolerable, the rebellion having grown too large and lively to be endured, for it was now threatening the rest of Athens' sway. Nor was the rebellion dependent on the Spartans and likely to collapse if Athens and Sparta made peace.

From the diplomatic missions groping for a permanent treaty all through the last year, Athens could see that Sparta was willing, in principle, to trade away her allies in the north in exchange for a treaty. But in practice Sparta had little control over the rebellious northern confederation, which predated the coming of Brasidas: the Spartans in the north were allies of the Chalcidians, not their lord. Nor would Brasidas himself, despite the chaperones the Spartans had sent, necessarily do as he was told by Sparta (an intransigence proven by his acceptance of Mende and the attack on Potidaea, both in time of truce).

Even if peace with Sparta could be achieved, therefore, the rumblings in the Athenian empire might not cease. No, regardless of what happened with Sparta, some signal act of terror was needed to bring the empire once again to heel. Such, at least, was the notion of Cleon (who seems to have been admirably consistent in his faith in atrocity), and so he prevailed upon the Athenians to appoint him to command a force for the north: thirty ships, twelve hundred Athenian hoplites (and a greater number from the allies), and three hundred cavalry. At more than twenty-four hundred hoplites, this was one of the largest armies that Athens had ever sent by sea in the war, a heavy mace to batter the northern rebels into submission.[70]

Cleon sailed first to besieged Scione on the western peninsula of the Chalcidice, not to reinforce the Athenians already there but to add hoplites from the besieging forces to his army. His plan was to take Torone on the middle cape by surprise. He landed near Torone and soon learned—joy!—that the inspiring Brasidas was not there and that the defenders were few. The city was imperiled because Brasidas had ambitiously extended the city wall to encompass part of the conurbation that lay outside the old circuit, and so there were simply not enough soldiers to man the wall and guard the harbor.[71]

Cleon attacked Torone from both directions at once, assailing the new wall from the landward side and sending ten triremes crowded with men into the haven. The Spartan commander of the town's garrison could not decide which front to defend and changed his purpose from wall to harbor at the worst moment: he was too late to defend the city, which was entered from the harbor by the men on the ships, and he lost the benefit of the new wall, being forced to fall back to the old one, which had been partially dismantled. The Athenians burst through this, killing some of the town's defenders in the fight. The rest soon surrendered. Poor Brasidas, who had been marching hard to save Torone, was only five miles away when the city fell. The women and children of the town were made slaves—and presumably auctioned on the spot, in the thrifty ancient manner, to traders who accompanied the campaign. The men of Torone and their Chalcidian and Peloponnesian allies, seven hundred in all, were carried back to Athens, the Spartan commander of the town no doubt joining in prison his countrymen captured on Sphacteria. If the decree that Cleon had passed for Scione is any guide, the men of Torone were marked down for execution. But before the Athenians could get around to killing them, Athens found that she needed to trade them one for one for captives of her own.[72]

Cleon's success at Torone raised his hopes, and now he had ambitions to win back Amphipolis, Brasidas' greatest prize in the north. Cleon sailed to Eion, at Strymon's mouth—it was but three miles downriver from Amphipolis, and ever since Thucydides had rescued it after the fall of the greater city, the Athenians had held it against Brasidas. From Eion Cleon tried, and failed, to win back Stagirus on the Aegean coast to the west, but he succeeded in storming a town that had defected to Brasidas on the coast to the east. From Eion, too, Cleon sent for King Perdiccas to join him with an army and sent to the Thracians to hire mercenaries.[73]

MAP 9.8 Cleon's Northern Campaign, 422 BC

Brasidas took a position on a hill near Amphipolis overlooking Eion in order to watch Cleon's movements, and he also called for help from the Chalcidians and the friendly Thracians round about. Those he could not enspell with his martial glory, he hired with silver. He had two thousand Greek hoplites and three hundred Greek cavalry. In hoplites, at least, he was outnumbered, and Thucydides thought Brasidas' mixed army inferior in quality to that of the Athenians.[74]

When Cleon thought the time was right, he marched upriver toward Amphipolis, keeping the river on his left, to challenge Brasidas to battle if the Spartan would accept. If not—and he did not expect the outnumbered Brasidas to do so—Cleon intended to mock Brasidas' craven unwillingness by drawing close to the city on the side that the river did not protect, a location that would give him also the opportunity to look over the ground and consider how a siege of the city might be undertaken. Perdiccas and the Thracian mercenaries had not yet arrived, but Cleon was confident enough to face Brasidas in the field, if not to escalade great Amphipolis itself.[75]

When Brasidas saw Cleon headed toward the city, the Spartan came down from his hill and retired within the walls of Amphipolis. Cleon was right: Brasidas did fear a stand-up battle. He could also not be sure that Cleon would not try to take the city at a rush. But Cleon marched right by

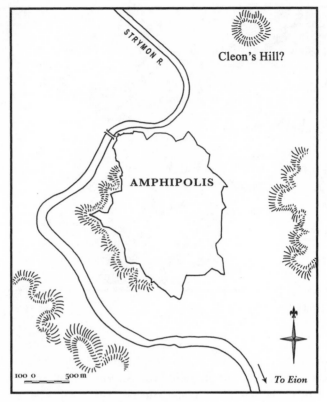

MAP 9.9 The Battle of Amphipolis, 422 BC

Amphipolis and occupied a high hill beyond the city to the north, and from there he continued his inspection. Brasidas, unwilling to risk a straight-up battle so outnumbered, massed his men at nearby gates in case an opportunity offered for a sally, for if he was outnumbered now, he would be even more so when Cleon's reinforcements arrived. He hoped, too, that a quick pounce might conceal the smallness of his numbers and the fact that much of his force was made up of townsfolk with contrived weapons.[76]

The Athenians saw this massing in Amphipolis from their hill, and as Cleon and his men descended, they could see the hooves of horses and the feet of men under the gates of the city (which suggests how close to the city the Athenians were and also that the Greeks were no great fitters of gates). From their previous vantage, the Athenians had also seen Brasidas sacrificing at the temple of Athena within the walls. From all this—which Cleon carefully confirmed with his own eyes—the Athenian commander suspected a sally. So he ordered the Athenians into battle formation with the city to their front; then, he ordered all his soldiers to turn in place ninety degrees to the left and to march in formation south toward Eion. First, the left wing would pass Amphipolis, then the center, and then the right: if Brasidas' army did come out, Cleon's soldiers, already arrayed for battle, would simply turn in place to face the enemy. So the Athenians set off for Eion. Nothing stirred within the city. After a while, and finally confident that Brasidas would not attack, Cleon wheeled the right wing of his army by ninety degrees so that it extended toward the city, with its shieldless flank closest to the walls. The Athenian army now formed a right angle, the left and center marching in a column along the road, with the old right wing perpendicular to that column, on the right and behind, but marching in the same direction toward Eion.[77]

Cleon was challenging Brasidas to battle in the most ostentatious and insulting way he could contrive. Once upon a time Brasidas had prevailed over the Athenians at Megara and reclaimed the loyalty of the city by offering battle when the Athenians had refused to accept his challenge. This facing-down of the Athenians at Megara had by now become part of Brasidas' legend, repeated throughout the north as reassurance that the Athenians would never dare to fight the Spartan hero. But now it was Brasidas who was reluctant to fight, and Cleon wanted to make that reluctance as evident as possible. Brasidas had refused to fight when the Athenians marched toward the city, withdrawing instead behind its walls. Now Brasidas was refusing to fight again when the Athenians marched home, ever so close to the walls of Amphipolis. One imagines the hoplites in Cleon's ranks making unusual gestures toward the city (although, of course, the sober Thucydides would never tell us such a thing).[78]

Cleon's wheeling of his right wing toward the city was intended to complete the humiliation of Brasidas. The Athenians would march past the gates of Amphipolis, yards away, exposing their vulnerable flank. No greater challenge could one Greek army offer to another, no greater insult. Cleon would show Amphipolis, and all of the north, that their adored Lacedaemonian paladin was a coward. Once upon a time men trailed their cloaks to provoke a challenge and to shame their opponent should no challenge be forthcoming. Cleon was trailing his army, and we can imagine his swagger as he went by.[79]

Cleon's maneuver cost Athens the north and Cleon his life. The Athenian was not wrong in his estimation of the meaning of his gesture, or how it would have been received by the northerners and the Greek world in general had it succeeded. His error was in assuming that Brasidas was in fact too outnumbered or too timid to come forth. That Brasidas was outnumbered was certainly true; timidity, however, does not seem to have been in the Spartan's constitution.

Watching from within Amphipolis as the Athenians paraded past, Brasidas grasped his tactical problem: if he attacked the Athenians where they were most vulnerable, his victory would be inconsequential. The most attractive point of attack, the projecting flank of the Athenian right wing, was also the trailing element of the Athenian army. If Brasidas waited for that body to reach the gates and attacked it there, the rest of the Athenian forces would already be a considerable way off and have ample time to form up and return to rescue their comrades—or simply to escape. So Brasidas could not wait until the right wing swept past his position like a broom: his plan, then, would be to attack first the more distant Athenian left and center, marching toward Eion one behind the other on the road. Besides, the Athenian right, so close to the walls, was the most obviously vulnerable and so was keyed-up for combat. But in the rest of the army, the looser order of a march inevitably prevailed, despite the fact that Cleon had disposed these troops to be able to turn and fight if attacked. Brasidas pointed out this confusion to his comrades: "These men won't stand against us," he said. "Look at the motions of their spears and heads. Men who do that never withstand an onset."[80]

Out the gate Brasidas rushed, with one hundred and fifty picked men, running the length of the Athenian right and crashing into the perpendicular Athenian center now spread out before him on the road. The center would have had plenty of time to form against him, but moments ago they had been luxuriating in the relaxed content that follows on seeing someone else—the dangling Athenian right wing—in peril. Their sense of their own unpreparedness bred panic, and they were shocked by the boldness of the attack. And so it was that Brasidas' one hundred and fifty routed the Athenian center, many times their number. Then the bulk of Brasidas' army emerged from another gate in Amphipolis' walls, falling upon the Athenian left wing, ahead on the road. They cut it off from the rest of the army, routed it, and drove the shattered Athenian mass toward Eion. By that time Brasidas' band had turned back to attack the uninjured Athenian right, which again outnumbered them, but so unnerved were the Athenians that they fell back to the hill Cleon had used earlier as a point of vantage. It was while harrying these Athenians that Brasidas himself was hit. The Athenians did not even notice as the Spartan's companions carried him mortally wounded out of the battle, bearing him unobtrusively, lest the Athenians take fire at having struck down the great Brasidas.[81]

Brasidas' main force now came up from routing the Athenian left, twice or three times charging up the hill where the Athenian right had taken refuge, but failing to dislodge the Athenians. The hoplites of the main body were then called off, and men with javelins, on horse and foot, were sent in their place. These finally broke the Athenians, who fled, keenly pursued by cavalry and light troops. When the fugitives counted themselves at Eion, six hundred were revealed to have been killed. One of them, struck down in flight by a Thracian peltast (Thucydides gloats), was Cleon. Of Brasidas' army only seven fell. Wounded Brasidas lived to hear of the victory, then passed over the River Styx. And in the place to which the ferryman brought him, where all the heroes of the Greeks sojourned, cunning Odysseus will have greeted him with an ironic smile, and swift-footed Achilles will have clasped his hand and named him by far the best of the Achaeans.[82]

After chasing off the Athenians, Brasidas' mourning army stripped the Athenian dead and set up their trophy. The Athenians retrieved their dead under truce and sailed back to Athens. The men of Amphipolis proclaimed their savior Brasidas a hero, one of the demigods, and buried him inside the city (where no mere mortal might lie), in a tomb in their marketplace, following his bier to burial in full armor. Sacrifices were decreed, and games in his honor. And the monuments to the founder of the city, the Athenian Hagnon, were torn down and his rites abandoned (for founders, too, were worshipped as heroes). The Amphipolitans made Brasidas their founder in Hagnon's place.[83]

We may wonder that in a triumph so sparing of victorious blood, Brasidas was one of the fallen. Since the days of Methone and Pylos he had always, of course, been brave. But we may suspect that his bravery had in recent months become mixed with a certain yearning for extinction. He can hardly have been unaware that his Spartan countrymen were bargaining away the lives and cities of his northern allies like sprats at a Piraeus fishmonger's. Soon the day would come when he would have to betray his friends at Sparta's command or pass into rebellion from Sparta, just as the doomed Pausanias, the victor of Plataea, had in the elder days. But the Spartan code afforded him an escape from such high, contrary cloudbanks of fate. Leading his handful against the Athenians, Brasidas went smiling to his death.

In honor of Brasidas' bravery, the Spartans appointed his ancient father one of the oath takers for the peace with Athens his victory yielded. His mother, a fearsome Spartan dame of the "come back with your shield or on it" school, was harder to please. "My son was a brave man," she said. "But many others were braver."[84]

The battle of Amphipolis was fought in the second half of October 422 BC. By early April of the next year, a treaty of peace had been made for a period of fifty years between the Athenians and the Spartans.

The coming of peace, Thucydides tells us, was aided by the deaths in the north of Cleon and Brasidas, both of whom had (he says) for personal reasons opposed a treaty. Aristophanes confirms their opposition: to him they were the twin pestles of the mortar in which brutal War crushed cities. Thucydides adds that in the absence of Cleon and Brasidas, powerful personages in both Athens and Sparta were likewise eager for peace for personal reasons. Cleon's Athenian political rival Nicias, for one, so successful a general in the later years of the war, yearned for a treaty because he wished the felicity of his success to abide unstained. It was as if he had been reading Solon's somber advice in Herodotus to judge no man blessed until he is dead. So adamant was Nicias' advocacy at Athens that the treaty came to be known by his name, as the Peace of Nicias. By contrast, King Pleistoanax of Sparta, whose recall many Spartans blamed for their woes in the latter years of the war (he was accused of having bribed the priestess at Delphi to secure his return to Sparta), favored peace because he wished to trade his stains for felicity.[85]

As in the truce of 423 BC, the interests of Apollo led the 421 BC treaty of peace. The document went on to say that Sparta and Athens and their allies were to stop fighting. The Lacedaemonian prisoners at Athens—the ones who had been held there since the fall of Sphacteria, with a few additions since—were to be restored to Sparta. And all the places Athens had captured in or around the Peloponnese—Pylos, Cythera, and Methana on the Argolid peninsula—were to be surrendered. In exchange, the Spartans were to return Amphipolis to Athens—but the people of Amphipolis might depart with their goods, much as Brasidas had allowed the town's Athenian loyalists to do. Other than Amphipolis, the allies of Brasidas in the north were divided into two groups: those simply left to Athens' mercy (including Scione, still under siege) and those given watery guarantees that they could formally be independent of Athens but were nevertheless obliged to pay her the tribute Aristides had imposed on all Athenian allies more than fifty years before, a baffling and likely unworkable compromise (for what happened if they did not pay?). Of course, with Brasidas dead and his army departed, the Athenians could in practice do in the north whatever their strength allowed.[86]

There was much absent from the treaty, and those absences were gravid with future conflict. The sixty ships Athens had failed to return in 424 BC were not to be returned to Sparta's allies. No article required Athens to restore to Megara her port of Nisaea. Nothing was said of Corinth's lost possessions in the northwest, Sollium and Anactorium. Simply put, Sparta was betraying her allies and breaking the agreement they had made at the beginning of the war: that all should possess, leaving the conflict, what they had going into it. And the treaty, it was stipulated in its text, could be changed by bilateral agreement between Athens and Sparta, without the approval of Sparta's allies.[87]

When they learned of the terms of the treaty, before it was sworn, Sparta's allies were furious, and many of them—including the most powerful: the Corinthians, Megarians, Boeotians, and Eleans—refused to be part of it. With them, at least in principle, Athens would still be at war. Some of them negotiated their own truces with Athens, which did not imply that they accepted the terms of the Peace of Nicias—the truce between Athens and Boeotia was renewed every ten days. Others, like Corinth, simply stopped fighting against Athens, although no formal truce was agreed.[88]

Sparta's allies felt betrayed, a betrayal that they had not expected as recently as 423 BC. This we can deduce from that fact that the oath swearers to the one year's truce of 423 BC, whose purpose had been to negotiate a wider peace, had included nearly all of Sparta's important Peloponnesian allies (including Corinth) and, beyond the Peloponnese, the Megarians. At that time Sparta's allies must have expected her to negotiate terms with Athens that they, too, would find satisfactory. Sparta had herself yearned for peace since her men were trapped on Sphacteria in 425 BC—all the more so since her men had been imprisoned at Athens and raids upon her territory from Pylos and Cythera made her fear the revolt of her helots. It was Sparta's loyalty to her allies that had prevented peace in 423 BC. Only now was Sparta willing to betray their interests. It was not hard to foresee the consequences of this betrayal: the most powerful members of Sparta's confederation would secede.

Something had changed at Sparta between 423 and 421 BC. Thucydides implies that the most potent new factor was that Sparta's thirty-year truce with nearby Argos was about to run out, and the Argives showed no signs of wishing to renew it without having restored to them Thyrea, that eternal symbol of the hegemony of the Peloponnese, the territory that Sparta had won in the Battle of Champions in the middle of the sixth century BC. Returning Thyrea would, of course, imply the superiority of Argos over Sparta in rank, and thus was quite out of the question. But if the treaty could not be renewed, then the Argives would be free to join the Athenians in their war against Sparta. And in such a combination Sparta could, perhaps for the first time, glimpse the destruction of her nation by external, rather than internal, enemies.[89]

Yet growing anxiety about Argos is not a fully satisfactory explanation for Sparta's change of mind. Given the history of relations between Sparta and Argos, the truculence of the Argives could have been predicted—indeed, relied upon. At least since Sparta began to seem vulnerable in 425 BC, the Spartans must have known that they might have to contend with Argos' entry into the war. And if peace with Athens was the only escape from peril (and given that Sparta could secure such a peace by betraying her allies),

Sparta might just as easily have betrayed her allies and settled with Athens in 423 BC, thereby sparing much suffering.

In fact, Sparta could now more easily abandon her allies because she felt that her allies had already abandoned her. Victorious Boeotia and her northern neighbor Phocis had scorned to join even the one-year truce with Athens. And then there was the infighting and the petty power grabbing: in the winter of 423/422 BC, Tegea and Mantinea had fought a private war against each other, and Mantinea had been devouring other states in Arcadia even while the greater war had been going on, in violation of the agreement between Sparta and her allies. Mantinea's ambition was becoming a serious problem: in the summer after the Peace of Nicias with Athens (421 BC), Sparta would march against Mantinea to try to make her disgorge some of her conquests. Elis had similarly been at war with Lepreum, a small Peloponnesian ally bordering Sparta's Messenia, and that war had become fierce enough that the Spartans, even as they fought Athens, had to send troops to protect Lepreum. Adding insult to it all was the fact that, before the one-year truce of 423 BC, wee Troezen had made a private peace with Athens.[90]

If Sparta's Peloponnesian allies were disobeying her, the powerful Boeotians were proving no more cooperative. In the fall of 422 BC, Boeotia had taken by treachery Panactum, a border fort of the Athenians. The Spartans, now so eager for peace, could hardly have approved: this was just the sort of act that, if it inspired revenge, might revive the war that had been temporarily lulled with the one-year truce. The Boeotians were also unwilling to return Plataea to Athens. To justify their refusal, they invoked the quibble they had been burnishing to a gleam since the very first night of the war: that Plataea had not been captured but had come over to them voluntarily. (Plataea had finally done so in 427 BC, it will be recalled, because her defenders were starving.) In fact, the Boeotians wanted to yield nothing at all to Athens: they had won the battle of Delium and so proved themselves Athens' superiors. Even the slightest gratification of Athens would imply that they were stepping down from this position. But this intransigence might also imply that Boeotia was unwilling to defer any longer to Sparta's interests, to consider Sparta her *hegemon*. These are just the failures of Sparta's allies to cooperate with her of which we know. It may not be an accident of Thucydides' reporting that when Sparta was at her nadir during the Athenian descents from Cythera in the spring of 424 BC—when she could not defend even the littoral of Laconia against the marauding Athenians— we hear of no help sent her by her Peloponnesian neighbors.[91]

When Sparta looked out from Laconia, she saw her alliance already in ruins, her allies no longer heeding her orders. Nor would the Greeks have expected anything different, under the circumstances. "The Lacedaemonians were disgraced and despised because of their misfortunes," says Thucydides. Obedience to a *hegemon* was obedience paid to rank; when rank was shattered, obedience was not paid. The recent behavior of her allies, then, had dispensed Sparta from the agreement to make no peace with Athens unless all her allies came out of the war with what they had carried into it.[92]

More puzzling than Sparta's rationale, perhaps, is the Athenian willingness to make peace in 421 BC. It was the Athenians, in the end, who had to be convinced. Negotiations were hard, extending over months, with many claims and counterclaims advanced. And as winter turned to spring in 421 BC and the season of fighting approached, the Spartans resorted to one final arm-twist to compel the Athenians to accept the treaty: they ordered their allies, so the Athenians would hear of it, to assemble the materials for a fortress in Attica. The Spartans would raise their own landlocked Pylos, their own wooden Cythera, against the Athenians. The deeper threat here, of course, was that the Spartans were finally prepared to sacrifice the prisoners from Sphacteria—for these would certainly be killed if the Peloponnesians invaded Attica.[93]

The Athenians probably needed a final shove toward peace because Athens' position, already strong, was likely to become even stronger. Sparta herself still writhed pleasingly beneath the pricks and prods of Pylos and Cythera. Boeotia, although triumphant against Athens at Delium, showed no eagerness to undertake a great adventure. And all Athens had to do was wait, smug and content, and soon great Argos would join the war. Why, then, make peace?[94]

The balance of power in Greece was tipping ever more in favor of the Athenians, but still the Athenians made peace. Their main reason for peace, Thucydides says, was fear that their defeats at Delium and Amphipolis would spark a wider revolt in the Athenian empire. We have seen how Sparta's defeats had brought her into contempt with her allies and how her confederation was dissolving as a result. And insofar as the Athenian alliance was still to some degree a hegemony, held together by Athens' allies' respect for Athens' superior rank rather then by fear of Athenian punishment, it was potentially subject to the same dissolution— or so, at least, the Athenians might have thought. It was perfectly Greek for the Athenians to imagine that although the power of Athens to coerce her allies was little abated, although charismatic Brasidas was dead and Perdiccas was (however briefly) a friend, and although the spate of defections in the north seemed to have eased, Athens' rule over her innumerable subjects was nevertheless rendered precarious by the shame of her defeats at Delium and Amphipolis.[95]

Defeat at Amphipolis also propelled Athens toward peace with Sparta for reasons other than her fear for her empire. Her claim to equality with

Sparta was in the balance. For to Greeks, the embarrassing defeat of an Athenian army at Amphipolis by a Spartan-commanded army rendered the Athenians petitioners once again. Sparta might now justly refuse to accept the equality of Athens in rank, a claim that—although sometimes superseded—had been Athens' objective in the war all along.

The prospect of the addition of proud Argos to the fight was, curiously, another incentive for Athens to pursue peace: for what confusion Argos would bring to the rankings of honor! What Athens had achieved against Sparta she had achieved as the unquestioned chief of her coalition. But Argos—impossibly proud, ancient Argos, which had once sent Agamemnon against Troy—would admit Athens as no more than an equal, if even that: in the war at mid-century, as we have seen, both the Spartans and the Argives seem to have regarded the Athenians as subordinate to hegemonal Argos. At best, if Athens and Argos destroyed Sparta together, an exhausted Athens and a fresher Argos might yet have to spar for hegemony. And that was a hopeful scenario. Less comfortable scenarios might be imagined that would leave the maritime power of Athens to the side, with Sparta and Argos competing for first place in rank (as so often in the past) and Athens relegated to a lesser position.[96]

Thus if, even after the shame of Athens' defeat at Amphipolis, Sparta would admit Athens to half her ancient glory, Athens must accept. And so it was that the treaty was sworn in the spring of 421 BC.[97]

The same motive that drove Athens to accept peace with Sparta can explain the strange coda to the treaty: for perhaps two weeks after the treaty was sworn, the Spartans and the Athenians added to it an alliance between the two states, also to last for fifty years. Astonishing. Two unfriendly powers, just emerging from ten years of bitter war, had formed an alliance against the world.[98]

That the Lacedaemonians should have wanted an alliance with Athens perhaps makes sense, if the anger and hurt of the Ten Years' War can be momentarily laid aside. Sparta was looking forward to war with Argos. Her confederation was already disintegrating before the peace was settled, and now that she had made what amounted to a separate peace with the Athenians, abandoning her allies, she feared (with justice, as it turned out) that her angry satellites might find Argos a more comfortable planet around which to swing. So Sparta might not have to fight Argos alone, but rather an Argive alliance, filled out with many of Sparta's own erstwhile allies. Alternatively, Sparta's former allies might join with Athens against her: that possibility Sparta's alliance with Athens foreclosed. But a greater mystery is why Athens herself should agree to such an alliance—why Athens should bind herself to her mortal enemy of the last ten years, guaranteeing to help her against Argos and any coalition Argos might assemble.[99]

So inexplicable have moderns found this alliance between Athens and Sparta that a learned German was driven to take up his red pen. There *was* no such alliance, he said; it was perhaps merely a proposal left lying around the council halls of Athens, and someone later wrote it into the text of Thucydides. And certainly in terms of power politics, such an alliance does seem a manifestation of mass Athenian dementia. In the world of rank, however, such an alliance made perfect sense—indeed, it was nearly inevitable.[100]

An equal and nearly perfectly symmetrical alliance, binding both Athens and Sparta to aid the other alike, was a far more definite expression of equality between states than a treaty of peace. The differing interpretations of the Thirty Years' Peace and its consequences for rank show what imperfect instruments Greek peace treaties were for settling the rank of states. The singular ability of alliances to express equality led Thucydides to have the Spartans offer such an alliance in the speech he wrote for them when they offered Athens an equal peace in 425 BC. But more important, once the Spartans had formally admitted the equality of Athens, it was in the vital interest of Athens that Sparta maintain her standing in the world. For as Sparta's equal, Athens must defend the position of Sparta against all others, including Argos. Were Sparta were to be brought down by any other power, then her equal would be brought down as well.

Now the homey metaphors Cimon used to get Athens to help Sparta against the helots in the 460s BC came horribly to life: truly was Athens bound by a yoke to her fellow ox; truly was Athens one leg and Sparta the other. By the logic of the war they had fought, and that of the peace they had just agreed upon, Athens and Sparta had now to join in protecting their shared supremacy. Like the last two Spartans at Thermopylae, their spears broken and their daggers lost in the entrails of enemies, Athens and Sparta had to stand back to back and defy the whole world with their claws.

EPILOGUE

L ESS THAN TWO WEEKS BEFORE libations were poured and oaths were sworn over the treaty of peace between Athens and Sparta, Aristophanes' play *Peace* was ushered onstage at Athens' festival of the Dionysia. To Athenians who had watched the playwright's lacerating earlier work—the *Acharnians* (425 BC), savaging the democracy at war; the *Knights* (424 BC), lambasting Cleon and the politicians; the *Clouds* (423 BC), pummeling the philosopher Socrates; and the *Wasps* (422 BC), attacking the jury courts and whacking Cleon again (of course)—this new play must have seemed curiously sweet and gentle. So Aristophanes himself felt, and he even made a joke of it: in the opening scene two slaves work frantically to feed dung cakes to a gigantic dung beetle (offstage), and when this byplay has lasted long enough for the lack of an explanation to have become funny, one of the slaves says, "By now some smart-ass kid in the audience'll be asking, 'What's the point of this? Why the beetle?' And the guy sitting next to him'll say: 'I think it's an allusion to Cleon, because he eats shit!'" But, amazingly, it was not.[1]

In fact, the giant beetle, despite its insatiable appetite for ordure (so that the audience was adjured to brick up their toilets lest the beetle be distracted), had a wholly virtuous use, which was to convey the hero (Aristophanes' usual stout, rural Athenian) to Olympus. There the hero sets about digging up the goddess Peace, who has been buried in a hole for the last ten years. The chorus, representing the farmers of Greece, then begins to pull Peace out with ropes, and the hero praises the Spartans for pulling hard, while he abuses the Boeotians, Megarians, and Argives for not pulling hard enough. Up Peace finally comes in the form of a statue. And then the hero returns to Athens, taking with him Peace's companions, who are lewdly attired personifications of Festival and Harvest Time, the first as a present for the Athenian democracy and the second to be his own bride. Now merchants arrive: first, a sickle maker bearing nuptial gifts to thank the hero for restoring peace, thereby bringing prosperity to his business; next, a crowd

Comic masks

of dealers in warlike appurtenances, moaning that peace has ruined them, whereupon the hero offers to buy a breastplate cheap to use as a chamber pot. When the merchants finally quit the stage, the hero auditions boys to sing at his wedding and reproaches the first for singing only martial songs— and thus the stripling is revealed to be the son of Lamachus, the gung-ho general whom Aristophanes had so roundly mocked in the *Acharnians*. So the hero hires instead the son of Athens' most famous coward, Cleonymus the Shield Thrower, whom by the time of *Peace* Aristophanes had subjected to years of joyful invective. Finally the hero leads his family and his bride out into the Attic countryside, freed from war, and the play ends in a joyful wedding song, "Hymen! Hymenaeo!"

A hardheaded modern sensibility will not find as much cause for joy in the peace that ended the Ten Years' War as Aristophanes did. For one thing, the treaty was such that Sparta's most important allies—Boeotia, Corinth, Megara, and Elis—refused to ratify it and were furious at Sparta for having made it. Certain conditions of the peace, moreover—the return of Amphipolis and Panactum to Athens and of Athenian prisoners held by Boeotia—involved other parties who could, and in some cases did, delay or thwart them.[2]

Some terms of the peace were, in fact, never fulfilled. The Spartans captured on Sphacteria were returned to Sparta. And eventually, after considerable wrangling, the Boeotians leveled the Athenian border fort at Panactum and handed its foundations back to the irritated Athenians. But in the Thraceward region, the rebels against Athens had no intention of being turned over to Athenian punishment, and the handful of Spartans there had not the power to compel them—nor did the Spartan commander in the area want to. So the Peloponnesians quietly departed from Amphipolis, and the Amphipolitans promptly barred their city against the Athenians. Thus the rebellion in the north continued, and the Athenians—deeming the Spartans to have failed to fulfill their side of the treaty—refused to give up Pylos and Cythera. The Spartans did, however, prevail upon the Athenians to remove the revolutionary Messenians from Pylos and garrison it themselves. Sparta's fear of her own slaves, current or former, had not abated.[3]

Oddly, these various failures to carry out the terms of the treaty did not result in a resumption of open war between Athens and Sparta. The peace, rather, was strangely resilient, almost rubbery, and bounced along sullenly for nearly seven years. This was possible because, for all its failings, the Peace of Nicias did, at least for a time, settle the most important question between the rivals: that of their relative rank. The peace did, as a later author said it was meant to, "stop the war, and put an end to the rivalry between them over honor." Athens, after all, had gone to war to vindicate her claim to equality in rank with Sparta; Sparta, to prove her superiority in rank over Athens. The treaty and alliance had asserted the equality of the parties. So Athens had won the war, and the two parties appear, at least for the moment, to have taken this settlement of their respective rank to heart.[4]

The Athenians had won the war of rank, and they had also won in more practical terms. Athens in 421 BC was certainly less powerful than she had been in 431 BC: she had lost perhaps a third of her total population in fighting and the plague, and her coffers were, if not empty, then certainly not piled with the six thousand talents of silver with which she had begun the war. Still, Athens' empire—the source of her power—was for the most part untouched, while Sparta's alliance—no less the source of hers—was in tatters; Sparta would have to spend the next years sewing and patching it. Sparta emerged from the Ten Years' War far less powerful relative to Athens than she had been going into it.[5]

But if Athens had won the war of rank and of power, still the rank of both Athens and Sparta had been much battered in the war, as we would expect of a conflict in which each side spent a decade belaboring the honor of the other. In an ideal Greek war, the total amount of honor in the system was conserved, and the winner of a hoplite battle gained the same amount of honor as the loser lost. But the Ten Years' War had not worked like that; much honor had been lost and little gained. In the eyes of the other Greeks, the same defeats that had reduced both Athens and Sparta to a mutual willingness to accept equality had also driven down the rank of both in comparison to that great, proud, well-rested power that had sat out the war: Argos. "The Athenians were scorned because of their defeat at Delium," is how a later author described the aftermath of the war, "and the Lacedaemonians were humbled in honor, because of the loss of their men on the island of Sphacteria." Both Athens and Sparta emerged from the war as losers in comparison with Argos' undiminished rank and power.[6]

Argos was quick to recognize her new position, as were many of the rest of the Peloponnesians. When Argos raised the banner of hegemony, Sparta's angry ex-allies gathered around, just as Greek thinking about the relationship between rank and hegemony suggested they should. Argos "had very high rank due to its ancient deeds, because before the return of the sons of Hercules, almost all of the greatest kings came from Argos." And the ancient renown of Argos was buttressed by her current strength—for, not having fought in the war, Argos was rich in both men and money. Once again that fatal combination of ancient glory and present power that the Greeks called *timē*, and we have called rank, proved hard for great states to ignore and for lesser states to resist.[7]

So it was that Sparta soon found herself at war with Argos for the hegemony of the Peloponnese. After a great deal of complicated diplomacy, Athens was drawn into this war on the side of the Argives, making a military alliance with Argos and the league of cities opposed to Sparta (420 BC). But Athens did not renounce her treaty with Sparta; nor did the alliance with Argos contain a provision to resolve the contradiction presented by Athens' being allied to two states that were fighting one another. The overt peace between Athens and Sparta continued. And this was to remain the tale until 414 BC: there were fenced-in moments of hostility between Athens and Sparta, and even fighting between their soldiers, but amid a strange general tranquility. Sparta did not invade Attica; nor did Athens raid Laconia. Athens' far-flung empire (excepting local revolts, which did not impinge on relations between the greater powers) was at peace. And if that quiet was sometimes broken by the clash of other cities' arms, the Peace of Nicias preserved at least the treasured right of Greeks to fight against their own enemies rather than those designated by their masters.[8]

Even in the face of aggression, neither Athens nor Sparta was prepared formally to renounce the treaty because each cherished certain aspects of it. The Athenians valued the equality the treaty expressed; the Spartans, the protection it afforded them against full-scale war with Athens while they fought other wars. Indeed, even when conditions arose that gave ample cause for resuming the war, both states tactfully refrained. Such was the case in the winter of 419/418 BC, when the Argives convinced the Athenians that the Spartans had, by a technicality, broken the treaty with Athens. The Athenians inscribed words to that effect on the stone that bore the agreement and restored the plundering Messenians to Pylos as revenge—but, nevertheless, the wider peace continued.[9]

Sparta willfully disregarded the attacks of Athens so as to preserve the peace. In 418 BC, the Athenians sent a thousand hoplites and three hundred cavalry to help Argos, and their bloodthirsty representative even scolded the Argives for having had made a truce with the Spartans. But the wider peace between Athens and Sparta continued. In that year, the same Athenians fought alongside the Argives and their allies at the great battle of Mantinea, where the Spartans defeated the anti-Spartan coalition. But elsewhere the peace with Athens perdured. In 416 BC Athens not only took Sparta's island colony of Melos, killing the men and selling the women and children into slavery, but the Athenians themselves also raided Messenia from Pylos and made off with an immense booty. Even so (Thucydides reports in some frustration), the Spartans, for their part, refused to deem the treaty broken, blandly authorizing instead merely private reprisals against the Athenians, as if the raiding out of Pylos had been undertaken by pirates who merely happened to live in Athens and had nothing to do with the Athenian state. The Spartans, with other enemies to battle (especially Argos) and their crumbled alliance to reassemble, had cunningly reverted to their strategy in the late 450s BC: that of scornfully ignoring Athenian provocations and of regarding Athens as a subordinate ally of Argos.[10]

And so this odd peace might have continued forever, but as time moved on, the equality of rank expressed in the treaty came less and less to express the relationship the Greeks could see. Sparta won her wars. At the battle of Mantinea (418 BC), she defeated Argos, Athens, and their allies—winning, according to Thucydides, "the greatest battle for a long time between Greeks, joined in by the most famous states." Sparta's rank rose, and in time her past humiliations were forgotten. "The reproach brought against them for cowardice because of the catastrophe on the island [Sphacteria], and generally for bad judgment and slowness, they had wiped out by a single act," says Thucydides of Mantinea. Sparta "had fallen into disgrace through bad luck," the Greeks now thought, but at Mantinea the Spartans showed that "they were still the same inside." In retrospect, the disaster at

Sphacteria seemed less the kind of straight-up, honorable defeat that adjusted the rank of states and more a trick, a "theft of war," which did not.[11]

The rank of Sparta was rising. That of Athens, so often a side victim of the brisk drubbings Sparta was administering during these years, was not. As time went on, a sage Athenian observer could guess that the Spartans yearned to cast off the treaty—and might warn the Athenians that no pretext should be given to them to do so. For the more Sparta pulled ahead of Athens in the eyes of the Greeks, the more Athens valued the treaty expressing her equality in rank. Such wise voices prevailed at Athens for years after Peace of Nicias. Athens would sometimes join alliances against Sparta, sometimes try to hurt Sparta, and sometimes to try to humiliate her—but Athens' aggression would always stop just before it became intolerable to Sparta. In this period of warlike peace, Athens was careful to keep below the threshold of acts that would destroy the treaty between Athens and Sparta and the priceless claim to equality it embodied.[12]

While the Athenians took care to maintain their truculent peace with Sparta, they also began to look around for some mighty deed they could perform that would raise their rank in the eyes of the Greeks without breaking the treaty. Their eye fell upon the third great power in the Greek world, Syracuse in Sicily. Athens' previous involvement in the west had ended in humiliation, when the western Greeks made peace and the Athenians had been told to pack up and go home. So Athens' pride had an untended wound in the west. For those and other reasons, the Athenians sent a great expedition to Sicily in 415 BC.[13]

By 414 BC, the tectonic shifts of rank beneath Athens and Sparta had fractured the equality expressed by the Peace of Nicias. Sparta, no longer accepting the equality of Athens, felt it was time to seek revenge for her humiliation in the Ten Years' War, revenge that would propel her again to her ancient position of ascendancy over Athens. Athens, naturally, felt she needed to push Sparta down and, indeed, had been seeking ever more brazen ways of doing so. And Athens was finally prodded by Argos into an act Sparta had to answer. Having long implored her Athenian allies to raid Laconia itself, Argos finally prevailed upon them in this year to do so. The Spartans, who had long attempted to fail to "notice" Athens, and so to avoid fighting her, could not ignore a raid on their home territory; indeed, by this time, they may have welcomed a chance to prove themselves over the victors of 421 BC. Sparta's response had, of course, been utterly foreseeable: that is why Argos pleaded for it and Athens, we are told, so long refused to undertake such an enterprise. Athens and Sparta were at last formally at war again.[14]

Athens quickly found herself fighting her new war against the Peloponnesians from a far less favorable position than she had held in the Ten

Years' War of 431–421 BC. For in 413 BC the Athenian expedition against Syracuse ended in disaster, and many of Athens' subject cities, thinking the power of Athens broken, revolted. The Great King of Persia shared the view that Athens was crippled, and he began to support impecunious Sparta with orient gold. Now Sparta had fleets and allies in the Aegean, and Athens' control of the mass of her imperial possessions, never seriously endangered in the Ten Years' War, was in peril.

After many vicissitudes, the Athenians lost the struggle for the Aegean at the sea battle of Aegospotami in 405 BC, and the Spartans laid the city of Athens under siege by land and sea. In March 404 BC, a starving Athens surrendered. Sparta's allies bayed that Athens should be destroyed: her men killed, her women and children sold into slavery, her great buildings thrown down. Such a fate was nothing the Athenians had not inflicted upon others. But the Spartans were still the men they had been at war's onset, when they fought Athens over superiority in rank; they still thought in terms of tit for tat, of returning good for good and bad for bad.[15]

The Spartans stayed their allies' swords. Great, they told their underlings, had been the services of Athens to Greece in the time of the war against the Persians. And so Athens was preserved. The shining Athens of Pericles and his vaunting temples, of the tragedians, of Thucydides the grim and of Aristophanes the crow—all was suffered to survive and transform itself by imperceptible degrees into the golden-autumn Athens of Plato, Menander, and the orators.

FROM THE PELOPONNESIAN WAR, the whole age of battles from 431 to 404 BC, the Spartans emerged the victors. But it was the Athenians who won the Ten Years' War (431–421 BC), the first spate of those troubles. And the Athenians won both the war itself and, no less necessary in a war of symbols, the simultaneous war to define victory and defeat.

In the war of rank, Athens' underdog position gave her an advantage over Sparta. Sparta had long been the champion, and Athens the contender—a dynamic that presented its own set of imperatives and restrictions. Sparta went to war to defend her ancestral primacy in rank, while Athens wished to assert her equality in rank with Sparta; at the outset, it was easier for Sparta to uphold a status quo than for Athens to prove herself to the watching world. But as the war took the form of a sequence of vengeances and counter-vengeances, Athens' task proved the easier—for she only had to avenge Sparta's attacks equally, while Sparta always had to stay one step ahead. As a result of this disparity in objectives, Sparta, in the early years of the war, was compelled to adopt a more aggressive, hazardous strategy. It was she who had to invade Attica, and it was she who had to rush to avenge any unexpected counterblow inflicted by the Athenians. This condemned Sparta to overextend herself to take revenge upon Athens and forced her into distant entanglements, especially commitments to parties that the Lacedaemonians could not easily help, like Mytilene and the oligarchs on Corcyra. And when Sparta failed to vindicate one guarantee, she took upon herself other unwise responsibilities to avenge that defeat.

While Sparta's allies proved a rich source of shame to her, Athens could be (and generally was) far more cautious about taking under her wing states she could not easily help. Before Sphacteria changed the war, the loss of Plataea was the only great shame that Athens suffered from an ill-advised guarantee of protection (although she did endure some minor embarrassments in the northwest, when the Peloponnesians ravaged Cephallenia and Zacynthus). After Sphacteria, victorious Athens was far more open to foreign entanglements, as Sparta had been earlier—and Athens was duly punished for that new willingness at Delium, a disaster that grew out of an attempt to back a rebellion in Boeotia. The power of both Athens and Sparta depended in large part upon their friends, but for most of the Ten Years' War, Athens was far shrewder about those to whom she was willing to extend her protection (in addition, of course, to being far more able to extend protection to distant allies because of her well-traveled navy). Here, in particular, we can credit the cautious strategy of Pericles, who told the Athenians they would win through if they stayed at home.

Despite changes in leadership (and Thucydides' eagerness for us to think badly of Athenian leadership after Pericles), Athens' strategy in the Ten Years' War was remarkably consistent, at least in its objective: she sought a higher rank than Sparta had been willing to acknowledge before the war. To be sure, that objective was sought by different methods, and to different degrees, at different stages; under Pericles, the Athenians sought to prove their equality in rank with Sparta by reciprocal and proportionate revenge. From late 427 BC until their isolation of the Spartans on Sphacteria, they sought the same goal but abandoned the limitations of reciprocity and proportion. Once they had isolated the Spartans on Sphacteria, and even more so after they had captured the men on the island, the Athenians elevated their ambitions. They began to seek superiority in rank over the Spartans rather than mere equality, and to this end they switched to a policy of coercion, rather than merely shaming, to force Sparta to acknowledge Athenian superiority.

Athens' coercion of Sparta, taking the form of the raids from Pylos and Cythera, was just that: coercion. It was still not intended to destroy Sparta but rather to make Sparta admit that Athens had won the war over rank. But suspecting that Sparta herself might never yield superiority, Athens attempted to appeal to the wider Greek world in late 425 and 424 BC by embarking upon a concerted policy of emulating her glorious deeds and accomplishments in the 450s and early 440s BC. When that strategy failed at Delium in late 424 BC, Athens returned to seeking equality with Sparta, a goal she achieved in the Peace of Nicias and accompanying alliance of 421 BC.

Athens' determination to win a higher rank is the echoing refrain of the Ten Years' War. The Athenians knew what they wanted and had set out to get it. The strategic objectives of Sparta, by contrast, were inconsistent. For the most part, she wanted to prove her superiority over Athens in rank— but sometimes the Spartans acted as if they wanted to destroy Athens, or at least the power of Athens, as when they begged their Italian and Sicilian allies for money and a fleet at war's outset, when they later tried to beg the Great King for money, and when they attempted to burn the dockyards at Piraeus. All of these undertakings were futile, but pursuing them encouraged Sparta to expand the scope of her alliance yet further, apt as she was to overestimate her new allies' ability and willingness to help her.

Sparta's far-flung alliances increased her vulnerability in the war over rank. Sparta must have regretted her link with Opuntian Locris, for example: although that territory north beyond Boeotia might have proved useful for the prosecution of a more aggressive strategy against Athens (and, indeed, the Athenians feared that the Locrians would raid Euboea), Opuntian Locris turned out to be nothing more than an occasional punching bag for the Athenians, to the shame of the Spartans. And the sole result of Sparta's extending the nimbus of her alliance to the Dorian states of Italy and Sicily was to provide Athens with more ways to shame Sparta—as indeed Athens did, when she embarrassed Sparta by attacking allies there whom Sparta could not help.

Sparta's publicized war aims only weakened her cause further. The Spartans fought the Ten Years' War under the slogan of "Freedom for the Greeks," the final ultimatum they had flung at the Athenians before the outbreak of the fighting. As we have seen, however, the Spartans—other than Brasidas himself—seem in fact to have been wholly uninterested in a program of general liberation in the Athenian empire. The Spartan admiral Alcidas, when he sailed for Mytilene in 427 BC, was hardly freeing the Greeks when he methodically massacred the citizens of Athens' subjects he had captured; and in the last years of the war, the Spartans proved happy, indeed eager, to deliver back to Athens those Greeks in the Thraceward region whom Brasidas had indeed freed. Despite its hollowness, Sparta's slogan constrained her by making it difficult to resist requests for aid from hard-to-help states like Mytilene—assuming, of course, that Sparta had the foresight to want to. And at the same time, the slogan created confusion about Sparta's aims in the war, creating a conflict between the war Sparta was in fact fighting (the war over rank) and the war she had claimed to be fighting at the outset (a war to free the Greeks by destroying the power of Athens).

The Athenians, at least initially, were perplexed by Sparta's goals in the war. That is why in 431 BC they set aside a thousand talents and the hundred best warships of the year to protect Athens against an enemy come by sea, an enemy that could blockade Athens and starve her out. Athens was worried that Sparta had far more ambitious, sinister designs than she in fact did at the time—and this confusion was costly for Athens, in treasure and speedy triremes. In the long term, however, it was the Spartans who were the most damaged by their unclarity of purpose: for, since the Spartans claimed be fighting a far more ruthless war against Athens than they actually were, they could never be sure that the Athenians would not take them at their word—that the Athenians would not, if opportunity offered, escalate the war in an attempt to destroy Sparta before Sparta destroyed them. This uncertainty about Athenian motives, produced by uncertainty about Spartan motives, had somber consequences. For it was a wrong Spartan guess about Athenian escalation that set off the sequence of events that made Spartan victory in the war impossible.

At the most basic level, the Athenians won the Ten Years' War because they captured the Spartans on Sphacteria in 425 BC. After that, Sparta was merely playing for a draw—which she eventually achieved after the Athenian defeats at Delium (424 BC) and Amphipolis (422 BC), and which was formalized by the Peace of Nicias (421 BC) and the alliance with Athens that followed. Good Athenian tactics and good luck delivered the one hundred and twenty Spartans into Athenian hands, but those Spartans were present on Sphacteria in the first place because of a Lacedaemonian strategic error.

The Spartans had critically misjudged the Athenians' intentions at Pylos in 425 BC. The Athenians had been forced into the Bay of Navarino by a storm and fortified the promontory of Pylos as much out of necessity as strategic cunning. But when the Spartans were informed of the Athenian fort in Messenia, some of them—King Agis and the advisors who accompanied him to Attica in particular; the Spartans at home had ignored the incursion—overreacted. They thought the nature of the war had changed and that the Athenians had escalated their fight from a war over honor to a war in which they were seeking to destroy Sparta by raising the helots in revolt. It is easy to see how Athens' change in strategy in 426 BC, her abandonment of the constraints of reciprocity and proportion in her attempts to shame Sparta, might have led Sparta to think that Athens had resolved to destroy her. Still, the Spartans were wrong: Athens had wanted to intensify the war over honor, not change the objective of the war, which, after all, they were winning. In a world where both sides assumed that escalation by one would result in escalation by the other, Spartan lack of clarity about their objectives produced a murkiness about Athenian objectives and allowed the Spartans to make a severe misjudgment about the type of war the Athenians were fighting—and so to lose the war entirely.

In addition to winning the war of battles, Athens won the war of ideas about what made up the rank of states and how that rank could be damaged. The greatly different abilities of Athens and Sparta at war's outset meant that neither state could answer the attacks of the other directly; the progress of the war was therefore necessarily a matter of interpretation. The Spartans were confined by their military limitations to one great shaming of Athens a year—an invasion of Attica—with perhaps a second adventure in the northwest. The Athenians, who did not dare to invade the Peloponnese or challenge the Spartans to a hoplite battle, could not hope to inflict one single, supreme shame upon Sparta—but they could administer many smaller ones, using the mobility provided by their fleet.

This disparity in the abilities of Athens and Sparta meant that determining who was winning the war over rank depended in large part on weighing against each other the values of different kinds of shaming. Athens' shame at a Peloponnesian invasion of Attica had to be weighed against Sparta's shame at Athens' reprisal raids from ships and Athenian attacks on Sparta's allies. Both sides agreed that a hoplite battle between Athens and the Peloponnesians would be the supreme arbiter of rank: we can tell that because the Athenians studiously avoided fighting one against the Spartans in Attica. But beneath that gold standard, the relative value of the methods available to the combatants was debatable. This debate constituted a second war, mostly invisible to us today, and likely also mostly invisible to the participants at the time, who fought it, for the most part, unconsciously. That the Athenians won this war we can tell by Sparta's own actions, such as honoring Brasidas after he saved Methone, which show that they were indeed shamed by the Athenian raids on Laconia and the Peloponnese. And we can tell the same from Sparta's sometimes rather desperate attempts to protect states like Potidaea and Mytilene before they fell to Athens and to avenge them afterwards, which shows that the Spartans were deeply humiliated by Athenian successes against allies to whom they had given guarantees.

The Spartans never got to fight the war they wanted, one that defined rank in terms favorable to the Spartans and so almost exclusively in terms of the hoplite courage in which the Spartans were supreme. In such an ideal war, the Spartan strategy would have been to invade Attica in 431 BC and to ravage the countryside when the Athenians declined to come out and fight, and then, having avenged the *hybris* of Athens and proved the superior rank of Sparta, simply to have called a halt to operations. Subsequent Athenian raids on Laconia and the Peloponnese, as well as attacks on Spartan friends further afield, could have been ignored as trivial impertinences and petty Athens scorned as unworthy of response. Such, of course, had been the strategy of Sparta toward Athens after her victory at Tanagra during the war at mid-century, and such was the strategy of Athens toward Corinth and Boeotia through most of the Ten Years' War. But things had changed since Tanagra. In the Ten Years' War, Sparta was drawn into a long cycle of revenges and counter-revenges because she did feel shame at what Athens did to her and her allies, even at the beginning of the war.

At the same time as she became more and more successful at shaming Sparta, Athens also saw her estimations of the value of shaming acts, as well as her definition of the make-up of *time*, prevail in the minds of the Greeks. Put positively, in terms of honor rather than shame, the Athenians managed over the course of the Ten Years' War subtly to shift the definition of *time*, of the rank of states, from a preponderant emphasis on *andreia*, the courage displayed particularly in hoplite battle, to place greater value on *charis* (helping friends and taking revenge upon enemies) and *metis* (the cunning displayed by tactics and trickery). Since *metis* and *charis* played to Athenian strengths, while Sparta was supreme in *andreia*, this change in the way the Greeks estimated *time* was decidedly to Athens' advantage.

The Athenians won this second war, this war about the very nature of honor, not with pamphlets or manifestos, not with publicity or propaganda, but rather through consistency. Although the rank of cities notionally existed in the minds of the Greeks at large, and Greece as a whole treasured the recipe of its making, Greece as a whole could neither be consulted nor persuaded by argument. Just as when two Greek states agreed on their respective rank and the rest of the Greeks registered their decision, Greece took its lead from the combatants themselves when evaluating the power of modes of shaming. The war over the definition of *time* chiefly depended, then, not on convincing the Greeks directly but upon appearing to have convinced the *enemy*. And the enemy appeared to be convinced when he endorsed the value of his opponent's acts by avenging them and when his own acts suggested a lack of confidence that his methods of shaming were indeed causing enough shame to avenge the shame being inflicted on him.

The Athenians never showed a lack of confidence in their ability to shame Sparta. Through the first five years of the war, they were rigorously consistent in underlining the value they placed on their acts of shaming; they raided the Peloponnese when the Spartans invaded Attica and failed to do so when the Spartans did not. The Athenians never let themselves get behind in the exchange of shame, which might imply that they were giving up the contest or that they could not compete because their methods of shaming were unequal to those of the Spartans; nor did they ever let themselves get ahead (except once, by mistake in 428 BC, an error they hastened to correct in 427 BC), lest that imply they thought they needed to catch up.

The Athenians never displayed uncertainty. It was the Spartans, by failing to invade Attica in 429 BC in order to attack Plataea to take revenge for the fall of Potidaea, who implied that they lacked confidence in the value of their invasions of Attica. And the Spartans' subsequent acts, such as their parading Mytilene at Olympia, signaled increasing frustration with their own methods. And so it was that in the eyes of the Greeks, the Spartans slowly yielded the battle over the definition of *timē* to the Athenians.

For their victorious consistency in the war of ideas, the Athenians had to thank the statesman and general whom Thucydides fondly called Athens' "first citizen." It was to Pericles that the Athenians owed their deft management not merely of the logistics but also of the rhythm of reprisal, of not only the reality but also the appearance of revenge; to him they owed their ability to control not only the events but also the story the Greeks told about the events. This was the legacy the dying Pericles left to the Athenians, and by the time Athens abandoned Pericles' policy of exactingly calculated revenge, after the fall of Plataea in 427 BC, it did not matter. The Athenian definition of honor had already prevailed.

We can put a name to one Greek who came to accept the Athenian definition of honor and its importance. His name was Thucydides, son of Olorus, the historian. But Thucydides moved toward this realization not from some more Spartan, hoplite definition of the honor of states but from the intellectual stance we today call realism, from a position that was inclined to regard honor as a secondary consideration in the action of nations. And, ironically, Thucydides is far more famous for his point of departure, his realism, than for the nonrealist analyses of international relations to which his intellectual quest eventually took him.

Realism is the theory of international relations that considers power, the dread of the power of others, and the quest for power that dread imposes impartially upon all as the primary drivers of the acts of states. "The growth of the power of Athens, and the alarm which this inspired in Lacedaemon, made war inevitable," wrote Thucydides, and he proceeded to organize his material about the prewar period to drive home that point, first arguing for a novel (to his Greek reader) definition of power, *dynamis*, measured in terms of ships and money. From there, Thucydides went on to describe the waxing of the power of Athens according to that definition and made sure that his characters, in the speeches he wrote, kept pointing (whatever the speakers' notional objectives) to the power of Athens so as to underscore its importance.[16]

While Thucydides' account of events before the outbreak of the war (Book I in our editions) is strongly realist, Thucydides' evaluation of the importance of power changes radically over the course of his history. At first, power is the key Thucydides offers to help us understand the origins of the Ten Years' War—but when the question of the sovereignty of power arises again, later in Thucydides' work, it has undergone a monstrous transformation. Power and fear of power are no longer used as thorough-going historical explanations by Thucydides but instead feature in revolting speeches by Thucydides' most repellent characters. "You hold your empire," Thucydides makes the appalling Cleon say to the Athenians in his speech urging the slaughter of the Mytileneans, "as a tyranny over plotting and unwilling subjects. And they obey you . . . because you rule them by virtue of your strength rather than their goodwill." Trying to justify a monstrous Athenian crime, an Athenian speaker offers the blasphemous formulation, "Of the gods we believe, and of men we know, that by a necessary law of their nature they rule wherever they can." These speakers in Thucydides are making claims not just about how things are, as Thucydides does in his own voice in Book I, but also about how things ought to be. To them it is not merely an unhappy fact that power makes nations act in certain ways, it is a good thing as well: like Socrates' interlocutor Thrasymachus in Plato's *Republic*, these speakers are advocates for the idea that might makes right.[17]

What is Thucydides trying to do by having his most loathsome characters bring forth cold realist theses? There is every reason to suppose that the gloating realist theory of international relations professed by Cleon and like-minded speakers in Thucydides had real advocates in Thucydides' day; we would not be wrong in assuming that Thucydides' speakers represent the views of actual participants in a late fifth-century BC debate about the role of power and morality in foreign relations. The younger Xenophon, who continued Thucydides' history after its abrupt end in 411 BC, certainly participated in this debate, and some of his writings appear to rebut positions like those Thucydides gives to Cleon and his ilk. Thucydides' own position in this discussion, moreover, is telegraphed with abundant clarity by the characters and the fates of the men to whom he ascribes such harsh realist views. If one seeks a lesson in international relations from Thucydides' account of the war itself (rather than his realist account of its origins), therefore, it may be that realism as a creed, realism as a policy, is both wicked and fruitless.[18]

Either Thucydides changed his mind about realism in the course of writing his history, or he was trying to draw a distinction between two varieties of realism: one a regrettable but true theory about how the world sometimes works (his own view, on this understanding), the other a creed and a guide to state action (a view that Thucydides apparently opposed). It is hard to be certain whether Thucydides had such a distinction in mind— but the notion that he did gains some support from the fact that not all the characters who offer realist analysis later in Thucydides are detestable. And, although the attractive characters in Thucydides (men like Pericles of Athens and Archidamus of Sparta) are usually not made to speak in the language of power but are, rather, allowed to speak in the language of conventional Greek ethics, Thucydides briefly has Pericles himself profess a mild, fatalistic realism. "Your empire," Pericles says to the Athenians, in the phrase that Thucydides deftly turns to poison in Cleon's mouth, "is, to speak somewhat plainly, like a tyranny. To take it perhaps was wrong, but to let it go is unsafe."[19]

Whatever the reason for the turn of Thucydides' text against realism, after Book I realism largely departs from Thucydides' own narrative and his own analysis and takes up residence in the speeches of evil characters. And Thucydides' near abandonment of realism as a tool to analyze events (as opposed to a way of characterizing villains) tells us something about the realism Thucydides was willing to vouch for. The useful form of realism, in his mind, was no grand theory of foreign relations but rather a means of explaining a special, hard case: the origins of the Peloponnesian War.

Beyond the special case of the outbreak of that war, however, Thucydides knew full well that realism was not a catchall explanation for the interactions of states. In the speeches Thucydides wrote, even in Book I, nonrealist expositions of motivations in the international area hugely outnumber realist analyses, and all through his work Thucydides happily offers nonrealist explanations for great events (the outbreak of the First Peloponnesian War, for example, as well as the Corcyrean revolution and the Peace of Nicias). The moderate realism that Thucydides avows in his own voice is rather like the unusually sized Allen Wrench one buys to assemble a single new piece of furniture, then leaves sitting unused on the shelf for years. To Thucydides, realist imperatives were only a part of what drove states; he did not think realism explained everything, or even everything that mattered.

After Book I Thucydides' own mild, analytic realism gives way to other speculations about the motivations of men in grim times. The most famous of these is his materialist theory of ethics, offered in his analysis of the revolution on Corcyra. "In peace and prosperity states and individuals have better sentiments, because they do not find themselves suddenly confronted with imperious necessities; but war takes away the easy supply of daily wants and so proves a teacher of violence that brings most men's characters to a level with their fortunes." Human goodness depends on having a full larder. When war empties larders, men become wicked. This is not a realist theory: it is a naïve theory about the origins of evil.[20]

Through his speeches, moreover, Thucydides also begins to develop another theory: one of the ranking of states. His interest in the rank of states is already evident in speeches in the heavily realist Book I, but it gathers steam in the two great addresses Thucydides gives to Pericles during the war—the Funeral Oration and the speech in defense of his strategy—and finally receives its most systematic exposition in the speech of the Spartans at Athens asking the Athenians for peace in 425 BC. It is fair to say that as Thucydides' narrative proceeds, his focus on rank eclipses his realism; not only does his analysis of events in terms of fear of power give way to an analysis in terms of rank, but he also devotes much more of his theoretical energy in speeches to the question of the rank of states.[21]

Thucydides understood the rank of states he analyzed as the Athenians understood it. When we look into the speech Thucydides writes for the Spartans in 425 BC, with its (almost Periclean) emphasis on caution and the great role of doing favors as a source of *timē*, we see that Thucydides is analyzing rank as it was defined by the Athenians during the war—not as a contest of *andreia*, the courage of outright hoplite battle, but especially as a contest of *charis*, the careful exchange of good for good and bad for bad. And in his narrative, Thucydides steadily elevates the other factor in Athenian *timē*, *mētis*, which plays an ever-increasing role in the story he tells, both in events like the escape of the Plataeans from Plataea and in debates like that between the Athenians and Boeotians over the Athenian dead at Delium.

Thucydides understood that a realist theory of international relations, a theory narrowly grounded in power, did not describe the world in which he lived. Thucydides had seen that states' histories were often more powerful drivers of their actions than was their power. He had seen prickly pride make states strive beyond their strength and exhaust themselves with little regard for its limits. He had seen that not only the power of a foe but the spirit, too, had to be conquered. He had seen that states and men often acted on the basis of wrath and revenge rather than sober calculation. And he was hardly the only Greek to see these things. For such, too, is the lesson of the revenge tragedies of ancient Athens—although tragedy teaches it another way. Characters in tragedy carry out revenge as if they were operating under remote control, wretched and fully aware of the doom they are bringing to themselves and all about them but unable to resist fate, the gods, or the simple, overwhelming logic of vengeance. In the end, the tragedians seem to be saying, revenge is stronger than humanity, stronger than reason; it is an irresistible force for chaos in the affairs of men. And Thucydides seems finally to have been moving toward a similar view.

Thucydides was too young to have heard the cackling of the Furies when the *Eumenides* of Aeschylus was brought forth upon the stage at Athens. But no Greek needed poetry to learn reverence for the spirits of revenge; nor did any Greek need to be told that the Furies were tireless, remorseless, and sharp of scent. Greeks learned it from their parents, and they learned it from their children; they learned it from neighbors, and they learned it from strangers; they learned it from friends, and they learned it from enemies. Cock an ear into the streets of Athens, and hear the song of the Furies. Cock an ear into the streets of Athens, and hear the song of wrath.

> Once spilled, a mother's blood cannot be picked back up:
> the wet juice of it, alas, goes down into the earth.
> From your body, living, you must make return,
> red gobbits from your limbs for me to gulp right down.
> I will draw from you to eat a loathsome draught to drink,
> and when I have squeezed you dry alive, I will drag you down
> > to death,
> to make you pay for mother-slaying the tortures of revenge.[22]

CHRONOLOGY OF EVENTS

All dates are BC. Dates preceded by a question mark (e.g., ?449) indicate that we have a relative, not an absolute, date for an event: we are to a greater or lesser degree confident of the order of events, but the actual year may be off by one or two. Dates given in the form "434/433 (winter)" signify that we are not sure which side of the turn of the modern year the event belongs on, it having been the practice of Thucydides to date by summers and winters.

BEFORE THE WAR

480 Invasion of Greece by Xerxes, the Great King of Persia, with his army and fleet.

480 Battle of Artemisium (Greeks and Persians fight an indecisive sea battle off Euboea).

480 Battle of Thermopylae (Persians defeat the Greeks in central Greece; heroic death of the Spartan Three Hundred).

480 Battle of Salamis (Greeks defeat the Persian fleet off Attica).

479 Battle of Plataea (Greeks defeat the Persian army in Boeotia).

479 Battle of Mycale (Greeks defeat the Persians by land and sea on the east coast of the Aegean).

?479 The Athenians rebuild the walls of Athens.

?478 Delian League founded (alliance of Athens and the Greek rebels against Persia).

?471 Exile of the Athenian politician Themistocles; Cimon becomes predominant at Athens.

?467 Battle of Eurymedon (Delian League defeats the Persians on land and sea on the south coast of Asia Minor).

?465 Earthquake in Laconia; rebellion of the Spartan helots.

?465 Cimon leads the Athenians to help Sparta against the helots; the helots are driven to take refuge on Mount Ithome in Messenia.

?462 Cimon again leads the Athenians to help the Spartans; the Spartans send the Athenians home; the Athenians are insulted.

?461 Athens make alliances with Argos and Thessaly; soon thereafter Megara leaves the Spartan alliance and joins Athens.

?461 Cimon exiled from Athens; Pericles soon becomes predominant at Athens.

?458 The Athenians attack Halieis in the Peloponnese and are defeated in battle by Corinth and her allies.

?458 The Athenians defeat the Peloponnesian allies at sea at the battle of Cecryphaleia.

?458 The Athenians defeat the Aeginetans by sea and besiege Aegina.

?458 The Athenians defeat the Corinthians in the Megarid.

?457 The Peloponnesians march into central Greece to rescue Doris from Phocis.

?457 Battle of Tanagra (Athenians challenge the Peloponnesians on their return from Doris; Peloponnesians are victorious).

?457 Battle of Oenophyta (Athenians defeat the Boeotians in battle; become masters of Boeotia, Phocis, and Opuntian Locris).

?457 Surrender of Aegina to Athens.

?457 The Athenians finish the long walls connecting Athens to her port, Piraeus.

?456 Athenian raiding expedition around the Peloponnese, led by Tolmides, who captures Cythera, raids Laconia, takes Chalcis in the northwest, and defeats Sicyon in battle.

?456 Athens settles the helots from Mount Ithome at Naupactus in the northwest.

?455 The Athenians make a futile expedition to Thessaly.

?454 Athenian raiding expedition in the Gulf of Corinth, led by Pericles; Athenians win a battle in the territory of Sicyon.

?454 The Athenian expedition against the Persians in Egypt ends in disaster; Delian League treasury moved to Athens.

?451 Five-year truce between Athens and Sparta, negotiated by Cimon upon his return from exile.

451 The Spartans force Argos to make a peace treaty for a term of thirty years.

?450 Death of Cimon fighting the Persians in the eastern Mediterranean.

?449 The Spartans free Delphi from the Phocians (the Second Sacred War); shortly thereafter, the Athenians place Delphi back in Phocian hands.

?449 The Athenians summon a pan-Hellenic congress at Athens; the plan meets Spartan opposition and fails.

447 Building of the Parthenon begins at Athens.

?447 Battle of Coronea (Boeotians defeat Athens and recover their independence).

446 Megara defects to the Peloponnesians; Euboea revolts from Athens.

446 The Peloponnesians under King Pleistoanax invade Attica; he negotiates with Pericles and returns to the Peloponnese.

446/445 (winter) Thirty Years' Peace between Athens and Sparta.

?443 The Athenians lead a pan-Hellenic colony to Thurii in southern Italy.

440–439 Samos rebels from Athens; the Peloponnesian League declines to help Samos against Athens.

?435 Megarian Decree (Athenians ban the Megarians from markets and harbors of Athens and her confederacy).

435 Corcyra and Corinth fight over control of Epidamnus, and Corcyra defeats Corinth in the sea battle of Leucimne.

433 Athens makes a defensive alliance with Corcyra.

433 Battle of Sybota (Corinthians defeat Corcyra and an Athenian squadron at sea but fail to exploit their victory).

433 Athens becomes suspicious of Corinthian subversion of Athens' subject city Potidaea in the Thracian Chalcidice.

432 Athens sends an expedition to try to replace King Perdiccas of Macedon with his brother Philip; it fails.

432 Having received a Spartan promise of protection, Potidaea revolts from Athens in alliance with other Chalcidian cities and Perdiccas, the king of Macedon; Corinth rushes help to Potidaea.

432 June(?) Battle of Potidaea (Athenians defeat rebels in the field and lay Potidaea under siege).

432 July(?) First conference at Sparta (pressed by their allies, the Spartans declare that Athens has broken the Thirty Years' Peace).

432 August(?) Second conference at Sparta (Sparta's allies agree to go to war against Athens).

432/431 (winter) Diplomacy between Athens and Sparta.

THE TEN YEARS' WAR

The First Year of the War

431 April(?) Boeotian surprise attack on Plataea fails.

431 May(?) Peloponnesian army gathers at the Isthmus of Corinth.

431 May(?) The Peloponnesians attack the Athenian border fort of Oenoe.

431 late June–late July(?) The Peloponnesians invade Attica under the command of King Archidamus of Sparta.

431 July–August(?) Athenian naval expedition around the Peloponnese raids Laconia, fails to capture Methone, raids Elis (one hundred Athenian ships and fifty allies).

431 August(?) The Athenian raiding fleet continues to northwestern Greece and captures Sollium and Astacus.

431 August(?) The Athenian fleet in northwestern Greece accepts the defection of Cephallenia.

431 September(?) The Athenians invade Megara; the Athenian fleet returning from the Peloponnese joins the land army.

431 The Athenians raid Opuntian Locris and establish a fort on the island of Atalanta for the protection of Euboea.

431 The Athenians expel the Aeginetans from Aegina; the Spartans settle them at Thyrea on the Spartan border with Argos.

431/430 (winter) A Corinthian fleet attacks Acarnania and fails to compel Cephallenia to rejoin the Peloponnesians.

The Second Year of the War

430 The Peloponnesians invade Attica for the second time under the command of King Archidamus of Sparta and ravage for forty days.

430 Plague breaks out at Athens.

430 Athenian naval raid of the close Peloponnese: Epidaurus, Troezen, Halieis, Hermione (one hundred Athenian ships and fifty allies).

430 The Athenian raiding fleet continues on to besiege Potidaea in the Chalcidice but fails to capture the city.

430 The Athenians send envoys to Sparta asking for terms of peace; peace is not achieved; Pericles is dismissed from his position as general and fined.

430 A Peloponnesian fleet ravages Zacynthus in the northwest.

430 Peloponnesian envoys to the Great King of Persia are arrested in Thrace, taken to Athens, and executed.

430/429 (winter) The Athenians station at Naupactus a fleet of twenty triremes under the command of Phormio.

430/429 (winter) Potidaea surrenders to the Athenians; its people are allowed to depart and are replaced with colonists from Athens.

The Third Year of the War

429 The Peloponnesians under King Archidamus of Sparta attack Plataea; failing to take Plataea by assault, they lay the city under siege.

429 The Athenians campaign against Spartolus in Bottice (near the Thracian Chalcidice) and are defeated by the Chalcidians.

429 The Peloponnesians and Ambracians campaign unsuccessfully against Acarnania in the northwest.

429 The Athenian general Phormio defeats with twenty ships a Peloponnesian fleet of forty-seven outside the mouth of the Gulf of Corinth.

429 The Athenian general Phormio defeats with twenty ships a Peloponnesian fleet of seventy-seven near Naupactus.

429 Death of Pericles from the plague.

429/428 (winter) The Peloponnesians attempt a surprise attack by sea on Piraeus; the expedition is diverted to Salamis, which the Peloponnesians loot.

429/428 (winter) Sitalces, king of the Odrysian Thracians, launches an enormous expedition into Macedonia and the Chalcidice; his campaign comes to nothing.

429/428 (winter) Phormio marches through Acarnania, expelling from its towns enemies of Athens.

The Fourth Year of the War

428 The Peloponnesians invade Attica for the third time under the command of King Archidamus of Sparta.

428 Mytilene on Lesbos revolts against the Athenians; the Athenians blockade Mytilene by sea.

428 Athenian naval raid of the Peloponnese (thirty ships).

428 mid-August. Envoys of Mytilene are produced at the Olympic Games to ask for Peloponnesian aid; it is granted.

428 A second Peloponnesian campaign against Attica in the autumn, planned for both land and sea, proves abortive.

428 The Athenians raid the near Peloponnese with an emergency fleet of one hundred ships.

428 Finally landing enough men, the Athenians blockade Mytilene by land.

428/427 (winter) Half the garrison of Plataea escapes to Athens.

The Fifth Year of the War

427 The Peloponnesians dispatch a fleet under Alcidas to help Mytilene.

427 The Peloponnesians invade Attica for the fourth time, under the command of Cleomenes, regent of Sparta.

427 Mytilene surrenders while the Peloponnesian fleet is still en route; Alcidas and his fleet return to the Peloponnese.

427 The Athenians vote to massacre all the men of Mytilene, then change their minds and kill only one thousand of them; the land of Mytilene is divided among Athenian allotment holders.

427 The Athenians under Nicias capture the island of Minoa off Megara.

427 Plataea surrenders to the Peloponnesians; the garrison is executed.

427 Oligarchs take over Corcyra and try to detach the island from the Athenian alliance.

427 Civil war breaks out on Corcyra between democrats and oligarchs; the democrats prevail.

427 The Peloponnesian fleet defeats the Corcyreans but cannot exploit its victory because of the arrival of an Athenian fleet.

427 Massacre of oligarchs by democrats on Corcyra.

427 The Athenians send a squadron to Sicily (twenty ships).

427/426 (winter) Return of the plague to Athens.

The Sixth Year of the War

426 The planned Peloponnesian invasion of Attica is aborted by bad omens (earthquakes).

426 An Athenian fleet (thirty ships) raids the Peloponnese under the command of Demosthenes, son of Alcisthenes.

426 An Athenian fleet attacks and ravages Melos.

426 The Athenian fleet from Melos continues on to Boeotia, where its marines meet soldiers from Athens and ravage Tanagra; the fleet goes on to raid Opuntian Locris.

426 Sparta founds the colony of Heraclea in Trachis.

426 The Athenians and allies under Demosthenes ravage the island of Leucas in the northwest.

426 The Athenians and allies under Demosthenes attack Aetolia in the northwest and are defeated.

426 Summoned by the Aetolians, the Peloponnesians march from Delphi on Naupactus in the northwest; Demosthenes saves Naupactus by bringing Acarnanian troops.

426/425 (winter) The Athenians purify the island of Delos.

426/425 (winter) The Ambracians and Peloponnesians who failed to take Naupactus attack Amphilochian Argos in the northwest.

426/425 (winter) The Acarnanians and Athenians under Demosthenes defeat the Peloponnesians and Ambracians at the battles of Olpae and Idomene in the northwest.

The Seventh Year of the War

425 The Peloponnesians send a fleet to Corcyra hoping to restore the oligarchs to power (sixty ships).

425 The Peloponnesians invade Attica for the fifth time, under the command of Agis, king of Sparta.

425 The Athenians send a fleet of reinforcements to Sicily with orders to deal with trouble at Corcyra on the way (forty ships).

425 The Athenian fleet headed for Corcyra and Sicily is compelled to take refuge from a storm at Pylos, in Messenia, on the southwestern coast of the Peloponnese, which they fortify.

425 King Agis of Sparta recalls the Peloponnesian fleet from Corcyra and returns home with the Peloponnesian army from Attica to challenge the Athenians at Pylos.

425 The Spartans fail to dislodge the Athenians left with Demosthenes at Pylos after the departure of the Athenian fleet for Corcyra.

425 The Athenian fleet returns to Pylos and defeats the Peloponnesian fleet in Navarino Bay, trapping Spartan citizen soldiers on the island of Sphacteria.

425 The Spartans sue for peace to recover the men on Sphacteria; there is a truce for twenty days, but terms of peace are not agreed upon.

425 The Athenians, under Demosthenes and Cleon, defeat the Spartans on Sphacteria and carry the survivors back to Athens as hostages.

425 The Athenian fleet sails on to Corcyra, where it helps the democrats defeat the oligarchs; the oligarchs are massacred; the Athenian fleet then sails on to Italy and Sicily.

425 The Athenians under Nicias land and fight a battle at Solygeia in the territory of Corinth; they then go on to the Argolid peninsula, raid Troezen, Halieis, and Epidaurus, and fortify the peninsula of Methana.

The Eighth Year of the War

424 An Athenian fleet under Nicias captures Cythera and raids the coast of Laconia.

424 The Athenian fleet under Nicias goes on to attack the Aeginetans inhabiting Thyrea, which the Athenians capture; the survivors are taken to Athens and executed.

424 A general peace is agreed in Sicily and Italy at the conference of Gela; the Athenian fleet in the west returns home.

424 The Athenians attack Megara by surprise with the help of traitors and take her port of Nisaea, but they are prevented from taking the city itself by the Spartan Brasidas.

424 Brasidas leads a makeshift army through Thessaly to help the rebels against the Athenians in the Thracian Chalcidice; he accepts the defection of the city of Acanthus.

424 The Athenians hope to attack Boeotia by surprise with the help of traitors, but their plot is betrayed, and the rising in Boeotia proves abortive.

424 Demosthenes gathers Athenian allies in the northwest, is turned back from Boeotia, attempts to raid Sicyon, and is defeated in battle.

424 The Athenians, ignorant of the failure of their plans elsewhere in Boeotia, march to fortify Delium.

424 Battle of Delium (the Boeotians defeat the Athenians).

424/423 (winter) Brasidas takes the Athenian subject city of Amphipolis on the coast of Thrace.

424/423 (winter) Brasidas accepts the defection of Torone in the Chalcidice.

The Ninth Year of the War

423 A one-year truce is struck between Athens and Sparta.

423 Brasidas accepts the defection of Scione in the Chalcidice before he knows of the truce and that of Mende after he has been informed of it.

423 Brasidas campaigns with King Perdiccas of Macedonia against the king's rebellious subjects in Lyncestis.

423 The Athenians under Nicias recapture Mende and lay Scione under siege.

423/422 (winter) Mantinea and Tegea, allies of Sparta, fight a battle against one another.

423/422 (winter) Brasidas attempts, and fails, to capture Potidaea.

The Tenth Year of the War

422 The truce between Athens and Sparta is extended to late July or August.

422 The Athenians purify Delos by expelling its entire population.

422 An Athenian force under Cleon sails for Thrace; Torone is recaptured.

422 The Boeotians take the Athenian border fort of Panactum.

422 The Athenians under Cleon land near Amphipolis.

422 Battle of Amphipolis (Brasidas defeats the Athenians; both Cleon and Brasidas are killed).

421 *April* Peace and alliance are made between Athens and Sparta; many Spartan allies secede from the Spartan alliance and join Argos.

A fuller chronology of events from 435 to 404 BC is given by G. Busolt, *Griechische Geschichte bis zur Schlacht bei Chaeroneia* vol. 3.2 (1904) pp. xxv–xxxv. Busolt assigns events to months (which is sometimes more than the evidence will allow and which I have not regularly attempted here). His is the basis of all subsequent chronologies. B. W. Henderson, *The Great War Between Athens and Sparta* (1927) pp. 493–6, offers a simplified form of Busolt's chronology in English. Especially useful are chronologies with references to the relevant passages of Thucydides, which can be found in the *Cambridge Ancient History*[1] vol. 5 (1927) facing p. 252, A. W. Gomme, *A Historical Commentary on Thucydides* vol. 3 (1956) pp. 716–21, and R. B. Strassler, *The Landmark Thucydides* (1996) pp. 556–75.

GLOSSARIES OF PEOPLE,
THINGS, AND PLACES

GLOSSARY OF PEOPLE

Alcidas. This unlucky Spartan admiral led the Peloponnesian fleet to the rescue of Mytilene in 427 BC but arrived in the eastern Aegean after the city had fallen. Later in that same year, Alcidas led a fleet to Corcyra to help the pro-Peloponnesian oligarchs and won a sea battle, but he fled at the report of a considerable Athenian fleet. Alcidas was one of the Spartans sent to found Heraclea in Trachis in 426 BC.

Archidamus, son of Zeuxidamus (reigned ?476–427 BC). This king of Sparta opposed as precipitous Sparta's 432 BC declaration of war against Athens, but nevertheless led Sparta's early expeditions into Attica (431, 430, 428 BC) and the Peloponnesian attack on Plataea in 429 BC. Later Greeks named the Ten Years' War from 431 to 421 BC the Archidamian War after him. Thucydides regarded Archidamus as wise; along with Pericles, he is one of Thucydides' heroes in the first years of the war.

Aristophanes (before 445–?386 BC). The leading playwright of Athenian Old Comedy, Aristophanes authored over forty plays. Of the eleven that survive, the *Acharnians* (425 BC), the *Knights* (424 BC), and the *Peace* (421 BC) are major sources for the later years of the Ten Years' War. Rude and scatological, the plays of Aristophanes mocked the Athenian democracy, its foibles, and its personalities: Cleon was one of Aristophanes' favorite targets.

Brasidas, son of Tellis (d. 422 BC). The Spartan Brasidas saved Methone from Athenian attack in 431 BC, was elected ephor in 430 BC, and continued to distinguish himself thereafter, especially at Pylos in 425 BC. In 424 BC Brasidas led a force of freed Spartan helots and Peloponnesian mercenaries into the north, where he revived the Chalcidian rebellion against Athens and captured Amphipolis. Brasidas died fighting Cleon and the Athenians at the battle of Amphipolis in 422 BC. He was a hero of Thucydides', and the historian lent epic coloring to his descriptions of Brasidas' deeds.

Cimon, son of Miltiades (*ca.* 510–?450 BC). The son of the victor of Marathon (490 BC), Cimon was the leading politician and general at Athens before the ascendancy of Pericles. Cimon defeated the Persians at Eurymedon in ?467 and led the Athenians to the aid of the Spartans after the revolt of the helots in, probably, ?465 and ?462 BC. Ostracized after the Spartans sent the Athenians home during the second expedition, Cimon was in exile during most of the First Peloponnesian War (?461–446/445 BC), but he returned in ?451 BC to make a truce between Athens and Sparta. He died fighting the Persians in the eastern Mediterranean in the next year. Strongly pro-Spartan (he named one of his sons Lacedaemonius), Cimon appears to have believed that Athens and Sparta could be equals in *timē* (s.v.).

Cleon, son of Cleanetus (d. 422 BC). This Athenian politician and general was an opponent of Pericles in the first years of the Ten Years' War, and after Pericles' death, Cleon and his rival Nicias became the leading political figures in Athens. Cleon advocated massacring the men of defeated Mytilene in 427 BC (although the Athenians did not do so) and, along with Demosthenes, captured the Spartans on Sphacteria in 425 BC. Cleon campaigned successfully in the north in 422 BC until dying, defeated by Brasidas, at the battle of Amphipolis. Cleon is one of the great puzzles of the war: hated passionately by both Thucydides and Aristophanes, he had a great following at Athens, but his good qualities are hidden from us.

Demosthenes, son of Alcisthenes (d. 413 BC). Along with Cleon and Nicias, Demosthenes was a major Athenian commander in the later years of the Ten Years' War. He was defeated in Aetolia in 426 BC but went on to save Naupactus in that year and, subsequently, as leader of the Acarnanians, defeated a Peloponnesian/Ambracian coalition at Olpae and Idomene, thereafter returning to Athens in triumph. In 425 BC he fortified Pylos and, along with Cleon, subsequently captured the Spartans on Sphacteria. In 424 BC he was involved in the Athenian plots against both Megara (partially successful) and Boeotia (a failure). He was a signatory to the Peace of Nicias in 421 BC. Not to be confused with Demosthenes, son of Demosthenes, the great Athenian orator of the fourth century BC.

Diodorus Siculus (first century BC). Author of a forty-book universal history from the age of myth to the time of Julius Caesar, of which large parts survive, including his account of the period 480–421 BC. See appendix pp. 425–6 for discussion of this author and the use made of him in this book.

Nicias, son of Niceratus (*ca.* 470–413 BC). An Athenian general and politician, Nicias came to prominence in Athens after the death of Pericles; he was often opposed to Cleon. Nicias captured Minoa off the coast of Megara in 427 BC but gave up his Pylos command to Cleon in 425 BC. Nevertheless, in 425 BC, he landed an army in the territory of Corinth and fought the battle of Solygeia, and then went on to attack the Argolid peninsula. In 424 BC Nicias captured Cythera, the large island off Laconia, and raided Laconia. After the death of Cleon (422 BC), Nicias was a strong advocate of peace with Sparta, which later Greeks called the Peace of Nicias (421 BC) after him.

Perdiccas, son of Alexander (reigned *ca.* 450–413 BC). This king of Macedonia encouraged the revolt of Potidaea and the Chalcidians (432 BC) against Athens when Athens supported the claims of his brother to his throne, but thereafter he changed sides a number of times during the war. In 424 BC Perdiccas invited Brasidas and his Peloponnesian army into the north, not least to help Perdiccas against a rebellious chieftain, but after an attempt to suppress that rebel failed in 423 BC, Perdiccas allied with the Athenians against Brasidas. We simply do not know enough about the politics of the north to tell whether Perdiccas' tergiversations were driven by policy or whether he was just pathologically treacherous.

Pericles, son of Xanthippus (*ca.* 495–429 BC). This Athenian politician and general came to prominence in Athens after the ostracism of Cimon (?461 BC). In ?454 BC he led a successful raid into the Corinthian Gulf during the First Peloponnesian War and made peace with Sparta in the winter of 446/445 BC. He subsequently opposed any yielding to Spartan demands in the diplomacy that led up to the outbreak of the Ten Years' War (431–421 BC). His was the initial strategy of Athens during the war, that of declining to defend the fields of Attica and raiding the Peloponnese from ships. He died from the plague in 429 BC. Pericles is associated with the cultural flowering of mid-fifth-century BC Athens, especially the building of the Parthenon.

Phormio, son of Asopius. This Athenian general secured the alliance of the Acarnanians with Athens at some point before the Ten Years' War. In the winter of 430/429 BC, he was sent with a squadron of twenty ships to establish an Athenian naval station at Naupactus at the mouth of the Corinthian Gulf. In 429 BC he won two naval victories over Peloponnesian fleets of, respectively, forty-seven and seventy-seven ships. In the following winter, Phormio marched through Acarnania, driving enemies of Athens out of the Acarnanian towns. Then Phormio vanishes, mysteriously, from history. Thucydides appears to have considered Phormio an exemplary commander.

Pleistoanax, son of Pausanias (reigned *ca.* 458 to *ca.* 408 BC). This ill-fated Spartan king led the Peloponnesian invasion of Attica in 446 BC, which ended the First Peloponnesian War. He was subsequently sent into exile for his conduct on that campaign (he was accused of having been bribed by Pericles). Restored to Sparta by command of the Delphic oracle in 427 or 426 BC, he was then blamed for Sparta's misfortunes during the rest of the Ten Years' War. Not surprisingly, Pleistoanax was an advocate of peace with Athens in 421 BC.

Plutarch (late first/early second century AD). Among the extensive works left by the Roman-era polymath Plutarch is a series of paired lives of eminent Greeks and Romans. His *Lives* of Aristides, Themistocles, Pericles, and

Nicias preserve many otherwise unknown details about the period 480–421 BC. Plutarch must be used with care: much further removed from the events of the fifth century BC even than Diodorus (s.v.), he tended to attribute character themes to the figures he described and to report, without any great discrimination, stories illustrating those themes.

Sitalces, son of Teres (d. 424 BC). This king of the Odrysian Thracians became an ally of Athens in 431 BC and brokered the return of Perdiccas to the Athenian side in that year. In 430 BC the Peloponnesians attempted to convince Sitalces to defect to their side and relieve the Athenian siege of Potidaea; this he declined to do, and the Peloponnesian envoys were betrayed into Athenian hands. In the winter of 429/428 BC, furious at Perdiccas, Sitalces invaded Macedonia with a gigantic host in an attempt to replace the Macedonian king with a relative, but he failed. To honor his alliance with Athens, his men also ravaged the land of the rebels from Athens in the Chalcidice. After the death of Sitalces in 424 BC, his heir, Perdiccas' brother-in-law, ceased to help the Athenians.

Thucydides, son of Olorus (c. 460 BC to after 404 BC). Other than what this Athenian historian and general tells us in his own work—of his Thracian connection, his generalship in 424 BC, his failure to save Amphipolis from Brasidas, and his exile until after the surrender of Athens in 404 BC—we know practically nothing of Thucydides, our main source for the period 479–411 BC. His comments on politics, especially in 411 BC, show that he was, like many rich Athenians, an oligarch, and his admiration for the democratic politician Pericles is premised on Pericles' exerting a firm control over the undisciplined Athenian democracy. For a detailed discussion of the method of Thucydides, see the appendix pp. 417–25.

GLOSSARY OF THINGS AND GREEK TERMS

andreia. The quality of courage in which Greek soldiers competed. Competition in *andreia* tended to simplify battle and make it into a contest with tacit rules. *Andreia* exists in tension and competition with *mētis*, cunning (s.v.).

Athenian empire. See Delian League.

charis. A favor, the sense of gratitude for a favor, and the moral excellence of giving back what is owed, either in the form of favor, if a favor has been received, or revenge, if *hybris*, or injury, has been received.

cleruchy. In contrast to a Greek colony (s.v.), when Athens sent out a cleruchy ("allotment"), the cleruchs ("shareholders") remained Athenian citizens. During the Ten Years' War, Athens established cleruchies on Aegina in 431 BC and Lesbos in 427 BC.

colony. When a colony was sent out from a Greek city, the colonists gave up their old citizenship and became citizens of the colony. But a colony was expected to maintain close and reverential ties to her mother city. By their nature colonies were inferior in rank (*timē*) to the cities of old Greece.

Delian League. In the wake of the Persian War (480–479 BC), when the Spartans proved uncommitted to protecting the Greek states located on the coast of Asia Minor, in the Thraceward region, and in the Aegean, most of which had revolted from Persia, those states chose Athens as their *hegemon* (s.v.), and a formal alliance was formed on the island of Delos, sacred to the Ionians (s.v.). Allies were allowed to contribute to the common defense by providing ships (which a few, powerful places chose to do) or money (the vast majority). Over time Athens came to rule her allies with increasing harshness, and in the later stages of its history, the Delian League is referred to as the Athenian empire.

democracy. The "rule of the people," the Greek constitutional form in which all male citizens decided the city's actions by voting in a sovereign assembly. In a Greek democracy, officeholders were characteristically chosen by lottery rather than election. In the fifth century BC, Athens was the most prominent democracy in Greece, and imperial Athens sometimes imposed democracies on her subjects.

Dorians. In myth, all the Hellenes were descended from Hellen, son of Deucalion, with the Dorian race, or tribe, or nation hailing from his son Dorus. The Greeks believed that the Dorians abode long in Doris in central Greece, but after the Trojan War, the sons of Heracles led them into the Peloponnese, where they settled (expelling the Ionians, in some versions). Sparta, Corinth, and most other Peloponnesian states were Dorian, as were their colonies (like Syracuse in Sicily). Most of the Dorians spoke the Doric dialect of Greek.

drachma. See talent.

ephor. At Sparta a board of five ephors ("overseers") was elected each year and served as the nonmilitary executive (Sparta's two kings commanded in war), received ambassadors, and exercised general supervision of the Spartan way of life.

general (*strategos*). In democratic Athens ten generals, who served an annual term, had supreme tactical authority over both Athens' army and its fleet, although the democracy made strategy directly by vote of the assembly. *Strategoi* were usually sent out to command expeditions in committees of two or more. The office of *strategos* was one of the few positions in the Athenian democracy whose incumbents were chosen by election rather than lottery.

hegemony (*hegemon*). A hegemony was a Greek alliance believed to be held together by the supreme *timē* of the ruling state (the *hegemon*), whose allies paid it voluntary obedience out of respect. The Greeks distinguished a hegemony from an empire (*archē*), whose subjects obeyed a leading state out of fear. But naturally it always appealing to describe one's own alliance as a hegemony and that of the enemy as an *archē*.

helot. A Spartan slave or serf. Traditionally the descendents of the pre-Spartan occupants of Laconia and Messenia, the wretched helots farmed the land held by Spartan citizens, who were themselves not allowed to practice any gainful occupation. The helots rebelled in ?465 BC, and many of the Messenian helots were besieged by the Spartans and their allies on Mount Ithome (see Messenia s.v.). Once the Athenians established posts at Pylos (425 BC) and Cythera (424 BC), many helots fled to them, and the Spartans feared another general rising. To get the most dangerous of the helots out of Laconia, the Spartans sent seven hundred of them into the north with Brasidas to serve as soldiers (424 BC).

honorary consul (*proxenos*). If individuals had *xenoi*, or guest-friends, cities had *proxenoi*, or honorary consuls. A citizen of one city would agree to extend hospitality and protection in his home city to the visiting citizens of the other. Relationships of *proxenia* were usually hereditary and conveyed great honor on the citizens who were *proxenoi*. In the absence of permanent ambassadors, *proxenoi*, although, of course, citizens of the city in which they lived, not the one they represented, provided basic diplomatic services.

hoplite. A heavy-armed Greek infantryman. Full hoplite equipment consisted of a large round shield, an engulfing helmet, a cuirass or breastplate made either of bronze or from layers of glued linen, leg-protecting grieves, a spear, and a dagger. By the time of the Peloponnesian War, many hoplites had given up the greaves and the cuirass (or traded bronze in for linen) and replaced the old all-protecting helmet with the lighter, conical *pilos* (see picture p. 273). Hoplites fight in the phalanx (s.v.).

hybris. Insult, or the disposition or propensity to insult, or an excessive self-opinion implying these (our "hubris" comes from this last sense). *Hybris* damages *timē* (s.v.) and produces anger in its victims and a desire for revenge. Successful revenge "quenches the *hybris*" of the insulting party and restores the *timē* of the avenger.

Ionians. In myth, all the Hellenes were descended from Hellen, son of Deucalion, with the Ionian race, or tribe, or nation hailing from Hellen's grandson Ion. According to tradition, the Ionians had once lived in the Peloponnese but were driven out in the period after the Trojan War (by the Dorians, in some stories). They fled to Athens and from there colonized many of the Aegean islands and the section of the coast of Asia Minor called Ionia. Most Ionians spoke the Ionian dialect of Greek, although the Athenian version, Attic, was distinct.

mētis. The admired quality of cunning intellect that, in wartime, manifested itself in trickery on the battlefield and ingenuity in siegecraft. Greeks competed in *mētis* and enjoyed competition in *mētis*: Thucydides often presents an event in the war or a diplomatic exchange as a contest in *mētis*. *Mētis* exists in tension and competition with *andreia*, courage (s.v.).

obol. See talent.

oligarchy. The "rule of the few," a Greek constitutional form where not all male citizens had the right to participate in decision making, the political class being conventionally separated from the rest by a property qualification. Offices were characteristically filled by election rather than by lottery (which was the method favored by democracies). Thebes, and most of Sparta's allies, were oligarchies.

Peloponnesian League. Sparta had assembled a Peloponnesian alliance in the mid-to-late sixth century BC, taking in most of the Peloponnese except for perpetually hostile Argos. In the fifth century, the alliance was extended to include Megara, Boeotia, and other central-Greek states. The members of the Peloponnesian League (the name is modern) were bound to Sparta by bilateral treaties that obliged them to "follow the Lacedaemonians wheresoever they may lead by land or sea." Sparta's allies were not bound to each other, however, and frequently made war upon each other. Incapable of coercing the mass of her allies at once, Sparta was obliged to consult them on joint actions.

peltast. A light-armed Greek infantryman. Named for the *peltē*, the traditionally crescent-shaped light shield they carried, peltasts were armed with a mix of javelins and longer, thrusting spears.

phalanx. Hoplites (s.v.) fought the enemy arrayed in a phalanx, or "roller," usually eight or more men deep. Details, including whether hoplites in the phalanx pushed against each other with their shields, are controversial. See pp. 307–13.

talent. Six obols made a drachma, and six thousand drachmas a talent. Life could be sustained on two or three obols a day; a skilled craftsman received a drachma a day. The famous Athenian "owl" coin was a tetradrachm, that is, a four-drachma coin, and so very valuable. Given the profound changes in economic structure between ancient Greece and modern times, comparisons of buying power are nearly meaningless, but a talent of silver had many of the same connotations that a million dollars does today.

timē. To the Greeks, both men and states were ranked against each other, and the stuff of that ranking was *timē*, literally "worth," but also partaking of English "honor" or "prestige." The Greeks often fought wars to defend or advance the *timē* of their states, and many Greek acts in war, especially ravaging the agricultural land of the enemy, attacked the enemy's *timē*.

trireme. An oared warship approximately one hundred and twenty feet in length, in which some one hundred and seventy rowers disposed on three levels propelled a ram through the water, to the discomfiture of enemy ships. The Athenians also shipped ten hoplites and four archers as marines, in addition to a small crew of boat handlers. The trireme was commanded, at Athens, by a trierarch, a rich man who contributed to the upkeep of the ship. A Greek trireme was reconstructed in the 1980s: see pictures on pp. 125–6, 157.

GLOSSARY OF PLACES

Acarnania. A region of northwestern Greece to the west of Aetolia and south of the Gulf of Ambracia, Acarnania had been brought into alliance with the Athenians before the war by Phormio. In 431 BC the Athenian raiding fleet, upon its arrival in the northwest, assisted Acarnania. In 429 BC Ambracia and the Peloponnesians launched an unsuccessful campaign against Acarnania (the campaign that led to Phormio's two great naval victories), and in 426 BC the same parties tried to conquer Acarnania's ally Amphilochian Argos (leading to their defeat by Demosthenes and the Acarnanians at Olpae and Idomene).

Aegina. This island in the Saronic Gulf was a traditional maritime rival of Athens. She joined the Corinthian side in the First Peloponnesian War, but was defeated at sea and besieged by Athens (?458 BC). Upon her surrender (?457 BC), Aegina was enrolled as a tribute-paying subject of Athens in the Delian League. Despite this status Aegina lobbied the Spartans in 432 BC to go to war against Athens, and the Athenians in consequence expelled the Aeginetans from Aegina in 431 BC. The Spartans settled the Aeginetans at Thyrea, where the Athenians attacked them in 424 BC, taking the town and carrying the men away to be executed in Athens.

Aetolia. A district of northwestern Greece to the east of Acarnania and west of Phocis, Aetolia was an ally of Sparta in the Ten Years' War. At the bidding of Naupactus, which lay on the border between Aetolia and Ozolian Locris, Demosthenes invaded Aetolia in 426 BC and was bloodily defeated. Later in that year the Aetolians summoned Peloponnesian help against Naupactus—which, however, they failed to take.

Ambracia. A Corinthian colony in the northwest of Greece to the north of Acarnania near the north coast of the Ambracian Gulf, Ambracia was an ally of Sparta in the Ten Years' War. Ambracia had a rivalry with Acarnania over Amphilochian Argos, which lay between them.

Amphipolis. A Thraceward colony of Athens established in 437 BC in a wind of the river Strymon. Rich and populous, Amphipolis also commanded the bridge over Strymon between Macedonia to the west and Thrace to the east. Amphipolis was captured by Brasidas in 424 BC, and Cleon was defeated and died trying to recover it at the battle of Amphipolis in 422 BC.

Arcadia. A mountainous region of the central Peloponnese, whose two major cities were Tegea and Mantinea. Tegea had been Sparta's first Peloponnesian ally, and all the Arcadians were allied to Sparta during the Ten Years' War. In the winter of 423/422 BC, Tegea and Mantinea fought a war against each other.

Argolid. See Argos.

Argos. A Greek city-state in the Peloponnese, north of Sparta and south of Corinth. Sparta's great traditional Peloponnesian rival, Argos fought the Spartans in the 450s BC but was bound to peace with Sparta for thirty years in 451 BC. Argos was neutral in the Ten Years' War, but the Spartans were motivated to make peace with Athens in 421 BC in part because their thirty-year treaty with Argos was about to expire and they feared that Argos would join Athens. The plain of Argos, usually but not always wholly under Argive control, was the Argolid.

Attica. The territory of the city-state of Athens, bordering Boeotia on the north and Megara on the west.

Boeotia. The territory to the north of Attica, ruled (with the important exception of Plataea) by the Boeotian League, an alliance of oligarchic city-states under the domination of Thebes. League policy was decided by a committee of eleven Boeotarchs. The Boeotian League was allied to Sparta in the Ten Years' War. Boeotia was invaded by Athens in 426 BC, and the Athenians tried (and failed) to foment a pro-Athenian and pro-democratic rising among the cities of Boeotia in 424 BC.

Bosporus. The more northerly of the two straits that form the sea passage from the Aegean into the Black Sea. The Hellespont is the more southerly.

Byzantium. A Greek city-state strategically located on the Bosporus, Byzantium revolted from Athens with Samos in 440 BC and returned to the Athenian alliance in 439 BC. The Athenians were acutely sensitive to threats to the Bosporus and Hellespont region because Athens was not self-sufficient in grain, and she imported much from the Black Sea region.

Cephallenia. This island in the Ionian Sea at the mouth of the Gulf of Corinth joined Athens in 431 BC and was raided by the Peloponnesians in an attempt to get it to join them in the winter of 431/430 BC.

Chalcidice. The Thracian Chalcidice is a wide peninsula extending from the northern coast of the Aegean Sea and terminating in three narrow peninsulas, Pallene, Sithonia, and Acte. This was an area of thick Greek settlement, all of whose cities had been members of Athens' Delian League. Under the influence of Perdiccas (s.v.), in 432 BC many of these cities revolted from Athens along with Potidaea and formed the Chalcidian League based at Olynthus. Brasidas added more cities to the league in 424 and 423 BC. Athens ultimately failed to suppress the Chalcidian revolt, and the Chalcidian League was a major force in Greek affairs in the early fourth century BC.

Corcyra. An island in the extreme northwest of Greece (today known as Corfu to English speakers). A Corinthian colony, the city-state of Corcyra had long been on bad terms with Corinth, and war broke out between them in 435 BC. Athens intervened in the war on the side of Corcyra, which enraged Corinth against Athens. Corcyra was an ally of Athens during the Ten Years' War (and contributed ships to her raiding circumnavigation of the Peloponnese in 431 BC), but 427 and 425 BC saw oligarch-versus-democrat civil wars on Corcyra, both eventually won by the democrats with the help of Athens.

Corinth. A city-state in the Peloponnese to the north of Argos and west of Megara, Corinth seems to have been a prime mover in the First Pelopon- nesian War (?461–446/445 BC). The Thirty Years' Peace (446/445 BC) satis- fied her wants, and we find Corinth in *ca.* 440 BC opposing suggestions that the Peloponnesians should go to war with Athens during the rebellion of Samos. But relations with Athens soured over Corcyra and Potidaea, and Corinth was a major advocate at Sparta in 432 BC for war against Athens. In 424 BC the Athenians invaded the territory of Corinth and fought the battle of Solygeia against the Corinthians. Furious at the Spartans for what they felt was betrayal, the Corinthians refused to join in the Peace of Nicias in 421 BC.

Corinthian Gulf. The long horizontal body of water that separates the Pelopon- nese from northwestern Greece. In the winter of 430/429 BC, the Athenians established a naval station at Naupactus to guard the narrow mouth of the Gulf. Phormio's two great naval victories of 429 BC were fought just outside and just inside the Gulf of Corinth. Outside the mouth of the Corinthian Gulf lay the two strategic islands of Zacynthus and Cephallenia.

Cythera. A considerable island off the southern coast of Laconia, ruled by Sparta, Cythera was seized by the Athenians as a base for raiding Laconia in ?456 and 424 BC.

Delium. See Tanagra.

Delos. A small Aegean island in the Cyclades chain, with an important temple of Apollo. Athens' Delian League (s.v.) was established on Delos, its con- claves were initially held there, and its treasure kept there until ?454 BC, when, we think, it was moved to Athens. In the winter of 426/425 and 422 BC the Athenians made attempts to purify Delos of religious pollution.

Delphi. Situated inland from the north shore of the Gulf of Corinth, Delphi was the seat of the oracle of Apollo and the most respected oracular shrine in Greece. Although located within the territory of Phocis, Delphi did not be- long to Phocis, and a committee of Greek states (the Amphictyonic League) was pledged to protect her independence.

Doris. A poor, hilly region in central Greece, Doris was, according to tradition, where the Dorians (s.v.) had dwelt before their invasion of the Peloponnese. Weak Doris could thus call upon the Dorians, especially the powerful Spar- tans, for protection when they were attacked by more powerful neighbors, and this involved the Spartans in central Greece in ?457 and 426 BC.

Eion. The port of Amphipolis at the mouth of the Strymon in the Thraceward region and probably Athens' major naval station in the area, Eion was saved for Athens by the arrival of Thucydides on the day in 424 BC when Brasidas captured Amphipolis three miles upstream. The Athenians subse- quently held Eion against Brasidas, and Cleon marched from there to fight the battle of Amphipolis in 422 BC.

Euboea. The long island off the east coast of Attica and Boeotia. The cities of Euboea were never happy members of Athens' Delian League and revolted in 446 BC, a revolt suppressed by Pericles. During the Ten Years' War, the Athenians removed many of their agricultural beasts to Euboea to protect them against Peloponnesian invasions of Attica.

Hellespont. The more southerly of the two straits that form the sea passage from the Aegean into the Black Sea. The Bosporus is the more northerly.

Ionia. The middle stretch of the coast of Asia Minor, which according to tradition had been colonized by the Ionians (s.v.). Major cities of Ionia included Ephesus, Smyrna, and Miletus. The cities of Ionia became members of the Delian League after the Persian War (480–479 BC) and were tribute-paying subjects of Athens during the Ten Years' War.

Ionian Sea. The zone of the Mediterranean that lies between the west coast of Greece and Italy and Sicily. Corcyra, Leucas, Cephallenia, and Zacynthus were the major Greek islands in the Ionian Sea. The Ionian Sea shares with the Adriatic to its north harsher and less predicable weather than the Aegean. The normal way to pass over the Ionian Sea from Greece to the west, both for merchant ships and triremes, was to cross over from Corcyra so as to sail the open sea as briefly as possible from Greece to the heel of Italy. Frustratingly, the Ionian Sea is nowhere near Ionia.

Isthmus of Corinth. This neck of land connects the Peloponnese to the Greek mainland. Corinth held the narrowest point, at the western end, where ships could be hauled from the Gulf of Corinth into the Saronic Gulf. Then, going east, came difficult-to-pass Mount Geranea, and then the Megarid, the plain of Megara.

Ithome. See Messenia.

Lacedaemon. The ancient Greek name for the state we call Sparta from its capital city. Those who inhabited it were the Lacedaemonians. Lacedaemon controlled two territories, Laconia and Messenia.

Laconia. The eastern of the two territories held by the city-state of Lacedaemon (Sparta). According to tradition, the Lacedaemonians had settled in Laconia when they and the rest of the Dorians (s.v.) conquered the Peloponnese after the Trojan War. They made those they found there into their helots (s.v.).

Leontini. See Syracuse.

Lesbos. This large island in the eastern Aegean was dominated by the rival cities of Mytilene and Methymna. The cities of Lesbos were members of the Delian League and (like Samos and Chios) supplied ships rather than money to the common defense. Most of the cities of the island joined with Mytilene in her revolt from Athens in 428 BC, and when that revolt was defeated, all of the island except for the territory of loyal Methymna became an Athenian cleruchy (s.v.).

Leucas. An island off Acarnania near the mouth of the Gulf of Ambracia, Leucas was attached to the mainland by a narrow sand spit (the Isthmus of Leucas) over which triremes could be dragged. A Corinthian colony and an ally of Sparta in the Ten Years' War, Leucas played a major role in the joint Peloponnesian/Ambracian invasion of Acarnania in 429 BC. The Athenian general Asopius, son of Phormio, was killed raiding Leucas in 428 BC, and Demosthenes raided Leucas again in 426 BC, although he refused the requests of the Acarnanians to besiege the town of Leucas itself.

Locri. See Syracuse.

Macedonia/Macedon. Located north of Thessaly and west of Thrace, Macedonia was a messy, divided kingdom in the late fifth century BC, with a rather curious king, Perdiccas. For its history, see Perdiccas (s.v.).

Mantinea. See Arcadia.

Megara. A Greek city-state on the Isthmus of Corinth bordered by Corinth to the west and Boeotia and Attica to the east, Megara was a member of the Peloponnesian League. She defected to Athens in ?461 BC, then back to the Peloponnesians in 446 BC. In ?435 BC Athens laid a trade embargo, the so-called Megarian Decree, upon Megara; this caused Megara in 432 BC to urge Sparta to go to war against Athens. During the Ten Years' War, Athens invaded Megara and ravaged the land every year from 431 through 425 BC. In 424 BC Athens attempted to seize Megara but captured only her southern port, Nisaea. The plain of Megara is called the Megarid.

Megarid. See Megara.

Mende. A city halfway down the Pallene peninsula in the Thracian Chalcidice, Mende was a subject of Athens until she revolted to Brasidas in 423 BC. She was recaptured by the Athenians later in that same year.

Messana. An important city and port in Sicily, just across the strait from Italy, Messana defected to the western Ionians (who were allied to Athens) in 426 BC, then back to the Dorians, led by Syracuse, in 425 BC. Messana then served as a major base for the Dorian attempt to capture Rhegium in 425 BC.

Messenia/Messenians. Messenia was the western of the two territories held by the city-state of Lacedaemon (Sparta). Unlike Laconia, which the Spartans claimed to have held since the coming of the Dorians into the Peloponnese, Messenia the Spartans thought they had conquered in wars of the eighth and seventh centuries BC. They made the inhabitants into helots (s.v.), but unlike the helots of Laconia, the Messenian helots maintained a strong sense of their preconquest identity and so were especially feared by the Spartans. The helot revolt of ?465 BC resolved itself into a siege of the Messenian helots on Mount Ithome in Messenia, from which the Spartans let them go in ?456. The Athenians settled the refugees at Naupactus, where they proved valuable allies to Athens during the Ten Years' War. When they secured their hold on Pylos in 425 BC, the Athenians garrisoned it with Messenians from Naupactus, who raided into Messenia.

Methymna. See Lesbos.

Minoa. See Nisaea.

Mytilene. See Lesbos.

Naupactus. A strategic city on the north coast of the Gulf of Corinth, near its mouth, bordering the Ozolian Locrians and Aetolians. When the Athenians carried the surviving Messenian helots away from Messenia in ?456 BC, they settled them at Naupactus. In the winter of 430/429 BC, the Athenians sent Phormio with a squadron to Naupactus, and the Athenians seem to have maintained a naval station there for the rest of the Ten Years' War. Phormio's second great naval victory in 429 BC was decided right off the harbor of Naupactus. In 426 BC a Peloponnesian force marching from Delphi tried to capture Naupactus in cooperation with the Aetolians but was prevented by the timely arrival of Demosthenes with Acarnanian troops.

Navarino Bay. See Pylos.

Nisaea. The Saronic Gulf port of Megara, Nisaea was connected to Megara with long walls erected by the Athenians in the 450s BC (when the Athenians and Megarians were allies). During the Ten Years' War, the Athenians blockaded Nisaea closely from nearby Salamis. In 429 BC the Peloponnesians launched their abortive raid upon Piraeus from Nisaea, and in 427 BC the Athenians tightened their blockade by capturing Minoa, an island off the harbor of Nisaea. When the Athenians attempted to capture Megara in 424 BC, they ended up securing only Nisaea, which they refused to give up in the Peace of Nicias (421 BC).

Oenoe. A confusingly frequent toponym in ancient Greece, this is the name of both a town in the Argolid, where the Spartans and Argives (with Athenian help) may have fought a badly attested battle in the 450s BC, and a fort on the Attica-Boeotia border that the Peloponnesians attacked in 431 BC.

Opuntian Locris. A region of central Greece to the north of Boeotia, Opuntian Locris had yielded to Athens after Oenophyta in ?457 BC but appears to have reestablished her independence after Coronea in ?447 BC. Allied to the Peloponnesians in the Ten Years' War, Opuntian Locris was attacked by the Athenians in 431 and 426 BC. Not to be confused with Ozolian Locris.

Ozolian Locris. A region in the northwest of Greece to the west of Phocis and east and south of Aetolia, Ozolian Locris was an ally of Athens during the Ten Years' War, although when invaded by the Peloponnesians in 426 BC, most of its towns temporarily chose to support the invaders. Demosthenes departed from Ozolian Locris on his disastrous Aetolian campaign in 426 BC. Naupactus lay on the border between Ozolian Locris and Aetolia. Not to be confused with Opuntian Locris.

Pallene. See Chalcidice.

Panactum. See Thebes.

Pegae. Pericles departed from this Corinthian Gulf port of Megara on his Corinthian Gulf raiding expedition in ?454 BC. When Megara defected to the Peloponnesians in 446 BC, a large Athenian force was stranded in Pegae, but the Athenians fought the Megarians with success before making their way back to Attica via Boeotia. In (probably) 424 BC, Pegae was seized by oligarchic exiles from Megara, who used it to plunder the Megarid: this civil war played its role in inspiring the conspiracy of the Megarian democrats to betray Megara to Athens in 424 BC.

Persian empire. Inland from the Greek strip of settlement on the coast of Asia Minor lay the empire of the Great King of Persia, which extended, so far as the Greeks were concerned, so vast a distance into the east as to pass beyond the knowledge of men. In the world known to the Greeks, the Great King also ruled the eastern coast of the Mediterranean and Egypt. In 480–479 BC, the Great King Xerxes had tried to conquer Greece, but the Persians had been defeated at Salamis (480 BC), Plataea, and Mycale (479 BC). After the defeat of the invasion, the Greeks in the Aegean and on the coast of Asia Minor who had been under Persian rule rebelled, and the Delian League (s.v.) was founded under Athenian auspices to defend them against Persian reconquest and to carry on the war against Persia. In the 450s and 440s BC, Athenian fighting with the Persians petered out (although we do not see the details clearly), and the Persians were neutral in the Ten Years' War. But the wealth of the King was legendary, and both sides made attempts to secure the King's aid at the outset of the war (the Spartans did so again in 430 BC), and during the war the Athenians repeatedly raided convenient Persian possessions in Asia Minor in search of loot.

Phocis. In this region of central Greece to the northwest of Boeotia, the folk had a reputation for taking what was not theirs. Delphi was an independent enclave within Phocis. Phocis was an ally of Athens between ?457 and ?447 BC, but was an ally of Sparta during the Ten Years' War.

Piraeus. The port and military harbor of Athens, connected to Athens by the long walls (finished ?457 BC) and home to Athens' fleet of three hundred triremes. In 429 BC a Peloponnesian surprise attack on the Piraeus failed.

Plataea. A small city-state in Boeotia, just over Mount Cithaeron from Attica, Plataea had been protected against Thebes by Athens since the late sixth century BC. Thebes' failed attack on Plataea in 431 BC kicked off the Ten Years' War. Most of Plataea's population was then evacuated to Athens. In 429 BC the Peloponnesians attacked Plataea and, failing to take her, laid her under siege. Plataea fell to the Peloponnesians in 427 BC, and the surviving Plataeans were given Athenian citizenship.

Potidaea. A city at the head of the Pallene peninsula of the Thracian Chalcidice. So narrow was the peninsula at this point that the walls of Potidaea went from coast to coast, blocking off all land access to Pallene except through Potidaea's gates. In 432 BC Potidaea, encouraged by Perdiccas (s.v.) of Macedonia, revolted from Athens. Laid under siege by the Athenians, a considerable Athenian expedition in 430 BC failed to capture Potidaea, although she finally fell in the winter of 430/429 BC. Potidaea's population was allowed to depart under the terms of the surrender, and Athens sent a colony to occupy the city. In 422 BC Brasidas tried, and failed, to take Potidaea from the Athenians.

Pylos. This rocky outcropping on the west coast of the Peloponnese, over-looking Navarino Bay and the island of Sphacteria, was named for the legendary home of the Homeric hero Nestor. In 425 BC an Athenian fleet was forced to take shelter from bad weather at Pylos and improved the already strong place into a fort. The Spartans tried, and failed, to capture it, eventually being defeated in the naval battle of Navarino Bay, after which the Athenians first isolated, and then captured, a group of Spartan hoplites on Sphacteria. In the wake of those successes, Athenians established at Pylos a permanent station of Messenians from Naupactus, who raided the interior of Messenia (their ancestral homeland) and encouraged the defection of Sparta's helots. Desire to recover Pylos was a major Spartan motivation for peace in 423 and 421 BC.

Rhegium. See Syracuse.

Samos. This island in the eastern Aegean became part of Athens' Delian League after the defeat of the Persians. Samos was one of the three great island allies of Athens (along with Chios and Lesbos) that continued to supply ships to the league rather than paying tribute of money to Athens. Samos revolted from Athens in 440 BC and surrendered after a siege in 439 BC.

Saronic Gulf. The bight of the Aegean Sea to the west of Attica (whose port of Piraeus was on the gulf), to the south of Megara (whose port of Nisaea was on the gulf), and to the east of the Peloponnese. Major islands in the Saronic Gulf were Salamis, an Athenian possession, and Aegina, a traditional rival of Athens.

Scione. A city at the tip of the Pallene peninsula in the Thracian Chalcidice and a subject of Athens, Scione revolted to Brasidas in 423 BC. Besieged by the Athenians later in that year, Scione finally fell to Athens after the Peace of Nicias in 421 BC. All her men were killed and her women and children sold as slaves.

Sicyon. A Peloponnesian city-state to the west of Corinth, Sicyon was an ally of the Corinthians and Spartans during the First Peloponnesian War (?461–446/445 BC) and an ally of Sparta during the Ten Years' War. Sicyon was raided by Tolmides in ?456 BC and Pericles in ?454 BC, and Demosthenes was defeated there in 424 BC.

Sparta. The capital city of the city-state of Lacedaemon (which moderns also call Sparta). The two territories Sparta controlled were Laconia and Messenia.

Sphacteria island. See Pylos.

Syracuse. A powerful Corinthian colony near the southeastern corner of Sicily, Syracuse was an ally of Sparta from the outset of the Ten Years' War. Like the other Greeks of the west, Syracuse made no contribution to the war in metropolitan Greece. But Syracuse found herself fighting Athens in the west when Athens intervened in an existing war between a western Ionian coalition led by Italian Rhegium and Sicilian Leontini, against a western Dorian coalition led by Syracuse and Italian Locri on the toe of Italy.

Tanagra. A city in southern Boeotia and a member of Thebes' Boeotian League, Tanagra was the site of Athens' great defeat by Sparta in ?457 BC (the battle of Tanagra). Athens made an incursion into Boeotia and ravaged the territory of Tanagra in 426 BC. Delium, the object of the Athenian incursion in 424 BC that culminated at the battle of Delium, lay in the territory of Tanagra.

Tegea. See Arcadia.

Thebes. The major city of Boeotia and *hegemon* of the Boeotian League, Thebes had been under Athenian control between ?457 and ?447 BC, but was an ally of Sparta during the Ten Years' War. Thebes' attack on Plataea kicked off the war, and Thebes had designs on a number of other border territories between Attica and Boeotia, including Oenoe and Oropus, which the Peloponnesians attacked in 431 BC, and Panactum, which the Thebans captured in 422 BC. Theban reluctance to return Panactum was an obstacle to the Boeotians' joining the Peace of Nicias in 421 BC.

Thessaly. The region of Greece south of Macedonia, horse-riding Thessaly was so divided among factions and magnates that she was not much use to either side during the Ten Years' War, although she was of somewhat more use to the Athenians. Some Thessalian cavalry helped the Athenians in Attica in 431 BC (but never seem to have come again), the Thessalians harried the Spartan colony of Heraclea in Trachis after its foundation in 426 BC, and although they failed to stop Brasidas when he marched north through their territory in 424 BC, the Thessalians stopped two subsequent attempts to send him reinforcements.

Thrace. The savage realm to the north of the Aegean, extending from the river Strymon (the border with Macedonia) in the west to the Hellespont and Bosporus in the east, and then far to the north toward the river Danube. For history, see Sitalces (s.v.).

Thyrea (also called the Thyreatis or Cynuria). A miserable scrap of land lying between Laconia, the territory of Sparta, and Argos, Thyrea was important because whichever of the two neighbors held it was considered to be superior in *timē* over the other.

Torone. A city located near the southern tip of the Sithonia peninsula of the Thracian Chalcidice and a member of Athens' Delian League, Torone was captured by Brasidas in the winter of 424/423 BC. Torone was recovered for the Athenians by Cleon in 422 BC.

Zacynthus. An island in the Ionian Sea, at the mouth of the Gulf of Corinth, Zacynthus was an ally of Athens during the Ten Years' War and was raided by the Peloponnesians in 430 BC in an unsuccessful attempt to get it to defect to the Peloponnesian side. In 425 BC an Athenian fleet bound for Corcyra was recalled from Zacynthus to Pylos upon news of the arrival of the Peloponnesian fleet there.

AUTHOR'S NOTE AND ACKNOWLEDGMENTS

This book recounts the origins and course of what its ancient Greek contemporaries called the Ten Years' War (431 to 421 BC), the first long eruption of the series of conflicts known as the Peloponnesian War (431 to 404 BC). The story is told here in a fashion intended to welcome the reader with no knowledge of the ancient Greeks, to interest the knowledgeable reader, and to give the professional historian or classicist plenty to think about. Given the importance of Thucydides to contemporary students of international relations, the author hopes that they, too, will find something of interest in these pages, or at least some cause for vexation.

"Why did ancient authors approve of the strategy and foreign policy of Periclean Athens when modern scholars can find so little in them to praise?" is, put sharply, the question that *Song of Wrath* seeks to answer. More broadly, it investigates the culture of ancient Greek foreign policy and military strategy, and so follows naturally from the author's previous book, *Soldiers and Ghosts. A History of Battle in Classical Antiquity* (2005), which concerned the culture and evolution of ancient military tactics. What did ancient states seek in their foreign relations? How did they go about gaining their goals, both in peace and (especially) in war?

Song of Wrath attempts to reconcile the older methods of diplomatic and military history with the cultural history now dominant in the universities. The older techniques could explain events well enough, but mostly by assuming that ancient statesmen and generals thought much like modern ones; the new methods, on the other hand, do better justice to ancient ways of thinking, but have not been systematically applied to explain great events. In recent years the study of Greek foreign relations has been transformed by considering their cultural aspect: fictive kinship between cities, friendship (*philia*), guest-friendship (*xenia*), notions of international justice, and relationships of reciprocity, of relative rank, and of revenge between states. The purpose of this book is to apply this new thinking to a continuous and well-reported stretch of Greek history, in order to test how robust this new approach is: to explain a

411

whole sequence of events, the diplomacy leading up to, and the unfolding of, a tremendous war.

This intellectual project determines the period covered by the book. The fighting and the causes of the Peloponnesian War have tended to be studied apart, the first as a topic in military history, and the second as a topic in diplomatic history, and both in isolation from the Greek culture that gave rise to them. But this artificial separation neglects the best evidence we have for the war's causes and the way it was carried on in its first ten years, when those causes were guiding the plans of the parties. The same cultural forces, moreover, drove both.

To accomplish this melding of culture, strategy, and diplomacy, *Song of Wrath* attempts to put back into the Peloponnesian War *to muthōdes*, the romance, that the austere Thucydides intentionally denied to himself and his reader (1.22.4). It tells Thucydides' story as if it were told by Herodotus, trying to restore the sense of history, place, and myth that the Greek reader of Thucydides would have possessed (sometimes by recounting local legends that may not even have been told at the time, in the certainty that even if those stories were not told, others just as curious were). Above all, *Song of Wrath* attempts to restore to the story the ancient Greek ethical world in which the Peloponnesian War unfolded, the world that Thucydides assumed his reader shared with him, and thus felt he had no need to describe at length. The author of *Song of Wrath* dreads the hubris of facile modern comparison; his expertise lies elsewhere. But the reader will see in the vision of the culture of ancient Greek foreign affairs unfolded here parallels to the attitudes and behavior of contemporary states, and especially the states and nonstate actors that most trouble and perplex the contemporary West.

I am happy to thank the University of Virginia for the leave from teaching that allowed the writing of this book, and the Alexander von Humboldt Stiftung, the Gerda Henkel Stiftung and the Loeb Classical Library Foundation for their generous support during those periods of leave. Most of the book was written in Heidelberg, amid the incomparable resources of the *Seminar für Alte Geschichte und Epigraphik*, and I am extremely grateful for the years of kindness the *Seminar* has shown me. I am much indebted, too, to the History Faculty of the Massachusetts Institute of Technology, which have long extended summer hospitality to me. This book, finally, would have been quite impossible without the University of Virginia's indispensable LEO service, which sped literature to me wherever in the world I happened to be.

"Editors don't edit anymore. Agents edit." So I had been told. And therefore after the whole manuscript had been lovingly read by M. H. Lendon and E. A. Meyer (the latter more than once), I prevailed upon my agent Rob McQuilkin to edit it again in his free time, which he did with his characteristic literary sensitivity. The evil rumor about press editors was, moreover, soon dispelled when I arrived in L. Heimert's idyllic grotto in the grounds of Basic Books: for not only did she generously acquire the book and ceaselessly encourage its author, but the manuscript itself received much love from her, and was then exhaustively line-edited, to its great advantage, by her assistant A. Littlefield. This chain of high-quality editing was completed by J. Kelland Fagan, the copy editor.

An all-star team of ancient historians—J. Lazenby, P. Krentz, H. van Wees, and E. Wheeler—were kind enough to read the whole manuscript for content. L. J. Samons II graciously commented on the parts close to his interests. I have for years discussed the issues addressed in this book with my old friend D. A. Cohen, who works on similar themes in the Middle Ages, and another old friend, J. C. Bedell, performed the friendly office of preserving me from foolishness. So long and joyful, moreover, has been my companionship—intellectual and otherwise—with E. A. Meyer, that it has become hard to tell my ideas from hers.

Countless queries on philological matters were answered by W. D. Furley, and nearly as many about triremes by B. Rankov. I also tormented with questions J. Dillery, J. Grethlein, T. Hölscher, P. Hunt, A. Krieger, J. Ma, M. M. Miles, N. Papazarkadis, P. J. Rhodes, M. Richardson, B. Strauss, J. Strauss Clay, A. Theocharaki, A. Tilley, K. Trampedach, C. Witschel, A. J. Woodman, and L. Wylie, and all cheerfully responded. Alas, the comparative material about the role of revenge in modern warfare unearthed for me by M. Cancian did not survive the collision between the multitude of those who edited this book (see above) and my prolixity about antiquity (*passim*).

Chapters 1 and 2 draw upon material from J. E. Lendon, "Athens and Sparta and the Coming of the Peloponnesian War," pp. 358–81 in L. J. Samons II (ed.), *The Cambridge Companion to the Age of Pericles*, 2007 © Cambridge University Press, reproduced with permission.

For permission to cite writings in advance of publication, I thank D. Lindsay, P. Lipke, R. Oldfield, B. Paarmán, A. Papalas, D. Pritchard, B. Rankov, and A. Taylor.

For checking the references I thank M. Powers and for the index K. Bowman.

As for the illustrations, it gives me particular pleasure once again to be able to thank S. Kim for her drawings. K. J. Hatzigeorgiou pointed me to the map of Greece I have often adapted in these pages. Elke Fuchs tenderly scanned and cleaned up images from rare books graciously made available to me by Heidelberg's *Institut für Klassische Archäologie*, for access to which I thank especially J.-A. Dickmann. And I am also grateful for having been invited to work on the maps in the scholarly peace of Heidelberg's friendly *Institut für Papyrologie*. Only once I had chosen the images for the book did I discover how intricate it is to trace up-do-date information on vases depicted in 19th-century volumes: here R. Gondek and T. J. Smith rescued me, the latter calling upon the formidable assistance of T. Mannack and F. Lissarrague.

Translations are mine except when indicated otherwise, but they cannot fail in many cases to echo the work of previous translators. To those I may have slighted I offer my grateful acknowledgments here.

J. E. Lendon
Charlottesville, 1 June 2010

SUGGESTIONS FOR
FURTHER READING

Thucydides, one of the greatest of all Great Books, can best be approached by English speakers in the splendid *Landmark Thucydides* edition of Robert B. Strassler (1996). This lightly modernizes the Richard Crawley translation (one of the finest translations of a classic into English) and adds marginal summaries, helpful notes, and especially the maps necessary to make the contemporary reader as comfortable with Thucydides' geography as an ancient Greek reader was.

Modern considerations of Thucydides are very many (see my appendix for discussion of some of them). One of the few that gives pleasure to read is Francis Cornford's *Thucydides Mythistoricus* (1907), which is also the foundational document for modern interpretation of the author. Perhaps the best general academic treatment is Simon Hornblower's *Thucydides* (1987). Less academic is Donald Kagan's *Thucydides: The Reinvention of History* (2009), which is accessible and full of good sense.

For modern histories of the whole Peloponnesian War in English, the most enjoyable is the furiously opinionated B. W. Henderson, *The Great War Between Athens and Sparta* (1927). More sober, but far safer, is Donald Kagan's four-volume opus, *The Outbreak of the Peloponnesian War* (1969), *The Archidamian War* (1974), *The Peace of Nicias and the Sicilian Expedition* (1981), and *The Fall of the Athenian Empire* (1987), or the one-volume abridgement of the whole, *The Peloponnesian War* (2003). Lawrence Tritle's concise *A New History of the Peloponnesian War* (2010) emphasizes the psychological impact of the war on its participants. For those who want only what follows the story told here, Mark Munn, *The School of History: Athens in the Age of Socrates* (2000), can serve as a sequel to the present book, since it takes up the story of the Peloponnesian War from 415 BC.

For military treatments of the war, the reader can choose between John Lazenby's chronological, academic-in-tone *The Peloponnesian War. A Military Study* (2004) or Victor Davis Hanson's vivid, thematic *A War Like No Other* (2006), which strives in particular to imagine the war as it was experienced by those fighting it. Sir Nigel Bagnall's *The Peloponnesian War* (2006) offers the perspective of a distinguished contemporary soldier but is full of careless errors.

For a concise introduction to classical Athens, see Mark Munn, *The School of History*, pp. 15–91; for the rise and decline of Athens' navy, John R. Hale, *Lords of the Sea* (2009) is delightful. For the institutions of the democracy, see D. Stockton, *The Classical Athenian Democracy* (1990). As a counter to the naïve awe of Athenian democracy usual among its modern students, L. J. Samons' neo-oligarchic *What's Wrong with Democracy?* (2004) is astringent and cleansing. For an introduction to ancient Sparta, on the other hand, see Paul Cartledge, *The Spartans* (2003).

On Greek warfare, V. D. Hanson's *The Wars of the Ancient Greeks* (1999) is a succinct, beautifully illustrated account. To get deeper into current thinking, look into Hans van Wees, *Greek Warfare: Myths and Realities* (2004), a book I rely on particularly, or the Greek chapters of the present author's *Soldiers and Ghosts: A History of Battle in Classical Antiquity* (2005), Louis Rawlings, *The Ancient Greeks at War* (2007), or the first volume of the *Cambridge History of Greek and Roman Warfare* (2007).

On relations between states in ancient Greece, consult Polly Low, *Interstate Relations in Classical Greece* (2007) or Peter Hunt's *War, Peace, and Alliance in Demosthenes' Athens* (2010).

APPENDIX

The Sources

THUCYDIDES

I would claim that the picture I have drawn is thoroughly based upon the evidence of our most reliable sources, Thucydides above all, and that anyone who dislikes that picture had better begin by trying to discredit Thucydides, if he can.

STE. CROIX 1972 P. 290

The veracity of Thucydides is not today the impervious bastion that it seemed to Geoffrey de Ste. Croix in 1972. Long was Thucydides regarded as nearly infallible; long did moderns offer him kneeling tribute with titles like *Thucydides and the Science of History* and *Clio Enthroned*. But terrible was the reaction when it came: for a time Thucydides was thought relentlessly mendacious, a bitter and lying polemicist. Yet just as some were enjoying having their illusions shattered, others were taking up the challenge laid down as long ago as 1907 by Francis Cornford's *Thucydides Mythistoricus*: to study Thucydides as an intellectual and a literary author. Now the great majority of students treat him so and thus are formally uninterested in the relationship of his account to real events (so a discussion of "the veracity of Thucydides" now seems rather quaint). But ironically, the unintended trajectory of this most recent thinking has been to restore much of our faith in the veracity of Thucydides' account. For the students of Thucydides as a literary author and an intellectual have found solutions to many of the puzzles in the work that made their angry predecessors suspect him as a devising liar. We are unlikely ever to get back to the Thucydides of *Clio Enthroned*, but the Thucydides of today's classical scholarship is certainly a Thucydides that today's historian, with a little care and knowledge, can use.

The best recent discussion of Thucydides' veracity (with which I would generally align myself) is Cawkwell (1997) pp. 1–19. The state of Thucydidean studies today can be tracked through the innumerable papers in Rengakos and Tsamakis (2006). The most recent catalogue raisonné of writings on Thucydides—and a fair and wise guide to the author—is Marincola (2001) pp. 61–104.

Scholarly Approaches to Thucydides

Current Thucydidean scholarship can be divided into four tendencies, although a number of them can jostle in the work of an individual scholar. These tendencies also represent the successive archeological strata of work on Thucydides over the last fifty years, for in classics, nothing ever dies.

First, there is a small, aging band of Thucydidean fundamentalists who still defend the near infallibility of the historian's narrative, his chronological rigor, and even the historical veracity of the speeches he writes for his characters. This was the prevailing view throughout much of the twentieth century, and Gomme's *Historical Commentary on Thucydides* is its memorial. The great polemicist of this school was the late W. K. Pritchett (see, e.g., Pritchett 1995b), but it also has more or less living adherents, e.g., A. B. Bosworth (2000) and C. M. J. Sicking (1995). There is a strong sense of fighting a losing battle here: Pritchett described his interventions "as like punching a feather pillow—an indentation is made, but soon refills, and the whole soft, spongy mass continues as before" (1992 p. 57).

Second, as a reaction to the long and deadening faith in Thucydides, there is a position of extreme skepticism—the classic work is V. Hunter, *Thucydides the Artful Reporter* (1973). More recently, we might take as representative E. Badian, *From Plataea to Potidaea* (1993). Badian maintains that Thucydides is a ruthless polemicist who will stop at nothing to make his case. Such extreme views have attracted able rebuttal, e.g., Rhodes (1994), and now seem very dated, a sort of adolescent tantrum.

The third group, strong now, studies Thucydides as a teacher. He has lessons to teach, especially about political science, and he structures his narrative to teach those lessons. H.-P. Stahl's *Thukydides: Die Stellung des Menschens im geschichtlichen Prozess* (1966; translated as Stahl 2003) is fundamental, and a great influence on the present author is Greg Crane's *Thucydides and the Ancient Simplicity* (1998). This Thucydides is not trying to falsify (indeed, doing so would make his teaching less effective), but he does not hesitate to array his narrative—emphasize some things, deemphasize others, leave things out, tell partial stories—to bring out points that he thinks important for his teaching. He feels no inclination to describe fully a second time an instance of a phenomenon he has described once, so similar events get short treatment. This approach, to my mind, is especially useful for understanding Thucydides' account of the origins of the war.

Finally, there are those who regard Thucydides as a storyteller—perhaps the leading school at the moment. We might take T. Rood, *Thucydides: Narrative and Explanation* (1998), as emblematic of this strain, and Simon Hornblower's three-volume *Commentary on Thucydides* (1991–2008) as its monument. These students are aware that writing narrative is not inherently easy or obvious and, moreover, that Thucydides was writing for an audience with certain expectations. The inherent problems of composing narrative and Thucydides' literary objectives often draw him away from presenting his material as we would (or as we think we would) and sometimes make him suppress things we want to hear, but he does not systematically falsify. This kind of interpretation is, I think, particularly helpful for understanding Thucydides' account of the course of the war (Book II onwards).

Thucydides' Narrative

Thucydides was writing in the first instance for a contemporary audience, an audience of men like him who had lived through the war he described and their sons. It is this fact, and not the professions that Thucydides makes about his own method (1.21–22), that convinces us of the overall veracity of Thucydides' account. Hundreds, if not thousands, of people witnessed most of the events he describes. And the potential jeers of that multitude are our guards against the likelihood that Thucydides was systematically fabulating or too frequently in error.

Of course, Thucydides was here and there in error in his facts (Cawkwell 1997 p. 8 n. 23 makes a list of such errors), being at the mercy of human informants and human himself. Yet it is reassuring that when we can compare a document he quotes (5.47 with Hornblower *ad loc.*) with a copy preserved on stone (Tod[2] 72 = *IG*[3] 47), they are extremely close. It is also reassuring that we can detect consistent patterns in his evidence—the detail he commands about the names of minor Corinthians but not Spartans, for example (Stroud 1994)—which suggests that the particulars of his narrative, when he gives them, come from documents or informants and are not invented (for then he would know as many, or as few, Spartan names as Corinthian).

Thucydides' sense of his public occasionally imperiled his dispassion. For like many an author, Thucydides wrote particularly for like-minded men, and for him those whom he calls "sensible men" (4.28.5) were of an oligarchic persuasion—thus suspicious of the Athenian democracy—and fellow haters of the Athenian politician Cleon. It is in his depiction of the acts of Cleon that the reader feels the greatest suspicion of Thucydides' narrative (Woodhead 1960 is still the best study): if his sense of audience generally kept Thucydides to the truth, pleasing the audience with which he most identified might sometimes tug him away from it.

Still, most of the apparent problems with Thucydides' narrative are the result of our own unsophisticated reading of him, not of his lying. And the more sensitive habits of reading offered by the Thucydides-as-storyteller school go a long way to exonerate him from general suspicion. Those who think that

Thucydides was a dishonest polemicist attach great significance to his provision of information outside its proper chronological place. In an article of superb ingenuity—we are letting one stand for many—T. E. Wick (1979) argued that bringing about the defection of Megara was a consistent aim of the Athenians in the early years of the war. Thucydides, however, not wanting his reader to think that Athenian attention to Megara called into question Thucydides' account of the origins of the war, systematically deemphasized what Athens did against Megara, giving the details out of place and without the emphasis they merited. Yet understanding the necessities of narrative explains Thucydides' treatment of his Megara material better. For Thucydides, like any storyteller, knows that the making of narrative requires that events often be recounted in the context of greater events that make sense of them, and also that a historian cannot break the logic of his story to put everything in its chronological place. For when, out of carelessness or unwise chronological scrupulosity Thucydides does exactly that (as at 3.99, where a single sentence about the Athenians in Sicily is shoehorned, in the interests of agonizing chronological accuracy, into an account of events in the northwest of Greece), he both renders the detail he inserts out of its narrative context incomprehensible and muddles in the reader's mind the story into which he inserts the out-of-context detail.

Thucydides structures his story for effect. He repeats his structures. Sometimes things we think important get left out, and sometimes—rarely, unlike Herodotus—trivial or merely appealing things get in. He misplaces events so that their significance is obscured, often holding them back until the last minute to build excitement, and he juxtaposes for ironical effect what a perfectly chronological writer (if such existed) would not (on all of this, Marincola 2001 pp. 70–1, gathering discussions). He acts, in short, like any historian must who has a sense of his audience. The peculiarities of his account (like his treatment of the Megarians) are not signs of systematic mendacity or carelessness but of the challenges of writing narrative.

The Speeches in Thucydides

Thucydides shared with nearly all the historians of antiquity the habit of writing speeches for his characters. In describing his method, Thucydides says that in composing such speeches he "[made] the speakers say what was in my opinion demanded of them by the various occasions, of course adhering as closely as possible to the general sense of what they really said" (1.22.1; for what on earth Thucydides meant by this, Marincola 2001 pp. 78–9 gathers the dispiriting literature). Contemporary scholarship endorses the first part of that statement—"what was in my opinion demanded of them"—nearly to the exclusion of the second—"adhering as closely as possible to the general sense of what they really said" (for the reasons to consider the speeches inauthentic, Hornblower 1987 pp. 55–65, who, however, is more optimistic about the historical value of the speeches than most, esp. p. 65). In fact, the conclusion that the speeches are mostly the work of Thucydides himself is inevitable: for the reader notices that the speeches are in conversation with one another, even when their supposed speakers were miles and months apart.

Thus Thucydides makes Pericles, speaking at Athens (1.140–4), answer point for point a previous speech of the Corinthians, speaking at Sparta (1.120–4; Rengakos 1996 gives a catalogue of the numerous links between speeches). There are also suspicious anachronisms in the speeches, as when the Corinthians in 432 BC threaten, and Pericles in 432 BC discounts, the possibility of the Peloponnesians building a fort in Attica (1.122.1; 1.142.3, with Ste. Croix 1972 p. 209), a strategy not employed until 413 BC. And some of the matter in the speeches seems quite inappropriate to their givers and hearers. It is hard to imagine a Spartan king delivering to a Spartan audience, as Archidamus is made to do, a rather arid theoretical discussion of ethics (1.84.3; Crane 1998 p. 208). At 4.17.2 Thucydides even has Spartan speakers apologize for giving a long, very unlaconic speech.

For these and similar reasons, there can be little question that nearly all passages of speech in Thucydides were of the author's free composition and that the "general sense of what they really said" is no more than the objective of a speech ("Pericles argued against giving in to the Spartans"). Perhaps Thucydides sometimes added some of the real remembered sentiments of a personage as a form of rich seasoning: this I suspect he does particularly in Pericles' Funeral Oration (2.35–46). But which bits are real and which invented we can never tell (Pelling 2000 p. 117). Was Thucydides' description of his method in writing speeches true when he wrote it, and did his practice later diverge (so Andrewes 1962 p. 67)? But the conclusion is nearly unavoidable that Thucydides' description of his method of composing speeches does not accord with his actual practice.

Because of the impossibility of separating the historical wheat from the chaff, today's historian must take an even more skeptical view of the authenticity of the speeches in Thucydides than the despairing indecision of much of current scholarship (Pelling 2000 pp. 116–20; Marincola 2001 pp. 79–80). But that hardly means that the speeches are of no historical use. They cannot be read as transcripts of what historical figures said at the time: they must instead be read as Thucydides' retrospective commentaries on what was happening at the time. Sometimes speeches are used to explain why Thucydides thought decisions were made, although none of the speakers can confidently be deemed to speak in Thucydides' own voice; sometimes to lay out possible strategies for the parties; sometimes to characterize major figures or states; sometimes to tug at the heartstrings; sometimes, perhaps, to do no more than offer the reader some stylistic variation to enliven a long passage of narrative.

But Thucydides' speeches, for the most part, are loyal to their context, to the historical frame in which they lie. So, if the tone of Pericles' Funeral Oration is confident, we are entitled to deduce that the feeling of Athens at the time allowed for a confident speech. And if a character urges an action in a speech, we are entitled to conclude that a contemporary might have urged such an action at the time, even if that particular individual did not. And if a character is made to think in a certain way in a speech (e.g., if the Corcyreans argue brass tacks and the Corinthians ethics), we are entitled to try to use those modes of thinking to explain the behavior of people at the time, even if we cannot be confident that those were the arguments made by those men on that occasion.

Every so often Thucydides has a character convey in a speech an apparent hard nugget of fact: the Corinthians, for example, claim that their vote prevented the Spartans from going to the assistance of Samos in *ca.* 440 BC (1.40.5, 1.41.2). These it is safe to regard with the same cautious confidence as facts in Thucydides' narrative, and for the same reason: Thucydides was writing for a contemporary audience, and unless there is some reason to suppose that he wished to undercut the speaker's argument by having him tell an obvious lie—and speakers in Thucydides are made to tell lies for this reason—Thucydides would detract from the point of his speech if he introduced a detectable untruth.

What Lies Between Speeches and Narrative: Thucydides' Opinions and His Descriptions of His Own Method

The problem Thucydides poses to today's historian is not so much whether to believe his bare narrative (usually safe) or the literal accuracy of the speeches he gives his characters (unsafe). It is what lies between: in places where Thucydides is present in the text, offering opinions and interpretations of events, but not in the form of a speech. Thucydides, unlike Herodotus, does not usually distinguish his opinions from his narrative of events and saw no need, as a historian today would, to mark one from the other with the ubiquitous modern "perhaps": events and opinions come forth in the same tone.

Because Thucydides does not distinguish events from interpretation, there is a real danger that a modern student may mistake one for the other. A famous instance is the thoughts Thucydides attributes to Cleon and Brasidas before the battle of Amphipolis in 422 BC (5.6–10)—the reader only realizes that these must be Thucydides' supposition when he discovers that both men died in the battle; there was, therefore, no way for Thucydides to find out what they had been thinking (Woodhead 1960 p. 308). The reader must always be alert for moments like these and always ask himself, How could Thucydides know this? And if it seems unlikely that Thucydides could, we are probably in the world of Thucydides' unadvertised opinion. The private thoughts and motives Thucydides attributes to characters should always, therefore, be treated with great caution and tested, as far as possible, against his plain narrative of events. For no more than anyone else could Thucydides know the hidden motives of men or the relationship of the plans they expressed in public to the plans they caressed in their hearts. So, too, his depictions of the reasons for the actions of states: when the Athenian assembly made a decision, many speeches will have been given on both sides and a vote taken. Who knows which arguments, if any, prevailed with the people?

The tendency in the past among modern historians of the fifth century BC has been to give far too much credit to Thucydides' opinions: to resolve his failure to distinguish between event and opinion as we would by assimilating the value of Thucydides' opinions to that of his narrative of events—hence the whole scholarly industry of attempting to squeeze the history of the pre-war years into Thucydides' opinion that the war was produced by Spartan fear of Athenian power, and that of attempting to compress the variety of Athens' martial activities in the first years of the war into the strictly defensive strategy Thucydides attributes to Pericles. But it is far easier simply to admit that here, as elsewhere, Thucydides' opinions were sometimes wrong. It is far better to regard Thucydides' opinions with respect, as those of a highly intelligent contemporary, but not with idolatry. We are free to disagree, and I have done so in this book; indeed, this book could not be written otherwise, since it relies upon Thucydides' account of events but often removes them from the matrix of his opinions.

Into this doubtful netherworld of Thucydidean opinion we must also, ironically, cast Thucydides' descriptions of his own methods. Just as modern historians have overvalued Thucydides' opinions by failing to distinguish them from the events he describes, so, too, they have sometimes tried to defend, for example, his speeches on the same grounds, by understanding his statement of method (1.22–3) as possessed of the same value as "the Athenians also fortified Atalanta, and placed a garrison there, when the summer was coming to an end" (2.32.1). "We may not ignore Thucydides' promise to stay as close as possible to the general purport of what the speaker really said (1.22.1). Whoever can believe that the Funeral Oration of Pericles is a free composition of Thucydides is free to believe that there was no public funeral in Athens in 431 BC or that the Spartans never invaded Attica during the war" (Kagan 1974 p. 65 n. 73). But it is not given to any man to look clearly into his own soul. Compare the purpose of any modern book with what the book actually achieves. There is a gap. But most authors, and talented authors in particular, think that they have achieved exactly what they set out to do. So the apparent contradictions between what Thucydides says he will do and what he does should not perplex. Thucydides was a man.

Thucydides and This Book

In 1911 George Grundy grumped about Thucydides' account of the Archidamian War:

It must be confessed that, taken as read, the story of the war leaves the reader with the impression that it was composed of a series of disconnected incidents and petty operations, and ended in a somewhat futile way. The historian never mentions explicitly any ground plan or plans upon which it was conducted except in the case of the strategy of Pericles, which only in part survived the statesman himself. It is true that in various speeches said to have been made before the war began certain intended designs are mentioned; but nothing is said about their application to the course of events, and some of them are obviously inapplicable to this Ten Years' War (p. 315; cf. Wade-Gery 1949 p. 903).

Grundy's answer—which is true as far as it goes—was that Thucydides was a philosophical historian, and such details did not interest him (p. 317). But I think they did not interest Thucydides chiefly because he took for granted that his Greek reader could supply for himself the logic of how events fit together. We must read Thucydides as if we were Greek and supply the assumptions of a Herodotus, an Aeschylus, a Xenophon, or a Demosthenes. "The operations around Peloponnese seem a series of disjointed raids, without plan or design," Grundy moans (p. 317). But Thucydides expected his reader to know what he just mentions in passing (1.142.4, 2.43.1), that the raids were intended for reprisal, and he expected his reader to take for granted the whole mechanics of how reprisal worked in war. Without contradicting Thucydides' narrative or the scant analysis he does supply, I have tried in this book to supply the logic that Thucydides felt he did not need to.

We can also expand on Grundy and propose a deeper reason for Thucydides' unhelpful quiet, for his reluctance to provide the muscles that move the bones of the events of his narrative. Thucydides was a political philosopher and shared many of the instincts of what we would now call a realist. This disposed him to look beyond relations of reciprocity (both revenge and reciprocating favors) to the more profound engines of power relations he perceived beneath (see esp. Crane 1998; Low 2007 pp. 222–33). This is especially evident in his account of the origins of the war (see below), but this disposition is likely also to exert a continuing influence over his account of the war itself. Thucydides tells his reader what Thucydides is interested in, and reciprocity was not one of his major themes (as it was, notoriously, a theme of Herodotus).

The account of the Ten Years' War given in this book seeks to supplement Thucydides' silences with Greek motivations that Thucydides took for granted or had no interest in relating. But the relationship of the account given in this book to Thucydides' description of the origins of the war is frankly adversarial. Here I argue against the explicit opinion of Thucydides that "the truest cause of the war was the growing greatness of the Athenians, and the fear that this inspired, which compelled the Lacedaemonians to go to war" (1.23.6). And in doing so I make common cause with the "Thucydides as teacher" strain of

Thucydides interpretation. For it seems to me—as it has to many others—that Thucydides was himself arguing, in a rather professorial way, for his interpretation of the war in a world that thought otherwise (e.g., Kagan 2009 pp. 35–74). His interpretation therefore dominates the speeches and (naturally) his expressions of opinion. It also affects which events he includes: Thucydides' "Archeology," his account of Greece's earliest days (1.2–21), is intended (at least in part) to convey his definition of "power" as the possession of ships and money (see Kallet-Marx 1993 pp. 21–36; Marincola 2001 p. 70 n. 47). And it affects the organization of the first book: his account of the period 479–435 BC (1.89–117) comes after his account of 435–432 BC and the conference at Sparta that decided upon war, in order to buttress Thucydides' contention that the Spartans decided for war not because they were convinced by their allies but because they were afraid of the power of Athens (1.88).

Yet other puzzles of Book I—the neglect of the Megarian Decree in its chronological place (1.67.4, 1.139.1–2), so howled about by scholars looking to convict Thucydides, the failure to explain the nature of the grievances of Aegina (1.67.2, 1.139.1), and the strange placement of the (long and sometimes rather fanciful) story of Themistocles and Pausanias (1.128–38) in the middle of the final exchange of ultimatums between Athens and Sparta (see Marincola 2001 p. 71)—are, I think, more naturally explained by storytelling motives and necessities than polemic. Thucydides could hardly, after all, hide the Megarian Decree from an audience consisting of many who had voted for it.

DIODORUS OF SICILY

Three centuries after Thucydides lived the encyclopedic Greek historian Diodorus of Sicily. There can be no doubt that he compiled his account of the period 479–421 BC with that of Thucydides before him; yet he also had access to other material lost to us, especially the historical works of the fourth-century BC historian Ephorus. I concur with Green *Diodorus* (pp. ix–xii, 29–31, 34–47) that Diodorus' testimony must be treated with respect, especially when (as often between 478 and 432 BC) he has material Thucydides does not. But not being a radical skeptic about the veracity of Thucydides, even though I admit with Green that there could in principle be points when the version of Diodorus is to be preferred to that of Thucydides and that one must weigh each case, I simply do not find myself preferring Diodorus very frequently, unlike Diodorus' great contemporary advocate, the ingenious J. H. Schreiner (e.g., 1997).

But the main use to which Diodorus is put in the present book is not as a source of additional information or as a stick with which to beat Thucydides. I value Diodorus primarily as an ancient Greek reader of Thucydides, who, in the process of putting Thucydides' account into his own words, interpreted him as an ancient Greek would: Diodorus did, naturally and unself-consciously, what this book does laboriously by applying to Thucydides today's scholarship about the culture of Greek foreign relations. Although far separated in time from classical Greece, Diodorus is, moreover, arguably closer in outlook than the quirky Thucydides himself to the mainstream of classical Greek thinking about foreign relations, represented especially by Herodotus, Xenophon, and Demosthenes (see Lendon 2006). So when Diodorus, as he so frequently does, interprets the events of fifth-century BC Greece in terms of the rank of states, he may offer a glimpse of how a fifth-century Greek other than Thucydides might have interpreted what he saw happening in the world around him.

ATHENIAN INSCRIPTIONS

It was the pleasant custom of the Athenian democracy to command that some of its official documents be carved upon blocks of stone. Many of these inscriptions survive, although often in a sadly beat-up state, and these inscriptions give information about Athens and her empire that we do not have from books copied and recopied over the centuries in manuscript, especially (in our period) Thucydides.

My habit in this book has been to note such documents in passing but rarely to make very much of them. This is a reversal of the normal practice of historians of fifth-century BC Greece for more than a century, but it arises from the growing realization of scholars that most Athenian inscriptions from our period cannot be compellingly dated.

Athenians usually dated by the name of the archon at Athens who gave his name to the year (the Eponymous Archon). His year of office ran from July to July, which is why archon dates are given in the form "434/3," meaning July 434 to July 433 BC. But Athenians did not begin consistently to preface their decrees with archon dates until after 421 BC. Sometimes an archon date appears in the body of the inscription, sometimes there is another official whose year in office we know because he appears in another document with an archon date in it, and sometimes a document is dated by the name of the year's first secretary of the Council of Five Hundred, whose year we may know. But time's hammer seems to have fallen with particular harshness upon those innocent men, with the result that the great majority of surviving inscriptions from our period cannot be dated with any certainty from strong internal evidence.

It used to be thought possible to divide the set of undated inscriptions at least into "early" and "late" by the presence or absence of the letter sigma carved in a certain way (the "three-bar sigma"), which was deemed to mark inscriptions earlier than 445 BC. On the basis of this criterion, plausible historical contexts were found for many of the undated inscriptions from the 460s through the 440s BC (Meiggs 1972 was the monument of this scholarship). But

Harold Mattingly (his articles are collected in Mattingly 1996) cried out for decades that better contexts could be found for many of them in the 420s and 410s (as, indeed, nineteenth-century scholars had often proposed). And then in 1990, Mortimer Chambers and his colleagues proved that an inscription bearing a three-bar sigma dated to 418/17 BC (Chambers *et al.* 1990). Mattingly was right! So now many of those documents that were dated by context before 445 may (but need not) date later. Rhodes (2008) and Papazarkadas (2009) give histories of the controversy and a sense of the compromises that may eventually result: Rhodes accepts the down-dating of many documents to the 420s and 410s but thinks that others still find a better context earlier, while Papazarkadas is inclined to move all the Athenian imperial documents down into the period after 435 BC. Kallet (2009) pp. 49–54 traces the scholarly consequences of the old and new datings.

I am pessimistic about both sets of dates, old and new, early and late, and indeed about the practicality of dating most internally undated inscriptions from historical context. The practice of both the old, "early" daters and now today's "late" daters is necessarily to associate an inscription with some great event of which we know from literary sources; so, for example, the Athenian regulations for Chalcis (chapter 2 n. 46) used to be dated to *ca.* 446 BC because Athens put down a rebellion in Euboea then; but Mattingly suggested 424/3 BC because a fragment of Philochorus mentions Athenian intervention on Euboea in that year. Disappointingly, however, few inscriptions bear a clear relationship to events we know about; few have an unequivocal hook to great events.

Take the best case: Athenian casualty lists. These often indicate where Athenian soldiers died, and since military campaigns are the kind of great events about which we learn in literary sources, casualty lists should be among the easiest of inscriptions to date from context. And, indeed, scholarly consensus has settled upon dates for two such fifth-century BC inscriptions, relating them to events we know about: (a) *IG* I³ 1144 listing losses at Thasos, Eion, and Byzantium (the date of Thuc. 1.100.2–3 = ?464 BC) and (b) Tod² 26 = ML 33 = *IG* I³ 1147 = Fornara 78, listing losses at Cyprus, Egypt, Phoenicia, Halieis, Aegina, and Megara (the date of Thuc. 1.105 = ?458 BC).

But three other lists that name locations where Athenians died in war we nevertheless cannot seem to date: those (c) listing losses in the Chersonese, Byzantium, and "other wars" (Tod² 48 = ML 48 = *IG* I³ 1162); (d) listing losses from Potidaea, Amphipolis, Thrace, Pylos, Sermylia, and Singos (*IG* I³ 1184; see Bradeen 1969 pp. 155–6 for inconclusive arguments about its date); and (e) the newly found "Athenian Metro casualty list" (Parlama 2000) listing losses at "Tanagra and Spartolus" (for discussion, Papazarkadas 2009 pp. 69–70; Matthaiou 2009 pp. 203–4). Item d is especially dispiriting, with no fewer than six locations listed and presumably coming from the Peloponnesian War itself, a period (unlike 479–432 BC) about which we have a great number of details from Thucydides. Still, scholars cannot agree on a year for it: our literary evidence is simply not fine-grained enough. And when we move from casualty lists to documents of other types, to treaties and imperial regulations and domestic decrees, the process of assigning them to an historical context becomes no easier than dating an undated scrap of the *New York Times* from the twentieth century two millennia from now with the help of a one-volume *Time-Life Book of the 20th Century*.

1. In the period of interest to us (479–421 BC), the following major documents have firm dates from internal evidence:

A series of fragmentary lists of payments of one-sixtieth of Athens' imperial tribute to Athena, the so-called Athenian tribute lists: *IG* I³ 259–84 = *ATL* with essential corrections by Paarmann (2007). These run from 454/3 to 439/8 (438/7–436/5 preserve practically no entries) and 435/4 to 427/6 or 426/5 BC.

Tribute reassessment (Tod² 66 = ML 69 = *IG* I³ 71 = Fornara 136; Chapter 4 n. 68): 425/4 BC.

Loans to the city from the sacred treasuries of Athens (the "*Logistai* inscription") (Tod² 64 = ML 72 = *IG* I³ 369 = Fornara 134; above chapter 4 n. 68): 426/5 to 423/2 BC.

Parthenon building accounts (Tod² 52 = ML 59 = *IG* I³ 436–51 = Fornara 120): 447/6–443/2 BC.

Propylea building accounts (Tod² 53 = ML 60 = *IG* I³ 462–6 = Fornara 118): 437/6–433/2 BC.

Athens' alliance with Rhegium (Tod² 58 = ML 63 = *IG* I³ 53 = Fornara 124; but it is unclear whether it was struck or renewed in this year; see Cataldi 1987; chapter 2 n. 76): 433/2 BC.

Athens' alliance with Leontini (Tod² 57 = ML 64 = *IG* I³ 54 = Fornara 125; but it is unclear whether it was struck or renewed in this year; see Cataldi 1987; chapter 2 n. 76): 433/2 BC.

Athenian relations with Methone, decree ii (Tod² 61 = ML 65 = *IG* I³ 61 = Fornara 128): 426/5 BC.

Honors for Potamodorus of Orchomenus (*IG* I³ 73; chapter 8 n. 26): 424/3 BC.

Proxeny decree for Callipus of Thessaly (*IG* I³ 92; see *SEG* L 45 for date; chapter 9 n. 85): 422/1 BC.

2. To the above list, we can add some items whose contents allow a fairly confident date from context (dates prefixed with a question mark indicate that we can associate the inscription with an event in Thucydides, but the absolute date of that event remains in some doubt).

Casualty list from fighting at Thasos, Eion, and Byzantium (*IG* I³ 1144), year of Thucydides 1.100.2–3: ?464 BC.

Casualty list of the Athenian Erechtheid tribe in Cyprus, Egypt, Phoenicia, Halieis, Aegina, Megara (Tod² 26 = ML 33 = *IG* I³ 1147 = Fornara 78), year of Thucydides 1.105: ?458 BC.

Athenian allies killed at Tanagra (Tod² 28 = ML 35 = *IG* I³ 1149): ?457 BC.

Monument for Pythion, who helped the Athenians escape from Megarian Pegae (Tod² 41 = ML 51 = *IG* I³ 1353 = Fornara 101; above p.
79): describes events in 446 BC, although the date of the inscription itself is unknown.

Expenses of the war against Samos (Tod² 50 = ML 55 = *IG* I³ 363 =
Fornara 113): 441–440 or 440–439 BC.

Treaty with Samos ending the Samian revolt (ML 56 = *IG* I³ 48 =
Fornara 115): 439/8 BC.

Expenses of the squadrons sent to Corcyra (Tod² 55 = ML 61 = *IG* I³
364 = Fornara 126): 433 BC.

Memorial for the Athenian dead at Potidaea (Tod² 59 = *IG* I³ 1179):
432 BC.

Resettlement of Potidaea (Tod² 60 = ML 66 = *IG* I³ 514 = Fornara 129):
429 BC.

3. The following are inscriptions of the first importance to which no compelling date can be assigned:

The later tribute lists, traditionally assigned to 421/0–415/4 BC (*IG* I³ 34,
285–90); for the uncertain dates, see Kallet 2004.

Athenian financial arrangements (the "Callias Decrees") (Tod² 51 = ML
58 = *IG* I³ 52 = Fornara 119; discussed chapter 2 n. 76).

Decree about appointment of tribute collectors (the "Cleonymus Decree") (ML 68 = *IG* I³ 68 = Fornara 133). For the uncertain date, Samons 2000 pp. 188–9. This inscription has come to be considered a
fixed point giving a context for dating other general imperial regulations to the period of Cleon (e.g., the Cleinias Decree, the "coinage"
or "standards" decree, see Papazarkadas 2009 pp. 72–3), but it cannot be certainly dated itself.

Decree requiring Athens' subjects to use her coinage, weights, and measures (the "coinage" or "standards" decree) (Tod² 67 = ML 45 = *IG* I³
1453 = Fornara 97). For the current state of this mystery, Papazarkadas 2009 p. 72.

Regulation of Tribute Collection (the "Cleinias Decree") (ML 46 = *IG* I³
34 = Fornara 98).

Athenian regulations for Chalcis (Tod² 42 = ML 52 = *IG* I³ 40 = Fornara
103); for the uncertain date, Papazarkadas 2009 pp. 73–4. And this
carries with it into uncertainty Athenian regulations for the other
Euboean cities of Eretria (*IG* I³ 39 = Fornara 102) and Hestiaea (*IG* I³
41).

Athenian treaty with Halieis (*IG* I³ 75); before 418 BC but otherwise un-datable; for the uncertain date, Thompson (1971); and this carries with it into uncertainty the decree on the salary of the priestess of Athena Nike (Tod² 73 = ML 71 = *IG* I³ 36 = Fornara 139), so impor-tant to archeologists for dating the temple of Athena Nike, and the honors to Heracleides of Clazomenae (ML 70 = *IG* I³ 227). Also, if Halieis cannot be dated, no useful date for the treaty with Hermione (*IG* I³ 31; cf. *IG* I³ 67) results from the stylistic parallel asserted by Mattingly 2000.

Athenian treaty between Athens and Perdiccas (*IG* I³ 89).

Athenian treaty with Hermione (*IG* I³ 31), perhaps between 429 and 425 BC; see Jameson (2000–2003) pp. 27–8; but Rhodes 2008 p. 505 despairs.

Athenian relations with Methone, decree i (Tod² 61 = ML 65 = *IG* I³ 61 = Fornara 128).

NOTES

On the notes: unidentified references are to Thucydides, whose books 2.1 to 5.25 are our main source for the Ten Years' War (Thucydides is systematically discussed in the appendix pp. 417–25); where unclarity would be created by failure to identify Thucydides, Thuc. = Thucydides. Diod. Sic. = Diodorus Siculus (first century BC), whose book 12.1–76 offers a briefer parallel account, heavily derivative of Thucydides, but often muddled (appendix pp. 425–6). When he just appears to echo Thucydides, I do not cite him. Other common, frequently used abbreviations of ancient authors and works are Hom. *Il.* = Homer, *Iliad*; Hdt. = Herodotus, *Histories* (fifth century BC); Ar. *Ach.* = Aristophanes, *Acharnians* (425 BC); Ar. *Eq.* = Aristophanes, *Knights* (424 BC); Ar. *Pax* = Aristophanes, *Peace* (421 BC); Xen. *Hell.* = Xenophon, *Hellenica* (fourth century BC); Xen. *Lac.* = Xenophon, *Constitution of the Lacedaemonians*; Arist. *Rhet.* = Aristotle, *Rhetoric* (fourth century BC); *Ath. pol.* = *Constitution of the Athenians* attributed to Aristotle (fourth century BC); Paus. = Pausanias, *Description of Greece* (second century AD); Plut. *Per.* = Plutarch, *Life of Pericles* (first/second century AD); Plut. *Cimon* = Plutarch, *Life of Cimon*. These and other less frequently used abbreviations of ancient works are taken from the *Oxford Classical Dictionary*[3]. As for the modern secondary literature, it is voluminous, the more so on the method of Thucydides, and I have tried to cite only especially important or recent contributions from which the interested can trace the wider literature on an issue. Modern authors with dates after their names appear in the bibliography. Modern authors without dates after their names (e.g., Gomme or Hornblower, both of which are commentaries on Thucydides) are listed in the abbreviations that preface the bibliography along with the abbreviations used for modern collections of evidence and other frequently cited modern works.

INTRODUCTION

1. For the story that begins this book, the 424 BC attack on the long walls of Megara from the temple of Ares, 4.66–73, with Geske 2005 n. 526 for literature. The Athenian general hiding in the temple was Demosthenes, son of

Alcisthenes. The Athenian hoplite force was 600 strong, 4.67.1. "Just slaughters," Soph. *El.* 36–7 (the Delphic oracle to Orestes).

2. Athenians much augmented in strength: by 4,000 hoplites and 600 horsemen who had marched through the night from Eleusis, 4.68.5.

3. The Nisaea armistice did not cover the Spartans present, who were presumably carried off to Athens (so Gomme *ad loc.* 4.69.3) to join the large body of Spartan prisoners the Athenians, at this stage in the war, already held.

4. Brasidas levied a force of 3,700 hoplites from Sparta's allies in the Peloponnese and added some of his own troops (4.70.1; but there is a muddle about the numbers, Gomme *ad loc.*). The Boeotians sent 2,200 hoplites (4.72.1). Brasidas' total force was around 6,000 (4.72.2).

5. The Athenians hoplites were "in line of battle near Nisaea and the sea" (4.72.2) but are surprised by the Boeotian horse, so they must have been in line of battle against the Megarians, challenging them to come out from their walls to fight: see below p. 6 for the significance of this gesture.

6. For discussion of the logic of the Athenian generals (4.73.4), see chapter 8 n. 66.

7. Norms of the classical Greek challenge to battle, 1.54.2, 2.20.1–3, 5.60.2, 8.27; Xen. *Hell.* 2.1.27, 6.5.21, with Pritchett 1974; van Wees 2004 p. 135; Wheeler 2007 p. 203. For Brasidas' logic for challenging, 4.73.1–3, with Rhodes IV–V.24 *ad loc.* 4.73.2. Brasidas deployed in a suitable place, *chōrion epitēdeion*, 4.73.1 (so Lazenby 2004 p. 86), a term that can also mean "advantageous place" (so Gomme *ad loc.* 4.73.2–3), but the whole point is that Brasidas is trying to shame the Athenians and so must offer battle in a position that allows the Athenians no excuse for declining to fight. The relative numbers of the Athenians and of Brasidas' forces cannot have guided the Megarian decision to rejoin the Peloponnesians because, if numbers had been a decisive consideration, the Megarians would have opened their gates to Brasidas earlier.

8. "Had won and the Athenians declined battle," 4.73.4.

9. "Always to be the best," Hom. *Il.* 6.208 = 11.784. This discussion of *timē* draws especially on Lendon 2000; 2005 pp. 20–38, 397; 2006 pp. 86–7. For *timē* as a physical object, Hom. *Il.* 1.159–60; cf. Hom. *Il.* 5.552–3, 17.419, with Lendon 2000 pp. 8–9.

10. "Where men win glory," battle, e.g., Hom. *Il.* 4.225; in assembly, e.g., *Il.* 1.490. On *timē* as a source of loyalty among men, Lendon 2000 p. 17; 2006 pp. 86–8.

11. For anger and revenge in Arist. *Rhet.* 1378a–80b, 1382a; for tragedy, Lendon 2000 n. 38 gathers the literature; in the Attic law courts, Cohen 1995. On revenge as a way of protecting/restoring rank-honor and the Greek vocabulary of revenge, Demont 1995 pp. 37–45. The nexus between *timē*, anger, and revenge has recently been much investigated by students of Greek emotions, esp. Harris 2001 pp. 131–200 and Konstan 2006 pp. 43–90. "Since never equal," Hom. *Il.* 1.278–9 trans. Lattimore; "best of the Achaeans," esp. 1.244; "I must be called," 1.293–4; "that dire wrath," 1.2–4. My understanding of the Greek

concept of *hybris* is that of Fisher 1992 as modified by Cairns 1996. For cross-cutting principles tending to discourage revenge in classical Greece, Herman 2006. There is a controversy (which can be followed through Fisher 2000, Herman 2006, Brüggenbrock 2006, and McHardy 2008) about the power of the revenge motive, as against those contradictory principles, among individuals in classical Athens, which I sidestep here, since my interest is in relations between states (but for my views, Lendon 2000 pp. 11–13—I agree with Fisher on the continuing importance of revenge in daily life).

12. Delphic oracle, Parke 1956 nr. 1 = Fontenrose 1978 nr. Q26. "Lacedaemonians were angry," e.g., Xen. *Hell.* 3.2.21, 3.2.23, 3.5.5. Orator, Demosthenes 8.57, 9.31, 18.138; cf. Thuc. 7.68.1. Greek cities as individuals, van Wees 2004 pp. 6–18; Lendon 2005 pp. 13–25 with 406–7 for literature; Hunt 2010 pp. 211–12.

13. For Greek war and revenge, Lendon 2000 n. 5 gathers the literature; Hunt 2010 pp. 197–201. For the beginnings of a movement to consider the role of emotion in modern international relations theory, see the literature collected by Löwenheim and Heimann (2008) n. 9. On the Greek international community as a semilawful realm (rather like the world of epic), Low 2007 pp. 77–128; Hunt 2010 pp. 215–36.

14. Catalogue of the causes of Greek war, van Wees 2004 pp. 19–33. Greek war and *timē*, Lendon 2000; van Wees 2004 pp. 19, 22–6; Rawlings 2007 pp. 14–16. The degree to which Greek warfare was like a game with rules ("agonistic" is the term of art) is controversial. I have tried to reconcile its agonistic and apparently nonagonistic aspects (by pointing out that the latter were agonistic, too) in Lendon 2005 pp. 78–90 with pp. 401–3 and 410–11 for literature; add now Dayton 2006.

15. For *hegemonia* in this sense, Wickersham 1994; for literature, Luppino-Manes 2000 pp. 18–20. For loyalty to *timē* among states, Lendon 2000 p. 17; 2006 pp. 87–8. It did not, of course, always work: Hunt 2010 p. 105.

16. On the Greek sense that a state's acts in the international arena were played out before an audience, Hunt 2010 pp. 208–12, 266.

17. "Who wrongs you first," Hesiod, *WD* 709–11; cf. Antiphon 4.b.2.

18. "Events of war," 2.11.4 (the Spartan king Archidamus is the speaker). Context all important: so, too, among men, Arist. *Rhet.* 1379b.

19. Achilles: contrast his reactions to insult in Hom. *Il.* 1.223–44 (verbal abuse); 1.348–57 (tears); 9.628–55 (nearly apology, in response to insulting words from Ajax). On the imponderables of the *hybris*-anger-revenge system and the role of irrational emotion, Lendon 2000 pp. 15–21, and the rest of the present book.

20. For the terms Peloponnesian War and Archidamian War and their first attestations, Ste. Croix 1972 pp. 294–5.

21. "Possession for all time," 1.22.4. For surveys of the study of Greek foreign relations in terms of Greek culture, van Wees 2004 pp. 3–43; Lendon 2006; Low 2007; Hunt 2010.

22. For kinship between states, Jones 1999; races or "tribes" (*ethnē*) of the Greeks, Hall 1997; Hornblower ii pp. 61–80; gratitude between states, chapter 3 n. 39; "friendship" between states, Mitchell 1997.

23. "It has always been the law," 1.76.2; "right, as the world goes," 5.89, both translated by Crawley (the translation in which international relations scholars often read Thucydides; see Eckstein 2003 pp. 757–67 on problems with realists and translations). For Thucydidean realism, see below pp. 381–5, with literature.

24. For "reputation" and "prestige" in international relations, the categories that come closest to Greek *timē*, see Busby 2005; both notions are embattled in the discipline, "reputation" being understood as the effect of past behavior on whether other nations will believe future promises and threats (even this is controversial in international relations) and "prestige," among the dominant realists, usually no more than an emanation of, or reputation (in the more conventional sense of the word) for, power and so not an object of study in its own right. Opponents of the realists—very much in the minority—who regard prestige as a national end in itself nevertheless often conceive it as a vague "opinion of others that makes us feel good about ourselves"—the kind of warm feeling weak nations like Canada seek (Wylie 2009): nothing, in other words, that anyone would ever go to war over. Thus, understood, state prestige is not something likely to be defended by revenge, and so the small international relations literature on revenge in the international arena (see Löwenheim and Heimann [2008]) does not link up with the international relations writing on national prestige. Markey 1999 is a *cri de coeur* for prestige (of which he has a muscular conception, similar to my "rank") to be taken seriously in international relations.

CHAPTER I:
ATHENS AND SPARTA: THE BIRTH OF A RIVALRY

1. For the Eleusinian Mysteries, and other festivals mentioned below, Deubner 1932 gathers the references; much more fun and full of fancy is Parke 1977. Sharks attack initiates, Plut. *Phoc.* 28.3.

2. Unknown gods, Paus. 1.1.4, with Frazer *ad loc.*, and, of course, *Acts* 17.23. Love Avenging (*Anterōs*), Paus. 1.30.1. Piglets, etc., were placed in holes at the Skira and dug up during the Thesmophoria.

3. Court for inanimate objects, Rhodes *Comm. Ath. pol.* pp. 649–50.

4. For this competitive understanding of Athenian litigation, see esp. Cohen 1995.

5. Fifth-century Athenian salaried officials, *Ath. pol.* 24.3, 27.3–4 (with Rhodes *Comm. Ath. pol. ad loc.*).

6. "Accursed race . . . demagogues," Eur. *Hec.* 254–5.

7. On competitive public benefaction at Athens, Kallet 1998 pp. 54–8, and esp. Lys. 21.1–5.

8. Democracy refuses building, *IG* I³ 49 = Fornara 117. No private sponsorship of religious festivals: contrast what the rich Nicias could do at a festival at Delos with his more restrained benefactions at Athens (Plut. *Nicias* 3.3–6). But as late as the 460s BC, private means could still be used to build public buildings and relieve poverty, Kallet 1998 pp. 48, 54.

9. *Stasis* "insatiate of evils," Aes. *Eum.* 976–80.

10. This summary discussion of Sparta draws on Lendon 1997a with fuller literature; for a collection of recent scholarship on Sparta, Thommen 2006. Nearly everything about ancient Sparta is controversial, and recent controversy has centered on how much it is safe to believe about Spartan customs and institutions attested only in Roman-period authors (esp. Plutarch) and not in fifth- or fourth-century BC sources (esp. Herodotus, Thucydides, and Xenophon's *Constitution of the Lacedaemonians* [= Xen. *Lac.*]). Some Anglophone scholars (esp. Kennell 1995; Hodkinson 2000; Flower 2002) attribute the Roman-period material to a third-century BC "invention of tradition," while some German scholars prefer a fifth-century BC invention of tradition (esp. Thommen 1996 and the essays in Luther *et al.* 2006). The French, by contrast, tend to defend the soundness of the tradition and so the applicability of most of the Roman-period evidence to fifth-century Sparta (esp. Ducat 2006a, but also many papers by the American T. Figueira). My sympathies are with the French school, and I have allowed myself (limited) use of unsupported Roman-period material in this section, while avoiding the great questions this controversy raises (e.g., whether the Spartans ever had equality in landholding). For Spartan control of *hybris*, Xen. *Lac.* 2.14, 3.2, 3.4, 13.5, with Fisher 1989. Sacrificing puppies to Enyalius, Paus. 3.14.9.

11. For Spartan competition, Xen. *Lac.* 4.2; Plato, *Resp.* 545a; Arist. *Pol.* 1271a; Plut. *Ages.* 5.3. "Sound from a stone," Xen. *Lac.* 3.5, with David 1999. Gymnopaedia at Sparta, Plato, *Leg.* 633c with Richer 2005 pp. 249–50. Boys accepting insults, Plut. *Lyc.* 12.4; *Quaest. Conv.* 631f. Laconic speaking, Herc. Lemb. 13 (Dilts 18 = Rose 373); Plato, *Prt.* 342e; Plut. *Lyc.* 18.3, 19–21.1, with Schmitz 2006. Lysander not being laconic enough, Plut. *Lys.* 14.4.

12. Spartan boys compete, Plut. *Lys.* 2.2; Plut. *Lyc.* 17.1–2; Paus. 3.14.8–10; to be named captains, Plut. *Lyc.* 16.5; competition in mockery, Herc. Lemb. (Dilts 18 = Rose 373); Plut. *Lyc.* 12.4, 15.2, 17.1; story of the boy and the fox, Plut. *Apop. Lac.* 234a–b; stealing, Xen. *Lac.* 2.6–9; Plut. *Lyc.* 17.3; Plato, *Leg.* 633b, with Link 2004. Stealing cheeses from Artemis, Xen. *Lac.* 2.9. For the festival in Roman times, [Plut.] *Inst. Lac.* 239c–d; Paus. 3.16.7–11. Or was it wheat the boys tried to steal? There is a textual problem: Paradiso 2007. Anyone with an ounce of romance in his soul hopes the cheeses will prevail. For competition in Spartan education, Ducat 2006a pp. 171–5.

13. For Spartan age divisions, Lipka 2002 pp. 141–7. On the Spartan "cavalry" and its selection, Figueira 2006. Selectors for the *hippeis* explain their decisions, Xen. *Lac.* 4.3.

14. For the Spartan "doers of good," the *agathaergoi*, Figueira 2006 pp. 57–8. Spartan hunting, Xen. *Lac.* 4.7, 5.3, 6.3–4; mess cooks, Athenaeus 141d–e.

Spartan gymnastics, Xen. *Lac.* 5.8–9. Spartans compete in obedience, Xen. *Lac.* 8.2, with Lendon 2005 pp. 75–6. Clubfooted king, Plut. *Ages.* 4.3. *Gerousia,* "of all contests," Xen. *Lac.* 10.3; cf. Plut. *Lyc.* 26.1. For election to the *Gerousia,* Birgalias 2007; for its proverbial competitiveness, Lipka 2002 pp. 182–3.

15. On the Spartan constitution the classic treatment in English remains Andrewes 1966; see recently Thommen 2003. On the ephors, Richer 1998. Unusual powers of the ephors, Xen. *Lac.* 8.4; Plato, *Leg.* 712d; Arist. *Pol.* 1270b. Skin of Epimenides, *Suda s.v.* Epimenides (= *FGH* 457 T2). "Shave off their mustaches," Plut. *Cleom.* 9.2. Oaths, Xen. *Lac.* 15.7. For the alleged contribution of Lycurgus, esp. Plut. *Lyc.* 5.6, 6.1–4, and on the evolution of his myth, David 2007. Stories about the role of Lycurgus in creating the Spartan constitution were many and contradictory, and modern students tend to believe none of them.

16. Spartan voting by shouting, Lendon 2001.

17. Spartan marriage, Plut. *Lyc.* 15.3, with Lupi 2000. Spartan husbands sneak out, Xen. *Lac.* 1.5; Plut. *Lyc.* 15.4; borrow wives, Xen. *Lac.* 1.7–8; Plut. *Lyc.* 15.6–7. Athletics for Spartan girls, Xen. *Lac.* 1.4; Plut. *Lyc.* 14.2. Spartan bachelors humiliated, Plut. *Lyc.* 15.1–2; cf. Athenaeus 555c–d.

18. Spartan messes, Xen. *Lac.* 5.2–7; Plut. *Lyc.* 10, 12; for the literature, Fornis and Casillas 1997. Spartan money, Xen. *Lac.* 7.5; Plut. *Lyc.* 9.1, with Figueira 2002. Spartans forbidden to work, Xen. *Lac.* 7.1–4; Plut. *Lyc.* 24.2.

19. Helot clothes and beatings, Myron *FGH* 106 F2 = Athenaeus 657d. Helot dances, made drunk, Plut. *Lyc.* 28.4. Declaration of war on helots, *krypteia,* Plut. *Lyc.* 28.1–4. On the *krypteia,* Ducat 2006a pp. 281–331. For recent discussions of the helots, see the essays in Luraghi and Alcock 2003. For the debate about how much the Spartans feared the helots, Cartledge 1991.

20. Number of Spartans in 480 BC, Hdt. 7.234.2. For the number of full Spartan citizens during the Peloponnesian War, see chapter 3 n. 10 and chapter 7 n. 38. For the *perioeci,* Mertens 2002, with literature; Ducat 2008.

21. Suicidal Spartan bravery and suicide, Xen. *Lac.* 9.6, with David 2004. "We lie here," Hdt. 7.228. Families of the Spartan dead, Xen. *Hell.* 4.5.10, 6.4.16.

22. "The Lacedaemonians conduct," Xen. *Lac.* 11.8. On Spartan drill, Lendon 2005 p. 108, with n. 26, and Hodkinson 2006 pp. 129–30, 133–40 on the question, which is controversial.

23. For Argos' perennial ambition for the *hegemonia* of the Peloponnese, 5.28.2, 5.69.1. Argive cults: Apollo Lycaeus (who was worshipped in many Greek cities), Paus. 2.19.3; Medusa, 2.21.5; blood, 2.24.1.

24. On Sparta's relations with her allies, Lendon 1994, brought up to date by Bolmarcich 2008. Sparta the *hegemon* of Greece, Hdt. 1.69, 5.49; Thuc. 1.18.2. Enyalius in chains, Paus. 3.15.7.

25. Greeks combine against Xerxes, Hdt. 7.145, 7.172. For the concept of *hegemonia,* see above p. 11.

26. Argos refuses to join coalition against Persia, Hdt. 7.148–52; whether the story is true does not matter; the issue is how Greek states might be thought to deal with one another. On the Sparta/Argos war of ?494 BC, see below p. 68.

27. "They would rather be ruled by the barbarians," Hdt. 7.149.

28. "Quenched the *hybris*," Hdt. 5.77 = ML 15 = Fornara 42 (*ca.* 506 BC). No help for the Athenians at Marathon: Herodotus tells the story that the Athenians sent a messenger to Sparta, but the Spartans insisted that a religious obligation kept them at home for the next twenty days (Hdt. 6.105–7).

29. Athens' mediocre rank: it could be challenged by Tegea, Hdt. 9.26–7 (on which see below pp. 40–1). In retrospect, ancient authors retrojected an Athenian sense of rivalry with Sparta into an earlier period (see below n. 45). Athens' fleet, Hdt. 7.144; of which 180 served at Salamis (8.44), the next largest contingent being Corinth, with forty (8.1, 8.43). Athens yields command at sea to Sparta, Hdt. 7.161.2, 8.2–3.

30. "Much would Agamemnon lament," Hdt. 7.159.

31. "The race of the Athenians," Hdt. 7.161.3; "spring gone out of the year," 7.162. It is unimportant whether the Gelon story (for which Cataldi 2005) is true: it shows how the Greeks understood the ranked relations between *poleis*. For the prestige of Athenian autochthony, Rosivach 1987 pp. 302–3; on the legend of autochthony at Athens and its age, Shapiro 1998. For the inferior rank of colonies, Thuc. 1.25.3–4, 1.34.1, and esp. 1.38.2–5.

32. Array of the Greeks at Plataea, Hdt. 9.28; cf. Hdt. 9.102.3 for an array in the same order at Mycale.

33. Argument of the Tegeans at Plataea, Hdt. 9.26.4–7.

34. Athenian response to the Tegeans, Hdt. 9.27.

35. Precedence from battle fought in a city's territory, Thuc. 5.47.7, 5.67.2.

36. "The most famous," Hdt. 9.64.1. Athenians vs. Thebans, Hdt. 9.67; Spartans bravest, 9.71.1–2.

37. Satisfaction and revenge for Leonidas, Hdt. 8.114, 9.64. Debate over additional revenge for Leonidas, Hdt. 9.78–9, with Asheri 1998 pp. 73–5.

38. Battle of Mycale, Hdt. 9.90–2, 9.96–106. Raised the ambitions: see n. 45 below for argument that this Athenian sense of equality with Sparta should not be dated further back.

39. "Of all men," Hdt. 8.124; cf. Thuc. 1.74.1, with Jordan 1988.

40. Peloponnesian wall in 480 BC, Hdt. 8.40.2. Destruction of Athens in 480 BC, Hdt. 8.53.2; Thuc. 1.89.3. The existence of a circuit of pre-Persian Athenian walls, long controversial, is now generally accepted, Weir 1995.

41. Second destruction of Athens in 479 BC, Hdt. 9.13.2. Athenians and Spartans quarrel, Hdt. 9.6–11.

42. Dates beginning with a "?" (most of those 478 to 432 BC) signify that although we are reasonably confident in the relative chronology, the actual calendar year in which a given event occurs may be off by a year or two. Because of Thucydides' summary coverage of this period, many dates are unclear or

controversial, and the very existence of some of the events described is impeached by some scholars. I accept the dates proposed by Busolt (3.1, see pp. xvii–xxii for his timeline) and only slightly modified by Gomme i pp. 389–413 (the "orthodox chronology"), except for the date of the end of the revolt of the helots, for which see chapter 2 n. 28.

43. Athenians begin to build walls, 1.89.3; Spartan request, 1.90.1–2. Pull down extra-Peloponnesian walls: Thucydides speculates (1.90.1) that Sparta's allies urged this upon her out of fear of the fleet and the *tolma*, the boldness, the Athenians had shown in the war; Diodorus' rank-minded interpretation (11.39.2) is that "seeing the great glory the Athenians had gained with their naval power, the Lacedaemonians suspected their increase, and decided to forbid the Athenians to rebuild their walls."

44. Themistocles and the walls, 1.90–3; but Fornara and Samons 1991 pp. 119–21 think the story a literary fiction, and although I have accepted Thucydides' account here, I would not be sorry if they were right. For then the story is a splendid example of the tit-for-tat way in which Greeks imagined relations between states working. More practically: could city walls be built so quickly? I assume piled rubble and a stockade, with the final stone walls finished later.

45. "Of equal weight," 1.91.7; cf. 6.82.3; Fornara and Samons 1991 p. 125 accept that Themistocles was even at this stage an advocate of Athenian equality with Sparta. But I suspect that Thucydides is retrojecting this Athenian sense of equality a little too far back, perhaps picking up from Herodotus (5.91.1), who retrojected this sense of Athenian rivalry with Sparta over rank into the sixth century and as a result could present Athens' yielding command of the allied fleet against Xerxes to the Spartans as an act of singular Hellenic patriotism (8.3). Later authors followed Thucydides in placing Athens' sense of rivalry with Sparta right after the war (*Ath. pol.* 23) or placed it after Salamis (Diod. Sic. 11.27.2), when "the Athenians were puffed up, and it became clear to everybody that they intended to compete with the Lacedaemonians for hegemony on the sea, so the Lacedaemonians, foreseeing what was about to happen, acted in rivalry for honor to humble their pride" (cf. 11.39.2, 11.59.1). Judging by the behavior of both sides, and Athens' lack of a hegemonal alliance parallel to that of Sparta before the foundation of the Delian League, my guess is that an Athenian sense of equality in rank with Sparta postdates the Persian War by some years, but my argument can accommodate such a sense being older.

46. Greeks sail to the Hellespont, Hdt. 9.106.4, 9.114.

47. Council on Samos, Hdt. 9.106.

48. Sestos, Hdt. 9.114–21; Thuc. 1.89.2.

49. Athenians go home from Sestos, Hdt. 9.121. The islanders had formally been admitted to the Greek alliance the previous year, Hdt. 9.106.4. Ropes to dedicate in their temples: but not in the Athenian stoa at Delphi (as used to be thought), which seems to have been built later, Walsh 1986.

50. Pausanias, Plut. *Arist.* 23.2 (cf. Hdt. 8.3.2; Thuc. 1.95.1–5). On Greek military discipline, Lendon 2005 pp. 72–7, with literature.

51. Athenian *hegemonia*, Hdt. 8.3.2; Thuc. 1.95.1, 6.76.3; *Ath. pol.* 24.1.

52. Spartans lose command of the fleet, 1.95. "No open anger," 1.92.

53. For friendship, *philia*, between Greek states, see introduction n. 22. For the reduced likelihood that anger will develop between persons in relaxed circumstances, Arist. *Rhet.* 1380b. Aristotle (*Rhet.* 1379b) says that anger is likely among (human) *philoi*, because one expects them to treat one better (but that is another way of saying one does not anticipate insults from them).

54. "Taking that glory," Diod. Sic. 11.59.1, dated to 475 BC; cf. *Ath. pol.* 23.2, the Athenians "became glorious among the Hellenes and took the *hegemonia* from the Lacedaemonians, who were unwilling to give it up." "It does not profit Sparta," Diod. Sic. 11.50. Some accept this story, found only in Diodorus; some do not: Luppino-Manes 2000 pp. 66–76. On Diodorus see appendix pp. 425–6.

55. The cleansing of Thebes, Hdt. 9.86–8. Spartan campaign to Thessaly, Hdt. 6.72; Paus. 3.7.9; Plut. *Mal. Herod.* 859d. For this campaign (and the puzzle of its date), Lewis 1992a pp. 97–9 and Lewis 1992c p. 499.

56. Attempted expulsions from the Amphictyony, Plut. *Them.* 20.3–4, with Sánchez 2001 pp. 98–103.

57. Sparta's Argive war in the 490s BC, Hdt. 6.77–83, with Scott 2005 pp. 571–88, preferring (with Forrest 1960 p. 222 and subsequent commentators) the version in Arist. *Pol.* 1303a and Plut. *Mul. Virt.* 245f, which holds that the Argives gave citizenship to their *perioeci*, rather than that the city was taken over by their slaves. Perhaps others of the Arcadians, Strabo 8.3.2.

58. Spartan wars against Tegea, Arcadians, Hdt. 9.35.2 (the list of battles); Paus. 3.11.7–8; Dipaea, Isoc. 6.99; Paus. 8.8.6. There is no hope of dating these wars, except after Plataea (479 BC) and before the rebellion of the helots (?465 BC). On these wars, Lewis 1992a pp. 101–6.

59. Revenge against Persia and assessment, 1.96.1. Aristides, iron blocks, *Ath. pol.* 23.5; Plut. *Arist.* 24–5.

60. Delian League campaigns down to Eurymedon, 1.97–9. Fate of Pausanias, 1.128.3, 1.131–4; for the date of the expulsion of Pausanias (a very obscure matter), Badian 1993a pp. 86–7.

61. Battle of Eurymedon, 1.100.1; palm tree, Paus. 10.15.4.

62. Delian League lost early luster: the old scholarly game of distinguishing successive flavors of Athenian imperialism from inscriptions is rendered impossible by new doubts about the dates of fifth-century Athenian inscriptions (see Kallet 2009 and appendix pp. 426–30). But Thuc. 1.97–9 implies that the change in the nature of the Athenian dominion was complete by the suppression of the rebellion of Naxos in ?467 BC. Athenians borrow techniques of ruling from the Persians: Raaflaub 2009. "Far the first in glory and courage," Diod. Sic. 12.2.1; cf. 11.71.5, 12.54.3, with appendix pp. 425–6

for how I use this author; Thuc. 2.64.3–5; Plut. *Cimon* 12.1; *Ath. pol.* 23.2, 24.1–2. "Got rid of the rule," Thuc. 6.82.3.

63. Cimon and the Spartans, Plut. *Cimon* 16 (with "that's not how they do it"). Themistocles, Thuc. 1.135.2–1.138.6. Diod. Sic. 11.54.2–3 interprets: "The Lacedaemonians, seeing that Sparta was humbled by the treason of Pausanias the general, and that the Athenians were esteemed because no citizen of theirs had been convicted of treason, were eager to ensnare the Athenians in similar calumnies. So, since Themistocles was in high repute among the Athenians, and had a great reputation for excellence, they accused him of treason"; cf. 11.55.5, "the Lacedaemonians were eager to slander and humble the city of the Athenians, and . . . the Athenians wanted to clear themselves of the charge brought against them." What was Themistocles doing in Argos that made the Spartans so angry? O'Neal 1981 gathers the discussions.

64. Earthquake at Sparta, 1.101.2; Plut. *Cimon* 16.4–7. For the controversy over the date of the revolt, Luraghi 2001 pp. 280–90. On the rebellion, Cartledge 2002 (1979) pp. 186–91.

65. "Ought not help" and "not let Hellas become lame," Plut. *Cimon* 16.8. For the origins and resonances of Cimon's idea of equality between Athens and Sparta, Sordi 1976.

66. "Perfect equality" (*epi tois isois kai omoiois*), Xen. *Hell.* 7.1.1, 7.1.14 (369 BC, after the Spartan catastrophe at Leuctra), with Luppino-Manes 2000 pp. 9–18, 161–92; cf. Hdt. 9.7; Thuc. 5.47.7. For the powerful draw of the notion of equality among Greek states, Hunt 2010 pp. 97–107. For the nexus of hegemony, equality, and revenge, esp. Thuc. 5.69.1.

67. First Athenian expedition to help the Spartans, Plut. *Cimon* 16.8; the second, Plut. *Cimon* 17.2; Thuc. 1.101.2–1.102.2. Badian 1993a pp. 89–94 is convincing that the Athenians made two expeditions (as Plut. *Cimon* 17 believed), but his attempt to redate the earthquake to 469 BC (reviving an old heresy) was enjoyably crushed by Pritchett 1995a pp. 5–24. Defeat helots in the field, Hdt. 9.35.2; Paus. 3.11.7–8.

68. "First open point of difference," *diaphora*, 1.102.3. Said nothing of their suspicions: so Thucydides was only guessing that the Spartans considered the Athenians "bold and revolutionary and of alien stock" (1.102.3); cf. Fornara and Samons 1991 p. 128; Badian 1993a p. 95. Athenians "took it ill," 1.102.4; cf. Plut. *Cimon* 17.2. Diod. Sic. 11.64.3 interprets: "The Athenians, thinking that they had been dishonored, then marched away. But afterwards, being estranged from the Lacedaemonians, they fanned the fires of their hatred (*echthra*) more and more. Therefore they took this as the beginning of their estrangement, and afterwards, when the cities wrangled [had *diaphorai*], they entered into great wars, and filled all of Greece with great woes"; cf. Paus. 1.29.9.

69. Forms of *hybris* between cities, summarizing Lendon 2000 p. 14 and Lendon 2007 p. 261, with references. For the contrast between modern and Greek motivations for war, Dawson 1996 p. 65; van Wees 2004 p. 25.

70. The Greek logic for why an inferior should not be angry when insulted is expressed at Arist. *Rhet.* 1378a, 1370b. As Konstan 2006 puts it, "if your position is inferior, it is no insult to be reminded of it" (p. 55, and see his discussion at pp. 55–65). To be able to call upon Sparta in the future: see Lendon 2006 pp. 91–5 and Hunt 2010 pp. 192–3 for this strategy of reciprocity among Greek states.

71. Senator of Rome, Cassius Dio 58.5.3 (explaining the behavior of the arriviste Sejanus).

72. Wolf and lamb fable, Babrius 89.

73. Spartan agreement to help Thasos, 1.101.1–2. I follow Badian's compelling impeachment of this story in Badian 1993b pp. 134–6 and Badian 1993a pp. 92–4 (dealing with the apparent chronological problem of Thucydides' discussing Thasos before the earthquake); cf. Fornara and Samons 1991 p. 127.

74. Cimon exiled, Plut. *Cimon* 17.2.

CHAPTER II:
THE COMING OF THE TEN YEARS' WAR

1. Reign of Pericles at Athens, *Ath. pol.* 27.1–28.1. For Pericles and his career, Podlecki 1998 and Lehmann 2008. For Pericles' manner, and the story of the ignored abuser, Plut. *Per.* 5.1–3; Pericles does not weep at funerals, 36.4–5 (death of second son: in fact, Pericles convinced the Athenians to legitimize his third son, who was later executed by the democracy, Plut. *Per.* 37); does not dine out, 7.4; thought arrogant, 5.3–4, 37.5.

2. For the theme virtues of Themistocles, Aristides, and Cimon, see Plutarch's *Lives* of each. Mentions especially in fifth-century comedy show that these qualities were not merely themes imposed by the Roman-period Plutarch or his sources, but the association of these politicians with these virtues will have encouraged myth-making about them, and many of the stories Plutarch uses to illustrate these virtues will have been the result.

3. Pericles' policies, Plut. *Per.* 9, 11.4–5, 19.1, 20.2, 23.2; *Ath. pol.* 27. On Athenian colonies, Meiggs 1972 pp. 260–2; on cleruchies, emphasizing the large tracts handed out to cleruchs, Moreno 2009. On Pericles' building program, Plut. *Per.* 12–14, and see below pp. 74–6; prosecution of Pericles' brainy friends, 31–2.

4. Pericles elected general fifteen years straight, Plut. *Per.* 16.3. "A democracy in name," Thuc. 2.65.9. Pericles' "worthiness" (*ep' axiōsei*); "rank and wisdom" (*axiōmati kai tēi gnōmēi*), 2.65.8. For parallel between rank of state and rank of Pericles, Frazier 2001. "Your empire . . . a tyranny," 2.63.2 (trans. adapts Crawley).

5. Megara defects to Athens, 1.103.4; cf. Plut. *Cimon* 17.1; Diod. Sic. 11.79.1–3. Archeological traces have been found of the Megarian long walls: Hornblower *ad loc.* 4.66.3; Rhodes IV–V.24 *ad loc.* 4.66.4. Piraeus walls,

Thuc. 1.93.3–6. Athenian long walls, 1.107.1, 1.108.3, on which Conwell 2008. Traditionally dated ?458–?457 BC on the basis of 1.107.1, the Athenian long walls were probably begun earlier, given how considerable a project this was (Conwell 2008 pp. 37–54). Thucydides was hardly being precise in his chronology at 1.107.1. Before 431 a third wall was built parallel to the north, Athens-Piraeus wall, presumably because the earlier south wall did not connect to the Piraeus defenses, and an enemy arriving by sea could therefore land between the two older walls.

6. Conflict between Argos and Corinth, Plut. *Cimon* 17.2. For the role of Corinth, Lewis 1981 (1997).

7. Athenian landing at Halieis, battles by land and sea, 1.105.1–2. For Sicyon, not mentioned by Thucydides, *SEG* XXXI 369, with Lewis 1981 (1997) n. 26. Dionysus at Sicyon, Paus. 2.7.5–6. I accept the argument of Holladay 1977 (2002) pp. 57–9 that Sparta was not involved in this first year of the war.

8. "Eyesore of the Piraeus," Plut. *Per.* 8.5; Athens and Aegina fighting in 480 BC, Hdt. 7.145.1. For the ?458 sea battle between Athens and Aegina, 1.105.2. Diodorus interprets the cause of this war thus: "after such successes, the Athenians, seeing that the Aeginetans were puffed up by their former deeds, and also opposed to them, decided to war them down" (11.78.3). Cult of Hecate at Aegina, Paus. 2.30.2.

9. Athenian siege and Peloponnesian reinforcement of Aegina, 1.105.2–3. Rocks off Aegina, Paus. 2.29.6, or any modern yachting pilot.

10. Battle in the Megarid between Athens and Corinth, 1.105.3–106.2. "Fierce hatred of the Corinthians for the Athenians," 1.103.4. On hatred in Greek foreign relations, Lendon 2000 p. 15; Lendon 2007 p. 262.

11. "Cyprus, Egypt, Phoenicia," ML 33 (= Tod² 26 = *IG* I³ 1147 = Fornara 78).

12. Battle of Oenoe, Paus. 1.15.1, 10.10.3–4. Taylor 1998 gathers the (huge) literature on the battle. Many do not think it even took place, and if it did, any date (or location, there being many Oenoes in Greece) is a guess. My guess follows Robert 1890 pp. 412–22 and Meiggs 1972 pp. 469–72.

13. *Eumenides* on the Athens/Argos alliance: Aes. *Eum.* 290–1, 397–402, 667–73, 762–74, with Quincey 1964 and Podlecki 1966 pp. 82–100. But such political readings of tragedy are now severely unfashionable, so Saïd 1998 (but at pp. 280–1 she kindly gathers political interpretations of the *Eumenides*), and it is easy to sympathize, because when the dates of plays are not known, and allusions craned for, the finding of political allusions can become impossibly subjective (e.g., Vickers 2008). So other than the firmly dated *Oresteia*, where the allusions are patent, I make little use of tragedy in this book. Setting of the *Agamemnon*: moved to Argos with great emphasis, Aes. *Ag.* 24, 281–311, 503–23, 810, 855. And cf. the hopes for Argos in Aeschylus' *Supplices* 625–709.

14. Peloponnesians rescue Doris, 1.107.2. As Fornara and Samons 1991 pp. 135–6 argue, the plight of Doris is a quite sufficient explanation for this expedi-

tion, and there is no call to replace Thucydides' account with that of Diod. Sic. 11.81.1–4, who has the expedition motivated by affairs in Boeotia, merely because the rescue of Doris seems quaint to us. Diodorus guesses that "the Thebans, having been humbled by the alliance they made with Xerxes, sought a way to regain their ancestral strength and glory. Therefore, because all the other Boeotians held the Thebans in contempt and would not pay heed to them, the Thebans asked the Lacedaemonians to help them gain the *hegemonia* of all Boeotia" (11.81.1–2; cf. Justin, *Epit.* 3.6.10). But, as Plant 1994 p. 269 notes, Diodorus' version is impeached by Spartan tolerance of Athens' conquest of Boeotia so soon after Tanagra. For the force of claims like that of Doris, see chapter 3 n. 39.

15. The Peloponnesian campaign culminating in the battle of Tanagra, 1.107.3–7, on which see Pritchett 1996. Athens gets help from Aegean allies, Paus. 5.10.4, where, in their victory dedication, the Spartans claim victory over Argives, Athenians, and Ionians. Recruiting allies strongly implies that the battle was an Athenian initiative (cf. Diod. Sic. 11.80.1, for what it is worth), as is the consensus of the sources (so Roisman 1993a p. 75). The fragmentary inscriptional version of this Spartan dedication (Tod[2] 27 = ML 36 = Fornara 80) seems to identify Corinthians as fighting on the Spartan side (*l.* 5). For Boeotians, see below n. 17. Thucydides reports contacts between the Spartans and antidemocratic plotters at Athens (1.107.4, 1.107.6), but because, as in the case of Thasos (above p. 55), this was a stillborn, secret plot, we should probably not believe in it (cf. Badian 1993a n. 50; Plant 1994 p. 262).

16. Battle of Tanagra, 1.107.7–1.108.1. Thessalians defect: this detail may be confirmed by the epitaph of one of the Thessalians (*SEG* XXXIV 560, with Helly 2004), who "brought no shame to the glory of his city," perhaps implying that others did, unless this is just a sounding litotes. Cimon comes to fight at Tanagra: Plut. *Per.* 10.1–2; *Cimon* 7.3–4, although this story has become tangled up with that of the alleged oligarchic conspiracy against the democracy, in which I do not believe (see above n. 15). Fighting over two days, Paus. 1.19.9 and Diod. Sic. 11.80.2–6—who preserves a more elaborate version of the same tradition (adding the Thessalian attack on the Athenian supplies). But Diodorus' account (11.80.2) is desperately muddled, and although attempts can be made to explain the confusion (e.g., Green *Diodorus* pp. 156–61 nn. 329, 332–3), they hardly rehabilitate it. Meager confirmation of this tradition may nevertheless lie in (1) *SEG* XVII 243, a dedication at Delphi by the Thessalian cavalry of spoils from Tanagra, and (2) Plato, *Menex.* 242b, which describes the subsequent battle of Oenophyta as lasting for two days. If Plato has confused Oenophyta and Tanagra, this may be an independent attestation of the two-day battle Pausanias and Diodorus claim. Shield from Tanagra at Olympia, above n. 15. Pausanias (1.29.9) saw a list of the Argives and their allies from Cleonae, whom the Athenians buried in the Ceramicus after the battle. What has been identified as a fragmentary list of the Argive dead survives (Tod[2] 28 = ML 35).

17. Boeotians at Tanagra, Paus. 1.29.9 and [Plato], *Alc. I.* 112c, but certainly not their whole levy of *ca.* 7,000 men (Thuc. 4.93.3), because it is unlikely that Athens would have dared to fight so large a combined force (*ca.* 11,500 + *ca.* 7,000); see Reece 1950 p. 75 (but his solution, that Boeotians made up most of Sparta's 10,000 allies, is not the obvious reading of Thuc. 1.107.2). Still, as Meiggs 1972 p. 418 notes, the Athenian expedition to Oenophyta makes more sense if we accept the presence of Boeotians at Tanagra. Battle of Oenophyta, Thuc. 1.108.3. Myronides "hairy-assed," Ar. *Lys.* 802; cf. *Eccl.* 303–4. Tactics of Myronides, Diod. Sic. 11.81.5–6; Front. *Strat.* 2.4.11, 4.7.21; Polyaen. *Strat.* 1.35.1–2; none of the stories are probably to be believed, alas.

18. Political divisions in Boeotia, 3.62.5, 4.92.6; Arist. *Rhet.* 1407a; Plato, *Menex.* 242b (cf. Busolt 3.1 p. 319); these may be reflected (whatever the other value of the tradition) in the Diodorus/Justin tradition about Boeotia in the Tanagra campaign, see above n. 14. Walls of Tanagra torn down, Thuc. 1.108.3. Tanagra had probably been friendly to the Spartans, Roisman 1993a pp. 81–4.

19. Surrender of Phocis, Opuntian Locris, 1.108.3. Walsh 1986 p. 331 associates the building of the Stoa of the Athenians at Delphi with this conquest of Phocis.

20. Athenian long walls finished, 1.108.3. Aegina surrenders to Athens, 1.108.4. Diod. Sic. 11.70.2 interprets: "This city [Aegina], often successful in sea battles, was puffed up and abundantly supplied with money and triremes, and, in sum, always at odds with the Athenians"; cf. 11.78.3–4: "With their pride crushed by the magnitude of the disaster, they were compelled to join the tribute-paying league of the Athenians." Somewhere—probably in ?458 or ?457 BC—must also be placed the surrender to Athens of Troezen on the Argolid peninsula, which we only know about because the Athenians had to give it up at the end of the war, 1.115.1, 4.21.3.

21. For the fact of Spartan passivity (cf. 1.118.2), Holladay 1977 (2002), but I offer different reasons for it. Thucydides also preserves a tradition that the Persians, alarmed by the war in Egypt (?459–454 BC), tried to bribe the Spartans into attacking Athens (1.109.2), a legend that, whether we believe it or not, certainly attests to Spartan inactivity during most of Athens' Egyptian expedition. Why were the Spartans inactive? Were they prevented from invading Attica by Athenian possession of Megara and garrisons on Geranea? Cf. 1.107.3. This is a venerable position (e.g., Bury 1900 p. 363), forcefully advocated by Ste. Croix 1972 pp. 190–5, which has attracted many followers. *Contra*, Holladay 1977 (2002) pp. 58, 61 and Holladay 1985 (2002) p. 161. This is unlikely because the Corinthians had passed Geranea twice to fight battles in the plain of Megara, and the Spartan expedition to Doris may have passed it as well, on its way north, and certainly passed it on the way home; unlikely also because the Athenians thought it necessary to endure the colossal expense of building (or finishing, depending on the chronology one adopts) their own long walls, despite holding Megara, which implies that Megara was not regarded as sufficient de-

fense against the most likely invaders of Attica, the Peloponnesians. Were the Spartans still pinned down by the rebellious helots on Ithome? So Fornara and Samons 1991 pp. 133–7, "which easily explains what otherwise would have been unpardonable remissness on Sparta's part when her allies came under Athenian attack" (p. 133). But that had not prevented them from marching to Doris: so Holladay 1977 (2002) p. 63, and the march to Doris also (p. 62) seems to preclude Sparta being inactive because of losses during the earthquake and the helot war. As Lewis 1981 (1997) p. 72 notes, the last years of the Ithome war may have been no great affair, just a matter of keeping a garrison around Ithome. By a strategic choice of what dates to accept, it is also possible to bring Ithome to a close just before Tanagra (Plant 1994 p. 267) and so explain Spartan passivity before that date. But what about after?

22. Private and separate wars, cf. Yates 2005 p. 70.

23. Pride makes alliance between Greek states problematic, esp. Xen. *Cyr.* 5.5.25–34, with Lendon 2006 pp. 93–5; Thuc. 6.80.4; but one does get glory as *hegemon* of an alliance, 7.56.3. Honor of fighting "alone," Ziolkowski 1981 pp. 116–17, 123; cf. Hdt. 9.27.5; Thuc. 5.109; Diod. Sic. 11.82, 12.2.1.

24. Old hostility between Athens and Aegina, Hdt. 6.49–50, 6.73, 6.87–93. Aegina's war against Athens private, Thuc. 1.105.2; help vs. helots, 2.27.2; end of war, see the terms of the peace in Ste. Croix 1972 pp. 293–4. Aegina was probably not formally an ally of Sparta: Figueira 1981. Sparta does not owe Boeotia, cf. Holladay 1977 (2002) pp. 55–7.

25. Dependencies of Argos revolt, Diod. Sic. 11.65; cf. Paus. 5.23.3, 8.27.1: at some point Argos gobbled up Tiryns as well. Battle of Tegea, Hdt. 9.35.2. Tegeans help Argos against Mycenae, Strabo 8.6.19, as did Cleonae. Argive anti-Spartan league, Forrest 1960 p. 229. Roisman 1993a p. 72 takes a surviving treaty between Argos and two small places in distant Crete (Tod² 33 = ML 42 = Fornara 89) as a sign that Argos was claiming hegemony over the Dorian Greeks.

26. Shield from Tanagra, see above (n. 15). Main battle for hegemony was between Sparta and Argos: Holladay 1977 (2002) p. 61 was puzzled by Sparta's "failure to act against Argos," while Reece 1962 p. 119 was puzzled at the seeming inactivity of Argos. The fact is, given our Athens-focused sources, we have no idea what transpired between those powers. It may be that two considerable battles (Oenoe, above, and perhaps a battle in 450 BC, below) have left no more than the slightest traces—so who knows what else has gotten lost?

27. Tolmides' raid of ?456 BC, 1.108.5; Scholiast to Aeschines 2.75 (Blass = 78 Dindorf); Paus. 1.27.5, with Lewis 1992a pp. 117–18. At the end of the war, Athens was compelled to renounce an alliance with Achaea, a coalition of small states in the Peloponnese, on the south coast of the Gulf of Corinth (Thuc. 1.115.1, 4.21.3), an alliance Pericles made use of in ?454 (1.111.3). The expedition of Tolmides is perhaps the best occasion for the formation of this alliance. "Humble the fame of the Spartans," Diod. Sic. 11.84.3; on naval raiding as revenge, p. 123.

28. Spartans settle with the rebels on Ithome, 1.103.1–3; "let go the suppliant of Zeus," 1.103.2. Ten years on Ithome: the date here is my one significant departure from the dates of Busolt and Gomme (see chapter 1 n. 42) because, since their time, the mass of opinion (led by Reece 1962) has turned against adducing a textual corruption—reading a rebellion of "four" rather than "ten" years—at 1.103.1. Tolmides and the Messenians, Diod. Sic. 11.84.7–8, with Lewis 1992a p. 118. When and how the Athenians got hold of Naupactus is obscure: see Badian 1993c.

29. On the etiquette of "noticing" and not "noticing" in an honor culture, the classic discussion is Bourdieu 1966 pp. 197–207; cf. Stewart 1994 pp. 64–7. Cf. Arist. *Rhet.* 1379b, on the liberty (in human relations) to ignore insults that touch on realms where one knows one is superior, and 1378b, for paying no mind as itself a form of insult. For "noticing" in relations between Greek states, Lendon 2000 p. 20.

30. Pericles' raid of ?454 BC, 1.111.2. Spartans come to help Sicyon, Diod. Sic. 11.88.2. Pericles' expedition then went on (Thuc. 1.111.3) to attack Oeniadae in Acarnania in the northwest. During the Peloponnesian War Oeniadae was hostile to the Acarnanians until compelled by force to join their league in 424 (2.102.2, 3.7.3–4, 4.77.2). Did the Acarnanians call upon Pericles for help against Oeniadae? If so, that would encourage us to place shortly before Pericles' expedition the undated Athenian expedition under the Athenian general Phormio into the northwest (2.68.7–8; on which Gomme *ad loc.* 3.105.1; Hale 2009 p. 350; and for literature Fantasia 2006), which secured for Athens the alliance of the Acarnanians. The purpose of that expedition, against Corinth's colony Ambracia, also fits well in this period (so Krentz and Sullivan 1987).

31. Athenian expedition to Thessaly, 1.111.1; Diod. Sic. 11.83.3–4 guesses that the Athenians "were blaming [the Thessalians] for their treachery."

32. Athenian disaster in Egypt, 1.104, 1.109–10, with Kahn 2008 for the controversy over the dates of the expedition and the size of the disaster. The moving of the treasury from Delos is deduced from the fact that the Athenian tribute lists (strictly, lists of the 1/60 of the tribute dedicated to Athena) begin in 454/3 BC. For the tribute lists, see appendix p. 428.

33. Cimon's truce, 1.112.1; Plut. *Cimon* 18.1. I do not believe that Cimon was recalled early, as some late sources suggest: Marshall 2002.

34. Cimon in Cyprus, 1.112.1–4; Diod. Sic. 12.3.1–3. Athenian war with Persia ends: was there a formal treaty—the so-called Peace of Callias—between Athens and Persia? Begin to trace the oppressive scholarly literature through Samons 1998.

35. Sparta makes peace with Argos, 5.14.4. For the suggestion that the treaty of 450 BC implies a lost battle, Unz 1986 p. 80.

36. Sacred War to Delphi, Athenian expedition, 1.112.5; Plut. *Per.* 21.2, and, perhaps, Plut. *Mal. Herod.* 859d, Strabo 9.3.15, and Paus. 10.14.7; on this exchange Busolt 3.1 pp. 419–20; Sánchez 2001 pp. 106–9. Tod² 39 = *IG* I³ 9 =

Fornara 82, sometimes adduced in this context, is too fragmentary to interpret or date reliably (Sánchez 2001 pp. 109–11).

37. Pan-Hellenic congress, Plut. *Per.* 17. Despite controversy in the 1970s (Stadter pp. 201–4 gathers the literature), this so-called Congress Decree now is generally accepted (Bloedow 1996) and dated where Busolt (3.1 p. 446) put it, in ?449 BC, although the date is hardly secure. The Congress Decree finds a parallel in, and therefore some support from, the undated Eleusinian First-Fruits Decree (Tod² 74 = ML 73 = *IG* I³ 78 = Fornara 140), which (*ll.* 24–6, 30–6) invites all the Hellenes to send first fruits to Eleusis. "Thinking big," Plut. *Per.* 17, *mega phronein*, on which Cairns 1996.

38. For the dimensions of Greek temples, Schmitt 1992. There were larger temples on Samos, in Greek Asia Minor, and in Sicily, where *campanilismo* in temple size had long prevailed. For the Periclean building program, Boersma 1970 pp. 65–75; Hurwit 1999 p. 158. For the Odeum as the Great King's pavilion or a hat, Plut. *Per.* 13.5–6.

39. For the controversy over whether the Greeks swore not to rebuild the temples destroyed by the Persians (an oath from which the Athenians presumably thought themselves released by the Congress Decree), Meiggs 1972 pp. 504–7, brought up to date by Krentz 2007 pp. 731–42.

40. Paying for the Parthenon, Plut. *Per.* 12. Whether Athena strictly needed to call upon tribute is controversial (see Fantasia p. 276). But there is no reason to suppose that the tribute was not called upon, as Plutarch says, and direct use of the tribute was probably necessary for the Periclean building program as a whole, as Samons 2000 pp. 41–2 argues. Controversy at Athens about the building program, Plut. *Per.* 12.2–3, a passage now generally accepted: Kallet 2005 n. 40. "Once the Athenians had greater wealth," Dem. 22.76; cf. Isoc. 15.234.

41. Tolmides argues with Pericles, Plut. *Per.* 18.2–3.

42. Athenian disaster in Boeotia, 1.113; Xen. *Mem.* 3.5.4; Diod. Sic. 12.6.2. Athena Itonia, Plut. *Ages.* 19.2; Paus. 9.34.1–2.

43. Boeotia, Phocis, Opuntian Locris, in 431 BC, 2.9.2. "The fame of Athens was cast down," Xen. *Mem.* 3.5.4 (discussing Delium in 424 as well); cf. Diod. Sic. 12.7.

44. Revolt of Megara in 446 BC, 1.114.1.

45. Gravestone of Pythion, ML 51 = Tod² 41 = Fornara 101; combining this with Diod. Sic. 12.5.2 to work out the story; cf. Busolt 3.1 pp. 426–7.

46. Peloponnesian invasion of Attica, 1.114.2, 2.21.1; Plut. *Per.* 22.2; Diod. Sic. 12.6.1. Suppression of Euboean revolt by Athens, 1.114.3; Plut. *Per.* 23.2; Diod. Sic. 12.7. Lewis 1992a p. 135 notes that "the real mystery is what Pericles said to induce his opponents to abandon the protection they were in effect providing for the Euboeans." Along with so many fifth-century Athenian inscriptions (see appendix pp. 426–8), those that used to be assigned to the end of this revolt, the Athenian regulations for Chalcis, Eretria,

and Hestiaea (*IG* I³ 39–41), cannot be reliably dated (Papazarkadas 2009 pp. 73–4; appendix p. 429) and so must be left out of discussion.

47. For the terms of the Thirty Years' Peace, 1.115.1, with Ste. Croix 1972 pp. 293–4 (for no special provision being made for Aegina, see below n. 92), adding, I would guess (with Gomme *ad loc.* 2.83.3), Athens' returning Chalcis in the northwest to Corinth, which is useful to explain why Corinth is better disposed to Athens in 440 BC, but subtracting (with Hornblower *ad loc.* 1.140.2), as a misreading of the Greek, Ste. Croix's suggestion that the treaty in some way formally recognized the legitimacy of the Athenian empire. Athenians look back fondly at the Thirty Years' Peace, Ar. *Ach.* 194–7; Ar. *Eq.* 1390–1. Pericles and Pleistoanax, "what was necessary," Plut. *Per.* 23.1; Scholiast to *Clouds* 859 = *FGH* 70 F193 = Fornara 104.

48. "Went as far as Eleusis," 2.21.1; cf. 1.114.2.

49. Thirty Years' Peace: lists of allies, 1.40.2; neutrals can join either side, 1.35.2; arbitration clause, 1.140.2, 7.18.2. "Equal" treaty, e.g., 5.15.2; Andoc. 3.11. "Unequal" treaty, e.g., Aeschin. 3.106; Isoc. 4.120–1, 4.175–82. "Follow the Spartans," Xen. *Hell.* 2.2.20, 4.6.2.

50. "Best not to puff," 6.11.6. "Wise 'em up," Lendon 2000 p. 14; 2006 pp. 85–6. On Churchill, Le Vien and Lord 1962 p. 40.

51. For the conventions of Greek battle, Lendon 2005 pp. 41–3, 401–2, 410–11, with literature and controversy.

52. "Thefts of War," Whitehead 1988. Relationship between spirits and rank, Lendon 2006, with nn. 28–9, on the lack of consequences for rank of winning by trickery; also Lendon 2005 p. 88. For victory giving the defeated no excuses, Andoc. 3.18.

53. Epitaph over Athenian war dead, *IG* I³ 1163, reading [*esodo*]*n* (*l.* 4) with ed.; [*d' apeneim' ho*] (*l.* 5), suggested to me by W. D. Furley; and [*touto men h*] (*l.* 6) with Peek. For the (uncertain) date of this epigram, Mattingly 1966 pp. 176–7, 191–2; Papazarkadas 2009 p. 76.

54. Pan-Hellenic colony to Thurii, Diod. Sic. 12.9–11; no help later, Diod. Sic. 12.23.2; cf. Kagan 1969 p. 164. On this obscure episode, Busolt 3.1 pp. 522–41; Kagan 1969 pp. 155–69; and for a gathering of the recent literature, Podlecki 1998 pp. 81–9.

55. For the rebellion of Samos from Athens, 1.115.2–1.117.3. The best discussions are Busolt 3.1 pp. 542–54 and Legon 1972; for literature, Landucci Gattinoni 1998 n. 1 and Podlecki 1998 p. 203 n. 4. Athenian offer to arbitrate between Samos and Miletus, Plut. *Per.* 25.1, with Quinn 1981 p. 11. Pericles descends on Samos, 1.115.3; Diod. Sic. 12.27.2–3; Plut. *Per.* 25.1.

56. Byzantium revolts, 1.115.5; and perhaps some other small places as well, Busolt 3.1 p. 544. On the importance of the passage to the Black Sea, Moreno 2007 argues that Black Sea grain (which passed through the Hellespont) was not in the fifth century crucial for feeding Athens. But his own list of references

to this trade, and to Spartan ambitions to stop it (pp. 337–8), appears to refute him. The degree to which Athens was dependent on imported grain is controversial (see Hunt 2010 p. 36 for literature), but the tenable positions extend from "considerably" to "abjectly."

57. Sophocles the poet (and the other generals) are listed by Androtion (*FGH* 324 F 38 = Fornara 110). I accept here the traditional date scholars have assigned to the *Antigone*, during, or shortly before, 442 BC, but Tritle 2010 p. 15 n. 48 gathers dissenters.

58. Samians sail against Miletus, Athenians watch for the Persians, 1.115.5–1.116.1.

59. Samians defeated at sea, besieged, 1.116.1–2.

60. Endgame at Samos, 1.116–17; cf. Plut. *Per.* 25–8, with many dubious details, effectively impeached by Karavites 1985. Cost of the Samian war, 1,400+ talents in Tod² 50 = ML 55 = Fornara 113; 1,200 talents in Nepos, *Timoth.* 1, both with Meiggs 1972 p. 192. The settlement with Samos, Thuc. 1.117.3; Diod. Sic. 12.28.3–4; and the (very fragmentary) ML 56 = Fornara 115.

61. Samian appeal to Sparta in *ca.* 525 BC, Hdt. 3.46–7. Spartans fail in *ca.* 525 BC, Hdt. 3.54–6. For the connection of that old debt to the 440 revolt, Cartledge 1982 pp. 260–3.

62. Powerful forces at Sparta wanted war, so Ste. Croix 1972 pp. 200–3. The Spartan invitation of the allies to vote was a practical, rather than a "constitutional," requirement of the Spartan alliance: Lendon 1994. Corinth prevents action, 1.40.5; cf. 1.41.2, 1.43.1. Involvement of the Peloponnesians in the Samian revolt may be confirmed by ML 56 *l.* 7, with Meiggs 1972 p. 190. Mytilene may also at this time have approached the Spartans for support were she to join the revolt, then decided not to when the Spartans were discouraging, Thuc. 3.2.1, 3.13.1, with Kagan 1969 p. 173. Sparta's allies prevent war with Athens: Ste. Croix 1972 p. 203 is right that the Spartans themselves were consistently willing to go to war with Athens at least from the time of the Samian appeal to them (?440 BC).

63. "Truest cause of the war," 1.23.6; "growing greatness," 1.88; to Sparta's allies, 1.118.2; *aitiai* and *diaphorai*, 1.23.5 (so Crawley translates). For the literature on the meaning of these terms and the relation of causes that Thucydides has in mind, Meyer 1997 pp. 23–35; Eckstein 2003. Samons 2004 p. 129 suggests attractively that the "truest cause" is the "why," and the grounds for complaint/points of difference are the "why then." For recent discussions of Thucydides' account of the outbreak of the war, Rood 1998 pp. 205–24 and Pelling 2000 pp. 82–111.

64. Accepting Thucydides' view of the cause of the war, Ste. Croix 1972, and for a collection of others, Meyer 1997 pp. 25–35.

65. Emphatic distinction, 1.23.5–6; not discussed at the time, 1.23.6; fear of power presses harder upon Spartans than allies 1.88; cf. 1.118.2.

66. Aristophanes' burlesque of war's cause, Ar. *Ach.* 515–39; "one pot," *Pax* 613. Plut. *Per.* 29.30 (guessing Ephorus from the similarity to Diod. Sic. 12.38–9; at 12.41.1 Diodorus attributes his account of the causes of the war to Ephorus).

67. Fear of power causes war: Thucydides was hardly alone in this type of analysis; cf. Polybius 1.10.5–6, 1.83.3–4, 2.13.4.

68. Thucydides was wrong about cause of war: so Kagan 1969, esp. pp. 345–6; vindicated against subsequent scholarly argument by Meyer 1997 pp. 27, 31–2 (whose arguments I adopt here). Additional Athenian power at sea: the adhesion of Corcyra to Athens (see below). But this is formally part of the *aitiai* and *diaphorai* (1.23.6 and following), rather than Athens' growing great and causing fear (1.88 and following), and so not, according to Thucydides, even part of the growth of Athens' power (Meyer 1997 p. 32).

69. Next resort for explanation of the war, cf. Sealey 1975, who maintained that Thucydides himself had originally conceived of the cause of the war in terms of a chain of vengeances—the "grounds for complaint" and "points of difference"—but had subsequently changed his mind to Sparta's fear of Athenian power and never fully reconciled the two positions in his narrative; see also Fornara and Samons 1991 p. 141. But evolution of Thucydides' thought in the other direction (from fear of power to chain of vengeances) is just as possible.

70. "At this time," Diod. Sic. 11.65.1–3; cf. Paus. 2.16.5.

71. "I have always held the same principle," 1.140.1; Pericles a "powerful man," 1.127.3. Spartans violated the peace, 7.18.2.

72. Athens' dispute with Megara: Plut. *Per.* 30.2–3 places the Megarian Decree in a sequence of vengeances; also Ar. *Ach.* 524–39, with Pelling 2000 pp. 103–11, 141–5, 151–8. Megarian Decree: Thuc. 1.67.4, 1.139.1–2; Fornara 122–3 gathers the other ancient evidence. For the date (the Megarian Decree is often placed in 433 or 432 BC), Brunt 1951 (1993), arguing that it should be before the Corcyrean affair (below) because of Thucydides' neglect of it, and there it helps to explain the existing tension to which Thucydides alludes in the Corcyrean debate (1.33.3, 1.35.4, 1.36.1, 1.44.2, and esp. 1.42.2, with Gomme and Hornblower *ad loc.*). For collections of literature on the Megarian Decree, Meyer 1997 p. 26; Pébarthe 2000 n. 130; adding Podlecki 1998 pp. 140–2. Athenian feelings high against Megara after 446, Legon 1968 p. 213.

73. Corcyra vs. Corinth, 1.25; "raised up," 1.25.4; cf. 1.38.2–5. Thucydides gives his descriptions of Corcyra an Homeric flavor, Mackie 1996 pp. 103–5. Old conflict between Corcyra and Corinth, 1.13.4; cf. Hdt. 3.49–53; Plut. *Them.* 24.1.

74. Epidamnus takes Corinth as mother city: justifiable because the actual founder of Epidamnus was a Corinthian whom the Corcyreans had summoned from their mother city according to custom, and some of those who had settled there had been Corinthian; Delphi approved the transfer as well (1.25.1–3). "Flew into a rage" and "insulting," 1.26.3, with Crane 1998 pp. 93–105. On the Corcyrean affair, Intrieri 2002 pp. 12–65 gathers the literature.

75. Corcyra has the better of the war, 1.26.3–1.30.4 (Corinth's anger, 1.31.1; cf. 1.38.5). Altars of Necessity and Force at Corinth, Paus. 2.4.6. Corcyreans plead at Athens, 1.31.1–1.44.1. Athenians send help to Corcyra, 1.44.1–1.45.3, 1.53; for the costs of this expedition (alas, the figures are mangled), Tod² 55 = ML 61 = Fornara 126.

76. Fear of power in the Corcyrean debate at Athens, 1.33.2, 1.35.5, 1.36.3, 1.44.2. On the speeches Thucydides writes for the Corcyrean and Corinthian envoys (1.32–43), Crane 1998 pp. 105–24; Rood 2006. For speeches in Thucydides, and how I have used them, appendix pp. 420–2. The Athenian decision to help Corcyra (or slightly before) is one traditional context for at least the first of the two so-called Callias Decrees (Tod² 51 = ML 58 = Fornara 119) regulating the treasuries of Athens. Scholars have quarreled over their dates for over a century (for the controversy, Samons 2000 pp. 122–38, 219–30: he locates the first document in early 432 BC and the second in 422/1). In the first decree a huge sum of money (3,000 talents) is noted as having been moved to the Athenian Acropolis; debts to the gods are ordered to be paid from it and the rest spent on Athens' dockyards and walls. Were the Athenians preparing for war? But I leave these documents out of consideration because (1) none of the dating arguments seem strong, and (2) given the lack of *comparanda*, the significance of the arrangements ordered is unclear: the Athenians may have done things like this frequently. Also often related to Corcyra are Athens' striking or renewals of her alliances with Rhegium (on the toe of Italy; Tod² 58 = ML 63 = Fornara 124) and Leontini (in Sicily; Tod² 57 = ML 64 = Fornara 125), firmly dated to 433/2. Can a secret history of Athens' interest in the west be deduced from these treaties (see esp. Wick 1976)? But Athens will have made or renewed many dozens of treaties a year, and it is mere accident that these happened to be inscribed (most treaties were not) and have survived. So we can deduce nothing about special Athenian interest in the west from them.

77. Battle of Sybota, 1.46.1–1.49.4 ("old, imperfect armament," 1.49.1), Crawley's translation. On this battle, Wilson 1987 pp. 35–64.

78. For where the Corcyrean pursuit ended up (a puzzle presented by Thucydides' account of this battle, Gomme *ad loc.* 1.50.3, 3.76), Wilson 1987 pp. 37–47. Corinthians prevail over the Corcyrean right: the Corinthians were on the left of their line (1.48.4, 1.49.6), and their allies on the right. This, too, is a puzzle (Wilson 1987 p. 45; Lazenby 2004 p. 24) because the state leading a coalition usually held the honorable right in a line of battle. But Hammond 1945 (1973) p. 33 saw that this resulted from a meeting engagement involving an evolution from a single-file north-south line of passage into a perpendicular east-west line of battle: since the Corinthians were leading (as their status required) north with the coast to their east, they necessarily ended up on the left when the fleet formed line of battle to the west. Athenians intervene at Sybota, 1.49.4–7.

79. Killing survivors on the wrecks after Sybota, 1.50.1. Revenge as a motive suggested by Hammond 1945 (1973) p. 35. Thuc. 1.54.2 has the Corcyreans

lose nearly 70 ships and the Corinthians about 30 at Sybota, but as Gomme (*ad loc.* 1.54.2) notes, that would make it most unlikely that the Corcyreans, reduced to *ca.* 60 ships, would continue to challenge the *ca.* 120 on the Corinthian side. The figure has become corrupt.

80. Array for second battle on day of Sybota, events at night, 1.50.3–1.51.5. Reinforcing squadron arrives: which means the battle lines of the aborted second battle must also have been oriented east-west, so that the Corinthians, to the south, would see the arriving ships from the south first (*pace* Hammond 1945 [1973] p. 55; Gomme *ad loc.* 1.51.2; Wilson 1987 pp. 51–2).

81. Day after Sybota, 1.52–3; supplies, 1.48.1.

82. "You act unjustly" and what follows, 1.53.2.

83. Trophies after Sybota, 1.54. Corinth feared to break the treaty: the Spartans thought the Corcyreans in the right against Corinth (1.28.1), so their support of Corinth could not be taken for granted.

84. "First ground of complaint" (*aitia*) and "another point of difference" (*diaphora*), 1.55.2–1.56.2.

85. On the origins of the Potidaean affair, 1.56.2–1.57.6, with Salmon 1984 pp. 292–6 for the political and Lazenby 2004 pp. 26–7 for the military aspects. The tribute lists may imply tensions between Athens and Potidaea earlier, Hornblower i pp. 97–9. On these obscure doings in Macedonia, Cole 1974; Badian 1993d pp. 172–9.

86. Potidaeans send envoys to Athens, Spartan promise to Potidaea, 1.58.1; cf. 1.71.4.

87. Revolt of Potidaea, Chalcidians, help of Perdiccas, Corinthians, 1.57–60. For the "Chalcidian League" now founded by the rebels, Psoma 2001.

88. Athens moves against Potidaea, Chalcidians and Perdiccas prepare, 1.61.1–1.62.3.

89. Battle, and subsequent siege, of Potidaea, 1.62.4–1.64.3. Alcibiades and Socrates at Potidaea, Plato, *Symp.* 220d–e. The poetic memorial to the Athenian fallen survives on a mutilated stone, Tod^2 59 = *IG* I^3 1179.

90. Potidaea a new *aitia*, 1.66.1.

91. Sparta's allies summoned to Sparta, 1.67.1. "I see war," Plut. *Per.* 8.5.

92. Sparta described as being hostile to Athens, both in Thucydides' narrative, 1.44.2, and speeches, 1.33.3, 1.140.2. Complaints against Athens, 1.67.2–4, 2.27.1. Aegina, cf. Plut. *Per.* 29.4. On the rights and wrongs of Aegina's claims (an exceedingly dark matter), Figueira 1990. Corinth's allies at Sybota, Thuc. 1.46.1.

93. Thucydides writes a set of four speeches for this Spartan debate (1.68–86), on which Bloedow 1981; Crane 1998 pp. 196–236, 258–85; and for the literature, Meier 2006 nn. 154, 166, 172, 175. The first two speeches, those of the Corinthians (1.68–71) and the Athenians (1.73–8), mostly address the question "Should we fight?" although "Assuming that we will fight, when should we do so?" also arises (1.71.1, 1.71.4, 1.78); in the latter two speeches,

those of Archidamus (1.80–5, from which I take his arguments in the text) and the ephor Sthenelaidas (1.86), the war is for the most part assumed, and "when?" is the primary issue (esp. 1.82–3, 1.85–6), although arguments for and against going to war at all are also rehearsed (see Moxon 1978 p. 9). Although Thucydides is opposed to interpreting the outbreak of the war in terms of revenge, revenge and related concepts creep into the debate—the *hybris* of the Athenians (1.68.2), the need to avenge (1.69.2, 1.86.2–3) and to act "worthily of Sparta" (1.86.5)—and the later Corinthian speech urging the allies to war: again, revenge (1.121.1, 5; cf. 1.141.7). On the Spartan vote for war, 1.87, with Flaig 1993 and Lendon 2001. Delphi, "if they made war," 1.118.3. Did Apollo respond so eagerly to curry favor because he had heard rumors of Peloponnesian plans to "borrow" his Delphic treasures to fund the war (1.121.3, 1.143.1)?

94. Spartans summon allies again, 1.119.1–1.125.1. On this meeting, Lendon 1994 esp. pp. 174–6, with literature on the speech Thucydides (1.120–4) writes for the Corinthians. "A war undertaken by an alliance," 1.82.6. Prewar agreement between Sparta and her allies, 5.30–1, with Busolt 3.2 p. 857; Lendon 1994 pp. 160–7.

95. "During that time," 1.126.1. Sparta's fear of power stronger than Athenian persuasion, 1.88. Meeting toward the end of the summer: for the date of the congress of Sparta's allies, one has a choice between the received text of Thucydides—attack on Plataea in early April 431 BC (because two months are left in the archon year, 2.2.1), the invasion of Attica eighty days after that, in June (2.19.1), and the battle of Potidaea seven months before, in October 432 (2.2.1), and so the Spartan vote for war and the congress of allies at Sparta in succession after that (so Thompson 1968, endorsed by Hornblower *ad loc.* 2.2.1). Or (with Gomme i pp. 421–5) one can adduce corruptions in the numbers in the manuscript and prefer a schedule that works better with the implications of Thucydides' account, especially his statement that the attack on Attica was "nearly a year" between the congress of allies at Sparta and the invasion of Attica (1.125.2), and the desperate haste that drives the Corinthians (1.67.1, 1.119, 1.120.1; cf. 1.86.3), who are presented as thinking an immediate invasion of Attica is possible (1.71.4). This implies that the campaigning season is not over, an implication supported by a sense that Greeks did not tend to have battles and major gatherings in the winter. On this dating, the battle of Potidaea dates to June 432, the Spartan decision to early July, the congress of allies to early August, and the attack on Plataea to early March 431. That puts the invasion of Attica in May. I accept with Thompson 1968 and Busolt (3.2 p. 799 n. 1) the numbers in the text that place Plataea in April 431 and the invasion of Attica in June, but concur with Busolt and Gomme that the "in the eighth month" figure must be corrupt: it pushes the battle of Potidaea and the meetings at Sparta too late into the year. I concur with Gomme and Busolt in putting the battle of Potidaea in June 432. The conference and declaration of

war are then dated by how long one thinks it took Greeks to organize two successive meetings at Sparta, but should be as early as possible (1) to get as "nearly" to a year to June 431 as possible, and (2) to account for the sense of Corinthian urgency, which implies that the campaigning season was not over. Gomme guesses early August for the congress of the allies; Busolt 3.2 p. 841 guesses late August or early September. I do not think July is out of the question. All the literature is gathered and discussed by Fantasia *ad loc.* 2.2.1.

96. Why so long a delay before actual hostilities? The Peloponnesians may have decided it was too late in the year to launch a campaign (although Thucydides represents the Corinthians as claiming that an immediate invasion of Attica was possible, 1.71.4). Alternatively, as Moxon 1978 pp. 12–13 argued, although Archidamus had been defeated in the Spartan assembly, the Spartans may nevertheless have adopted the strategy he advocates in the speech Thucydides gives him (1.80–5) of delaying the start of hostilities, either because they had a change or heart or because Archidamus, the only available king, used his powerful constitutional position as war leader to delay their action: even once the campaign was underway, he was, Thucydides says, still looking for ways to delay crossing the Attic border (2.18.3–5).

97. Spartans demand Athenians drive out curse, 1.126–7; "in any respect," 1.126.1; cf. 1.82.1. Athenians "retort," 1.128.1; cf. 1.135.1, 1.139.1. Marr 1998 and Rhodes 2005 p. 86 ingeniously speculate that both these Spartan curses attached to the Spartan king Archidamus, which would again emphasize the reciprocity of the Athenian response.

98. "They commanded the Athenians," 1.139.1. Ar. *Ach.* 536–9; Andoc. 3.8; Aeschin. 2.175; Diod. Sic. 12.39.4; and Plut. *Per.* 29.5 confirm the special importance of the Megarian Decree to the Spartans.

99. Athens refused to "submit" (*hupakouō*) to Sparta's demands, 1.139.2. Turn Megarian Decree to wall, Plut. *Per.* 30.1; Ar. *Ach.* 537. Advice of Pericles, Thuc. 1.140.5–1.141.1 (for Pericles' speech [1.140–4], Bloedow 1981 pp. 131–5, with Meier 2006 n. 94 for the literature). "Not yield," 1.140.1. "Learn to deal with you as equals," 1.140.5; cf. 2.64.3; and 1.34.1 where the Corcyreans claim to be the "equals" of the Corinthians. Thucydides has Pericles propose in his speech a set of aggressive tit-for-tat retorts to the Spartan demands: Athens will retract the Megarian Decree *if* Sparta abolishes her laws forbidding foreigners in Sparta; Athens will let her allies be autonomous *if* the Spartans do the same (1.144.2). "Simple rudeness" is how Lewis 1992b p. 379 describes them. We do not know if such retorts were included in the formal Athenian reply (or indeed how much credit is to be given to them, since they are presented in a speech). But if they are historical, they suggest Athens' intractability over her rank. On the intransigence of Pericles, Samons 2004 p. 127. Aristophanes (*Ach.* 541–54) confirms the Athenian hard line. "Nothing at command," 1.145. Equals cannot yield to commands, 1.141.1, 5.111.4; cf. 1.77.4.

100. Spartans regret rejecting arbitration, 7.18.2–3. Corcyra offers Corinth arbitration, 1.28.2; cf. 1.34.2, 1.39.1–2. For the connection of refusal to accept arbitration and rage at another party's getting above themselves, cf. 4.122.5. Accepting arbitration humiliating, [Dem.] 7.8.

101. Let the Greeks be autonomous, 1.139.3; cf. 2.8.4. For this as a Spartan slogan rather than a serious demand (which explains why Thucydides presents Pericles as more concerned with the Megarian Decree, the main complaint of the previous embassy), Nesselhauf 1934 p. 293. For the antecedents and afterlife of the slogan, Prandi 1976; Price 2001 pp. 128–38, 145–7. In fact, during the Ten Years' War, the Spartans showed no interest in a program of general liberation of the Athenian empire.

102. Power and prosperity thought to lead to *hybris*, e.g., 3.39.4, 3.45.4, 4.18.2; Hdt. 5.91; Dem. 1.23, with Romilly 1977 pp. 46–7.

103. Athens' pretension justified in Thucydides' speeches, 2.41, 2.61.4, 2.63–4. Sparta wants a bone, Samons 2004 p. 249 n. 31. Nothing unusual, nothing improper: it follows that I concur with Eckstein 2006 pp. 72–5 (n. 143 for literature arguing the contrary) and Hunt 2010 pp. 51–61 (n. 1 for literature) in not granting causal importance to an exceptional Athenian militarism born of democracy. Athens was not provably more militaristic than other Greek states, and any Greek state, in her circumstances, would have acted as she did.

CHAPTER III:
THE WAR OF REVENGE, 431–430 BC

1. Copaïc eels, Ar. *Ach.* 880–94; *Pax* 1003–14. Lost cities of Copaïs, Paus. 9.24.1–2; Strabo 9.2.16–18, 9.2.35; for the archeological evidence, Buck 1979 p. 3. The best description of Lake Copaïs before it was drained in the 1890s is that of Frazer vol. 5 pp. 112–13.

2. Plataea founded by Thebes, 3.61.2; this origin denied by the Plataeans, Paus. 9.1.1–2. On relations, Hammond 1992 pp. 143–5.

3. Attack on Plataea, 2.2–6; cf. 3.65–6. On how Thucydides tells the story, Stahl 2003 pp. 65–73 and Pelling 2000 pp. 67–9. [Dem.] 59.98–101 has a slightly muddled adaptation of Thucydides' version of the story, on which Pelling 2000 pp. 61–7. Attack after a sacred day, Thuc. 3.56.2; moon, 2.4.2. For the date of the attack on Plataea, see chapter 2 n. 95. Hdt. 7.233 gives 400 rather than Thucydides' 300 Theban invaders.

4. On the alleged Plataean oath to spare the Thebans and its possible consequences, West 2003 vs. Hornblower 2007. For the killing of the Thebans as revenge, 3.56.2.

5. Theban quibble about Plataea: reasoning from 3.52.2 and 4.17.2. Sparta's agreement with her allies, 5.31.5 and see above p. 101. Plataea put the Spartans in the wrong, 7.18.2.

6. Boeotians at Athens arrested, 2.6.2. The Athenians knew the value of such hostages, 1.113.2.

7. Treaty "glaringly violated," 2.7.1. The argument of Price 2001 p. 287 that Thebes was not an ally of Sparta, and so the glaringly violated treaty was a purely local one, seems unlikely in light of 7.18.2. Soft, winking words, cf. 3.65.2–3. The same excuse was offered by the Corinthians at Potidaea, 1.60.

8. On the Athenian and Spartan alliances, 2.9, and for Sparta and her alliance, see p. 33.

9. On Athens and her alliance, see pp. 47–51. Athens' 300 ships, 2.13.8; Xen. *An.* 7.1.27. Athens' land army, Thuc. 2.13.6–8; the garrisons were 16,000 strong, made up of older and younger men; these figures (Fantasia *ad loc.* 2.13.6–7 gathers the literature) are successfully defended by van Wees 2004 pp. 241–3. For a full discussion of Athens' resources, Busolt 3.2 pp. 867–91. For the cleruchs of Lemnos and Imbros, 3.5.1, 4.28.4, 5.8.2, 7.57.2, with Meiggs 1972 pp. 424–5.

10. Approximately 6,000 Laconian hoplites at the battle of Mantinea in 418 BC, reached by very fancy ciphering from Thuc. 5.68.3, see Hornblower *ad loc.*; van Wees 2004 pp. 243–9; of these 6,000, some 40 percent will have been full Spartan citizens (van Wees p. 84; see below chapter 7 n. 38). For the full force of Sparta's alliance, Busolt 3.2 p. 860 guesses 30,000 for two-thirds of the full levy of each state (Kagan 1974 p. 19 n. 9, himself accepting Busolt's estimate, lists others). Plutarch (*Per.* 33.4), with what justification we cannot guess, gives two-thirds of the full Peloponnesian strength at 60,000. For a full discussion of the military resources of the Spartan alliance, Busolt 3.2 pp. 854–67.

11. Requests for aid by the combatants, 2.7. Gomme *ad loc.* 2.7.2 wonders whether 500 ships is a textual corruption; Diod. Sic. 12.41.1 seems to have read 200 in the version available to him. Mainland Greeks ignorant of the west, esp. 6.1.1.

12. Spartans in Attica in 446 BC, 1.114.2, 1.115.1. Yield to prevent being ravaged, 4.84.1, 4.87.2 (with a statement of the principle); Xen. *Hell.* 4.6.4–4.7.1; cf. Thuc. 2.71.1; expectation that the victim will yield after ravaging, 2.66.2, 3.88.4, 3.91.3; Xen. *Mem.* 2.1.13.

13. On the difficulty of doing economic damage by ravaging, Hanson 1998 (1983). Even Hanson's severest critic, Thorne 2001, who attempted to defend the general economic efficacy of ravaging, admitted that it could have no decisive effect upon mercantile Athens (pp. 252–3). We are in fact told (*Hell. Oxy.* 17.5) that the Peloponnesians did little damage to the Attic countryside during this Ten Years' War.

14. For losses in Greek battle, Krentz 1985a; Dayton 2006 pp. 80–102.

15. For the rank consequences of ravaging, Lendon 2007 n. 14, adding Dem. 1.27; Lycurg. *Leoc.* 47; Isoc. 8.77. The idea goes back to Ober 1985 p. 34; cf. van Wees 2004 p. 123.

16. "In a few years," 5.14.3; "some of the Greeks," 7.28.3.

17. Athenian and Peloponnesian preparations for the invasion of Attica, 2.10–17. Thucydides writes a speech for the Spartan king Archidamus (2.11), on which see Hunter 1973 pp. 11–21. Spartan envoy to Athens, 2.12; "great evils," 2.12.3, with Hornblower *ad loc.*

18. Attack on Oenoe, 2.18.1–2.19.1, with Gomme *ad loc.* 2.18.1. On the question "Why attack Oenoe?" Bloedow 1983 p. 30 gathers the literature. For the location of Oenoe, Munn 2002 n. 6. And Munn discusses how Oenoe might or might not be regarded as part of Attica, and so when exactly Thucydides thought the war formally began (Plataea? Oenoe? Eleusis?), on which also Hornblower i pp. 236–7; Price 2001 pp. 277–89; Fantasia pp. 228–9. Boeotian claim on Oenoe: deducing from Hdt. 5.74; Thuc. 8.98; a situation similar to Oropos to the east, see Hornblower *ad loc.* 2.23.3.

19. War only came to exist upon invasion of Attica: Price 2001 pp. 283–4 is sound. Boeotian cavalry in Attica, 2.12.5.

20. "Yielding anything" (*endōsein ti*), 2.18.5. For rams at Oenoe (Thucydides says *mēchanai*, "engines"), see Hornblower *ad loc.* 2.18.1.

21. Peloponnesian march into Attica, 2.19–20. Fields of Eleusis, Paus. 1.38.6, with Frazer *ad loc.*

22. Archidamus draws up for battle, 2.20.1, accepting and explaining *es machēn taxamenon* ("drew up for battle"), sometimes doubted by editors (see Gomme *ad loc.*).

23. "Deeming themselves worthy," 2.11.8. For possible arguments that refusing to fight under these circumstances was not humiliating (the need to make them shows that it was), below p. 134.

24. Controversy at Athens about response to invasion, 2.21.

25. No assembly at Athens, 2.22.1. How did Pericles prevent it? See Bloedow 1987.

26. Pericles offers to surrender his property, 2.13.1; Plut. *Per.* 33.2. Cleon, Plut. *Per.* 33.6–34.1.

27. Athenian cavalry patrols: Ober 1985 (1996) and Spence 1990 (2007) argued for aggressive use of cavalry to limit the damage done by Peloponnesian ravagers in Attica. But Samons 2004 p. 250 pointedly wonders why, if the cavalry was so important in Attica, Pericles took 300 of them on his raiding expedition in 430 BC, when the Peloponnesians were still ravaging the Attic countryside. Athenian and Thessalian cavalry vs. Boeotian, 2.22.2–3. Thucydides' account of the presence of the Thessalians "according to the ancient alliance" (2.22.3) is puzzling because of the catalogue of Thessalian towns he then gives. The implication is that Thessaly was divided in its loyalties, and this is confirmed by the march of Brasidas in 424 (4.78). As Gomme *ad loc.* notes, the Thessalians are not listed among the Athenian allies in 2.9.4 and never come to help the Athenians again. Pausanias (1.29.6) saw at Athens the tomb of the Thessalians who died on this occasion.

28. Peloponnesians march west through Attica, 2.23. On Greek logistics, van Wees 2004 pp. 104–8. On Oropus, see Hornblower *ad loc.* 2.23.3. Ravaging Plataea, 2.12.5. Length of time in Attica: Kagan 1974 p. 57 gathers the estimates.

29. Athenian defensive measures after the 431 BC Peloponnesian invasion, 2.24. For the strategy of Pericles, 2.65.7; cf. 1.144.1, 2.13.2, and for discussion below p. 168–71. Wars of extermination arise from revenge, Lendon 2000 p. 15; van Wees 2010.

30. 431 BC Athenian raiding expedition, 2.23.2. For Athens' allies in the northwest, 2.7.3. Acarnanian slings, 2.81.8.

31. Athenian raiding in the 450s BC, 1.108.5, 1.111.2–3, and see pp. 69–70. "Humble the fame of the Spartans" (*tapeinōsein de tēn tōn Spartiatōn doxan*), Diod. Sic. 11.84.3. "Reprisal" (*timōrian*) and "revenge" (*timōreisthai*), Thuc. 2.42.4; cf. 1.142.4. Aristophanes, Ar. *Ach.* 221–36; cf. 509–11; *Pax* 626. Compare raiding Laconia in 394, Xen. *Hell.* 4.8.6–7. Scholars (Grundy 1948 [1911] pp. 331, 335; Adcock 1927 p. 198; Lewis 1992b pp. 381, 388) have noticed the revenge theme in the texts but have been at a loss to understand it: was it to raise Athenian morale?

32. Damage caused by Athenians less, but hardly trivial, if the vast crews of the triremes participated in the ravaging. There was a tradition that the Athenians did more damage than the Spartans, Justin, *Epit.* 3.7.4–5; Polyaen. *Strat.* 1.36.1; cf. Plut. *Per.* 34.2, who vaguely implies that the damage was equal. [Xen.] *Ath. pol.* 2.4 discusses the insolent ease of ravaging from the sea. Athenians can claim to cause more pain, 1.143.4. Speed important in revenge, 3.38.1, a principle going back to Homer, Lendon 2000 p. 10. "Not go long unpaid," Hom. *Il.* 14.483–4. Why so many ships and such expense, especially if (as argued here) this was essentially a symbolic act? Rhodes II *ad loc.* 2.25.1 gathers the opinions, and see below p. 293 for discussion of the need that ravaging be laborious. But the Athenians may also have felt that they needed to take enough ships to win a sea battle. The Peloponnesians had a fleet of at least 100 ships (2.66), and the last time the Athenians had faced Corinth and her allies at Sybota, the Peloponnesian fleet was of 150 (1.46.1). The Athenians could not at this stage of the war know that the Peloponnesians would not challenge them to battle; nor could they be certain how great their advantage in quality was. After the first two years, when the Athenians raided with 150 ships (100 of their own, 50 belonging to allies), they contented themselves with fewer.

33. Athenian revenge on those who began the war, cf. 1.78.4. "Deal with you as equals," 1.140.5; for the history of this concept, see chapter 1 n. 66.

34. Or, "since Sparta had been the aggressor, a draw formally acknowledging the status quo was equivalent to an Athenian victory," Raaflaub 2007 p. 101; cf. Cartledge 2002 (1979) p. 202.

35. Itinerary of the Athenian raid, 2.25. "Doing ill," 2.25.1. Diod. Sic. 12.43.1 adds, on what basis we do not know, that the Athenians raided Acte,

perhaps meaning Sparta's allies on the Argolid peninsula (see Gomme *ad loc.* 2.25.1).

36. On the Greek trireme, Morrison *et al.* 2000, on the basis of the construction and sea trials of the reconstructed trireme *Olympias*. See Basch 1987 pp. 265–302 for a catalogue of pre-*Olympias* reconstructions of the Greek trireme (and his is the fullest collection of ancient images of triremes and pre-trireme craft). Papalas (forthcoming) offers the fullest catalogue to date of criticisms made of the *Olympias* design; the most systematic attack on *Olympias* is that of Tilley 2004. For an optimistic evaluation of *Olympias*' sailing qualities (she was tested in rather gentle conditions), Lindsay (forthcoming).

37. Tight quarters and arrangements for eating, Casson 1995. Triremes anchor (rather than pull up on shore) for the night, Harrison 1999. On the water needs of a trireme, the rowers of the reconstructed *Olympias* needed one liter per rower per hour (Coates and Morrison 1993 p. 108; for watering ancient warships, Sleeswyk and Meijer 1998). With 170 rowers and eight-hour rowing days, that is nearly a ton and a half a day; *Olympias* weighs only 27.5 tons. Xen. *Hell.* 6.2.27–30 is the fullest account of triremes landing on a hostile shore to see to their needs: even in a hurry, when the men slept on the boats, triremes might land for two meals a day. Athenian attack on Pheia, 2.25.3–5.

38. Athenian attack on Methone, 2.25.1–2, with Hornblower *ad loc.* Brasidas elected ephor, Xen. *Hell.* 2.3.10. For the sights of Methone, Paus. 4.35, with Frazer *ad loc.*

39. For the exchange of good offices between states, Low 2007 pp. 36–54; van Wees 2004 pp. 10–12; Hunt 2010 pp. 192–7. For the honor of helping, Missiou 1992 pp. 111–39; Azoulay 2004 pp. 52–60, 76–8. For the dishonor of failing to help, Lendon 2006 pp. 91–5; Hunt 2010 p. 193. Attacking Methone, although a Lacedaemonian possession, could also shame Sparta for her inability to help her friends, for the folk of Methone were exiles from Nauplia in the Argolid, driven out by the Argives (Paus. 4.24.4, 4.35.2) and settled at Methone by the Spartans.

40. Athenian fleet in the northwest, 2.30. The location of Sollium has not been established, but it is generally thought to lie on the Plagia peninsula stretching toward Leucas, Berktold and Faisst 1993.

41. Athenians against Opuntian Locris, 2.26.

42. Athenian expulsion of Aeginetans, 2.27.1.

43. Settlement of Aeginetans by Sparta, 2.27.2. Aeginetan complaints to Sparta, 1.67.2. Spartan gratitude, cf. 4.56.2. On Spartan gratitude here and elsewhere in the war, see esp. Missiou 1998. Diod. Sic. 12.44.3 adduces a different reciprocity: revenge upon the Athenians because they had settled the Messenians at Naupactus. Battle of Champions at Thyrea, Hdt. 1.82, with Lendon 2005 pp. 39–57. Argos wants Thyrea, Thuc. 5.14.4. Settling Aeginetans to mollify the Argives: so Figueira 1988 pp. 528–9, arguing, at pp. 525–6, that the Aeginetans were granted the status of *perioeci* by the Spartans. In the summer of 431 BC, the

Athenians also made a treaty with Sitalces, a mighty king in Thrace (2.29). On this, in the context of later fighting in the north, see below pp. 326–7.

44. 431 BC Athenian invasion of Megara, 2.31. Athens/Megara borderlands, Paus. 1.39.2–3.

45. Athenians invade Megara twice per year, 4.66.1; Plut. *Per.* 30.3, on which chapter 6 n. 9.

46. Sore pain to Megara, 4.66.1; Paus. 1.40.4. Lack of help from allies, Thuc. 4.72.2. Decree about attacking Megara, Plut. *Per.* 30.3.

47. Pericles' funeral oration, 2.35–46; Grethlein 2005 pp. 41–2 gathers the gigantic literature on this speech.

48. Athenian reasoning that they are not losing, 2.39, on which Krentz 1997 p. 69.

49. On the importance of the fair fight for rank, chapter 2 n. 52. For the importance of fighting alone to establish rank, chapter 2 n. 23. Spartan logic, 2.39.3. Pericles urges rededication, 2.43.

50. Corinthians in the northwest of Greece, 2.33.

51. Second Peloponnesian invasion of Attica, 2.47, 2.55, 2.57.

52. Spartans spare northeast of Attica, Diod. Sic. 12.45.1; Decelea, Hdt. 9.73. There is no reason to think (*pace* Hornblower *ad loc.* 3.26.3) that the Peloponnesians ever ravaged these areas during the Ten Years' War. Leda's egg at Sparta, Paus. 3.16.1.

53. "Ravaged the whole country," 2.57.2. Destruction of wealthy houses, 2.65.2; on Athenian affection for their rural temples, 2.16.2. Will 1975 p. 302 (picked up by van Wees 2004 p. 36) emphasizes the desire to protect holy sites as a motive for the invaded to come out and fight. For need to defend tombs and temples, also Hunt 2010 pp. 141–3.

54. Peloponnesians see smoke, question runaway slaves, 2.57.1. The plague and its effects, 2.47.3–2.54.5. For medical speculations on the nature of the plague, Schmitz 2005 pp. 54–9 gathers the literature. There will be more by now, likely just as futile. For Thucydides' description of the plague, the literature is gathered by Meier 2006 n. 113. For the long-term effects of the plague on Athens' war effort, Hanson 2005 pp. 78–82. What are believed to be mass graves into which the dead from the plague were thrown have recently been discovered during the construction of the Athens metro: Tritle 2010 p. 49.

55. "Those claiming excellence," 2.51.5. For the conditions of the poor, 2.17.

56. Apollo to help "asked or unasked," 1.118.3. For the religious understanding of the plague, 2.54, 2.64.1; cf. Paus. 10.11.5, with Furley 1996 pp. 79–80; Rubel 2000 pp. 120–45.

57. Pericles' raiding expedition in 430 BC, 2.56; Plut. *Per.* 35.

58. Asclepius and the goats, Paus. 2.26.4. Attack Epidaurus for access to Asclepius: Mikalson 1984 p. 220 (endorsed by Fantasia *ad loc.* 2.56.4). On the establishment of the Athenian shrine to Asclepius at Athens soon after the Ten Years' War, see further Rubel 2000 pp. 244–9.

59. Troezen: hole, Paus. 2.31.2; olive tree, 2.31.10. Mount Cuckoo, 2.36.2; Hermione, 2.35.4–7, 10. The source for these anecdotes, and many of the other local rites, customs, and myths recounted in this book, is Pausanias, who lived in the second century AD. It is rarely possible to establish the antiquity of what Pausanias describes. I offer these details to give the reader a sense of place, and if these local oddities did not exist in the late fifth century BC, others just as odd did.

60. "Oh Prasiae!" Ar. *Pax* 242.

61. On the revolt of Potidaea, see above pp. 97–100. Expense of the siege of Potidaea, 2.70.2. "Ambition for honor" (*philotimoumenos*), Diod. Sic. 12.46.2.

62. 430 BC Athenian expedition to Potidaea, 2.58.

63. 430 BC Peloponnesian expedition against Zacynthus, 2.66; for the Spartan motivation, cf. the next year, 2.80.1.

64. 430 BC political situation at Athens, 2.59. Spread and timing of plague, 2.54.5; Plut. *Per.* 36.3.

65. "Much ill," Plut. *Per.* 34.2.

66. Athenians send envoys to Sparta, 2.59.2. Diod. Sic. 12.45.5 says that the Spartans "took no heed" of them, but this is presumably only a gloss on Thucydides' vague "the envoys were ineffectual" (2.59.2).

67. Pericles' 430 BC speech, 2.60–4, on which Romilly 1963 pp. 147–52; recent literature is gathered by Meier 2006 pp. 142–4. "Obedience" and "submission," 2.61.1, 2.62.3. As code words, cf. 1.141.1, 1.143.1, 3.10–11, and esp. 2.63.1. For slavery used in this metaphorical sense in Thucydides, cf. 5.29.3, 5.69.1, 5.100; Gomme *ad loc.* 5.9.9. For mobilization of the slavery metaphor in fourth-century speeches about foreign affairs, Hunt 2010 pp. 109–17.

68. No further Athenian offers of peace, fine, reelection of Pericles (presumably for the next year; not a special election, Kagan 1974 p. 93), 2.65. Charge of corruption, Plato, *Gorg.* 516a (also implied by the defense on this point Thucydides has him make at 2.60.5–6). Fine, Diod. Sic. 12.45.4; Plut. *Per.* 35.3–4. On the legal process (very obscure), Stadter *ad loc.* 35.4; Fantasia *ad loc.* 2.65.3, with literature.

69. Peloponnesian mission to the Great King, Sitalces, killing of the envoys, 2.67. Relationship between Argos and Persia, Hdt. 7.150–1.

70. The story of the curse on the Spartan envoys is at Hdt. 7.133–7. Characteristically, Thucydides does not tell it. The Spartans kept trying to interest the Persians in helping them (4.50), but without success in the Ten Years' War.

CHAPTER IV: ODYSSEUS' WAR, 429–428 BC

1. Fall of Potidaea, 2.70.

2. Connection between Potidaea and invasions of Attica, 2.70.1.

3. Garrison of Plataea, 2.78.3. Did fear of the plague discourage an invasion of Attica this year (so Kagan 1974 p. 102 and others)? But, as Thucydides

points out (2.57), it had not made the Peloponnesians cut short their invasion the previous year, the longest of the war. On the question of "why Plataea in 429 BC?" Bloedow 1983 p. 42 gathers the literature.

4. Plataea allied to Athens, Hdt. 6.108; Thuc. 3.55.1. The exact date of the alliance is controversial (see Badian 1993f p. 117). Spartan honors to Plataea after the battle of Plataea, 2.71.2–3, 3.58.4–5, 3.68.1–2; Paus. 9.2.5–6; Plut. *Arist.* 20.4–6.

5. Colloquy between Archidamus and the Plataeans, 2.71–73.2, with Pelling 2000 pp. 72–4.

6. Plataeans refuse the Spartan offer, 2.73.2–74.1.

7. Archidamus' reply to the Plataeans, 2.74.2; revenge (*timōria*), 2.74.3.

8. Peloponnesian assault on Plataea, 2.75–8, and (brief and embroidered), [Dem.] 59.101–2. The figure of seventy days given in the manuscript for the construction of the Peloponnesian ramp (Thuc. 2.75.3) is corrupt, Gomme and Hornblower *ad loc.*

9. On *andreia*, Smoes 1995 and the papers collected in Rosen and Sluiter 2003. For *mētis*, Lendon 2005 p. 411 gathers the literature; for *mētis* and craftsmanship, Lendon 2005 p. 112 n. 32.

10. On this divine intervention at Plataea (2.77.6) and Thucydides' attitude to it, Hornblower 2007 p. 145.

11. Fortifications around Plataea fully described at 3.21. Mid-September, 2.78.2.

12. Revenge must be reciprocal and proportionate, Hdt. 1.2, 9.64; Thuc. 3.66.2–4, 3.82.3, 7; Arist. *Rhet.* 1367a, 1378b, with Lendon 2000 pp. 16, 17. Excessive revenge, Hdt. 4.205. Athena *axiopoinos*, Paus. 3.15.6.

13. Winter 430/29 BC raiding expedition to Asia Minor, 2.69. This is the first sending of "silver-collecting" (*argurologoi*) ships, on which Kallet-Marx 1993 pp. 136–7, 160–4, who argues that they have nothing to do with the regular collection of tribute (a view endorsed by Hornblower ii p. 95). These were plundering raids (Kallet 1998 n. 8). Similar expeditions also go out in the winters of 428/7 and 425/4 and the summer of 424, and at least the second is also a plundering expedition (3.19), which also ends in disaster. For a detailed account of these expeditions, Keen 1993; and, for the Lycian point of view (an inscription survives, apparently showing official Persian involvement in the resistance), Thonemann 2009 pp. 171–9. Pausanias saw at Athens the tomb of the leader of this expedition, Paus. 1.29.7.

14. Ambracian plea to Sparta, 2.80.1.

15. "After that the Athenians," Spartan domino theory, 2.80.1. Cephallenia in 431 BC, 2.30.2; Ozolian Locris in 426 BC, 3.101.2.

16. Phormio stationed at Naupactus, 2.69. Why so small a force? see below p. 168.

17. War in Ambracia, 2.80–3.

18. For Phormio's first battle in 429 BC, 2.83–4.

19. For the trireme, chapter 3 n. 36. *Periplous*: for this interpretation, White-head 1987. For the circling dogfight of triremes, Shaw 1993 p. 99: ramming triremes did not need a great speed differential to do damage (pp. 99–100; cf. Oldfield [forthcoming]).

20. The *diekplous*: this interpretation builds upon Lazenby 1987, trying to answer the objection of Holladay 1988 (2002) that the *periplous* and *diekplous*, although mentioned as alternatives, seem too much alike in the reconstructions of Whitehead and Lazenby, but not accepting Holladay's suggestion that shear-ing the oars off opposing ships was the objective of the maneuver—although it will have happened incidentally often enough—a tactic for which there seems to be no evidence before Polyb. 16.4.14 and Diod. Sic. 11.18.6, 13.78.1 (Lazenby 1987 p. 169 does not believe in oar shearing). Cf. the Byzantine Anonymous (*Naumachia Syntaxthena para Basileiou Patrikiou kai Parakoimoumenou*; ed. and trans in Pryor and Jeffreys 2006), who (7.4), for what it is worth, defines *diekplous* as "when ships charge through the center of the enemy and then turn around and charge again" (cf. Schol. to Thuc. 1.49.3 [Hude p. 44]). Triremes' inability to move sideways: tried with the reconstructed *Olympias*, but not suc-cessful, Morrison *et al.* 2000 p. 248.

21. Greeks form circle at Artemisium, 480 BC, Hdt. 8.11. Persian ships more maneuverable, Hdt. 8.10.

22. The drift speeds of the reconstructed trireme *Olympias* have been mea-sured (Taylor [forthcoming]): in a 20-knot breeze, 3.4 knots with the boat stern to wind and 2.6 knots with the wind on the beam.

23. Spartan fleet at Leucas in 429 BC, Phormio asks for help, 2.80.2–3, 2.84.5–2.85.4. Why were so few ships sent? asks Kagan 1974 pp. 112–13. See below p. 168.

24. Diversion of Phormio's reinforcement to Crete, 2.85.5–6.

25. Why Crete? On this famously baffling episode, Herman 1989, with Geske 2005 p. 16 n. 9 for literature; cf. Fantasia *ad loc.* 2.85.5. Figueira 1988 pp. 538–42, noting that the Athenian target, Cydonia, was an Aeginetan col-ony, guesses that some of the Aeginetans the Athenians expelled in 431 BC had removed here and were troubling Athenian shipping.

26. Seventy-seven Peloponnesian ships: perhaps a textual corruption and the number Thucydides wrote was fifty-seven, Hornblower *ad loc.* 2.86.4. The strait at the mouth of the Gulf: Thucydides errs by giving the distance of seven stades (three-quarters of a mile) unless his text has been corrupted, Gomme *ad loc.* 2.86.3.

27. For this second sea battle of Phormio in 429 BC, 2.86–92. Thucydides writes speeches for the Peloponnesian commanders (2.87) and Phormio (2.89), on which Romilly 1956 pp. 138–50; Hunter 1973 pp. 43–60.

28. Phormio's victories: Pausanias (10.11.6; with Walsh 1986 pp. 326–8) saw dedications from these victories in the Stoa of the Athenians at Delphi. And this battle is perhaps the best context for an Athenian dedication at

Dodona (Dieterle 2007 pp. 92–3): "The Athenians, victorious in the sea-battle, dedicated this having taken it from the Peloponnesians."

29. Attempted raid on Piraeus, 2.93–4. For other interpretations of this episode, Falkner 1992; Badian 1999 pp. 4–5. For the lack of a ready squadron at Athens, see below pp. 166–7.

30. The raid on Salamis shows that a single night's sack could constitute a "ravaging" (*eporthoun*), 2.93.4.

31. Thucydides records two other events in this year, 429 BC: the Thracian king Sitalces' invasion of Macedonia and the Thracian Chalcidice (2.95–101), on which pp. 326–8, and an expedition of Phormio into Acarnania (2.102–3), p. 232.

32. Telling details about triremes, 2.93.1, 2.94.2–3.

33. Why no squadron ready at Piraeus? Because the Athenians did not expect an attack, says Thucydides (2.93.1, 3), showing that there was no permanent squadron: the Athenians would only have launched one if they expected an attack. Teredo worm, Ar. *Eq.* 1308; Lipke (forthcoming); Hale 2009 pp. 24–5. Become slow if left in water, 7.12.3; Morrison *et al.* 2000 pp. 276–9. Speed disadvantage from growths, etc.: Oldfield (forthcoming) shows that speed differentials well under a knot were enough to achieve a successful ramming, so even a small loss of speed could be disastrous.

34. Recaulking dry triremes, Morrison *et al.* 2000 pp. 182–8.

35. Phormio's reinforcement diverted to Crete, 2.85.5; 428 BC, 3.3.2; 425 BC, 4.2.3. Two weeks in 427, Busolt 3.2 p. 1046; thirty days in 406, Xen. *Hell.* 1.6.24.

36. Athenian reserve of 100 triremes, 2.24.2: note that Thucydides says that trierarchs were appointed for them, not that crews were hired. *Salaminia* and *Paralus*, 3.33.1, 3.77.3, 6.53.1, 6.61.4, 8.74.1. *Ath. pol.* 24.3 refers to twenty "guard ships" that the Athenians employed during the war, but the scant other references to such ships (see Rhodes *Comm.* Ath. pol. *ad loc.*) place them away from Athens (e.g., at Naupactus in 425 BC, Thuc. 4.13.2), and the other figures the *Ath. pol.* gives seem to be for Athens' peacetime establishment (Rhodes *Comm.* Ath. pol. pp. 305–6) or something else entirely.

37. Three years, Kagan 1974 p. 40 (and the method of calculation is his, p. 38, although his estimate, at 1,600 talents, is even higher; Busolt 3.2 p. 1016 arrived at the same estimate for how long Athens could support Pericles' strategy on a different basis); five or six years, Podlecki 1998 p. 145. Fantasia *ad loc.* 2.13.3–5 gathers and discusses the recent literature.

38. Pericles not such a fool: so it appeared to Thucydides, at any rate, who says that Pericles' estimate of the strength of Athens for the war was correct (2.65.5). Sixty ships for eight months, Plut. *Per.* 11.4. For this not being Athenian practice in war, cf. Samons 2000 p. 307; Pritchard 2007 n. 2. Thuc. 3.17.2 (even if not an interpolation, see Hornblower *ad loc.*) does not imply that Athens normally had 100 ships guarding "Attica, Euboea, and Salamis" but rather that these ships were sent out in response to the expected Peloponnesian attack by sea. The

theory offered here about naval wages explains an apparent anomaly in 3.17.2, the statement that the naval expenses of 428 BC were exceptionally high because the Athenians briefly had 250 ships at sea. They do not seem so high if one assumes that the fleets Athens sent out in the first years of the war were paid for eight months; but if they were not, 428 will indeed have seen the highest naval wage costs of the war. Athenians anxious about lack of naval practice, 3.115.4, with Gomme *ad loc*. For the lengths of Athenian naval expeditions from 431 to 426, Rosivach 1985 pp. 45–51, adjusted as necessary for 431 in accord with chapter 2 n. 95. Two talents per month per trireme, Gabrielsen 2008 p. 59.

39. The use of small squadrons on extended service continued: twenty ships to the west in 427 BC, 3.86; seven ships at Thasos in 424 BC, 4.104.5.

40. Death of Pericles and Thucydides' epitaph for him, 2.65.6–13, on which Westlake 1968 pp. 37–42; Will 2003 pp. 213–22. Recent literature is gathered by Meier 2006 pp. 144–8.

41. "If they would keep quiet," 2.65.7; cf. 1.144.1. "They should prepare for the war," 2.13.2. Krentz 1997 pp. 62–5 traces the precedents for this strategy at Athens.

42. Pflugk-Hartung 1884; Delbrück 1890. Henderson 1927 pp. 47–68 gave an enjoyable summary of this controversy in English. Mere Athenian survival will bring the Spartans to treat, Adcock 1927 pp. 195–6; Spartan league will collapse, Brunt 1965 (1993); "far too optimistic," Kagan 1974 p. 25.

43. "Firm up their friendships," 2.7.3, with Gomme and Hornblower *ad loc.*, translating the difficult *perix tēn Peloponnēson katapolemēsontes* with Wilson 1987 p. 131. Scholars reluctant to emphasize the raiding: but recent students have come to recognize that "we shall have to consider some possible indications that . . . Pericles may have had more offensive ideas than Thucydides allows" (Lewis 1992b p. 386; cf. Schubert and Laspe 2009). Blockade, Busolt 3.2 pp. 898–900. Blockade theory fashionable, e.g., Grundy 1948 (1911) pp. 315–83; finally killed off by Ste. Croix 1972 pp. 214–20. Ravaging to cause economic hardship, Westlake 1945 (1969); cf. Ste. Croix 1972 pp. 208–10. Raiding as a signaling strategy, Kagan 1974 pp. 35–41; the Vietnam connection is made in Kagan 2005 p. 6.

44. Spartan strategy: there is a dispiriting literature. Like Grundy 1948 (1911) p. 33 before him, Brunt 1965 (1993) felt that the Spartans placed all their confidence in ravaging Attica and did not diverge from that strategy until after the disaster of 425 BC. That seems impossible given the range of Sparta's activity in the years after 431. On the other hand, Kelly 1982 (2007) has argued that the Spartans always primarily pursued a naval strategy—also absurd. Did Spartan strategy therefore *evolve* in a more adventurous direction, as early as 430 (so Kagan 1974 pp. 93–4, 99), and steadily more after, or as late as 426 (Lewis 1992b p. 390)? Or did the Spartans gyrate between ravaging and a more adventurous strategy, depending on the political situation at home (Cawkwell 1975; Moxon 1978)? See chapter 8 n. 64 for discussion of the problems with such "faction" theories.

45. Building forts on enemy territory (*epiteichismos*) contemplated before the war, 1.122.1, 1.142.2–4.

46. Athens prevents Mytilene from controlling Lesbos, Diod. Sic. 12.55.1. Mytilene's previous contacts with Sparta and preparations, 3.2.1–2 (cf. 3.13.1). For how Thucydides tells the story of the revolt of Mytilene, Stahl 2003 pp. 103–16.

47. Complaints at Athens, 3.2.3. For the old rivalry between Mytilene and Methymna, Mason 1993 (with p. 228 for the feud with Tenedos). For the links between Mytilene, Sparta, and Boeotia in time of myth, Egan 1983. Why did the *proxenoi* complain, since they were in the Greek way themselves citizens of Mytilene? Arist. *Pol.* 1304a tells a tangled tale of personal motives; see Hornblower *ad loc.* 3.2.3.

48. Envoys from Athens to Mytilene, 3.3.1. 428 BC Athenian expedition to Mytilene, using the fleet assigned to ravage the Peloponnese, 3.3.2–3.

49. 428 BC Peloponnesian invasion of Attica, 3.1.

50. Cavalry in 431 BC, 2.22.2; wide ravaging in 430 BC, 2.55, 2.57.

51. Athenian coup de main at Mytilene fails, 3.3.4–5.

52. Athenian ultimatum to Mytilene, 3.3.3, 3.4.1. Boeotian and Spartan envoys to Mytilene, 3.5.2. Thucydides hints that the Mytileneans always intended to revolt from the Athenians (3.2.1–2) and that their actions were temporizing, since they were unprepared when the Athenians preempted them. But their actions suggest more limited aims. Wilson 1981 p. 147 attributes Mytilenean caution to the ruling oligarchs' lack of confidence in the loyalty of the *demos*.

53. Fighting at Mytilene, Mytileneans ask to send envoys, 3.3.2–4; Wilson 1981 pp. 150–1 guesses "40 ships at least" for the Mytileneans, which sounds about right, and at pp. 147, 151, he suggests that the feebleness of their fleet was the consequence of political disunity.

54. Mytilenean envoys to Athens, Sparta, 3.4.4–6. Athenians camped along the shore to the north: Thucydides says (3.4.5) "at Malea, to the north of the town," but other ancient authors (see Gomme *ad loc.* 3.6.2; Wilson 1981 pp. 152–6) agree in identifying Cape Malea with the promontory to the south of the city. So there is some muddle. But other than Mytilene itself, by far the best harbor in the vicinity is that near what is now the fishing village of Panagiouda, three miles north of Mytilene, and that is where we should assume the Athenians made their base (so Wilson 1981 p. 154).

55. Mytilenean envoys return from Athens, fighting outside Mytilene, 3.5.1–2. Wilson 1981 pp. 144–8 speculates on the numbers involved: the Mytileneans were few because the oligarchs did not trust the *demos* with arms (p. 146). On the soldiers from Imbros and Lemnos, chapter 3 n. 9.

56. Laconian and Theban envoys arrive at and depart from Mytilene, Mytileneans await reinforcements, 3.5.2. Athenians summon allied ships (presumably from Chios, Quinn 1981 p. 30 with 3.10.5); blockade, 3.6.

57. Mytilenean envoys arrive at Sparta, 3.8. For the date, Gomme *ad loc.*, who comments on the delay before the Olympics, and Busolt 3.2 pp. 912, 1006–7. Ar-

rival in mid-July represents quite a leisurely schedule, and late June is hardly impossible. Roisman 1987 p. 387 gathers explanations for Spartan delay, noting that it was really far greater, since the Spartans had known of the Mytilenean intention to revolt before it happened (Thuc. 3.5.2). The Olympics of 428 BC, 3.8: accepting the argument of Hornblower *ad loc.* that there is no reason to suppose that the Athenians were excluded, as some scholars have held.

58. In a speech, Thucydides attributes to Archidamus (1.81.3) awareness of the dangers of accepting responsibility for islanders who rebelled from Athens.

59. In the temple of Zeus, 3.14.1, *pace* Gomme *ad loc.*, taking "nearly" with "as suppliants" rather than "in the temple." Plea of the Mytileneans to the Peloponnesians: Thucydides writes a speech for them (3.9–3.14), of which the classic discussion is Macleod 1978 (1983) pp. 64–8; see also Price 2001 pp. 132–41.

60. 428 BC Athenian ravaging fleet, 3.7.1–3. For the doings of this fleet in the northwest, see below pp. 232–3. Athenian financial stringency: so Thucydides has the Mytileneans say in their speech, 3.13.3, and Athenian actions suggested the same; cf. 3.19.

61. Peloponnesian plan to aid Mytilene, 3.15. Thucydides has the Mytileneans in their speech say that this will make the Athenians withdraw their ships (3.13.4), and Peloponnesian actions suggest the same.

62. Fighting on Mytilene, 3.18. Taking Methymna will release small allies: so Wilson 1981 p. 157 reasons.

63. Peloponnesian preparations, 3.15; "haul-ways," not LSJ's "windlasses," is the correct translation of Thucydides' *holkoi* (3.15.1; Rankov [forthcoming]); Athenian reaction, 3.16.1–2; for the crews see Rhodes III *ad loc.* Athenian show of force, an *epideixis* ("display"), 3.16.1. For the summary passage that follows in Thucydides, 3.17, often thought an interpolation, see above n. 38.

64. Athenian raid on the way back from the northwest, 3.16.2; only eighteen ships, since twelve had remained at Naupactus (3.7.3), but Thucydides rather carelessly still calls them thirty (3.16.2); cf. Gomme *ad loc.*

65. Athenian setback in the northwest, 3.7.4–5 (on which see below p. 233).

66. Mytilene besieged by land, 3.18.3–5.

67. Money raising for Mytilene in 428 BC, 3.19, with Kallet-Marx 1993 pp. 134–8; Thonemann 2009 pp. 176–9; see above nn. 13, 38. Richest Athenians excused from the emergency fleet, 3.16.1. For Lysicles, Gomme *ad loc.* 3.19.1. For the Samian exiles at Anaea, Fantasia 1986 pp. 133–9.

68. Athenian finances during the Ten Years' War are a dark matter: see esp. Samons 2000 and Pritchard 2007 for the state of the question. The major evidence is the "*Logistai* Inscription" (Tod² 64 = ML 72 = IG I³ 369 = Fornara 134), which indicates that from 433 to 426 BC the Athenians borrowed *ca.* 4,800 talents from the treasuries of their gods, an average of some 685 talents per year, heavily concentrated in the first years of the war (ML 72 = ATL iii pp. 341–4). ATL's annual guesstimates (pp. 342–3) are loans of 1,145 talents in 432/1; 1,370 talents in 431/0; 1,300 talents in 430/29; 600 talents in 429/8;

200 talents in 428/7; 100 talents in 427/6—but what we really know is that the Athenians borrowed a great deal near the beginning of the 431–426 period and much less later. From 426/5 to 423/2 they borrowed, on average, 202 talents per year. These figures suggest that they had progressively solved their financial problems (partially, of course, by sending out smaller expeditions). Blamire 2001 p. 110, on the basis of the declining loans, revived an old guess that the tribute was substantially raised in 428/7, and given Athens' attested financial stress in 428 and the lack of as powerful evidence for such stress afterwards, this reconstruction is appealing. Calculations like those of Samons 2000 p. 209—subtracting the money borrowed from Athena from the 6,000 talent reserve of 431 (2.13.3), holding back the 1,000 talent reserve, coming up with a sad remnant of, say, 400 talents in 421, and crying ruin—even if justified in method, ignore the fact that the reserve alone would have paid for five more years of war at the rate the Athenians were borrowing by 426/5–423/2, as well as the fact that the Athenians were so close to breaking even that it would not have been difficult for them to fund the war indefinitely at the 426/5–423/2 rate with a modest further increase in revenue. No objection to a theory of Athens' income nearing expenses by 427 is presented by the reassessment decree of 425/4 (Meritt and West 1934 = Tod² 66 = ML 69 = Paarmann 2007 IIA pp. 79–82, IIB pp. 137–59 = Fornara 136, discussed in *ATL* iii pp. 70–80, Samons 2000 pp. 173–83; the literature is gathered by Geske 2005 nn. 592, 597–8; two other such inscriptions survive but are undated and too fragmentary to be very useful), which lists in extenso the tribute the Athenians hoped to receive from their empire and mentions that it was to be increased. But (1) the reassessment decree lists a vast number of places never present on lists of actual payments: between 380 and 400 cities were assessed, while the total number of cities that ever actually paid in a given year was never more than 175 (ML p. 194). (2) The decree lists also Melos, which we know was not paying, having declined to surrender to the Athenians in 426 (Thuc. 3.91.1–3), and was still refusing to join her empire in 416. (3) The figures claimed are high, sometimes twice or thrice those given for actual payments in the tribute lists (ML p. 193). "Strangest of all omissions in Thucydides is that of the increase in the tribute in 425–424 BC," complains Gomme (iii p. 500). Not really. Because of the poor state of the tribute list inscriptions for the war years, we have no idea whether or by how much Athens raised her tribute before 425/4 (Kallet-Marx 1993 pp. 164–70, 191–4). And we are also ignorant as to whether the tribute called for in this reassessment was ever actually collected or even asked for. The lack of correspondence between the sums in the reassessment and the sums listed in other inscriptions as actually paid should be accepted as just that (Kallet 2004 p. 494). But why? The decree describes a procedure whereby the assessors' assessments were expected to be challenged before a court at Athens. I would guess that the assessments reflect Athens' initial bargaining position, before a process of negotiation through the

courts (rather like challenging one's property tax assessment in the modern United States; cf. ML p. 197; Samons 2000 pp. 180–1). No doubt a similarly optimistic list was produced every time the tribute was reassessed, but this is the only useful list we have. The reassessment decree tells us nothing about either the amounts of Athens' tribute or at what point in the progress of increase of tribute the reassessment of 425/4 lies (for what it is worth, Plut. *Arist.* 24.3 says that after the death of Pericles, the tribute was increased "little by little" to 1,300 talents per year; cf. Andoc. 3.8–9, for 1,200 talents per year after the peace of Nicias, but see Samons 2000 p. 231). Lack of financial stress from 427 to 421 (see esp. Kallet-Marx 1993 pp. 179–80, 183, 202–3, but see the counter-argument of Samons 2000 p. 209–11): it does not appear that the Athenians ever, during the Ten Years' War, had to dip into the 1,000-talent reserve fund they established in 431 (2.24.1; Samons 2000 p. 166) or (so far as we can see) to melt down precious dedications to the gods (2.13.4), as they would in the last years of the Peloponnesian War (Samons 2000 pp. 276–7, 281–90); nor did they take domestic austerity measures like reducing or eliminating the salaries paid to jurors and officials (most of these salaries would be briefly abolished, for both political and financial reasons, under the oligarchy of the 400 in 411 [*Ath. pol.* 29–30; Samons 2000 p. 259]); nor did they reduce the pay of rowers, as they would by 412 (Thuc. 8.45.2; but after 415 BC, 6.8.1, 6.31.3). To the contrary, in the later years of the Ten Years' War, Cleon raised jury pay from two to three obols (Ar. *Eq.* 797–800; schol. *Vesp.* 88, 300), and public building, although not on the scale of the period before the war, never ceased (Kallet-Marx 1993 pp. 153–4, 203). The sending of plundering, "silver-collecting" ships (above n. 13) is, however, attested in the winter of 425/4 and the summer of 424.

69. For the escape from Plataea, 3.20–4. [Dem.] 59.103, who gives a summary account of this episode, says that the escapers were chosen by lot.

70. Ladders the right length, Gomme *ad loc.* 3.20.3. Inner ditch, cf. 2.78.1. One foot bare: a famous moment when the rationalizing Thucydides gives a naturalistic explanation ("so as not to slip in the mud") for a superstitious practice; Hornblower *ad loc.* 3.22.2 collects discussions.

71. Sentries on tops of towers: unmentioned in Thucydides, but why otherwise attack the towers from the exterior (3.23.1)? Shot arrows, threw javelins, reading 3.23.2 with Harrison 1959. For the topography, Pritchett 1982.

72. For *andreia* and *mētis*, see above n. 9. Some of the Plataean stratagems on this occasion were canonized in the Greek stratagem literature, Polyaen. *Strat.* 6.19.2–3.

73. Helmsmen compete in skill, 7.70.3, with Lendon 2005 p. 105; cf. Plato, *Leg.* 707a–b. Competition of generals (on land) in *mētis*, Lendon pp. 85–6; martial skill (on land) and *mētis* pp. 109–13. Van Wees 2004 pp. 229–30 collects the (scanty) evidence of trireme command being regarded as agonistic. At Thuc. 7.69.2, trierarchs are urged to compete in courage.

74. Paches at Notion, 3.34; Polyaen. *Strat.* 3.2. This episode entered the tradition as a classic *ruse de guerre*, Wheeler 1984 p. 270. On the Greek admiration for guile in warfare, Lendon 2005 pp. 78–90, with pp. 411–12 for literature; on Thucydides' taste for stories of this kind, Heza 1974, with p. 234 on Paches at Notion.

CHAPTER V: THE DYING OF THE BRAVE, 427 BC

1. Salaethus at Mytilene, 3.25. Food running short: it was soon exhausted, 3.27.1.

2. Peloponnesian fleet leaves from the Gulf of Corinth, a guess: Roisman 1987 p. 394 and Wilson 1981 p. 159 suppose the fleet was to leave from Cyllene, a frequent point of departure for the Peloponnesians (Fantasia *ad loc.* 2.84.5), but Cyllene is no great place to stage a spring expedition since it has no protection from the north.

3. Cleomenes, 3.26.2. For the deduction about Archidamus, Gomme *ad loc.* 3.26.2.

4. "Opposed the Lacedaemonians," 1.127.3.

5. 427 BC Peloponnesian invasion of Attica, 3.26.2–4.

6. Alcidas and his slow fleet, 3.16.3–4, 3.26.1, 3.27.1, 3.29.1; the need for secrecy will have discouraged the Peloponnesians from hauling the ships over the Isthmus of Corinth. For the southerly route, 5.110.1, 8.39.3–4, with Wilson 1981 p. 160, who offers guesses as to why the fleet was slow; cf. Roisman 1987 pp. 392–3.

7. Surrender of Mytilene, 3.27–8. A spear butt probably dating to this victory survives from Athens, inscribed "The Athenians from the Lesbians to the Dioscuri" (Camp 1978 = *SEG* XXVIII 24). If the date is right, given the equestrian associations of Castor and Pollux, this dedication may imply the presence of Athenian cavalry on this campaign, which is not otherwise attested (Camp 1978 p. 194).

8. Paches' pledge to the Mytileneans, 3.28. Escape of Salaethus, 3.35.1.

9. Alcidas finds out that Mytilene has fallen and turns back, 3.29–31. Chios had a fleet of more than sixty triremes in 412 BC (8.6.4; cf. 1.116.2, 1.117.2, 2.56.2).

10. Thucydides writes a short speech for one of Alcidas' captains (3.30), urging that the fleet sail to Mytilene despite its fall, on which Lateiner 1975. Alcidas wise not to continue to Mytilene: so Roisman 1987 p. 398.

11. Alcidas kills prisoners at Myonessus (I speculate about his reasons for doing it ashore), 3.32.1. Myonessus and pirates, Aeschin. 2.72; Livy 37.27.4. Those on the sea regarded as enemies by the Spartans, 2.67.4, with Gomme *ad loc.* 3.32.1.

12. Alcidas at Ephesus, lectured by Samian exiles, 3.32.2–3. Why Ephesus? Thucydides does not say. Water and rest? So Gomme *ad loc.* 3.33.1. But he had

just stopped at Myonessus (so Roisman 1987 p. 401). Roisman guesses Alcidas was making a rendezvous with the Samian exiles—but then why not at the exiles' stronghold only some fifteen miles to the south? I guess he needed food and chandlery goods. Alcidas' visit to Ephesus has been adduced as a possible context for the so-called Spartan War Fund inscription, which bears no date (*IG* V[1].1 = ML 67 [who date it to 427 BC] = Fornara 132). But the date of this document is too uncertain to build an interpretation on: see Smarczyk 1999 and Bleckmann 2002.

13. Urging wider revolt, Persian help, in Mytilenean speech, 3.13.6–7; cf. Diod. Sic. 12.55.2. Exiles urge seizing a city on the coast, Thuc. 3.31. Causing revolts among Athens' allies had also been mentioned in the speeches Thucydides placed before the war, 1.81.3, 1.122.1. For other reasons these were bad ideas, Roisman 1987 pp. 397–400.

14. Raising a general revolt not part of the Spartan plan, cf. Lewis 1992b pp. 390–1.

15. Alcidas flees, Paches follows, 3.33; Ionia unwalled: accepting Hornblower's *ad loc.* 3.33.2 interpretation.

16. Alcidas gets back to the Peloponnese, 3.69.1. Paches and Salaethus, 3.35.

17. Envoys from Mytilene, 3.28.1, 3.36.5. Decision about Mytilene in Athenian assembly, 3.36.1–3. I borrow here some of these imagined Mytilenean pleas from Thucydides' speech of Diodotus (3.42–8): see below n. 19.

18. Athenian repentance, 3.36.4–6. "Create a desolation," Eur. *Tro.* 97.

19. For the Mytilenean debate, 3.37–40 (Cleon) and 3.42–8 (Diodotus), on which see esp. Macleod 1978 (1983) pp. 68–77; Price 2001 pp. 89–101 and Gärtner 2004 for the literature. For the theme of revenge in the speech of Cleon, Andrews 2000 pp. 47–50.

20. Athenian moral revulsion: they thought that "their plan was savage [the Greek word (3.36.4) is *ōmos*, 'raw' or 'savage'] and monstrous, to destroy the whole city rather than merely the guilty"; cf. 3.49.1. For this divergence between the arguments of the speeches Thucydides gave his speakers and Thucydides' narrative depiction of the debate, Andrewes 1962 p. 71.

21. Trireme race to Mytilene, 3.49.

22. "By just so much," 3.49.4. For the fate of Paches, who in one tradition kills himself with his own sword at a hearing about his generalship (Plut. *Nic.* 6; Plut. *Arist.* 26.5) and in another was executed for violating two women of Mytilene whose husbands he had killed (*Anth. Pal.* 7.614), see Westlake 1975 (1989).

23. "Those most guilty," 3.50.1.

24. Fate of Mytilene, 3.50, with Gauthier 1966 on the allotments. On the cleruchs being absentee (an old controversy), Moreno 2009 p. 213.

25. Why settle cleruchs at a time of financial need? So asks Kagan 1974 pp. 164–5. The Athenians had also made a cleruchy of Aegina in 431 BC (2.27.1), but their treasury was fuller then. On the taxation of cleruchs, Samons 2000 p. 201; Moreno 2009 pp. 212–14.

26. Why the Athenians want Minoa, 3.51.1.

27. Nicias, son of Niceratus: his manner, Plut. *Nic.* 2.3–4; mining wealth, 4.2; generous and pious, 3.2–4.1, with Geske 2005 pp. 76–84; careful in war, 6.3.

28. Nicias at Minoa, 3.51; Plut. *Nic.* 6.4, with Geske 2005 pp. 18–26.

29. For the capture of Minoa as coherent with previous Athenian strategy, cf. Kagan 1974 p. 171.

30. Salaethus promises to lift the siege of Plataea, 3.36.1.

31. Number of defenders in Plataea, 2.78.3–4, 3.68.3.

32. Surrender of Plataea, 3.52.1–2, guessing at the role of the Thebans from the speech of the Plataeans (3.53–9), 3.68, and 5.17.2, where the Thebans do in fact refuse to return Plataea in 421 BC for this reason. For the significance of the persistence of the quibble about Plataea, cf. Gomme *ad loc.* 3.52.2.

33. Trial of the Plataeans, 3.52.3–5, with Hornblower *ad loc.* 3.52.4 for parallels for the balancing of good and evil deeds.

34. For Aeimnestus, the father of Lacon, at Plataea, Hdt. 9.72.2, with Rhodes III *ad loc.* 3.52.5.

35. For the speeches Thucydides writes for the Plataeans (3.53–9) and the Thebans (3.61–7), the most important discussions are Macleod 1977 (1983) and Price 2001 pp. 103–25 (with literature).

36. Fate of the Plataeans, Plataea, 3.68. Dignified no, Diod. Sic. 12.56.5, rather than mentioning or inventing services to the Spartans, as the uncharitable Hornblower suggests *ad loc.* 3.68.2.

37. Plataea handed over to the Thebans, who give it to the Megarian exiles: we do not, with Classen, delete "Thebans" at 3.68.3; see Gomme *ad loc.* Pausanias and the temple of Hera at Plataea, Hdt. 9.61.3.

38. Athenians give citizenship to the Plataeans, esp. [Dem.] 59.103–4, with Kapparis 1995; Pelling 2000 pp. 65–6, 74–7. This is a mare's nest, because Thucydides has both the Plataeans (3.55.3) and the Thebans in their speeches (3.62.2) indicate that the Plataeans were already, in some sense, Athenian citizens before this grant; nor does he mention the grant of citizenship after the fall of Plataea. The simplest solution is to suppose (with many scholars, Hornblower *ad loc.* 3.55.3) that the earlier block grant of citizenship (in 519? 509? 480 BC?) was conditional upon its recipients relocating to Athens, with those who then declined to do so remaining Plataeans and so requiring naturalization in 427.

39. For the (rare) naturalization of individuals in fifth-century BC Athens, Osborne 1987 pp. 12–13, 16. For the limitation of Athenian citizenship to those with two citizen parents, Patterson 1981.

40. Corcyrean envoys at Athens, 427 BC, 3.71.2–3.72.1.

41. Corcyrean prisoners at Corinth, return to Corcyra, 1.54.2–1.55.1, 3.70.1. According to 3.70.1, the Corcyrean *proxenoi* at Corinth notionally stood surety for them to the gigantic sum of 800 talents, but there is presumably something wrong with this number, Gomme *ad loc.* Several years spent scheming: a guess.

Wilson 1987 pp. 91–2 discusses the date, and Intrieri 2002 p. 72 n. 18 gathers the discussions. We do not know exactly when the prisoners were sent home, but there is no reason to suppose, with Gomme *ad loc.* 3.70.1, that the return of the prisoners was recent. For how Thucydides tells the story of the civil war at Corcyra and the interventions of the Athenians and Peloponnesians, Rood 1998 pp. 115–17. For the literature on the episode, Intrieri 2002 pp. 67–119.

42. Oligarchic undertakings at Corcyra, 3.70.2–3; "trying to enslave," 3.70.3.

43. Trial of Peithias and the oligarchic leaders, 3.70.3–5. Peithias was a "voluntary" (3.70.3, presumably rather than hereditary, see Hornblower *ad loc.*) *proxenos* of Athens, a status attested nowhere else.

44. Peithias' plan for the Athenian alliance: Corcyra's compact with Athens was still notionally the defensive alliance of 433 BC (1.44.1), and her help ravaging the Peloponnese in 431 (2.25.1) may have gone beyond their strict duty under the treaty. Now it was to be transformed into a full alliance (3.70.6). Massacre in the Corcyrean council, 3.70.6.

45. Corcyrean assembly, Athenian reaction, 3.71.1–3.72.1, 3.80.2. Trireme carries democratic refugees to Athens, deduced from 3.71.2 (with Gomme *ad loc.*; Wilson 1987 p. 94), which places democratic refugees already in Athens when the envoys of the oligarchy arrive. Athenians depart from Naupactus, 3.75.1.

46. Democrat vs. oligarch fighting on Corcyra, 3.72.2–3.73.1. Oligarchic coup planned in advance, cf. Wilson 1987 p. 90.

47. Democratic counterattack, 3.74. Did one or two days pass between the two combats? I guess one with Classen *ad loc.* and Wilson 1987 p. 90, but Gomme *ad loc.* guesses two. For the topography of the city of Corcyra, Intrieri 2002 p. 16 n. 19 and p. 196 n. 146 gathers the literature: little is certain.

48. Athenian ships approach, Nicostratus arrives on Corcyra, negotiates, 3.75.1. Thucydides just says "the ten most guilty" were to be put on trial, and I suspect the number of ten was suggested by the need to find five democrats to match the five ringleaders among the oligarchs (3.70.4).

49. Nicostratus cannot get away, new troubles, 3.75.2–4.

50. Corcyrean oligarchs go to the island, 3.75.5.

51. Naupactus uncovered: I try to answer, with the peril of Naupactus (hinted at by Thucydides 3.69.2), Wilson's incredulity that Nicostratus planned to depart (1987 p. 104).

52. Peloponnesian fleet arrives at Corcyra, 3.69, 3.76.

53. Loss of Mytilene cancelled out: 3.69.2 rather vaguely implies a causal relationship between the Peloponnesian failure at Mytilene and the attempt to gain Corcyra.

54. Preparations for 427 BC sea battle off Corcyra, 3.77. Corcyrean slave rowers, 1.55.1.

55. Sea battle of Corcyra, 3.78. Gomme *ad loc.* 3.77.3 gathers suggestions for when the *Salaminia* and *Paralus* left Athens.

56. Corcyreans prepare defenses, Peloponnesians ravage, 3.80. The setting up of the trophy is not reported but likely: Thucydides is working hard to make the reader forget that Alcidas actually won the battle, although outnumbered; see Roisman 1987 pp. 408–9. Democrats negotiate with the oligarchs: Gomme *ad loc.* 3.80.1 suggests that oligarchs were needed as hoplite marines; more likely in this case as experienced captains? Hoplites would not have been so easy to kill when they disembarked (3.81.2). Lassitude of Alcidas: what could he have done? asks Roisman (1987 pp. 409–10; cf. Badian 1999 pp. 5–6). Whatever it was Alcidas originally planned to do, for he must have expected to have to capture a city in turmoil. And he had two defected triremes full of Corcyreans, not to mention plenty of highly motivated allies within the city, to help him get into Corcyra.

57. Athenian fleet reported approaching, 3.79–80. On Eurymedon's name, see Hornblower *ad loc.* 3.80.2.

58. Peloponnesian flight from Corcyra, 3.81.1.

59. Corcyrean democrats slaughter oligarchs, 3.81.2–5.

60. No food or drink for oligarchs: not in Thucydides, but that is how these things usually worked (cf. 1.134.2).

61. Thucydides on *stasis*, 3.82–3, on which, in general, see Macleod 1979 (1983) p. 53; Price 2001 pp. 11–67; and for the literature, Intrieri 2002 pp. 121–69. Much of the useful discussion of the passage arises from the question of whether the following 3.84 is an interpolation in the text, as most, ancient and modern, accept; Luginbill 2000 gathers the literature. "Teacher of violence," 3.82.2; "ancient simplicity," 3.83.1; all trans. Crawley adapted.

62. "As long as the nature of mankind" and "imperious necessities," 3.82.2; "carried to a still greater excess," 3.82.3, all trans. Crawley adapted; the list of the features of *stasis* paraphrases 3.82.4–6.

63. Athenian expedition to Sicily, 3.86; Gorgias goes to Athens, Diod. Sic. 12.53.2–5. Two coalitions in the west: although Camarina, a Dorian city, was allied to the Ionians (3.86.2). It is unclear whether the Athenian alliances with Rhegium (Tod² 58 = ML 63 = IG I³ 53 = Fornara 124) and Leontini (Tod² 57 = ML 64 = IG I³ 54 = Fornara 125) were made or renewed in 433/2 BC; see Cataldi 1987. For Athenian relations with the west between the outbreak of the war and 427 (a very murky matter involving a possible expedition of an Athenian general to Naples, FGH 566 F 98), Cataldi 1989. This 427 western expedition has recently been proposed as the original context for the Athenian treaty with Egesta: it is argued that 418/17, the date of the inscription, was a renewal (IG I³ 11, with Matthaiou 2004; Papazarkadas 2009 p. 75).

64. Why prod Syracuse? Westlake 1960 (1969) pp. 394–6 gathers references to Athenian concern about Sicilian intervention in the war in Greece. "Wanted to prevent importation of grain," 3.86.4. Thucydides also suggests (3.86.4) that the Athenians were testing the strength of Sicily in hope of conquest, but this labors under the suspicion of being retrospective from the perspective of the great, disastrous 415–413 BC Sicilian expedition; see Gomme *ad loc.*; Lazenby

2004 p. 58. For other Thucydidean allusions to Athenian interest in the west, 1.36.2, 1.44.3. Economic interpretation of Athenian interest in the west, esp. Grundy 1948 (1911) pp. 324–32; *contra* Ste. Croix 1972 pp. 214–20.

65. Peloponnese self-sufficient in grain, 1.143.4; cf. Lazenby 2004 p. 58; which is not to say, of course, that cheap grain was not imported (Hdt. 7.147), merely that the Peloponnesian states were not normally as reliant upon it as Athens was. Trade during the war between Athens and Corinth, MacDonald 1982, with n. 30, for evidence of Athenian trade with other enemy states during the war. Merchant ships cross the Ionian sea at Corcyra: Kiechle 1979 gathers the evidence. Gomme 1933 (1939) drew far too strong a contrast between triremes creeping along the shore and sailing ships dancing freely over the deeps: see now Morton 2001 pp. 51–2, 143–72.

66. The Athenians in Sicily, 427 BC, 3.86.5; winter of 427/6, 3.88; summer of 426 BC, 3.90 (where he says his account of affairs in the west will be selective, and he did not lie; Messana, 3.90.4), 3.99; winter of 426/5 BC, 3.103, 3.115; also Diod. Sic. 12.53–4; Justin, *Epit.* 4.3.4–7 (deeply confused). But for the history of this expedition, there is also a fragmentary papyrus, *PSI* 1283, a fragment of a lost history of Sicily (discussed, with literature, by Ameruoso 1999). For full discussion of the sources, Scuccimarra 1985. Bosworth 1992 (with an English translation of the papyrus, p. 48) attempts to reconcile the sources and construct a narrative. Laches returns to Athens: Hornblower *ad loc.* 3.86.1 and Cataldi 1996 pp. 45–54 collect the literature for the (unresolvable) dispute about whether he was prosecuted by Cleon on his return.

67. No blockade in the west: Westlake 1960 (1969) p. 397, followed by Kagan 1974 p. 189, thinks that the Athenians concentrated their efforts at the strait of Messina to block grain shipments to the Peloponnese. But given the currents in the strait (see below p. 280), this was the last place in the whole Mediterranean to set up a blockade; cf. 7.25.1.

68. Return of the plague, 3.87, with Rhodes III *ad loc.* for the numbers.

69. Peace offer: Ar. *Ach.* 652–4, and at 194–7 nostalgia is expressed for the Thirty Years' Peace of 445 BC, which hints at the terms Sparta offered. The *Acharnians* was performed early in 425, and so this must refer to events before then, but not, I think, so far back as the Athenian peace offer of 430, as Kagan 1974 pp. 82–3 (he collects the literature at n. 42 and p. 193 n. 26), 193 argued.

70. For seeing *hybris* in the enemy and in one's own actions in retrospect, Lendon 2000 p. 16.

71. No longer than three years, 7.28.3.

CHAPTER VI: THE NEW SPEAR, 426 BC

1. Athens against Melos in 426 BC, 3.91.1–3; Diod. Sic. 12.65.1–3, with Geske 2005 pp. 45–53. For the relations between Athens and Melos, Seaman 1997 pp. 385–418, defending Thucydides' statement that Melos did not yield

as a result of this 426 invasion. For the size of the 426 fleet, compare the one that actually took Melos in 416, only thirty-eight ships; for explanations of the size of the 426 fleet, Rhodes III *ad loc.* 3.91.3. Thera, also a Spartan colony, listed as neutral at the beginning of the war (2.9.4), was subordinate to Athens by the date of ML 68 = *IG* I³ 68 = Fornara 133, the so-called Cleonymus Decree, alas of uncertain date (see appendix p. 429). Nor do our literary sources mention when Thera yielded to the Athenians.

2. Earthquake prevents 426 BC Peloponnesian invasion of Attica, 3.89; Diod. Sic. 12.59.1. 426 BC Athenian expedition around the Peloponnese, Thuc. 3.91.1. Thucydides' account is so summary that he neglects to mention the actual ravaging during the circumnavigation, unless that ravaging has fallen into the textual crux of 3.94.1 (on which see Gomme *ad loc.*). But in Thucydides' usage, "around the Peloponnese" (which is all Thucydides says here) usually implies a raiding expedition in summer—2.25.1 and 2.30.1 (clear), 3.3.2 (implied), 3.7.1–2 (clear), 3.91.1 and 3.94.1 (implied), 7.20.1 (clear from 7.20.2)—but not, probably, in winter (2.69.1, 3.105.3, and 7.17.2; cf. Xen. *Hell.* 5.4.62–3).

3. Busy Athenian capture of merchant ships: Polyaen. *Strat.* 5.13.1 has a Corinthian trireme skipper, Ariston, son of Pyrrhichus (an individual referred to at Thuc. 7.39.2), protecting three grain transports. If there is any truth to the story at all, it may refer to this expedition.

4. 426 BC Athenian incursion into Boeotia, 3.91.3–6, with Geske 2005 pp. 53–8 for literature.

5. Sights of Tanagra, Paus. 9.20–2.

6. Ravaging and fight at Tanagra, 3.91.3–5. The recently discovered "Athens Metro Casualty List" may refer to casualties at this battle, see appendix p. 427. On the excellent quality of the hoplites who served with the fleet, 3.98.4.

7. Athenian withdrawal from Boeotia and 426 BC attack on Opuntian Locris, 3.91.5–6.

8. First Athenian incursion into Boeotia: did the Boeotians expect an Athenian attack at the beginning of the war? They are reported (*Hell. Oxy.* 17.3) to have emptied some small, hard-to-defend cities and incorporated their populations into that of Thebes. But there is a problem with dating this event, Salmon 1978 pp. 81–6.

9. No protection for Megara, 4.72.2. 426 BC, in the context of the more aggressive strategy of the Athenians, is a good moment to guess that the Athenians made their transition from ravaging Megara once a year (2.31.3, with Gomme *ad loc.*) to twice a year (4.66.1), accepting that this contradicts Plutarch (*Per.* 30.3), who thought that the Athenians invaded twice a year from the very beginning of the war. Athenian passivity on land: Hanson 2005 p. 81 attributes it to loss of manpower caused by the plague.

10. "Noticing," see chapter 2 n. 29.

11. For the relationship between the incursion into Boeotia and the fall of Plataea, Lewis 1992b p. 410.

12. Casual Boeotian raiding of Attica in 426 BC or early 425, Ar. *Ach.* 1022–31, 1076–1225 (425 BC).

13. "Bring home the seed of Zeus' son," 5.16.2.

14. Temple of Zeus Lycaeus, Paus. 8.2.6, 8.38.4–6.

15. Return of Pleistoanax to Sparta (5.16.2–3), from which we know that Pleistoanax returned between the summer of 427 BC and the summer of 426 (see Hornblower *ad loc.* 5.16.2), but connecting his return to the earthquakes is my speculation.

16. Colony to Heraclea in Trachis, 3.92; Diod. Sic. 12.59.3–5, with Hornblower *ad loc.* 3.92 and Falkner 1999a.

17. Additional Spartan motivations for the colony in Trachis, 3.92.4. Thucydides also says that Heraclea was attractive as a stopping-off point on the road to Thrace; I suspect that this is a retrojection of later Spartan interest in Thrace (424 BC); cf. Hornblower ii pp. 255–6 and Rhodes IV–V.24 *ad loc.* 4.78.1. Thucydides goes on to say (3.93) that the colony never in fact proved a hazard to Euboea.

18. For the names of the founders of Heraclea, 3.92.5, with Hornblower *ad loc.* and Lazenby 2004 p. 268 n. 46. Heracles in Trachis, Diod. Sic. 12.59.4, with Hornblower *ad loc.* 3.92.1.

19. Athens purifies Delos, 3.104, with Hornblower *ad loc.*, a note so gigantic it is best read with Rhodes III *ad loc.*'s metacommentary on it; also Smarczyk 1990 pp. 504–25. Diod. Sic. 12.58.6 connects the purification with the recurrence of the plague, a connection commentators have accepted.

20. Explanations for name "Ozolian" Locris, Paus. 10.38.1–3; Phocian hellebore, 10.36.7.

21. Northwesterners carry weapons, 1.5.3. Call for a relative of Phormio, 3.7.1. We do not know what became of Phormio, who never commands again after 429 BC: see Hornblower *ad loc.*

22. Phormio in Acarnania in 429 BC, 2.102–3. Oeniadae, 2.82, 2.102.2, 3.94.1, 3.114.2; attacked by Asopius, 3.7.3.

23. Sollium, 2.30.1, and see chapter 3 n. 128. Rivalry over Amphilochian Argos, 2.68, and see chapter 2 n. 30 for a guess about the date of Phormio and the Acarnanians' recapture of Amphilochian Argos.

24. Naupactus embattled: the Messenians of Naupactus dedicated at Delphi a triangular pillar the height of four men, celebrating their victory over (the text is fragmentary) either Kalydon to their west or Aetolian Kallion to the northeast: *SEG* XIX 392 = *SEG* XXXII 550 = Jacquemin and Laroche 1982 pp. 192–204.

25. Demosthenes' ravaging fleet of 426 BC, 3.91.1 (his colleague, Procles, son of Theodorus, quickly vanishes from Thucydides' account until he shows up again to die, 3.98.4). Thucydides and Demosthenes: Roisman 1993b pp. 11–22 collects the literature. The case for Thucydides belittling Demosthenes—unanswerable, I think, despite Roisman—is made by Woodcock 1929 pp. 93–108. I suggest a reason below. On how Thucydides tells the story of Demosthenes' activities in the northwest, Stahl 2003 pp. 129–38.

26. Leucas hostile to the Acarnanians, 3.94.2; 429 BC, 2.80.3–5. Death of Asopius, 3.7.4.

27. Demosthenes against Leucas, 3.94.1–2. For Demosthenes' attack on Leucas as retribution for the death of Asopius, Treu 1956 p. 424.

28. Demosthenes' plan against Aetolia, 3.94.3–3.95.1; "do a favor," 3.95.1. Thucydides (3.95.1) attributes to Demosthenes a further hope (a "wild speculation," as Lewis 1992b p. 410 calls it) that once he had conquered and added the Aetolians to his strength, he would be able to advance through Ozolian Locris into Doris, into Phocis, and then into Boeotia. Here, Thucydides, no doubt encouraged by his distaste for Demosthenes (cf. Woodcock 1929 p. 95), has either believed too easily slanders in the wake of the disastrous end of this expedition or credited some gasconade Demosthenes delivered to encourage his troops. For (1), Athens bordered Boeotia directly; there was no need to invade her by such a roundabout path. And (2), Thucydides later says (3.96.2) that Demosthenes intended a limited expedition into Aetolia, followed by a retreat on Naupactus and then a second expedition into Aetolia. "If Thucydides is right, this passage is a fatal obstacle to the view that Demosthenes intended to reach Boeotia in this campaign" (Rhodes III *ad loc.*). (3) Demosthenes' attack on Aetolia was premised on the military feebleness of the Aetolians (3.94.4), so what use would they have been on a march into Boeotia? Rejecting Demosthenes' Boeotian plan, we necessarily reject, too, the argument that this campaign was part of a pincer movement against Boeotia, of which the Tanagra incursion (3.91.3–6) was another part: Rhodes III *ad loc.* 3.95.1 collects writings by scholars who have so argued.

29. Messenian description of Aetolia, 3.94.3–5. Names of Aetolian women, Pritchett 1991 n. 7.

30. Demosthenes' preparations for Aetolia, 3.95.

31. Demosthenes invades Aetolia, 3.96–8. For the topography of this campaign, Pritchett 1991, although without inscriptions (rare in this region), the identification of locations is largely guesswork.

32. Ambush of Athenians in Aetolia, 3.97.3, assuming (although Thucydides does not say so) that Demosthenes' force had moved away from Aegitium, the last town they took before they were attacked. I have imagined the mechanics of this combat as similar to those at Lechaeum in 390 BC, Xen. *Hell.* 4.5.10–17; Lendon 2005 pp. 93–4, 412. Athenian archers: presumably the 120 archers carried by Demosthenes' thirty ships.

33. For Athenian generals' dread of the angry democracy, esp. 7.48.3–4.

34. "So great a number," 3.98.4, but 120 was hardly an army, which makes the remark even odder. And it is curious that they should be "the best" (see Gomme *ad loc.*) since seagoing hoplites were usually of humble origin and not the sort of people a Greek aristocrat would describe as "best." For what it is worth, late authors (gathered by Moysey 1991 pp. 33–4) give Thucydides a son named Timotheus.

35. Aetolian pleas for help to Sparta and Corinth, 3.100.1, the one to supply the troops and the other, presumably, the transport.

36. Peloponnesian march from Delphi to Naupactus, 3.100.2–3.102.2; for the route, Gomme *ad loc.* 3.102.5.

37. Demosthenes arrives at Naupactus, siege abandoned, 3.102.3–5. Where did Demosthenes' ships (3.102.4) come from? Classen *ad loc.* guessed Acarnanians (although, as Gomme *ad loc.* notes, we never hear of an Acarnanian fleet). Gomme guessed that they were the thirty Athenians, but Thucydides implies that these had already gone home (3.98.5). I guess the squadron of twelve ships that Athenians normally seem to have kept at Naupactus all year round, last seen at Corcyra with Nicostratus in 427 BC (3.75.1 and esp. 4.13.2, with Strassler 1990 n. 27; Rhodes IV–V.24 *ad loc.* 4.13.2). Presumably Demosthenes expected to return with these ships well before the Peloponnesians reached Naupactus; otherwise, he could simply have sent his crews to the walls. Was Demosthenes still technically an Athenian general when he rescued Naupactus (see Hornblower *ad loc.* 3.102.3; Rhodes III *ad loc.* 3.98.5 for the controversy)? I suspect so, because I find it hard to believe that Athenian generals on distant service did not retain their powers until relieved on the spot by others (cf. Fornara 1971 pp. 74–5).

38. Plea of the Ambracians to attack Amphilochian Argos, 3.102.6: the Spartan domino theory, expressed as the hope that an attack on Amphilochian Argos and Acarnania would make the rest of the area join the Spartans, resurfaces here. See above pp. 154–5.

39. Peloponnesians wait for the Ambracians, 3.102.5–7.

40. Ambracians attack Amphilochian Argos, Acarnanians call for Demosthenes, 3.105. On Demosthenes' position, 3.105.3, 3.107.2, and above n. 37. On the topography of this campaign (requiring much guesswork), Hammond 1936/1937 (1973) and Pritchett 1992. Ambracian mercenaries, 3.109.2; presumably the same Epirotes the Ambracians had recruited in 430 (2.68.9) and 429 (2.80).

41. Peloponnesians march to Olpae, 3.106. The Aetolians did not accompany the Peloponnesians, which suggests that the Aetolians felt as jilted by their departure as the Acarnanians had by that of Demosthenes from Leucas (cf. Gomme *ad loc.* 3.102.6).

42. Athenians arrive at Amphilochian Argos, 3.107.1–3. Athenian hoplites: mentioned at 3.107.4, with Gomme *ad loc.* I assume that Demosthenes came by sea with the twenty Athenian ships, although Thucydides does not make his route clear at 3.107.1–2. Gomme *ad loc.* and Pritchett 1992 p. 54 thought that he came by land.

43. Deployments at Olpae, 3.107.3–4. Host army has a right to the right wing, see chapter 1 n. 35. Eurylochus' contingent (3.107.4): we are not told who made it up, but Lazenby 2004 p. 64 soundly guesses the 600 colonists from Heraclea in Trachis (3.100.2), who included Spartan *perioeci* and even some former Spartan citizens (3.92.5).

44. Battle of Olpae, 3.108. Demosthenes' ambuscade achieved immortality in Polyaenus' book of military stratagems (*Strat.* 3.1.2).

45. Negotiations after the battle of Olpae, 3.109.

46. Disgrace the Peloponnesians and Spartans, 3.109.2, with Gomme *ad loc.* *Diabalein,* meaning to slander or discredit, indicates that the Peloponnesians would lose both the confidence of the northwesterners and honor.

47. Peloponnesians try to creep away from Olpae, 3.111.

48. For dividing the enemy at Olpae as a precaution against the advancing Ambracians, Kagan 1974 p. 214.

49. Battle of Idomene, 3.110, 3.112.

50. Herald comes to Demosthenes and his allies, 3.113. "How many of yours?" 3.113.3–6, with some paraphrasing. Does the circumstantial detail here imply that Thucydides was present? So Gomme *ad loc.* 3.113.6 and others. But there might as easily be literary explanations for it: Lateiner 1977a pp. 47–9; Stahl 2003 pp. 133–5.

51. "Greatest disaster," 3.113.6. Settlement between Acarnanians and Ambracians, 3.114.2–4; for alliances immediately following treaties of peace, see Mosley 1974 and below pp. 264 and 360–7.

52. Division of the booty after the victory in the northwest, everybody goes home, 3.114.1–2. Golden statues at Athens, *IG* I³ 468, with Pritchett 1992 pp. 74–6.

53. Aristophanes' *Acharnians*: Henderson's Loeb translation is excellent (and often adapted below). Dicaeopolis, or "Chastiser of the City": so W. D. Furley suggests to me the name should be rendered from the verb *dikaioō* rather than the adjective *dikaios* (which would make his name "Just City," which is how it is usually rendered). For discussion of other views, Olsen *ad loc.* 406. "They made us," Ar. *Ach.* 73–5. "No gold for you," *l.* 104, but my translation does no justice to the broken Greek Aristophanes gives to the Persian. Henderson translates, "No gettum goldum, gapey-arse Ioni-o." But does this proctal gaping mean "accustomed to and available for buggery" or "afflicted with anal incontinence"? Olson *ad loc.* tries to resolve this essential point.

54. "Throw," Ar. *Ach.* 281; "basket," *l.* 333.

55. "What rents of garments," Ar. *Ach.* 423–4. Pitiful costume: specifically that of Telephus, the king disguised as beggar of Euripides' lost 438 BC tragedy the *Telephus.* Much of the humor of this part of the play resided in allusions to the *Telephus*: Pelling 2000 pp. 141–5. "Our men," *ll.* 515–16. This is the comic history of the origins of the war we looked at above, p. 88.

56. "The meat of these piglets," Ar. *Ach.* 795–6; "The Dog's Asshole," *l.* 863, with Olsen *ad loc.*, for erudite discussion of possible meanings.

57. "Bring me my sausage," Ar. *Ach.* 1118–19; "fare-thee-well," *ll.* 1143–5; the rhyme is Henderson's; "oh ah!" *ll.* 1190 vs. 1198.

58. Aristophanes against peace, Ar. *Ach.* 652–4; the peace we have guessed was proposed by the Spartans in the winter of 427/6 BC (see above pp. 214–15). Mocks the Megarians, *l.* 757. Is Aristophanes advocating peace? See Pelling 2000 pp. 158–63 for the debate.

59. Combatants in the war reluctant to give up when ahead: so Ar. *Pax* 211–19; cf. Ar. *Eq.* 668–73. Giving up unthinkable: Worthington 1987 points out

that in the *Knights* of early 424 BC, Cleon is not severely abused for preventing peace the previous year, although he would have been an obvious target if Aristophanes had been in favor of the peace.

CHAPTER VII: AS HONORABLE AS CIRCUMSTANCES PERMIT, 425 BC

1. Situation on Corcyra before 425 BC, 3.85. Peloponnesian plans for Corcyra, 4.2.3.

2. Situation in Sicily/Italy in the winter of 426/5 BC, Syracuse prepares fleet, 3.115.3.

3. Athenians need to practice their fleet, 3.115.4, with Gomme *ad loc.*; cf. 1.142.6–9, 2.89. For Athens' peacetime naval practice see above p. 59.

4. Agis in Attica, 425 BC, 4.2.1.

5. Athenian fleet leaves Athens, 4.2.2. Demosthenes' mission: all Thucydides says is "at the request of Demosthenes they said that he might use the ships, however he wanted, around the Peloponnese" (4.2.4), that is, probably for raiding (for "around the Peloponnese," see chapter 6 n. 2). Demosthenes not a general: for his formal position (was he or was he not a general elect?), Gomme *ad loc.* 4.2.4; Hornblower *ad loc.* 3.102.3.

6. Demosthenes argues with the generals, generals hear about the Peloponnesians at Corcyra, 4.3.1. Decaying situation in the west, 4.1. Samons 2006, esp. n. 2, gathers the literature on the Pylos campaign. For Demosthenes' plan, see below n. 8.

7. Athenians driven into Pylos, 4.3.1; late storms, 4.6.1. For Thucydides' muddled account of the topography of the area (not important here), Bauslaugh 1979; Pritchett 1994 pp. 167–9; Hornblower *ad loc.*; Rhodes IV–V.24 *ad loc.*; Rubincam 2001. On where various stages of the fighting occurred, which has inspired controversy, Pritchett 1965a and 1994 are fundamental; Hornblower ii p. 150 gathers the literature. Lazenby 2004 p. 270 n. 12 and Hornblower *ad loc.* 4.8.5 dismiss the heresy of Wilson 1979 pp. 76–82, while Pritchett 1994 pp. 149–51, 153–4 and Samons 2006 n. 11 refute that of Strassler 1988.

8. Demosthenes' plea to fortify Pylos, and argument, 4.3.2–4.4.1. Demosthenes' original plan (a guess from 4.3.3): which means that his original request to the generals to put in at Pylos, before the storm, must have been for a mere raid, perhaps intended also for reconnaissance. That the fleet brought no tools (4.4.2; Strassler's 1990 p. 113 argument against this point is ingenious but unsuccessful) shows that Demosthenes did not originally intend to fortify Pylos without stopping somewhere else first. Demosthenes' plan borrowed from Corcyra: Westlake 1983 (1989, 2007) points out that the aggressive use of fortification in the territory of other cities probably grows out of its venerable use in civil strife. Cf. the Megarian oligarchs when they seized Pegae, Megara's Corinthian Gulf port, probably in 426 BC (4.66.1).

9. Demosthenes has no explicit directive from home to fortify: as implied, again by the lack of tools (4.4.2), but also by the facts that Demosthenes was merely a private citizen, the generals resisted him, and the Messenians, upon whom he could call in a private capacity as the savior of Naupactus, were to be the main actors in his plan (4.3.3). If Pylos were taken by the Peloponnesians: as it was, in 409/8 BC, Diod. Sic. 13.64.5, with Strassler 1990 p. 121.

10. 400 hoplites on the Athenian fleet: there is probably no need to deduce more from the presence of taxiarchs, or infantry officers (4.4.1), as Gomme did *ad loc.* 4.9.2, since taxiarchs could serve as subordinate naval commanders, Xen. *Hell.* 1.6.29. The *hormē*, or "impulse" (4.4.1), I think, was one of fear (cf. Rood 1998 pp. 29–30) and not random or inexplicable, and here we can do no more than notice the vast literature on the "luck-of-Pylos" theme (beginning with Cornford 1907 pp. 82–109; see Hornblower ii pp. 149–50 for a catalogue), arguing that Thucydides makes too much of fortune in this passage and his description of the fighting at Pylos in general (*contra* Rood 1998 pp. 24–39). "In every way," 4.4.3. Athenians fortify Pylos, 4.4.2.

11. Athenian fleet departs, Demosthenes stays, Spartans are unconcerned, 4.5. Demosthenes sends to Naupactus: Thucydides does not report this message, no doubt sent north with the fleet, but it must be implied from the arrival of boats loaded with Messenians and full of makeshift weapons (4.9.1, with Gomme *ad loc.*).

12. Peloponnesians in Attica, 4.6. For war over rank vs. war about existence, 5.101. Diod. Sic. 12.61.2 understands the Spartan reaction in terms of rank: "they considered it a disgrace for men not brave enough to defend Attica when it was being ravaged to fortify and hold a place in the Peloponnese." Hopes of Demosthenes: only raiding, not inspiring helot rebellion, is implied by 4.3.3; cf. 3.112.4.

13. The help of rebellious slaves: which is not to say that Greek cities and individuals did not often use their own slaves in war, a phenomenon that probably occurred more than we hear about: Hunt 1998.

14. Peloponnesians return home from Attica, 4.6.

15. Summons of Peloponnesians to Pylos and recall of the Peloponnesian fleet, 4.8.1–2. Message to the Peloponnesian fleet: Lazenby's (2004 p. 70) theory that this was sent straight from Sparta when the occupation of Pylos was reported is hard to reconcile with 4.8.2. Strassler's (1990) suggestion that messengers left for Corcyra when the Athenian fleet left Piraeus (p. 114) obliges him to come up with reasons for the fleet to cool its heels for two weeks before arriving at Pylos (p. 118).

16. Two boats of Messenians arrive at Pylos, 4.9.1, reading *etuchon paragenomenoi* ("happened to arrive") with Gomme *ad loc.*: the fact of arrival at that moment, not the fact of arrival *per se*, was fortuitous.

17. Arrival of the Spartan army and Peloponnesian fleet at Pylos, Demosthenes calls for help, 4.8.2–3. About a week after the Athenian fleet departs: Strassler 1990 pp. 124–5. Demosthenes' plea for help: prompted by hearing of

the approach of the Peloponnesian fleet, since Demosthenes must have been expecting to face the Spartan land forces (4.9.3, with Lazenby 2004 p. 69, answering the puzzlement of Gomme *ad loc.*) and to evacuate with his ships if his position became untenable. Athenian repairs at Zacynthus: so I suppose, to explain (cf. 6.104.2) why the Athenian fleet, by Strassler's 1990 minimum estimate (p. 124) a week gone from Pylos, had not made it further than Zacynthus (4.8.3), which has puzzled commentators (Gomme *ad loc.*; Strassler 1990 p. 121). Cf. Wilson 1979 p. 67.

18. Plan of the Spartans at Pylos, 4.8.5–7. Fall of Pylos expected in hours not days: deducing from 4.8.4–8, trying to answer Samons 2006 p. 535.

19. Scholars (e.g., Gomme *ad loc.* 4.8.6) have rejected Thucydides' account of the Peloponnesian plan because they allege that the Peloponnesians did not have enough ships to occupy the straits to the north and south of Sphacteria (see the authors cited below in this note). There may be reasons to reject Thucydides' account (the arguments of Samons 2006 are very strong), but impracticality is not one of them. Samons 2006 n. 45 gathers the literature on spacing between triremes. "4 ft. 3 in.," Wilson 1979 p. 74. Morrison *et al.* 2000 p. 59 suggest ten feet (and they should know better). Of the proposals by academics for the Peloponnesian array, only Bauslaugh's (1979 p. 4) "option B" with *ca.* 140 feet between the ships is possible in the real world. Triremes in motion (which would have far finer control of their relative positions) could, of course, get far closer together, a fact upon which the *diekplous* maneuver no doubt relied. Thucydides' "block up" (4.8.5) and "close" (4.8.7) the straits of Navarino Bay are, of course, not to be taken too literally. Thucydides has expressed himself obscurely, but I do not think that by "intended to close up the entrances with serried ships with their prows facing outwards" (4.8.7, for "serried," the puzzling *buzēn*, Pritchett 1994 p. 148), he is trying to describe anything other than a normal line of battle. Certainly the Spartans did not intend to sink their ships in the passages (so Gomme thought *ad loc.* 4.8.7; destroyed by Wilson 1979 pp. 73–5) or, I think (as Strassler 1988 p. 202 suggests), to cram the ships so close together as to create a sort of Xerxes-over-the-Hellespont bridge or boom of boats (that would indeed have required more ships than the Spartans had). Pritchett 1994 pp. 148–9 offers later parallels that suggest that ships *buzēn* were capable of motion. And Thucydides at least imagines this disposition could have been taken up on the day of battle, even if it was not (4.13.4), which shows that it was nothing as elaborate as a boom made out of triremes.

20. One salty sort: Shaw 1993 p. 103. Gap between obstructions at Syracuse, 7.38.3; and other passages imply that wide spacing was normal, 2.86.5, 2.89.8, 7.23.3, as does the canonization of the *diekplous* tactic, which would hardly have been possible if triremes lined up very close together; cf. 7.70.4.

21. Triremes at anchor in formation, 2.90.1; Xen. *Hell.* 1.1.17, 1.6.18, 21. Forty feet for the anchor line: this is a minimum anchor road, for the sake of argument; a modern harbormaster would be appalled.

22. What advantage from a line with large gaps? So ask Strassler 1988 p. 202 and Samons 2006 p. 531; my reply follows Samons', p. 535. Well-known tactic against outflanking, Hdt. 8.60; Thuc. 1.74.1. "A confined space," Thuc. 2.89.8; cf. 7.36.4. Second line vs. *diekplous*, Xen. *Hell.* 1.6.31.

23. Hope that the Athenians will decline to attack, 4.8.8. I interpret Thucydides' statement that the Spartans thought that they "would likely take the place [i.e., Pylos] by siege without sea-battle or danger" to mean they hoped to make a sea battle unattractive to the Athenians, not that they hoped to make it physically impossible.

24. Spartan station on Sphacteria, 4.8.7–9; preventing landings is, I suggest (trying to answer Samons 2006 pp. 532–4), the most likely meaning of Thucydides' rather vague "fearing lest [the Athenians] would make war upon them from there." And it worked, 4.13.3, with Rood 1998 p. 33.

25. Spartan preparations for attack on Pylos, 4.8.4, 9.

26. Demosthenes' preparations to defend Pylos, 4.9. Demosthenes' force: I guess forty Messenian hoplites plus thirty hoplites from his three remaining ships plus any rowers for whom the Messenians had brought full panoplies. For other counts, Lazenby 2004 p. 271 n. 16. Thucydides gives Demosthenes a speech of encouragement (4.10), on which Hunter 1973 pp. 66–9. Spartans and Peloponnesians attack Pylos, 4.11.1–4.13.1. Trireme thirteen feet above the sand: Morrison *et al.* 2000 p. 194.

27. "Allow the enemy," 4.11.4. Heroism of Brasidas at Pylos: is there an epic tone here? So Badian 1999 p. 7; Howie 2005 pp. 212–14.

28. "It was the special glory" (*doxēs*), 4.12.3.

29. New Spartan plan, send ships for wood, 4.13.1. Ascend by ladders: this is no more than a guess as to what 4.13.1 was intended to mean.

30. Athenian ships arrive at Pylos, 4.13.2–3, accepting, with nearly all editors, "50" instead of the "40" that appears in the manuscript; see Gomme *ad loc.* 4.13.2. But Wilson 1979 p. 93 and Lazenby 2004 p. 72 accept "40." Peloponnesian fleet lined up in order of battle (*pace* Samons 2006 p. 535): so I deduce from 4.13.3—"they [the Athenians] . . . saw the ships in the harbor, and not sailing out"—the fact that the Athenians were indeed discouraged and that what the Peloponnesians did on this day is contrasted both with "sailing out against [the Athenians] into the open water" and with what the Spartans actually did the next day (which was to remain deep within the harbor). If the Peloponnesians did adopt this array on this occasion, that explains how Thucydides knew about it (since they did not use it the next day, 4.13.4). But my interpretation requires Thucydides to use "in the harbor" (*en tōi limeni*) sloppily in different senses in 4.13.3 and 4.13.4.

31. Athenians withdraw to Prote, 4.13.3.

32. The day of the sea battle at Pylos, 4.13.3–4. Began to deploy inside Navarino Bay: trying to make sense of 4.13.4, with the help of Samons 2006 pp. 535–6. But Thucydides seems to think that the Spartans still intended to deploy in the passages on the day of the battle but somehow failed to do so.

33. Blocking the passages a short-term strategy, 4.8.8.

34. For the habits of "fair and open" battle (phrase is from Xen. *Hell.* 6.5.16), Lendon 2005 p. 341 n. 4, drawing especially on Pritchett 1974 but accepting, with Krentz 2002 pp. 27–8 and van Wees 2004 pp. 134–5, that these were not rules, merely how things often happened. Lendon 2005 pp. 78–90 tries to show how such customs and their subversion could coexist.

35. Competitive tunnel vision, Lendon 2005 p. 89.

36. Battle in, and on the edges of, Navarino Bay, 4.13.3–4.14.5. Why the Peloponnesians were not ready is a famous puzzle, since the Athenians could be seen approaching from a great distance: see esp. Westlake 1974 (1989) pp. 212–17; Wilson 1979 pp. 81, 90; and Rood 1998 pp. 33–4.

37. After the battle in Navarino Bay: Thucydides says that both sides returned to their camps (4.14.5), but the Athenians did not have a proper camp, which worried Gomme and Hornblower *ad loc.* What he must mean is that they anchored in the shelter of the land in Navarino Bay near Pylos and took turns coming close to shore to get water and cook their meals on the promontory (as they do at 4.26.1–3).

38. Blockade of Sphacteria, 4.14.5. Approximately 172 out of 420 full Spartan citizens: estimating from the proportion of survivors (4.38.5) 120 Spartans out of 292 soldiers (= 41 percent). All were members of the Spartan army (citizens, *perioeci*, and whatever else), because chosen by lot from its *lochoi*, or divisions (4.8.9). For the total Spartan citizen population (estimating 41 percent of *ca.* 6,000, the Spartan army in 418 BC = *ca.* 2,460), see chapter 3 n. 10. High-born Spartans trapped on Sphacteria, 5.15.1.

39. Spartans ask Athenians for a truce, 4.15. Westlake 1974 (1989) p. 221 is right that the Spartans "considered peace to be desirable on other grounds in addition to the needs of the local situation at Pylos."

40. Terms of the truce at Pylos, 4.16.

41. 425 BC speech of the Spartans at Athens, 4.17–20, on which Hornblower ii p. 171 gathers the literature; add Crane 1998 pp. 187–92 (upon whom I have drawn here); Howie 2005 pp. 219–25; Romilly 2005. For the Spartan apology for their speech, 4.17.2–3 (cf. 4.84.2), with Hornblower *ad loc.*

42. Spartan speech a chance for Thucydides to analyze: I have untangled the argument of this speech as it touches on honor, shame, and rank and, for the sake of clarity, ignored the Spartans' other, intertwined argument, which is a lecture on the perils of *hybris* and reliance on good fortune, on which Hunter 1973 pp. 74–83. "Honor and fame" (*timē kai doxa*), 4.17.4. "Greatest reputation" (*axiōma megiston tōn Hellēnōn*), 4.18.1. Peace will protect Spartan honor against further loss (*pro aischrou tinos*), 4.20.2. "Honorable [*kosmon*] as circumstances permit," 4.17.1.

43. Athenians elevated in honor (*dokēsin*), 4.18.5, with Hornblower *ad loc.*; *doxēs*, 4.20.2–3. Honor both alike (*hoti hupdeesteron on ta megista timēsei*), 4.20.4.

44. Proposed alliance, 4.19.1; as Rhodes IV–V.24 notes, this shows that the Spartans were prepared to betray their own allies; cf. 4.20.4. In fact the Ten Years' War ended in just such an alliance, 5.23. See above p. 244 for the alliance between Ambracia and her former enemies in 426 BC.

45. No revenge, grace, 4.19.2–4, 4.20.3. On the need to renounce vengeance if peace is to be achieved, cf. 4.62.3–4, 4.63.2. For placing the other in debt for favors as a tool of Greek foreign policy, Lendon 2006 pp. 91–5. Implacable revenge, 4.20.1; cf. 4.19.4.

46. Equality in honor between Athens and Sparta: so Romilly 1963 pp. 177–8 compares this to Cimon's description of Athens and Sparta as the two legs, or two oxen, of Greece (Plut. *Cimon* 16.8); see p. 52. Pericles, 1.140.5–1.141.1. Spartans expect the Athenians to accept, 4.21.1; to the extent that they are willing to give up the fleet, Kagan 1974 p. 233. The men on the island as the peace term, 4.19.1; cf. 4.17.4, the vague "keep what you have, but gain honor [*timēn*] and glory [*doxan*] as well."

47. "Be king equally with me," Hom. *Il.* 9.616. On honoring and granting honor, Lendon 1997b pp. 47–50, 56–8, 78–81.

48. Athenians reject the Spartan terms, 4.21.

49. Athenian reply, 4.21.3 (where Thucydides also makes the connection to reversing the Thirty Years' Peace). According to Philochorus (*FGH* 328 F 128), three votes of the assembly were needed.

50. Plataea not asked for, as Gomme notes, *ad loc.* 4.21.3, "it was simply and solely 'back to pre-445'." Megara: Lewis 1992b p. 387 says that the request for Nisaea and Pegae is "a demand for Megara as a whole." Then why not ask for Megara?

51. Men on the island must surrender: Gomme *ad loc.* 4.21.3 "it was, one might almost say, expressly to avoid such a dishonor that they had proposed discussing peace."

52. "Grasping for more," 4.21.2. Spartans beg and wheedle in their speech, 4.18.1, 4.19.1–2, 4.20.2.

53. Spartan envoys ask to confer with a committee, 4.22.1.

54. The Spartan envoys and Cleon, 4.22.2; a story to be regarded with suspicion given Thucydides' hatred of Cleon.

55. Spartans cannot discuss betraying their allies before assembly, 4.22.3. Truce terminated, bickering over ships, 4.23.1. Length of truce, 4.39.2.

56. Double siege after the end of the truce, 4.23.2. Conditions at Pylos, 4.26.1–4. Eating on the island, 4.30.2.

57. Smuggling supplies to Sphacteria, 4.26.6–9. "Each side," 4.26.9.

58. Athenians worry about winter, 4.27.1. Scholars guess (Wilson 1979 p. 126; Rhodes IV–V.24 *ad loc.* 4.27.1) that these Athenian anxieties arose around the end of July/beginning of August. Various ancient authors gave different dates from mid-September through November for the end of the season of safe sailing, Simonsen 2003 pp. 260–2; Morton 2001 pp. 259, 285–6.

59. Growing confidence at Sparta, 4.27.2. Exchange between Cleon and Nicias (I have simplified the details here), 4.27.3–4.28.5. I accept Flower's (1992) argument that the story makes better sense if we assume that Nicias had already been appointed to the command, although Thucydides implies the opposite. For this assembly, also Geske 2005 pp. 32–42 (against Flower), 85–92, 165–7 (a bibliographical essay).

60. "Sensible men" (*sōphrones*), 4.28.5.

61. For Thucydides' description of this assembly as character assassination of Cleon, Westlake 1968 pp. 69–73. For Cleon's behavior here in terms of *mētis*, Murari Pires 2003 pp. 137–40. Lazenby 2004 p. 75 is moving in the same direction: he thinks Cleon engineered the whole affair; Geske 2005 pp. 88–9 argued that Nicias outmaneuvered Cleon. Cleon's reinforcement, 4.28.4. Cleon chooses Demosthenes, 4.29.1–2. For Demosthenes' mysterious transformation into a real general, an old and insoluble puzzle, Gomme *ad loc.* 4.2.4, 4.29.1. How Cleon could "choose" Demosthenes as his colleague and what happened to the authority of the other generals in Navarino Bay is unknown.

62. Demosthenes prepares to attack Sphacteria, 4.29.2–4.30.3. Was this fire an accident, or did Demosthenes (who had fire used against him in Aetolia, 3.98.2) order it set, and has Thucydides represented it as an accident to belittle Demosthenes (so Woodcock 1929 p. 101; Howie 2005 n. 79 for literature)? Food hoarded on Sphacteria, 4.39.2.

63. Demosthenes gains confidence, 4.30.3.

64. Cleon arrives, Athenian ultimatum about the men on the island, 4.30.4–4.31.1. Hesiod, *Works and Days* 663–77, with Morton 2001 p. 256.

65. Athenian invasion of Sphacteria, 4.31.1–4.32.2. For the numbers of the Athenian force (which present various problems), Wilson 1979 pp. 104–5; Lazenby 2004 pp. 76–7.

66. Battle on Sphacteria, 4.32.3–4.33.2. "They cast stones," Eur. *Andr.* 1128–36 (of Neoptolemus), with thanks to W. D. Furley. Spartans flag, 4.34.1–2.

67. "Leaders over leaders," 5.66.4. Spartan withdrawal to fort on Sphacteria, 4.34.3–4.35.2.

68. Fight for the fort on Sphacteria, 4.35.3–4.36.3.

69. Thucydides' comparison to Thermopylae, 4.36.3, with Rood 1998 p. 37.

70. Athenian request that the Spartans surrender, 4.37.

71. Spartan commander negotiates with Spartan authorities, 4.38.1–3. "Nothing dishonorable," 4.38.3.

72. Spartans surrender, 4.38.3. "Of all the events," 4.40.1.

73. Athenians had flagrantly breached Greek customs of warfare, cf. Crane 1998 p. 233. "Brave men all killed?" 4.40.2, adapting Hornblower's *ad loc.* translation. For the meaning of this joke, Rhodes IV–V.24 *ad loc.* and Link 2005.

74. Not a "stand-up battle," 4.38.5.

75. Reasons for Greek amazement, 4.40.1. "The glory of the Lacedaemonians" (*Lakedaimoniōn tetapeinōmenōn tēi doxēi*), Diod. Sic. 12.75.5. For Spartan disgrace, see also Thuc. 5.75.3.

76. Honors for Cleon at Athens, Ar. *Eq.* 281–3, 702, 709, 776, 1404–5; but there was evidently controversy regarding to whom the credit should go, 54–7, 355, 742–3, 1201. "Cleon's undertaking," Thuc. 4.39.3.

77. Statue of victory on the Athenian acropolis, Paus. 4.36.6. Shields taken from the Spartans, at Athens, Paus. 1.15.4; cf. Ar. *Eq.* 846–9. One survives: *IG* I³ 522 = Shear 1937 pp. 346–8. Messenian statue, for the inscription, Tod² 65 = ML 74. Paus. 5.26.1 says the Messenians attributed this to the Sphacteria victory. For the monument itself, Hölscher 1974. For the Messenian monument at Delphi, sometimes associated with this Olympia monument, chapter 6 n. 24. Messenians to garrison Pylos, 4.41.2. For the reassessment of the tribute of the Athenian empire (Tod² 66 = ML 69 = *IG* I³ 71 = Fornara 136) soon after these events, and in the past regarded of as great historical importance, see chapter 4 n. 68.

78. Prisoners taken to Athens, 4.38.4, 4.41.1 (panoplies lost in 426 BC, 3.114.1).

79. Events on Corcyra at end of 425 BC, 4.46.1–3. On this new fighting on Corcyra, Intrieri 2002 pp. 115–19. Not the same island: Gomme *ad loc.* 4.46.3.

80. Athenian generals unhappy, 4.47.2.

81. Corcyrean oligarchs tricked, imprisoned, 4.46.4–4.47.3.

82. Corcyrean oligarchs tricked, killed, 4.47.3–4.48.1.

83. Corcyrean oligarchs kill themselves/are killed, 4.48.2–6. For the curse of suicide, Parker 1983 pp. 41–2; van Hooff 1990 pp. 63, 106–7 gathers *comparanda*. Civil war on Corcyra over: but Diod. Sic. 13.48 describes yet another outbreak that he dates to 410 BC, on which Wilson 1987 pp. 112–14.

84. Athenians leave Corcyra, 4.48.6.

85. Situation in Sicily/Italy at the beginning of 425 BC, 4.1. Plans of the Syracusans and allies, 4.24.

86. Engagement in the strait of Messina, 4.25.1–3. Thucydides implies that the Syracusans did not want to fight here because it was considered so dangerous, 4.25.1. For the currents, 4.24.4, with Hornblower *ad loc.*, which shows they were on Thucydides' mind, although their exact role in the battle is my speculation. For the difficulties of navigation here, e.g., Purdey 1826 pp. 135–6. Swirling north in the current: deduced from the fact that the Syracusans ended up at Cape Pelorus, to the north of Messana (4.25.3, with Gomme on the text *ad loc.*). For a battle in the Hellespont where the current played a great role, cf. Diod. Sic. 13.39.4–5.

87. Second day of fighting in the strait of Messina, 4.25.3–6.

88. Tow against the current: the obvious reason for the tow, which Thucydides (4.25.5) does not explain. Syracusans attack: the obscure term Thucydides (4.25.5) uses for the Syracusan motion, *aposimōsantōn*, meaning "render snub-nosed," has given the most acute pleasure to commentators: see Gomme and Hornblower *ad loc.*

89. Leontini and Messana, 4.25.7–12.

90. Eurymedon and his reinforcements show up, 4.48.6.

91. Peace in Sicily, 4.58–65. Thucydides (4.59–64, see Hornblower *ad loc.*) writes a speech for one of the delegates to this conference, Hermocrates of Syracuse, an important figure during the Sicilian expedition (415–413 BC, Thuc., Books VI–VII), whose speech here looks forward to those events. For the literature Hornblower ii p. 221 and Scuccimarra 1985 p. 26.

92. For the prosecution of the Athenian generals returned from the west, Cataldi 1996. Not disrupted the peace, Gomme *ad loc.* 4.65.2. We reject, as an artifact of the later Sicilian disaster, Thucydides' description of the conviction of the generals by the Athenians because the Athenians hoped to "subdue" Sicily and were furious that they had failed to do so (4.65.3–4; cf. 3.86.4). On the usual charges made against Athenian generals, Hamel 1998 pp. 140–57.

93. Spartan prisoners as hostages, 4.41.1.

94. Spartan cowards, Xen. *Lac.* 9.1–6; Plut. *Ages.* 30.3 (cloaks, beards) with Ducat 2006b. What happened to the captured Spartans when they returned to Sparta, 5.34.2; connections of captured Spartans, 5.15.1.

95. Messenian garrison on Pylos, 4.41.2–4, with Wilson 1979 pp. 127–9. A payment of thirty talents in October 425 BC to Demosthenes (*l.* 18 of Tod² 64 = ML 72 = *IG* I³ 369 = Fornara 134) probably reflects the settlement of the Messenians at Pylos.

96. Athenian descent on the territory of Corinth, 4.42.1, on which see Stroud 1971, with Geske 2005 pp. 100–6, with full literature. Polyaen. *Strat.* 1.39 has Nicias make a first landing by night and set troops in ambush, but Thucydides knows nothing of this. Corinth untouched before: a contrast with the rest of the Peloponnese emphasized by 3.16.1, about the second Athenian raiding expedition of 428 BC, when "putting out, they made a display along the Isthmus [i.e., the territory of Corinth] and descents wherever they wanted on the Peloponnese." Horse transports in 425 BC, 2.56.2. Taking of Anactorium in 425 BC, 4.49, and see chapter 8 n. 61 for a speculation about the purpose of this campaign.

97. Thucydides does not tell us why the Athenians invaded the Corinthiad: Hornblower ii. 197 gathers suggestions. Battle against Corinthians in ?458 BC, 1.105.1.

98. Corinthians prepare for Athenian attack, 4.42.3.

99. Battle of Solygeia in the Corinthiad in 425 BC and legend about Solygeia, 4.42.2–4.44.2. Corinthians leave half their army (4.43.4): their willingness to split their force on this occasion bespeaks their superiority in numbers. Pheia in 431 BC, 2.25.3. Athenian cavalry praised, Ar. *Eq.* 595–610.

100. End of battle of Solygeia, 4.44.2–5.

101. Athenians must apply for the bodies they have left behind, 4.44.6; Plut. *Nic.* 6.5–6 explains the consequences for the honor of the sides. Second Athenian landing in territory of Corinth, Thuc. 4.45.1.

102. Absurdities, 1.54.2, 1.105.6, 2.22.2, 2.92.5, 4.72.4, 4.134.2.

103. Nicias raids the Argolid peninsula, fortifies Methana, 4.45.2. Kagan 1974 p. 255 guessed rather desperately that the purpose of this expedition was to encourage Argos to join the war. Second year of the war, 2.56.4–5; whether these areas had been raided thereafter is hard to say, since Thucydides describes so many Athenian raids as merely going "around the Peloponnese" (see chapter 6 n. 2). Troezen: we know that by 423 BC Troezen had made a private peace with Athens (4.118.4); fragmentary treaties without dates between Athens and Halieis (*IG* I³ 75) and Athens and Hermione (*IG* I³ 31), as well as fragments perhaps of the Troezen treaty itself (*IG* I³ 67, with Mattingly 2000 pp. 131–40), survive. By associating these with this 425 raid, scholars usually argue that the cities of the peninsula made private treaties with Athens at this time. But I am not confident enough of the dates of the treaties to include them in a narrative (see appendix p. 430). Troezen 446/5 BC, 1.115.1.

CHAPTER VIII: THE BRONZE DREAM, 424 BC

1. Spartan envoys to Athens and Spartan motivation for peace, 4.41.3–4. Peace refused three times, Ar. *Pax* 665–7; cf. *Eq.* 794–6. Spartan peace offers on the basis of equality (*epi tēi isēi*), 5.15.2. The rank-minded Diodorus tells the story that the Spartans offered to exchange their men for Athenian prisoners man for man and thought that the Athenians' refusal proved that they considered the Spartans better men than they were (12.63.2).

2. Cythera a known danger to Sparta, Hdt. 7.235. Cythera seized during 450s BC, Paus. 1.27.5; Scholiast to Aeschines, 2.75 (Blass = 78 Dindorf).

3. Nicias against Cythera, 424 BC, 4.53.1–4.54.3, with Geske 2005 pp. 106–11 for literature. For the 100 talents and the date, Tod² 64 *ll.* 20–1 = ML 72 = *IG* I³ 369, with Gomme *ad loc.* 5.53.1. *Perioeci*: Thuc. 4.53.2 mentions a garrison, but it has no place in his narrative. Either it was defeated with the rest or, perhaps, if it had been made up of full Spartan citizens, it had been withdrawn to avoid another Sphacteria (so Busolt 3.2 p. 1126).

4. Nicias' discussions with the people of Cythera, 4.54.3. Tribute, hostages from Cythera, 4.57.4–5; the tribute, four talents, was large (see Hornblower *ad loc.*).

5. Nicias' raid on Laconia, 424 BC, and Spartan paralysis, 4.54.4–4.56.1. Spartans organize cavalry and archers, 4.55.2. The Spartans never got over their scorn of horse fighting, and Spartan cavalry was still poor in the next century, Xen. *Hell.* 6.4.19.

6. Sparta receives appeals from the north, 4.79.2–3.

7. Brasidas enrolls helots, 4.80. Pay mercenaries when they arrived: it can be deduced from 4.80.1, 4.80.5, and 4.83.5–6 that Brasidas was not given much, if any, treasure at the outset. Thucydides does not imply that the cautionary massacre of 2,000 helots he mentions when describing the outset of this expedition (4.80.3–4) is contemporary (see Hornblower *ad loc.*).

8. Spartan law about shields, Critias fr. 37 (D–K); cf. Ar. *Eq.* 849. Brasidas around Corinth and Sicyon, 4.70.1, 4.74.1.

9. Homeric looting, vaunting, Lendon 2000 pp. 5–6, 9; and for vaunting (*euchomai*), the references are gathered there at n. 26. "Carrion birds," Hom. *Il.* 11.453–4.

10. For the Athenian logic in refusing to fight, below n. 66. The suggestion that the Peloponnesians should have sent a smaller force to offer a challenge more likely to be met is that of Krentz 1997 p. 68.

11. Athenians attack Thyrea, 424 BC, 4.56.2, with Figueira 1988 pp. 529–38. On the battle of champions at Thyrea, see chapter 3 n. 43.

12. Surrender of Aegina in ?457 BC, 1.108.4.

13. Athenian storming of Thyrea, 424 BC, 4.57, with Rhodes IV–V.24 *ad loc.* Figueira 1988 pp. 531–2 guesses that the Aeginetans at Thyrea were practicing piracy against the Athenians from this fort. "Old eternal hatred," 4.57.4.

14. Athenians invaded Megara not once but twice: joining Classen and Gomme (*ad loc.* 2.31.3) in trying to reconcile 2.31.3 (431 BC), where the Athenians are said to invade once a year and sometimes only with their cavalry, with 4.66.1 (424 BC), where the Athenians invade twice a year (with which Plut. *Per.* 30.3 agrees) with their whole forces. I have suggested above (chapter 6 n. 9) a switch in 426.

15. On the constitution of Megara, Hornblower *ad loc.* 4.66.1. Exiles from Megara, 3.68.3, assuming, with most commentators, that these are the same exiles who appear in Pegae in 4.66.1.

16. Intrigue at Megara, 4.66, with Geske 2005 n. 526 for literature.

17. Peloponnesian garrison in Nisaea, 4.66.

18. Athens built Megara's long walls in the 450s BC, 1.103.4.

19. Plan to take the long walls, 4.67.3; the taking of Minoa in 427 BC (3.51.2) was aimed at blocking privateering out of Nisaea. Raids from Boeotia, Ar. *Ach.* 1018–36, 1071–7; border guards, 4.67.2, with Hornblower *ad loc.* 4.67.5, 8.92.2, 5.

20. Athenians surprised at Megara, Megara had never received help before, 4.72.2.

21. "Because the danger was not foreign to them," 4.72.1; see Gomme, Hornblower, and Rhodes IV–V.24 *ad loc.* for interpretations. For the sense of mutual protection against Athens among the rest of the Peloponnesian alliance, cf. 4.70.1.

22. Athenian logic for not attacking Brasidas, 4.73.4, and see below n. 66.

23. End of the story at Megara, 4.74. Loss of Nisaea in 409 BC, Diod. Sic. 13.65.1. Megarians tear down their long walls, 4.109.1.

24. Athenian negotiations with malcontents in Boeotia, 4.76.1–3. For the literature on this campaign, Geske 2005 n. 552. Aristophanes makes puzzling allusions to Athenian dealings with Boeotia after 426 BC, *Ach.* 155–60; *Eq.* 479.

25. Desire for democracy motivates the Boeotian conspiracy, 4.76.2. Mythic history of Orchomenus, Paus. 9.34–7.

26. Heracles the Nose-Docker, Paus. 9.25.4; also Paus. 9.26.1, 5 (with 9.37.1) for other monuments. The plot against Boeotia, 424 BC, Thuc. 4.76. Orchomenus in 424: *IG* I³ 73 (with Hornblower *ad loc.* 4.76.3), an Athenian decree firmly dated to 424/3, honors and makes a grant of money to one Potamodorus and his son, Athenian *proxenoi* at Orchomenus. Presumably they had been involved in the conspiracy and needed assistance after its failure.

27. "Things would transpire," 4.76.5.

28. For the location of Delium, see Hornblower *ad loc.* 4.76.4 for controversy. No matter: as long it was in the territory of Tanagra, which bordered Attica, the decision to fortify it is puzzling. Delium easy for the Athenians to get if they wanted, cf. Roisman 1993b p. 47.

29. "Convenient refuges," 4.76.5. In this sentence, Thucydides has shifted the point of view to the Boeotian rebels (cf. Classen *ad loc.*), so these fortified places were strongholds for the rebellion, not outposts for the Athenians to ravage from, like those around the Peloponnese, as most have thought (e.g., Busolt 3.2 p. 1141; Gomme *ad loc.* 4.90.4; Rhodes IV–V.24 *ad loc.* 4.76.3). That Demosthenes simply left Boeotia after he failed at Siphae (on this puzzle, Roisman 1993b pp. 50–1), rather than raiding the coast from his ships, argues the same.

30. Plot in Boeotia betrayed, 4.89. Demosthenes' movements before Siphae, 4.77. Boeotian conspirators advance the day of action: here and below I expand Thucydides' puzzling account (on which Hornblower *ad loc.* 4.77.1; Gomme, Hornblower, and Rhodes IV–V.24 *ad loc.* 4.89.1), triangulating from (1) the planned simultaneity of the Athenian descents on Delium and Siphae (4.76.4, 4.77.1), along with Thucydides' statement that a "failure" (rather, I think, than *LSJ*'s "mistake") was made in respect of the date (that is, Demosthenes did not forget the date agreed, as "mistake" implies—Hornblower *ad loc.* 4.77.1 points out how peculiar that would be—but the planned-for simultaneity was not achieved); the fact that (2) Demosthenes arrived *before* the date agreed with Hippocrates (4.89.1); and (3) the fact that the plan was anyway betrayed by a Phocian (4.89.1), and Boeotian troops preempted the risings of Siphae and Chaeronea even before Demosthenes' early arrival (4.89.2). Number of hoplites with Demosthenes, 4.101.3, *pace* Gomme *ad loc.*, who wants an additional 400; number of triremes, 4.76.1.

31. Demosthenes told to help with Oeniadae, 424 BC: I see no other way of interpreting the perplexing 4.77.2; see Gomme and Hornblower *ad loc.*; Roisman 1993b p. 48. Demosthenes gathers northwestern allies, adds Agraeans to force, 4.77.2; cf. 4.101.3. Risings in Boeotia prove abortive, 4.89.

32. Demosthenes at Sicyon, 4.101.3–4. "A thing of immortal make," Hom. *Il.* 6.180–82 (trans. Lattimore).

33. Athenians under Hippocrates invade Boeotia, 424 BC, 4.90.1. Hippocrates ignorant: his ignorance that the Boeotian army was anywhere nearby (4.93.2) implies the more general ignorance argued for by Gomme *ad loc.* 4.90.1. Athenian allies: the *xenoi* in Thucydides, on whom Hornblower *ad loc.* 4.90.1.

34. Athenians fortify Delium, the temple tumbledown, 4.90.2.

35. Athenians finish fortifying Delium and depart for home, 4.90.4. Hippocrates with cavalry, 4.93.2; garrison, 4.100.5. Ravaging is mentioned in the speech Thucydides gives to Pagondas, 4.92.1.

36. Boeotians gather against Hippocrates, 4.91. Cavalry from Opuntian Locris, 4.96.8.

37. Pagondas wants the Boeotians to fight the Athenians, 4.92, with Hornblower *ad loc.*

38. Speech of Pagondas before the battle of Delium, 4.92, with Hornblower *ad loc.* Boeotians decide to fight, 4.93.1.

39. On the battle of Delium, Lendon 2005 pp. 78–90, with 410 for literature on the topography. Dispositions of Hippocrates before Delium, 4.93.2.

40. Dispositions of Pagondas before Delium, 4.93.1, 4.93.3–4. According to Diod. Sic. 12.70.1, a picked unit with the Homeric-revival name "charioteers and chariot-riders" formed the first line of the whole army (Lendon 2005 p. 85), a story unobjectionable if they are regarded instead as advancing in front of the Thebans alone, as the 300-strong Sacred Band (of which this unit may have been some sort of predecessor) did at Leuctra in 371 BC (Plut. *Pel.* 23.2–4 and Diod. Sic. 15.55.2–15.56.2, with Lendon 2005 pp. 108–10). But Toher 2001 makes an ingenious argument that the "charioteers and chariot-riders" never existed. For the danger of being outflanked when a deep formation is used, Xen. *Hell.* 4.2.13; *An.* 4.8.11. Streams on the Delium battlefield, Thuc. 4.96.2. Peltasts with the Boeotians: assuming (*pace* Gomme *ad loc.* 4.93.3) that they are mercenaries (as Athens' were, 4.28.4) gives some sense to Thucydides' distinguishing them from the rest of the *psiloi* (light-armed troops). No Athenian light-armed, 4.94.1.

41. On the great *othismos* ("push") controversy, Rawlings 2007 p. 95 and Schwartz 2009 p. 188 gather the literature. My treatment here comes closest to the compromise positions of Wheeler 2007 pp. 209–11; Rawlings 2007 pp. 93–7; Schwartz 2009 pp. 198–200; Matthew 2009: yes, there was pushing, but a lot else happened as well. Push of shields, 4.96.2; Xen. *Hell.* 4.3.19 = *Ages.* 2.12. Push on backs, esp. Xen. *Mem.* 3.1.8.

42. Hoplite pushing impossible: so esp. Krentz 1985b; Goldsworthy 1997; van Wees 2004 pp. 184–91; they go on to offer the psychological explanation given below. Metaphorical "pushing" in Greek warfare, e.g., 4.35, and the references are gathered by Krentz 1985b pp. 55–7. Wounded men removed: van Wees 2004 p. 189 n. 26 gathers the evidence. "At length of a spear" (*eis doru*), Xen. *Hell.* 4.3.17, 7.1.31; cf. Plut. *Tim.* 28.1. And for the importance of the spear to the hoplite, Eur. *HF* 190–4. Hoplite shield flicking, suggested by van Wees 2004 p. 190.

43. "Little by little" (*ōsamenoi kata brachu*), 4.96.4; cf. Xen. *Cyr.* 7.1.33–4. "One more step," Polyaen. *Strat.* 2.3.4; cf. 3.9.27. "Pressure of knees," Amm. Marc. 16.12.37, with Lendon 2005 p. 262; Gomme *ad loc.* 4.96.2 for other Roman parallels. For apparently rather literal pushing in the Hellenistic period,

see esp. Polyb. 18.30.4 (cf. Pritchett 1985 pp. 67–8; Wheeler 2007 pp. 210–11); Asclep. *Tact.* 5.2. For "turning to flight" in Greek battle, Pritchett 1985 pp. 69–71.

44. Rather overestimates the force: so deep formations would not always prevail right away, as van Wees 2004 p. 190 complained they should if the mass push were real. Hoplite equipment impractical for individual combat, recently argued by Schwartz 2009 (who introduced Inspector Olsen into the controversy, pp. 53–4, 155–6); "size of a bridge table," p. 35. On the abandonment of various parts of the archaic hoplite panoply during the course of the fifth century BC, Hannah 2010.

45. Korean riot footage also illustrates what a fearsome offensive weapon the edges of even a large, awkward shield can be; cf. Eur. *Phoen.* 1404–15.

46. Hoplites drawing together, for an attack, Xen. *Hell.* 4.3.18; to receive attack, Hdt. 9.18; Thuc. 2.4, 5.10; Xen. *Hell.* 7.4.22; both sides, Thuc. 5.71.1. Hoplites undrilled or poorly drilled: my view in Lendon 2005 p. 108–9, but see the challenge in Wheeler 2007 pp. 205–8. For massing in the *Iliad*, Lendon 2005 pp. 28–32.

47. Hoplites clump up with those to their sides, 5.71.1, with van Wees 2004 p. 187. Spartans walk rather than run, 5.70.

48. Advance of Boeotians and Athenians at the battle of Delium, 4.96.1. Speech of Hippocrates, 4.95, with Hornblower *ad loc.* Athenian sacrilege, 4.92.7, 4.97.3.

49. Fighting at the battle of Delium, 4.96.2–4.

50. Thespians at Thermopylae, Hdt. 7.222, 7.226. Cult of Love at Thespiae, Paus. 9.27.1; at Sparta, Athenaeus 561e. Thespians: what is thought to be their tomb has been discovered and excavated, and the bodies counted, *IG* VII 1888; see Hornblower *ad loc.* 4.96.3 (also, perhaps, a tomb of the Tanagrans, *IG* VII 585). It is an irony that, in the winter of 423/2 BC, the Thebans dismantled the city wall of Thespiae, whose loyalty they suspected (4.133.1).

51. End of the battle of Delium, 4.96.5–4.97.1.

52. Socrates retreats from Delium, Plato, *Symp.* 221a–c. Number of dead at battle of Delium, 4.101.2. Light-armed soldiers and builders killed, making sense of Thucydides' (4.101.2) statement that "many light-armed troops and baggage-bearers" were killed.

53. Thebans and the loot, Diod. Sic. 12.70.5 (Hornblower *ad loc.* 4.97.1 does not believe in the Delia festival, thinking it a doublet for the recently reestablished Athenian festival of Apollo on Delos, but it is equally possible that it was a one-up response to the Athenian Delia). Ransom: so I suppose, trying to answer Gomme's (*ad loc.* 4.97.1) puzzle, "it is difficult to guess what rich things the Athenians had taken with them for a very brief campaign."

54. Rescue of Athenian fugitives by sea, 4.96.8. Meeting of the heralds, 4.97.2–4.

55. Athenians and Boeotians argue over the bodies from Delium, 4.98–9, with Lateiner 1977b pp. 101–3; Orwin 1994 pp. 90–6; and Hornblower *ad loc.*

56. Euripides' *Suppliants*: see Hornblower *ad loc.* 4.97.2 for the debate.

57. Boeotian preparations to attack Delium, summoning of allies, 4.100.

58. Retaking of Delium by the Boeotians, 4.101.1–2. The Athenian dead from Delium: Pausanias (1.29.13) saw their memorial at Athens. This is one of the contexts suggested for the elegy quoted at p. 82.

59. "The fame of Athens," Xen. *Mem.* 3.5.4 (a passage already adduced in its relationship to Coronea, see p. 78); cf. Diod. Sic. 12.70.3; Hanson 2005 p. 135. Worse to lose to the Boeotians, cf. Aeschin. 3.88. For a modern parallel to the shame of being defeated by an enemy you hold in contempt, Löwenheim and Heimann 2008 p. 715.

60. For the events in the 450s BC, 1.103–11, and see above pp. 60–72. Divisions in Boeotia, 4.92.6; cf. 1.113.1–2. Capture of Cythera, 424: perhaps a relative of Tolmides, the general Autocles, son of Tolmaeus (4.53.1), Davies 1971 nr. 2717. Cleon negotiating with Argos, Ar. *Eq.* 465–7 (spring 424). Match of events in the 450s and 420s: a literary scholar might rejoin that the two seem similar because Thucydides' account of 425–424 had for some reason contaminated his account of the 450s (or vice versa). But the Athenians in 425–424 seem to imitate actions in the 450s that Thucydides' account of the 450s does not mention. Thus, the Athenians attack Troezen in 425 (4.45.2), but Thucydides does not mention Athens' interest in Troezen in the 450s, except accidentally when he reports on the terms of the Thirty Years' Peace (1.115.1).

61. Athenians burn Spartan arsenal in Laconia: an even stronger parallel if Falkner 1994 is right that Laconian Asine, rather than Gytheum, was the port that Tolmides burned in the 450s BC, for Nicias attacked Asine from Cythera (4.54.4). Moreover the 425 expedition of the Athenians and Acarnanians to capture Anactorium (4.49.1), which the Corinthians had held since 433 (1.55.1), may recall Tolmides' capture of Chalcis (1.108.5), which the Athenians perhaps had to give up in the Thirty Years' Peace, see chapter 2 n. 47. According to *IG* II² 403, Athena's share of the proceeds from the Anactorium expedition (if the editors have it right) were added to those from the northwestern campaign of the previous year, as well as to those from the final extermination of the oligarchs on Corcyra, and paid for a statue of Athena Nike. Pericles' expedition in ?454, Thuc. 1.111.2–3. Tolmides, too, raided Sicyon (1.108.5) and was defeated there. Oeniadae in 424: Oeniadae had, of course, been attacked before in the war, in 428 (3.7.3), and an attack had been contemplated in 429 (2.102.2).

62. Corinthians, 4.42.3; Aeginetans, 4.57.1 (deducing from the fact that they were building a fort on the coast); Sicyon, 4.101.3–4 (deducing from the Sicyonians' attack on the Athenians before all the Athenians ships had even arrived). The Spartans expected an Athenian attack on Laconia once they had captured Cythera, 4.55.1, but that would have required no special foreknowledge.

63. Any aggressive strategy will appear similar: so Kagan 1974 pp. 258–9, who thought that the new strategy of Cleon was to make Athens safe from invasion in future by capturing Megara and making Boeotia friendly. But how

does that explain Athens' other acts? Other students speak more vaguely of, e.g., "an ever more ambitious strategy" (Lazenby 2004 p. 79).

64. Analysis of post-Periclean Athenian strategy in political-party terms to explain its apparent inconsistency originated in nineteenth-century Germany (Beloch 1884 pp. 19–46; Busolt 3.2 *passim* and esp. p. 1053). In English, Adcock 1927 (esp. p. 204) popularized the distinction between a Periclean "Tory" (although he did not use the word) party of farmers and the rich, led by Nicias, and a left-wing party of Cleon, that of "the sailors and craftsmen and traders . . . who sought to convert what was in essence a defensive war into a war of definite triumphant aggression" (p. 204; cf. 236), and this method of analysis was dominant into the 1970s (Holladay 1978 [2002]; Kagan 1974 was its final monument). Such analysis has since quietly been abandoned, because of (1) the growing realization that, given our ignorance of the internal politics of the contending states, the assignment of politicians to factions is quite arbitrary; and (2) a growing sense that Athenian politics did not work that way anyway (esp. Sealey 1958 [1967]; Holladay 1978 [2002]; cf. Thompson 1973 for Sparta, which had been subjected to the same kind of analysis). Contemporary scholars emphasize instead the remarkable consensus of the Athenians on great matters (esp. Ober 1989). Thucydides calls the actors in his story the "Athenians" and "Lacedaemonians" and rarely lifts the lid on their internal disagreements. But "perhaps inability to trace party-history in detail should not be regretted. Thucydides says very little about Athenian parties. He mentions party-differences where they influenced conduct of the Archidamian War, that is, he mentions difference of policy between Cleon and Nicias in 422. The proper inference is that party-differences had very little effect on the policies carried out before 422" (Sealey 1958 [1967] p. 70).

65. Athenian reply to Spartan envoys, 425 BC, 4.21.3.

66. Athenian logic for not fighting, 4.73.4. Gomme, Hornblower, Rhodes IV–V.24 *ad loc.*, Roisman 1993b p. 44, and Lazenby 2004 p. 87 all complain that Thucydides' suggestion that the Athenian generals, in declining battle, reasoned that "they had got most of what they wanted" does not accord with Athenian hopes for getting hold of Megara. But in the previous year it was Nisaea (along with Pegae), not Megara, that they wanted (4.21.3). Handing over Megara itself to the Athenians was primarily the goal of the democratic cabal at Megara (4.66.3), not of the Athenians. Roisman 1993b pp. 45–6 gathers (and adds to) speculations about why the Athenians withdrew.

67. Pericles pays jurors, Arist. *Pol.* 1274a; *Ath. pol.* 27.4; Cleon, Ar. *Eq.* 797–800; Schol. *Vesp.* 88, 300. For an up-to-date survey of Athenian building from 430 to 420 BC, Shear 2007 pp. 92–6. For suggestions of a building boom in and after 425, Boersma 1970 p. 85; Mikalson 1984 pp. 222–3; Miles 1989 pp. 227–35; Rubel 2000 pp. 262–306. Temple of Athena Nike: not datable on epigraphic grounds (see appendix p. 430 on the Halieis treaty, *IG* I³ 75); nevertheless Athens' victory over Sparta at Sphacteria seems the best context for a temple to Victory

(Boersma 1970 p. 85). Improved the wall system at Athens: Ar. *Eq.* 817–8 alludes to Cleon's "walling off" or building a "cross-wall" (*diateichisma*), which archeologists are happy to think refers to an actual construction (e.g., Boersma 1970, nr. 10), but commentators on the play (e.g., Sommerstein 1981 *ad loc.*) are just as confident is a metaphor for Cleon's dividing the people. Temple "of the Athenians" at Delos, Boersma 1970 nr. 36; Rubel 2000 p. 301; stoa at Brauron, Rubel 2000 p. 302; Theater of Dionysus, Boersma 1970 nr. 84; Nemesis at Rhamnous, Miles 1989 pp. 221–7; Rubel 2000 pp. 298–300.

68. Currently fashionable reconstruction: that of Mattingly, whose essays are collected in Mattingly 1996. Mattingly's assignment of the Cleonymus and the Coinage/Standards Decrees (see appendix p. 429 for references) to this period is endorsed by Rhodes 2008 and Papazarkadas 2009 pp. 72–3.

69. In the *Knights*, Cleon is associated with a very aggressive strategy, promising Demos control of Arcadia (*ll.* 797–8). "Oh Athens," Ar. *Eq.* 1329–30. Golden cricket, Thuc. 1.6.3. "He lives," Ar. *Eq.* 1323; "Aristides and Miltiades," *l.* 1325. All this crowning with violets is presumably an allusion to Pindar's description of Athens as violet-crowned (fr. 64), which is another link to the mid-century past.

70. "Greetings," Ar. *Eq.* 1333–4; "isn't she pretty," *ll.* 1390–1 (mine is a feeble translation of one of the most contrived puns in Aristophanes).

CHAPTER IX:
THE BLOODY MARCH OF PEACE, 424–420 BC

1. Thracian tattoos, Hdt. 5.6; food throwing, Xen. *An.* 7.3.21–3; messages to the gods, Hdt. 4.94.

2. For Thrace in the late fifth century BC, 2.29, 2.97–8, with Archibald 1998 pp. 93–125. Thucydides and the north, 4.105.1, with Hornblower *ad loc.* On Thucydides' family, Hornblower *ad loc.* 4.104.4.

3. For Macedonia in the late fifth century BC, 2.99.1–2.100.2, with Hammond and Griffith 1979 pp. 115–36.

4. For the Macedonian/Argive connection, 2.99.3; Hdt. 8.137–9.

5. For the cities of the Thracian Chalcidice and Bottice, Flensted-Jensen 2004.

6. On Amphipolis and its importance, 4.102, 4.108.1, with Flensted-Jensen 2004 pp. 819–20; eels, Mitchell 1991 pp. 174–5.

7. Athens, Perdiccas, and the Chalcidians before the war, 1.56.2–1.61.2, and see pp. 98–9 with literature. We reprise the story here to give context to later events.

8. Song of the maidens of Bottice, Plut. *Them.* 16.2.

9. Athenians colonize Potidaea, 2.70.4. According to Diod. Sic. 12.46.7, 1,000 colonists. Tod² 60 = ML 66 = *IG* I³ 514 = Fornara 129 is a dedication the colonists made on the Athenian acropolis before they left. *IG* I³ 62 *l.* 8 also

refers to these colonists. Athenians fail to take Spartolus, 429 BC, 2.79, with Rhodes II *ad loc.* The recently found "Athenian Metro Casualty List" (Parlama 2000; and see appendix p. 427) may refer to this defeat.

10. Athens' 425 BC adventure in the north, 4.7. The town the Athenians attempted to capture is unlocated (Hornblower *ad loc.*).

11. Athenians take Therme, 1.61.2; trade Therme, 2.29.6. Perdiccas supports the Peloponnesians in the northwest, 2.80.7—if we can believe this story, since the aid was both secret and futile.

12. Sitalces becomes an Athenian ally, 2.29.1–5, with Luppino 1981. Official sanction at Athens for the cult of the Thracian god Bendis may have something to do with this alliance (Archibald 1998 p. 97 n. 16; Rubel 2000 pp. 239–43), but it cannot be exactly dated. Sitalces brokers alliance between Athens and Perdiccas, 2.29.5–7.

13. Winter of 429/8 BC expedition of Sitalces into Macedonia, 2.95.1–2.96.1, 2.98.1–2.101.6. Badian 1993b regards Thucydides' account with a pervasive doubt that I do not share. Perdiccas' promise to Sitalces, 2.95.1.

14. Telling of the Thracian host, 2.96, 2.98.3–4. Archibald 1998 p. 119 is inclined to believe Thucydides' number.

15. Sitalces enters Macedonia, 2.99.1, 2.100; goes against Chalcidice, 2.101.1–5. "Not believing," 2.101.1.

16. Betrothal of Seuthes, 2.101.5–6. Death of Sitalces, 4.101.5, with Ar. *Ach.* 141–50, 156–8 on his friendship to Athens in 425 BC; but after Sitalces' death, the same Thracians Aristophanes imagined sent as gifts must be hired (5.6.2, in 422). Kingdom of Sitalces plays no more role: Archibald 1998 pp. 120–1.

17. Terror inspired by Sitalces' expedition, 2.101.2–3.

18. "Enforce one promise," 2.95.1. Ancient simplicity, 3.83.1, and see above p. 211.

19. Pleas to Sparta from the north in 424 BC, Spartan logic, 4.79–80. Relations between Athens and Perdiccas: the second Methone Decree (Tod² 61 = ML 65 = *IG* I³ 61 = Fornara 128), firmly dated to 426/5, refers to problems.

20. Brasidas' march through Thessaly, 4.78.1–4.79.1, with Gomme *ad loc.* for the route and Badian 1999 p. 11 on the confrontation at the river. For all 1,700 as private "guests," Kagan 1974 p. 290. Brasidas marched through Thessaly in three days: assuming that Thuc. 4.78.5 has structured his account by daily marches. "Cargoes of lies," Hermippus fr. 63 *l.* 8 (*PCG*) = Athenaeus 27e.

21. Athenians react to Brasidas' coming to the north, 4.82. Brasidas in Lyncestis, 4.83.

22. Brasidas outwitted the slyest of men: to Thucydides, Brasidas is an Odysseus figure (Badian 1999 p. 33), or he partakes of both Achilles and Odysseus (Howie 2005 pp. 270–6). For the particular quality of *xunesis* ("intelligence") that Thucydides attributes to Brasidas (4.81.2), Hornblower *ad loc.*

23. Brasidas takes Acanthus, 4.84, 4.88.1; for the archeological remains, Flensted-Jensen 2004 pp. 823–4. Thucydides writes Brasidas a speech (4.85–7, with Hornblower *ad loc.*). Brasidas takes Stagirus, 4.88.2.

24. Northern reaction to Delium, 4.108.5, 5.14.2.

25. History of Athenian involvement in Amphipolis and description of the city, 4.102. Brasidas and Argilus, 4.103.4 (and the guess why the Athenians suspected them is Hornblower's *ad loc.*). Brasidas' new allies Acanthus and Stagirus were colonies of Andros (Meiggs 1972 p. 335; Hornblower *ad loc.* 4.84.1), as was Argilus, and all were presumably friendly to each other. Badian 1999 pp. 16–19 guesses that getting hold of a link in this Andrian chain was why Brasidas first went to Acanthus.

26. Brasidas' march on Amphipolis, Amphipolitans react, 4.103.1–4.104.3. Busolt 3.2 p. 1151 puts the taking of Amphipolis in December 424 BC.

27. Summoning of the fleet from Thasos, 4.104.4–5. Westlake 1962 (1969) p. 286 collects speculations as to why the general was at Thasos. Thasos will not have been the squadron's regular winter station: the harbor is too exposed from the north. Better-sheltered Eion (4.108.1) seems to have been the Athenian base. Gomme *ad loc.* 4.104.5 rightly thought seven ships "a small force; if there were other ships in Thucydides' command, where were they?" But see above p. 168 for discussion of the small size of Athenian squadrons on extended duty.

28. Brasidas' offer to Amphipolis, 4.105.

29. Controversy in Amphipolis, Amphipolis surrenders, 4.106.1–3. Athenians in Amphipolis: so Thucydides says at 4.105.2 and 4.106.1. Probably not a garrison from Athens (as Rhodes IV–V.24 *ad loc.* 4.105.2 argues)—or taking Amphipolis would have been far harder (so Westlake 1962 [1969] p. 281)— but Amphipolitans of Athenian origin (so Hornblower *ad loc.* 4.106.1). The general Eucles seems to have had few or no Athenian troops with him, Westlake 1962 (1969) pp. 280–1. It would take time to assemble a force: trying to reconcile 4.106.1, the Athenians expect no speedy relief (which, given the summons to Thasos, puzzled Westlake 1962 [1969] p. 283; Badian 1999 p. 22), with 4.105.1, Brasidas fears the coming of the squadron from Thasos.

30. Thasos squadron arrives at Eion, 4.106.3–4. Brasidas attacks Eion, 4.107.1–2.

31. Towns and Thracians defect to Brasidas in wake of his taking Amphipolis, 4.107.3. We learn later (5.6.4) that other Thracians, too, became Brasidas' friends.

32. Brasidas seeks to fulfill Spartan promise to liberate the Greeks, 4.108.2; messages to Brasidas from would-be rebels and their motivation, 4.108.3–6. Perdiccas at Amphipolis, 4.107.3.

33. Boreas kin to the Athenians, Paus. 1.19.5. Athenian winter measures in the north, 4.108.6.

34. Exile of Thucydides, 5.26.5, with Gomme iii pp. 584–7. We do not know what happened to Eucles, the general who actually lost Amphipolis.

35. Brasidas builds triremes, 4.108.6. Brasidas in Acte, 4.109. Busolt 3.2 p. 1160 dates this expedition to the end of February 423 BC.

36. For the remains of Torone, Cambitoglou 2001. For the products and features of Torone, Henry 2004 pp. 57–63, 89–92.

37. Brasidas' assault on Torone begins, 4.110.1–4.111.2. Brasidas' men got lost: trying to make sense of Thucydides' statement that those outside the walls "wondered at the delay" (4.111.2), which puzzled Gomme *ad loc.*, and that Brasidas' men had to be "led around" (ibid.) to the postern. Why, if this were the intended way in, were they not already there? Wrong side of the town in Torone: see Cambitoglou 2001 vol. 1 pp. 67, 73.

38. Brasidas takes Torone, 4.111.2–4.113.3. Around to the rear gate: read very literally, Thucydides 4.111.2 may mean that the conspirators broke open a second postern and led the men around to that. Proverb, Henry 2004 pp. 93–4.

39. Athenians retreat to the Oil Bottle at Torone, 4.113.2: *lekythos*, a usual Greek pottery shape.

40. Negotiations, Brasidas addresses the Toroneans, both sides fortify, 4.114.

41. Taking of the Oil Bottle, 4.115.1–4.116.1.

42. Brasidas thanks Athena, 4.116.2; for the temple of Athena, Cambitoglou 2001 vol. 1 p. 74. Brasidas' plotting in the winter of 424/3 BC, 4.116.3.

43. Brasidas takes Scione, 4.120–1. End of March: for the date, 4.120.1 and 4.122.6, with 4.118.12 and Hornblower *ad loc.* For the remains of Scione, Flensted-Jensen 2004 p. 842. For Scione's Peloponnesian connection, Hornblower *ad loc.* 4.120.1.

44. For the honors to Brasidas at Scione, Hornblower *ad loc.* 4.121.1.

45. Brasidas' plans against Mende and Potidaea, and Brasidas hears of the truce, 4.121.2–4.122.2.

46. Sparta's requirements for peace: since Sparta's allies (other than the Boeotians) were willing to concur in the truce (4.119.2), the Spartans must not yet have been contemplating the betrayal of their allies enacted by the treaty of 421 BC. For Sparta's prewar agreement with her allies, p. 101.

47. "On the basis of equality" (*epi tēi isēi*), 5.15.2. Athenian fears from loss of Amphipolis, 4.108.1. For the importance of the Hellespont for Athenian grain imports, see chapter 2 n. 56.

48. Chios told to pull down its walls, 4.51.

49. Exiles from Lesbos in Asia Minor, 4.52.2–3, 4.75.1. Exiles from Samos in Asia Minor, 4.75.1; cf. 3.19.2 and 3.32.2 with Fantasia 1986.

50. Thucydides on Athenian motivation for the truce, 4.117.1–2; and for momentum, cf. 4.108.4–6.

51. Terms of the truce of 423 BC, 4.118; ship size, 4.118.5, with Gomme *ad loc.*

52. Continuing Spartan fear of helot revolt, 5.14.3–4.

53. Equality of honor necessary for peace, cf. Ar. *Pax* 211–14. Military parity perilous: adding explanatory logic to the famously baffling and textually corrupt 4.117.2 (see Classen, Gomme, and Hornblower *ad loc.*). I delete *kai kratēsein* with most eds., and W. D. Furley suggests to me the supplement *komisasthai <ē> hōs eti Brasidas ēutuxei*.

54. Spartans refuse reinforcements to Brasidas, 4.108.6–7. Thucydides also says the leaders at Sparta were jealous of Brasidas.

55. Scione excluded from truce, Brasidas lies about Scione, Athenians react, 4.122. Euboea: a scholiast to Aristophanes (= Philochorus *FGH* 328 F 119) mentions an Athenian expedition in 424/3 BC, but Gomme iii p. 592 suspected that he was confused.

56. Mende revolts to Brasidas, 4.123.1–2.

57. Athenians prepare to go against Pallene, and Brasidas prepares Pallene to resist, 4.123.3–4.

58. Brasidas' second march into Lyncestis, 4.124.1–4.125.1, with Hammond 1972 pp. 104–8. Gomme *ad loc.* 4.124.1 suggests that Perdiccas threatened to cut off Brasidas' supplies to force him to join the campaign.

59. Retreat of Brasidas from Lyncestis, 4.125.2–4.128.3. Lazenby 2004 p. 274 n. 45, citing Thuc. 7.30.2, suggests that Brasidas may have learned some of his tactics from the Thracians. Speech of Brasidas to his army in Lyncestis, 4.126, with Hornblower *ad loc.* and Hunter 1973 pp. 23–30.

60. Brasidas wins through to the realm of Perdiccas, and results, 4.128.3–5.

61. Athenians against Mende, 4.129, with Geske 2005 pp. 132–41 for literature.

62. Second day at Mende, 4.130.1.

63. Third day at, and fall of, Mende, 4.130.2–7. Hornblower *ad loc.* 4.130.4 assumed Polydamidas was a Spartan, but 4.132.3 counts against this.

64. Athenians against Scione, 4.131; leave a garrison and go home, 4.133.4 Scione finally falls after the peace in 421 BC, 5.32.1. An undated and fragmentary text of a treaty that seems to represent the reconciliation of Athens to some towns in Bottice may (or may not) date to around this time, Tod² 68 = *IG* I³ 76, with Mitchell 1991 pp. 179–80, and Geske 2005 p. 140 for literature.

65. Perdiccas allies with Athens (4.132.1), which may (or may not) be the same as an undated treaty that survives on stone (*IG* I³ 89); see Gomme *ad loc.* 4.132.1, with Geske 2005 p. 140 for literature.

66. Perdiccas, Thessaly, and the Peloponnesian reinforcements, 4.132.2, with Gomme *ad loc.* Kagan 1974 pp. 315–6, drawing on Busolt, argues that the inspectors were to control, not to help, Brasidas. Brasidas' promises, 4.86.1, 4.88.1 (with Hornblower *ad loc.* on both), 4.108.2–3. Against the promises (*paranomōs*), 4.132.3, with Gomme *ad loc.*

67. War between Tegea and Mantinea, 4.134; and, as Gomme *ad loc.* notes, any territory changing hands as a result of such a war would be in contravention of the prewar agreement between Sparta and her allies. Hornblower *ad loc.* collects monuments that may be from this war. Troezen makes a separate peace with Athens, 4.118.4. The epigraphically preserved treaties between Athens and Halieis (*IG* I³ 75) and Hermione (*IG* I³ 31), also on the Argolid peninsula, may be contemporary or not: see appendix p. 430.

68. Brasidas' attempt on Potidaea, 4.135.1. Thucydides does not say why Brasidas went against Potidaea, but the relief of Scione, the completion of whose investment is described at 4.133.4, seems the natural reason.

69. Extension of the truce, exile of the Delians, 5.1.1, with Hornblower *ad loc*. For the return of the Delians, in the next year, at the order of Delphi, 5.32.1. Diod. Sic. 12.73.1 says that Athens accused the Delians of colluding with the Spartans, and some have followed him, esp. Jordan 1986 pp. 137–8, citing the landfall of Alcidas at Delos in 427 BC (Thuc. 3.29.1—but he does not strictly say they landed, merely that they were seen); Smarczyk 1990 pp. 520–1. I reject this theory with Rubel 2000 p. 155; Hornblower and Rhodes IV–V.24 *ad loc*. 5.1.1. Why ever would the weak islander Delians ally with Spartans or allow themselves to be thought to do so? First two terms of the truce of 423 BC concern Apollo, 4.118.1–4. The agreement about Delphi appears originally to have been a separate document from the truce (so Rhodes IV–V.24 *ad loc*.). Rivalry over Delphi during Cimon's truce, 1.112.5; Plut. *Per.* 21.2; cf. Plut. *Them.* 20.3–4 and above p. 73.

70. Cleon sails north, 5.2.1. See Busolt 3.2 p. 1175 on the strength of this force.

71. Cleon arrives at Scione, goes to Torone, 5.2.2–4.

72. Cleon takes Torone, 5.2.2–5.3.5. Captives auctioned on the spot: for this practice, Hornblower *ad loc*. 5.3.4.

73. For the Amphipolis campaign, 422 BC, 5.3.6, 5.6–11. On the battle of Amphipolis and its topography, Pritchett 1965b pp. 30–48; answered by Jones 1978 pp. 71–104; answered by Pritchett 1980. I accord with Pritchett except where noted below. For how Thucydides tells the story, Howie 2005 pp. 231–60. Cleon fails at Stagirus, summons allies, 5.6.1–2. Did Thucydides fail to mention other significant conquests of Cleon's? No: see Mitchell 1991 pp. 176–81, with literature; Rhodes IV–V.24 *ad loc*. 5.2.1.

74. Brasidas takes his position on hill, calls for help, 5.6.3–5. The numbers of the armies at Amphipolis: Thucydides got himself into a muddle: compare 5.6.3, 5.8.2, 5.8.3, and 5.9.3 and see Gomme *ad loc*. 5.8.2 and Hornblower *ad loc*. 5.6.3 and 5.8.2. Athenian army of higher quality, 5.8.2.

75. Cleon marches out from Eion, 5.7. Thucydides has Cleon driven to advance by the contempt of his soldiers for his military incapacity (5.7.2). But "since his first appearance as a general in 425 BC his record of achievement had been amazing" (Kagan 1974 p. 324). Thus Gomme and Hornblower *ad loc*. 5.7.2 quite properly discard this opinion, but we are left with no explanation for why Cleon moved when he did.

76. Brasidas enters Amphipolis, his plans, Cleon ascends hill, 5.8. Thucydides (5.8–9) presents Brasidas' plans for his sally as more definite than they probably were. Both Brasidas and Cleon died in the battle and could hardly tell Thucydides what they had planned (so Woodhead 1960 p. 308). The speech Thucydides gives Brasidas (5.9, with Hornblower *ad loc*.) is a manifesto of what Everett Wheeler (1988 pp. 162–5) has called the "Odyssean" strain of Greek generalship, the valuation of guile; see also Lendon 2005 pp. 85–90. For the relation of the speech to the action, Hunter 1973 pp. 30–40.

77. Athenians and Cleon watch Amphipolis, Brasidas, 5.10.2–3; Cleon deploys to march back to Eion past Amphipolis, 5.10.3 (I discard as the product of Thucydides' bias the suggestion [5.10.3] that Cleon did not want a battle before his reinforcements arrived: he had gone out seeking one). "Having wheeled (*epistrepsas*) the right wing and so exposed its uncovered side to the enemy, he led off the army" (5.10.4). Despite Pritchett 1980 pp. 334–5 (endorsed by Hornblower and Rhodes IV–V.24 *ad loc.*; Lazenby 2004 p. 103), *epistrepsas* means "wheel," that is, a body of men pivoting on a corner rather than each man turning in place (cf. Asclep. *Tact.* 10.4–5; Kagan 1974 p. 328). Of course, *all* the Athenian soldiers marching south past Amphipolis (on their right) revealed their uncovered side to the enemy (Gomme *ad loc.* 5.10.3). But Thucydides distinguishes Cleon's uncovering of the right wing from the situation of the rest of the army. So the right wing must be uncovered in some more dangerous sense: having wheeled out of line of march, its uncovered flank was much closer to the enemy in the city.

78. Megara part of the legend of Brasidas, 4.85.7, 4.108.5.

79. Trailing his army: the metaphor is that of Woodhead 1960 p. 307. For similar taunting behavior at sea, Xen. *Hell.* 1.5.12.

80. Brasidas' plan of attack at Amphipolis, 5.9.6–7, 5.10.1, 5. "These men won't stand," 5.10.5. The oddity here is that after depicting Cleon foolishly wheeling his right and making it vulnerable (5.10.4), leading the reader to expect an attack on the right, Thucydides seems to describe Brasidas' forces attacking the center and the left (5.10.6, 8), defeating the reader's expectation.

81. Brasidas attacks the Athenians, is wounded, 5.10.6–8. Where were the gates from which Brasidas' forces came? On the basis of what was then archeologically attested, Pritchett 1980 pp. 305–6 located them on the north face of the city, facing the bridge over the Strymon. But northern gates give Brasidas' men rather a long approach, considering that the attack was to be a surprise, and one would think that a "Thracian Gate" (5.10.7)—so one of them is called—should face east into Thrace rather than north (so Jones 1978 p. 94). Since then at least one (later) gate has been found on the (incompletely excavated) eastern face of the city (Lazaridis 1993, esp. the map pp. 22–3), and there were probably more. The two gates Brasidas' forces came out of will have been on the eastern face of the city, on the wall paralleling (and close to) the road the Athenians took to Eion, and not too close together, since the attack by the two forces could be described as *amphoterōthen* ("from both sides") (5.10.7).

82. End of the battle of Amphipolis, deaths of Cleon and Brasidas, 5.10.8–11; Athenian dead, 5.11.2. Diod. Sic. 12.74.2, in an account of the battle that otherwise conveys little conviction, has Cleon die well, and Woodhead 1960 pp. 309–10 hints that in this detail his version might be preferred to that of Thucydides; cf. Kagan 1974 p. 330. Pausanias (1.29.13) saw at Athens a monument to the Athenians at Amphipolis.

83. Trophy, funeral, and honors for Brasidas, 5.10.12–5.11.3, with the massive note of Hornblower *ad loc.* 5.11.1.

84. Brasidas' father, 5.19.2, with Rhodes IV–V.24 *ad loc.* "My son was a brave man," Diod. Sic. 12.74.3–4; Plut. *Lyc.* 25.5, probably not, alas, to be believed.

85. Brasidas and Cleon, Pleistoanax and Nicias, 5.16.1–5.17.1; Ar. *Pax* 270, 283–4. For Nicias' motive, Geske 2005 pp. 153–61. The importance of Brasidas is also implied by the fact that a Peloponnesian mission of reinforcement to the north (winter 422/1 BC) turned back when it heard of his death, assuming that peace would result (5.13). The Thessalians also obstructed these Peloponnesian reinforcements (5.13), and Papazarkadas 2009 p. 75 associates with this event *IG* I³ 92, a firmly dated Athenian proxeny decree for a Thessalian made at the proposal of the Athenian generals.

86. For the terms of the Peace of Nicias, 5.18, with Gomme iii pp. 670–2; Hornblower *ad loc.* 5.18.5–6 on the distinctions between the northern cities. Places Athens had captured to be returned: also Atalanta, the island Athens had fortified off Opuntian Locris (2.32, 3.89.3), and Pteleum, about which we know nothing. Oddly, there is no mention of Troezen in the treaty Thucydides preserves, although it had featured in the one-year truce (4.118.4), unless words have fallen out of the treaty at 5.18.7 (which Gomme *ad loc.* suspected for other reasons).

87. Peloponnesian fleet not to be returned: noticed by Legon 1969 p. 325. Corinth's resentment over the non-return of Sollium and Anactorium, 5.30.2. Treaty can be amended without Sparta's allies, 5.18.11; this provision a matter of resentment, 5.29.2–3; Diod. Sic. 12.75.4; with Andrewes and Lewis 1957 p. 177.

88. The hostility of some of Sparta's allies was known before the treaty was sworn: Aristophanes (*Pax* 466, 481, 500–2) names the Boeotians and the Megarians as against the peace. Athens' 421 BC truce with Boeotia, 5.26.2, with Hornblower *ad loc.*; lack of truce with Corinth, 5.32.5–7.

89. Thucydides on Sparta's motivations for peace, 5.14.3–4; Argos, 5.14.4. For the Argive longing for hegemony, chapter 1 n. 23.

90. Boeotia and Phocis not in the 423 BC truce, 4.118.2. At 4.119.2 Elis is not represented among the oath swearers of the truce, although Epidaurus and Sicyon, smaller places, are, so it may also have held itself back from the truce, or there may be a problem with the text of Thucydides. War between Tegea and Mantinea, above pp. 252–4. Mantinea against Arcadia, 5.29.1; Sparta against Mantinea in the summer of 421 BC, 5.33. Elis and Lepreum, 5.31.2–5, with Falkner 1999b. Troezen's treaty with Athens, 4.118.4.

91. Boeotians take Panactum, 5.3.5, with Hornblower *ad loc.* Boeotians will not yield Plataea, 5.17.2.

92. "Disgraced and despised," 5.28.2.

93. Sparta's allies told to prepare to build a fort in Attica, 5.17.2.

94. Why should Athens make peace now? So Kagan 1974 p. 339, and he opts for war weariness (pp. 339–41). But why more so in 421 than in 423 BC?

Lewis 1992b p. 431, dismissing attempts to show that Athens was almost out of money (gathered by Geske 2005 n. 611, and see my chapter 4 n. 68) thinks that because of Delium and Amphipolis, Athens was running out of hoplites.

95. Athens fears revolt after Amphipolis (and Thucydides mentions Delium, too), 5.14.1–2.

96. Argos comes in for abuse in Ar. *Pax* 475–7, 493 for not being willing to make peace. On the problems alliances presented to rank, pp. 67–8.

97. Admit Athens to half Sparta's glory: Ar. *Pax* 1082 reflects this equality; Athens and Sparta are to "rule Greece in common."

98. Alliance two weeks after Peace of Nicias: so Andrewes in *HCT* V.25–VII p. 22. Alliance between Athens and Sparta, 5.22.3–5.25.1. Two unfriendly powers, 5.27.2.

99. Sparta wants alliance because of fear of Argos, worry that former allies might join Athens, 5.22.2.

100. Learned German refused to believe in the alliance, Schwartz 1919 pp. 46–62, refuted by Dover in *HCT* VIII pp. 428–31. For puzzlement at the alliance, see also Gomme *ad loc.* 5.22.3; Legon 1969 p. 330 (intended to coerce Sparta's allies); Lazenby 2004 p. 107 (the Athenians afraid of the Boeotians); Kagan 1981 pp. 27–8 (appealing because it recalled Cimon's notion of two equal hegemonies, which is relatively close to the argument here). For the terms of the alliance, 5.23. The only unsymmetrical element is that Athens must help Sparta against the helots, 5.23.3. Sparta's offer of alliance in 425 BC, 4.19.1.

EPILOGUE

1. "By now some smart-ass," Ar. *Pax* 43–8, abridged.

2. Kagan 1974 pp. 345–6 gathers modern appreciations of the Peace of Nicias.

3. The prisoners from Sphacteria, 5.24.2. At 5.34.2 Thucydides notes that they were temporarily disenfranchised. Panactum, Athenian prisoners in Boeotian hands, 5.35.5, 5.36.2, 5.39.1–3, 5.40.2, 5.42. Amphipolis not returned, 5.21; Cythera and Pylos, 5.35.3–4.

4. Nearly seven years of peace, 5.25.3. But it is part of Thucydides' argument that the period 432–404 BC was a single twenty-seven-year war to minimize the significance of the peace (5.25.3–5.26.3) and to emphasize suspicion between Athens and Sparta (5.35.2–8, 5.42.2–5.43.1). "Rivalry between them" (*philotimias*), Diod. Sic. 12.72.5.

5. The practical outcome of the war: Busolt's (3.2 p. 1197) formulation remains the best.

6. "Athenians were scorned" (*Athenaiōn kataphronoumenōn . . . Lakedaimoniōn tetapeinōmenōn tēi doxēi*), Diod. Sic. 12.75.5.

7. "Had very high rank" (*mega axiōma*), Diod. Sic. 12.75.6. Diodorus was probably expanding Thucydides 5.28.2, which contrasts the disgrace of Sparta, "badly spoken of and scorned by virtue of her misfortunes," with Argos, "in the best state in all respects."

8. Athens forms an alliance with Argos and her coalition, 5.43–7.

9. Athens writes on the treaty, Messenians return to Pylos, 5.56.1–3; "but otherwise they kept quiet," 5.56.3.

10. Athenians to Argos, 5.61.1–2; Athenians at the battle of Mantinea, 5.67.2, 5.74. Thucydides identifies this as a potential casus belli with Sparta (5.26.2), as he does Athens' involvement in the Epidaurian war (5.55.4). Melos, 5.116.3–4; Pylos, 5.115.2.

11. "Greatest battle," 5.74.1; "reproach," 5.75.3; "theft of war," Paus. 1.13.5; cf. Thuc. 6.18.2.

12. Sage Athenian observer (Nicias), 5.46.1, 6.11.6. Spartan desire for revenge, 6.10.2, 6.11.6.

13. Athenian motivation for Sicily, esp. 6.18.4.

14. Laconia in 414 BC, 6.105, 7.18.3–4; Andoc. 3.31.

15. Spartan motive for not destroying Athens in 404 BC, Xen. *Hell.* 2.2.19–20.

16. "The growth of the power of Athens," 1.23.6, in Crawley's slight overtranslation (I offer my own translation pp. 86–7, and see there for discussion and references). On Thucydides and realism, Constantineau 1997 pp. 21–112; Crane 1998; Eckstein 2003, 2006 pp. 48–57. For the realism of Thucydides, Book I, see also appendix p. 424.

17. "You hold your empire," 3.37.2; "of gods we believe," 5.105.2 (all trans. Crawley). For more such passages, 6.85.1; 1.76.2 and 5.89 quoted above pp. 16–17. That Thucydides did not himself endorse such views is now conventional: see Lebow 2001 p. 549.

18. For the Greek intellectual context of Thucydidean realism, Crane 1998 pp. 72–5, 237–57; Hunt 2010 pp. 155–80. For the intervention of Xenophon, Lendon 2006, esp. 95–7.

19. "Your empire," 2.63.2. On the two different levels of realism in Thucydides, Crane 1998 pp. 36–71 and 237–93. For Thucydides' drift away from realism, Ober 2001 (2009).

20. "In peace and prosperity," 3.82.2, trans. Crawley adapted.

21. Rank in Book I: especially the speech of the Corinthians at Athens (1.37–43), the speech of the Athenians at Sparta (1.73–8; although it also contains famous realist passages), the speech of Sthenelaidas (1.86), and the first speech of Pericles (1.140–4). Pericles' Funeral Oration (2.35–46); last speech (2.60–4; see also the speech of Archidamus, 2.11). Speech of the Spartans at Athens in 425 BC (4.17–20). Direction is given to literature on all these speeches where they are mentioned in the main narrative above.

22. Aes. *Eum.* 261–8, with thanks to W. D. Furley, as also for the epigraph of the book.

BIBLIOGRAPHY

ABBREVIATIONS

Standard abbreviations are used for ancient authors and works, from the *Oxford Classical Dictionary*[3] where possible, and sometimes expanded for clarity's sake. I have used the following abbreviations for modern collections of ancient evidence and frequently cited modern works, especially commentaries on ancient texts.

ATL = B. D. Meritt, H. T. Wade-Gery, and M. F. McGregor, *The Athenian Tribute Lists,* 4 vols. (Cambridge MA and Princeton, 1939–1953).

Busolt = G. Busolt, *Griechische Geschichte bis zur Schlacht bei Chaeroneia* vol. 3.1 (Gotha, 1897); 3.2 (Gotha, 1904).

Classen = J. Classen and J. Steup (eds.), *Thukydides*[3–5], 8 vols. (Berlin, 1900–1922).

Fantasia = U. Fantasia, *Tucidide. La guerra del Peloponneso, Libro II* (Pisa, 2003).

FGH = F. Jacoby (ed.), *Fragmente der griechischen Historiker* (Leiden, 1923–1958).

Fornara = C. W. Fornara, *Archaic Times to the End of the Peloponnesian War* (Baltimore, 1977).

Frazer = J. G. Frazer, *Pausanias's Description of Greece,* 6 vols. (London, 1898).

Gomme = A. W. Gomme, *A Historical Commentary on Thucydides* vols. 1–3 (Oxford, 1945–1956).

Green *Diodorus* = P. Green, *Diodorus Siculus Books 11–12.37.1* (Austin, 2006).

HCT V.25–VII = A. W. Gomme, A. Andrewes, and K. J. Dover, *A Historical Commentary on Thucydides, Volume IV, Books V.25–VII* (Oxford, 1970).

HCT VIII = A. W. Gomme, A. Andrewes, and K. J. Dover, *A Historical Commentary on Thucydides, Volume V, Book VIII* (Oxford, 1981).

Hornblower = S. Hornblower, *A Commentary on Thucydides*, 3 vols. (Oxford, 1991–2008).

IG = *Inscriptiones graecae* (Berlin, 1873–).

LSJ = H. G. Liddell, R. Scott, and H. Stuart Jones, *A Greek-English Lexicon*[9] (Oxford, 1940).

ML = R. Meiggs and D. Lewis, *A Selection of Greek Historical Inscriptions to the End of the Fifth Century BC*, rev. ed. (Oxford, 1988 [[1]1969]).

Olsen = S. D. Olsen, *Aristophanes* Acharnians (Oxford, 2002).

Rhodes *Comm. Ath. pol.* = P. J. Rhodes, *A Commentary on the Aristotelian* Athenaion Politeia (Oxford, 1981).

Rhodes II = P. J. Rhodes, *Thucydides History II* (Warminster, 1988).

Rhodes III = P. J. Rhodes, *Thucydides History III* (Warminster, 1994).

Rhodes IV–V.24 = P. J. Rhodes, *Thucydides History IV.1–V.24* (Warminster, 1998).

SEG = *Supplementum epigraphicum graecum* (Leiden, 1923–).

Stadter = P. A. Stadter, *A Commentary on Plutarch's* Pericles (Chapel Hill, 1989).

Tod[2] = M. N. Tod, *A Selection of Greek Historical Inscriptions to the End of the Fifth Century BC*[2] (Oxford, 1946 [[1]1933]).

MODERN WORKS CITED
(SEE ALSO ABBREVIATIONS)

Adcock 1927 = F. E. Adcock, "The Archidamian War," *Cambridge Ancient History*[1] vol. 5 (Cambridge, 1927) pp. 193–253.

Ameruoso 1999 = M. Ameruoso, "In margine a P.S.I. XII 1283 (=Pack[2], 1343): Un nuovo Antioco?" *Zeitschrift für Papyrologie und Epigraphik* 128 (1999) pp. 133–49.

Andrewes 1962 = A. Andrewes, "The Mytilene Debate: Thucydides 3.36–49," *Phoenix* 16 (1962) pp. 64–85.

Andrewes 1966 = A. Andrewes, "The Government of Classical Sparta," in E. Badian (ed.), *Ancient Society and Institutions* (Oxford, 1966) pp. 1–20.

Andrewes and Lewis 1957 = A. Andrewes and D. M. Lewis, "Note on the Peace of Nicias," *Journal of Hellenic Studies* 77 (1957) pp. 177–80.

Andrews 2000 = J. A. Andrews, "Cleon's Hidden Appeals (Thucydides 3.37–40)," *Classical Quarterly* 50 (2000) pp. 45–62.

Archibald 1998 = Z. H. Archibald, *The Odrysian Kingdom of Thrace* (Oxford, 1998).

Asheri 1998 = D. Asheri, "Platea vendetta delle Termopoli: Alle origini di un motivo teologico erodoteo," in M. Sordi (ed.), *Responsabilità perdono e vendetta nel mondo antico* (Milan, 1998) pp. 65–86.

Azoulay 2004 = V. Azoulay, *Xénophon et les grâces du pouvoir* (Paris, 2004).

Badian 1993a = E. Badian, "Toward a Chronology of the *Pentecontaetia* down to the Renewal of the Peace of Callias," in id., *From Plataea to Potidaea* (Baltimore, 1993) pp. 73–107.

Badian 1993b = E. Badian, "Thucydides and the Outbreak of the Peloponnesian War: A Historian's Brief," in id., *From Plataea to Potidaea* (Baltimore, 1993) pp. 125–62.

Badian 1993c = E. Badian, "Athens, the Locrians and Naupactus," in id., *From Plataea to Potidaea* (Baltimore, 1993) pp. 163–9.

Badian 1993d = E. Badian, "Thucydides and the *Archē* of Philip," in id., *From Plataea to Potidaea* (Baltimore, 1993) pp. 171–85.

Badian 1993e = E. Badian, *From Plataea to Potidaea: Studies in the History and Historiography of the* Pentecontaetia (Baltimore, 1993).

Badian 1993f = E. Badian, "Plataea Between Athens and Sparta: In Search of Lost History," in id., *From Plataea to Potidaea* (Baltimore, 1993) pp. 109–23.

Badian 1999 = E. Badian, "The Road to Acanthus," in R. Mellor and L. Tritle (eds.), *Text and Tradition: Studies in Greek History and Historiography in Honor of Mortimer Chambers* (Claremont, 1999) pp. 3–35.

Basch 1987 = L. Basch, *Le musée imaginaire de la marine antique* (Athens, 1987).

Bauslaugh 1979 = R. A. Bauslaugh, "Thucydides IV 8.6 and the South Channel at Pylos," *Journal of Hellenic Studies* 99 (1979) pp. 1–6.

Beloch 1884 = K. J. Beloch, *Die Attische Politik seit Perikles* (Leipzig, 1884).

Berktold and Faisst 1993 = P. Berktold and G. W. Faisst, "Die Lage von Sollion," *Chiron* 23 (1993) pp. 1–11.

Birgalias 2007 = N. Birgalias, "Le gérousia et les gérontes de Sparte," *Ktema* 32 (2007) pp. 341–9.

Blamire 2001 = A. Blamire, "Athenian Finance, 454–404 BC," *Hesperia* 70 (2001) pp. 99–126.

Bleckmann 2002 = B. Bleckmann, "Nochmals zur Datierung von IG V 1,1," *Ktema* 27 (2002) pp. 35–8.

Bloedow 1981 = E. F. Bloedow, "The Speeches of Archidamus and Sthenelaidas at Sparta," *Historia* 30 (1981) pp. 129–43.

Bloedow 1983 = E. F. Bloedow, "Archidamus the 'Intelligent' Spartan," *Klio* 65 (1983) pp. 27–49.

Bloedow 1987 = E. F. Bloedow, "Pericles' Powers in the Counter-Strategy of 431," *Historia* 36 (1987) pp. 9–27.

Bloedow 1996 = E. F. Bloedow, "'Olympian' Thoughts: Plutarch on Pericles' Congress Decree," *Opuscula Atheniensia* 21 (1996) pp. 7–12.

Boersma 1970 = J. S. Boersma, *Athenian Building Policy from 561/0 to 405/4 BC* (Groningen, 1970).

Bolmarcich 2008 = S. Bolmarcich, "The Date of the 'Oath of the Peloponnesian League'," *Historia* 57 (2008) pp. 65–79.

Bosworth 1992 = A. B. Bosworth, "Athens' First Intervention in Sicily: Thucydides and the Sicilian Tradition," *Classical Quarterly* 42 (1992) pp. 46–55.

Bosworth 2000 = A. B. Bosworth, "The Historical Context of Thucydides' Funeral Oration," *Journal of Hellenic Studies* 120 (2000) pp. 1–16.

Bourdieu 1966 = P. Bourdieu, "The Sentiment of Honour in Kabyle Society," in J. G. Peristiany (ed.), *Honour and Shame: The Values of Mediterranean Society* (Chicago, 1966) pp. 193–241.

Bradeen 1969 = D. W. Bradeen, "The Athenian Casualty Lists," *Classical Quarterly* 19 (1969) pp. 145–59.

Brüggenbrock 2006 = C. Brüggenbrock, *Die Ehre in den Zeiten der Demokratie: Das Verhältnis von athenischer Polis und Ehre in klassischer Zeit* (Göttingen, 2006).

Brunt 1951 (1993) = P. Brunt, "The Megarian Decree," *American Journal of Philology* 72 (1951) pp. 269–81. Reprinted with addenda in id., *Studies in Greek History and Thought* (Oxford, 1993) pp. 1–16.

Brunt 1965 (1993) = P. A. Brunt, "Spartan Policy and Strategy in the Archidamian War," *Phoenix* 19 (1965) pp. 255–80. Reprinted in id., *Studies in Greek History and Thought* (Oxford, 1993) pp. 84–111.

Buck 1979 = R. J. Buck, *A History of Boeotia* (Edmonton, 1979).

Bury 1900 = J. B. Bury, *A History of Greece to the Death of Alexander the Great* (London, 1900).

Busby 2005 = J. W. Busby, "Prestige and Reputational Concerns of Major Powers Under Unipolarity," 2005 Annual Meeting of the American Political Science Association, pp. 1–58.

Cairns 1996 = D. Cairns, "*Hybris*, Dishonour, and Thinking Big," *Journal of Hellenic Studies* 106 (1996) pp. 1–32.

Cambitoglou 2001 = A. Cambitoglou (ed.), *Torone I: The Excavations of 1975, 1976, and 1979*, 3 vols. (Athens, 2001).

Camp 1978 = J. Camp, "A Spear Butt from the Lesbians," *Hesperia* 47 (1978) pp. 192–5.

Cartledge 1982 = P. Cartledge, "Sparta and Samos: A Special Relationship?" *Classical Quarterly* 32 (1982) pp. 243–65.

Cartledge 1991 = P. Cartledge, "Richard Talbert's Revision of the Sparta-Helot Struggle: A Reply," *Historia* 40 (1991) pp. 379–81.

Cartledge 2002 (1979) = P. Cartledge, *Sparta and Laconia*² (London, 2002; ¹1979).

Casson 1995 = L. Casson, "The Feeding of Trireme Crews," *Transactions of the American Philological Association* 125 (1995) pp. 261–9.

Cataldi 1987 = S. Cataldi, "I prescritti dei trattati ateniesi con Reggio e Leontini," *Atti della accademia delle scienze di Torino, 2. classe di scienze morali, storiche e filologiche* 121 (1987) pp. 63–72.

Cataldi 1989 = S. Cataldi, "La spedizione di Diotimo in Italia e i *Sikeloi*," *Rivista di filologia e di istruzione classica* 177 (1989) pp. 129–80.

Cataldi 1996 = S. Cataldi, "I processi agli strateghi ateniensi della prima spedizione in Sicilia e la politica cleoniana," in M. Sordi (ed.), *Processi e politica nel mondo antico* (Milan, 1996) pp. 37–63.

Cataldi 2005 = S. Cataldi, "Tradizioni e attualità nel diologo dei messaggeri Greci con Gelone (Erodoto VII 157–62)," in M. Giangiulio (ed.), *Erodoto e il "modello erodoteo"* (Trent, 2005) pp. 123–71.

Cawkwell 1975 = G. Cawkwell, "Thucydides' Judgment of Periclean Strategy," *Yale Classical Studies* 24 (1975) pp. 53–70.

Cawkwell 1997 = G. Cawkwell, *Thucydides and the Peloponnesian War* (London, 1997).

Chambers *et al.* 1990 = M. H. Chambers, R. Galluci, and P. Spanos, "Athens' Alliance with Egesta in the Year of Antiphon," *Zeitschrift für Papyrologie und Epigraphik* 83 (1990) pp. 38–57.

Coates and Morrison 1993 = J. Coates and J. Morrison, "Summary of Lessons Learned," in J. T. Shaw (ed.), *The Trireme Project: Operational Experience 1987–90, Lessons Learnt* (Oxford, 1993) pp. 108–9.

Cohen 1995 = D. Cohen, *Law, Violence, and Community in Classical Athens* (Cambridge, 1995).

Cole 1974 = J. W. Cole, "Perdiccas and Athens," *Phoenix* 28 (1974) pp. 55–72.

Constantineau 1997 = P. Constantineau, *La doctrine classique de la politique étrangère* (Paris, 1997).

Conwell 2008 = D. H. Conwell, *Connecting a City to the Sea: The History of the Athenian Long Walls* (Leiden, 2008).

Cornford 1907 = F. Cornford, *Thucydides Mythistoricus* (London, 1907).

Crane 1998 = G. Crane, *Thucydides and the Ancient Simplicity* (Berkeley and Los Angeles, 1998).

David 1999 = E. David, "Sparta's *Kosmos* of Silence," in S. Hodkinson and A. Powell (eds.), *Sparta: New Perspectives* (London, 1999) pp. 117–46.

David 2004 = E. David, "Suicide in Spartan Society," in T. J. Figueira (ed.), *Spartan Society* (Swansea, 2004) pp. 1–24.

David 2007 = E. David, "Xénophon et la mythe de Lycurgue," *Ktema* 32 (2007) pp. 297–310.

Davies 1971 = J. K. Davies, *Athenian Propertied Families, 600–300 BC* (Oxford, 1971).

Dawson 1996 = D. Dawson, *The Origins of Western Warfare: Militarism and Morality in the Ancient World* (Boulder, 1996).

Dayton 2006 = J. C. Dayton, *The Athletes of War: An Evaluation of the Agonistic Elements in Greek Warfare* (Toronto, 2006).

Delbrück 1890 = H. Delbrück, *Der Strategie des Perikles* (Berlin, 1890).

Demont 1995 = P. Demont, "Secours et vengeance: Note sur *timōria* chez Hérodote," *Ktema* 20 (1995) pp. 37–45.

Deubner 1932 = L. Deubner, *Attische Feste* (Berlin, 1932).

Dieterle 2007 = M. Dieterle, *Dodona* (Hildesheim, 2007).

Ducat 2006a = J. Ducat, *Spartan Education: Youth and Society in the Classical Period*, trans. E. Stafford, P.-J. Shaw, and A. Powell (Swansea, 2006).

Ducat 2006b = J. Ducat, "The Spartan 'Tremblers'," in S. Hodkinson and A. Powell (eds.), *Sparta and War* (Swansea, 2006) pp. 1–55.

Ducat 2008 = J. Ducat, "Le statut des périèques lacédémoniens," *Ktema* 33 (2008) pp. 1–92.

Eckstein 2003 = A. M. Eckstein, "Thucydides, the Outbreak of the Peloponnesian War, and the Foundation of International Systems Theory," *International History Review* 25 (2003) pp. 757–74.

Eckstein 2006 = A. M. Eckstein, *Mediterranean Anarchy, Interstate War, and the Rise of Rome* (Berkeley and Los Angeles, 2006).

Egan 1983 = R. B. Egan, "Thucydides and the Kinsmen of the Mytileneans (3.2.3)," *L'antiquité classique* 52 (1983) pp. 232–4.

Falkner 1992 = C. L. Falkner, "Thucydides and the Peloponnesian Raid on Piraeus in 429 BC," *Ancient History Bulletin* 6 (1992) pp. 147–55.

Falkner 1994 = C. Falkner, "A Note on Sparta and Gytheum in the Fifth Century," *Historia* 43 (1994) pp. 495–501.

Falkner 1999a = C. Falkner, "Sparta's Colony at Herakleia Trachinia and Spartan Strategy in 426," *Échos du monde classique/Classical Views* 43 (1999) pp. 45–57.

Falkner 1999b = C. Falkner, "Sparta and Lepreon in the Archidamian War," *Historia* 48 (1999) pp. 385–94.

Fantasia 1986 = U. Fantasia, "Samo e Anaia," in [no ed.], *Serta historica antiqua* (Rome, 1986) pp. 113–43.

Fantasia 2006 = U. Fantasia, "Formione in Acarnania (Thuc. II 68, 7–8) e le origini della guerra del Peloponneso," *Incidenza dell'antico* 4 (2006) pp. 59–98.

Figueira 1981 = T. J. Figueira, "Aeginetan Membership in the Peloponnesian League," *Classical Philology* 76 (1981) pp. 1–24.

Figueira 1988 = T. J. Figueira, "Four Notes on the Aiginetans in Exile," *Athenaeum* 66 (1988) pp. 523–51.

Figueira 1990 = T. J. Figueira, "*Autonomoi kata tas spondas* (Thucydides 1.67.2)," *Bulletin of the Institute of Classical Studies* 37 (1990) pp. 63–88.

Figueira 2002 = T. J. Figueira, "Iron Money and the Ideology of Consumption in Laconia," in A. Powell and S. Hodkinson (eds.), *Sparta: Beyond the Mirage* (London, 2002) pp. 137–70.

Figueira 2006 = T. J. Figueira, "The Spartan *Hippeis*," in S. Hodkinson and A. Powell (eds.), *Sparta and War* (Swansea, 2006) pp. 57–85.

Fisher 1989 = N. R. E. Fisher, "Drink, *Hybris*, and the Promotion of Harmony in Sparta," in A. Powell (ed.), *Classical Sparta: Techniques Behind Her Success* (London, 1989) pp. 26–50.

Fisher 1992 = N. R. E. Fisher, *Hybris* (Warminster, 1992).

Fisher 2000 = N. R. E. Fisher, "*Hybris*, Revenge and *Stasis* in the Greek City-States," in H. van Wees (ed.), *War and Violence in Ancient Greece* (London, 2000) pp. 83–123.

Flaig 1993 = E. Flaig, "Die spartanische Abstimmung nach der Lautstärke: Überlegungen zu Thukydides 1.87," *Historia* 42 (1993) pp. 139–60.

Flensted-Jensen 2004 = P. Flensted-Jensen, "Thrace from Axios to Strymon," in M. H. Hansen and T. H. Nielsen (eds.), *An Inventory of Archaic and Classical Poleis* (Oxford, 2004) pp. 810–53.

Flower 1992 = H. Flower, "Thucydides and the Pylos Debate," *Historia* 41 (1992) pp. 40–57.

Flower 2002 = M. A. Flower, "The Invention of Tradition in Classical and Hellenistic Sparta," in A. Powell and S. Hodkinson (eds.), *Sparta: Beyond the Mirage* (London, 2002) pp. 191–217.

Fontenrose 1978 = J. Fontenrose, *The Delphic Oracle* (Berkeley, 1978).

Fornara 1971 = C. Fornara, *The Athenian Board of Generals from 501 to 404* (Wiesbaden, 1971).

Fornara and Samons 1991 = C. W. Fornara and L. J. Samons II, *Athens from Cleisthenes to Pericles* (Berkeley and Los Angeles, 1991).

Fornis and Casillas 1997 = C. Fornis and J.-M. Casillas, "An Appreciation of the Social Function of the Spartan *Syssitia*," *Ancient History Bulletin* 11 (1997) pp. 37–46.

Forrest 1960 = W. G. Forrest, "Themistokles and Argos," *Classical Quarterly* 10 (1960) pp. 221–41.

Frazier 2001 = F. Frazier, "Prestige et autorité de l'homme d'état chez Thucydide," *Ktema* 26 (2001) pp. 237–56.

Furley 1996 = W. D. Furley, *Andokides and the Herms* (London, 1996).

Gabrielsen 2008 = V. Gabrielsen, "Die Kosten der athenischen Flotte in klassischer Zeit," in F. Burrer and H. Müller (eds.), *Kriegskosten und Kriegsfinanzierung in der Antike* (Darmstadt, 2008) pp. 46–73.

Gärtner 2004 = T. Gärtner, "Die Mytilene-Debatte im thukydideischen Geschichtswerk," *Gymnasium* 111 (2004) pp. 225–45.

Gauthier 1966 = P. Gauthier, "Les cléruches de Lesbos et la colonisation athénienne au Vᵉ siècle," *Revue des études grecques* 79 (1966) pp. 64–88.

Geske 2005 = N. Geske, *Nicias und das Volk von Athen im Archidamischen Krieg* (Stuttgart, 2005).

Goldsworthy 1997 = A. Goldsworthy, "The *Othismos*, Myths and Heresies: The Nature of Hoplite Battle," *War in History* 4 (1997) pp. 1–26.

Gomme 1933 (1939) = A. W. Gomme, "A Forgotten Factor of Greek Naval Strategy," *Journal of Hellenic Studies* 53 (1933) pp. 16–24. Reprinted in id., *Essays in Greek History and Literature* (Oxford, 1939) pp. 190–203.

Grethlein 2005 = J. Grethlein, "Gefahren des *logos*: Thukydides' 'Historien' und die Grabrede des Perikles," *Klio* 87 (2005) pp. 41–71.

Grundy 1948 (1911) = G. B. Grundy, *Thucydides and the History of His Age²* vol. 1 (Oxford, 1948; ¹London, 1911).

Hale 2009 = J. R. Hale, *Lords of the Sea: The Epic Story of the Athenian Navy and the Birth of Democracy* (New York, 2009).

Hall 1997 = J. M. Hall, *Ethnic Identity in Greek Antiquity* (Cambridge, 1997).

Hamel 1998 = D. Hamel, *Athenian Generals: Military Authority in the Classical Period* (Leiden, 1998).

Hammond 1936/1937 (1973) = N. G. L. Hammond, "The Campaigns in Amphilochia During the Archidamian War," *Annual of the British School at Athens* 37 (1936/1937) pp. 128–40. Slightly updated as "Military Operations in Amphilochia," in id., *Studies in Greek History* (Oxford, 1973) pp. 471–85.

Hammond 1945 (1973) = N. G. L. Hammond, "Naval Operations in the South Channel of Corcyra, 435–433 BC," *Journal of Hellenic Studies* 65 (1945) pp. 26–37. Reprinted as "Naval Operations of Corcyra," in id., *Studies in Greek History* (Oxford, 1973) pp. 447–70.

Hammond 1972 = N. G. L. Hammond, *A History of Macedonia* vol. 1 (Oxford, 1972).

Hammond 1992 = N. G. L. Hammond, "Plataea's Relations with Thebes, Sparta, and Athens," *Journal of Hellenic Studies* 112 (1992) pp. 143–50.

Hammond and Griffith 1979 = N. G. L. Hammond and G. T. Griffith, *A History of Macedonia* vol. 2 (Oxford, 1979).

Hannah 2010 = P. Hannah, "The Warrior *Loutrophoroi* of Fifth-Century Athens," in D. Pritchard (ed.), *War, Democracy and Culture in Democratic Athens* (Cambridge, 2010) pp. 266–303.

Hanson 1998 (1983) = V. D. Hanson, *Warfare and Agriculture in Ancient Greece²* (Berkeley and Los Angeles, 1998 [¹Pisa, 1983]).

Hanson 2005 = V. D. Hanson, *A War Like No Other: How the Athenians and Spartans Fought the Peloponnesian War* (New York, 2005).

Harris 2001 = W. V. Harris, *Restraining Rage: The Ideology of Anger Control in Classical Antiquity* (Cambridge, 2001).

Harrison 1959 = E. L. Harrison, "The Escape from Plataea: Thucydides 3.23," *Classical Quarterly* 9 (1959) pp. 30–3.

Harrison 1999 = C. M. Harrison, "Triremes at Rest: On the Beach or in the Water?" *Journal of Hellenic Studies* 119 (1999) pp. 168–71.

Helly 2004 = B. Helly, "Épigramme funéraire pour Thétimos, fils de Ményllos, d'Atrax," *Zeitschrift für Papyrologie und Epigraphik* 148 (2004) pp. 15–28.

Henderson 1927 = B. W. Henderson, *The Great War Between Athens and Sparta* (London, 1927).

Henry 2004 = A. S. Henry, *Torone: The Literary, Documentary and Epigraphical Testimonia* (Athens, 2004).

Herman 1989 = G. Herman, "Nikias, Epimenides and the Question of Omissions in Thucydides," *Classical Quarterly* 39 (1989) pp. 83–93.

Herman 2006 = G. Herman, *Morality and Behaviour in Ancient Athens: A Social History* (Cambridge, 2006).

Heza 1974 = E. Heza, "Ruse de guerre—trait caractéristique d'une tactique nouvelle dans l'oeuvre de Thucydide," *Eos* 62 (1974) pp. 227–44.

Hodkinson 2000 = S. Hodkinson, *Property and Wealth in Classical Sparta* (London, 2000).

Hodkinson 2006 = S. Hodkinson, "Was Classical Sparta a Military Society?" in id. and A. Powell (eds.), *Sparta and War* (Swansea, 2006) pp. 111–62.

Holladay 1977 (2002) = A. J. Holladay, "Sparta's Role in the First Peloponnesian War," *Journal of Hellenic Studies* 97 (1977) pp. 54–63. Reprinted in A. J. Podlecki (ed.), *Athens in the Fifth Century and Other Studies in Greek History: The Collected Papers of A. James Holladay* (Chicago, 2002) pp. 105–17.

Holladay 1978 (2002) = A. J. Holladay, "Athenian Strategy in the Archidamian War," *Historia* 27 (1978) pp. 399–427. Reprinted in A. J. Podlecki (ed.), *Athens in the Fifth Century and Other Studies in Greek History: The Collected Papers of A. James Holladay* (Chicago, 2002) pp. 61–84.

Holladay 1985 (2002) = A. J. Holladay, "Sparta and the First Peloponnesian War," *Journal of Hellenic Studies* 105 (1985) pp. 161–2. Reprinted in A. J. Podlecki (ed.), *Athens in the Fifth Century and Other Studies in Greek History: The Collected Papers of A. James Holladay* (Chicago, 2002) pp. 119–22.

Holladay 1988 (2002) = A. J. Holladay, "Further Thoughts on Trireme Tactics," *Greece amd Rome* 35 (1988) pp. 149–51. Reprinted in A. J. Podlecki (ed.), *Athens in the Fifth Century and Other Studies in Greek History: The Collected Papers of A. James Holladay* (Chicago, 2002) pp. 183–4.

Hölscher 1974 = T. Hölscher, "Die Nike der Messenier und Naupaktier in Olympia," *Jahrbuch des Deutschen Archäologischen Instituts* 89 (1974) pp. 70–111.

Hornblower 1987 = S. Hornblower, *Thucydides* (London, 1987).

Hornblower 2007 = S. Hornblower, "Thucydides and Plataian Perjury," in A. H. Sommerstein and J. Fletcher (eds.), *Horkos: The Oath in Greek Society* (Bristol, 2007) pp. 138–47.

Howie 2005 = J. G. Howie, "The *Aristeia* of Brasidas: Thucydides' Presentation of Events at Pylos and Amphipolis," *Papers of the Langford Latin Seminar* 12 (2005) pp. 207–84.

Hunt 1998 = P. Hunt, *Slaves, Warfare, and Ideology in the Greek Historians* (Cambridge, 1998).

Hunt 2010 = P. Hunt, *War, Peace, and Alliance in Demosthenes' Athens* (Cambridge, 2010).

Hunter 1973 = V. J. Hunter, *Thucydides the Artful Reporter* (Toronto, 1973).

Hurwit 1999 = J. M. Hurwit, *The Athenian Acropolis* (Cambridge, 1999).

Intrieri 2002 = M. Intrieri, Biaios Didaskolos: *Guerra e stasis a Corcira fra storia e storiografia* (Soveria Mannelli, 2002).

Jacquemin and Laroche 1982 = A. Jacquemin and D. Laroche, "Notes sur trois piliers Delphiques," *Bulletin de correspondance hellénique* 106 (1982) pp. 191–218.

Jameson (2000–2003) = M. J. Jameson, "Athens and Phaselis, IG I³ 10 (EM 6918)," *Horos* 14–16 (2000–2003) pp. 23–9.

Jones 1978 = N. Jones, "The Topography and Strategy of the Battle of Amphipolis in 422 BC," *California Studies in Classical Antiquity* 10 (1978) pp. 71–104.

Jones 1999 = C. P. Jones, *Kinship Diplomacy in the Ancient World* (Cambridge, MA, 1999).

Jordan 1986 = B. Jordan, "Religion in Thucydides," *Transactions of the American Philological Association* 116 (1986) pp. 119–47.

Jordan 1988 = B. Jordan, "The Honors for Themistocles After Salamis," *American Journal of Philology* 109 (1988) pp. 547–71.

Kagan 1969 = D. Kagan, *The Outbreak of the Peloponnesian War* (Ithaca, 1969).

Kagan 1974 = D. Kagan, *The Archidamian War* (Ithaca, 1974).

Kagan 1981 = D. Kagan, *The Peace of Nicias and the Sicilian Expedition* (Ithaca, 1981).

Kagan 2005 = D. Kagan, "Perikles As General," in J. M. Barringer and J. Hurwit (eds.), *Periklean Athens and Its Legacy* (Austin, 2005) pp. 1–9.

Kagan 2009 = D. Kagan, *Thucydides: The Reinvention of History* (New York, 2009).

Kahn 2008 = D. Kahn, "Inaros' Rebellion Against Artaxerxes I and the Athenian Disaster in Egypt," *Classical Quarterly* 58 (2008) pp. 424–40.

Kallet 1998 = L. Kallet, "Accounting for Culture in Fifth-Century Athens," in D. Boedeker and K. A. Raaflaub (eds.), *Democracy, Empire, and the Arts in Fifth-Century Athens* (Cambridge, MA, 1998) pp. 43–58.

Kallet 2004 = L. Kallet, "Epigraphic Geography: The Tribute Quota Fragments Assigned to 421/0–415/4 BC," *Hesperia* 73 (2004) pp. 465–96.

Kallet 2005 = L. Kallet, "Wealth, Power, and Prestige: Athens at Home and Abroad," in J. Neils (ed.), *The Parthenon* (Cambridge, 2005) pp. 35–65.

Kallet 2009 = L. Kallet, "Democracy, Empire, and Epigraphy in the Twentieth Century," in J. Ma, N. Papazarkadas, and R. Parker (eds.), *Interpreting the Athenian Empire* (London, 2009) pp. 43–66.

Kallet-Marx 1993 = L. Kallet-Marx, *Money, Expense, and Naval Power in Thucydides' History 1–5.24* (Berkeley and Los Angeles, 1993).

Kapparis 1995 = K. Kapparis, "The Athenian Decree for the Naturalisation of the Plataeans," *Greek, Roman and Byzantine Studies* 36 (1995) pp. 359–78.

Karavites 1985 = P. Karavites, "Enduring Problems of the Samian Revolt," *Rheinisches Museum für Philologie* 128 (1985) pp. 40–56.

Keen 1993 = A. G. Keen, "Athenian Campaigns in Karia and Lykia During the Peloponnesian War," *Journal of Hellenic Studies* 113 (1993) pp. 152–7.

Kelly 1982 (2007) = T. Kelly, "Thucydides and the Spartan Strategy in the Archidamian War," *American Historical Review* 87 (1982) pp. 25–54. Reprinted in E. L. Wheeler (ed.), *The Armies of Classical Greece* (Aldershot, 2007) pp. 393–422.

Kennell 1995 = N. Kennell, *The Gymnasium of Virtue: Education and Culture in Ancient Sparta* (Chapel Hill, 1995).

Kiechle 1979 = F. K. Kiechle, "Korkyra und der Handelsweg durch das Adriatische Meer im 5. Jh. v. Chr.," *Historia* 28 (1979) pp. 173–91.

Konstan 2006 = D. Konstan, *The Emotions of the Ancient Greeks: Studies in Aristotle and Classical Literature* (Toronto, 2006).

Krentz 1985a = P. Krentz, "Casualties in Hoplite Battles," *Greek, Roman and Byzantine Studies* 26 (1985) pp. 13–20.

Krentz 1985b = P. Krentz, "The Nature of Hoplite Battle," *Classical Antiquity* 4 (1985) pp. 50–61.

Krentz 1997 = P. Krentz, "The Strategic Culture of Periclean Athens," in C. D. Hamilton and P. Krentz (eds.), Polis *and* Polemos: *Essays on Politics, War, and History in Ancient Greece in Honor of Donald Kagan* (Claremont, 1997) pp. 55–72.

Krentz 2002 = P. Krentz, "Fighting by the Rules: The Invention of the Hoplite Agôn," *Hesperia* 71 (2002) pp. 23–39.

Krentz 2007 = P. Krentz, "The Oath of Marathon, Not Plataia?" *Hesperia* 76 (2007) pp. 731–42.

Krentz and Sullivan 1987 = P. Krentz and C. Sullivan, "The Date of Phormion's First Expedition to Akarnania," *Historia* 36 (1987) pp. 241–3.

Landucci Gattinoni 1998 = F. Landucci Gattinoni, "Pericle e Samo: Spirito di vendetta or volontà di pacificazione?" in M. Sordi (ed.), *Responsabilità perdono e vendetta nel mondo antico* (Milan, 1998) pp. 87–96.

Lateiner 1975 = D. Lateiner, "The Speech of Teutiaplus (Thuc. 3.20)," *Greek, Roman and Byzantine Studies* 16 (1975) pp. 175–84.

Lateiner 1977a = D. Lateiner, "Pathos in Thucydides," *Antichthon* 11 (1977) pp. 42–51.

Lateiner 1977b = D. Lateiner, "Heralds and Corpses in Thucydides," *Classical World* 71 (1977) pp. 97–106.

Lazaridis 1993 = D. Lazaridis, *Amphipolis* (Athens, 1993).

Lazenby 1987 = J. F. Lazenby, "The *Diekplous,*" *Greece and Rome* 34 (1987) pp. 169–77.

Lazenby 2004 = J. F. Lazenby, *The Peloponnesian War. A Military Study* (London, 2004).

Le Vien and Lord 1962 = J. Le Vien and J. Lord, *Winston Churchill: The Valiant Years* (New York, 1962).

Lebow 2001 = R. N. Lebow, "Thucydides the Constructivist," *American Political Science Review* 95 (2001) pp. 547–60.

Legon 1968 = R. P. Legon, "Megara and Mytilene," *Phoenix* 22 (1968) pp. 200–25.

Legon 1969 = R. P. Legon, "The Peace of Nicias," *Journal of Peace Research* 6 (1969) pp. 323–34.

Legon 1972 = R. Legon, "Samos in the Delian League," *Historia* 21 (1972) pp. 145–58.

Lehmann 2008 = G. A. Lehmann, *Perikles* (Munich, 2008).

Lendon 1994 = J. E. Lendon, "Thucydides and the 'Constitution' of the Peloponnesian League," *Greek, Roman and Byzantine Studies* 35 (1994) pp. 159–77.

Lendon 1997a = J. E. Lendon, "Spartan Honor," in C. D. Hamilton and P. Krentz (eds.), Polis *and* Polemos: *Essays on Politics, War, and History in Ancient Greece in Honor of Donald Kagan* (Claremont, 1997) pp. 105–26.

Lendon 1997b = J. E. Lendon, *Empire of Honour: The Art of Government in the Roman World* (Oxford, 1997).

Lendon 2000 = J. E. Lendon, "Homeric Vengeance and the Outbreak of Greek Wars," in H. van Wees (ed.), *War and Violence in Ancient Greece* (London, 2000) pp. 1–30.

Lendon 2001 = J. E. Lendon, "Voting by Shouting in Sparta," in E. Tylawsky and C. Weiss (eds.), *Essays in Honor of Gordon Williams* (New Haven, 2001) pp. 169–75.

Lendon 2005 = J. E. Lendon, *Soldiers and Ghosts* (New Haven, 2005).

Lendon 2006 = J. E. Lendon, "Xenophon and the Alternative to Realist Foreign Policy: *Cyropaedia* 3.1.14–31," *Journal of Hellenic Studies* 126 (2006) pp. 82–98.

Lendon 2007 = J. E. Lendon, "Athens and Sparta and the Coming of the Peloponnesian War," in L. J. Samons II (ed.), *The Cambridge Companion to the Age of Pericles* (New York, 2007) pp. 258–81.

Lewis 1981 (1997) = D. M. Lewis, "The Origins of the First Peloponnesian War," in G. S. Shrimpton and D. J. McCargar (eds.), *Classical Contributions: Studies in Honor of Malcolm Francis McGregor* (Locust Valley, 1981) pp. 71–8. Reprinted in id., *Selected Papers in Greek and Near Eastern History*, ed. P. J. Rhodes (Cambridge, 1997) pp. 9–21.

Lewis 1992a = D. M. Lewis, "Mainland Greece, 479–451 BC," *Cambridge Ancient History*² vol. 5 (Cambridge, 1992) pp. 96–120.

Lewis 1992b = D. M. Lewis, "The Archidamian War," *Cambridge Ancient History*² vol. 5 (Cambridge, 1992) pp. 370–432.

Lewis 1992c = D. M. Lewis, "Chronological Notes," *Cambridge Ancient History*² vol. 5 (Cambridge, 1992) pp. 499–505.

Lindsay (forthcoming) = D. Lindsay, "*Olympias* Under Sail, and Other Performance Matters: A Practical Seaman's Perspective," in B. Rankov (ed.),

Trireme Olympias: *The Final Report. Sea Trials 1992–4. Conference Papers 1998* (Oxford).

Link 2004 = S. Link, "Snatching and Keeping: The Motif of Taking in Spartan Culture," in T. J. Figueira (ed.), *Spartan Society* (Swansea, 2004) pp. 1–24.

Link 2005 = S. Link, "Die Spartanische Kalokagathia—nur ein böser Witz? Zur Deutung von Thuk. 4, 40, 2," *Tyche* 20 (2005) pp. 77–86.

Lipka 2002 = M. Lipka, *Xenophon's Spartan Constitution* (Berlin, 2002).

Lipke (forthcoming) = P. Lipke, "Triremes and Shipworm," in B. Rankov (ed.), *Trireme* Olympias: *The Final Report. Sea Trials 1992–4. Conference Papers 1998* (Oxford).

Low 2007 = P. Low, *Interstate Relations in Classical Greece* (Cambridge, 2007).

Löwenheim and Heimann 2008 = O. Löwenheim and G. Heimann, "Revenge in International Politics," *Security Studies* 17 (2008) pp. 685–724.

Luginbill 2000 = R. Luginbill, "Paragraph 3.84 and Thucydides' History," *Ancient History Bulletin* 16 (2000) pp. 151–74.

Lupi 2000 = M. Lupi, *L'ordine delle generazioni: Classi di età e costumi matrimoniale nell'antica Sparta* (Bari, 2000).

Luppino 1981 = E. Luppino, "La *summachia* tra Atene e Sitalce: Un episodio del primo anno della guerra de peloponneso (Thuc., II, 29, 1–7)," *Rivista storica dell'antichità* 11 (1981) pp. 1–14.

Luppino-Manes 2000 = E. Luppino-Manes, *Egemonia di terra ed egemonia di mare* (Alessandria, 2000).

Luraghi 2001 = N. Luraghi, "Der Erdbebenaufstand und die Entstehung der messenischen Identität," in D. Papenfuss and V. M. Strocka (eds.), *Gab es das griechische Wunder? Griechenland zwischen dem Ende des 6. und der Mitte des 5. Jahrhunderts v. Chr.* (Mainz, 2001) pp. 279–301.

Luraghi and Alcock 2003 = N. Luraghi and S. E. Alcock, *Helots and Their Masters in Laconia and Messenia* (Cambridge, 2003).

Luther *et al.* 2006 = A. Luther, M. Meier, and L. Thommen (eds.), *Das frühe Sparta* (Stuttgart, 2006).

MacDonald 1982 = B. R. MacDonald, "The Import of Attic Pottery to Corinth and the Question of Trade During the Peloponnesian War," *Journal of Hellenic Studies* 102 (1982) pp. 113–23.

Mackie 1996 = C. J. Mackie, "Homer and Thucydides: Corcyra and Sicily," *Classical Quarterly* 46 (1996) pp. 103–13.

Macleod 1977 (1983) = C. W. Macleod, "Thucydides' Plataean Debate," *Greek, Roman and Byzantine Studies* 18 (1977) pp. 227–46. Reprinted in id., *Collected Essays* (Oxford, 1983) pp. 103–22.

Macleod 1978 (1983) = C. Macleod, "Reason and Necessity: Thucydides iii. 9–14, 37–48," *Journal of Hellenic Studies* 93 (1978) pp. 64–78. Reprinted in id., *Collected Essays* (Oxford, 1983) pp. 88–102.

Macleod 1979 (1983) = C. Macleod, "Thucydides on Faction (3.82–83)," *Proceedings of the Cambridge Philological Society* 205 (1979) pp. 52–68. Reprinted in id., *Collected Essays* (Oxford, 1983) pp. 123–39.

Marincola 2001 = J. Marincola, *Greek Historians* (Oxford, 2001).

Markey 1999 = D. Markey, "Prestige and the Origins of War: Returning to Realism's Roots," *Security Studies* 8 (1999) pp. 126–73.

Marr 1998 = J. Marr, "What Did the Athenians Demand in 432 BC?" *Phoenix* 52 (1998) pp. 120–3.

Marshall 2002 = B. Marshall, "The Return of Kimon (Once Again)," *Ancient History* 32 (2002) pp. 144–60.

Mason 1993 = H. J. Mason, "Mytilene and Methymna: Quarrels, Borders, and Topography," *Échos du monde classique/Classical Views* 37 (1993) pp. 225–50.

Matthaiou 2004 = A. P. Matthaiou, "*Peri tēs IG I³ 11*," in id. and G. E. Malouchou (eds.), *Attikai Epigraphai. Praktika sumposiou eis mnēmēn Adolf Wilhelm* (Athens, 2004) pp. 99–122.

Matthaiou 2009 = A. P. Matthaiou, "Attic Public Inscriptions of the Fifth Century BC in Ionic Script," in L. Mitchell and L. Rubenstein (eds.), *Greek History and Epigraphy. Essays in Honour of P. J. Rhodes* (Swansea, 2009) pp. 201–12.

Matthew 2009 = C. A. Matthew, "When Push Comes to Shove: What Was the *Othismos* of Hoplite Combat?" *Historia* 58 (2009) pp. 395–415.

Mattingly 1966 = H. B. Mattingly, "Athenian Imperialism and the Foundation of Brea," *Classical Quarterly* 16 (1966) pp. 172–92.

Mattingly 1996 = H. B. Mattingly, *The Athenian Empire Restored* (Ann Arbor, 1996).

Mattingly 2000 = H. B. Mattingly, "The Athenian Treaties with Troizen and Hermione," *Historia* 49 (2000) pp. 131–40.

McHardy 2008 = F. McHardy, *Revenge in Athenian Culture* (London, 2008).

Meier 2006 = M. Meier, "Probleme der Thukydides-Interpretation und das Perikles-Bild des Historikers," *Tyche* 21 (2006) pp. 131–67.

Meiggs 1972 = R. Meiggs, *The Athenian Empire* (Oxford, 1972).

Meritt and West 1934 = B. D. Meritt and A. B. West, *The Athenian Assessment of 425 BC* (Ann Arbor, 1934).

Mertens 2002 = N. Mertens, "*Ouk homoioi, agathoi de*: The *Perioikoi* in the Classical Lakedaimonian Polis," in A. Powell and S. Hodkinson (eds.), *Sparta: Beyond the Mirage* (London, 2002) pp. 285–303.

Meyer 1997 = E. A. Meyer, "*The Outbreak of the Peloponnesian War* after Twenty-Five Years," in C. D. Hamilton and P. Krentz (eds.), Polis *and* Polemos: *Essays on Politics, War, and History in Ancient Greece in Honor of Donald Kagan* (Claremont, 1997), pp. 23–54.

Mikalson 1984 = J. D. Mikalson, "Religion and the Plague at Athens, 431–423 BC," in [no ed.], *Studies Presented to Sterling Dow on His Eightieth Birthday* (Durham, NC, 1984) pp. 217–25.

Miles 1989 = M. M. Miles, "A Reconstruction of the Temple of Nemesis at Rhamnous," *Hesperia* 58 (1989) pp. 131–249.

Missiou 1992 = A. Missiou, *The Subversive Oratory of Andokides* (Cambridge, 1992).

Missiou 1998 = A. Missiou, "Reciprocal Generosity in the Foreign Affairs of Fifth-Century Athens and Sparta," in C. Gill, N. Postlethwaite, and R. Seaford (eds.), *Reciprocity in Ancient Greece* (Oxford, 1998) pp. 181–97.

Mitchell 1991 = B. Mitchell, "Kleon's Amphipolitan Campaign: Aims and Results," *Historia* 40 (1991) pp. 170–92.

Mitchell 1997 = L. Mitchell, "*Philia, eunoia* and Greek Interstate Relations," *Antichthon* 31 (1997) pp. 28–44.

Moreno 2007 = A. Moreno, *Feeding the Democracy: The Athenian Grain Supply in the Fifth and Fourth Centuries* BC (Oxford, 2007).

Moreno 2009 = A. Moreno, "'The Attic Neighbour': The Cleruchy in the Athenian Empire," in J. Ma, N. Papazarkadas, and R. Parker (eds.), *Interpreting the Athenian Empire* (London, 2009) pp. 211–21.

Morrison *et al.* 2000 = J. S. Morrison, J. F. Coates, and N. B. Rankov, *The Athenian Trireme*² (Cambridge, 2000).

Morton 2001 = J. Morton, *The Role of the Physical Environment in Ancient Greek Seafaring* (Leiden, 2001).

Mosley 1974 = D. J. Mosley, "On Greek Enemies Becoming Allies," *Ancient Society* 5 (1974) pp. 43–50.

Moxon 1978 = I. Moxon, "Thucydides' Account of Spartan Strategy and Foreign Policy in the Archidamian War," *Rivista storica dell'antichità* 8 (1978) pp. 7–26.

Moysey 1991 = R. A. Moysey, "Thucydides, Kimon, and the Peace of Kallias," *Ancient History Bulletin* 5 (1991) pp. 30–5.

Munn 2002 = M. Munn, "Thucydides on Plataea, the Beginning of the Peloponnesian War, and the 'Attic Question'," in V. B. Gorman and E. W. Robinson (eds.), *Oikistes: Studies in Constitutions, Colonies, and Military Power in the Ancient World, Offered in Honor of A. J. Graham* (Leiden, 2002) pp. 245–69.

Murari Pires 2003 = F. Murari Pires, "Thucydide et l'assemblée sur Pylos (IV.26–28): Rhétorique de la méthode, figure de l'autorité et détours de la mémoire," *Ancient History Bulletin* 17 (2003) pp. 127–48.

Nesselhauf 1934 = H. Nesselhauf, "Die diplomatischen Verhandlungen vor dem Peloponnesischen Kriege," *Hermes* 69 (1934) pp. 286–99.

O'Neal 1981 = J. L. O'Neal, "The Exile of Themistocles and Democracy in the Peloponnese," *Classical Quarterly* 31 (1981) pp. 335–46.

Ober 1985 = J. Ober, *Fortress Attica: The Defense of the Athenian Land Frontier, 404–322 BC* (Leiden, 1985).

Ober 1985 (1996) = J. Ober, "Thucydides, Pericles, and the Strategy of Defense," in id. and J. W. Eadie (eds.), *The Craft of the Ancient Historian: Essays in Honor of Chester G. Starr* (Lanham, 1985) pp. 171–88.

Reprinted in id., *The Athenian Revolution: Essays on Ancient Greek Democracy and Political Theory* (Princeton, 1996) pp. 72–85.

Ober 1989 = J. Ober, *Mass and Elite in Democratic Athens: Rhetoric, Ideology, and the Power of the People* (Princeton, 1989).

Ober 2001 (2009) = J. Ober, "Thucydides Theoretikos/Thucydides Histor: Realist Theory and the Challenge of History," in D. R. McCann and B. S. Strauss (eds.), *War and Democracy: A Comparative Study of the Korean War and the Peloponnesian War* (Armonk, 2001) pp. 273–306. Reprinted in J. Rusten (ed.), *Oxford Readings in Thucydides* (Oxford, 2009) pp. 434–78.

Oldfield (forthcoming) = R. Oldfield, "Collision Damage in Triremes," in B. Rankov (ed.), *Trireme Olympias: The Final Report. Sea Trials 1992–4. Conference Papers 1998* (Oxford).

Orwin 1994 = C. Orwin, *The Humanity of Thucydides* (Princeton, 1994).

Osborne 1987 = M. J. Osborne, *Naturalization in Athens* vols. 3–4 (Brussels, 1987).

Paarmann 2007 = B. Paarmann, Aparchai *and* Phoroi: *A New Commented Edition of the Athenian Tribute Quota Lists and Assessment Decrees* (Diss. Fribourg, 2007).

Papalas (forthcoming) = A. Papalas, "The Reconstructed Trireme *Olympias* and Her Critics," in B. Rankov (ed.), *Trireme* Olympias: *The Final Report. Sea Trials 1992–4. Conference Papers 1998* (Oxford).

Papazarkadas 2009 = N. Papazarkadas, "Epigraphy and the Athenian Empire: Reshuffling the Chronological Cards," in J. Ma, N. Papazarkadas, and R. Parker (eds.), *Interpreting the Athenian Empire* (London, 2009) pp. 67–88.

Paradiso 2007 = A. Paradiso, "Ravir des fromages à l'autel d'Orthia," *Ktema* 32 (2007) pp. 311–25.

Parke 1956 = H. W. Parke, *The Delphic Oracle* vol. 2 (Oxford, 1956).

Parke 1977 = H. W. Parke, *Festivals of the Athenians* (Ithaca, 1977).

Parker 1983 = R. Parker, *Miasma: Pollution and Purification in Early Greek Religion* (Oxford, 1983).

Parlama 2000 = L. Parlama, "Palaiologou Shaft: 452 Marble Memorial Stele," in id. and N. Stampolidis (eds.), *Athens, the City Beneath the City: Antiquities from the Metropolitan Railway Excavations* (Athens, 2000) pp. 396–9.

Patterson 1981 = C. Patterson, *Pericles' Citizenship Law of 451/0 BC* (Salem, 1981).

Pébarthe 2000 = C. Pébarthe, "Fiscalité, empire athénien et écriture: Retour sur les causes de la guerre de Péloponnèse," *Zeitschrift für Papyrologie und Epigraphik* 129 (2000) pp. 47–76.

Pelling 2000 = C. Pelling, *Literary Texts and the Greek Historian* (London, 2000).

Pflugk-Hartung 1884 = J. von Pflugk-Hartung, *Perikles als Feldherr* (Stuttgart, 1884).

Plant 1994 = I. M. Plant, "The Battle of Tanagra: A Spartan Initiative?" *Historia* 43 (1994) pp. 259–74.

Podlecki 1966 = A. J. Podlecki, *The Political Background of Aeschylean Tragedy* (Ann Arbor, 1966).

Podlecki 1998 = A. J. Podlecki, *Perikles and His Circle* (London, 1998).

Prandi 1976 = L. Prandi, "La liberazione della Grecia nella progaganda spartana durante la guerra del Peloponneso," in M. Sordi (ed.), *I canali della propaganda nel mondo antico* (Milan, 1976) pp. 72–83.

Price 2001 = J. J. Price, *Thucydides and Internal War* (Cambridge, 2001).

Pritchard 2007 = D. Pritchard, "Costing the Armed Forces of Athens During the Peloponnesian War," *Ancient History* 37 (2007) pp. 125–35.

Pritchett 1965a = W. K. Pritchett, "Pylos and Sphakteria," in id., *Studies in Ancient Greek Topography* vol. 1 (Berkeley and Los Angeles, 1965) pp. 6–29.

Pritchett 1965b = W. K. Pritchett, "Amphipolis," in id., *Studies in Ancient Greek Topography* vol. 1 (Berkeley and Los Angeles, 1965) pp. 30–48.

Pritchett 1974 = W. K. Pritchett, "The Challenge to Battle," in id., *The Greek State at War* vol. 2 (Berkeley and Los Angeles, 1974) pp. 147–55.

Pritchett 1980 = W. K. Pritchett, "Amphipolis Restudied," in id, *Studies in Ancient Greek Topography* vol. 3 (Berkeley and Los Angeles, 1980) pp. 298–347.

Pritchett 1982 = W. K. Pritchett, "The Roads of Plataea," in id., *Studies in Ancient Greek Topography* vol. 4 (Berkeley and Los Angeles, 1982) pp. 88–102.

Pritchett 1985 = W. K. Pritchett, "The Pitched Battle," in id., *The Greek State at War* vol. 2 (Berkeley and Los Angeles, 1985) pp. 1–93.

Pritchett 1991 = W. K. Pritchett, "Demosthenes' Campaign in Southern Aitolia in 426 BC," in id., *Studies in Ancient Greek Topography* vol. 7 (Amsterdam, 1991) pp. 47–82.

Pritchett 1992 = W. K. Pritchett, "Demosthenes' Amphilochian Campaign in 426 BC," in id., *Studies in Ancient Greek Topography* vol. 8 (Amsterdam, 1992) pp. 1–78.

Pritchett 1994 = W. K. Pritchett, "Thucydides and Pylos," in id., *Essays in Greek History* (Amsterdam, 1994) pp. 145–77.

Pritchett 1995a = W. K. Pritchett, "Thucydides' *Pentekontaetia*," in id., *Thucydides' Pentekontaetia and Other Essays* (Amsterdam, 1995) pp. 1–131.

Pritchett 1995b = W. K. Pritchett, *Thucydides' Pentekontaetia and Other Essays* (Amsterdam, 1995).

Pritchett 1996 = W. K. Pritchett, "Thucydides' Campaign of Tanagra," in id., *Greek Archives, Cults, and Topography* (Amsterdam, 1996) pp. 149–72.

Pryor and Jeffreys 2006 = J. H. Pryor and E. M. Jeffreys, *The Age of the Dromon: The Byzantine Navy ca. 500–1204* (Leiden, 2006).

Psoma 2001 = S. Psoma, *Olynthe et les Chalcidiens de Thrace* (Stuttgart, 2001).

Purdey 1826 = J. Purdey, *The New Sailing Directory for the Mediterranean Sea, the Adriatic Sea or Gulf of Venice, the Archipelago and Levant, the Sea of Marmara, and the Black Sea* (London, 1826).

Quincey 1964 = J. H. Quincey, "Orestes and the Argive Alliance," *Classical Quarterly* 14 (1964) pp. 190–206.

Quinn 1981 = T. J. Quinn, *Athens and Samos, Lesbos, and Chios: 479–404 BC* (Manchester, 1981).

Raaflaub 2007 = K. Raaflaub, "Warfare and Athenian Society," in L. J. Samons II, *The Cambridge Companion to the Age of Pericles* (New York, 2007) pp. 96–124.

Raaflaub 2009 = K. Raaflaub, "Learning from the Enemy: Athenian and Persian 'Instruments of Empire'," in J. Ma, N. Papazarkadas, and R. Parker (eds.), *Interpreting the Athenian Empire* (London, 2009) pp. 89–124.

Rankov (forthcoming) = B. Rankov, "Slipping and Launching," in D. Blackman and B. Rankov and K. Baika, H. Gerding, J. McKenzie, J. Pakkanen (eds.), *Shipsheds of the Ancient Mediterranean* (Cambridge).

Rawlings 2007 = L. Rawlings, *The Ancient Greeks at War* (Manchester, 2007).

Reece 1950 = D. W. Reece, "The Battle of Tanagra," *Journal of Hellenic Studies* 70 (1950) pp. 75–6.

Reece 1962 = D. W. Reece, "The Date of the Fall of Ithome," *Journal of Hellenic Studies* 82 (1962) pp. 111–20.

Rengakos 1996 = A. Rengakos, "Fernbeziehungen zwischen den Thukydideischen Reden," *Hermes* 124 (1996) pp. 396–417.

Rengakos and Tsamakis 2006 = A. Rengakos and A. Tsamakis, *Brill's Companion to Thucydides* (Leiden, 2006).

Rhodes 1994 = P. J. Rhodes, "In Defence of the Greek Historians," *Greece and Rome* 41 (1994) pp. 156–71.

Rhodes 2005 = P. J. Rhodes, *A History of the Classical Greek World* (Oxford, 2005).

Rhodes 2008 = P. J. Rhodes, "After the Three-Bar Sigma Controversy: The History of Athenian Imperialism Reassessed," *Classical Quarterly* 58 (2008) pp. 500–6.

Richer 1998 = N. Richer, *Les éphors: Études sur l'histoire et sur l'image de Sparte* (Paris, 1998).

Richer 2005 = N. Richer, "Les gymnopédies de Sparte," *Ktema* 30 (2005) pp. 237–62.

Robert 1890 = C. Robert, "Archäologische Nachlasse," *Hermes* 25 (1890) pp. 412–50.

Roisman 1987 = J. Roisman, "Alcidas in Thucydides," *Historia* 36 (1987) pp. 385–441.

Roisman 1993a = J. Roisman, "The Background of the Battle of Tanagra and Some Related Issues," *L'antiquité classique* 62 (1993) pp. 69–85.

Roisman 1993b = J. Roisman, *The General Demosthenes and His Use of Military Surprise* (Stuttgart, 1993).

Romilly 1956 = J. de Romilly, *Histoire et raison chez Thucydide* (Paris, 1956).

Romilly 1963 = J. de Romilly, *Thucydides and Athenian Imperialism* (Oxford, 1963) (trans. P. Thody, from *Thucydide et l'impérialisme athénien* [Paris, 1951]).

Romilly 1977 = J. de Romilly, *The Rise and Fall of States According to Greek Authors* (Ann Arbor, 1977).

Romilly 2005 = J. de Romilly, "Le discours des Lacédémoniens (IV, 17–20) et la tendance à généralité dans l'histoire de Thucydide," in id., *L'invention de l'histoire politique chez Thucydide* (Paris, 2005) pp. 89–94.

Rood 1998 = T. Rood, *Thucydides: Narrative and Explanation* (Oxford, 1998).

Rood 2006 = T. Rood, "Rhetoric, Reciprocity and History: Thucydides' Corcyra Debate," in [no ed.], *III International Symposium on Thucydides* (Alimos, 2006) pp. 65–73.

Rosen and Sluiter 2003 = R. M. Rosen and I. Sluiter, *Andreia: Studies in Manliness and Courage in Classical Antiquity* (Leiden, 2003).

Rosivach 1985 = V. Rosivach, "Manning the Athenian Fleet, 433–426 BC," *American Journal of Ancient History* 10 (1985) pp. 41–66.

Rosivach 1987 = V. Rosivach, "Autochthony and the Athenians," *Classical Quarterly* 37 (1987) pp. 294–305.

Rubel 2000 = A. Rubel, *Stadt in Angst: Religion und Politik in Athen während des Peloponnesischen Krieges* (Darmstadt, 2000).

Rubincam 2001 = C. Rubincam, "The Topography of Pylos and Sphakteria and Thucydides' Measurements of Distance," *Journal of Hellenic Studies* 121 (2001) pp. 77–90.

Saïd 1998 = S. Saïd, "Tragedy and Politics," in D. Boedeker and K. A. Raaflaub (eds.), *Democracy, Empire, and the Arts in Fifth-Century Athens* (Cambridge, MA, 1998) pp. 275–95.

Salmon 1978 = P. Salmon, *Étude sur la confédération béotienne (447/6–386)* (Brussels, 1978).

Salmon 1984 = J. B. Salmon, *Wealthy Corinth* (Oxford, 1984).

Samons 1998 = L. J. Samons II, "Kimon, Kallias and Peace with Persia," *Historia* 47 (1998) pp. 129–40.

Samons 2000 = L. J. Samons II, *Empire of the Owl* (Stuttgart, 2000).

Samons 2004 = L. J. Samons II, *What's Wrong with Democracy? From Athenian Practice to American Worship* (Berkeley and Los Angeles, 2004).

Samons 2006 = L. J. Samons II, "Thucydides' Sources and the Spartan Plan at Pylos," *Hesperia* 75 (2006) pp. 525–40.

Sánchez 2001 = P. Sánchez, *L'Amphictione des Pyles et de Delphes* (Stuttgart, 2001).

Schmitt 1992 = R. Schmitt, *Handbuch zu der Tempeln der Griechen* (Frankfurt, 1992).

Schmitz 2005 = W. Schmitz, "Göttliche Strafe oder medizinisches Geschehen— Deutungen und Diagnosen der 'Pest' in Athen (430–426 v. Chr.)," in M. Meier (ed.), *Pest: Die Geschichte eines Menschheitstraumas* (Stuttgart, 2005) pp. 44–65.

Schmitz 2006 = W. Schmitz, "Die Macht über die Sprache: Kommunikation, Politik und soziale Ordnung in Sparta," in A. Luther, M. Meier, and L. Thommen (eds.), *Das frühe Sparta* (Stuttgart, 2006) pp. 89–111.

Schreiner 1997 = J. H. Schreiner, *Hellanikos, Thukydides, and the Era of Cimon* (Aarhus, 1997).

Schubert and Laspe 2008 = C. Schubert and D. Laspe, "Perikles' defensiver Kriegsplan: Ein thukydideische Erfindung?" *Historia* 58 (2009) pp. 373–394.

Schwartz 1919 = E. Schwartz, *Das Geschichtswerk des Thukydides* (Bonn, 1919).

Schwartz 2009 = A. Schwartz, *Reinstating the Hoplite: Arms, Armour and Phalanx Fighting in Archaic and Classical Greece* (Stuttgart, 2009).

Scott 2005 = L. Scott, *Historical Commentary on Herodotus Book 6* (Leiden, 2005).

Scuccimarra 1985 = G. Scuccimarra, "Note sulla prima spedizione ateniense in Sicilia (427–424 a.C.)," *Rivista storica dell'antichità* 15 (1985) pp. 23–52.

Sealey 1958 (1967) = R. Sealey, "Athens and the Archidamian War," *Proceedings of the African Classical Associations* 1 (1958) pp. 61–87. Reprinted in id., *Essays in Greek Politics* (New York, 1967) pp. 75–110.

Sealey 1975 = R. Sealey, "The Causes of the Peloponnesian War," *Classical Philology* 70 (1975) pp. 89–109.

Seaman 1997 = M. G. Seaman, "The Athenian Expedition to Melos in 416 BC," *Historia* 46 (1997) pp. 385–418.

Shapiro 1998 = H. A. Shapiro, "Autochthony and the Visual Arts in Fifth-Century Athens," in D. Boedeker and K. A. Raaflaub (eds.), *Democracy, Empire, and the Arts in Fifth-Century Athens* (Cambridge, MA, 1998) pp. 127–51.

Shaw 1993 = J. T. Shaw, "Steering to Ram: The *Diekplous* and *Periplous*," in id. (ed.), *The Trireme Project: Operational Experience 1987–90, Lessons Learnt* (Oxford, 1993) pp. 99–104.

Shear 1937 = T. L. Shear Sr., "The Campaign of 1936," *Hesperia* 6 (1937) pp. 333–81.

Shear 2007 = J. L. Shear, "Cultural Change, Space, and the Politics of Commemoration in Athens," in R. Osborne (ed.), *Debating the Athenian*

Cultural Revolution: Art, Literature, Philosophy, and Politics, 430–380 BC (Cambridge, 2007) pp. 91–115.

Sicking 1995 = C. M. J. Sicking, "The General Purport of Pericles' Funeral Oration and Last Speech," *Hermes* 123 (1995) pp. 404–25.

Simonsen 2003 = K. Simonsen, "Winter Sailing," *Mouseion* 3 (2003) pp. 259–68.

Sleeswyk and Meijer 1998 = A. W. Sleeswyk and F. Meijer, "The Water Supply of the Argo and Other Oared Ships," *Mariner's Mirror* 84 (1998) pp. 131–8.

Smarczyk 1990 = B. Smarczyk, *Untersuchungen zur Religionspolitik und politischen Propaganda Athens im Delisch-Attischen Seebund* (Munich, 1990).

Smarczyk 1999 = B. Smarczyk, "Einige Bemerkungen zur Datierung der Beiträge zu Spartas Kriegskasse in IG V,1 1," *Klio* 81 (1999) pp. 45–67.

Smoes 1995 = É. Smoes, *Le courage chez les Grecs, d'Homère à Aristote* (Brussels, 1995).

Sommerstein 1981 = A. H. Sommerstein, *Aristophanes* Knights (Warminster, 1981).

Sordi 1976 = M. Sordi, "Atene e Sparta dalle guerra persiane al 462/1 a.C.," *Aevum* 50 (1976) pp. 25–41.

Spence 1990 (2007) = I. G. Spence, "Perikles and the Defence of Attika During the Peloponnesian War," *Journal of Hellenic Studies* 110 (1990) pp. 91–109. Reprinted in E. L. Wheeler (ed.), *The Armies of Classical Greece* (Aldershot, 2007) pp. 359–77.

Stahl 2003 = H.-P. Stahl, *Thucydides: Man's Place in History* (Swansea, 2003), translating *Die Stellung des Menschen im geschichtlichen Prozess* (Munich, 1966).

Ste. Croix 1972 = G. E. M. de Ste. Croix, *The Origins of the Peloponnesian War* (Ithaca, 1972).

Stewart 1994 = F. H. Stewart, *Honor* (Chicago, 1994).

Strassler 1988 = R. B. Strassler, "The Harbor at Pylos, 425 BC," *Journal of Hellenic Studies* 108 (1988) pp. 198–203.

Strassler 1990 = R. B. Strassler, "The Opening of the Pylos Campaign," *Journal of Hellenic Studies* 110 (1990) pp. 110–25.

Stroud 1971 = R. S. Stroud, "Thucydides and the Battle of Solygeia," *California Studies in Classical Antiquity* 4 (1971) pp. 227–47.

Stroud 1994 = R. S. Stroud, "Thucydides and Corinth," *Chiron* 24 (1994) pp. 267–304.

Taylor 1998 = J. G. Taylor, "Oinoe and the Painted Stoa: Ancient and Modern Misunderstandings?" *American Journal of Philology* 119 (1998) pp. 223–43.

Taylor (forthcoming) = A. Taylor, "The Slow Trireme Experience in *Olympias* in 1994," in B. Rankov (ed.), *Trireme* Olympias: *The Final Report. Sea Trials 1992–4. Conference Papers 1998* (Oxford).

Thommen 1996 = L. Thommen, Lakedaimonion Politeia: *Die Entstehung der spartanischen Verfassung* (Stuttgart, 1996).

Thommen 2003 = L. Thommen, *Sparta. Verfassungs- und Sozialgeschichte einer griechischen Polis* (Stuttgart, 2003).

Thommen 2006 = L. Thommen, "Einleitung: Überlegunge zum frühen Sparta," in A. Luther, M. Meier, and L. Thommen (eds.), *Das frühe Sparta* (Stuttgart, 2006) pp. 9–14.

Thompson 1968 = W. E. Thompson, "The Chronology of 432/1," *Hermes* 96 (1968) pp. 216–31.

Thompson 1971 = W. E. Thompson, "The Athenian Treaties with Haliai and Dareios the Bastard," *Klio* 53 (1971) pp. 119–24.

Thompson 1973 = W. E. Thompson, "Observations on Spartan Politics," *Rivista storica dell'antichità* 3 (1973) pp. 47–58.

Thonemann 2009 = P. Thonemann, "Lycia, Athens and Amorges," in J. Ma, N. Papazarkadas, and R. Parker (eds.), *Interpreting the Athenian Empire* (London, 2009) pp. 167–94.

Thorne 2001 = J. A. Thorne, "Warfare and Agriculture: The Economic Impact of Devastation in Classical Greece," *Greek, Roman and Byzantine Studies* 42 (2001) pp. 225–53.

Tilley 2004 = A. Tilley, *Seafaring on the Ancient Mediterranean: New Thoughts on Triremes and Other Ancient Ships* (Oxford, 2004).

Toher 2001 = M. Toher, "Diodorus on Delion and Euripides' *Supplices*," *Classical Quarterly* 51 (2001) pp. 178–82.

Treu 1956 = M. Treu, "Der Stratege Demosthenes," *Historia* 5 (1956) pp. 420–47.

Tritle 2010 = L. A. Tritle, *A New History of the Peloponnesian War* (Malden, 2010).

Unz 1986 = R. Unz, "Chronology of the *Pentekontaetia*," *Classical Quarterly* 36 (1986) pp. 68–85.

Van Hooff 1990 = A. J. van Hooff, *From* Autothanasia *to Suicide: Self-Killing in Classical Antiquity* (London, 1990).

Van Wees 2004 = H. van Wees, *Greek Warfare: Myths and Realities* (London, 2004).

Van Wees 2010 = H. van Wees, "Genocide in the Ancient World," in D. Bloxham and D. Moses (eds.), *The Oxford Handbook of Genocide Studies* (Oxford, 2010) pp. 239–58.

Vickers 2008 = M. Vickers, *Sophocles and Alcibiades: Athenian Politics in Ancient Greek Literature* (Ithaca, 2008).

Wade-Gery 1949 = H. T. Wade-Gery, "Thucydides," *Oxford Classical Dictionary*[1] (Oxford, 1949) pp. 902–5; ([2]1970) pp. 1067–9; ([3]1996) pp. 1516–19.

Walsh 1986 = J. Walsh, "The Date of the Athenian Stoa at Delphi," *American Journal of Archaeology* 90 (1986) pp. 319–36.

Weir 1995 = R. G. A. Weir, "The Lost Archaic Wall Around Athens," *Phoenix* 49 (1995) pp. 247–58.

West 2003 = S. West, "*Horkou pais estin anōnymos*: The Aftermath of Plataean Perjury," *Classical Quarterly* 53 (2003) pp. 438–47.

Westlake 1945 (1969) = H. D. Westlake, "Seaborne Raids in Periclean Strategy," *Classical Quarterly* 39 (1945) pp. 75–84. Reprinted in id., *Essays on the Greek Historians and Greek History* (Manchester, 1969) pp. 84–100.

Westlake 1960 (1969) = H. D. Westlake, "Athenian Aims in Sicily, 427–424 BC," *Historia* 9 (1960) pp. 385–401. Reprinted in id., *Essays on the Greek Historians and Greek History* (Manchester, 1969) pp. 101–23.

Westlake 1962 (1969) = H. D. Westlake, "Thucydides and the Fall of Amphipolis," *Hermes* 90 (1962) pp. 276–87. Reprinted in id., *Essays on the Greek Historians and Greek History* (Manchester, 1969) pp. 123–37.

Westlake 1968 = H. D. Westlake, *Individuals in Thucydides* (Cambridge, 1968).

Westlake 1974 (1989) = H. D. Westlake, "The Naval Battle at Pylos and Its Consequences," *Classical Quarterly* 24 (1974) pp. 211–26. Reprinted in id., *Studies in Thucydides and Greek History* (Bristol, 1989) pp. 60–77.

Westlake 1975 (1989) = H. D. Westlake, "Paches," *Phoenix* 29 (1975) pp. 107–16. Reprinted in id., *Studies in Thucydides and Greek History* (Bristol, 1989) pp. 50–9.

Westlake 1983 (1989, 2007) = H. D. Westlake, "The Progress of *Epiteichismos*," *Classical Quarterly* 33 (1983) pp. 12–24. Reprinted in id., *Studies in Thucydides and Greek History* (Bristol, 1989) pp. 34–49, and E. L. Wheeler (ed.), *The Armies of Classical Greece* (Aldershot, 2007) pp. 379–91.

Wheeler 1984 = E. L. Wheeler, "Sophistic Interpretations and Greek Treaties," *Greek, Roman and Byzantine Studies* 25 (1984) pp. 253–74.

Wheeler 1988 = E. L. Wheeler, "*Polla kena tou polemou*: The History of a Greek Proverb," *Greek, Roman and Byzantine Studies* 29 (1988) pp. 153–84.

Wheeler 2007 = E. L. Wheeler, "Battle: A. Land Battles," in P. Sabin, H. van Wees, and M. Whitby (eds.), *The Cambridge History of Greek and Roman Warfare* vol. 1 (Cambridge, 2007) pp. 186–223.

Whitehead 1987 = I. Whitehead, "The *Periplous*," *Greece and Rome* 34 (1987) pp. 178–85.

Whitehead 1988 = D. Whitehead, "*Klope polemou*: 'Theft' in Ancient Greek Warfare," *Classica et Mediaevalia* 39 (1988) pp. 43–53.

Wick 1976 = T. E. Wick, "Athens' Alliances with Rhegion and Leontinoi," *Historia* 25 (1976) pp. 288–304.

Wick 1979 = T. E. Wick, "Megara, Athens, and the West in the Archidamian War: A Study in Thucydides," *Historia* 28 (1979) pp. 1–14.

Wickersham 1994 = J. Wickersham, *Hegemony and Greek Historians* (Lanham, 1994).

Will 1975 = E. Will, "La territoire, la ville et la polorcétique grecque," *Revue historique* 253 (1975) pp. 297–318.

Will 2003 = W. Will, *Thukydides und Perikles* (Bonn, 2003).

Wilson 1979 = J. B. Wilson, *Pylos 425 BC: A Historical and Topographical Study of Thucydides' Account of the Campaign* (Warminster, 1979).

Wilson 1981 = J. Wilson, "Strategy and Tactics in the Mytilene Campaign," *Historia* 30 (1981) pp. 144–63.

Wilson 1987 = J. B. Wilson, *Athens and Corcyra: Strategy and Tactics in the Peloponnesian War* (Bristol, 1987).

Woodcock 1929 = E. C. Woodcock, "Demosthenes Son of Alcisthenes," *Harvard Studies in Classical Philology* 39 (1929) pp. 93–108.

Woodhead 1960 = A. G. Woodhead, "Thucydides' Portrait of Cleon," *Mnemosyne* 13 (1960) pp. 289–317.

Worthington 1987 = I. Worthington, "Aristophanes' *Knights* and the Abortive Peace Proposals of 425 BC," *L'antiquité classique* 56 (1987) pp. 56–67.

Wylie 2009 = L. Wylie, "Valuing Reputation and Prestige: Canadian Foreign Policy and the International Criminal Court," *American Review of Canadian Studies* 39 (2009) pp. 112–30.

Yates 2005 = D. Yates, "The Archaic Treaties Between the Spartans and Their Allies," *Classical Quarterly* 55 (2005) pp. 65–76.

Ziolkowski 1981 = J. E. Ziolkowski, *Thucydides and the Tradition of Funeral Speeches at Athens* (New York, 1981).

ILLUSTRATION CREDITS

FIGURES

121   3.1 Greek cavalryman. From M. M. Collignon, "Cavalier athénien et scènes de la vie guerrière," *Monuments grecs publiés par l'association pour l'encouragment des études grecques en France*, 14–16 (Paris, 1885–88) pp. 1–23, pl. 5 "Coup Attique du Musée du Louvre." Pistoxenos Painter (ARV: 860.9), (Athenian red-figure) cup from Vulci, *ca.* 475–425 BC, Louvre G108.

124   3.2 Greek warship under sail. Drawing by SeungJung Kim from kylix, London, British Mus. B436.

125   3.3 Reconstructed trireme under sail. Drawing by SeungJung Kim after photo: Paul Lipke/Trireme Trust.

126   3.4 Lines of the reconstructed trireme *Olympias*. Drawing: John Coates/Trireme Trust.

140   3.5 The Athenian hero Theseus clad as a hoplite in linen cuirass. From E. Gerhard, *Auserlesene Griechische Vasen-bilder*, 4 vols. (Berlin, 1839–58) Taf. 158 top. Methyse Painter (ARV: 633.6, 1663), (Athenian red-figure) calyx krater, *ca.* 475–425 BC, from Vulci, Bologna PU285.

156   4.1 Greek warship, possibly a trireme. Drawing by SeungJung Kim from Exekias Dinos, Rome, Villa Giulia 50599.

157   4.2 Trireme ramming. Drawing by SeungJung Kim after photo: Rosie Randolph/Trireme Trust.

178   4.3 Ancient Olympia, artist's reconstruction. From A. Boetticher, *Olympia: Das Fest und seine Stätte* (Berlin, 1883) Tav. XV "Ansicht von Olympia: Reconstruction."

189   5.1 Tegean hoplite, late fifth century BC. Spartan hoplites probably used similar equipment. From E. Pottier, "Un guerrier Tégéate," *Bulletin de Correspondance Hellénique* 4 (1880) pp. 408–15, pl. VII (p. 408) "Un guerrier Tégéate."

271   7.1 Hoplite and light-armed soldier throwing a stone. From E. Gerhard, *Auserlesene Griechische Vasen-bilder*, 4 vols. (Berlin, 1839–58) Taf. 164 top. Group of Polygnotos (undetermined) (ARV: 1051.13, 1680), (Athenian red-figure) stamnos, *ca.* 475–425 BC, from Vulci, Vatican, Mus. Greg. 690. Amazonomachy.

273   7.2 Greek soldier in a *pilos* helmet, the kind that Thucydides says the Spartans wore. Such helmets provided poor protection against missiles. Fourth-century BC relief from M. J. de Witte, "Pollux et Lycée sur une bronze de Dodone," *Monuments grecs publiés par l'association pour l'encouragment des études grecques en France* 6 (1877) pp. 9–10, pl. 2 "Bas-relief du plaque de bronze trouvé à Dodone."

277   7.3 The *Nike* of Paeonius, commissioned by the Messenians of Naupactus to celebrate the victory over the Spartans at Sphacteria. From A. Boetticher, *Olympia: Das Fest und seine Stätte* (Berlin, 1883) Tav. IX "Nike des Paionius."

285   7.4 Detail of Athenian cavalry from the Parthenon Frieze. From *A Description of the Collection of Ancient Marbles in the British Museum*, Part VIII (London, 1839) Plate LI, right section.

287   7.5 Greek cavalryman. From E. Gerhard, *Auserlesene Griechische Vasen-bilder*, 4 vols. (Berlin, 1839–58) Taf. 290 middle. Dokimasia Painter (ARV: 414.34), (Athenian red-figure) stamnos, *ca.* 500–450 BC, Northwick, Spencer-Churchill (previously in the Ashmolean Mus. 1965.121).

308   8.1 Hoplites running in three lines. The charge of a phalanx will have looked similar. From E. Gerhard, *Auserlesene Griechische Vasen-bilder*, 4 vols. (Berlin, 1839–58) Taf. 258 top. Corinthian black-figure oinochoe. Whereabouts unknown. Formerly Rome, Alibrandi Collection. R. Wachter, *Non-Attic Greek Vase Inscriptions* (Oxford, 2001), 323, and 345 no. COR 59; R. Arena, *Le iscrizione corinzie su vasi* (Rome, 1967), no. 48.

309   8.2 Hoplites fighting with spears. From E. Gerhard, *Auserlesene Griechische Vasen-bilder*, 4 vols. (Berlin, 1839–58) Taf. 165 bottom. Polygnotos (ARV: 1031.38), (Athenian red-figure) neck amphora (twisted handles), *ca.* 475–425 BC, London, British Mus. E272. Amazonomachy.

310   8.3 Hoplite with detailed representation of armor. From E. Gerhard, *Auserlesene Griechische Vasen-bilder*, 4 vols. (Berlin, 1839–58) Taf. 169 bottom. Altamura Painter (ARV: 594.54), (Athenian red-figure) amphora (type B), *ca.* 475–425 BC, from Vulci, London, British Mus. E263. Menelaus and Helen.

321   8.4 The Temple of Athena Nike on the Athenian Acropolis, likely commissioned by the Athenians to celebrate their victory over the Spartans at Sphacteria. From A. Boetticher, *Die Acropolis von Athen* (Berlin, 1888) Tav. XXXIII "Tempel der Nike."

332   9.1 Centaur with female captive. From *A Description of the Collection of Ancient Marbles in the British Museum*, Part II (London 1815) Plate XV.

339   9.2 Torone from the sea, present state, with the Oil Bottle in the foreground. Drawing by SeungJung Kim after photo in Alan S. Henry, *Torone, The Literary, Documentary and Epigraphical Testimonia* (Athens, 2004) p. xx.

342   9.3 What Brasidas would have looked like when adorned with the ribbons of an athletic victor. From E. Gerhard, *Auserlesene Griechische Vasen-bilder*, 4 vols. (Berlin, 1839–58) Taf. 275 top right. Kleophrades Painter (ARV: 183.9, 1632), (Athenian red-figure) Panathenaic amphora, *ca.* 500–450 BC, Boston, MFA 10.178. Athletic victor.

370   Comic masks. From *A Description of the Collection of Ancient Marbles in the British Museum*, Part II (London 1815) Frontispiece.

MAPS

Maps not otherwise identified below are adapted from L. L. Poates, in C. D. Shaw, *Stories of the Ancient Greeks* (Boston, 1903).

3   Megara and Its Environs, 424 BC (adapted from J. B. Bury, *A History of Greece to the Death of Alexander the Great* [London, 1900] fig. 62 p. 167)

20   1.1 Attica (adapted from J. B. Bury, *A History of Greece to the Death of Alexander the Great* [London, 1900] fig. 62 p. 167)

28   1.2 The Peloponnese (adapted from J. B. Bury, *A History of Greece to the Death of Alexander the Great* [London, 1900] fig. 50 p. 126)

61   2.2 The Long Walls Between Athens and Piraeus, completed ?457 BC (adapted from J. B. Bury, *A History of Greece to the Death of Alexander the Great* [London, 1900] fig. 114 p. 376)

92   2.7 Northern Greece, Including Epidamnus, Corcyra, and Potidaea (adapted from J. B. Bury, *A History of Greece to the Death of Alexander the Great* [London, 1900] fig. 31 p. 85)

95   2.8 War Around Corcyra, 435–433 BC (detail adapted from J. B. Bury, *A History of Greece to the Death of Alexander the Great* [London, 1900] fig. 31 p. 85)

110   3.1 Boeotia (adapted from J. B. Bury, *A History of Greece to the Death of Alexander the Great* [London, 1900] fig. 60 p. 161)

205   5.2 The Corcyrean Revolution, 427 BC (detail adapted from J. B. Bury, *A History of Greece to the Death of Alexander the Great* [London, 1900] fig. 31 p. 85)

213   5.3 The Athenian Expedition to Southern Italy and Sicily, 427 BC (drawing by Elke Fuchs after J. B. Bury, *A History of Greece to the Death of Alexander the Great* [London, 1900] fig. 34 p. 97)

253   7.2 Navarino Bay, with Pylos and Sphacteria (adapted from B. W. Henderson, *The Great War Between Athens and Sparta* [London, 1927], map facing p. 193, "Map: Pylos and Sphacteria," itself after G. B. Grundy, "An Investigation of the Topography of the Region of Sphakteria and Pylos," *Journal of Hellenic Studies* 16 [1896] pp. 1–54, plate 3, "Pylos and Environs.")

280   7.3 The War in the West, 425 BC (drawing by Elke Fuchs after J. B. Bury, *A History of Greece to the Death of Alexander the Great* [London, 1900] fig. 34 p. 97)

335   9.4 Amphipolis and Environs (drawing by SeungJung Kim after D. Lazaridis, *Amphipolis* [Athens 1997] pp. 62–3)

INDEX